Dimensions of Learning
Teacher's MANUAL

Robert J. Marzano
and
Debra J. Pickering
with
Daisy E. Arredondo
Guy J. Blackburn
Ronald S. Brandt
Cerylle A. Moffett
Diane E. Paynter
Jane E. Pollock
Jo Sue Whisler

2nd Edition

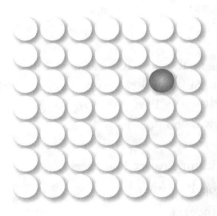

Association for Supervision and Curriculum Development
Alexandria, Virginia USA

Mid-continent Regional Educational Laboratory
Aurora, Colorado USA

Association for Supervision and Curriculum Development
1703 N. Beauregard St. • Alexandria, VA 22311-1714 USA
Telephone: 1-800-933-2723 or 703-578-9600 • Fax: 703-575-5400
Web site: http://www.ascd.org • E-mail: member@ascd.org

McREL

McREL (Mid-continent Regional Educational Laboratory)
2550 S. Parker Road, Suite 500 • Aurora, Colorado 80014
Telephone: 303-337-0990 • Fax: 303-337-3005
Web site: http://www.mcrel.org/

Barbara B. Gaddy, Editor/Project Manager
Jeanne Deak, Desktop Publisher
Sarah Allen Smith, Indexer

Printed in the United States of America.

ASCD publications present a variety of viewpoints. The views expressed or implied in this book should not be interpreted as official positions of the Association.

ISBN: 0-87120-321-9

ASCD stock no. 197133   S6/97
ASCD member price: $24.95   nonmember price: $29.95

To order additional copies of this book, please contact ASCD.

01 00 99 98   5 4 3 2

About the Authors

Robert J. Marzano is Deputy Executive Director, McREL Institute, Mid-continent Regional Educational Laboratory, 2550 S. Parker Rd., Suite 500, Aurora, Colorado 80014.

Debra J. Pickering is Senior Program Associate, Mid-continent Regional Educational Laboratory, 2550 S. Parker Rd., Suite 500, Aurora, Colorado 80014.

Daisy E. Arredondo is Associate Professor, Educational Leadership Studies, West Virginia University, 606 Allen Hall, P.O. Box 6122, Morgantown, West Virginia 26506.

Guy J. Blackburn is Educational Policy Analyst, Oakland Schools, 2100 Pontiac Lake Rd., Waterford, Michigan 48328.

Ronald S. Brandt is former Executive Editor, Association for Supervision and Curriculum Development, 1250 N. Pitt St., Alexandria, Virginia 22314. He is now a writer and consultant.

Cerylle A. Moffett is former Professional Development Program Manager, Association for Supervision and Curriculum Development. She is now an independent consultant, CMA Associates, 916 DeWolfe Drive, Alexandria, Virginia 22308.

Diane E. Paynter is Senior Program Associate, Mid-continent Regional Educational Laboratory, 2550 S. Parker Rd., Suite 500, Aurora, Colorado 80014.

Jane E. Pollock is Senior Program Associate, Mid-continent Regional Educational Laboratory, 2550 S. Parker Rd., Suite 500, Aurora, Colorado 80014.

Jo Sue Whisler is Senior Program Associate, Mid-continent Regional Educational Laboratory, 2550 S. Parker Rd., Suite 500, Aurora, Colorado 80014.

Dimensions of Learning Teacher's Manual

Chapter 3. Dimension 3: Extend and Refine Knowledge

Chapter 4. Dimension 4: Use Knowledge Meaningfully

Chapter 5. Dimension 5: Habits of Mind

Chapter 6. Putting It All Together

Acknowledgments

We would like to express our sincere appreciation to those individuals from the following school districts who contributed ideas and suggestions to this second edition of the *Dimensions of Learning Teacher's Manual*:

Ashwaubenon School District, Green Bay, Wisconsin

Berryessa Union School District, San Jose, California

Brisbane Grammar School, Queensland, Australia

Brockport Central School District, Brockport, New York

Brooklyn School District, Brooklyn, Ohio

Broome-Tioga Boces, Binghamton, New York

Cherry Creek Public Schools, Aurora, Colorado

Colegio International de Caracas, Caracas, Venezuela

Douglas County Schools, Douglas County, Colorado

George School District, George, Iowa

Green Bay Area Public Schools, Green Bay, Wisconsin

Ingham Intermediate School District, Mason, Michigan

Kenosha Unified School District #1, Kenosha, Wisconsin

Kingsport City Schools, Kingsport, Tennessee

Lakeland Area Education Agency #3, Cylinder, Iowa

Lakeview Public Schools, St. Clair Shores, Michigan

Loess Hills AEA #13, Council Bluffs, Iowa

Lonoke School District, Lonoke, Arkansas

Love Elementary School, Houston, Texas

Maccray School, Clara City, Minnesota

Monroe County ISD, Monroe, Michigan

Nicolet Area Consortium, Glendale, Wisconsin

Northern Trails AEA #2, Clear Lake, Iowa

North Syracuse Central School District, North Syracuse, New York

Prince Alfred College, Kent Town, South Australia

Redwood Elementary School, Avon Lake, Ohio

Regional School District #13, Durham, Connecticut

Richland School District, Richland, Washington

St. Charles Parish Public Schools, Luling, Louisiana

School District of Howard-Suamico, Green Bay, Wisconsin

South Washington County Schools, Cottage Grove, Minnesota

Webster City Schools, Webster City, Iowa

West Morris Regional High School District, Chester, New Jersey

The following members of the Dimensions of Learning Research and Development Consortium worked together from 1989 to 1991 to advise, consult, and pilot portions of the model as part of the development of Dimensions of Learning.

ALABAMA

Auburn University
Terrance Rucinski

CALIFORNIA

Los Angeles County Office of Education
Richard Sholseth
Diane Watanabe

Napa Valley Unified School District
Mary Ellen Boyet
Laurie Rucker
Daniel Wolter

COLORADO

Aurora Public Schools
Kent Epperson
Phyllis A. Henning
Lois Kellenbenz
Lindy Lindner
Rita Perron
Janie Pollock
Nora Redding

Cherry Creek Public Schools
Maria Foseid
Patricia Lozier
Nancy MacIsaacs
Mark Rietema
Deena Tarleton

ILLINOIS

Maine Township High School West
Betty Duffey
Mary Gienko
Betty Heraty
Paul Leathem
Mary Kay Walsh

IOWA

Dike Community Schools
Janice Albrecht
Roberta Bodensteiner
Ken Cutts
Jean Richardson
Stan Van Hauen

Mason City Community Schools
Dudley L. Humphrey

MASSACHUSETTS

Concord-Carlisle Regional School District
Denis Cleary
Diana MacLean

Concord Public Schools
Virginia Barker
Laura Cooper
Stephen Greene
Joe Leone
Susan Whitten

MICHIGAN

Farmington Public Schools
Marilyn Carlsen
Katherine Nyberg
James Shaw
Joyce Tomlinson

Lakeview Public Schools
Joette Kunse

Oakland Schools
Roxanne Reschke

Waterford School District
Linda Blust
Julie Casteel
Bill Gesaman
Mary Lynn Kraft
Al Monetta
Theodora M. Sailer
Dick Williams

NEBRASKA

Fremont Public Schools, District 001
Mike Aerni
Trudy Jo Kluver
Fred Robertson

NEW MEXICO

Gallup-McKinley County Schools
Clara Esparza
Ethyl Fox
Martyn Stowe
Linda Valentine
Chantal Irvin

NEW YORK

Frontier Central Schools
Janet Brooks
Barbara Broomell

PENNSYLVANIA

Central Bucks School District
Jeanann Kahley
N. Robert Laws
Holly Lomas
Rosemarie Montgomery
Cheryl Winn Royer
Jim Williams

Philadelphia School District
Paul Adorno
Shelly Berman
Ronald Jenkins
John Krause
Judy Lechner
Betty Richardson

SOUTH CAROLINA

School District of Greenville County
Sharon Benston
Dale Dicks
Keith Russell
Jane Satterfield
Ellen Weinberg
Mildred Young

State Department of Education
Susan Smith White

TEXAS

Fort Worth Independent School District
Carolyne Creel
Sherry Harris
Midge Rach
Nancy Timmons

UTAH

Salt Lake City Schools
Corrine Hill

MEXICO

ITESO University
Ana Christina Amante
Laura Figueroa Barba
Antonio Ray Bazan
Luis Felipe Gomez
Patricia Rios de Lopez

PROGRAM EVALUATOR

Charles Fisher

Introduction

Overview

Dimensions of Learning is an extension of the comprehensive research-based framework on cognition and learning described in *Dimensions of Thinking: A Framework for Curriculum and Instruction* (Marzano et al., 1988), published by the Association for Supervision and Curriculum Development (ASCD). Dimensions of Learning translates the research and theory explained in *Dimensions of Thinking* into a practical framework that K-12 teachers can use to improve the quality of teaching and learning in any content area. The Dimensions of Learning Research and Development Consortium, which worked on the model for two years, was made up of more than ninety educators, including the author team from the first edition of this manual. Under the leadership of Dr. Robert Marzano of the Mid-continent Regional Educational Laboratory (McREL), these educators helped to shape the basic program into a valuable tool for reorganizing curriculum, instruction, and assessment.

Implicit in the Dimensions of Learning model, or framework, are five basic assumptions:

1. Instruction must reflect the best of what we know about how learning occurs.

2. Learning involves a complex system of interactive processes that includes five types of thinking—represented by the five dimensions of learning.

3. The K-12 curriculum should include the explicit teaching of attitudes, perceptions, and mental habits that facilitate learning.

4. A comprehensive approach to instruction includes at least two distinct types of instruction: one that is more teacher directed, and another that is more student directed.

5. Assessment should focus on students' *use* of knowledge and complex reasoning processes rather than on their recall of information.

In addition to this teacher's manual, Dimensions of Learning is supported by a number of resources designed to help educators fully understand (1) how these five assumptions affect teachers' work in the classroom and, as a consequence, students' learning and (2) how the Dimensions of Learning framework can be used to restructure curriculum, instruction, and assessment:

- *A Different Kind of Classroom: Teaching with Dimensions of Learning* (Marzano, 1992) explores the theory and research underlying the framework through a variety of classroom-based examples. Although teachers need not read this book to use the model, they will have a better understanding of cognition and learning if they do. Staff developers also are encouraged to read this book to strengthen their delivery of the Dimensions of Learning training.

- *Observing Dimensions of Learning in Classrooms and Schools* (Brown, 1995) is designed to help administrators provide support and feedback to teachers who are using Dimensions of Learning in their classrooms.

- *Dimensions of Thinking* (Marzano et al., 1988) describes a framework that can be used to design curriculum and instruction with an emphasis on the types of thinking that students should use to enhance their learning.

- The *Dimensions of Learning Trainer's Manual* (Marzano et al., 1997) contains detailed training scripts, overhead transparencies, and practical guidelines for conducting comprehensive training and staff development in the Dimensions of Learning program.

- *Assessing Student Outcomes: Performance Assessment Using the Dimensions of Learning Model* (Marzano, Pickering, & McTighe, 1993) provides recommendations for setting up an assessment system that focuses on using performance tasks constructed with the reasoning processes from Dimensions 3 and 4.

We recommend that those who plan to train others to use Dimensions of Learning first participate in the training offered by ASCD or McREL or by individuals recommended by these organizations. In some cases, experienced staff development trainers with an extensive background in the teaching of thinking may be able to learn about each dimension through self-study or, ideally, through study with peers. We strongly recommend, however, that before conducting training for others, these individuals use the Dimensions of Learning framework to plan and teach units of instruction themselves. In short, Dimensions of Learning is best understood and internalized through practical experience with the model.

- *Implementing Dimensions of Learning* (Marzano et al., 1992) explains the different ways that the model can be used in a school or district and discusses the various factors that must be considered when deciding which approach to use. It contains guidelines that will help a school or district structure its implementation to best achieve its identified goals.

- Finally, the Dimensions of Learning Videotape Series (ASCD, 1992) introduces and illustrates some of the important concepts underlying the Dimensions of Learning framework. Videotaped classroom examples of each dimension in action can be used during training, in follow-up sessions for reinforcement, or during Dimensions of Learning study-group sessions.

Together, these resources guide educators through a structured, yet flexible, approach to improving curriculum, instruction, and assessment.

What Is Dimensions of Learning?

Dimensions of Learning is a comprehensive model that uses what researchers and theorists know about learning to define the learning process. Its premise is that five types of thinking—what we call the five dimensions of learning—are essential to successful learning. The Dimensions framework will help you to

- maintain a focus on learning;

- study the learning process; and

- plan curriculum, instruction, and assessment that takes into account the five critical aspects of learning.

Now let's take a look at the five dimensions of learning.

Dimension 1: Attitudes and Perceptions

Attitudes and perceptions affect students' abilities to learn. For example, if students view the classroom as an unsafe and disorderly place, they will likely learn little there. Similarly, if students have negative attitudes about classroom tasks, they will probably put little effort into those tasks. A key element of effective instruction, then, is helping students to establish positive attitudes and perceptions about the classroom and about learning.

Dimension 2: Acquire and Integrate Knowledge

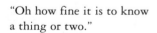

"Oh how fine it is to know a thing or two."

—Molière

Helping students acquire and integrate new knowledge is another important aspect of learning. When students are learning new information, they must be guided in relating the new knowledge to what they already know, organizing that information, and then making it part of their long-term memory. When students are acquiring new skills and processes, they must learn a model (or set of steps), then shape the skill or process to make it efficient and effective for them, and, finally, internalize or practice the skill or process so they can perform it easily.

Dimension 3: Extend and Refine Knowledge

Learning does not stop with acquiring and integrating knowledge. Learners develop in-depth understanding through the process of extending and refining their knowledge (e.g., by making new distinctions, clearing up misconceptions, and reaching conclusions). They rigorously analyze what they have learned by applying reasoning processes that will help them extend and refine the information. Some of the common reasoning processes used by learners to extend and refine their knowledge are the following:

- Comparing
- Classifying
- Abstracting
- Inductive reasoning
- Deductive reasoning
- Constructing support
- Analyzing errors
- Analyzing perspectives

Dimension 4: Use Knowledge Meaningfully

The most effective learning occurs when we use knowledge to perform meaningful tasks. For example, we might initially learn about tennis rackets by talking to a friend or reading a magazine article about them. We really learn about them, however, when we are trying to decide what kind of tennis racket to buy. Making sure that students have the opportunity to use knowledge meaningfully is one of the most important parts of planning a unit of instruction. In the Dimensions of Learning model, there are six reasoning processes around which tasks can be constructed to encourage the meaningful use of knowledge:

- Decision making
- Problem solving
- Invention
- Experimental inquiry
- Investigation
- Systems analysis

"Knowledge changes knowledge."

"Information isn't knowledge until you can use it."

Dimension 5: Habits of Mind

The most effective learners have developed powerful habits of mind that enable them to think critically, think creatively, and regulate their behavior. These mental habits are listed below:

Critical thinking:

- Be accurate and seek accuracy

- Be clear and seek clarity

- Maintain an open mind

- Restrain impulsivity

- Take a position when the situation warrants it

- Respond appropriately to others' feelings and level of knowledge

Creative thinking:

- Persevere

- Push the limits of your knowledge and abilities

- Generate, trust, and maintain your own standards of evaluation

- Generate new ways of viewing a situation that are outside the boundaries of standard conventions

Self-regulated thinking:

- Monitor your own thinking

- Plan appropriately

- Identify and use necessary resources

- Respond appropriately to feedback

- Evaluate the effectiveness of your actions

The Relationship Among the Dimensions of Learning

It is important to realize that the five dimensions of learning do not operate
in isolation but work together in the manner depicted in Figure A.1.

FIGURE A.1

HOW THE DIMENSIONS OF LEARNING INTERACT

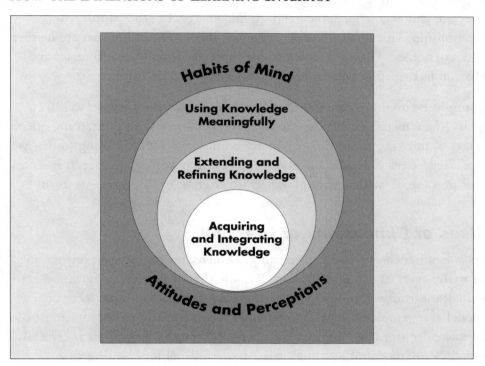

Briefly, as the graphic in Figure A.1 illustrates, all learning takes place
against the backdrop of learners' attitudes and perceptions (Dimension 1)
and their use (or lack of use) of productive habits of mind (Dimension 5). If
students have negative attitudes and perceptions about learning, then they
will likely learn little. If they have positive attitudes and perceptions, they
will learn more and learning will be easier. Similarly, when students use
productive habits of mind these habits facilitate their learning. Dimensions
1 and 5, then, are always factors in the learning process. This is why they are
part of the background of the graphic shown in Figure A.1.

When positive attitudes and perceptions are in place and productive habits
of mind are being used, learners can more effectively do the thinking
required in the other three dimensions, that is, acquiring and integrating

knowledge (Dimension 2), extending and refining knowledge (Dimension 3), and using knowledge meaningfully (Dimension 4). Notice the relative positions of the three circles of Dimensions 2, 3, and 4. (See Figure A.1.) The circle representing meaningful use of knowledge subsumes the other two, and the circle representing extending and refining knowledge subsumes the circle representing acquiring and integrating knowledge. This communicates that when learners extend and refine knowledge, they continue to acquire knowledge, and when they use knowledge meaningfully, they are still acquiring and extending knowledge. In other words, the relationships among these circles represent types of thinking that are neither discrete nor sequential. They represent types of thinking that interact and that, in fact, may be occurring simultaneously during learning.

It might be useful to consider the Dimensions of Learning model as providing a metaphor for the learning process. Dimensions of Learning offers a way of thinking about the extremely complex process of learning so that we can attend to each aspect and gain insights into how they interact. If it serves this purpose, it will be a useful tool as we attempt to help students learn.

Uses of Dimensions of Learning

As a comprehensive model of learning, Dimensions can have an impact on virtually every aspect of education. Because the major goal of education is to enhance learning, it follows that our system of education must focus on a model that represents criteria for effective learning, criteria that we must use to make decisions and evaluate programs. Although Dimensions is certainly not the only model of learning, it is a powerful tool for ensuring that *learning* is the focus of what we do as educators. It should validate current efforts in schools and classrooms to enhance learning, but should also suggest ways of continuing to improve. Although individuals, schools, and districts should use the model to meet their own needs, it might be helpful to understand a number of possible ways in which the Dimensions of Learning model might be used.

A Resource for Instructional Strategies

At the most basic level, this manual has been used as a resource for research-based instructional strategies. Although there are many effective strategies included in the manual, it is important to remember that the manual is not the model. As the strategies are used, they should be selected and their effectiveness measured in terms of the desired effect on learning. The implication is that even at this basic level of use, it is important for teachers to understand each dimension as they select and use strategies.

"We were thrilled to discover that Dimensions of Learning is not an 'add-on' but, instead, a framework that enhances teaching and learning across the curricula within our classrooms."

—First-grade teacher
in Connecticut

A Framework for Planning Staff Development

Some schools and districts see Dimensions as offering an important focus during their planning of staff development and as a way of organizing the diverse inservice experiences offered in the district. The matrix in Figure A.2 (see next page) graphically represents this organization. Down the left-hand side is an outline of the components of the Dimensions model. Planning for professional development begins here, whether for individuals or an entire staff. The first question staff developers would ask is, "What part of the learning process needs to be improved?" After answering that question, resources for seeking the improvement are identified across the top of the matrix. These resources might includes programs, strategies, individuals, or books that can be used to achieve the desired learning goal. There might be many resources available that complement and supplement each other and could, therefore, all be offered to those seeking the improvement in learning. When any resource is identified, the matrix allows for indicating clearly which aspects of the learning process might be enhanced if people were to select and use that resource. Notice that the focus is on the learning process rather than on the resource.

A Structure for Planning Curriculum and Assessment

One reason that the Dimensions of Learning model was created was to influence the planning of curriculum and assessment, both at the classroom and the district level. It is particularly suited to planning instructional units and creating assessments that are clearly aligned with curriculum, including both conventional and performance instruments.

Within each dimension there are planning questions that can help to structure the planning so that all aspects of the learning process are addressed: for example, "What will I do to help students maintain positive attitudes and perceptions?" or "What declarative knowledge are the students learning?" Although it is important for the planner to ask powerful questions, sometimes the answer may be that very little or nothing at all will be planned to address that part of the model. It is not important to plan something for every dimension; it is important to ask the questions for every dimension during the planning process. More detailed explanations and examples are included throughout this manual and in each planning section.

Those who use the Dimensions model to influence their assessment practices quickly realize instruction and assessment are closely integrated but that both conventional and performance-based methods of assessment have a role. Specific recommendations for assessment are included at the end of this manual.

> "The Dimensions model validates so much of what we were already doing in our classrooms. It gives us a common structure and vocabulary with which to discuss and plan professional activities throughout the school."
>
> —An elementary school principal

MATRIX FOR PLANNING STAFF DEVELOPMENT

Resources for Improvement / Dimensions of Learning Outline								
Attitudes & Perceptions								
I. Classroom Climate								
A. Acceptance by Teachers and Peers								
B. Comfort and Order								
II. Classroom Tasks								
A. Value and Interest								
B. Ability and Resources								
C. Clarity								
Acquire & Integrate Knowledge								
I. Declarative								
A. Construct Meaning								
B. Organize								
C. Store								
II. Procedural								
A. Construct Models								
B. Shape								
C. Internalize								
Extend & Refine Knowledge								
Comparing								
Classifying								
Abstracting								
Inductive Reasoning								
Deductive Reasoning								
Constructing Support								
Analyzing Errors								
Analyzing Perspectives								
Use Knowledge Meaningfully								
Decision Making								
Problem Solving								
Invention								
Experimental Inquiry								
Investigation								
Systems Analysis								
Habits of Mind								
Critical Thinking								
Creative Thinking								
Self-Regulated Thinking								

A Focus for Systemic Reform

The most comprehensive use of the Dimensions model is as an organizational tool to ensure that the entire school district is structured around and operating with a consistent attention to learning. The model provides a common perspective and a shared language. Just as curriculum planners ask questions in reference to each dimension during planning, people in every part of the school system ask similar questions as they create schedules, select textbooks, create job descriptions, and evaluate the effectiveness of programs.

These four uses of the model are offered only as examples. There is no reason to select only from among these four options; the purpose of the model is to help you define and achieve your goals for student learning. The model is a structure that should allow for and encourage a great deal of flexibility.

Using This Manual

Understanding the Dimensions of Learning model can greatly improve your ability to plan any aspect of education. This manual is designed to help teachers and administrators study learning through the Dimensions model and to provide guidance for those who are using the model to achieve their specific individual, school, and district goals. The sections of the manual, as well as the format used to organize the information and recommendations, are described below.

1. There is a chapter for each dimension that includes an introduction, suggestions for helping students to engage in the thinking involved in that dimension, classroom examples to stimulate reflection and suggest ways of applying the information, and a process for planning instruction in the particular dimension.

2. The margins throughout the manual contain information that should help you think about the ideas highlighted in each dimension and pursue further study. You will find

    • bibliographic references (shortened in some cases because of space), which provide suggestions for further reading;

    • quotes from documents that were used as references for the section;

    • interesting and relevant quotes or thoughts, offered as ideas for reflection;

    • descriptions of implementation activities that have been used in schools or districts;

- suggested materials that might be used in planning classroom activities or that contain other strategies related to the dimension; and

- graphics that depict ideas addressed in the dimension.

3. The chapter "Putting It All Together" walks the reader through the entire planning process and offers suggestions, different planning sequences, and examples from units of study planned using the Dimensions of Learning framework. This chapter also discusses critical issues related to assessment techniques that can be used to collect data on students' performance in each of the dimensions; rubrics to facilitate consistent, fair teacher judgment and to promote student learning; and ideas for assigning and recording grades.

The strategies and resources highlighted throughout this manual are only a small percentage of those that could have been included in support of each dimension. If cost had not been a consideration, this manual would have been published as a loose-leaf notebook so that users could add their own strategies and resources. Gathering additional ideas and suggestions should be a goal for every professional educator. Hopefully, what is offered here will contribute to the resources that master teachers already have gathered and provide a beginning for those new to the profession.

Dimension 1

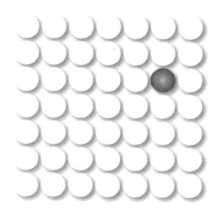

Dimension 1
Attitudes and Perceptions

Introduction

Most people recognize that attitudes and perceptions influence learning. As learners, we all have experienced the impact of our attitudes and perceptions related to the teacher, other students, our own abilities, and the value of assigned tasks. When our attitudes and perceptions are positive, learning is enhanced; when they are negative, learning suffers. It is the shared responsibility of the teacher and the student to work to maintain positive attitudes and perceptions or, when possible, to change negative attitudes and perceptions.

The effective teacher continuously works to influence attitudes and perceptions, often so skillfully that students are not aware of her efforts. Subtle though this behavior may be, it is a conscious instructional decision to overtly cultivate specific attitudes and perceptions. In the next two sections, you will find strategies and techniques for enhancing two types of attitudes and perceptions: those related to the climate of the classroom and those related to classroom tasks. You will find strategies, techniques, recommendations, and classroom examples to refer to when you are planning to

- elicit positive attitudes and perceptions from learners and

- teach the learner how to maintain positive attitudes and perceptions or change negative or detrimental ones.

"I read once, 'Billiard balls react. People respond.' This reminds me that although I recognize that I did not cause my students to have some of the negative attitudes that they bring to school, I *am* responsible for having a repertoire of effective strategies for eliciting positive attitudes that enhance students' learning."

—A mathematics teacher in Missouri

This dimension includes two main sections as described below.

I.   Helping Students Develop Positive Attitudes and Perceptions About Classroom Climate

   • Feel accepted by teachers and peers

   • Experience a sense of comfort and order

II. Helping Students Develop Positive Attitudes and Perceptions About Classroom Tasks

   • Perceive tasks as valuable and interesting

   • Believe they have the ability and resources to complete tasks

   • Understand and be clear about tasks

Helping Students Develop Positive Attitudes and Perceptions About Classroom Climate

Educators recognize the influence that the climate of the classroom has on learning. A primary objective of every teacher, then, is to establish a climate in which students

- feel accepted by teachers and peers and

- experience a sense of comfort and order.

The following strategies are designed for teachers to use to help students enhance their attitudes and perceptions and to help students develop their *own* strategies for enhancing attitudes and perceptions.

1. Help students understand that attitudes and perceptions related to classroom climate influence learning.

Students vary in the degree to which they understand the relationship among attitudes, perceptions, and learning. Emphasize with students that

- attitudes and perceptions related to classroom climate are critical to learning, and

- it is the shared responsibility of the students and the teacher to keep attitudes as positive as possible.

Help students understand that it is important to maintain a climate that positively affects learning and that this means much more than simply "good behavior." There are many ways to help build this understanding:

- Share with students how your own learning (from kindergarten to where you are today) has been influenced by your attitudes and perceptions related to acceptance and to comfort and order. Include in your discussion strategies you use, or have used, as a learner to maintain positive attitudes and perceptions and how those strategies have worked to enhance your learning. Then ask students to share their experiences and the effectiveness of strategies they have used.

- Present a variety of hypothetical situations in which an individual student's negative attitude is affecting his or her learning. Ask students to discuss why the student might have a negative attitude and to suggest ways in which the situation might be resolved.

An elementary school principal regularly displays positive quotes about learning on bulletin boards and posters throughout the school (e.g., "Attitudes are the mind's paintbrush"). He periodically asks students what they think each quote means and how the idea might enhance their learning.

McCombs & Whisler (1997) *The Learner-Centered Classroom and School*

For strategies for "invitational learning," see Purkey (1978) *Inviting School Success.*

Combs (1982) *A Personal Approach to Teaching*

• Help students become aware of fictional, historical, or famous people who have enhanced their own learning by maintaining positive attitudes. Newspaper articles, books, films, or television programs are good resources for examples.

Feel Accepted by Teachers and Peers

Everyone wants to feel accepted by others. When we feel accepted, we are comfortable, even energized. However, when we do not feel accepted, we are often uncomfortable, distracted, or depressed. The stakes are particularly high in the classroom. Students who feel accepted usually feel better about themselves and school, work harder, and learn better. Your job as a teacher begins with helping students to feel accepted by both you and their peers. There are a number of ways you can accomplish this.

2. Establish a relationship with each student in the class.

We all like to experience being "known." A simple gesture such as being greeted by name can be validating. Students are no different. Establishing relationships with them communicates that you respect them as individuals and contributes to their successful learning. There are many ways to establish these relationships:

• Talk informally with students before, during, and after class about their interests.

• Greet students outside of school, for instance at extracurricular events or at stores.

• Single out a few students each day in the lunchroom and talk to them.

• Be aware of and comment on important events in students' lives, such as participation in sports, drama, or other extracurricular activities.

• Compliment students on important achievements in and outside of school.

• Include students in the process of planning classroom activities; solicit their ideas and consider their interests.

• Meet students at the door as they come into class and say hello to each child, making sure to use his or her first name.

- Take time at the beginning of the school year to have students complete an interest inventory. Use this information throughout the year to connect and converse with students about their interests.

- Call students before the school year begins and ask a few questions about them to begin to establish a relationship.

- Call parents and share anecdotes that focus on something about which parents and students can be proud.

3. Monitor and attend to your own attitudes.

Most teachers are aware that when their attitudes toward students are positive, student performance is enhanced. However, they are sometimes unaware of favoring or having higher expectations for certain students. Increasing awareness of, monitoring, and attending to your own attitudes can contribute to students feeling accepted. The following process might be helpful when you are aware of a negative attitude:

1. Before class each day, mentally review your students, noting those with whom you anticipate having problems (either academic or behavioral).

2. Try to imagine these "problem" students succeeding or engaging in positive classroom behavior. In other words, replace your negative expectations with positive ones. This is a form of mental rehearsal. It's useful to review the positive images more than once before beginning the instructional day.

3. When you interact with students, try consciously to keep in mind your positive expectations.

4. Engage in equitable and positive classroom behavior.

Research suggests that even those teachers who are most aware of their interactions with students unwittingly can give more attention to high achievers than to low achievers and call on one gender more than the other. It is important to do what is necessary to ensure that all students are attended to positively so that they are likely to feel accepted. To this end, there are several classroom practices that are useful:

- Make eye contact with each student in the room. You can do this by scanning the entire room as you speak. Freely move about all sections of the room.

Good (1982) "How Teachers' Expectations Affect Results"

Rosenshine (1983) "Teaching Functions in Instructional Programs"

Covey (1990) *The 7 Habits of Highly Effective People*

Rosenthal & Jacobson (1968) *Pygmalion in the Classroom*

Kerman, Kimball, & Martin (1980) *Teacher Expectations and Student Achievement*

Sadker & Sadker (1994) *Failing at Fairness*

Grayson & Martin (1985) *Gender Expectations and Student Achievement*

Hunter (1976) *Improved Instruction*

Rowe (1974) "Wait-time and Rewards as Instructional Variables, Their Influence on Language, Logic and Fate Control"

Gardner (1983) *Frames of Mind*; Gardner (1993) *Multiple Intelligences*

McCarthy (1980) *The 4MAT System*

Wlodkowski & Ginsberg (1995) *Diversity and Motivation*

Dunn & Dunn (1978) *Teaching Students Through Their Individual Learning Styles*

Gregorc (1983) *Student Learning Styles and Brain Behavior*

- Over the course of a class period, deliberately move toward and be close to each student. Make sure that the seating arrangement allows you and students clear and easy access to move around the room.

- Attribute the ownership of ideas to the students who initiated them. (For instance, in a discussion you might say, "Dennis has just added to Mary's idea by saying that. . . .")

- Allow and encourage all students to be part of class discussions and interactions. Make sure to call on students who do not commonly participate, not just students who respond most frequently.

- Provide appropriate "wait time" for all students, regardless of their past performance or your perception of their abilities.

5. Recognize and provide for students' individual differences.

All students are unique. They come to the educational setting with varying experiences, interests, knowledge, abilities, and perceptions of the world. As research and experience tell us, people also vary in their preferred styles of learning and thinking; their types and degree of intelligence; their cultural backgrounds that include varying perspectives and customs; and their particular needs due to background, physical or mental attributes, and learning deficits or strengths. Teaching that recognizes and provides for such differences results in students feeling more accepted because of greater personalization. The result is increased and improved student learning. The following strategies can help teachers recognize and provide for students' individual differences:

- Use materials and literature from around the world.

- Design a classroom setup that accommodates varying physical needs.

- Plan varied classroom activities so that all students have opportunities to learn in their preferred style.

- Allow students choice in projects so that they may use their strengths and capitalize on their interests as they demonstrate their learning.

- Include in your lessons examples of successful people talking about how they recognized and capitalized on their differences.

6. Respond positively to students' incorrect responses or lack of response.

Students participate and respond when they think it is okay to make mistakes or to not know an answer, that is, when they know that they will continue to be accepted in spite of errors or lack of information. How you respond to a student's incorrect response or lack of response is an important factor in creating this sense of safety for students. When students give wrong answers or no answer, dignify their responses by trying one of the following suggestions:

- Emphasize what was right. Give credit to the aspects of an incorrect response that are correct and acknowledge when the student is headed in the right direction. Identify the question that the incorrect response answered.

- Encourage collaboration. Allow students time to seek help from peers. This can result in better responses and can enhance learning.

- Restate the question. Ask the question a second time and allow time for students to think before you expect a response.

- Rephrase the question. Paraphrase the question or ask it from a different perspective, one that may give students a better understanding of the question.

- Give hints or cues. Provide enough guidance so that students gradually come up with the answer.

- Provide the answer and ask for elaboration. If a student absolutely cannot come up with the correct answer, provide it for him and then ask him to say it in his own words or to provide another example of the answer.

- Respect the student's option to pass, when appropriate.

7. Vary the positive reinforcement offered when students give the correct response.

Praise is perhaps the most common form of positive reinforcement teachers provide when students give correct responses. There are times, however, when praise can have little effect—or even a negative effect—on students' perceptions of their contributions to the class. For example, students may perceive praise as empty, patronizing, or automatic, especially when they are frequently correct and accustomed to praise; enthusiastic praise of a correct response may communicate to other students that the issue is closed and cut off other answers; some students might be embarrassed when singled out, praised, or otherwise reinforced publicly.

Hunter (1969) *Teach More Faster!*

Brophy (1982) *Classroom Organization and Management*

Brophy & Good (1986) "Teacher Behavior and Student Achievement"

There are alternative ways to respond to correct answers that can reinforce and validate students:

- Rephrase, apply, or summarize students' responses. ("That would also work if. . . .")

- Encourage students to respond to one another. ("What do you think? Is Juan correct?")

- Give praise privately, particularly to students who may be embarrassed by being acknowledged in front of their peers. ("Ian, today in class I was very pleased when you. . . .")

- Challenge the answer or ask for elaboration. ("Devon, that seems to contradict. . . .")

- Specify the criteria for the praise being given so that students understand why they are being praised. ("Barb, that answer helps us to see a new way of. . . .")

- Help students analyze their own answers. ("How did you arrive at that answer?")

- Use your tone of voice to ensure that students understand what is being reinforced.

- Use silence along with nods or other body language, such as eye contact, that encourages students to elaborate on their answers.

8. Structure opportunities for students to work with peers.

Opportunities to work in groups toward a common goal, when structured appropriately, can help students feel accepted by their peers. Be sure to set up groups that help foster positive peer relations and that enhance student achievement. There are a number of strategies that will increase the success of group work:

Johnson, Johnson, & Holubec (1994) *New Circles of Learning*

Slavin (1983) *Cooperative Learning*

Kagan (1994) *Cooperative Learning Structures*

Shaw (1992) *Building Community in the Classroom*

- Teach students the skills necessary for group interactions.

- Identify learning goals in advance and make them very clear for students.

- Monitor the group to suggest additional information, resources, or encouragement as necessary.

- Structure the learning experience so that every student in the group has a responsible role in completing the task.

- Make sure that each student in the group is acquiring the targeted knowledge.

9. Provide opportunities for students to get to know and accept each other.

Some students make friends and are accepted more readily than others. Other students have a difficult time accepting peers who are different from themselves. Take the time to provide opportunities for students to get to know each other, to see that in spite of some apparent differences they are alike in many ways. Encourage them to establish relationships with individuals and groups other than those with whom they already have friendships. Teachers commonly provide opportunities for students to get to know each other at the beginning of the school year. Providing opportunities at other times of the year can have positive effects especially when students understand that the goal is to improve learning for all. Some specific strategies might include the following:

Canfield & Wells (1976) *100 Ways to Enhance Self-concept in the Classroom*

- Ask each student to interview another student at the beginning of the year and then introduce that student to the rest of the class.

- Have students make posters representing their backgrounds, hobbies, and interests. Students might include pictures of themselves from birth to the present. Then hang these posters around the classroom, or ask students to present them to the class.

Smuin (1978) *Turn-ons: 185 Strategies for the Secondary Classroom*

- Encourage all students to share about themselves and their heritage. This activity might be particularly interesting for students if there are others in the class from different countries and cultures.

- Have each student write his or her name on a sheet of paper. Ask them to pass their papers around and write one positive comment on each of the other students' sheets. Encourage students to avoid repeating a comment that is already included on the page. Return the completed "positive-o-grams" to their "owners" to keep.

Whisler & McCombs (1992) *Middle School Advisement Program*

- Have students design and make a "nameplate" that represents their likes and dislikes with a collage, pictures, or drawings. These can be placed on students' tables or desks during the first weeks of school.

- Use structured "get-to-know-you" activities periodically throughout the year.

10. Help students develop their ability to use their own strategies for gaining acceptance from their teachers and peers.

Students need to accept increasing responsibility for gaining acceptance from teachers and peers. However, many students will need opportunities to identify and practice using strategies for gaining acceptance. You might

Carkhuff (1987) *The Art of Helping*

Attitudes & Perceptions

✔ *Helping Students Develop Positive Attitudes and Perceptions About Classroom Climate*

"People develop feelings that they are liked, wanted, acceptable, and able from having been liked, wanted, accepted, and from having been successful."

—Arthur W. Combs

periodically ask students to identify and discuss potential strategies and then record them in a way that can be regularly updated and used (e.g., on bulletin boards or overheard transparencies or in notebooks). Remember to emphasize with students that using strategies to gain acceptance positively influences the learning environment for everyone.

Suggested strategies for students to use in **gaining acceptance from their teachers** include the following:

- If you are developing negative attitudes toward a teacher, make an appointment to meet with him or her one-on-one. Frequently, a personal interaction will establish a more positive relationship.

- Treat teachers with respect and courtesy. When talking with them, make eye contact and use appropriate language.

- If a teacher seems angry or irritable in class, don't take it personally. Teachers are human; they have good days and bad days just like everyone else.

- Work hard. Regardless of your level of achievement, when a teacher perceives you are trying to learn, the relationship between you and the teacher will likely be a positive one.

Suggested strategies for students to use in **gaining acceptance from their peers** include the following:

- Be interested rather than interesting. When you are first getting to know people, spend more time asking them about themselves rather than telling them about yourself.

- Compliment people on their positive characteristics.

- Avoid reminding people about their negative qualities or about bad things that have happened to them.

- Treat people with common courtesy. Treat them as you would like to be treated or as you would treat an honored guest.

Experience a Sense of Comfort and Order

A student's sense of comfort and order in the classroom affects his or her ability to learn. Comfort and order as described here refer to physical comfort, identifiable routines and guidelines for acceptable behavior, and psychological and emotional safety.

A student's sense of comfort in the classroom is affected by such factors as room temperature, the arrangement of furniture, and the amount of physical activity permitted during the school day. Researchers investigating learning styles (e.g., Carbo, Dunn, and Dunn, 1986; McCarthy, 1980, 1990) have found that students define physical comfort in different ways. Some prefer a noise-free room; others prefer music. Some prefer a neat, clutter-free space; others feel more comfortable surrounded by their work-in-progress.

Teachers can draw on the extensive research available on classroom management (e.g., Anderson, Evertson, and Emmer, 1980; Emmer, Evertson, and Anderson, 1980) to guide them in addressing issues about classroom order. This research shows, for example, that explicitly stated and reinforced rules and procedures create a climate that is conducive to learning. If students do not know the parameters of behavior in a learning situation, the environment can become chaotic.

Most educators understand the importance of involving students in making decisions about the classroom climate. When students are involved in decision making, individual needs are more likely to be met. The following subsections cover strategies for establishing a sense of comfort and order in the classroom.

11. Frequently and systematically use activities that involve physical movement.

Many students will be more comfortable if they do not have to remain in one position for a long time. There are many ways to allow—even encourage—movement during regular classroom instruction:

- Periodically take short breaks in which students are allowed to stand up, move about, and stretch.

- Set up classroom tasks that require students to gather information on their own or in small groups, using resources that are away from their desks.

- Systematically switch from activities in which students must work independently at their own desks to activities in which they must organize themselves in small groups in different areas of the room.

- When students' energy level begins to wane, take an exercise break for two to five minutes to change the routine.

> "The physical setting of a high school should nurture a student in much the same way that the clean, safe interior of a home makes the youngster feel comfortable and secure."
>
> —NASSP (1996) *Breaking Ranks: Changing an American Institution,* p. 34.

Carbo, Dunn, & Dunn (1986) *Teaching Students to Read Through Their Individual Learning Styles*

12. Introduce the concept of "bracketing."

Bracketing is a process of maintaining focus and attention by consciously blocking out distractions. In the first step, the learner recognizes that it is time to pay attention. Next, the learner acknowledges his or her distracting thoughts and mentally frames or "brackets" them. Finally, the learner makes a commitment to avoid thinking about the distracting thoughts. Bracketing can be accomplished in a variety of ways. You might suggest to students that they

- Use self-talk. ("I won't think about it now.")

- Designate a later time to think about it. ("I will think about it at the end of class.")

- Mentally picture pushing the distracting thoughts out of their head.

Bracketing contributes to a sense of comfort in the classroom because it helps students to focus on one idea or task at a time. To help students understand and practice bracketing, you might use the following strategies:

- Model bracketing by talking through the process during an appropriate transition time (e.g., after lunch or before recess). You might say that you are "changing channels" in preparation for beginning a new task.

- Provide personal examples and ask students to share their examples of when bracketing was productive or not very useful.

- Share with students examples, testimonials, or videos of well-known, accomplished people (e.g., Olympic athletes, performers, and political leaders) explaining how they have used strategies similar to bracketing to stay focused.

- Use examples from literature in which students might find explicit references or infer that a character bracketed information to persevere or stay focused.

- If a student's distracting thoughts are consuming or urgent, suggest that he focus on the thoughts for a minute or two and then "put them in a box" to retrieve after class. You can use this box figuratively, or you might have a box on your desk for this purpose.

13. Establish and communicate classroom rules and procedures.

Well-articulated classroom rules and procedures are a powerful way of conveying a sense of order to students. This can be accomplished in a number of ways:

- Generate clear rules and standard operating procedures for the classroom (either independently or collaboratively with the class). Figure 1.1 lists some categories for which rules and procedures are commonly specified.

- Have students discuss what rules and procedures they think would be appropriate for the classroom.

- Communicate rules and procedures by discussing their meaning or rationale, providing students with a written list, posting them in the classroom, role playing them, or modeling their use.

- Specify when rules and procedures apply and how they may vary depending on the context (e.g., "At the beginning of class. . . ." or "During exams. . . .").

- When a situation occurs that requires an exception to the rules, acknowledge the change and explain the reasons for the exception.

- When providing students with feedback about their behavior, identify the specific behavior that was consistent with the rules of the class. In addition, let students know how they contributed to their own success and to the success of others.

- Enforce rules and procedures quickly, fairly, and consistently.

✔ *Helping Students Develop Positive Attitudes and Perceptions About Classroom Climate*

Fisher et al. (1978) *Teaching Behaviors, Academic Learning Time and Student Achievement*

Evertson et al. (1981) *Organizing and Managing the Elementary Classroom*

FIGURE 1.1

CATEGORIES FOR CLASSROOM RULES

1. Beginning class
2. Room/school areas
3. Independent work
4. Ending class
5. Interruptions
6. Instructional procedures
7. Noninstructional procedures
8. Work requirements
9. Communicating assignments
10. Checking assignments in class
11. Grading procedures
12. Academic feedback

Maslow (1968) *Toward a Psychology of Being*

Edmonds (1982) "Programs of School Improvement: An Overview"

Carbo, Dunn, & Dunn (1986) *Teaching Students to Read Through Their Individual Learning Styles*

Hanson, Silver, & Strong (1986) *Teaching Styles and Strategies*

14. Be aware of malicious teasing or threats inside or outside of the classroom, and take steps to stop such behavior.

Personal safety is a primary concern for everyone. It is difficult to learn when you feel physically or psychologically unsafe. There are several things you can do to help your students feel safe:

- Establish clear policies about the physical safety of students. The clearer you can be about policies regarding physical safety, the stronger the message will be to students. Policies and rules should include a description of the consequences of threatening or harming others.

- Make sure your students know that you are looking out for their safety and well-being. Be certain that they understand that you will take action on their behalf.

- Pinpoint the students who are threatening or teasing others and those who are being threatened or teased. Talk with the students to find out why this is happening.

- Occasionally patrol the perimeter of the school, looking for threatening aspects of the environment. Check areas within the school where students could be threatened (e.g., bathrooms or hallways).

- If necessary, meet with parents to discuss problems.

- Establish an environment in which "put downs" are not acceptable.

15. Have students identify their own standards for comfort and order.

Teachers may spend much of their time in their classrooms prompting students to meet agreed-upon standards for comfort and order. However, the goal is for students to learn to identify their own standards for comfort and order based on their preferences and understandings about accepted social behavior.

Some classroom activities can help students take on more responsibility for their own comfort and order, while being attentive to the needs of those around them as well:

- Ask students to describe in some detail how they would arrange their personal space (e.g., their desk area or work space) to achieve a sense of comfort and order. This description might include a checklist that students could refer to later. From time to time, ask students to assess the extent to which they are keeping their personal space up to the standards they have identified.

- Periodically place a group of students in charge of "room arrangement." Make it the group's job to enhance the appearance or arrangement of the classroom in some way.

- Discuss with students how to change their standards for comfort and order depending on the situation. For example, a student may need the environment to be very quiet while studying but may enjoy music while working on an art project. You might prompt students to examine different activities (e.g., doing homework, cleaning up a room, and fixing a bike) in order to find out what they need to make themselves comfortable.

- Suggest that students ask other people to describe their needs or strategies for creating comfort and order. Sometimes ideas from others can validate strategies or help students generate new ones.

Classroom Examples

The following classroom examples are offered to stimulate reflection on how to apply the ideas covered in this section of Dimension 1 in your classroom.

Each year Mrs. Frost developed classroom rules and had her elementary students write them on individual tablemats, which they then decorated to their liking. Although the tablemats were meant to help students experience ownership of the rules, it seemed to her that she was the only one who "owned" them. The students were constantly finding new ways to bend them, and much of Mrs. Frost's time was spent enforcing them. Feeling frustrated, she talked with a colleague who suggested that she allow students to devise their own set of rules and decide on the consequences for breaking them. Two days later, Mrs. Frost found her colleague to share how well it worked. "The students added rules I had not thought of," she explained, "and some of their consequences are harsher than mine. In addition, one child came up with a great title for the list: Respect yourself, respect others, and respect property."

• • •

Mr. Vosburg decided he needed some new ways to get more students to participate in classroom discussion. Many students seemed to "fade into the background" during discussions or to offer ideas only when called on. After some reflection, he realized that he knew many strategies that addressed this problem; he just did not use them very often. He decided to make a conscious effort to use these strategies, such as recording students' ideas on the board and writing their names next to the ideas, remembering students' ideas and referring to them at a later time (e.g., "Yesterday, Colleen said that she disagreed with. . . ."), and challenging students ideas more vigorously, especially with students who would find these challenges more reinforcing than praise (e.g., "But wait, Sandy. That doesn't make sense if. . . ."). As Mr. Vosburg had hoped, when students realized that their ideas were making an impression on him, they began to participate more enthusiastically and thoughtfully.

• • •

Mr. Berger noticed that students in his high school history classes often referred to each other as "that kid sitting in the back" or "the guy with the vest on" or "that girl who always wears a ponytail." He decided to create some opportunities for students to get to know one another in the hopes that in the future they would interact more frequently. He started by having students play a rhyming "name game," one that is usually played in elementary school. The students thought it was funny to play a "kid's" game, but they also began to know and use each other's names. Mr. Berger was very pleased when he noticed that once students began to address each other by name, they were more likely to ask each other for information and check with each other when they needed some help.

Helping Students Develop Positive Attitudes and Perceptions About Classroom Tasks

The second area of attitudes and perceptions is related to the tasks that learners are asked to perform. First, learners must perceive that tasks are valuable or interesting or they will not put much effort into them. Second, students must believe they have the ability and resources to complete tasks or they will not attempt the tasks because the risk is too great. Third, students must clearly understand what they are being asked to do; if students do not understand a task but try it anyway, their efforts probably will be unfocused and ineffective. The following strategies are a few of the many ways in which a teacher can help students develop and maintain positive attitudes and perceptions about tasks.

1. Help students understand that learning is influenced by attitudes and perceptions related to classroom tasks.

It is important for students to understand that their attitudes and perceptions about classroom tasks significantly influence what they learn from those tasks. It is also important for them to understand that maintaining positive attitudes and perceptions toward tasks is a shared responsibility between teachers and students. If students develop these understandings, they are more likely to appreciate the efforts teachers make to keep students' attitudes and perceptions as positive as possible. They also are more likely to develop and use their own strategies for maintaining positive attitudes and perceptions as they work on assigned tasks.

Learning is influenced by the degree to which students perceive tasks as valuable and interesting, believe that they have the ability and resources to complete tasks, and understand and are clear about tasks. There are many ways to help students understand these influential attitudes and perceptions:

- Share with students how your own learning (from kindergarten to where you are today) has been influenced by your attitudes and perceptions related to tasks you have been assigned. Share strategies you use, or have used, to maintain positive attitudes and perceptions and thus to improve your learning. Then ask students to share their experiences and the strategies that have worked to enhance their learning.

One principal uses Back to School Night as an opportunity to present the Dimensions of Learning model. He highlights the faculty's role in helping students to acquire, integrate, extend, and use knowledge and elicits parents' help in enhancing students' attitudes toward learning. Throughout the year, the school newsletter includes suggestions for parents to enhance students' attitudes.

- Present hypothetical situations in which students' attitudes are negatively influencing learning and ask students to discuss how learning might be enhanced if the situation were resolved.

- Help students become aware of how fictional, historical, or famous people maintain positive attitudes toward tasks. People in newspaper articles or characters in books, films, or television programs can provide opportunities to discuss both positive and negative examples.

Perceive Tasks as Valuable and Interesting

2. Establish a sense of academic trust.

One way of ensuring that students perceive their assigned tasks as valuable is to establish with them a relationship referred to as "academic trust." This means that students consider tasks to be valuable because they trust that the teacher only assigns tasks that are valuable. In an environment of academic trust, students are less likely to challenge tasks that they do not immediately see as valuable because they have the confidence that they will eventually understand why the tasks are important.

Like any trusting relationship, academic trust can only be developed over time. It requires that students have consistent experiences with teachers in which they eventually see the value of assigned tasks.

3. Help students understand how specific knowledge is valuable.

If students do not initially see value in learning about specific knowledge, sometimes all they need is an explanation of why the knowledge is valuable. For example, it may be difficult for students to understand why learning about the Cuban missile crisis is important. However, the teacher might use the details of the crisis to help students understand how the relationship between the United States and the former Soviet Union has evolved over time.

There are a number of other ways to help students understand the value of specific knowledge:

- Explain to students how this information will be useful to them later as they learn even more complex concepts, make interdisciplinary connections, or as they complete a task. (You may want to "preview" an upcoming task, pointing out how the knowledge they are learning will be useful as they complete the task.)

"Teachers should have the ability to develop activities for students that—while embodying the learning objectives—are clearly linked to intellectual products that the students value."

—NASSP (1996)
Breaking Ranks: Changing an American Institution, p. 15.

- Help students relate the information to real-life experiences in which the information can be used.

- Have students identify and share with one another why *they* think specific information or tasks might be worthwhile or important to their learning.

4. Use a variety of ways to engage students in classroom tasks.

Few would dispute that when students are highly engaged in tasks, they learn more. Constructing tasks that are interesting and engaging is a challenge, especially given the diversity among learners in terms of interests and abilities. There are numerous ways to construct and present tasks that can increase the numbers of students who find the task interesting:

- Construct tasks that are "authentic," that is, related to life outside of school or in the workplace. Students who clearly see the relevance and use of tasks are more likely to be engaged in them.

- Make sure that tasks represent an intellectual challenge. It is not uncommon to observe students, at all levels of achievement, becoming immediately immersed in seemingly unimportant tasks (e.g., solving a riddle, looking for a solution to a hypothetical situation, or clarifying a confusing idea) simply because they are engaged in a perceived challenge. Classroom tasks can have a similar effect if the intellectual challenge is there.

- Allow for student choices. There are a number of ways to provide students with choices yet maintain the academic rigor of a task. For example, you might give students several tasks or product ideas from which to choose in order to demonstrate specific knowledge; you also might allow students to select their own specific content to exemplify or illustrate a generalization or principle.

- Exhibit a sense of enthusiasm about the material you present. If you are excited about the content, students may share your enthusiasm.

- Provide anecdotes and interesting "asides" related to the information being presented. Although students may not initially be interested in the content, you might pique their interest with an anecdote.

Brookover et al. (1979) *School Social Systems and Student Achievement*

Strong, Silver, & Robinson (1995) "What Do Students Want?"

Wlodkowski & Ginsberg (1995) *Diversity and Motivation*

McCombs & Whisler (1997) *The Learner-Centered Classroom and School*

Markus & Ruvulo (1990) "Possible Selves: Personalized Representations of Goals"

Markus & Wurf (1987) "The Dynamic Self-concept: A Social Psychological Perspective"

5. Create classroom tasks that relate to students' interests and goals.

Students are more likely to perceive tasks as valuable if the tasks somehow relate to their interests and goals. Consequently, teachers often seek out information about students' interests and goals as a way to help them see value and to engage them in learning. For example, if a teacher presenting a unit on ratios and proportions knows that students in her class are interested in music and sports, she could explain how ratios and proportions are used in music performances and sports events.

Over time, teachers might want to give students the opportunity to generate their own tasks based on their personal interests. For example, after introducing three types of graphs in a math lesson, the teacher might have students select something of interest to them to illustrate the use of the three types. One student might select the shooting percentages of her favorite basketball players; another might graph the number of months that various books are on the best-seller list.

Teachers can find out about students' interests and goals through ongoing conversations or by directly eliciting this information. Figure 1.2 shows an example of an interest inventory that teachers might ask students to complete.

FIGURE 1.2

STUDENT INVENTORY

1. If you could be anything in the world, what would it be?
   _____
   _____

2. Where would you like to go if you could go anywhere?
   _____
   _____

3. If you could live during any period in history, when would it be?
   _____
   _____

4. What projects are you currently working on?
   _____
   _____

5. What projects would you like to work on?
   _____
   _____

Believe They Have the Ability and Resources to Complete Tasks

6. Provide appropriate feedback.

The kind of feedback students receive as they are working on tasks can have a significant influence on the extent to which they believe they can be successful. Many good teachers are accustomed to giving students the kind of feedback that encourages them and expresses confidence in their ability (e.g., "Good job.", "Keep going.", "I knew you could do it.", "Don't stop now."). However, at times students may need more specific feedback that identifies exactly what they did well and what they need to improve. This may require breaking the task into smaller parts and helping students see their strengths and weaknesses in each part. For example:

- "Your opening paragraph clearly states the thesis of the essay. Your closing summarizes nicely. Let's look at the support offered in your third paragraph."

- "The stance you take before you swing provides exactly the stability you need. Don't change your swing, but as you lean back. . . ."

- "This part of the assignment was strong. Because you went back and checked your answers, you. . . ."

The type of feedback needed varies as a function of the specific student, the task, and even the mood of the day. However, the purpose of feedback is always to build students' confidence in their ability to complete challenging, complex assignments.

Brophy & Good (1986) "Teacher Behavior and Student Achievement"

7. Teach students to use positive self-talk.

One of the most powerful ways in which students can develop positive attitudes about their abilities is to replace their negative self-talk with positive self-talk. The first step in this process is to become aware of negative self-talk. Students might keep a journal for a few days, noting all the negative things they say about themselves and about school (e.g., "I dislike this class. I can't do this very well."). Once they have identified specific negative comments they make to themselves in specific situations, they can try to change their negative self-talk to positive self-talk (e.g., "I enjoy this class. I'm good at it."). It is important to note that students initially do not have to believe their positive self-talk for it to help them be successful.

Covington (1985) "Strategic Thinking and the Fear of Failure"

Covington et al. (1974) *The Productive Thinking Program*

Whisler & Marzano (1988) *Dare to Imagine*

"Your mind can amaze your body if you just keep telling yourself, I can do it, I can do it, I can do it."

—Jon Erickson

Covington (1985) "Strategic Thinking and the Fear of Failure"

Covington et al. (1974) *The Productive Thinking Program*

Hunter (1982) *Mastery Teaching*

Covey (1990) *The 7 Habits of Highly Effective People*

8. Help students recognize that they have the abilities to complete a particular task.

When students believe that they do not have the abilities needed to complete a task, sometimes they simply need to understand that, in fact, they do. This means more than being a cheerleader for students; it means helping them understand that they have the knowledge. Students may be overwhelmed and distracted from the knowledge embedded in the task, particularly when tasks are presented in complex contexts or are long-term projects. There are a number of ways to help them to recognize their own knowledge:

- Explain more clearly exactly what knowledge is needed for the task.

- Provide students with evidence that they have demonstrated the knowledge in the past (e.g., through work in a portfolio or scores on previous assignments).

- Break the task into smaller parts in a way that helps students see that they have the knowledge for each step and, therefore, are able to complete the task.

- Provide students with a spontaneous miniquiz in which they are asked to demonstrate the knowledge in a simpler context. When they are successful, refocus them on the more complex task.

9. Help students understand that believing in their ability to complete a task includes believing that they have the ability to get the help and the resources needed.

When students are encouraged to believe in their abilities, it is possible for them to misunderstand and think that they are only successful when they can complete a task on their own. It is important for all students to understand that both in school and in life, identifying and seeking help appropriately is a characteristic of a confident learner.

Students at all ability levels may need prompting and modeling to improve their abilities in this area; however, interestingly, high-achieving students may need even more. High achievers can put heavy pressure on themselves to be successful without anyone's help. In fact, they may perceive seeking help as a weakness. Take and make opportunities to discuss, model, and reinforce the act of seeking appropriate help to complete a task.

Understand and Be Clear About Tasks

10. Help students be clear about the directions and demands of the task.

Although the need for students to be clear about the directions and demands of the task seems obvious, achieving this clarity can be difficult. Ask parents who help their children with homework and you will hear examples of their frustrated attempts to understand tasks, not only when their only source is their children's interpretation of the directions, but also when they have the assignment sheet in hand. Experienced teachers who know that completing the task as assigned will enhance students' learning use techniques to ensure clarity, including the following:

- Ask friends, colleagues, or family members to read assignment sheets and explain their understanding of the assignments before giving them to students.

- As you review directions with students, have them mentally rehearse the more complex parts to help them identify and clear up confusions.

- Have students explain the tasks to each other, articulating and clearing up confusions.

- Ask students if they understand what they are being asked to do.

- Show students examples of work turned in by other students.

11. Provide students with clarity about the knowledge that the task addresses.

Sometimes students are asked to engage in tasks without knowing what knowledge the task is requiring them to use. It is possible for students to complete tasks by focusing more on the product to be handed in than on the knowledge being used. This might result in the task having little positive effect on learning. For example, students making a miniature colonial quilt may enjoy making the quilt but lose sight of the fact that they are developing an understanding of how people use available resources to survive. In short, teachers need to ask themselves what knowledge a task is intended to teach and then communicate this clearly to students so that they know what they are supposed to be learning as a result of doing the task.

Emmer, Evertson, & Anderson (1980) "Effective Management at the Beginning of the School Year"

12. Provide students with clear expectations of performance levels for tasks.

To be successful learners, students need to know what standards of performance are expected of them. As students mature and grow as learners, they will learn to generate their own personal standards for excellence. However, teachers need to provide performance standards to students when they are beginning a task so that they know and understand the criteria others will use to evaluate their work.

Students also need to understand the characteristics of performances that exceed the standards and be able to describe those performances that do not meet the standards. There are a number of formats that can be used to communicate these criteria to students, the most common of which are checklists and rubrics. An example of each of these is provided in Figure 1.3.

FIGURE 1.3

SAMPLE CHECKLIST AND RUBRIC: TERM PAPER

Checklist (Sample Items)	Completed
cover page with title	✔
bibliography	✔
appropriate page setup: • 1-inch margins • 12-point font	✔ ✔

Rubric

4 Thesis was clearly stated and was supported with information and examples that reflected insight into its meaning; selected examples and information strongly elaborated on the thesis and added an original perspective.

3 Thesis was clearly stated and supported with appropriate information and examples.

2 Thesis was stated but parts of it were unclear and/or some information and examples offered in support were not clearly related to the thesis or reflected misconceptions or confusions.

1 Thesis was unclear and/or information and examples offered did not support the thesis.

Classroom Examples

The following classroom examples are offered to stimulate reflection on how to apply the ideas covered in this section of Dimension 1 in your classroom.

Mr. Snow was tired of hearing that teachers should try harder to link assignments to children's interests. He had a great deal of content to cover and hated those "fluffy" units that had no content, that simply engaged students in self-exploration. He also was not going to dress up like George Washington and put on a show for students like one teacher did. With this attitude, he reluctantly attended the required inservice on the topic of student attitudes. To his surprise, he realized that he had misinterpreted the message. The presenter explained that linking assignments to students' interest should not compromise academic rigor: "Just have them find examples of grammar rules in articles about topics they like. Have them create three kinds of graphs using data they care about. Ask them to apply scientific principles to situations they see every day. Have them create analogies to show, for example, how the cell is like other systems they see around them. Always hold students accountable for the knowledge but let them help you identify ways to make it more interesting." Mr. Snow of course had used many of the suggested techniques in the past, but he acknowledged to himself that he had not done it as much lately. He also admitted that he could probably use some new ideas.

• • •

One of Mrs. Fitzsimmons's brightest students experienced intense anxiety when he took tests and when he was called on in class. In an attempt to help him, Mrs. Fitzsimmons suggested that he use the strategy of positive self-talk. She even provided him with a process: (1) keep a journal to record the negative self-talk you notice before, during, and after a difficult task; (2) identify and write down positive self-talk that replaces the negative messages; and (3) practice saying the positive things to yourself during tasks. The student listened to Mrs. Fitzsimmons respectfully as she explained her idea, but it was clear that he was not persuaded to try the process. Mrs. Fitzsimmons was disappointed that she had not helped him. However, two years later, the student came to visit her. After some polite small talk, he shared with her that his anxieties had gradually worsened. Recently he had become so desperate that he tried the process she had suggested to him so long ago. "I just wanted you to know that it's working!" he explained. "I came back to say thanks." Mrs. Fitzsimmons smiled as she remembered how often teaching involves delayed gratification.

• • •

The students in Mr. Young's class had just turned in their projects for the semester. As he looked them over, Mr. Young became concerned and disappointed. Although it appeared that some students had worked very hard, most of the projects were nothing more than fancy products that, at best, were related only tangentially to the knowledge he had been trying to emphasize in the semester. His first reaction was that he could not give students low grades, inasmuch as they had worked hard. But then he decided to get tough and send the message that he would not compromise his standards.

The day the students received their grades, most of them were upset. When Mr. Young explained why he had given the low grades, one student responded, "That isn't fair. We did what we thought you wanted." At first, Mr. Young was defensive. Why did students have to be told that their projects had to demonstrate knowledge? But as he listened to the students' complaints, he had to acknowledge that he had not been clear when assigning the projects. After more discussion, the students and Mr. Young reached a compromise: In the future, he would try to clearly specify what knowledge the students should be demonstrating with their projects; the students agreed they would put more energy into demonstrating knowledge than into creating a "pretty project."

Unit Planning: Dimension 1

Planning for Dimension 1 requires asking and answering the following overarching question:

What will be done to help students develop positive attitudes and perceptions?

What follows is a step-by-step process that will guide you in answering this question. Each step asks you to answer a key question or provide specific information. There is a space on the planning guide (see page 42) in which to record your ideas, notes, decisions, and planned activities. A sample planning guide has been filled out for a hypothetical social studies unit about Colorado. (This unit topic was chosen because, with some changes, it could be used for a unit about any state or region and at any developmental level. You will find the entire unit in the planning section at the end of Chapter 6, "Putting It All Together.")

Step 1

> Are there any goals or concerns related to students' **attitudes and perceptions**
> - in general?
> - related to this specific unit?

To answer these questions, do the following:

- Identify any concerns and goals, *in general*, that you may have. For example, perhaps students recently have been expressing their frustrations about the relevance of their schoolwork, a particular student has given up trying, or you have noticed that lately you have been overly concerned with content coverage and less concerned with students.

- Identify goals and concerns that you may have *related to this specific unit*. For example, perhaps you know that the assignments in the upcoming unit are going to be challenging for students or your experience tells you that students might not find the topics immediately interesting.

Step 2

> What will be done to address these goals or concerns?

This question has two parts as follows:

Step 2a

> Specifically, will anything be done to help students ...

Classroom Climate

- feel accepted by teachers and peers?

- experience a sense of comfort and order?

Classroom Tasks

- perceive tasks as valuable and interesting?

- believe they have the ability and resources to complete tasks?

- understand and be clear about tasks?

Answer this question by identifying the aspect of attitudes and perceptions that will help you address your goals and concerns.

Step 2b

> Describe what will be done.

Describe the specific activities, experiences, and strategies that you will use to address your goals and concerns. You might want to consider the strategies suggested in this section of the manual:

Classroom Climate

1. Help students understand that attitudes and perceptions related to classroom climate influence learning.

2. Establish a relationship with each student in the class.

3. Monitor and attend to your own attitudes.

4. Engage in equitable and positive classroom behavior.

5. Recognize and provide for students' individual differences.

6. Respond positively to students' incorrect responses or lack of response.

7. Vary the positive reinforcement offered when students give the correct response.

8. Structure opportunities for students to work with peers.

9. Provide opportunities for students to get to know and accept each other.

10. Help students develop their ability to use their own strategies for gaining acceptance from their teachers and peers.

11. Frequently and systematically use activities that involve physical movement.

12. Introduce the concept of "bracketing."

13. Establish and communicate classroom rules and procedures.

14. Be aware of malicious teasing or threats inside or outside of the classroom, and take steps to stop such behavior.

15. Have students identify their own standards for comfort and order.

Classroom Tasks

1. Help students understand that learning is influenced by attitudes and perceptions related to classroom tasks.

2. Establish a sense of academic trust.

3. Help students understand how specific knowledge is valuable.

4. Use a variety of ways to engage students in classroom tasks.

5. Create classroom tasks that relate to students' interests and goals.

6. Provide appropriate feedback.

7. Teach students to use positive self-talk.

8. Help students recognize that they have the abilities to complete a particular task.

9. Help students understand that believing in their ability to complete a task includes believing that they have the ability to get the help and the resources needed.

10. Help students be clear about the directions and demands of the task.

11. Provide students with clarity about the knowledge that the task addresses.

12. Provide students with clear expectations of performance levels for tasks.

Dimension 1 Planning Guide

Unit: _Colorado_

Step 1

Are there any goals or concerns related to students' _attitudes and perceptions_
- in general?
- related to this specific unit?

Step 2

What will be done to address these goals or concerns?

Specifically, will anything be done to help students. . .	Describe what will be done.
Classroom Climate ☑ feel accepted by teachers and peers? ☑ experience a sense of comfort and order?	_I am going to work on slowing down and giving students a chance to answer my questions; I need to do more restating and rephrasing of the questions._ _I will go over the rules of bus behavior and the general rules for field trips; I think I'll have students generate some additional rules and suggestions for making the field trip successful._
Classroom Tasks ☑ perceive tasks as valuable and interesting? ☐ believe they have the ability and resources to complete tasks? ☐ understand and be clear about tasks?	_The assignments will give students the opportunity to apply knowledge to regions of their choice._

I think I have been in a rut lately when responding both to students' incorrect answers and to their correct or thoughtful answers.

The last field trip was not fun for anyone; it seemed unorganized and many rules for bus behavior were forgotten.

Students might be getting tired of studying Colorado.

Dimension 2

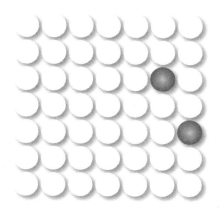

Dimension 2
Acquire and Integrate Knowledge

Introduction

Before planning to help students acquire and integrate knowledge, it is important to clarify the type of knowledge that is the target of the lesson or unit. Many cognitive psychologists believe that knowledge can be organized into two basic categories: *declarative knowledge* and *procedural knowledge*. Here are some examples of each type of knowledge:

Declarative Knowledge

The learner *knows or understands*

- democracy
- a numerator
- an amoeba
- the conventions of punctuation
- the rules of basketball
- that when oppression meets resistance, conflict results
- that George Washington was the first president of the United States

Procedural Knowledge

The learner *is able to*

- add and subtract
- write a paragraph
- shoot free throws
- read a bar graph
- set up an experiment
- search a database
- read music

Many districts are working to identify academic standards and benchmarks, which specify the declarative and procedural knowledge that students should have by the end of grades 2, 5, 8, and 12. This work then serves as a resource for teachers as they plan curricular units that specify the content knowledge that students must acquire and integrate.

Learning *procedural knowledge* requires the learner to perform a process or to demonstrate a skill, that is, to take some kind of action. Some of the actions are primarily mental (e.g., add and subtract); some are primarily physical (e.g., shoot free throws). Whether mental or physical, when we perform these actions, we go through a series of steps: first we do one thing, then another, then another. This is the case even with complex processes like writing, reading a bar graph, and setting up an experiment. Although the sequence of steps is not always linear, there are steps that we must perform in the skills and processes that make up procedural knowledge.

In contrast, learning *declarative knowledge* does not require the learner to perform a series of steps with the mind or body. This kind of information is information that the learner must know or understand. When we think of democracy, we do not perform one step first, then another, and then another. Rather, we recall the attributes of democracy (e.g., one person, one vote; decisions are made by the group versus by an individual). Similarly, when we think of an amoeba, we think about its characteristics (e.g., it is a one-celled animal), and when we think of the conventions of punctuation, we think of a set of rules used in the written language (e.g., capitalize the first letter of the first word in each sentence). In short, declarative knowledge is the information—facts, concepts, and generalizations—within content knowledge.

The Importance of Understanding the Nature of Knowledge

Anderson (1990) *Cognitive Psychology and Its Implications*

Anderson (1995) *Learning and Memory*

Although studying the distinctions between the types of knowledge is somewhat of a technical endeavor, many educators would argue that it is necessary in order to effectively plan and implement curriculum, instruction, and assessment. Clearly, to help students learn, we must not only understand the learning process, we must understand the nature of knowledge. We must be as good at identifying the knowledge students are learning as we are at planning interesting educational activities. We must understand how teaching and assessing declarative knowledge is different from teaching and assessing procedural knowledge. We must make informed decisions about what knowledge is worth acquiring and integrating, extending and refining, and using meaningfully. The following explanations and descriptions are offered as a resource for those who are unfamiliar with these distinctions and, especially, for those who are using the Dimensions of Learning model as a structure for planning and implementing curriculum, instruction, and assessment.

The Relationship Between Declarative and Procedural Knowledge

Because we as educators are concerned with students' ability to use the knowledge that they are learning, helping students acquire procedural knowledge is sometimes seen as the ultimate goal of education. This reflects the common misconception that procedural knowledge is the most important type of knowledge, a conclusion that perhaps results because examples of procedural knowledge typically begin with the phrase "is able to" and because the uses of procedural knowledge are apparent (e.g., it is easy to identify how we use the ability to write a paragraph). In addition, people tend to think that if students are involved in an activity or something "hands-on," procedural knowledge is being used. Activities and hands-on experiences (e.g., making a model of the solar system) are often methods that are used to help students learn or demonstrate declarative knowledge. The uses of declarative knowledge, although sometimes not as apparent, are numerous and important.

Most tasks involving the use of knowledge require both declarative and procedural knowledge. Completing a decision-making, problem-solving, or experimental-inquiry task, for example, requires learners to perform the steps of the specific process (procedural knowledge). But it is the declarative knowledge—what learners know or understand about the topic—that often is the primary factor in students' successfully completing tasks and obtaining useful results. For example, students who are asked to conduct an experiment to determine the makeup of an unknown substance in chemistry class must be *skilled* in the scientific process. However, their research will be significantly influenced by their *understanding* of the properties of chemicals.

Acquiring a skill without understanding the various concepts related to the skill could result in students' acquiring knowledge that is of limited use. For example, if students are skilled at solving linear and quadratic equations, but do not understand the distinctive characteristics of these equations or when to use a specific type of equation, they are missing the critical knowledge— the declarative knowledge—that is necessary to know how and when to use these skills.

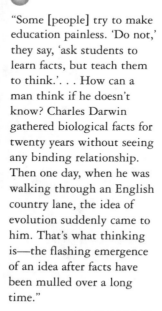

Levels of Generality and the Organization of Knowledge

Within the general categories of declarative and procedural knowledge, there are even finer distinctions that can guide the process of identifying the knowledge that all students should have the opportunity to learn. We can understand these distinctions by examining how declarative and procedural knowledge can be organized to create a hierarchy from specific to general knowledge.

Declarative Knowledge

Declarative knowledge can be organized into patterns that highlight different relationships among pieces of information. Organizational patterns are used to ensure that students do not see information as isolated pieces, sometimes call "infobits." When, instead, students see that the pieces of information can be connected to form patterns, they are more likely to use and retain the information. Six of the most common organizational patterns are explained below.

1. Descriptions. At the most specific level, declarative knowledge can be organized as *descriptions* of specific persons, places, ideas, things, or events. Information might be organized as simple descriptions when students are initially learning the meaning of *vocabulary terms* or when they are gathering key *facts* related to very specific content knowledge.

> *Vocabulary Terms.* Knowing a vocabulary term means understanding the meaning of a word at a very general level. This means organizing information to show the most important characteristics of the word as well as to identify some examples or experiences that further describe it. In other words, students need to have enough information to describe the word accurately, but at a somewhat surface level of understanding, and have no serious misconceptions about its meaning.

> *Facts.* Facts can be organized to describe very specific persons, places, living and nonliving things, and events. They commonly articulate information such as the following:

- characteristics of a specific person (e.g., The fictitious character of Robin Hood lived in Sherwood Forest.)

- characteristics of a specific place (e.g., Denver has a very dry climate.)

- characteristics of specific living and nonliving things (e.g., My dog, Tuffy, is a golden retriever; the Empire State Building is more than 100 stories high.)

- characteristics of a specific event (e.g., Construction began on the Leaning Tower of Pisa in 1174.)

2. Time Sequences. Important events that occur between two specific points in time can be organized into a *time sequence.* For example, the events from a story or biography can be organized into a time sequence.

3. Process/Cause-Effect Relationships. Process/cause-effect relationships organize information into a causal network leading to a specific outcome or into a sequence of steps leading to a specific product. The information that explains how we digest food, for example, can be organized into a process pattern. The events leading to the fall of the Roman Empire can be organized into a causal network.

4. Episodes. Episodes are specific events that have (1) a setting (e.g., a particular time and place), (2) specific participants, (3) a particular duration, (4) a specific sequence of events, and (5) a particular cause and effect. For example, "Watergate" could be organized as an episode if it is important for students to know the facts about the time and place, how long it lasted, who was involved, the sequence of events, the causes, and the specific effects on the country.

5. Generalizations/Principles. Generalizations are statements for which examples can be provided. "Mysteries often use the technique of foreshadowing" is a generalization. *Principles* are generalizations that articulate rules or relationships that can be applied to a number of specific situations. "Water seeks its own level" is a scientific principle. In some cases, it is easy to confuse generalizations with facts. Facts identify characteristics of specific persons, places, living and nonliving things, and events, whereas generalizations make statements about *classes or categories* of persons, places, living and nonliving things, and events. In addition, generalizations identify characteristics about abstractions; specifically, information about abstractions is always stated in the form of generalizations. The following are examples of the various types of generalizations:

"We're drowning in information and starving for knowledge."

—Rutherford D. Rogers

- characteristics of classes of persons (e.g., It takes at least two years of training to become a fireman.)

- characteristics of classes of places (e.g., Large cities have high crime rates.)

- characteristics of classes of living and nonliving things (e.g., Golden retrievers are good hunting dogs; firearms are the subject of great debate.)

- characteristics of classes of events (e.g., The Super Bowl is one of the premier sporting events of the year.)

- characteristics of abstractions (e.g., Love is one of the most powerful human emotions.)

6. Concepts. Concepts, the most general way of thinking about knowledge, are commonly single words or phrases that label entire classes or categories of persons, places, living and nonliving things, and events (e.g., *dictatorship, civil rights, equilibrium, perspective, artificial intelligence*, and *poetry*). Whereas generalizations are statements about general classes or categories, concepts are words or phrases that label the general classes or categories. "Governments are established to both regulate and provide services" is a generalization. *Government* is a concept.

Because concepts can be confused with vocabulary terms, it might be useful to examine the distinctions between them. The difference between concepts and vocabulary terms is in the approach used to teach them. If *dictators*, for example, were approached as a simple vocabulary term, students would be expected to have a general, but accurate, understanding of what the word means. In other words, students could generate mental images of the word or connect it to experiences in which the word applies. However, if the word were approached as a concept, students would be expected to develop an in-depth understanding of the word. This would include being able to articulate the key characteristics of the concept and being able to generate a number of examples that illustrate each characteristic. Students would need to understand, for example, that one characteristic of dictators is that they tend to silence or persecute their opposition. They should then be able to provide examples of dictators, such as Mussolini and Hitler, who imprisoned or banished their dissenters.

The ways of organizing declarative knowledge described above are listed in an order that represents a hierarchy, from the most specific to the most general. This level of generality refers to the degree to which the knowledge transfers, that is, the degree to which it can be applied to many different, specific situations. If, for example, students are studying a concept, such as *culture*, which is at the highest level of generality, this general information about culture will help them organize and therefore understand specific information about the cultures of many different countries. It will also help them organize and understand specific information about the cultures of organizations. If, however, students are studying facts, such as the specific characteristics of the Empire State Building, this information will not necessarily help them when they are learning specific facts about other buildings, the Taj Mahal, for example.

Procedural Knowledge

The terms *skills* and *processes* are commonly used to identify types of procedural knowledge. Although they are not part of a strict hierarchy, skills and processes do represent levels of generality of procedural knowledge. A skill typically refers to a specific set of steps performed in a fairly strict order and, ideally, without much conscious thought. Adding, subtracting, typing, and strumming a guitar are examples of skills. A process is a more general set of steps that is performed with more conscious thought and careful consideration of what needs to be done next. Skills might be embedded within the steps of a process. In fact, the most general processes, called *macroprocesses*, describe procedural knowledge that is commonly comprised of a number of skills. Reading for comprehension, driving a car, and giving a speech are examples of macroprocesses.

When specifying the procedural knowledge that students are to learn in a specific lesson or unit, identifying only general processes is not sufficient. One goal of a unit might be, for example, to help students learn to read for comprehension. However, reading is such a general process that more specific procedural knowledge also needs to be designated; for example, students might be learning to create mental pictures as they read or to figure out the meaning of a word they do not know. As is true of declarative knowledge, the more clearly the procedural knowledge is specified, the more likely it is that students will acquire that knowledge.

Acquiring and Integrating Declarative and Procedural Knowledge

Understanding these two types of knowledge—declarative and procedural—not only influences how teachers identify knowledge for lessons and units, it also should help them select appropriate instructional strategies. Different strategies are appropriate for each type of knowledge because students learn each type differently. Learning declarative knowledge requires three phases: *constructing meaning*, *organizing*, and *storing*. Learning procedural knowledge requires phases that are somewhat parallel with those in declarative knowledge: *constructing models*, *shaping*, and *internalizing*. The relationships among the phases within each type are different, as represented in Figures 2.1 and 2.2. The emphasis that you place on the various phases can vary greatly depending on the specific goals you set for the lesson or unit. More detailed explanations of each phase, along with suggestions for instruction and planning, are included in the remainder of this chapter. A discussion of assessment for all of the dimensions can be found in Chapter 6, "Putting It All Together."

FIGURE 2.1

THE PHASES OF DECLARATIVE KNOWLEDGE

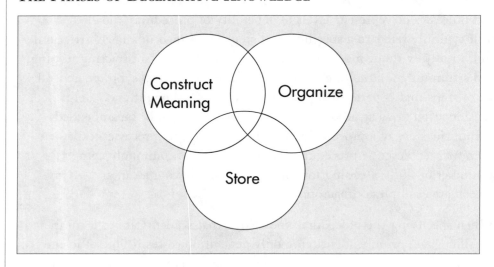

FIGURE 2.2

THE PHASES OF PROCEDURAL KNOWLEDGE

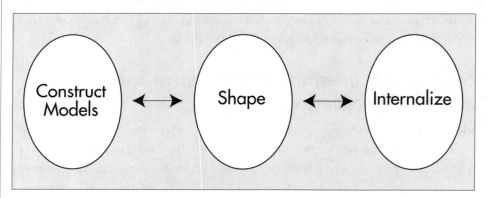

Dimension 2
Acquire & Integrate Knowledge

*Helping Students Acquire
and Integrate Declarative
Knowledge*
✔ *Construct Meaning*

Helping Students Acquire and Integrate Declarative Knowledge

As explained in the introduction to this dimension, declarative knowledge includes information the learner must know or understand. Knowing and understanding requires the learner both to acquire new information and integrate that information with what has been previously learned. This process of acquisition and integration has been the topic of much theorizing and experimentation in an attempt to understand how to help students learn more effectively. Although there is still much that is not understood, the three phases—construct meaning, organize, and store—define more precisely what the learner must do to be successful. The explanations of these phases and the accompanying strategies should help teachers to plan experiences that will lead to more efficient and effective learning.

Construct Meaning for Declarative Knowledge

An important phase in learning declarative knowledge is constructing meaning. Experienced educators know that if students are to understand the information they are receiving, they must actively do something "in their heads." Students must construct meaning by recalling prior knowledge and linking it with new knowledge, making and verifying predictions, and filling in unstated information. If students are watching a documentary film on sharks, for example, they are using what they already know to make sense of the new information about sharks. Their prior knowledge enables them to predict what they might see in the documentary and to then verify those predictions as they view the film. They might also correct their misconceptions, fill in unstated information, and identify areas that are confusing. All of these activities exemplify the *active* process of constructing meaning that needs to occur as students are trying to understand the information.

Fortunately, human beings tend to construct meaning naturally as they are exposed to information, as they read the newspaper in the morning, for example, or listen to the radio. However, in the classroom, students often need prompting to use, and to improve on, their ability to construct meaning. There are many techniques and strategies that can be used to help students learn to construct meaning during structured classroom experiences and during independent assignments. The following sections provide suggestions to use as students are constructing meaning while they are initially acquiring and integrating knowledge.

Acquire & Integrate Knowledge

*Helping Students Acquire
and Integrate Declarative
Knowledge*
✔ *Construct Meaning*

"It sounds like a simple
proposition: we construct
our own understandings
of the world in which we
live. . . . Our experiences
lead us to conclude that
some people are generous
and other people are cheap
of spirit, that representational
government either works or
doesn't, that fire burns us if
we get too close, that
rubber balls usually bounce,
that most people enjoy
compliments, and that
cubes have six sides."

—Brooks & Brooks (1993)
In Search of Understanding,
p. 4.

1. Help students understand what it means to construct meaning.

The strategies in this section can help students construct meaning and thereby enhance their learning. However, any time students are using a strategy, success is much greater if they understand the effect the strategy should have on their learning. Further, students will be much more likely to use the strategies on their own if they are able to recognize situations in which the strategies are needed. Thus, we suggest that teachers provide experiences for students that will help them to understand the importance of constructing meaning as they acquire declarative knowledge. Suggestions for achieving this understanding include the following:

- Lead a discussion with students about the differences between simply looking at or hearing words and seeking understanding. You might ask students to read a passage (such as the one below) that has been intentionally written to hinder the constructing meaning process. Then give the passage a title ("Doing Laundry"), and have students read it again, noting how differently they process the information when they have a cue (i.e., the title) that elicits prior knowledge.

  The procedure is actually quite simple. First, you arrange items into different groups. Of course, one pile may be sufficient depending on how much there is to do. If you have to go somewhere else due to a lack of facilities, that is the next step; otherwise, you are pretty well set. It is important not to overdo things. That is, it is better to do too few things at once than too many. In the short run, this may not seem important, but complications can easily arise. A mistake can be expensive as well. At first, the whole procedure will seem complicated. Soon, however, it will become just another facet of life. It is difficult to foresee any end to the necessity for this task in the immediate future, but then, one never can tell.

  After the procedure is complete, you arrange the materials into different groups again. Then you can put them into their appropriate places. Eventually, they will be used again, and the whole cycle will then have to be repeated. However, that is part of life.

- When you use strategies that help students construct meaning, review why you are using these strategies.

- When students are about to receive new information, cue them to select a strategy that helps them construct meaning. After using the strategy, have them discuss if and how it helped them understand the information.

2. Use the three-minute pause.

Jay McTighe, of the Maryland Assessment Consortium, recommends that teachers regularly use the three-minute pause. This means stopping every ten or fifteen minutes during a classroom activity and asking students to reflect on and verbalize about something they have learned. Students may work in pairs or small groups or talk together as a class. This pause changes the mode in which students are operating by asking them to move from listening and observing (input) to reflecting and talking (output).

To set up the three-minute pause, you can give students very loose directions (e.g., "Talk about what you have been thinking during this activity") or directions that are very structured (e.g., "Answer the following question. . . ."). The degree to which your directions are structured should depend on the complexity of the content about which students are constructing meaning and the level of experience that students have had with the three-minute pause. Below are some examples of what you might ask students to do. Then give students three minutes, or fewer, to go through the process.

- "Summarize what you have learned."

- "Identify one thing you already knew and one thing that was new to you."

- "Describe something you found interesting."

- "Identify one thing that was confusing, and try to clear it up."

- "Answer the following question. . . ."

3. Help students experience content using a variety of senses.

It is a fairly well-accepted principle that if students have the ability to create detailed mental images of information they are receiving, they can improve their comprehension and retention of the information. Further, the more senses they use to create those images, the better the results. These images can make a distant historical example seem more real and transform an abstraction that is difficult to understand into something more concrete. To help students cultivate this skill, when they are reading a book, viewing a film, listening to a discussion or lecture, or observing a demonstration, encourage them to use all five senses.

Richardson (1983) "Images, Definitions and Types"

Suhor (1984) "Toward a Semiotics-based Curriculum"

Sight
- Ask students to imagine and describe what the information looks like.

- Ask students to think of the information as a motion picture in their minds.

Dimension 2
Acquire & Integrate Knowledge

Helping Students Acquire
and Integrate Declarative
Knowledge
✔ *Construct Meaning*

Smell

- Ask students to imagine and describe the smells associated with the information.

Taste

- Ask students to imagine and describe the tastes associated with the information.

Touch

- Ask students to imagine and describe the sensations of touch associated with the information.

Hearing

- Ask students to imagine and describe the sounds associated with the information.

Creating mental images is a skill that you can help students to practice and refine. After asking them to create images, have several students describe their images aloud. Give them feedback about how well their images depict the content being learned and about any misconceptions the images reveal (e.g., "That is a good start for your picture. But remember, you want a picture of the electrons outside the nucleus."). To help students clarify and sharpen their images, also provide feedback about the details in their images (e.g., "What did you hear, smell, or taste?" "What color were the. . . ?"). After giving this specific feedback aloud to several students, ask students to pair up and share their images to practice giving each other the same types of feedback. In this way, students will improve both their learning of the content and their ability to create images that construct meaning.

4. Help students to construct meaning for vocabulary terms.

Marzano & Arredondo (1986) *Tactics for Thinking*

Marzano & Marzano (1988) *A Cluster Approach to Elementary Vocabulary Instruction*

The most specific way to organize knowledge, as described in the introduction to this dimension, is to identify vocabulary terms. Vocabulary development is a major focus in many classrooms because teachers know that the words students are able to use while listening, speaking, reading, and writing will influence their success in any academic area. However, the most commonly used approaches to teaching vocabulary are probably not the most effective.

Teachers often ask students to look up a word in a dictionary or glossary, copy the definition, and then use it in a sentence to show that they understand the meaning. Although this type of activity might help students learn some words, it does not necessarily encourage students to *construct meaning* for words. When we understand words for which we have constructed meaning,

Dimension 2
Acquire & Integrate Knowledge

*Helping Students Acquire
and Integrate Declarative
Knowledge*
✔ *Construct Meaning*

we do not understand them as definitions. We understand them because we have constructed meaning as result of our experiences with them. The following strategy, adapted from *Tactics for Thinking* (Marzano & Arredondo, 1986), is the type of approach that is consistent with the belief that in order to truly understand vocabulary words and other types of declarative knowledge, the learner must construct meaning for this knowledge.

1) Provide students with a direct or indirect experience for the new word through a field trip, classroom activity, discussion, or some personal examples of your experience with the word.

2) Have students *describe* (rather than *define*) the new word in terms of their experiences.

3) Using the information generated in steps 1 and 2, ask students to form a strong mental image of the new word.

4) Ask students to say the word to themselves and mentally picture the word spelled correctly.

5) Systematically review the word, adding and deleting information.

5. Present students with the K-W-L strategy.

The K-W-L strategy, developed by Donna Ogle (1986), is a powerful way to help students construct meaning. This process can be presented to students as a simple three-step strategy:

Ogle (1986) "K-W-L: A Teaching Model That Develops Active Reading of Expository Text"

- Before reading, listening, observing, or acting, students identify what they *know (K)* about the topic.

- Next, they list what they *want (W)* to know about the topic.

- After the activity, students identify and list what they have *learned (L)*. This list may include new and unpredicted knowledge, answers to questions from the W column, and knowledge that validates or invalidates items from the K column.

You can help students become familiar with the K-W-L strategy by asking them to create their own worksheets. Figure 2.3 shows the beginnings of a K-W-L worksheet prepared by a student before watching a film about sharks.

FIGURE 2.3

K-W-L WORKSHEET: FILM ABOUT SHARKS

KNOW	WANT	LEARNED
They are mean.	Do they live only in oceans?	
They live in water.	Where are there the most?	
They have sharp teeth.	How big are they?	

Some teachers adapt the K-W-L strategy by changing "what I know" to "what I *think* I know" and "what I want to know" to "what I *think I'm going to find out*." Both of these changes seem to increase students' level of participation and input into the learning process. Other teachers add an additional *W* to the end of the strategy to prompt students to determine "what I want to know now." This step emphasizes that learning is an ongoing process.

6. Create opportunities for students to discover or figure out the new information for themselves.

Joyce & Weil (1986) *Models of Teaching*

When teachers want students to understand a concept or principle, they often use *inquiry* or *inductive* models of presenting information to increase the level of students' involvement and understanding. When teachers use these models, they explicitly ask students to use their prior knowledge as they try to understand new information. As a result, students not only gain new knowledge, but deepen their understanding of their prior knowledge.

For example, a science lab teacher might ask students to conduct experiments and then ask them to construct an explanation for their results. A language arts teacher might give students examples and nonexamples of the concept of simile and then ask them to try to figure out the defining characteristics. The approach in the latter example is a basic model from which Bruce Joyce and Marsha Weil developed a "concept attainment" process, described in *Models of Teaching* (1986). We have developed five phases from those described by Joyce and Weil.

For a discussion of inquiry models, see also Bruner, Goodnow, & Austin (1956) *A Study of Thinking*.

Dimension 2
Acquire & Integrate Knowledge

*Helping Students Acquire
and Integrate Declarative
Knowledge*
✔ *Construct Meaning*

Phase I

The first step in presenting a concept is to provide examples and nonexamples. Assume that a teacher wants to present the concept of *compound words*. First he generates pairs of examples and nonexamples. Examples have all of the defining attributes or characteristics of the concept; nonexamples do not have all of these attributes. The teacher then presents examples and nonexamples to students one at a time. For the concept of *compound words*, he might make the following presentation to students: "This is an example of a compound word: *boyfriend*. This is not an example: *boy*. This is an example: *railroad*. This is not an example: *car*." As the teacher presents pairs of examples and nonexamples, students try to figure out the defining characteristics of the concept. The teacher then asks students to view these initial ideas as hypotheses.

Phase II

The second step is to present more pairs of examples and nonexamples so that students can test their initial hypotheses about the defining characteristics of the concept. At the end of this phase, the teacher asks students to orally state their hypotheses and explain how they arrived at them. Here is one example of a hypothetical student response, again using the compound words illustration:

> *I think that the example words are made up of two words. Sometimes the meaning of the combined word comes from the two words, but a lot of times it doesn't. At first I thought the two words made up the meaning of the combined word all of the time, but then I noticed that. . . .*

Phase III

The next step is to present more examples and nonexamples. The teacher keeps presenting pairs of examples and nonexamples until the majority of students are able to state the defining characteristics of the concept.

Phase IV

In this phase of the process, the teacher asks students to identify examples and nonexamples on their own. This can be done in two steps. The teacher might first have students pick examples and nonexamples from a list he has provided. Using the compound words illustration, he might say, "Here's a word. Is it an example of the concept? *Railroad*. Here's another word. Is it an example of the concept? *Rebound*." Next, the teacher might have students find their own examples and nonexamples of compound words and report back to the entire class.

Dimension 2
Acquire & Integrate Knowledge

*Helping Students Acquire
and Integrate Declarative
Knowledge*
✔ *Construct Meaning*

Phase V

During the last phase of the process, the teacher asks students to develop a written or oral description of the concept that includes the key or defining characteristics. In addition, the teacher gives students the name of the concept and asks them to include it in their definitions. (*Note:* In some versions of the concept attainment process, the name of the concept is provided.)

The following example illustrates how another teacher might use the phases of the concept attainment process:

Assume that a social studies teacher wants to present the concept of *Eurocentrism*. She explains to students that the concept she will illustrate can be thought of as a "perspective." She also explains that the examples validate this perspective; the nonexamples do not. The teacher explains to her students that their job is to figure out what perspective is illustrated by the examples, but not by the nonexamples. She has developed about twenty pairs of examples and nonexamples, including the following:

Examples	*Nonexamples*
• *Middle East*	• *United States*
• *The Orient*	• *Japan*
• *The West*	• *Canada*
• *The East*	• *China*
• *Columbus discovered America.*	• *Columbus invaded a new land and enslaved the indigenous people.*

As the teacher presents these to students during the first four phases of the concept attainment process, students gradually realize that ideas such as "The West," "The East," and "Columbus discovered America" make sense only from the perspective of Europe as the center of civilization. By the time the teacher explains that this concept is called *Eurocentrism*, students are able to write clear definitions of it.

7. Use instructional techniques that provide students with strategies to use before, during, and after they receive information.

Some reading theorists have conceptualized the reading process as consisting of three phases: before reading, during reading, and after reading. These phases apply whether students are reading, listening to, or viewing information. In each phase, learners do certain things to create meaning from the new information they are receiving.

Several instructional techniques provide students with strategies to use before, during, and after they receive information. Using these techniques in the classroom communicates to students that during the learning process, they have a responsibility to do much more than simply pick up a book and read a text or sit down and watch a film. Students are expected to develop and use strategies (e.g., accessing what they already know, asking and answering questions, and creating and changing mental pictures) that increase their understanding of the information they are receiving.

Below are two instructional techniques that follow the before, during, and after structure: Reciprocal Teaching and SQ3R: Survey, Question, Read, Recite, and Review.

Reciprocal Teaching

Reciprocal teaching is a technique that actively engages both teacher and students in the use of prior knowledge. The following is an adaptation of the reciprocal teaching strategy:

a. *Summarizing.* After students have silently or orally read a short section of a passage, a single student acting as teacher (i.e., the student leader) summarizes what has been read. Other students, with guidance from the teacher, may add to the summary. If students have difficulty summarizing, the teacher might point out clues (e.g., important items or obvious topic sentences) that aid in the construction of good summaries.

b. *Questioning.* The student leader asks some questions to which the class responds. The questions are designed to help students identify important information in the passage. For example, the student leader might look back over the selection and ask questions about specific pieces of information. The other students then try to answer these questions based on their recollection of the information.

c. *Clarifying.* Next, the student leader tries to clarify confusing points in the passage. He might point these out or ask other students to point them out. For example, the student leader might say, "The part about why the dog ran into the car was confusing to me. Can anyone explain this?" Or, the student leader might ask other students to ask clarification questions. The group then attempts to clear up the confusing parts. This might involve rereading parts of the passage.

d. *Predicting.* The student leader asks for predictions about what will happen in the next segment of the text. The leader can write the predictions on the blackboard or on an overhead, or all students can write them down in their notebooks. Keeping those predictions in mind,

Palincsar & Brown (1985) "Reciprocal Teaching: Activities to Promote Reading with Your Mind"

Palincsar et al. (1986) *Teaching Reading as Thinking*

Research reported on by Reeve, Palincsar, and Brown (1987, "Everyday and Academic Thinking") shows that reciprocal teaching results in students' improved performance on classroom comprehension tests (from 20% to 80% correct) and on standardized comprehension tests (average gain of two years).

Robinson (1961) *Effective Study*

the class then silently or orally reads the text. Then a new student is selected to be the teacher (i.e., the student leader), and the process begins again. During each successive summarizing stage, the student leader addresses the predictions that were made.

SQ3R: Survey, Question, Read, Recite, and Review

SQ3R is a five-step study plan to help students construct meaning while reading. It uses the elements of questioning, predicting, setting a purpose for reading, and monitoring for confusion. Developed by Francis Robinson (1961), SQ3R helps students understand and recall what they have read. As described in *Teaching Reading in the Content Areas: If Not Me, Then Who?* (Billmeyer, 1996), SQ3R includes the following steps:

1. *Survey*
   - Think about the title: "What do I know?" "What do I want to know?"
   - Glance over headings and/or skim the first sentences of paragraphs.
   - Look at illustrations and graphic aids.
   - Read the first paragraph.
   - Read the last paragraph or summary.

2. *Question*
   - Turn the title into a question.
   - Write down any questions that come to mind during the survey.
   - Turn headings into questions.
   - Turn subheadings, illustrations, and graphic aids into questions.
   - Write down unfamiliar vocabulary words and determine their meaning.

3. *Read actively*
   - Read to search for answers to questions.
   - Respond to questions and use context clues for unfamiliar words.
   - React to unclear passages, confusing terms, and questionable statements by generating additional questions.

4. *Recite*
   - Look away from the answers and the book to recall what was read.
   - Recite answers to questions aloud or in writing.
   - Reread text for unanswered questions.

5. *Review*
   - Answer the major purpose question.
   - Look over answers and all parts of the chapter to organize information.
   - Summarize the information learned by drawing flow charts, writing a summary, participating in a group discussion, or by studying for a test.

Dimension 2
Acquire & Integrate Knowledge

*Helping Students Acquire
and Integrate Declarative
Knowledge*
✔ *Organize*

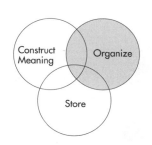

Organize Declarative Knowledge

In addition to constructing meaning, learning declarative knowledge involves organizing information, that is, identifying the important pieces of information and putting them together to see the possible relationships, or patterns, in these pieces. In the introduction to this dimension, we explained the importance of students' recognizing patterns in information. We also discussed ways that information can be organized when you are identifying the declarative knowledge for specific lessons and units of study. However, even if you have organized the information for students during planning, there is no assurance that students will recognize patterns in that information. The strategies included in this section are suggested as ways to help students see the patterns that have been identified as important and to help them recognize patterns for themselves as they encounter blocks of information. Keep in mind that using these strategies also frequently helps students to construct meaning and to store, or remember, the information they are learning.

1. Help students understand the importance of organizing information.

Students may sometimes feel anxious and overwhelmed when they are receiving a large quantity of information. It might help if they understand that organizing information is an essential phase of learning and that recognizing and using patterns in information can reduce their anxieties and enhance the learning process. Before teaching organizing strategies, help students to understand that the purpose of the strategies is to enable them to figure out what is important and to recognize the relationships among the pieces of information. If they believe that this process of organizing will help them understand, use, and retain the information, they will be more likely to use the strategies. Approaches for increasing students' awareness and understanding of the importance of organizing information might include the following activities:

1. Ask students to look for patterns in their environment, emphasizing that patterns help us to sort through and understand stimuli we are receiving.

2. Pantomime some behavior patterns (e.g., two people meeting, shaking hands, then departing; someone walking, opening a door, and jumping back in fear) so that students see how easy it is for them to recognize and respond to familiar patterns of behavior.

3. Present a picture with hidden outlines of familiar objects and ask them to find the objects in the picture (e.g., using *Where's Waldo?*). Point out that when they are familiar with the pattern of the object, they can recognize it even in complex environments.

4. Present information to students as it might appear in a text, then present the same information in a graphic organizer. Emphasize that students can better recognize the information in the text once they have become familiar with the pattern.

All of these are ways of emphasizing that just as patterns around us help us to cope with our world, organizing information helps us to understand, use, and retain that information.

2. Have students use graphic organizers for the identified organizational patterns.

Heimlich & Pittelman (1988) Semantic Mapping

Most declarative information can be organized into one of the six patterns identified in the introduction to this dimension: descriptions, time sequences, process/cause-effect relationships, episodes, generalizations/principles, or concepts. (You may wish to review the descriptions of these patterns on pages 46-49.) Each of these organizational patterns can be depicted in a graphic organizer that can be used in the classroom in two ways: in teacher-structured and student-structured lessons. If, during planning, the teacher has organized the information into a pattern, he or she can provide the students with the appropriate graphic organizer, either with the information filled in or blank so that students can fill in the information as it is presented. In more student-structured situations, the information is presented and students are asked to choose the organizer that helps them make the most sense of the information. Below are suggested graphic organizers for the six common organizational patterns included in this dimension.

One district regularly schedules evening sessions for parents at which teachers demonstrate strategies for Dimension 2 and make suggestions about how parents can use the strategies to help their children with their homework. Parents find the various graphic organizers particularly helpful.

a. ***Descriptive patterns*** can be used for *vocabulary terms* or for *facts*. Specifically, descriptive patterns represent information that has been organized around vocabulary terms. Descriptive patterns also represent facts that have been organized to describe characteristics about specific persons, places, things, and events. The information organized into a descriptive pattern does not need to be in any particular order. For example, information about the Empire State Building or about the term *urban* might be organized as a simple descriptive pattern. A descriptive pattern can be represented graphically as shown below.

van Dijk (1980)
Macrostructures

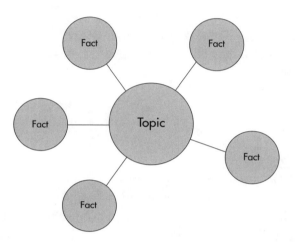

b. ***Time sequence patterns*** organize events in a specific chronological order. For example, the information in a biography about Edgar Allan Poe can be organized as a sequence pattern. A time sequence pattern can be represented graphically as shown below.

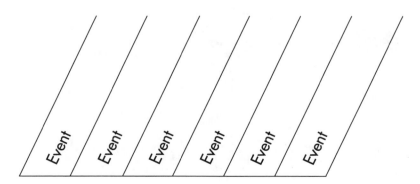

c. *Process/cause-effect patterns* organize information into a causal network leading to a specific outcome or into a sequence of steps leading to a specific product. For example, information about the process of digesting food might be organized as a process/cause-effect pattern. A process/cause-effect pattern can be represented graphically as shown below.

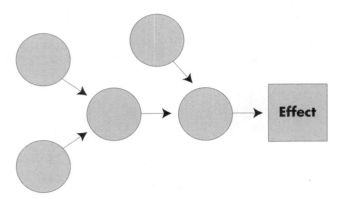

d. *Episode patterns* organize a large quantity of information about specific events, including (1) a setting (time and place), (2) specific people, (3) a specific duration, (4) a specific sequence of events, and (5) a particular cause and effect. For example, the information about Watergate might be organized into an episode pattern using a graphic like that shown below.

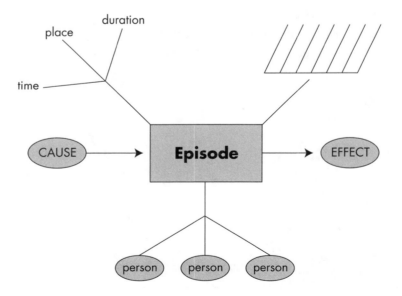

Dimension 2
Acquire & Integrate Knowledge

*Helping Students Acquire
and Integrate Declarative
Knowledge*

✔ *Organize*

e. *Generalization/principle patterns* organize information into general statements with supporting examples. For instance, for the statement "Mysteries often use the technique of foreshadowing," examples can be provided and represented in a graphic like that shown below.

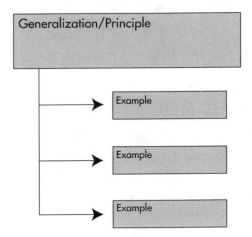

f. *Concept patterns*, the most general of all patterns, organize information around a word or phrase that represents entire classes or categories of persons, places, things, and events. The characteristics, or attributes, of the concept, along with examples of each, should be included in this pattern. The concept of *culture*, for example, could be organized into a graphic like that shown below.

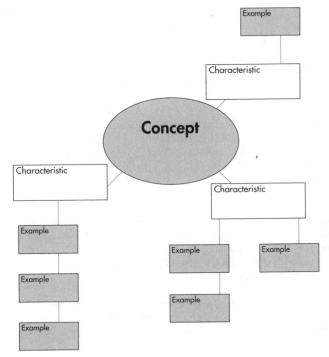

Dimension 2

Acquire & Integrate Knowledge

*Helping Students Acquire
and Integrate Declarative
Knowledge*

✔ *Organize*

To reiterate, the same block of information often can be organized into a number of different patterns. Figures 2.4, 2.5, 2.6, and 2.7 contain a passage about dictators and graphics showing how this concept can be organized into different patterns. Notice that the learner would focus on different information as a function of the pattern used.

FIGURE 2.4

DICTATORS RISE TO POWER

The United States was not the only nation to suffer from the Great Depression. The nations of Europe also were hard hit. Moreover, many Europeans had been trying to repair the damage to their countries caused by World War I.

Because of the hardships under which they were forced to live, some Europeans were willing to listen to leaders who promised to make their nations rich and powerful again. Some of these leaders brought about total changes in their countries. Their actions also caused another world war.

Dictators rise to power. In the 1920s and 1930s, new leaders formed governments in Italy and Germany. The governments formed in these countries were dictatorships. In a dictatorship, the leader or leaders hold complete authority over the people they rule. The people living in a dictatorship have only those rights that their leader, the dictator, chooses to give them. Dictators alone make all the important decisions in their nations. The decisions made by the dictators of Italy and Germany contributed to the beginning of World War II.

Mussolini takes over in Italy. After World War I, many Italians wanted to feel pride in the strength of their country once again. Benito Mussolini, the founder and organizer of the Fascist Party, convinced the Italians that he and his party could strengthen the nation. To succeed, the Fascists had to take control of the economy, the government, and many other parts of Italian life.

In 1922, the Fascists took control of the Italian government, creating a dictatorship with Mussolini as leader. Italians who were against Mussolini or his government were either thrown into prison or were forced to leave the country.

Mussolini planned to increase Italy's power and wealth by taking over weaker nations. He turned to Africa and, in 1935, attacked Ethiopia. By early 1936, the Italian army overran this East African country and added it to the Italian empire.

Hitler becomes dictator in Germany. After losing World War I, Germany continued to struggle with severe economic problems throughout the 1920s. These difficulties and the memory of their defeat in World War I brought many Germans to the Nazi Party. Its leader, Adolf Hitler, promised to make Germany the most powerful country in the world. In 1933, the Nazis won control of the German government. Hitler became Germany's dictator and silenced anyone who opposed him.

The people against whom Hitler directed his greatest hatred were the Jewish citizens of Germany. He unfairly blamed them for all of Germany's problems. By constantly repeating these false accusations, Hitler aroused public opinion in Germany against its Jewish citizens. Then he took away all civil rights and property of the Jews. Next, the police rounded up Jewish men, women, and children and sent them to concentration camps or prison camps.

Hitler promised the Germans that he would add to the territory of their nation. He immediately put the country to work making weapons and other war materials. The first nation he moved into was Austria in 1938. Hitler annexed Austria, he explained, because most of its people were Germans.

FIGURE 2.5

CONCEPT PATTERN: DICTATORS RISE TO POWER

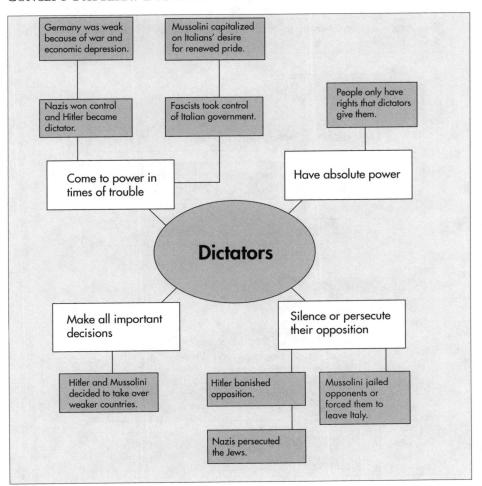

FIGURE 2.6

TIME SEQUENCE PATTERN: DICTATORS RISE TO POWER

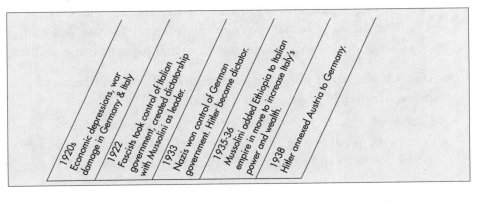

FIGURE 2.7

GENERALIZATION/PRINCIPLE PATTERN: DICTATORS RISE TO POWER

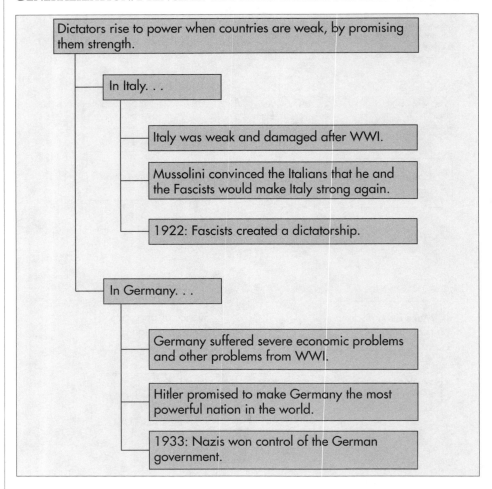

3. Provide students with advance organizer questions.

A good organizational strategy to use, particularly if you want to provide students with strong guidance in organizing information, is to present questions prior to exposing students to new information. You can structure these questions around the six types of organizational patterns just described:

Ausubel (1968) *Educational Psychology*

*   *Questions to ask when you want to emphasize descriptive patterns about specific people, places, things, and events:*

    *   *Facts about a specific person:* Describe important points about Columbus. What was his personality like? What important things did he do? Why did he do them? What happened as a result?

- *Facts about a specific place:* Describe the important characteristics of Denver. Where is it? How big is it? What are its unique features? What important events have occurred there?

- *Facts about a specific thing:* Describe the important characteristics of the space shuttle. What does it look like? What is it used for? Why was it made? What important things has it been involved in?

- *Facts about a specific event:* Describe the important characteristics of the Watergate break-in. Where did it happen? When did it happen? Who was involved? Why did it happen? What happened as a result of it?

- *Question to ask when you want to emphasize a specific time sequence pattern:*
  - What is the sequence of movements in Beethoven's Ninth Symphony?

- *Questions to ask when you want to emphasize a process or a cause-effect pattern:*
  - What are the steps involved in making a cake? How does each step relate to the others?
  - What were the causes of the Persian Gulf War? How does each cause relate to one or more of the others?

- *Questions to ask when you want to emphasize an episode pattern:*
  - Who were the participants, what was the sequence of events, and what were the effects of the Duke of Windsor's abdication of the throne of England in the 1930s?

- *Question to ask when you want to emphasize a generalization/principle pattern with examples:*
  - What are three illustrations of the principle that water rises to its own level?

- *Questions to ask when you want to emphasize a concept pattern with examples and defining characteristics:*
  - What are three examples of modern dictators? Explain why they are examples. What are the defining characteristics of dictators?

Dimension 2
Acquire & Integrate Knowledge

*Helping Students Acquire
and Integrate Declarative
Knowledge*
✔ *Organize*

4. Present note-taking strategies that use graphic representations.

A useful way of highlighting the various patterns that students can use to organize information is to introduce a note-taking format like the sample page from a set of notes shown in Figure 2.8. Students structure their notes by dividing the page in half with a vertical line and then leaving a strip at the bottom that cuts across the entire page. On the left side of the page, students take notes in whatever fashion they wish; one common method is simply to indent less important ideas. Periodically, students stop and make a graphic representation of their notes on the right side of the page. This note-taking method takes extra time but forces students to consider the information a second time. At the end of their note taking, or periodically throughout the process, students record summary statements of what they have learned in the space at the bottom of the page.

FIGURE 2.8

NOTE TAKING WITH GRAPHICS: THE FIVE SENSES
(ONE OF SEVERAL PAGES)

Notes

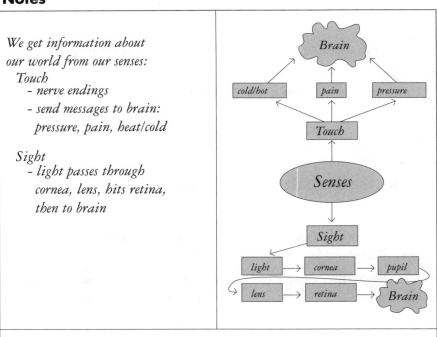

5. Have students create physical and pictographic representations of information.

Creating physical representations and pictographs of information is an organizational strategy that works for many students. Physical representations, as the name implies, are physical models or enactments of information. For example, students in a science class might create a physical representation by making a three-dimensional model of an atom, using ping-pong balls and straws. When creating physical enactments of information, students act out the information. For example, elementary students might create a physical enactment of the solar system by having one student stand in the center of the room with a flashlight and be the sun, while other students representing the planets walk (rotate) around him.

Students also can organize information through pictographs. A pictograph is a drawing that uses symbols and symbolic pictures to represent important information. For example, after watching a film about Colorado's natural resources, a student might use the pictograph in Figure 2.9 to organize information.

FIGURE 2.9

PICTOGRAPH: COLORADO'S NATURAL RESOURCES

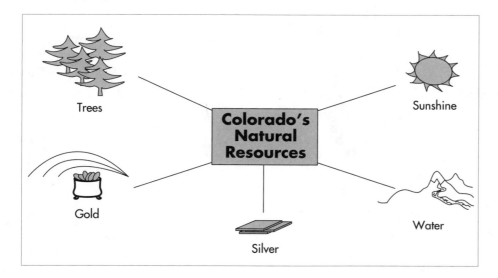

Dimension 2
Acquire & Integrate Knowledge

*Helping Students Acquire
and Integrate Declarative
Knowledge*
✔ *Organize*

One group of teachers
regularly clips out graphs
and charts from *USA Today*
to show students how
graphs and charts are used
every day to organize and
communicate both simple
and complex information.

6. Have students use graphs and charts.

Quantitative information is commonly organized into graphs and charts. Although they are often associated with mathematics, graphs and charts can also be used in other subject areas. For example, a literature teacher might ask her high school students to compare three short stories by creating pie graphs that represent the relative emphasis on character, plot, and setting. Before doing the pie graphs, she asked students to create graphs for three movies that placed differing emphases on character, plot, and setting. Figure 2.10 depicts one student's perspective relative to the movies *The Remains of the Day*, *Mission Impossible*, and *The Sound of Music*.

FIGURES 2.10

PIE CHARTS: COMPARING PLOT, CHARACTER, AND SETTING IN MOVIES

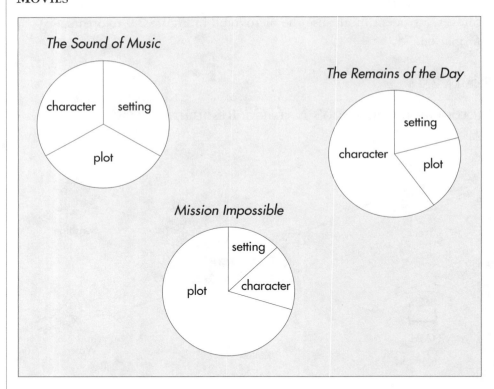

Dimension 2
Acquire & Integrate Knowledge

*Helping Students Acquire
and Integrate Declarative
Knowledge*
✔ *Store*

Store Declarative Knowledge

To easily access and use information, often we must consciously store it in memory. Constructing meaning and organizing the information often positively influence what we remember, but sometimes we need to use storage strategies in order to retain important pieces of information. For instance, even if you create mental pictures of something you have read and make an outline of the information, you might have to do something to help you remember key points if you want to recall them at a later date.

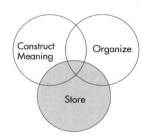

Some educators believe that memorizing should be deemphasized in the learning process. They reason that it is more important for students to focus on understanding (not recalling) information, to learn where to find information, and to learn how to access it. Although recall may not be the primary goal of most learning situations, it is easy to list situations in the classroom, in the workplace, and even during leisure activities in which there is the need to recall information without looking it up. As educators, we must make careful decisions about what we want students to recall and then provide them with effective and efficient strategies for storing important information.

Reviewing information a number of times is the least effective, and most commonly used, information-storage strategy. The most powerful memory strategies are those that use "imagery." For example, to help us recall information we might

- imagine a mental picture of the information,

- imagine physical sensations associated with the information, and

- imagine emotions associated with the information.

If you want to create an image about George Washington, you might first picture Washington on his horse (mental picture). You then might imagine the smell of the leather saddle and the feeling of sitting on the horse (physical sensations). In addition to creating images, it also helps to "talk to yourself" about the information you are trying to remember; for example, "George Washington was the first president. He kept his army together at Valley Forge." Finally, you might try to conjure up feelings of patriotism (emotions). There are many powerful classroom strategies based on the use of imagery.

Lindsay & Norman (1977)
Human Information Processing

1. Help students understand the process of storing information.

Because students sometimes spend a disproportionate amount of study time memorizing information, it is important for them to gain two key understandings before learning additional memory strategies. First, students should spend most of their time engaged in constructing meaning and organizing information, not only because these processes will enhance their *understanding* of information, but because using these processes will also enhance their *memory* of the information. Second, when it is appropriate to instantly recall something, the efficient use of storage strategies can significantly reduce the time it takes to commit the information to memory. To help students grasp the importance of these two points, take the time to discuss the process of storing, and provide experiences that will help them decide when and how to use strategies for storing information. These experiences might include one or more of the following:

- To help students understand how the construction of meaning influences storing, present two blocks of information: one for which students will use strategies for constructing meaning and organizing, the other for which they will not. Test students' recall immediately and then again after a period of time. It is likely that they will recall the information that they processed with the strategies better than that processed without strategies.

- To show the power of storing strategies, have students memorize some information using repetition; then have them recall similar information using storing strategies that they have learned. Test their recall immediately, then again after a period of time. Compare students' recall of the two sets of information.

- To ensure that students appropriately use storing strategies, when presenting declarative knowledge discuss what should be remembered and if the use of storing strategies might be necessary.

2. Present students with the strategy of using symbols and substitutes.

Hayes (1981) *The Complete Problem Solver*

Although it is easy to create images for some types of information, it is difficult to do this with other types. For example, creating images for factual information about George Washington is fairly easy because you can picture him, his horse, his army, and so on. But what about abstract information like the basic elements of water: two hydrogen atoms and one oxygen atom? To create images of these elements you can use symbols and substitutes:

Dimension 2
Acquire & Integrate Knowledge

*Helping Students Acquire
and Integrate Declarative
Knowledge*
✔ *Store*

A *symbol* is anything (an event, a person, a place, or a thing) that suggests to you the information you are trying to remember. For example, an oxygen bottle used in scuba diving might symbolize *oxygen* to you.

A *substitute* is a word that sounds like the information you want to remember and is easy to picture. You can use substitutes when you cannot think of a symbol or any other way of picturing information. For example, the word *hydrant* sounds like h*ydrogen*, and it is easy to picture.

You now have one symbol and one substitute to use with *oxygen* and *hydrogen* respectively. To remember that water is two parts hydrogen and one part oxygen, you could imagine two hydrants floating in water balancing an oxygen tank. You might also generate physical sensations and emotions and talk to yourself about the information.

3. Use the link strategy with students.

The link strategy is almost always used with symbols and substitutes. It simply involves linking one image to another in a chain or story. For example, suppose a student wants to remember the 13 original colonies: Georgia, New Jersey, Delaware, New York, North Carolina, South Carolina, Virginia, New Hampshire, Pennsylvania, Connecticut, Rhode Island, Maryland, and Massachusetts. Because it is difficult to mentally picture the states themselves, the student will probably have to use symbols and substitutes. For example, a Jersey cow sounds like *New Jersey*, and the Empire State Building could be a symbol for *New York*. The name Georgette sounds like *Georgia*, and the words *Christmas carol* sound like *Carolina*, so they could be used as substitutes.

The student would then link the mental pictures provided by the symbols and substitutes into one continuous story. For example, the student might first picture Georgette (*Georgia*), the Jersey cow (*New Jersey*). Next she would imagine Georgette (a Jersey cow) putting on a pair of yellow underwear (which sounds like *Delaware*) as she stands on top of the Empire State Building (*New York*). Georgette then begins singing Christmas Carols (*North*

Hayes (1981) *The Complete Problem Solver*

and South Carolina). Under her left "arm" Georgette is holding a Virginia ham (*Virginia, New Hampshire*). In her right "hand" she has a pen (*Pennsylvania*). With the pen, Georgette is connecting dots (which sounds like *Connecticut*). These dots join to form a picture of a road (*Rhode Island*). On the road is Marilyn Monroe (*Maryland*) on her way to mass (*Massachusetts*).

4. Use highly structured systems for storing information with students.

There are many highly structured systems to help students store information. Four of them are discussed here.

Ross & Lawrence (1968) "Some Observations on Memory Artifice"

a. **The rhyming pegword method.** The rhyming pegword method is a simple system that can be used to remember information that is or can be organized in a list format. It begins with visualizing the following rhymes:

1 is a *bun*	6 is a *pile of sticks*
2 is a *shoe*	7 is *heaven*
3 is a *tree*	8 is a *gate*
4 is a *door*	9 is a *line*
5 is a *hive*	10 is a *hen*

The words *bun, shoe, tree, door, hive, sticks, heaven, gate, line*, and *hen* are easy to remember because they rhyme with the numbers 1 through 10. If a student wants to put information in slot #1 (1 is a bun) of the framework, she would do so by forming a mental image of the information she wants to remember that also includes a bun, because bun is the "pegword" for the first slot of the framework. For example, assume the student wants to put the following information about Christopher Columbus into slot #1:

- *He landed in America in 1492.*
- *He sailed with three ships.*
- *The popular opinion was that he would sail off the end of the world.*

To form a mental image of this information that includes the pegword *bun*, she might imagine a bun sailing across the ocean. Christopher Columbus would be standing at the bow of the bun. Two other buns (ships) would also be sailing. She might then picture the end of the world with water rushing off it like a waterfall. She could even put the date 1492 in the picture. The student might also say to herself, "Columbus landed in America in 1492. He sailed with three ships."

To continue, if the student wants to put information about notable jazz musicians into slot #2 during a unit on the history of jazz music, she would form images representing that information and make sure that the images contained a shoe (e.g., she might form an image of Louis Armstrong and Chuck Mangione trying on red shoes). Continuing this process, she could put ten different sets of information into the rhyming pegword system—simply by including a pegword in her image for each set. To retrieve the information, all the student would have to do is count one through ten. Each number would remind her of its corresponding pegword. In turn, each pegword would remind her of the images that contain the information she wants to remember.

A common question is whether students can use this method effectively to memorize the multiplication tables. The answer is that students have used this method to help them recall the troublesome facts. For example, if the student cannot recall the answer to 7 x 8, he might create a picture of angel from heaven (pegword for 7) swinging on a gate (pegword for 8) and the number 56 emblazoned on the front of the gate. In his picture, the gate is making a creaking noise that sounds like 56, 56, 56.

b. *The number/key word method.* At first the number/key word method seems complex. However, it is actually quite simple and very powerful. In this system each digit from 0 through 9 is associated with a unique sound (always the sound of a consonant).

Hayes (1981) *The Complete Problem Solver*

Digit	Sound	Reason for using sound
0	*s*	*Zero* begins with *z*, which is like a backwards *s*.
1	*t*	*T* has one vertical bar.
2	*n*	*N* has two vertical bars.
3	*m*	*M* has three vertical bars.
4	*r*	The word *four* ends with *r*.
5	*l*	*L* is the Roman numeral for 50.
6	*j* or *ch*	Turn the letter *j* around and it resembles a 6; *ch* and *j* make similar sounds.
7	*k*	Turn the letter *k* around and it can look like a 7.
8	*f*	When the letter *f* is written in script, it looks like an 8.
9	*p*	Turn the letter *p* around and it looks like a 9.

Dimension 2
Acquire & Integrate Knowledge

*Helping Students Acquire
and Integrate Declarative
Knowledge*
✔ *Store*

These letter/digit associations are used to develop a list of easy-to-remember key words for as many slots as you like. For example, let's assume you would like to build a framework for 30 slots. Each slot has a number (1 through 30), but we also need a very concrete key word for each slot. You create these key words by using the letter/digit association. Consider the slot 21:

$$21 = NT$$

Those two digits are associated with the sounds *N* and *T*, in that order. A word that also contains those same sounds in the same order is NET. Therefore, finding key words for any number is simply a matter of finding a word that has the same sounds in the same order as the digits (e.g., 307 = M-S-K = MASK).

Using this system you can create key words for as many slots as you like. You might think that the key words would be hard to remember, but they are not. Once you have established which key words you want to associate with which numbers, all you have to do is recall the consonant sounds associated with each digit in the number, and that will automatically remind you of the key word. Below is a set of key words for the numbers 1-30. You can use this list or establish key words on your own. Of course, you can go beyond 30. With a list of 100 key words you could easily memorize 100 pieces of information.

1 = T = Tea	16 = TJ = TaJ Mahal
2 = N = kNee	17 = TK = TKo (Technical Knockout —boxing)
3 = M = Maypole	18 = TF = TurF
4 = R = Rug	19 = TP = TeePee
5 = L = Law	20 = NS = NoSe
6 = J = Jaw	21 = NT = NeT
7 = K = Key	22 = NN = NuN
8 = F = Free	23 = NM = NaMe
9 = P = Pie	24 = NR = NeaR
10 = TS = TosS	25 = NL = NaiL
11 = TT = TreaT	26 = NCH = NiCHe
12 = TN = ToN	27 = NK = NecK
13 = TM = TiMe	28 = NF = kNiFe
14 = TR = TRay	29 = NP = NiP
15 = TL = TaLe	30 = MS = MouSe

Dimension 2
Acquire & Integrate Knowledge

*Helping Students Acquire
and Integrate Declarative
Knowledge*
✔ *Store*

After students decide how long the framework should be, they can use this system as they would the rhyming pegword system: attach a mental picture of an item they wish to recall to the mental picture of the key word for that slot. For example, if a student is using the number/key word method to recall the presidents of the United States, she would create a mental picture, for example, of Abraham Lincoln standing in front of the Taj Mahal to recall that he was the sixteenth president of the United States.

c. **The number/picture system.** Like the rhyming pegword system, the number/picture system allows students to associate information with digits. It operates on the principle that each of the digits *1-9* and *0* actually look like objects that are easy to imagine:

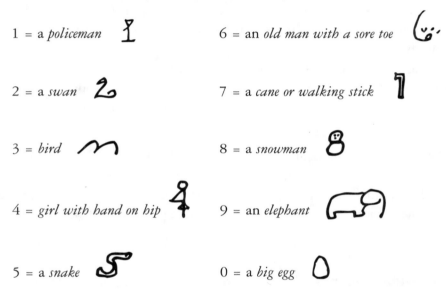

1 = a *policeman*

2 = a *swan*

3 = *bird*

4 = *girl with hand on hip*

5 = a *snake*

6 = an *old man with a sore toe*

7 = a *cane or walking stick*

8 = a *snowman*

9 = an *elephant*

0 = a *big egg*

Like the bun, shoe, tree, and door from the rhyming pegword system, the policeman, the swan, the bird, and so on are easy-to-remember cues with which to associate information you want to remember. The number/picture system provides ten cues or ten slots. If a student wants to place information in the first slot, she would form an image of the information and include a policeman in that image—the cue for that slot—and so on.

d. **The familiar place system.** One of the easiest memory strategies to use is the familiar place system. First, you imagine a place that is very familiar to you, like your bedroom. Then, you mentally go around your room and identify familiar objects in the order in which they appear in your room. You might first select the door to your room. Then, moving

Hayes (1981) *The Complete
Problem Solver*

Dimension 2
Acquire & Integrate Knowledge

*Helping Students Acquire
and Integrate Declarative
Knowledge*
✔ *Store*

to the right, the mirror on the dressing table, the chair, the plant to the right of the chair, the window, the bed, and so on. In this framework, then, you would have selected six objects to associate information with, or six "slots" to put things into: (1) door, (2) mirror, (3) chair, (4) plant, (5) window, (6) bed. Of course, you could keep going around your room and produce as many slots as your room would allow.

The objects in your framework should always represent slots with which you associate information you want to recall. For example, assume you want to remember key ideas about ancient philosophers. You would first picture your doorway in your mind. In your mental picture, you would open the door and see Socrates dressed in argyle knee "socks." You would then see him surrounded by students dressed in togas. He is holding a copy of a book, and you hear him asking questions. Given that the second slot is your mirror, you might picture Plato standing in a cave with a plate spinning on his head. The point is that the objects in your framework become slots with which you associate particular information you want to recall. As long as you have broken information into meaningful chunks, you can store these chunks in the slots of your framework.

A variation of the familiar place framework is to imagine a route that you commonly take (e.g., the way you drive home). To identify slots, select familiar objects or places you pass along the way: (1) the stop sign at the corner, (2) the school on the left side of the road, (3) the restaurant, and so on.

5. Provide students with mnemonics for important content.

A *mnemonic* is a word, phrase, rhyme, or similar device that provides a cue to the information to be remembered. For example, the colors of the spectrum (red, orange, yellow, green, blue, indigo, and violet) become easier to remember when you realize the first letter of each color spells the name *Roy G. Biv*. Similarly, the five Great Lakes (Huron, Ontario, Michigan, Erie, and Superior) can be arranged so that their first letters spell the word *homes*.

With a little ingenuity, teachers and students can devise mnemonic devices for a variety of types of declarative information.

Dimension 2
Acquire & Integrate Knowledge

*Helping Students Acquire
and Integrate Declarative
Knowledge*

✔ *Classroom Examples*

Classroom Examples

The following classroom examples are offered to stimulate reflection on how to apply the ideas covered in this section of Dimension 2 in your classroom.

In previous years, a favorite unit in the first grade was the unit on birds. Students read about birds, listened to stories about birds, studied parts of birds and their behavior, went bird watching, created a class "Bird Book," and wrote individual reports about different types of birds. Although the teachers liked the unit, they realized that they had done a better job of identifying activities than they had of identifying the declarative knowledge students would be learning. Therefore, they began to list the information about birds that they hoped students would learn. Next, they began to organize this list of declarative knowledge using the common organizational patterns (i.e., facts, generalizations, concepts, and so on). As a result of planning in this way, they decided they had too many facts and that the unit would be stronger if they organized the information under a key concept and a generalization, as follows:

At the end of the unit, students will

- *understand the characteristics of living things (key concept) and*

- *understand that animals have characteristics that help them live in different environments (generalization).*

Using these organizational patterns, the teachers restructured the bird unit. They kept many of the activities that the students loved but made sure that each activity increased students' understanding of the identified declarative knowledge.

• • •

One goal of Mrs. Garron's fifth-grade unit on Mayans and Aztecs was to help students understand why and how civilizations throughout history have experienced a rise and then a fall. She decided to use the mental imagery strategy to help students develop this understanding. From the text and supplementary materials in her file, she pulled out details that would help students create images of the Mayan and Aztec civilizations. She then guided students through the process of creating detailed mental pictures of the thriving cities. Finally, she provided details that helped students change their images by creating mental pictures of the demise of these cultures. Students created pictures of the people fighting among themselves over gold, of military attacks on the cities, and of barren fields that had been farmed too heavily. As students created these images, Mrs. Garron noticed that they were highly engaged and interested in the task. They also asked questions that indicated they were beginning to understand the information.

In a later unit, when Mrs. Garron presented pictures of ghost towns in the western United States, she asked students to recall their pictures of the demise of the Mayans and Aztecs and to use that information to offer possible reasons that the towns had become ghost towns. She was thrilled when students easily transferred that knowledge to the examples from American history, thus demonstrating their understanding and retention of the information from the previous unit.

• • •

A team of health education teachers decided to organize their content around some key concepts and generalizations. For example, they wanted students to see that almost all topics in health (e.g., exercise, diet, blood sugar, and stress) can be studied from the perspective of balance. They wanted students to be able explain the ideal balance related to each topic, define specific conditions that result when things are out of balance, and describe ways that people reestablish balance. To help students see this common pattern, they organized the information they would use to teach each topic in the following ways:

Describe optimal balance for <u>blood sugar</u>

Describe the condition(s) related to too little <u>blood sugar</u>.

Describe the condition(s) related to too much <u>blood sugar</u>.

• • •

Out of frustration, a study group of students in a high school chemistry class decided to take the time to memorize some troublesome chemical symbols that they kept forgetting. They used some memory strategies they had learned in other classes, and their work paid off. For iron (Fe), for example, they created the mental image of the giant from <u>Jack and the Beanstalk</u> in his home with his wife ironing his huge overalls and complaining loudly, "<u>Fe</u>, Fi, <u>Fe</u>, Fum, ironing these pants is just plain dumb." For gold (Au), they created a mental picture of an old gold miner running after a thief who is carrying away a big pile of his shiny gold. The miner is yelling, "HEY YOU! HEY YOU! Bring back my gold!"

Unit Planning: Dimension 2, Declarative Knowledge

Planning to teach declarative knowledge requires asking and answering the question:

What will be done to help students acquire and integrate declarative knowledge?

There are four basic steps included in the process of answering this question, three of which require answering some additional questions:

Step 1: What declarative knowledge will students be in the process of acquiring and integrating? As a result of this unit, students will know or understand. . . .

Step 2: What experiences or activities will be used to help students acquire and integrate this knowledge?

Step 3: What strategies will be used to help students construct meaning for, organize, and/or store this knowledge?

Step 4: Describe what will be done.

There is a place on the Dimension 2 Planning Guide: Declarative Knowledge (see page 92) to record the responses to the planning questions and to describe what will be done to help students acquire and integrate the identified declarative knowledge. A sample page from the planning guide for this dimension has been filled out—using these planning questions—for a hypothetical social studies unit about Colorado. (This unit topic was chosen because, with some changes, it can be used for a unit about any state or region and at many developmental levels. The entire Colorado unit planning guide, for all of the dimensions, can be found in Chapter 6, "Putting It All Together." The chapter also includes general recommendations for assessment.) The following sections walk you through the four steps required to plan declarative knowledge and provide recommendations and points to keep in mind as you plan.

Dimension 2

Acquire & Integrate Knowledge

*Helping Students Acquire
and Integrate Declarative
Knowledge*
✔ *Unit Planning*

Step 1

> What declarative knowledge will students be in the process of **acquiring and integrating**? As a result of this unit, students will know or understand...

Identifying the declarative knowledge for a unit is often one of the most difficult parts of planning. This is because of the quantity of declarative knowledge that you might include in a unit and because you should be careful to include *only important knowledge*. To aid you in this part of the process, notice that this section, Step 1, walks you through the identification process and provides worksheet and graphic formats you may use as you make decisions. After you identify the important declarative knowledge, transfer each piece of knowledge to the planning guide and continue the planning process, Steps 2, 3, and 4. (See, for example, a page of the planning guide for declarative knowledge for the Colorado Unit on page 92. The entire unit can be found at the end of Chapter 6.)

Answering this key question in Step 1 of the planning process requires additional steps. These steps will vary as a function of the requirements and philosophy of your school or district. You may have a great deal of autonomy in identifying the knowledge students are to acquire, or you may need to closely follow *standards* and *benchmarks* from your state, district, or school. (Standards are statements of the information and skills that all students should learn before they graduate. Benchmarks translate standards into what students should know and be able to do at various developmental levels.) Suggestions and examples are provided for both situations: when you are planning with standards and benchmarks and when you are planning without them.

a. Identify the title or focus for the unit. This might be a theme (e.g., survival, heroes); a topic (e.g., Colorado, Civil War, Romeo and Juliet); a concept (e.g., *force, energy, revolution*); a principle or generalization (e.g., "Art both influences and reflects life"); or any other unifying idea that brings meaning to the unit.

b. Brainstorm a list of information that you might include in the unit. The purpose of this step is to begin to think about the important declarative knowledge that could be a focus for the unit. If you are in a district with standards and benchmarks, identify the benchmarks that might be addressed in the unit.

c. Identify and organize the declarative knowledge that students will learn. As you decide what information should be included from the list that you brainstormed, consider the question, "Are any of the following organizational patterns important in the unit?"

Dimension 2
Acquire & Integrate Knowledge

*Helping Students Acquire
and Integrate Declarative
Knowledge*
✔ *Unit Planning*

- concepts
- generalizations/principles
- episodes
- process/cause-effect relationships

- time sequences
- descriptions
  - vocabulary terms
  - facts describing specific persons, places, things, events

This identification and organization of information might be recorded on a declarative knowledge worksheet, then displayed graphically. There are two versions of the worksheet, along with their corresponding graphics, that simply show how the planning process looks different when you are guided by standards and benchmarks, and when you are not. Each process requires the following steps:

Without standards and benchmarks (see Sample Worksheet and Unit Planning Graphic: Colorado Unit, pages 86 to 87):

- Identify any organizational patterns that are important in this unit.
- Identify the important declarative knowledge that will be organized into these patterns.
- When necessary, identify any additional or specific knowledge that provides support for, examples of, or further explanations of more general knowledge.

With standards and benchmarks (see Sample Worksheet and Unit Planning Graphic: Colorado Unit, pages 88 to 89):

Identify the benchmarks that will be the focus of the unit, then do the following:

- Identify any organizational patterns that are important in this unit.
- For each benchmark, identify the important declarative knowledge that will be organized into these patterns.
- When necessary, identify any additional or specific knowledge that provides support for, examples of, or further explanations of more general knowledge.

Note that with both of these approaches, you are asked to identify more specific information that "provides support for, examples of, or further explanations of" the more general knowledge. This emphasizes that much of the more *specific* information already organized into vocabulary terms, facts, time sequences, process/cause-effect relationships, and episodes in a unit can be organized to support more *general* concepts and generalizations/principles.

Sample Worksheet: Colorado Unit
Declarative Knowledge <u>Without</u> Standards and Benchmarks

Step 1

What declarative knowledge will students be in the process of ***acquiring and integrating***? As a result of this unit, students will know or understand. . . . (Use worksheet below to answer this question.)

Identify any organizational patterns that are important in this unit:	Identify the important declarative knowledge that will be organized into these patterns. When necessary, identify any additional or specific knowledge that provides support for, examples of, or further explanations of more general knowledge.
Concepts?	*Topography, natural resources, climate, culture* *—facts about Colorado that are examples of each of these concepts*
Generalizations/ principles?	*Topography, natural resources, and climate influence the culture of a region.* *—examples from Colorado (e.g., Mountains and snow influence winter sports culture.)*
Episodes?	
Processes/cause-effects?	
Time sequences?	*Story of the Colorado Gold Rush, 1859-1900*
Descriptions: facts, vocabulary terms?	*Facts describing how Molly Brown, Zebulon Pike, and Alferd Packer interacted with their environments* *Vocabulary terms: tourism, urban*

Unit Planning Graphic: Colorado Unit
Declarative Knowledge (Without Standards and Benchmarks)

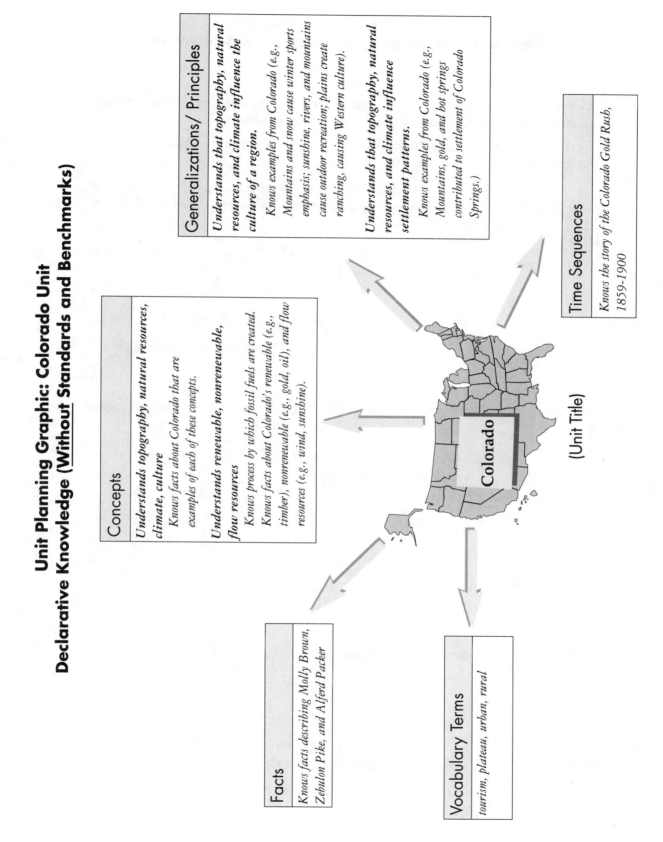

Generalizations/ Principles

Understands that topography, natural resources, and climate influence the culture of a region.

    Knows examples from Colorado (e.g., Mountains and snow cause winter sports emphasis; sunshine, rivers, and mountains cause outdoor recreation; plains create ranching, causing Western culture).

Understands that topography, natural resources, and climate influence settlement patterns.

    Knows examples from Colorado (e.g., Mountains, gold, and hot springs contributed to settlement of Colorado Springs.)

Concepts

Understands topography, natural resources, climate, culture

    Knows facts about Colorado that are examples of each of these concepts.

Understands renewable, nonrenewable, flow resources

    Knows process by which fossil fuels are created.
    Knows facts about Colorado's renewable (e.g., timber), nonrenewable (e.g., gold, oil), and flow resources (e.g., wind, sunshine).

Time Sequences

Knows the story of the Colorado Gold Rush, 1859-1900

Colorado

(Unit Title)

Facts

Knows facts describing Molly Brown, Zebulon Pike, and Alferd Packer

Vocabulary Terms

tourism, plateau, urban, rural

87

Sample Worksheet: Colorado Unit
Declarative Knowledge <u>With</u> Standards and Benchmarks

Step 1

What declarative knowledge will students be in the process of **acquiring and integrating**? As a result of this unit, students will know or understand. . . . (Use worksheet below to answer this question.)

Identify any organizational patterns that are important in this unit:	For each benchmark, identify the important declarative knowledge that will be organized into these patterns. When necessary, identify any additional or specific knowledge that provides support for, examples of, or further explanations of more general knowledge.
	Benchmark Understands the interactions between humans and their physical environment within a region
Concepts?	*Topography, natural resources, climate, culture* *—facts about Colorado that are examples of each of these concepts*
Generalizations/ principles?	*Topography, natural resources, and climate influence the culture of a region.* *—examples from Colorado (e.g., Mountains and snow influence winter sports culture.)*
Episodes?	
Processes/cause-effects?	
Time sequences?	*Story of the Colorado Gold Rush, 1859-1900*
Descriptions: facts, vocabulary terms?	*Facts describing how Molly Brown, Zebulon Pike, and Alferd Packer interacted with their environments* *Vocabulary terms: tourism, urban*

Unit Planning Graphic: Colorado Unit Declarative Knowledge (With Standards and Benchmarks)

Geography Standard 1, Benchmark 2(D): Understands the interactions among humans and their physical environment within a region

Concepts: Understands topography, natural resources, climate, culture

Knows facts about Colorado that are examples of each of these concepts

Generalizations/Principles: Understands that topography, natural resources, and climate influence the culture of a region.

Knows examples from Colorado (e.g., Mountains and snow influence winter sports culture.)

Facts: Knows how Molly Brown, Zebulon Pike, Alfred Packer's interacted with their physical environments.

Vocabulary Terms: tourism, plateau

Geography Standard 2, Benchmark 5(D): Understands the reasons for human movement within and among regions.

Generalizations/Principles: Understands that topography, natural resources, and climate influence settlement patterns.

Knows examples from Colorado (e.g., Mountains, gold, and hot springs contributed to the settlement of Colorado Springs.

Vocabulary Terms: urban, rural

Colorado

(Unit Title)

Other declarative knowledge not related to benchmarks:

Knows the story of the Colorado Gold Rush, 1859-1900.

Geography Standard 3, Benchmark 2(D): Understands characteristics and locations of renewable and nonrenewable resources

Concepts: Understands renewable resources, nonrenewable resources, and flow resources

Knows process by which fossil fuels are created

Knows facts about Colorado's renewable (e.g., timber), nonrenewable (e.g., gold, oil), and flow resources (e.g., wind, sunshine).

89

Dimension 2

Acquire & Integrate Knowledge

*Helping Students Acquire
and Integrate Declarative
Knowledge*

✔ *Unit Planning*

Step 2

> What **experiences** or **activities** will be used to help students acquire and integrate this knowledge?

For each major piece of knowledge, identify how students will have access to the knowledge. (For this step and for Steps 3 and 4, refer to the filled-in planning guide for the Colorado Unit, page 92.) Will they have direct, active experiences (e.g., field trips, simulations) or indirect experiences (e.g., reading the text, viewing a film, listening to lecture or discussion)? Some activities or experiences that might be included are

- read text
- go on field trip
- conduct experiment
- observe demonstration
- engage in discussion

- view film
- do independent research
- participate in simulation
- interview sources

Step 3

> What strategies will be used to help students **construct meaning** for, **organize**, and/or **store** this knowledge?

Because we know that rich experiences and activities do not guarantee that students will learn what you want them to, select strategies to use with these activities that will increase the likelihood that they will construct meaning, organize, and store the knowledge. Keep in mind that these three phases of learning declarative knowledge overlap (i.e., strategies that help them construct meaning also might help them organize and store). However, it is important to ask yourself questions relating to each phase. (See page 91 for questions and a summary of strategies included in this chapter.)

Step 4

> Describe what will be done.

Provide a brief description of how the strategies will be used in conjunction with the identified experiences and activities.

Dimension 2
Acquire & Integrate Knowledge

*Helping Students Acquire
and Integrate Declarative
Knowledge*
✔ *Unit Planning*

Summary of Strategies for Use in Step 3 of Planning for Declarative Knowledge

What will be done to help students *construct meaning* for this knowledge? Strategies might include the following:

1. Help students understand what it means to construct meaning.

2. Use the three-minute pause.

3. Help students experience content using a variety of senses.

4. Help students to construct meaning for vocabulary terms.

5. Present students with the K-W-L strategy.

6. Create opportunities for students to discover or figure out the new information for themselves.

7. Use instructional techniques that provide students with strategies to use before, during, and after they receive information.

What will be done to help students *organize* this knowledge? Strategies might include the following:

1. Help students understand the importance of organizing information.

2. Have students use graphic organizers for the identified organizational patterns.

3. Provide students with advance organizer questions.

4. Present note-taking strategies that use graphic representations.

5. Have students create physical and pictographic representations of information.

6. Have students use graphs and charts.

What will be done to help students *store* this knowledge? Strategies might include the following:

1. Help students understand the process of storing information.

2. Present students with the strategy of using symbols and substitutes.

3. Use the link strategy with students.

4. Use highly structured systems for storing information with students.

5. Provide students with mnemonics for important content.

Dimension 2 Planning Guide: Declarative Knowledge

Unit: _Colorado_

Step 1	Step 2	Step 3	Step 4
What **declarative knowledge** will students be in the process of **acquiring and integrating**? As a result of this unit, students will know or understand. . .	What **experiences** or **activities** will be used to help students acquire and integrate this knowledge?	What strategies will be used to help students **construct meaning** for, **organize**, and/or **store** this knowledge?	Describe what will be done.
Concept: Topography —Natural and artificial features including land forms, bodies of water, road, bridges, etc. Facts describing Colorado's topography will deal with the Rocky Mountains, sand dunes, rivers, plains, plateaus, canyons.	Text, pp. 8–10	K-W-L	_On a class K-W-L chart, we all will generate the K and the W related to topography. We will then read the text, watch the film, and read physical maps. After each experience, we will fill out the L of the chart. We will use the information from the K-W-L chart to start a class pictograph of examples of topography._
	Film: "From Sea to Shining Sea"		
	Read physical maps	Physical/pictographic representation	
	Independent study: Regional cake		_Each student will make a cake depicting topography from a region of his or her choice. Students will find information independently. After the regional cake assignment, as a class, we will add to our pictograph._
Concept: Natural Resources —Materials found in nature that are useful, necessary, or attractive Facts describing Colorado's natural resources will deal with snow, gold, soil, sunshine, forests, oil, mountains.	Film: "From Sea to Shining Sea"	3–minute pause	_Several times during the film, I will stop and ask students to identify one type of natural resource. After the film, I will ask them to try to create mental pictures of examples of natural resources and identify what they see, smell, feel, etc. We then will start our pictographs of natural resources, a class one and individual ones. After reading the natural resource maps, we will add information to the pictographs._
	Read natural resource maps	Use all senses	
	Field Trip: Argo Gold Mine	Pictograph	_During the field trip, students will have their pictographs with them so they can add examples of the natural resources that we observe._

Helping Students Acquire and Integrate Procedural Knowledge

Acquiring and integrating procedural knowledge requires students to develop the ability to perform and use critical skills and processes, both physical skills and processes, like typing, and mental skills and processes, like solving an equation. Helping students successfully acquire procedural knowledge at every developmental level is especially important because learning complex skills and processes is often dependent on how well simpler skills and processes have been learned. For example, students will have trouble learning to design a building if they have not mastered the skills of measuring to a scale. The fact that each piece of procedural knowledge can be so important and the fact that students master skills and processes at such different rates means that we as educators must understand the phases of acquiring and integrating procedural knowledge—construct models, shape, and internalize—and be able to structure experiences so that all students can be successful.

Construct Models for Procedural Knowledge

The first phase of learning a skill or process is to develop a rough model of the steps involved. For example, when you first learned to hit a golf ball, someone probably showed you what to do before you actually tried a shot on your own. Your instructor may have demonstrated the proper grip, the proper stance, how to shift your weight, and so on. Likewise, when you first learned long division, someone probably showed you the steps in the process. In short, when we learn a new procedure, we need a place to start; we need a model. Without an initial model, learning a skill or process can be chaotic and time consuming because it is essentially a trial-and-error process. Helping students construct models is essential if students are to efficiently and effectively learn procedural knowledge.

When helping students to construct models, it is important to be aware of and sensitive to the fact that a process or skill you are teaching is new to them, although you use it automatically. When helping students to construct a model of the steps, be careful not to omit important steps or make assumptions about students' abilities to perform the procedures embedded in a single step.

There are several ways that you can help students construct models. It is advantageous to use more than one approach when helping students construct a model for the steps involved in any procedure. By doing so, you

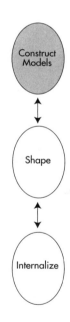

are likely to reach more students because one technique may "connect" for one student and not for another. In addition, you will be addressing more than one learning-style preference by using more than one strategy.

1. Help students understand the importance of constructing models for procedural knowledge.

Anderson (1990) *Cognitive Psychology and its Implications*

Anderson (1995) *Learning and Memory*

It can be beneficial for students to understand that acquiring procedural knowledge begins with constructing a model, or a set of steps, for the skill or process. Like acquiring declarative knowledge by constructing meaning, developing procedural knowledge requires learners to "construct" the steps in their heads by observing others performing the skill or process, by reading an instruction manual, or by figuring out the steps for themselves. Simply watching someone else perform the skill or process, and then mimicking his or her actions, leads to inefficient learning. Help students to understand the importance of constructing models by

- explaining the process of constructing models and providing examples from your learning experiences;

- helping students to think of examples from their own lives when they had to learn a specific set of steps to be successful; and

- setting up an experiment with students in which you teach them a skill without helping them construct a model, then teach another skill with specific strategies for constructing models. Ask students to compare the learning experiences in terms of how confident they feel about using the skill, how long they can remember how to use it, and the extent to which they can use it in different contexts.

2. Use a think-aloud process to demonstrate a new skill or process.

Suhor (1984) "Toward a Semiotics-based Curriculum"

This is a simple yet powerful technique for building an initial model. It involves verbalizing your thoughts as you demonstrate the skill or process. It is important, of course, that your thinking include all the important parts of the skill or process. For example, a teacher using a think-aloud process to help students develop a model of two-column addition might write a problem on the board and then say,

Let's see. The first thing I have to do is add up the numbers in the ones column: 2 plus 3 equals 5, and 7 more equals 12. That's 12 ones, which equals 1 ten and 2 ones. I write down the 2 ones and take the 1 ten over to the tens column. I think I'll write the 1 at the top of the tens column so I don't forget it.

3. Provide or construct with students a written or graphic representation of the skill or process they are learning.

For some students, watching a teacher model a skill or process will not sufficiently prepare them to construct a clear, accurate model for themselves. They may also need a written or graphic representation that describes or depicts each step. Depending on the skill or process, these representations could be in the form of one or several of the following: a set of written steps (see Figure 2.11), a flow chart (see Figure 2.12), or a series of pictures or symbols (see Figure 2.13).

Gagne (1989) *Studies of Learning: 50 Years of Research*

FIGURE 2.11

A SET OF WRITTEN STEPS FOR READING A BAR GRAPH

> a. *Read the title of the graph. Get a sense of the information that will be in it.*
>
> b. *Look at the horizontal line at the bottom of the graph. Identify what is being measured on it.*
>
> c. *Look at the vertical line on the left side. What is being measured on it? Look at the scale that is used.*
>
> d. *For each of the items measured on the horizontal line, identify its "height" on the vertical line and interpret that height.*
>
> e. *Make a statement that summarizes the important information in the bar graph.*

FIGURE 2.12

A FLOW CHART FOR THE PROCESS OF INVENTION

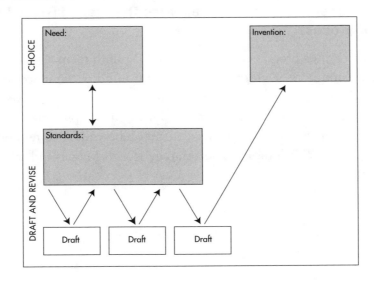

FIGURE 2.13

A SERIES OF PICTURES OR SYMBOLS FOR SERVING A TENNIS BALL

Perhaps Chinese and Japanese restaurants should consider providing customers with more specific directions on how to use chopsticks. Instead of simply including a picture of someone using chopsticks, the directions should include the following specific steps:

1. *Grasp one chopstick in the valley between the thumb and forefinger.*

2. *Stabilize this chopstick with the upper part of the thumb and the lower part of the ring finger.*

3. *Place other chopstick between tips of thumb and forefinger. Do NOT stabilize it. Rest chopstick on end of middle finger.*

4. *Adjust small ends of chopsticks to make them even.*

5. *Move second chopstick back and forth, making small ends touch.*

6. *Use step 5 to grasp a bite of food.*

4. Help students see how the skill or process they are learning is similar to and different from other skills or processes.

To help students develop a sense of the new skill or process, it can be useful to show them how some steps are similar to the steps of another skill or process that they have already learned. You might also point out how the previously learned skill might seem similar, but is really different. For example, while teaching students to swing a baseball bat, a teacher might review the steps of swinging a golf club, which were learned in a previous lesson. The goal is to emphasize the steps that are similar, but also to explain which steps are different and how having a skill in one might cause errors in using the other skill. (e.g., being able to swing a golf club might cause you to incorrectly swing a baseball bat).

5. Teach students to mentally rehearse the steps involved in a skill or process.

A model of a skill or process can be reinforced through mental rehearsal, which means simply reviewing the steps in your mind without actually performing them. For example, you might rehearse the steps involved in hitting a golf ball by going over them in your mind and picturing yourself doing each part of the process. In effect, mental rehearsal helps reinforce the basic model of a skill or process. This strategy is well-known and widely used by athletes.

Shape Procedural Knowledge

Constructing an initial model for a new skill or process is just the first step in learning procedural knowledge. Once you actually begin to use the skill or process, you will probably alter your initial model. You will start to find out what works and what does not work and, in response, you will modify your approach, adding some things and dropping others. You may also become aware of variations in using the process, potential problem areas, common errors, and how to use the process or skill in different contexts—like driving on a wet road versus driving on a dry road, or driving on a highway versus driving in a parking lot. This is called *shaping*. For example, after you constructed an initial model for performing long division, you began to discover some shortcuts and "tricks" that made the process work better for you. Similarly, after you first learned how to create text on your word processor, you began to identify ways that you could use the word processor more efficiently.

The importance of shaping a new skill or process cannot be exaggerated, and yet it is often shortchanged or even ignored. It is perhaps the most crucial part of learning a new skill or process because without it, errors can creep in and become internalized and, therefore, difficult to correct. It is also during this phase that students attend to their conceptual understanding of skills and processes so that they are not focused on simply learning a set of steps. Lack of attention to this aspect of learning procedural knowledge is a primary reason for students' failure to effectively use basic skills and processes. When planning for procedural knowledge, classroom activities for shaping should be included. To help with this planning, the following sections offer suggestions of strategies and techniques that can help students shape procedural knowledge.

1. Help students understand the importance of shaping procedural knowledge.

As we have just discussed, it is essential for teachers to understand the importance of shaping. Similarly, students might see more value in assignments that are designed to encourage shaping if they understand this phase in acquiring procedural knowledge. The idea that shaping is a process of making a skill or process "your own" might appeal to some students and help them to understand and use some of the strategies in this section. Facilitating this understanding can be done a number of ways including the following:

- Take the time to explain to students the process of shaping.

"Hours of learning time and energy can be saved. . . and achievement results will reach a higher level more rapidly if students' initial practice is guided and monitored by the teacher."

—Hunter (1982)
Mastery Teaching, p. 71.

For more on the importance of shaping, see Healy (1990) *Endangered Minds*.

Acquire & Integrate Knowledge

Helping Students Acquire and Integrate Procedural Knowledge

✔ *Shape*

- Share with students your own personal experiences with shaping a skill or process, and encourage them to identify and share their own.

- Ask students what happens when they practice a skill that they are performing incorrectly.

- Encourage students to offer suggestions for improving or adapting skills and processes. Explain why this is an important part of the culture of the classroom.

- Look for, and encourage students to look for, real-life examples of people shaping a skill or process and, therefore, improving their ability to use it.

2. Demonstrate and create opportunities for students to practice using the important variations of the skill or process.

Every skill or process has variations, the understanding of which is important to the successful use of the skill or process. For example, to skillfully perform three-column addition, you must understand a number of variations in that process: what to do when you have to carry from the first column to the second, what to do when you do *not* have to carry from the first column to the second and so on, what to do if the numbers are presented horizontally rather than in a column. Helping students shape a new skill or process requires illustrating these important variations. For example, to shape the process of three-column addition, a teacher might use a single problem but keep changing it to illustrate all the variations. To highlight the variations, the teacher might ask questions like the following: "What would happen if the 4 were a 7? Now, how many ones and how many tens would I have? Now suppose in the tens column I had two tens from the ones column. What would happen?"

In addition to working through one or two examples and asking what-would-happen-if questions, the teacher should create opportunities for students to practice using all of the variations. After working through the single example with all the variations, the teacher might give students problems to work out that exemplify all of the variations they have seen demonstrated.

3. Point out common errors and pitfalls.

It is easy for errors to creep into a skill or process during the early phases of learning. If these errors are not identified and corrected during the shaping process, they may be practiced and become difficult to correct later. Whether the targeted skill is using a lathe (where errors could result in injury) or a

Dimension 2
Acquire & Integrate Knowledge

*Helping Students Acquire
and Integrate Procedural
Knowledge*
✔ *Shape*

skill necessary for writing (where errors result in poor communication), it is important to help students identify and correct errors. This should happen during the shaping process in a number of ways:

- Identify and demonstrate some common errors. As you demonstrate the errors, think out loud to model the process of noticing and correcting errors.

- Demonstrate the skill process and make obvious and subtle errors. Ask students to observe closely and try recognize and describe the errors. Then have them suggest corrective measures.

- As students are working, provide feedback that will help them become aware of and correct errors they are making.

- Ask students to interview people who have mastered the skill or process. Emphasize that they should focus their interview questions on the parts of the skill or process where errors are commonly made so that they can avoid such pitfalls.

- Encourage students to share with peers the parts of the skill or process that they find difficult and elicit suggestions from peers for avoiding mistakes.

- When necessary, help students develop a new model for the part of the skill or process that is proving to be troublesome for them.

4. Help students develop the conceptual understanding necessary to use the skill or process.

Part of the shaping process is helping students to understand the skill or process, that is, to know its various uses and to understand any important concepts related to the skill or process. Technically, this means that it is important to make sure that students have the declarative knowledge they need to use the procedural knowledge. If students learn to do an analysis of variance in statistics, for example, but do not understand the concept of variance, the skill becomes relatively useless. Likewise, if students are learning to find points on a map, but do not understand the various uses of maps, their acquired skill is of limited value to them. To make sure students understand what they need to use a skill, consider the following suggestions.

a. Describe a variety of situations or contexts in which students can use a specific skill or process.

Teachers can help students understand that most skills or processes vary according the situation or context in which they are being used. For example, the skills involved in driving a car change somewhat when

Dimension 2
Acquire & Integrate Knowledge

*Helping Students Acquire
and Integrate Procedural
Knowledge*
✔ *Shape*

there is wet pavement rather than dry pavement; hemming a pair of pants requires slight variations in some of the steps as a function of the fabric used; and map reading skills may need to be slightly adapted to different types of maps.

Students will use a skill much more proficiently if, during shaping, they are provided with different situations or contexts that require them to use the skill, and then are cued to notice what adaptations and adjustments they must make in each setting.

b. *Check for students' level of understanding of key concepts and principles (declarative knowledge) related to the skill or process.*

When initially planing for procedural knowledge, it is, of course, important to identify and plan for teaching the declarative knowledge students will need in order to learn and use the identified skills and processes. However, even when this declarative knowledge has been taught, it is important to periodically check students' level of understanding of important concepts as they are learning the skills and processes. Practicing a skill or process that has little meaning is not an effective use of students' time. During shaping,

*   review important concepts and ask students to identify any that are confusing;

*   as they begin to practice the skills and processes, periodically ask students to explain to you, or to each other, what they are doing and why they are doing it; and

*   listen to their explanations to detect confusions, misconceptions, or lack of important knowledge. When necessary, postpone having students practice the skill or process and, instead, provide additional opportunities for them to *understand* what they are learning *to do*.

Internalize Procedural Knowledge

The last aspect of learning a new skill or process is internalizing it. For some skills and processes, this means learning them to the point where you can use them without much conscious thought. This level of skill is called *automaticity* because you use the skill or process automatically. In fact, some skills and processes have to be used automatically if they are to be truly useful. Imagine how difficult driving a car would be, for example, if the skill of using the brake were not an automatic response. If you always had to think about when and how to use the brake, there might be serious consequences.

You cannot achieve automaticity in all skills and processes, but you can develop fluency in them. For example, the process of editing is never automatic, but good editors are quite fluent in the language of editing. Although good editors have to think about what they are doing, they have internalized the necessary skills to the degree that they can use them with relative ease.

For a process to be learned to the level of automaticity or fluency, extensive practice is required. Because learning procedural processes is time consuming, it is important to identify those processes and skills that students truly need to internalize versus those with which students simply need to be familiar. A good deal of time and effort should then be devoted to helping all students internalize those skills and processes identified as needing this level of learning. It important to understand that students can often pass a test without internalizing the skill or process. If it is important for students to internalize a skill so that they can, for example, use it in six months, teachers must provide students with the time and experiences necessary to internalize it. Teachers often give students enough time and practice to learn a process or skill well enough to pass a test but not enough time to actually internalize it. The following sections highlight some things you can do to help students internalize procedural knowledge.

1. Help students understand the importance of internalizing procedural knowledge.

Achieving automaticity or fluency with a skill or process requires practice, something students often resist. It might be helpful, even motivating, for students to understand the internalizing phase of acquiring procedural knowledge.

You can easily point out examples from students' lives in which they internalized skills (e.g., riding a bike, forming letters, and throwing a ball)

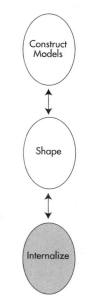

Dimension 2
Acquire & Integrate Knowledge

*Helping Students Acquire
and Integrate Procedural
Knowledge*
✔ *Internalize*

and emphasize that they achieved this level of mastery because of practice. Students might be able to remember that during the process of learning a skill, like riding a bike, they could think of nothing else because the learning process consumed all of their mental energy. Yet now they can ride a bike, talk to a friend, and enjoy the scenery all at the same time because the skills of riding a bike have been internalized and there is mental energy left to do other things simultaneously. Help students to understand that many, although not all, skills they are learning in school need to be acquired so that they can use these skills with relative ease.

Suggestions for building this understanding might include the following:

- Explain internalizing, and provide students with examples from your own life.

- Teach students a skill without having them internalize it. Give them a test, wait for a period of time, and then announce you are going to test them again. Many students will protest that they cannot perform the skill now, even though they passed the test. Discuss with them what is required to internalize a skill, that is, to be able to use it in the future.

- Use examples from daily life, current events, movies, or books that exemplify the process of internalizing. For example, in the movie *Karate Kid*, the teacher had the boy wax cars ("Wax on. Wax off.") to internalize the specific hand movements that he would use later in more complex karate moves.

2. Help students set up a practice schedule.

"Practice makes permanent, not perfect."

When students are first learning a new skill or process, they should practice it immediately and frequently; that is, they should engage in *massed practice*. For example, in a computer technology class period, you might have students construct a model for the process of operating a spread-sheet program by demonstrating the process and making a flow chart. After students have spent time shaping the process, have them begin massed practice. Pairs of students might work at the computer and practice the process of operating the spread-sheet program as many times as possible before the end of a period. You might also provide time for students to practice the next day—perhaps not for as long a period of time as on the previous day, but for a substantial amount of time. You could gradually increase the intervals of time between practice sessions. Instead of practicing every day, you could have students practice every other day, then every third day, and so on. This is called *distributed practice*, lengthening the intervals of time between practice sessions. Over time, students would naturally internalize the new skill.

In general, then, practice sessions should initially be spaced close together and then gradually spaced further and further apart. Figure 2.14 shows the relationship between massed and distributed practice.

FIGURE 2.14

RELATIONSHIP BETWEEN MASSED AND DISTRIBUTED PRACTICE

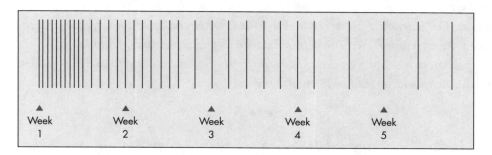

3. Have students chart and report on their speed and/or accuracy when practicing new skills or processes.

When developing some skills, the emphasis is on accuracy; when developing others, the emphasis is on accuracy and speed. One way of helping students to develop new skills and processes is to have them keep a record of their progress as they practice. If they are working on accuracy, they can divide a series of problems, for example, into several clusters, and then chart the number they solved correctly for each cluster. If they are working on accuracy and speed, they can create a chart that indicates how many problems they were able to solve correctly in a given period of time, and then try to beat that time for the next cluster. If accuracy suffered when speed increased, they can decide if they should slow down again to achieve accuracy.

When students are keeping speed and accuracy charts, you should remind them that they are internalizing the skill, that is, they are practicing so that the skill becomes permanent and automatic. The charts can help answer the question that students often pose, "If I know how to do these problems, why do I have to do 20 of them?"

Classroom Examples

The following classroom examples are offered to stimulate reflection on how to apply the ideas covered in this section of Dimension 2 in your classroom.

Mrs. Fox had been teaching a unit on percents. Her students were doing well computing percentages in different types of problems. She decided to give them some story problems so that they could apply their new skills. To her dismay, most of the students were unable to solve all of the problems. As a result of conferencing with some of her students, she realized that she had not taught the declarative knowledge associated with the procedures of calculating percentages. Her students did not understand when to use which type of calculation nor what the problems actually meant. For example, when asked to determine what percentage of the original price the sale price represented, most students did not know which procedure, formula, or calculation to use. She then decided to identify the important concepts and information related to percentages and teach that to her students.

• • •

Ms. Hallfield was trying to help students understand and use analogies. She decided to teach students how to solve analogy problems (e.g., Man is to boy :: king is to_____. Answers: a. child b. prince c. queen d. son). Although she demonstrated these problems through a think-aloud technique, she realized that many of her students were not improving their ability to solve them. She recalled a conversation she had with a friend, an athletic coach, who had described how clearly students must know each step of a process. She decided to present students with a set of written steps for solving the analogy problems (see below), even though she thought the steps were fairly obvious. She was surprised to see how much these steps helped some of her students.

1. *Describe the relationship between the two elements in the first set. Verbalize the entire first step, emphasizing the phrase that describes the relationship.*

    For example: "A is similar to B," or "A is the opposite of B," or "A causes B."

2. *Verbalize the given element in the second set along with the relationship phrase in Step 1.*

    For example: Step 1: "A causes B."

    Step 2: "C causes_____."

3. *Finish the second set with an element that has that relationship with the given element.*

• • •

Coach Elway, the physical education teacher, had given his student teacher the responsibility of teaching students to pass a football. The student teacher, Kevin, demonstrated throwing a spiral and then asked students to spend the rest of the class period practicing this throw. Because of students' limited success in demonstrating this skill, Kevin sought out Coach Elway for advice. Coach Elway explained that Kevin should have spent more time working with students on each step of the process of throwing the ball and helping them shape the process before asking them to practice.

• • •

Shirley's father said to Mrs. Cliburn, the piano teacher, "Why does she have to keep playing the same scales and technique lessons over and over again? She's becoming bored and the rest of us are frustrated, to say the least." Mrs. Cliburn smiled and patiently replied, "The great pianists practice many hours each day. Shirley can play the Chopin nocturne she wants to play only after she has mastered the fundamentals. She must practice, practice, practice."

Dimension 2
Acquire & Integrate Knowledge

*Helping Students Acquire
and Integrate Procedural
Knowledge*
✔ *Unit Planning*

Unit Planning: Dimension 2, Procedural Knowledge

Planning to teach procedural knowledge requires asking and answering the following question:

What will be done to help students acquire and integrate procedural knowledge?

There are three basic steps included in the process of answering this question, two of which require answering additional questions.

Step 1: What procedural knowledge will students be in the process of acquiring and integrating? As a result of this unit, students will be able to...

Step 2: What strategies will be used to help students construct models for, shape, and/or internalize this knowledge?

Step 3: Describe what will be done.

There is a place on the Dimension 2 Planning Guide: Procedural Knowledge (see page 112) to record the responses to the planning questions and to describe what will be done to help students acquire and integrate the identified procedural knowledge. This planning guide has been filled out— using these planning questions—for a hypothetical social studies unit about Colorado. (This unit topic was chosen because, with some changes, it could be used for a unit about any state or region and at many developmental levels. The entire Colorado unit planning guide, for all of the dimensions, can be found in Chapter 6, "Putting It All Together." The chapter also includes general recommendations for assessment.) To help you use the planning process, the following sections walk you through each step and provide recommendations and points to keep in mind as you plan.

Step 1

> What procedural knowledge will students be in the process of **acquiring and integrating**? As a result of this unit, students will be able to. . . .

Answering this first key question in the planning process requires additional steps. These steps will vary as a function of the requirements and philosophy of your school or district. You may have a great deal of autonomy in identifying the knowledge students are to acquire, or you may need to closely follow standards and benchmarks from your state, district, or school. Suggestions and examples are provided for both situations: when you are planning with standards and benchmarks and when you are planning without them.

As you identify the skills or processes that students will be learning, you might record them on the procedural knowledge planning worksheet, then organize them graphically. There are two versions of the worksheet, along with their corresponding graphics, simply to show how the planning process looks different when you are guided by standards and benchmarks and when you are not. Each process requires the following steps:

Without standards and benchmarks (see Sample Worksheet and Unit Planning Graphic: Colorado Unit, page 109):

- Identify the important procedural knowledge (skills and processes).
- When necessary, identify specific skills that support more general processes.

With standards and benchmarks (see Sample Worksheet and Unit Planning Graphic: Colorado Unit, page 110):

Identify the procedural knowledge benchmarks that will be the focus of this unit, then do the following:

- For each benchmark, identify the important procedural knowledge (skills and processes).
- When necessary, identify specific skills that support more general processes.

The goal during planning for either of these situations is to identify exactly what students will be learning to do. It is important to remember, especially when you are guided by benchmarks that identify very general processes, to be fairly specific when identifying the skills and processes students will learn. If the identified procedural knowledge is too general, such as "students will know how to engage in the research process," it will be

Dimension 2

Acquire & Integrate Knowledge

*Helping Students Acquire
and Integrate Procedural
Knowledge*
✔ *Unit Planning*

difficult to generate a single model, or set of steps. Most general processes contain many supporting, specific skills and processes, each with its own set of steps. Therefore, if you start with a very general process, make sure that you also identify skills or processes that are specific enough to generate steps that students can use when they are constructing models for, shaping, and internalizing the procedural knowledge.

Step 2

> What will be done to help students **construct models** for, **shape**, and **internalize** the procedural knowledge?

To answer this question, first decide how proficient students should become in using each skill or process. In some cases, you may simply want to introduce the skill or process and help students construct models and shape the skill or process. In other cases, you may want to help students through each phase of learning procedural knowledge so that they internalize the skill or process.

You might want to consider the strategies from this chapter of the manual as you answer the questions related to each of these phases of learning procedural knowledge. (See page 111 for questions and a summary of these strategies.)

Step 3

> Describe what will be done.

Briefly describe how these strategies will be used to help students acquire the identified procedural knowledge.

Sample Worksheet: Colorado Unit
Procedural Knowledge <u>Without</u> Standards and Benchmarks

What procedural knowledge (skills and processes) will students be in the process of **acquiring and integrating**? As a result of this unit, students will be able to. . . . (Use worksheet below to answer this question.)

Identify the important procedural knowledge (skills and processes).
When necessary, identify specific skills that support more general processes.
read and interpret physical maps
read and interpret natural resource maps

Unit Planning Graphic: Colorado Unit
Procedural Knowledge <u>Without</u> Standards and Benchmarks

Skills/Processes (P)
Knows how to read and interpret physical and natural resource maps

Sample Worksheet: Colorado Unit
Procedural Knowledge <u>With</u> Standards and Benchmarks

What procedural knowledge (skills and processes) will students be in the process of **acquiring and integrating**? As a result of this unit, students will be able to. . . . (Use worksheet below to answer this question.)

For each benchmark, identify the important procedural knowledge (skills and processes).
When necessary, identify specific skills that support more general processes.

Benchmark: Uses thematic maps
 	
    read and interpret physical maps
 	
    read and interpret natural resource maps

Unit Planning Graphic: Colorado Unit
Procedural Knowledge <u>With</u> Standards and Benchmarks

Geography Standard 6, Benchmark 1(P): Uses thematic maps
Knows how to read and interpret physical maps
Knows how to read and interpret natural resource maps

Summary of Strategies for Use in Step 2 of Planning for Procedural Knowledge

What strategies will be used to help students *construct models* for the procedural knowledge?

1. Help students understand the importance of constructing models for procedural knowledge.

2. Use a think-aloud process to demonstrate a new skill or process.

3. Provide or construct with students a written or graphic representation of the skill or process they are learning.

4. Help students see how the skill or process they are learning is similar to and different from other skills or processes.

5. Teach students to mentally rehearse the steps involved in a skill or process.

What strategies will be used to help students *shape* the procedural knowledge?

1. Help students understand the importance of shaping procedural knowledge.

2. Demonstrate and create opportunities for students to practice using the important variations of the skill or process.

3. Point out common errors and pitfalls.

4. Help students develop the conceptual understanding necessary to use the skill or process.

What strategies will be used to help students *internalize* the procedural knowledge?

1. Help students understand the importance of internalizing procedural knowledge.

2. Help students set up a practice schedule.

3. Have students chart and report on their speed and/or accuracy when practicing new skills or processes.

Dimension 2 Planning Guide: Procedural Knowledge

Step 1	Step 2	Step 3
What **procedural knowledge** will students be in the process of **acquiring and integrating**? As a result of this unit, students will be able to. . .	What will be done to help students **construct models** for, **shape**, and **internalize** the knowledge?	Describe what will be done.
read and interpret physical maps.	*Note: These strategies will be used to teach both types of maps.*	*I will talk through the steps of reading a map, demonstrating the steps with each type. I will give them a set of written steps for reading any map.*
read and interpret natural resource maps.	*Think-aloud* *Set of written steps* *Practice with variations* *Internalizing is not a goal.*	*Working in groups, students will receive several variations in format (taken from different textbooks) for both physical and natural resource maps. There will be questions for the group and then for individual students to answer as a way of becoming familiar with each variation. This assignment also will reinforce the learning of the concepts of topography and natural resources.*

Dimension 3

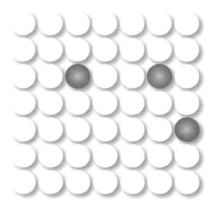

Dimension 3
Extend and Refine Knowledge

Introduction

Learning declarative and procedural knowledge requires much more than simply recalling information or mechanically performing a procedure. The most effective learning occurs when students develop an in-depth understanding of important knowledge so that they can use that knowledge in school and in life. To develop this understanding, learners extend and refine the knowledge they initially acquire. This occurs as learners examine and analyze knowledge and information in a way that helps them make new connections, discover or rediscover meanings, gain new insights, and clarify misconceptions.

For example, when first learning about the concept of *free enterprise*, a student might understand it well enough to generate a definition and some examples. However, broadening that understanding requires him to do more than recite the definition or generate additional examples. It requires him to compare free enterprise to other economic structures or to figure out how the principles of free enterprise can be applied to predict what might happen in new, specific situations. In other words, deepening understanding requires thinking about the information by using reasoning processes that are more complex than those used when knowledge simply is being recognized or reproduced. It necessitates using processes that change—extend and refine—the knowledge.

The principal and faculty at a middle school agreed to focus schoolwide on one complex reasoning process each month. Letters were sent to parents explaining the definition and steps of the process and asking for their support in reinforcing the process at home. Hall bulletin boards, dedicated to the various grade levels and content areas, displayed students' work related to the targeted reasoning process.

Helping Students Develop Complex Reasoning Processes

The eight complex reasoning processes identified in Dimension 3 are offered as resources for teachers as they are helping students to extend and refine their knowledge. It is not sufficient to simply ask students questions or give them assignments that require these types of reasoning processes; educators need to directly teach the processes. The following reasoning processes can be used to deepen students' understanding of what they are learning.

- *Comparing:* Identifying and articulating similarities and differences among items

- *Classifying:* Grouping things into definable categories on the basis of their attributes

- *Abstracting:* Identifying and articulating the underlying theme or general pattern of information

- *Inductive reasoning:* Inferring unknown generalizations or principles from information or observations

- *Deductive reasoning:* Using generalizations and principles to infer unstated conclusions about specific information or situations

- *Constructing support:* Building systems of support for assertions

- *Analyzing errors:* Identifying and articulating errors in thinking

- *Analyzing perspectives:* Identifying multiple perspectives on an issue and examining the reasons or logic behind each

Each of these reasoning processes is used unconsciously by people every day. We compare things. We draw conclusions inductively. We analyze other people's perspectives during informal interactions and in learning situations. However, when teachers require students to use these processes as a means of extending and refining knowledge, they must teach the steps involved in the processes so that students use them deliberately and rigorously.

As schools and districts begin to plan for teaching these processes, they should keep in mind some general principles of implementation:

- Although the eight complex reasoning processes should be systematically and rigorously taught, no single teacher should take on all eight in one semester or school year. If students are to learn and internalize these processes, they must have time to shape and

"Constructing support, analyzing errors, and analyzing perspectives. I call these the thinking skills of marriage."

—A teacher in Iowa

practice them over time. When students are first learning the processes, you should introduce only three or four new processes in any one year.

- Students of all ages are capable of learning and using all of these types of thinking processes. Younger students, of course, may require more guidance and modeling than older students. In addition, they need to apply the processes to developmentally appropriate content. When older students are learning the processes, the same principles apply. They need guidance and modeling in the early stages of learning the processes and may need more guidance later as they use the processes with increasingly complex content.

- It is more likely that students will increase their ability to use different types of thinking if teachers across all grade levels and content areas are using a common language, providing similar experiences, and setting consistent expectations that communicate to students that they will be held accountable for specific reasoning abilities. Although there is nothing magical about the list of reasoning processes highlighted in this Dimension, having a list that is used throughout the district can be magical. Students may develop the ability to reason at a level that is rarely demonstrated in classrooms today.

For each of the eight reasoning processes identified in Dimension 3, the following sections are included:

1. *Help students understand the process.* This section discusses how to introduce the process to students and how to help them understand the function or goal of the process.

2. *Give students a model for the process, and create opportunities for them to practice using the process.* This section introduces the complex reasoning process itself: the model for the steps involved in using the process. Examples of specific ways to guide students through the thinking involved in the process are presented.

3. *As students study and use the process, help them focus on critical steps and difficult aspects of the process.* This section identifies critical steps and difficult components of the process as well as specific examples and suggestions about how to deal with these elements.

> "More than anything else, learning the critical attributes for each of the complex reasoning processes made me realize how much thinking I was doing for my students. I was doing the majority of the work for them!"
>
> —An elementary teacher

A curriculum writing committee created a database of focused, high-quality classroom tasks in various content areas at different grade levels based on the complex reasoning processes. Teachers could access this database and use the tasks directly or use them as models to create their own tasks.

4. *Provide students with graphic organizers or representations of the model to help them understand and use the process.* Graphic organizers and representations help students understand and visualize the process. Examples of these organizers or representations are included in this section.

5. *Use teacher-structured and student-structured tasks.* This section addresses the importance of modeling and guiding the use of the process, first through the use of teacher-structured tasks. Suggestions are provided for how to move from teacher-structured to student-structured tasks, shifting students from highly structured tasks to tasks that students create as they become more proficient and confident at using the process.

Comparing

> *Comparing* is the process of identifying and articulating similarities and differences among items. Stated more simply, it is the process of describing how things are the same and different.

Almost daily, we compare things—classes we take, books we read, the food we eat, the experiences we have. In fact, it is difficult not to compare. The effect of this everyday process of comparing is that we see things differently, we gain insights, we change perspectives. You might think you had a bad day, for instance, until you hear of a friend's day that was much worse. "Compared to hers," you might conclude, "my day wasn't so bad after all." If you read two books by the same author and then compare them, you might discover something in one of them that you missed when you first read it. Comparing, then, influences our perceptions of our world. (In some classrooms, comparing refers only to similarities; the term *contrast* is used to refer to differences.)

Comparing is done in the classroom for the same reasons: to gain insights, to see distinctions, to change perspectives. When students are asked to use comparing with content knowledge, however, they need to go beyond loose, everyday comparing. They need to be taught and held accountable for rigorously using the process to ensure that their learning is enhanced as a result of the comparison. The following sections review activities and strategies that will help students understand and fully master the process of comparing.

1. Help students understand the process of comparing.

As common as the process of comparing is, it is still useful to introduce the basic concept to students, especially young students. You can do this by presenting examples of the different ways in which people use comparing. For example, you might describe a time when you compared a movie you saw with the book of the same title and gained a new appreciation for the book. Then you might have students identify comparisons they have made (e.g., two classes they are taking; a place they have visited and their own home). Finally, help students become aware of how often comparisons are used in daily life and in the world around them. For example, you might ask students to listen to the various news media and notice how often people, current events, or celebrations are compared during newscasts.

For more on comparing:

Beyer (1988) *Developing a Thinking Skills Program*

Mullis, Owen, & Phillips (1990) *America's Challenge: Accelerating Academic Achievement*

Stahl (1985) *Cognitive Information Processes and Processing Within a Uniprocess Superstructure/Microstructure Framework*

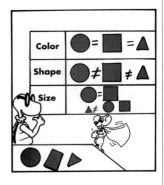

2. Give students a model for the process of comparing, and create opportunities for them to practice using the process.

a. *Give students a model for the process of comparing.*

Even when students understand comparing, it is important to provide them with steps to follow as they use the process with content knowledge. The following steps are recommended:

1. Select the items you want to compare.
2. Select the characteristics of the items on which you want to base your comparison.
3. Explain how the items are similar and different with respect to the characteristics you selected.

The process might be stated in simpler terms for young students:

1. What do I want to compare?
2. What is it about them that I want to compare?
3. How are they the same? How are they different?

b. *Create opportunities for students to practice using the process.*

Explain and demonstrate each of the steps in the comparison process to students. You can do this in a think-aloud fashion. You might say,

Let me see. I want to compare an apple and an orange. That's the first step in the process. The next step is to pick the characteristics I'm going to compare. I think I'll pick size, shape, taste, and nutritional content.

Once you have modeled the steps, make them available to students by having students copy them or by displaying them on the board or on a piece of chart paper. Then create some opportunities for students to have fun using the steps with nonacademic topics so that they become comfortable with the process.

3. As students study and use the process of comparing, help them focus on critical steps and difficult aspects of the process.

As you increasingly hold students accountable for engaging in the comparing process, provide focused instruction and practice in order to help them avoid common errors and pitfalls. The following key points review some common problems and suggestions for solving or avoiding common errors.

Key Points

1) Comparing is the reasoning process that is probably the most commonly used in K-12 classrooms. It is a powerful way of helping students examine key attributes of important content knowledge, and students seem to become comfortable with the three steps fairly quickly. Because of its power and ease of use, however, it can be overused. Thus, it is important in the planning process to carefully consider the questions: Why are students doing this comparison? Are the items that they are comparing important to this content knowledge? Is comparing the best process to use to help students extend and refine this knowledge?

2) One key to a rigorous comparison is to identify characteristics that are meaningful and interesting. For example, comparing wars on the characteristic of "the kinds of horses that were ridden" might be interesting but will not add much to students' learning. Conversely, "the extent to which the conflict involved foreign countries" and "the extent to which economic factors caused the wars" are characteristics that might lead to increased understanding.

For students to become skilled at identifying meaningful and interesting characteristics, they may need extensive modeling and feedback as they practice. You can provide this support in different ways:

- *Brainstorm ideas for characteristics as a class*, especially the first few times you give students a comparison task or when the content is particularly difficult for them. You might then ask students to select characteristics from the brainstormed list or to come up with their own.

- *Use expanded comparison*. This means that using a comparison matrix, students are provided with several characteristics, then asked to expand the matrix by adding additional characteristics of their own that are as meaningful and interesting as those provided. It is important to provide students with good initial characteristics and with feedback on their additions.

3) Make sure that students understand that the purpose of doing a comparison task in the classroom is to extend and refine knowledge. To reinforce this, after they have completed the comparison, ask questions about what they learned, for example, "What insights did you gain?", "What new connections did you make with other content?", or "What did you discover or rediscover as a result of doing the comparison?"

"No wonder my students couldn't provide me with strong comparisons! I had never taught them step 2. It's determining the characteristics that allows students to make a comparison truly meaningful."

—A fifth-grade teacher

4. Provide students with graphic organizers or representations to help them understand and use the process of comparing.

A powerful way to help students understand the process of comparing is to show them how to represent their thinking in a graph or picture. Figures 3.1 and 3.2 suggest ways of organizing the information that is being compared.

A *Venn diagram* is an organizer that is best used when you want to highlight the fact that the two things being compared have some things in common (these characteristics go in the area of intersection) but not others (these go in the nonintersecting part of each circle). When several characteristics are identified in the comparison, you may want to use a separate Venn diagram for each set of characteristics. For example, Figure 3.1 is an example of how a first-grade teacher might lead her students in a comparison of different cultures on the characteristics of holidays and celebrations, and food.

FIGURE 3.1

VENN DIAGRAMS

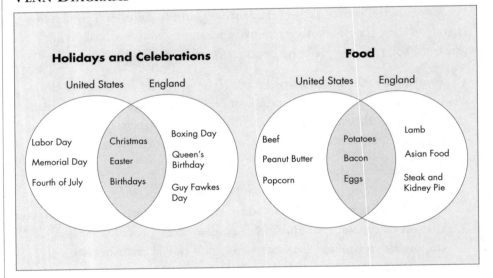

Figure 3.2 is a matrix that can help students organize their information as they perform each step of the comparing process.

FIGURE 3.2

COMPARISON MATRIX

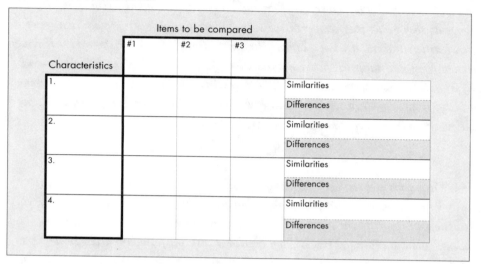

5. Use teacher-structured and student-structured tasks.

When students are just beginning to use the comparison process and whenever you have a very specific academic goal in mind, you might give students highly structured comparison tasks. A teacher-structured task presents students with the items to be compared and the characteristics on which they are to be compared. Students then describe how the items are similar and different, using the characteristics the teacher has selected. When the comparison is completed, students are asked to summarize what they learned. For example, students might be given a list of cities, including their own, and asked to compare them on size, job opportunities, cultural opportunities, crime rates, and air quality. This process would be structured for students to make sure that they begin to understand characteristics of different types of communities.

When students have become adept at using the process of comparing, have them structure their own tasks. You might ask them to generate the items to be compared or the characteristics on which to base their comparison or both. Students should then work independently or in groups to identify similarities and differences among the items. Even though students are working more independently, you might still need to monitor their work to make sure they are rigorously engaged in comparisons that will enhance their learning of important content knowledge.

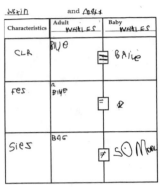

Comparison matrix by kindergartners

Classroom Examples

The following classroom examples are offered to stimulate reflection on how to apply the ideas covered in this section of Dimension 3 in your classroom.

Students in Mr. Johanssen's kindergarten class were studying about how living things grow and change. To help increase their understanding of how different animals change as they grow, they compared the baby or young stage with the adult stage of several different animals. For example, students identified similarities and differences between frogs and tadpoles, between butterflies and caterpillars, between whales and calves, and between horses and colts. The characteristics they used in their comparison included size, color, skin covering, and body shape. Students were surprised to discover how much some animals change as they grow.

• • •

Mrs. Wasson noticed that her geography students seemed to use maps readily in the classroom but were reluctant to use maps that were unfamiliar to them. She led a class discussion on the different types of maps and their purposes. To extend and refine students' understanding, Mrs. Wasson created a task the following week in which she asked them to identify features of map projections that make them useful and then to choose three different types of map projections (e.g., Mercator, Robinson, and Mollweide). After students compared their selected maps on these features, Mrs. Wasson asked them to explain how the map projections were similar and different with respect to the characteristics they selected. Students began to develop a more in-depth understanding of the different uses of each map projection.

• • •

For the first semester of the school year, Ms. Norford decided to focus on helping her health education students understand the social, economic, and political effects of disease on individuals, families, and communities. She created a task to enhance students' understanding and to strengthen students' use of the process of comparing. Students were to compare the similarities and differences between Typhoid Mary, a cook who infected twenty-two or more New York residents between 1900 and 1907, and Ryan White, a child who contracted the HIV virus in the 1980s. Students were required to select elements of the disease (e.g., symptoms and treatments), aspects of the affected communities (e.g., the public's attitude toward the disease), and characteristics having to do with how well the individuals reacted to having the disease (e.g., how well they accepted it, whether they sought treatment, and whether they told others).

Classifying

> **Classifying** *is the process of grouping things into definable categories on the basis of their attributes. Stated more simply, it is the process of grouping things that are alike into categories.*

Classifying is a process used every day to organize our world. The average kitchen, for example, is organized by classifying the foods, the cooking utensils, and the dinnerware into categories based on attributes such as the frequency with which we use them, their size, or their storage requirements. Stores, schools, libraries, and homes all have items classified in some way, and although we take these classification systems for granted, they influence our perceptions and our behavior. Imagine changing the way we group students entering school, or food in a grocery store, or books in a library. Changing classification systems would change our world.

Just as classifying influences our perceptions in everyday life, using classifying in the classroom can influence what students see about the knowledge they are acquiring. In fact, one reason that classifying is a powerful way to extend and refine knowledge is that consciously putting things into different categories influences how we perceive the items. When a round, purple object is grouped with other round objects, you notice it is round; when it is grouped with other purple objects, you notice it is purple. Because the process of classifying and reclassifying focuses students on different attributes of items they are studying, it is a process that extends and refines students' knowledge.

If you want classifying to have this effect of extending and refining knowledge, however, you need to do more than just say to students, "Classify this information." As an extending and refining activity, classifying is often a challenging process, and many students need careful guidance to fully master it. We recommend using the activities below because they help students first to understand the process of classifying and then to fully explore and develop their classifying skills.

1. Help students understand the process of classifying.

Although classifying is a natural human behavior, it is a good idea to introduce the concept to students so that they understand the process and see that consciously classifying items can influence their learning. Start by identifying various ways in which classifying is used and what advantages classifications provide. For example, you might discuss with students how classifying things in their drawers at home helps them to find things quickly.

For more on classifying:

Beyer (1988) *Developing a Thinking Skills Program*

Jones, Amiran, & Katims (1985) "Teaching Cognitive Strategies and Text Structures Within Language Arts Programs"

Mervis (1980) "Category Structure and the Development of Categorization"

Nickerson, Perkins, & Smith (1985) *The Teaching of Thinking*

Smith & Medin (1981) *Categories and Concepts*

Taba (1967) *Teacher's Handbook for Elementary Social Studies*

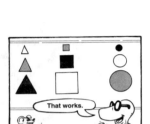

To help students gain an appreciation for the extent to which classifying influences perceptions and behavior, you might also have students try to imagine how their perceptions or behavior would change if certain classification systems we take for granted were changed (e.g., if the food in a grocery store was classified into three price ranges or if department stores classified clothes according to size only). Have students select an item (e.g., a tiger) and place it in several different categories (e.g., with a group of cats, then with a group of wild animals, then with other striped items). Ask them to notice what attributes they see in the same item as they change the group it is in.

2. **Give students a model for the process of classifying, and create opportunities for them to practice using the process.**

   a. *Give students a model for the process of classifying.*

   Although some classifying can be done loosely, students need to learn a set of steps for the process of classifying. Below is one set of general steps that students can use.

   1. Identify the items you want to classify.
   2. Select what seems to be an important item, describe its key attributes, and identify other items that have the same attributes.
   3. Create the category by specifying the attribute(s) that the items must have for membership in the category.
   4. Select another item, describe its key attributes, and identify other items that have the same attributes.
   5. Create this second category by specifying the attribute(s) that the items must have for membership in the category.
   6. Repeat the previous two steps until all items are classified and the specific attributes have been identified for membership in each category.
   7. If necessary, combine categories or split them into smaller categories and specify the attribute(s) that determine membership in the category.

The process might be stated in simpler terms for young students:

> 1. What do I want to classify?
> 2. What things are alike and could be put into a group?
> 3. How are these things alike?
> 4. What other groups can I make and how are the things alike in each group?
> 5. Does everything now fit into a group?
> 6. Would it be better to split up any of the groups or put any groups together?

b. Create opportunities for students to practice using the process.

When presenting the steps in the classifying process, you should demonstrate each, perhaps with a think-aloud technique. For example, while demonstrating the process, you might say,

I'm going to classify the fifty states. I think I'll start with New York. What other states are like New York and why?

Once the students are familiar with the steps, have them practice using them. Ask them to classify then reclassify things around them, for example, the books in the classroom, the furniture, the items in their desk. Each time, hold students more accountable for the rules that describe the categories and the reasons for placing each item into a specific category.

3. As students study and use the process of classifying, help them focus on critical steps and difficult aspects of the process.

As students learn to classify, there are several parts of the process that may need special attention and focused instruction if the process is to realize its potential to help students extend and refine knowledge. As you help students with the classifying process, keep in mind the following points:

Key Points

1) In the second step of the process of classifying, students group items based on a specific attribute. When they get to step 4, they create another category and again specify the attribute. In order to focus the classification process, it is important that this second attribute, as well as each subsequent attribute, be related to the first. For example, if students are classifying the states and the first attribute is "has a predominantly warm climate," the second attribute should be something like "has a predominantly cold climate" or "has a climate with a balance

"Although I have certainly had students classify many times in my class, I discovered that I was using classifying only to sort items accurately rather than to extend and refine their knowledge."

—A teacher in Arkansas

of warm and cold weather." Switching to an attribute such as "is densely populated" will create confusion and decrease the likelihood that students will increase their understanding of the items and the attributes they are studying.

2) Classifying is the process of placing items into groups on the basis of their attributes. In the second step of the process, students are required to select an important item and identify other items that share the same attribute. In this early stage of classifying, it is important for students to focus on attributes that are important and meaningful to the content. The selected attributes should cause the student to discover something in the items or to make connections among items that they had not previously made. If the attributes are not interesting or important, the students might accurately place items into groups but without any apparent positive effect on learning.

3) As students begin to place the items into categories, it is important that they understand the defining characteristics of the categories well enough to justify placement of the items. Sometimes the reasons for placing the items will be apparent, for example, if the categories are based on the attribute of color. However, as the content becomes more complex, explaining the reasons for the placement of items might be the most challenging part of the process. It is important to ask students for this explanation. For example, the following is a sample of an item on an open-book final exam in a high school history class:

Below is a list of wars and military conflicts that we have studied this year. Create a classification system with at least three categories. Explain the rule or defining characteristics of each. Place each war into a category and explain to what extent it has the defining characteristics of that category.

French Revolution	*Spanish American War*
American Revolution	*World War I*
French and Indian War	*World War II*
Vietnam	*Desert Storm*

4) Having students classify and then reclassify is often a key to helping them notice unique distinctions among items that they could miss if they classify items only once. It might help students if you provide different contexts for different classifications; for example, you might ask students to classify a list of plants as if they were gardeners, then reclassify them as if they were doctors who treat people with allergies.

4. Provide students with graphic organizers or representations to help them understand and use the process of classifying.

For many students, a graphic organizer or representation may help them to understand and use the process of classifying. Figure 3.3 depicts two examples of graphic representations that students might use.

FIGURE 3.3

GRAPHIC ORGANIZERS FOR CLASSIFYING

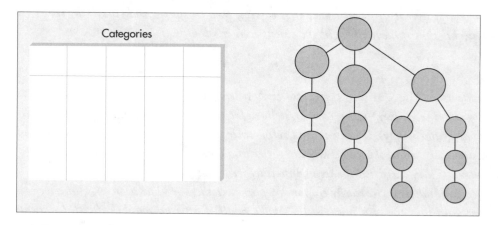

5. Use teacher-structured and student-structured tasks.

Even when students have been introduced to classifying and understand the steps involved, they still may feel a bit unsure of themselves. At this early stage, or any time the teacher has a very specific academic goal in mind, use teacher-structured classification tasks, that is, tasks in which the teacher specifies the items to be classified and the categories into which they are to be classified. Ask students to place the given items in the given categories to increase or demonstrate their understanding of the content. For example, in a literature class you might give students a list of book titles and ask them to categorize them based on whether the major conflict was (a) man versus man, (b) man versus society, or (c) man versus himself. The goal is to increase students' understanding of the types of conflicts found in literature and to focus their study on specific titles.

As students become more comfortable with classifying, you might use more student-structured classification tasks to allow students to direct more of their own learning. In these tasks, you might provide students with a list of the items to be classified, but ask them to identify their own categories and explain the rules they used to form the categories. Alternatively, you might ask students to generate the items to be classified and the categories. It is important any time that students are structuring their classifying task that you ask them to identify what they learned in the classifying process.

Classroom Examples

The following classroom examples are offered to stimulate reflection on how to apply the ideas covered in this section of Dimension 3 in your classroom.

Mrs. Martinez's primary students were learning about the different ways that objects can be described and classified. To extend and refine their understanding, she asked them to select a dozen objects from bins she kept in the classroom and to group together items that were alike. Students selected a wide range of things, including buttons, rocks, paper clips, magnets, and rubber balls. Mrs. Martinez had her students classify the objects several different times, first by size, then by shape, and finally by the material that students thought the objects were made of.

• • •

Students in Ms. Shreiber's class were given a set of vocabulary terms related to geography (e.g., bay, basin, canyon, delta, glacier, harbor, mesa, peninsula, plateau, tundra, and valley). To extend and refine their understanding of the Earth's physical features, she asked them to create categories into which to place each term. Students automatically classified the terms into categories that they had studied in the text, such as landforms created by erosion, by plate tectonics, or glaciation. Ms. Shreiber concluded that the task involved the simple recall of information. She directed students to reclassify the items as if they were Martians seeing these physical features for the first time.

• • •

Students in Mr. Rory's class were studying the various ways that authors develop and use characters in literature. To help extend and refine students' knowledge, Mr. Rory gave them a list of thirty characters from several literary works, then asked them to form categories for these characters and explain the rules used to form the categories. He was pleased with the depth of students' understanding and with the range of categories that they created. A few students, for example, created categories based on the attribute of "types of character flaws"; others used the attribute of "the kinds of changes (e.g., physical, emotional, or psychological) that the characters experienced as the stories evolved."

• • •

Students in Ms. Hussey's science class were studying the basic properties of matter, specifically the elements that make up living and nonliving substances: hydrogen, helium, lithium, beryllium, boron, carbon, nitrogen, oxygen, fluorine, sodium, potassium, mercury, strontium, iodine, chlorine, radium, chromium, iron, neon, and lead. They also had been learning how elements are grouped according to similar properties. Ms. Hussey asked her students to classify these elements (assuming them to be at room temperature) into the traditional categories of solids, liquids, and gases. Students had no problem completing this task. In order to extend their knowledge of the elements, Ms. Hussey then asked students to reclassify the elements into a set of completely new categories. She was pleased with the different ideas that students generated for categories (e.g., "economically valuable" versus "not valuable," "replenishable" versus "not replenishable," and the like) and the wide variety of new connections that students made between and among the elements.

• • •

Mrs. Ranahan wanted to be sure that her mathematics students understood the basic characteristics of the real number system and its subsystems. With this goal in mind, she had been distinguishing the following categories of numbers: counting numbers, whole numbers, integers, rational numbers, and real numbers. She thought students had a fairly good understanding of these categories and, thus, of the real number system and its subsystems. As an extending and refining activity she

- *gave them the beginning of a list of numbers (0, 2, 11, 15, 1/2, -7, 0.75, $\sqrt{48}$, π),*

- *asked them to add to this list other examples of numbers that represent the categories of numbers so that their final list included 30 numbers, and*

- *asked them to place each number from their list of 30 into the five categories.*

Mrs. Ranahan then asked students to reclassify the numbers using their own rules for categories.

Abstracting

> *Abstracting is the process of identifying and articulating the underlying theme or general pattern of information. Stated more simply, it is the process of finding and explaining general patterns in specific information or situations.*

The process of abstracting builds on an ability we all need to function daily: the ability to recognize patterns. We must recognize and use patterns in structures, designs, behaviors, and natural phenomena in order to understand and respond to the stimuli bombarding us in a complex world. Similarly, recognizing patterns in the incredible amount of information we receive, whether in school or in daily activities, allows us to organize and use this information more readily. Abstracting takes this ability a step further by providing a process for identifying less-obvious general patterns in specific information we see and hear and then using these general patterns to see similarities between blocks of information that at first seem to be quite different. Because abstracting forces a level of analysis that goes deeper than literal interpretations, the result of using the process should be an increased understanding of each block of information. The benefit of this increased understanding should be clear both for students in the classroom and for anyone attempting to make sense of the information they receive every day.

Like comparing and classifying, abstracting helps students in the classroom analyze similarities and differences in information they are studying. It is especially effective in helping them understand unfamiliar information by recognizing that it contains patterns similar to information that is more familiar; for example, if students are studying a war that occurred in ancient Greece, they might understand it better if they can see how it follows a similar pattern to a fairy tale they know well. Conversely, abstracting can help students gain new insights into what is familiar by analyzing the familiar with patterns extracted from something unfamiliar; for example, students may gain insights into their own culture by relating familiar customs and rituals to a general pattern that they extracted while studying customs and rituals from a culture foreign to them.

Another reason to teach the process of abstracting is that it is the reasoning process underlying metaphor and analogy. You are abstracting when you create a metaphor—for example, "love is a rose"—to help explain an abstraction (love) by relating it at an abstract level to something more concrete (rose). Similarly, you are abstracting when you use an analogy to understand something (e.g., "The Earth is to the Sun as the electron is to the nucleus."). Developing an understanding of the ability to use abstracting, therefore, can help students to understand and generate metaphors and analogies.

For more on abstracting:

Anderson (1993) *Rules of the Mind*

Anderson (1995) *Learning and Memory*

Gick & Holyoak (1980) "Analogical Problem Solving"

Gick & Holyoak (1983) "Schema Induction and Analogical Transfer"

Holland et al. (1987) *Induction: Processes of Inference, Learning and Discovery*

Ortony (1980) "Metaphor"

"Analogies, it is true, decide nothing. But they can make one feel more at home."

—Sigmund Freud

Because abstracting allows us to see how two seemingly different things are connected, it is a very powerful tool for extending and refining knowledge in the classroom. You can help students develop their abstracting skills by including the following activities in your classroom.

1. Help students understand the process of abstracting.

Because of its complexity, abstracting should be introduced to students using content with which they are familiar. For example, you might explain how abstracting can help us to identify the general pattern of some common fables, such as "The Grasshopper and the Ant" or "The Emperor's New Clothes," and relate the general patterns to current events or to something happening at school. Gradually increase the complexity of stories or start with a current event and demonstrate making connections. Ask students to help you go through the same process by identifying how two stories or situations are really alike. Push them to make connections among increasingly dissimilar situations.

Once students have heard and generated several clear examples of abstracting, you can explain its main function: to distill information into its most basic form, then connect it to information that on the surface appears unrelated, or to create something new that follows the same general pattern. Although they should be able to do this with simple information without using a step-by-step process, explain that in academic situations the information they are analyzing is often longer, more complex, or unfamiliar. In these situations, a process will serve them well. Additionally, explain that using the process can help them increase their understanding of information as they make connections that are more subtle and would be missed without a rigorous use of the process.

Finally, students might gain an appreciation for this process if they understand situations in which abstracting has been used. Discuss examples with them and encourage them to look for examples in and out of school. Movies and plays are sometimes created as a result of an author abstracting from history or literature; for example, *My Fair Lady* is a story following the same general pattern as the myth *Pygmalion*, and *West Side Story* was abstracted from *Romeo and Juliet*.

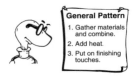

General Pattern
1. Gather materials and combine.
2. Add heat.
3. Put on finishing touches.

I can use the same pattern again here...

... and again here.

2. Give students a model for the process of abstracting, and create opportunities for them to practice using the process.

a. Give students a model for the process of abstracting.

Presenting a general model for the process of abstracting is a good way to help students become comfortable with the process. The steps of the model might include the following:

> 1. Identify what is considered important or basic to the information or situation with which you are working.
> 2. Write that basic information in a more general form by
>   - replacing words referring to specific things with words referring to more general things, and
>   - summarizing information whenever possible.
> 3. Find new information or a situation to which the general pattern applies.

This process might be stated in simpler terms for young students:

> 1. What is important here?
> 2. How can I say the same thing in a more general way?
> 3. What else has the same general pattern?

b. Create opportunities for students to practice using the process.

The various steps in the process should be demonstrated to students, preferably in think-aloud fashion. Provide students with the specific information and then let them observe your thinking. For example, you could give students the following passage:

Two rival tribes lived on opposite sides of a river. Over the years they began to trade with one another, with one tribe giving the other grain in return for cattle. As the quantity and quality of their trade increased, they began to interact more at a social level. As a result of their social interaction, they began to realize that they had differing beliefs about what they would do if the river dried up. Even though there was little chance that the river would actually dry up, the tribes became irritated and impatient with each other because of their differences. Their disagreements soon began to interfere with their trade. Over time, they stopped their trade and eventually went to war.

After telling this story, demonstrate the process of identifying the literal information of the story. The result might be the following:

- *Two tribes*
- *Lived across the river*
- *Exchanged cattle for grain*
- *Increased social interaction*
- *Learned of differences in beliefs about what should be done if the river dried up*
- *Two tribes became irritated with each other*
- *Stopped trading with each other and eventually went to war*

Next, show students how to translate the literal information into a more abstract form. Identify each specific and talk through how you are generating the general pattern.

- *Two groups of people or two entities live in relatively close proximity but are separated or antagonistic in some way.*
- *The two groups or entities begin to interact.*
- *Because of this interaction, they discover some type of conflict.*
- *They end up even less connected or more antagonistic than they were previously.*

Then link the general pattern to some other situation that would not seem similar at the literal level. For example, you might help students to see that the abstract pattern about the two tribes is similar to the relationship between a particular man and woman in a book they've been reading in class; or it might fit the type of interaction observed between two organisms in nature.

Next, provide students with a passage or story. As a class or in small groups, have them practice each step of the abstracting process. Provide feedback and push them to connect their general pattern to increasingly more interesting, specific information. Build in a number of practice sessions before applying the process to academic content.

3. As students study and use the process of abstracting, help them focus on critical steps and difficult aspects of the process.

The word *abstracting* can be intimidating to students who seem to interact more easily with concrete information. However, if they use the steps of the process to provide them with structure, they will see that abstracting is not as elusive as it might sound and they should develop increasing confidence

"When the students turned in their reports, I was very disappointed. I had asked them to explain how the situation in the Middle East followed the same pattern as another event in history, but their reports were less than acceptable. I began to realize that I had asked them to engage in abstracting but I had never taught them how."

—A high school teacher in Ohio

in their ability to generate and use abstract relationships. Keep in mind the following key points and recommendations as you help students understand and use the process.

Key Points

1) Ironically, it is the first step of the process, the one requiring the identification of the important or basic *literal* information, that poses the biggest challenge for many students. Mistakes range from missing key parts of the literal information to identifying virtually every detail as important. Students' ability to successfully complete this step will depend on the complexity of the information or situation and on their experience and practice in summarizing. They may need focused practice and feedback on just this part of the process, and, even with practice, they may require support in completing this step accurately.

2) As students are translating the literal to the abstract, they often have questions about how general the language in the pattern should be. Unfortunately, there is no clear-cut answer or way to measure the level of generality. The objective is to be general enough that connections can be made between seemingly different information but not so general that everything seems to connect to everything else. If the literal statement in the following example was rephrased as shown, the translation would be considered too general:

Literal	General
The colonists rebelled by staging the Boston Tea Party.	*Someone did something to someone else.*

The following translation, however, could lead to more insightful connections:

Literal	General
The colonists rebelled by staging the Boston Tea Party.	*A small group of people rebelled against oppression from an authority.*

Experience and common sense, then, should be your guide for defining the levels of abstraction that will extend and refine knowledge.

3) As students apply their general pattern to new specifics, the obvious connections will emerge first. In order to maximize the potential for abstracting to extend and refine knowledge, push students for more obscure connections. It is worth the effort to encourage and reinforce students' more rigorous use of the model, especially when they make

> "An unintended result of teaching abstracting was that students found out that at an abstract level they had a lot more in common with others than they thought."
>
> —A middle school teacher

powerful connections that cross the disciplines. For example, if students can see that the relationship between producers and consumers in nature is similar at an abstract level to producers and consumers in an economy, they may gain a better understanding of both.

4. Provide students with graphic organizers or representations to help them understand and use the process of abstracting.

For many students, using a graphic organizer will help them to understand the process of abstracting and guide them through the steps of the process. Figure 3.4 illustrates a simple organizer to use with abstracting.

FIGURE 3.4

GRAPHIC ORGANIZER FOR ABSTRACTING

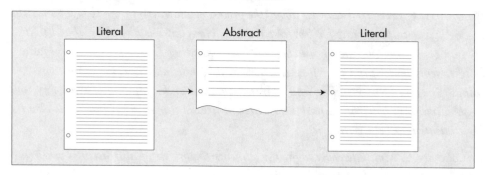

This three-part graphic allows students to record both the literal information as well as the abstract pattern. The literal information of the two items being associated are listed in the two outside panels, The abstract pattern that connects them is listed in the middle panel. (When using this graphic with your students, you might want to label the three sections "Specific, General, Specific.")

5. Use teacher-structured and student-structured tasks.

When students are just beginning to use the process of abstracting, and even later when there are very specific academic goals identified in the curriculum, students might need to engage in abstracting tasks that are highly structured. In these tasks, you may select the information to be abstracted, guide them through identifying the literal information, and even lead them through generating the abstract pattern. Students would then be asked to find another situation to which the abstract pattern applies.

As students become comfortable with using the process, have them structure more and more of the task. You might begin this by providing them with the original information but having them independently engage in each step of the abstracting process. Although it is still important to monitor them as they work, your goal is to help them to become more proficient and confident in their use of each step of the process. In this way, as different students generate slightly different general patterns, they will be more likely to make connections that never occurred to you. Students eventually should begin to identify for themselves the situations in which abstracting can help them to extend and refine their knowledge.

Classroom Examples

The following classroom examples are offered to stimulate reflection on how to apply the ideas covered in this section of Dimension 3 in your classroom.

When Mrs. Cleaver first learned about the process of abstracting, she thought that the process was not appropriate for her first graders. However, one day she realized that she had been using abstracting in class without intending to. She had been trying to help students understand that just as letters stand for sounds, numbers stand for things. She had been extending and refining students' understanding of symbol systems by showing them how things that seem different are similar at a general level—and her students had been getting it.

The next week, Mrs. Cleaver taught her students the process of abstracting by using some fairy tales that had plots following the same general pattern. From then on, she periodically challenged her students to look for general patterns as they learned. She was amazed at what her students observed. One student noticed that digits can be put together to make a new number in the same way that letters can be put together to make a new word. With further prompting from Mrs. Cleaver, students noticed that if they changed the order of the letters of some words, their meaning changed. For example, tap became pat. Similarly, if they turned around the order of the digits in a number, it, too, had a new meaning. For example, 453 became 354.

Mrs. Cleaver started a bulletin board on which she listed the general statements discovered by the class, along with specific examples from students. Periodically she added a general statement to see if students could apply it to specifics, for example, "If you put things together 'any old way', you don't get much meaning, but if you put things together in an organized way, you make patterns that have meaning." She hoped that students would see that words in random order say nothing, but in an organized sequence, they make a sentence; numbers in a random order do not have any meaning, but if you follow a pattern like counting by two's, you get meaning. Mrs. Cleaver had to admit that students were beginning to see connections everywhere, even connections she had not noticed.

• • •

Students in Mr. Lucas's language arts class were just beginning to use the process of abstracting. To help them extend and refine their understanding of themes in myths and epics, he presented them with a task that he thought would interest them. Using the movie <u>Star Wars</u>, Mr. Lucas helped students identify the important or basic elements of the movie and create a general pattern from this specific information:

1. *A young man has special talents.*

2. *He is destined for possible greatness.*

3. *He must forge his character through a series of tests and trials of body and will.*

4. *He is helped by wise advisors in a battle between good and evil.*

5. *He comes close to death and destruction.*

6. *He overcomes limitations.*

7. *He is triumphant.*

Mr. Lucas then asked students to apply this pattern to <u>The Odyssey</u> and to an epic, myth, or legend that they had studied in previous units (e.g., Native American literature or ancient legends).

• • •

Mr. Hillman explained to his students that a computer virus is so named because someone noticed that this phenomenon in computers behaves, at an abstract level, like a virus in nature. He asked students to use the process of abstracting to trace the thinking that led to the name <u>computer virus</u>.

Inductive Reasoning

> *Inductive reasoning is the process of inferring unknown generalizations or principles from information or observations. Stated more simply, it is the process of making general conclusions from specific information or observations.*

For more on inductive reasoning:

Anderson (1990) *Cognitive Psychology and Its Implications*

Lipman, Sharp, & Oscanyan (1980) *Philosophy in the Classroom*

Negin (1987) *Inferential Reasoning for Teachers*

Wason & Johnson-Laird (1972) *Psychology of Reasoning*

Most of us informally use induction every day. For example, we are using induction when we observe the way the cashier at the supermarket greets the customers and rings up the items, and we conclude that he is in a bad mood. We are reasoning inductively when we infer that a potential employer during an interview is looking for someone who is assertive and confident. In both of these situations, the conclusions reached inductively have helped us understand a situation and respond appropriately.

We have all also experienced the consequences of reaching conclusions inductively that turned out not to be true. We might misinterpret evidence, for example, and, as a result, wrongfully accuse someone of stealing something. We might misread nonverbal cues and attribute the wrong motives to an action or comment. The power of inductive reasoning, and the reason it is important for students to learn, is that it is a reasoning process that enables us to figure out things that are not explicit or overt. However, the limitation of inductive reasoning is that no matter how carefully we use the process, the conclusions we draw may or may not be true.

Some would argue that this characteristic of inductive reasoning—the fact that conclusions reached inductively may or may not be true—is the reason that students should understand and learn to use the process. There are times in our lives when it is important to realize that conclusions drawn inductively should be used cautiously. In certain situations, before conclusions are accepted at any level, they should be validated with as much information as possible. People might be less likely to form stereotypes, for example, if they understood that they are often based on conclusions drawn from too little information or from too few observations. When people serve on a jury, they need to realize that they are often being asked to reach verdicts inductively. If they understand inductive reasoning, they may be more careful about listening to all of the available information before reaching their conclusions. Situations like these remind us how important it is for students to develop an understanding of and ability to use this process.

In the classroom, we cue students to reason inductively any time we ask them to identify what is not explicitly stated or when we ask them to read between the lines. By teaching them the process of inductive reasoning, we increase the likelihood that they will be able to learn more than what is obvious. And, by holding them accountable for rigorously using the process, we increase the chances that they will generate valid, accurate conclusions, both in the classroom and in life.

The following suggestions should help in planning for students to learn about inductive reasoning and to develop the ability to use the process.

1. Help students understand the process of inductive reasoning.

Students need some introduction to the concept of inductive reasoning because it is so commonly used yet often misunderstood. Giving students a concrete example is the best introduction. Try this one: Walk into class, slam the door, throw your books on the desk, and then fold your arms across your chest. After a moment, ask students what conclusions they formed when they observed your actions. Then explain to them that the mental process they were using is called inductive reasoning, which is reasoning that uses specific observations to draw general conclusions. Ask them to identify other possible explanations of the behavior in order to emphasize that their conclusions may or may not be true.

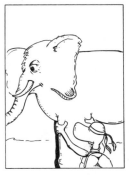

You might ask students to identify other examples of induction. For example, you might ask students to observe a newscast and identify the inductions made by the announcer. Or you could have a discussion about the uses and necessity of induction in daily life (e.g., "What would life be like if we could not induce anything?").

Finally, explain to students that inductive reasoning will help them extend and refine knowledge by increasing their ability to make connections and see patterns in the information available to them in class and anywhere in life.

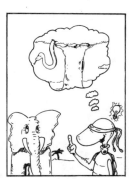

2. Give students a model for the process of inductive reasoning, and create opportunities for them to practice using the process.

a. Give students a model for the process of inductive reasoning.

Although induction is a natural mental process, it is still necessary to provide students with a model they can use when applying induction to content. The steps of the model might include the following:

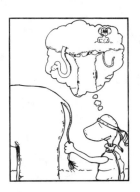

> 1. Focus on specific pieces of information or observations. Try not to assume anything.
> 2. Look for patterns or connections in the information you have identified.
> 3. Make a general statement that explains the patterns or connections you have observed.
> 4. Make more observations to see if your generalization holds up; if it does not, change it as necessary.

The general set of steps may be presented in simpler terms for young students:

1. What specific information do I have?
2. What connections or patterns can I find?
3. What general conclusions or predictions can I make?
4. When I get more information, do I need to change my general conclusions or predictions?

b. ***Create opportunities for students to practice using the process.***

When you present this strategy to students, you might model each step in think-aloud fashion. For example, you might say,

Right now I'm looking out the window and watching a man mowing his lawn. It's the middle of the day, and the man appears to be in his sixties or seventies. I see him at home quite a bit. Let me put all this information together. It could be that he is retired. What else do I see or know that would support or refute that conclusion?

You can list the steps on a wall chart so that students can follow along as you speak.

Another way of providing opportunities for practice is to take students on *induction outings.* An induction outing is simply a situation in which students go outside the classroom to observe and draw conclusions based on their observations. For example, a teacher might ask students to walk around the school or the neighborhood and make specific observations (e.g., "The house on the corner has a lot of athletic equipment in the garage and the backyard."). Students would then make inductions from those observations (e.g., "The people who live in the house on the corner are very interested in sports."). After reporting their inductions, students describe their observations and explain the reasoning that led to their conclusions. Gradually hold students more accountable for making pure observations and for having more than one or two observations for their conclusions.

3. As students study and use the process of inductive reasoning, help them to focus on critical steps and difficult aspects of the process.

As students learn to engage in inductive reasoning, there are several parts of the model that may need special attention and focused instruction. Keep the following points in mind as you help students to increase their understanding of and ability to use the inductive reasoning process.

Key Points

1) Sometimes the statements that students offer as inductions are not really conclusions generated as a result of seeing connections or patterns in information or observations. Often, especially when students are initially learning induction, their "conclusions" actually are

   - *restatements* of the original information ("I conclude that the characters were really angry because they said they were mad."),

   - *descriptions of the observation* ("I conclude that the salt melted the ice."), or

   - *opinions* ("I conclude that the people were wrong to protest.").

   Students need multiple opportunities to practice generating conclusions that represent *connections or patterns* among observations or pieces of information. They also need modeling and feedback during these practice sessions.

2) As students practice inductive reasoning, make sure they are basing their conclusions on observations and information rather than assumptions and opinions. This, of course, requires that students understand the differences between an observation and an assumption or an opinion. For example, if a student concludes that Edgar Allan Poe was probably obsessed with death and if he bases that conclusion on the "observation" that "Poe's poems were weird," it must be pointed out to him that the conclusion is based on an opinion, not on a pure observation.

   It is difficult to make pure observations, that is, objective observations not confounded by opinions, assumptions, or biases. Sometimes our opinions, assumption, and biases are obvious and we can be careful to avoid using them to draw our conclusions. However, sometimes it is not so obvious that our observations are confounded by or represent our opinions, assumptions, and biases. Students will need practice and feedback to become proficient at making observations that are objective.

   Tweney, Doherty, & Mynatt (1981) *On Scientific Thinking*

3) One of the most important requirements of good inductive reasoning is that conclusions are based on as many observations or as much specific information as possible. Although one can never be sure that conclusions are true, the conclusions have more validity when they are supported well. Consistently push students to look for more information and observations to support their initial conclusions.

"The temptation to form premature theories upon insufficient data is the bane of our profession."

—Sherlock Holmes (Arthur Conan Doyle)

Extend & Refine Knowledge

*Helping Students Develop
Complex Reasoning Processes*
  ✔ *Inductive Reasoning*

4. Provide students with examples of graphic organizers or representations to help them understand and use the process of inductive reasoning.

For many students, using a graphic organizer will help them understand the process of inductive reasoning and guide them through the steps of the process. Figure 3.5 helps to emphasize that students need to make a number of observations before drawing a conclusion.

FIGURE 3.5

GRAPHIC ORGANIZER FOR INDUCTIVE REASONING

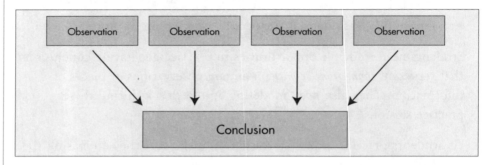

"Inductive reasoning can be done at the kindergarten level. I design tasks around very simple content, but my students are starting to understand how much they can figure out by using what they observe."

—A primary teacher

Figure 3.6 is an example of an inductive reasoning matrix, which is a way of organizing large blocks of information to facilitate making inductions. The induction is most easily applied to concepts. The horizontal rows of the induction matrix contain the concepts to be considered. In general, these concepts should all belong to a common category (e.g., types of government). The columns of the matrix contain questions to be answered about each concept. Note that conclusions can be drawn for both rows and columns. Once students answer all of the column questions (e.g., "Who governs?") for each of the four types of governments (e.g., democracy), they can draw conclusions about each form of government (row conclusions). They can also draw conclusions about governance, decision making, and early forms of government (column conclusions). Finally, they can construct a summary conclusion that combines the elements of the row and column conclusions.

FIGURE 3.6

INDUCTIVE REASONING MATRIX

	Who governs?	How are decisions made?	What are some early examples?	CONCLUSIONS
Democracy				
Republic				
Monarchy				
Dictatorship				
CONCLUSIONS				SUMMARY CONCLUSIONS

5. Use teacher-structured and student-structured tasks.

When students are first learning to engage in inductive reasoning and any time that the content is complex, it is appropriate to use highly structured induction tasks and to monitor students closely as they are completing the tasks. They may need help in making the initial observations or selecting important pieces of information, in seeing the connections or patterns, and in generating logical conclusions from these patterns. For example, if you are on a field trip to a local pond, and you want students to draw some conclusions about the living things around the pond, you might focus them on observations of specific phenomena and dictate descriptions of these phenomena for them to record in their learning logs. After returning to the class, you might lead them in a discussion that focuses on specific observations and help them generate some conclusions.

Eventually, as students become more accustomed to making inductions, you should be able to provide much less structure. In fact, one of the goals of teaching students inductive reasoning is to help them begin to discover subtle connections and patterns within content even when they are not explicitly directed to do so. For example, the next time you go on a field trip, you may simply encourage students to make their own observations and see what they conclude from what they have observed.

Classroom Examples

The following classroom examples are offered to stimulate reflection on how to apply the ideas covered in this section of Dimension 3 in your classroom.

Ms. Krueger presented her fifth-grade students with the following task:

> *Fossil remains tell us about the plant or animal that formed them. Fossils also tell us about the environment in which the plant or animal lived. You will be given a variety of photographs, diagrams, and other representations of fossils from the Mesozoic Era (e.g., lungfish, lizards, dinosaurs, insects, seaweeds, and land plants). Observe the features of the fossils (e.g., backbone or not, number of legs used for walking, presence of wings, body surface covering) which would help the plant or animal survive in a particular environment. Look for patterns or connections in the information you have identified. What do these patterns tell you about the environment in which these plants or animals lived (e.g., water or land, danger from other creatures, amount of seasonal changes)?*

• • •

Mrs. Smith asked students in her literature class to select a favorite character from a favorite book and look for patterns and connections in the character's actions, attitudes, and relationships. She then asked students to use the patterns and connections to draw conclusions about the character's personality, using information from the book to support their conclusions. Students then presented their conclusions and supporting information in "articles" that appeared in the class's newsletter, "The Book Nook."

• • •

As part of their study of political satire, students in Ms. Chung's high school literature class read <u>Gulliver's Travels</u>. *Periodically, she asked them to infer what might have been occurring in England at the time the story was written.*

• • •

Mrs. O'Riley was planning a unit to address a topic that was included in national documents covering standards in health literacy. These standards emphasized that students should understand a variety of consumer influences and how those influences affect decisions regarding health resources, products, and services. Students were aware that advertisers try to influence consumers to purchase their products by appealing to consumers' concern for their health. To increase their understanding of how advertisers attempt to influence consumers' decisions, Mrs. O'Riley gave students the following task:

> *We are surrounded by images and messages telling us how to be healthier and stronger, how to run faster and to jump higher, how to live longer. Who are*

the creators of these images and messages targeting? What do the creators of these advertisements think their audience wants and is willing to believe?

Choose an advertisement that promotes a product it claims will improve your health in some way (e.g., a super-energy-drink advertisement from an exercise magazine, a live-longer vitamin advertisement from a health magazine, or a television infomercial about an exercise machine). Study the advertisement carefully, noting various aspects, such as health-promoting claims, prices, and layout. Based on your observations, draw a conclusion about the creators of the advertisement. What do you think advertisers believe about what people want in relation to their health? What do advertisers seem to think people will believe about what might help them to achieve their goals (e.g., "The people who created this advertisement must believe that . . . .")? Support your conclusions with information and observations from the advertisement you studied.

Deductive Reasoning

Deductive reasoning is the process of using generalizations and principles to infer unstated conclusions about specific information or situations. Stated more simply, it is the process of using general statements to come to conclusions about specific information or situations.

For more on deductive reasoning:

Copi (1972) *Introduction to Logic*

Johnson-Laird (1983) *Mental Models*

Klenk (1983) *Understanding Symbolic Logic*

We all use deductive reasoning every day to make sense of our world. This happens every time we apply a general principle to a new specific situation and, as a result, understand something about that new situation. We are using deductive reasoning when, for example, we tell ourselves we should not eat that piece of chocolate cake because we know that cake often contains ingredients that can make us gain weight. We are reasoning deductively when we conclude that the airplane we are on has a fire extinguisher because it belongs to the general category of commercial airplanes, and we know that all commercial airplanes carry fire extinguishers. Both of these examples emphasize how commonly we need to use deductive reasoning to cope with new situations every day.

As simple as the above examples are, it is interesting that deductive reasoning is a process that many people find intimidating. One possible reason for this is that when people think of deductive reasoning, they immediately associate it with formal logic, a subject many people struggled with or successfully avoided in school. Although it is true that deduction is integral to formal logic, it is not true that deduction should be taught only in logic classes. All students should have the opportunity to develop the ability to reason deductively, not only because it is important in everyday life, as exemplified above, but because it is important to learning.

In academic situations, deductive reasoning is a key to achieving one of the major goals of learning: the ability to transfer knowledge from one situation to the next. When students are learning how to apply general principles to new specific situations, they are learning to transfer knowledge. If, for example, students are studying the characteristics of living things during a unit on plants, they should be able to transfer that knowledge deductively to their study of animals; or, if they understand some general principles of force and motion, they should be able to predict what will happen in an experiment in which those principles apply. This transfer of knowledge is dependent, of course, on understanding the general principles, but transfer also requires the ability to apply the principles deductively to the new specific situations.

Like any reasoning process, developing an understanding of the process of deductive reasoning and practicing the skills associated with it will enable anyone to use deduction in daily situations or while engaged in academically rigorous tasks. Although the topic of deduction can include the study of many types of arguments and rules of formal logic, the scope of information in the following sections will be limited to two major areas: (1) using deductive reasoning in a general sense, and (2) categorical syllogisms.

1. Strategies 1 through 5 provide recommendations for using deductive reasoning in a general sense, that is, learning to apply general principles to new specifics in order to increase understanding of the new information and to make predictions about the new situations. If students have these experiences, they should begin to develop the understanding needed to be aware of how deductive reasoning helps them in everyday life and with academic content.

2. A resource section (see pages 155-159) is provided for those who would like to provide students with a greater understanding of one particular type of deductive reasoning: categorical syllogisms.

1. Help students understand the process of deductive reasoning.

It is important for all students to understand deductive reasoning in a general sense, that is, to understand that deductive reasoning is a process of using general information to draw conclusions or to make predictions about specific situations. Illustrate the definition by providing examples of how they use deductive reasoning daily; for example, students can predict what they will see if they go to a specific grocery store because they know some general characteristics of grocery stores that always apply. Likewise, they can predict that they will not do well on a test if they are not familiar with the material that's on the test.

Once students begin to understand how the process is used in simple, everyday examples, you will want to increase their understanding of deductive reasoning so that they can apply the process to content knowledge. Given the common confusion between inductive and deductive reasoning, directly comparing the two types of thinking is a good way to begin. Explain that

> *deductive reasoning is the process of using general information to draw conclusions about specific information or situations, and*

> *inductive reasoning is the process of using specific pieces of information to draw general conclusions.*

When Sherlock Holmes said, "Brilliant deduction, my dear Watson," should he have said, "Brilliant induction, my dear Watson"?

Give students several examples of each type of reasoning. For example, explain that you are reasoning deductively when you apply the principles related to gravity and predict that you will fall to the ground if you step off the roof. Likewise, if you understand the principles of force and motion and have the right information related to a specific shot in billiards, you can predict the path of the billiard ball.

Contrast examples of deduction with examples of induction. For example, a detective reasons inductively by examining the clues at the scene of a crime and drawing a conclusion, such as the robber probably was someone the victim knew. That conclusion might be based on the following observations:

  a. *There were no signs that someone broke in.*

  b. *Only the places where valuables were kept were disturbed.*

  c. *The dog did not bark during the time of the robbery.*

There are other conclusions that could be drawn from these observations, but the pattern seems to lead to the detective's conclusion. A good detective, and someone who is skilled at *inductive reasoning*, will then look for other information to determine if the conclusion holds up.

You may need to demonstrate the difference between induction and deduction a number of times by presenting students with examples like those above. Try to make the examples as relevant and meaningful as possible. Over time, ask students to identify whether the examples provided are conclusions arrived at inductively or deductively.

2. **Give students a model for the process of deductive reasoning, and create opportunities for them to practice using the process.**

  a. *Give students a model for the process of deductive reasoning.*

   There are some very general steps or guidelines that apply to most deductive situations:

   1. Identify the specific situation that is being considered or studied.
   2. Identify the generalizations or principles that apply to the specific situation.
   3. Make sure that the specific situation meets the conditions that have to be in place for those generalizations or principles to apply.
   4. If the generalizations or principles do apply, identify what is known about the specific situation, that is, what conclusions can be drawn or what predictions can be made.

These general guidelines may be stated in simpler terms for young students:

1. What specific topic am I studying?
2. What general information do I already have that might help me understand my specific topic?
3. Am I sure the general information applies to the specific topic I am studying?
4. If it does, how did the general information help me understand the specific topic?

b. Create opportunities for students to practice using the process.

Before asking students to practice using the general guidelines for deduction, demonstrate them in a think-aloud fashion, using situations in which you can highlight each guideline. You might say,

I am a weather forecaster and I see a tornado on the radar. I ask myself, "What do I know about tornadoes?" I recall all the general principles related to tornadoes and determine if the tornado I am observing has the characteristics that would make those principles apply. If the tornado does have those characteristics, I can make predictions about what the tornado will do, and I can decide whether to sound any alarms.

Or,

I am trying to determine the length of a side of a triangle, given the other two sides. I know that for right triangles, the square of the hypotenuse is equal to the sum of the squares of the other two sides. First, I have to determine if the triangle I am studying is a right triangle. If it is, I can apply the principle and calculate the length of the unknown side.

Once students become familiar with these guidelines, ask them to practice using the steps of deductive reasoning by pairing up with other students and using the think-aloud technique. They can use principles from their content, such as math and science, or they may begin to identify generalizations they take from everyday situations, such as, "If I clean the house before mom gets home from work, and nothing else negative happens, the evening at home will be very pleasant."

3. As students study and use the process of deductive reasoning, help them focus them on critical steps and difficult aspects of the process.

To help students to become increasingly proficient at using deductive reasoning, it is important for the teacher to develop an understanding of key aspects of the process and to make sure that students are learning academic content that lends itself to the use of deductive reasoning. To plan the necessary experiences, the following key points are offered as guides.

Key Points

1) Deductive reasoning is the process of applying general information, in the form of generalizations and principles, to new specific situations. Obviously, if students are to use this process, they must be learning important content generalizations and principles that they can apply. Although this is obvious, sometimes the reality is that students spend a large percentage of their time memorizing factual information; consequently, developing an in-depth understanding of generalizations and principles is not a major emphasis in the curriculum. If students are to learn the process of deductive reasoning, the curriculum—both the written curriculum and what is actually delivered in the classroom—must emphasize the learning of clearly articulated generalizations and principles.

2) The third step of the process of deduction asks students to make sure that the specific situations meet the conditions that have to be in place for the generalization or principle to apply. It is important for students to understand that sometimes the wording of the generalization or principle does not include all conditions. The implication is that students might need to restate the generalization or principle to make sure the conditions are clearly articulated. For example, if a student is working from a principle that states, "If two magnets are placed near each other, they will be pushed apart," the student must add the condition that this is only true if the two common poles of the magnets (two north or two south poles) are brought together.

3) Some educators would assert that it is not as effective to present important generalizations and principles to students as it is to ask them to discover this knowledge. However, directly teaching important knowledge, and then asking students to apply that knowledge, can be just as effective as discovery methods. Using deductive reasoning to apply knowledge requires students to develop an understanding of both the concepts within a principle and the conditions that make it applicable.

"It was easy to teach my students that deductive reasoning was going from the general principle to the specific topic—just the opposite of inductive reasoning. It was difficult to teach them that a general principle only applies if the specific topic meets certain conditions."

—An eighth-grade teacher

It also requires that this understanding be sufficient to help them determine if the general statement applies to the new situation. If students are required to apply their understanding to increasingly complex and diverse situations, they may develop a level of understanding that equals—or even exceeds—what could be attained with inductive instructional approaches.

4. Provide students with graphic organizers or representations that will help them understand and use the process of deductive reasoning.

Below are two graphic organizers that may help students to understand the steps involved in deductive reasoning. These organizers also can be used to help some students organize their information and follow the steps of the process. Figure 3.7 provides places to describe the specific situation, the generalization or principle, the conditions that must be in place, and any conclusions or predictions that are made. It also emphasizes that the goal is to determine if there is a match between the specific situation and the generalization or principle.

FIGURE 3.7

GRAPHIC ORGANIZER FOR DEDUCTIVE REASONING

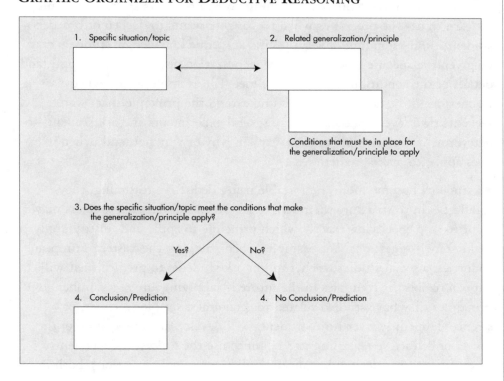

1. Specific situation/topic

2. Related generalization/principle

Conditions that must be in place for the generalization/principle to apply

3. Does the specific situation/topic meet the conditions that make the generalization/principle apply?

Yes?   No?

4. Conclusion/Prediction

4. No Conclusion/Prediction

Figure 3.8 organizes that information in a matrix with columns that follow the steps of the process. It allows for the application of several principles to a single, specific situation and for the generation of a number of predictions or conclusions.

FIGURE 3.8

DEDUCTIVE REASONING MATRIX

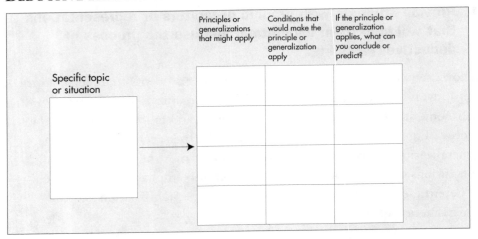

5. Use teacher-structured and student-structured tasks.

Sometimes students should be provided with very structured tasks that require them to use deductive reasoning. When students are just beginning to learn to use the process or when the teacher wants to deepen or broaden students' understanding of very specific academic knowledge, students may be given the specific situations, the generalization or principles to apply, and details of the conditions that must be met. For example, in a science class, a teacher might be helping students understand the principle that "water seeks its own level." She may set up several experiments and ask students to determine if the principle applies, explain why or why not, and, when it does apply, to make predictions.

As students become more comfortable using deductive reasoning, they should begin to structure their own tasks. To encourage this, teachers may want to stop specifying exactly which principle to apply and, instead, only make some suggestions. For example, when studying the Eastern European countries, a social studies teacher might ask students to predict what will happen to specific countries in the future by applying any of a number principles they have studied related to economics, sociology, civics, or science. Hopefully, over time, students will develop an appreciation of the power of deductive reasoning and begin to use the process independently when trying to understand or make predictions in new situations, both in the classroom and in daily life.

Classroom Examples

The following classroom examples are offered to stimulate reflection on how to apply the ideas covered in this section of Dimension 3 in your classroom.

During a unit on plants, Ms. Isaacs's kindergartners were learning about what plants need to survive and the different ways in which they get what they need. After several lessons, Ms. Isaacs placed three green plants on a shelf by a window. She placed one plant in the middle. She placed the other two plants on either side with a box over each one. She explained that all of the plants would receive the same amount of water. Ms. Isaacs asked students to predict what each of the plants would probably look like after a week and draw a picture that showed what they predicted.

• • •

Elementary students in Mr. Caraveo's class were learning how human beings breathe. A guest speaker came to the class to demonstrate the Heimlich maneuver. Knowing that they had already studied respiration, the speaker asked Mr. Caraveo's students to apply what they had learned to the following hypothetical situation:

> *Your friend is having a coughing fit. You ask him if he is all right, but he is coughing too hard to answer. Should you administer the Heimlich maneuver?*

• • •

Mrs. Williamson presented her business students with the following task:

> *If a country in eastern Europe became a free-market system, what can we predict would happen in that country?*

• • •

Ms. Touchett's high school physics class had been studying momentum. They had learned about Newton's first law and its applications in understanding car crashes and had just finished a discussion of the law of conservation of momentum in inelastic collisions. Ms. Touchett gave her students the following task to help them extend and refine their knowledge about momentum:

> *In a car crash, the severity of damage to vehicles and passengers is related to the change in velocity of the vehicles. When a heavy truck and a lighter car collide head-on, the wreckage travels in the direction that the truck was headed before the crash due to its greater momentum. The truck's velocity decreases slightly, but the car's velocity changes direction as well as speed. The car's change in velocity is much greater than the truck's. This is the reason that the truck driver often suffers less severe injuries than the driver of the car. The weight of the truck protects its driver in such a crash, but contributes to the damage to the car and its driver.*

Understanding this principle, or any principle of physics, can be important to understanding many activities in life. An Olympian hurdler once explained that he jumped the hurdles in a very unconventional way. He did violate conventions of running hurdles, he explained, but he did not violate the principles of physics. Clearly, science helped him understand his sport. Just as the principle of momentum was used to explain car-truck collisions, use it to explain at least two phenomena in sports (e.g, football, baseball, boxing, or tennis). Include in your explanation what happens, why it happens, and what equipment is used because of what happens. Just as auto manufacturers try to understand physics to help them devise new ways of keeping drivers safe, explain how understanding this principle of physics might suggest the need for new equipment in the sport.

Categorical Syllogisms

One type of deductive reasoning is represented in the form of *categorical syllogisms*. This section includes explanations and recommendations that can be used when planning to increase students' understanding of this type of deductive reasoning.

At a very basic level, you are making a categorical argument when you draw a conclusion from premises. For example, you are reasoning categorically when your thinking follows this pattern:

a. *All commercial airplanes have a fire extinguisher on board.*

b. *The airplane I am on is a commercial airplane.*

c. *Therefore, this airplane has a fire extinguisher on board.*

This type of argument is called a *syllogism*. Statements *a* and *b* are premises. Statement *c* is the conclusion. Syllogisms always have two premises and a conclusion. In everyday reasoning, the form of categorical syllogisms is usually hidden. The following argument, for example, is based on a hidden categorical syllogism: I know this airplane has a fire extinguisher because it is a commercial airplane. Underlying this statement are premises *a* and *b* and conclusion *c*. Note that the conclusion has to be true; we are sure of it. Again, this is the defining characteristic of all forms of deductive reasoning: Given that the premises are true, the conclusion has to be true. There are at least four powerful ways that categorical syllogisms can be used in the classroom. These four ways are usually used together.

1. *Help students see hidden categorical syllogisms in their reasoning and that of others.*

   One of the most powerful awarenesses students can have is that people often unknowingly use categorical syllogisms in their reasoning. You can foster this awareness by asking students to transform certain conclusions they or others make into the form of a categorical syllogism (two premises and a conclusion). This is called *standardizing* an argument. Although it is not absolutely necessary, you might want to teach students some of the formal rules for categorical syllogisms. One has already been mentioned: They have two premises and a conclusion. Additionally, the two premises can have only three elements. In the example above the three elements are

   • *commercial airplanes*

   • *contain fire extinguishers*

   • *the airplane (that the speaker is in)*

Additionally, one of the three elements is transferred between the other two. In this case, the element "contain fire extinguishers" is transferred from the element "commercial airplanes" to "the airplane I am in." Finally, the elements in a categorical syllogism are modified by such terms as "all," "some," and "none."

Once students have been introduced briefly to these general rules for categorical syllogisms, they can usually find statements that are based on an underlying categorical syllogism and standardize these statements, that is, rewrite them as categorical syllogisms.

2. *Provide students with a graphic way of representing syllogisms.*

Categorical syllogisms are so abstract that some people have difficulty following the reasoning that supports them. Euler diagrams, which use circles to represent membership in a set, can help make that reasoning more concrete. In an Euler diagram, each of the three elements in a categorical syllogism is represented by a circle. Circles are inside, outside, or overlapping one another based on the relationships expressed in the categorical syllogism. To illustrate, consider the following:

- *All mammals breathe air.*
- *All whales are mammals.*
- *Therefore, all whales breathe air.*

The three elements in this syllogism are

- A = *mammals*
- B = *breathe air*
- C = *whales*

If we represent each element with a circle, the first premise looks like this:

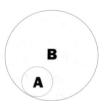

The second premise tells us that the circle for whales, C, goes inside the circle for mammals, A. Therefore, the entire categorical syllogism can be represented as follows:

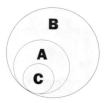

Once students have standardized statements into syllogistic forms, they can use Euler diagrams to help understand and test the validity of the reasoning represented by the syllogism.

3. *Present students with the various forms of valid and invalid categorical syllogisms.*

   Although categorical syllogisms can take many forms, only a few forms yield valid conclusions. For example, the following form of categorical syllogism generates no valid conclusion:

   • All A are B

   • All C are B

   • Therefore, _____.

   Again, the Euler diagram can help students see that there are many possibilities:

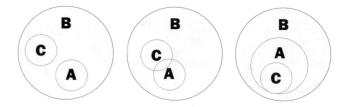

Because all three of these representations are equally possible, you cannot reach a definite conclusion. Figure 3.9 lists all the forms that categorical syllogisms can take and the valid conclusions that are possible.

FIGURE 3.9

VALID CONCLUSIONS FROM SYLLOGISTIC ARGUMENTS

SECOND PREMISE	FIRST PREMISE			
	All A are B	**Some A are B**	**No A are B**	**Some A are not B**
All B are C	All A are C	Some A are C Some C are A	Some C are not A	
Some B are C			Some C are not A	
No B are C	No A are C No C are A	Some A are not C		
Some B are not C				
All C are B			No A are C No C are A	Some A are not C
Some C are B			Some C are not A	
No C are B	No C are A No A are C	Some A are not C		
Some C are not B	Some C are not A			

SECOND PREMISE	FIRST PREMISE			
	All B are A	**Some B are A**	**No B are A**	**Some B are not A**
All B are C	Some A are C Some C are A	Some A are C Some C are A	Some C are not A	Some C are not A
Some B are C	Some A are C Some C are A		Some C are not A	
No B are C	Some A are not C	Some A are not C		
Some B are not C	Some A are not C			
All C are B	All C are A		No C are A No A are C	
Some C are B	Some C are A Some A are C		Some C are not A	
No C are B	Some A are not C	Some A are not C		
Some C are not B				

Of the sixty-four forms of categorical syllogisms listed in Figure 3.9, only twenty-seven yield valid conclusions. Once students are aware of this fact, they are better able to identify an invalid argument.

4. *Have students examine the truth of the premises in categorical syllogisms.*

A categorical syllogism may be logically valid but untrue. This occurs when the form of the syllogism is valid but the premises are not true or cannot be accepted in any absolute way. For example, the following categorical syllogism is logically valid:

- *All thieves are products of broken homes.*
- *Bill is a thief.*
- *Therefore, he is the product of a broken home.*

Saying that the syllogism is logically valid means that the conclusion follows from the premises. The premises themselves, however, must also be examined. In this example, the first premise, "All thieves are products of broken homes," is not true; therefore, the conclusion may not be true. An important awareness about categorical syllogisms, then, is that they can be logically valid but not true. You analyze the validity of a syllogism by looking at its logic. You analyze the truth of a syllogism by looking at the premises themselves. This is a powerful awareness for students. After they have analyzed the validity of a categorical syllogism, they can then consider its truth by examining the premises.

Once students become familiar with categorical syllogisms, introduce them to conditional syllogisms. One good source for this is Virginia Klenk's *Understanding Symbolic Logic* (1983).

**For more on constructing
support:**

Goldman, Berquist, &
Coleman (1989) *The Rhetoric
of Western Thought*

Kinneavy (1991) "Rhetoric"

Toulmin, Rieke, & Janik
(1981) *An Introduction to
Reasoning*

Constructing Support

*Constructing support is the process of building systems of support for
assertions. Stated more simply, it is the process of providing support for statements.*

There are times in all of our lives when we feel strongly enough about
something to want to take action. That action often includes trying to
influence or persuade others by constructing supportive arguments for a
particular position and then expressing those arguments orally or in writing.
To successfully construct arguments requires two kinds of knowledge: first,
an understanding of and the ability to use persuasive techniques and, second,
an understanding of the information needed to construct a powerful
argument. Understanding and successfully using persuasive techniques will
be useful to students throughout their lives. However, while developing the
ability to construct support, they should also be increasing their
understanding of the content information they are using in their arguments.
Thus, students should learn to construct support, not just because it is a life
skill but because it is another type of reasoning that can lead to their
extending and refining knowledge.

This twofold benefit of learning to construct support suggests that we
should make sure that the process is not relegated to speech and debate
classes only. These classes, of course, provide students with the opportunity
to develop knowledge and skills related to persuasion, but many students do
not take speech and debate classes. All content areas can have issues surface
about which it would be beneficial for students to take positions and
construct support. If educators used the process of constructing support
across the disciplines, more students would have the opportunity to develop
this ability and use the process in many different contexts with different
types of content information.

Another benefit of using the process of constructing support in the
classroom is that taking a position on an issue often increases students'
engagement, particularly when you give students some choice in selecting a
position they want to support. Teachers sometimes complain that students
display very little affect in the classroom, that apathy—sometimes even
lethargy—is evident. Part of the reason is that students become so focused
on simply taking in information that they begin to passively accept
everything they read and hear. Students may be more interested in and
motivated to study the knowledge related to issues when you encourage
them to identify issues about which people have different opinions and then
to take and defend their own positions. Constructing support, then, can
enhance students' learning simply by injecting new energy—even passion—
into the classroom.

If the process of constructing support is to be used across the disciplines, there needs to be some consistency in how it is defined and used. The definitions and suggestions included here can serve as a resource for teachers who want to help students develop a way of increasing their understanding of and ability to use this process.

1. Help students understand the process of constructing support.

Introduce the concept of constructing support by presenting a well-designed argument on some issue that will interest the students, such as requiring school uniforms. Before you present the argument, however, explain to students that you will be trying to persuade them that your idea is a good one. Ask them to look for specific strategies you are using to persuade them. At the end of your presentation, ask students to list their observations on the board. Then use this list to explain that constructing support involves planning an argument and using techniques like those listed. Ask them to add additional techniques and strategies as they become aware of them.

Once students begin to understand that constructing support is a process that takes planning and practice, try to help them gain an appreciation for how frequently it is used in our society. Encourage them to begin noticing when individuals are trying to persuade or influence others, either in their everyday life, in news reports, in their interactions with classmates, or in the content they are studying. Ask students to try to determine how successful the individuals were in each situation. Periodically ask students to share their examples, and then lead a class discussion around questions such as, "Why was it important to the individual to persuade or influence others?" and "What were the consequences or rewards if the individual was successful? If she or he was unsuccessful?" Students should begin to conclude that the ability to construct support can be very important not only to an individual but to many people or even to a society.

2. Give students a model for the process of constructing support, and create opportunities for them to practice using the process.

a. Give students a model for the process of constructing support.

There is no single strategy for constructing support. Below is one set of general steps that students can use when they are faced with situations that may require them to construct support.

1. Identify whether you are stating facts or opinions.
2. If you are stating an opinion, determine whether the situation warrants support.
3. When the situation warrants it, construct a supportive argument through the use of a variety of devices, such as facts, evidence, examples, or appeals.

The process might be presented in simpler terms for young students:

1. Am I stating a fact or an opinion?
2. If I am stating an opinion, do I need to offer support?
3. What will I include (Facts? Examples? Evidence? Appeals?) when I provide my support?

b. Create opportunities for students to practice using the process.

Before asking students to practice using these steps, model and demonstrate the various components of the process, preferably in a think-aloud fashion. For example, you might show students how you constructed support for your opinion that the school year should be lengthened, making sure to include each aspect of the process:

Let's see, I'm stating my opinion that the school year should be lengthened. Is it worth supporting further? Yes. I think this is an important issue for students. I'd better construct a good argument that includes facts related to effects on student achievement in other places and perhaps examples of parents' reactions. I think I also need to remind the audience of the traditions in this country that make education a high priority and then show them how lengthening the school year can serve that priority.

Have students practice the steps of this process with issues that interest them. You might ask them to demonstrate using the steps in a think-aloud manner in pairs and groups. At first, the issues should be simple, everyday issues that students might care about (e.g., constructing support to convince their parents to get a puppy or to buy them a new stereo or game). Gradually increase the complexity of the issues and the requirements for finding information to construct their arguments.

3. As students study and use the process of constructing support, help them focus on critical steps and difficult aspects of the process.

Although students' understanding of the position being taken will influence the strength of the argument, the success of the argument will also depend on the extent to which they understand concepts related to the process of constructing support. As students develop this understanding and practice using the process, keep the following recommendations and explanations in mind.

Key Points

1) It is important for students to understand the difference between facts and opinions for two reasons. First, constructing support is necessary for opinions, not facts. Second, when we support an opinion, facts can strengthen the arguments. Students need to understand that, according to researchers who study the nature of knowledge, facts are statements that can be verified, whereas opinions reflect someone's beliefs and may be accompanied by reasons for those beliefs. For example, the statement, "The month of May generally has more precipitation than April" is a fact. It is not a statement with which you agree or disagree; it is a statement that can be confirmed or disproved by checking the precipitation records with the weather service. The statement, "John Doe would make the best governor" is an opinion; it is a statement with which others may agree or disagree. It cannot be verified, therefore it is a statement for which support is needed.

    When students are distinguishing between facts and opinions, emphasize two points. First, although the word fact is often used to label something that is true, from a technical perspective a fact is a statement that is verifiable; it does not have to be true. Facts can be false. "The moon is made of green cheese" is a fact; that is, it is verifiable. When asking students to identify facts, make sure that they are clear about how you are defining "fact."

    Second, statements do not fall neatly into the categories of fact and opinion. In actuality, facts and opinions can be more accurately viewed as a continuum, with facts that can be empirically verified at one end (e.g., "Ten convicted felons were executed last year") and pure opinions at the other (e.g., "Capital punishment is wrong"). When students are confused, it might be because they are dealing with a statement somewhere near the middle of the continuum (e.g., "Capital punishment has been shown to deter crime").

To help students understand the difference between fact and opinion, you will need to give clear examples of each plus some that are in the middle. Discuss the characteristics of facts and opinions, highlighting those described above, and write them on the board. Then ask students to identify statements in information they read or hear that tend to be more on the fact side of the continuum and statements that tend to be more on the opinion side of the continuum. These opinions can be potential topics for teaching the process of constructing support.

2) The final step of the process of constructing support includes choosing from a list of devices that people use to develop a persuasive argument: facts, evidence, examples, and appeals. Although the first three devices will be more familiar to students, the last device, appeals, may be relatively new to them. It refers to the formal art of persuasion, dating back to the early Greeks, in which four basic persuasive techniques were identified, called the four appeals. Specifically, these included appeals using personality, tradition, rhetoric, and reason. Although appeals using reason are commonly emphasized in school, students should be aware of the other types of appeals so that they can use them when constructing their own arguments and recognize them in support offered by others. The four different types of appeals are explained below.

Personality. When the appeal is through personality, the speaker or writer tries to get you to like him. To accomplish this, he might use many personal stories or act very interested in you. Congeniality is another common element of this appeal.

Tradition or accepted beliefs. The appeal through tradition or accepted beliefs might be boiled down to "do the right thing." The power of the argument comes from the fact that there is a general acceptance of the beliefs or values alluded to. For example, you are appealing to tradition or accepted belief when you demonstrate that your position has been accepted by Americans since the beginning of the 20th century.

Rhetoric. An appeal through rhetoric aims to persuade through the beauty and style of language. It relies on the use of impressive phrases, idioms, and even gestures. The power of the argument comes from the power of the construction of the language.

Reason. An appeal to reason is an appeal to logic. The speaker makes claims and systematically provides evidence for the claims.

Illustrate each of the four types of appeals to students, using clear examples in which only one type of appeal is used. (This might be

"I always have done a good job teaching persuasion with an emphasis on using evidence, appeals to reason. I remember studying other types of appeals in my college rhetoric course, but I didn't think about teaching them to my students."

—A speech competition teacher

difficult because people commonly use more than one type of appeal in their persuasive arguments.) Additionally, ask students to create their own examples of each type of appeal. Finally, ask students to identify the types of appeals used in persuasive arguments in and outside the content area.

3) Although all four appeals are frequently used, the appeal to reason is the staple of a democratic society. There is no single way to appeal to reason, but there are some commonly accepted components that such an appeal includes:

- *Evidence.* Information that leads to a claim. For example, "Last night five crimes were committed within two blocks of one another."

- *Claim.* The assertion that something is true. For example, "The crime rate in our city is escalating dramatically."

- *Elaboration.* Examples of or explanations for the claim. For example, "The dramatic increase can be seen by examining the crime rates in the downtown area over the past twenty years."

- *Qualifier.* A restriction on the claim or evidence counter to the claim. For example, "The crime rate has stabilized in some areas, however."

As the example above illustrates, an appeal to reason is usually initiated by presenting evidence, such as incidents, events, and statistics, that leads to a conclusion. The evidence is designed to lead to a conclusion that is then clearly stated in the claim. If the evidence is strong and presented well, there is already support for the claim once it is stated. The claim then is the statement for which further support is offered. Elaborations lay out the case in detail providing definitions of key terms, specific examples, and additional evidence. Qualifiers state the restrictions on the claim. They can be statements about the situations to which the claim does not apply or they can be statements about the underlying assumptions of the claim.

To ensure that students understand the various components of the appeal to reason, present clear examples. Then have students identify the various components in information they read or hear (e.g., in editorials or news broadcasts). Finally, have students construct supporting arguments that use an appeal to reason for claims they have identified.

4. Provide students with graphic organizers or representations to help them understand and use the process of constructing support.

Some students will benefit from using a graphic organizer as they construct an appeal to reason. Figure 3.10 is one example of a graphic organizer you might suggest that students use to carefully consider the types of appeals that they will include in their support. Note that the organizer emphasizes the use of appeals through reason.

FIGURE 3.10

GRAPHIC ORGANIZER FOR CONSTRUCTING SUPPORT

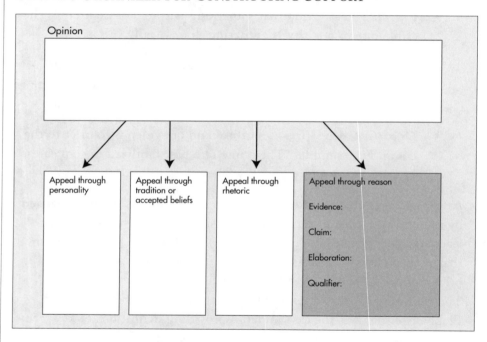

5. Use teacher-structured and student-structured tasks.

Tasks that require students to construct support may be highly structured by teachers, especially when students are just beginning to learn to construct support or any time that a specific academic goal would be served by focusing students on a specific issue. You may provide the description of the issue and even the opinion that is to be supported and then specify the types of support that should be used. However, because part of learning to construct support is being able to determine which opinions warrant support, students need to be involved in structuring the tasks as often as possible. In student-structured tasks, ask students to select the issue, the side of an issue they wish to support, and the types of support they will include.

Classroom Examples

The following classroom examples are offered to stimulate reflection on how to apply the ideas covered in this section of Dimension 3 in your classroom.

Mr. Santiago's history students were studying the foreign policy of the United States during the 20th century. To extend and refine their understanding of time and place as context for historical events, Mr. Santiago divided the class into two groups and gave the groups the following tasks:

Group 1: *President Woodrow Wilson has just asked you to give him your opinion as to whether the United States should join the League of Nations. As a nonpartisan foreign policy advisor, you recognize that a strong position can be made either for the United States to join or for the United States to return to a policy of isolationism. The President has asked you to give a speech stating your position at his next foreign policy meeting. Your speech should discuss the changing role of the United States in world affairs in the early 20th century.*

Group 2: *It is 1999. The new Secretary of State has taken a position against the policy of isolationism. The President wants to hear your perspective. Take a position for or against isolationism in which you clearly articulate your reasons.*

• • •

Students in Ms. Girardi's life skills class were researching different occupations that might be entered directly upon graduation from high school. As part of their study, they researched the types of preparation and training needed for these occupations and the educational opportunities available to prepare for these occupations. Ms. Girardi asked her students to take a position on whether or not a traditional college education is important to one's future ability to function and experience success in the world of work.

• • •

Mrs. Cimino's students protested when she introduced them to the process of long division. They thought it was a waste of time to learn the process, arguing that "everyone" has calculators and that "no one" ever does long division by hand. Some students added that they really did not need to know the multiplication facts for the same reason. Because the topic generated so much interest and "passion," Mrs. Cimino decided to have students take a position—for or against the importance of learning the computation processes—and present their arguments, which were to include an appeal to reason, to the class.

• • •

Mr. Hill asked his French foreign language students to identify a current issue in the French culture. He asked them to take a position on the issue and then develop and present a persuasive argument in French to the class.

Analyzing Errors

> *Analyzing errors is the process of identifying and articulating errors in thinking. Stated more simply, it is the process of finding and describing errors in thinking.*

For more on analyzing errors:

Gilovich (1991) *How We Know What Isn't So*

Johnson-Laird (1985) "Logical Thinking: Does It Occur in Daily Life?"

Perkins, Allen, & Hafner (1983) "Difficulties in Everyday Reasoning"

Toulmin (1958) *The Uses of Argument*

"The cuckoo who is on to himself is halfway out of the clock."

—Wilson Mizner

The process of analyzing errors can be useful to us every day as we are bombarded with information attempting to persuade us to believe something or to act in a particular way. Television, radio, and newspaper advertisements try to convince us to buy one product over another. Politicians try to convince us that their platforms will provide better conditions and services. Marketing agencies try to persuade us to make decisions in response to mail and telephone solicitations. As potential consumers, people may notice misrepresentations and detect errors in the information that is being presented, but sometimes they are persuaded to believe or act in ways that they later regret or want to rethink. It is important for us, as consumers and citizens, to develop the ability to recognize and analyze possible errors in the reasoning of those communicating with us and in our own reasoning as we receive these messages.

When we are influenced by flawed information or arguments, the consequences are frequently insignificant (e.g., we may buy one brand of cereal instead of another), but they may also be so significant that they influence our quality of life or impact life-and-death situations. The rigor with which we should analyze information for errors is dependent on the extent to which the information is intended to affect us. The higher the stakes, the higher the level of rigor that is needed. Recognizing these high-stakes situations and increasing the level at which we attend to and analyze information will decrease the possibility of suffering negative consequences.

When students study and use the process of analyzing errors in the classroom, they are likely to develop the disposition of attending to and analyzing information. They are also likely to gain a better understanding of the kinds of errors that people commonly make. This can enable them to detect even subtle or skillfully crafted errors in reasoning. Gaining this understanding and skill clearly benefits students in "real life." It also has immediate academic benefits: Engaging in error analysis can force students to carefully scrutinize content information, thus helping them to extend and refine their knowledge.

1. Help students understand the process of analyzing errors.

Students need to understand why the process of analyzing errors is important in the so-called information age. Talk them through a typical day in the life of a typical citizen, and try to list the types of information that this citizen must process. Put a check by each item that represents a time that the citizen should stop and look for errors in the underlying thinking.

To help students maintain an awareness of the importance of pausing to consider errors in thinking, periodically present examples of information that contain obvious as well as subtle errors. Advertisements are, of course, a rich source of examples and are commonly used, but also include examples from editorials, speeches, and articles in print and nonprint media. When appropriate, you might tape or purchase transcripts of radio and television talk shows to illustrate the errors that people make when they are discussing issues about which they feel passionate. In addition, provide examples from everyday situations that students can relate to (e.g., a school friend who states, "Everybody is doing. . . ."). Use these examples as a focus for discussing the reasons people make errors in their thinking and the consequences of people not recognizing these errors.

2. Give students a model for the process of analyzing errors, and create opportunities for them to practice using the process.

a. *Give students a model for the process of analyzing errors.*

The steps for the process of analyzing errors are deceptively simple, although teaching the process is a challenge because it requires that students have an understanding of the types of errors that people make. (For detailed information on types of errors in thinking, see pages 173-176.) The process includes the following steps:

1. Determine if the information being presented is important or is intended to influence your beliefs or actions.
2. If the information is important or intended to influence you, identify statements or claims that are unusual, violate what you know to be true, or seem wrong.
3. Look for errors in the thinking underlying the statements or claims you have identified.
4. If you find errors, seek clarification or more accurate information.

The process might be presented in simpler terms for young students:

> 1. Is the information I am receiving important or does it try to influence my thinking or my actions?
> 2. Does something seem wrong with any of the information?
> 3. What is wrong?
> 4. How can I get more or better information?

b. Provide students with the opportunity to practice using the model.

Whenever possible, take advantage of opportunities to model the process by thinking aloud. You might say,

Wait. This information is trying to convince me to. . . . Something is funny here. This isn't like what I have heard before. I need to ask for another reason to. . . .

As you talk through the process, focus students on the steps by using an overhead transparency or posting the steps where students can see them.

Each time you model the process, try to include a different type of error. This will help increase students' understanding of the types of errors to look for when they are receiving information.

3. As students study and use the process of analyzing errors, help them focus on critical steps and difficult aspects of the process.

The degree of success that students will have in using the process of analyzing errors is dependent on their knowledge and their disposition. They must have the ability to recognize situations in which the process of analyzing errors is needed, an understanding of the types of errors in thinking that are commonly made, and a willingness to analyze information that is being received.

To help you plan for developing students' ability to analyze errors, two resources are provided: (1) a teacher resource section, which defines and gives examples of four types of errors in thinking, and (2) the following explanations of key points to keep in mind while planning for classroom lessons and for schoolwide implementation of this process.

Key Points

1) When providing students with feedback on their ability to engage in the process of analyzing errors, make sure that you reinforce their efforts to analyze the information, even when they are not sure what type of error is being made. Putting a precise label on an error is not as important as determining that an error has been made. If students first develop the tendency to look for errors in information they are receiving, they are more likely to then develop an understanding of the types of errors that are made.

2) The in-depth study of errors in thinking (e.g., faulty logic, weak references, and attacks) is often the content of formal logic classes, and logic is not a class that students commonly take. Thus, the average student may not encounter this knowledge. However, when students are engaged in the process of error analysis, their understanding of these types of errors will influence their ability to recognize errors and respond appropriately when errors are detected. For example, when students understand specific types of faulty logic, such as "false cause" or "begging the question," they will be more likely to recognize these errors and dismiss arguments that include such errors. They also will know to withhold any conclusions or actions in response to these arguments until more relevant and accurate information is provided by the source.

   In order to help students build distinctions among types of errors, first try to expose them to a broad range of examples and provide them with easy access to resources (articles, books, and glossaries) that will help them label the types of errors they are encountering. Periodically select, or ask students to select, a specific type of error for focused study and ask students to look for and generate examples. If teachers do this across grade levels and subject areas, students gradually will develop an ability to analyze errors far beyond that of students in most classrooms today.

3) Educators sometimes avoid teaching the process of analyzing errors because they are concerned that students will learn to challenge all information they receive. Help students to understand that it is as important to be skilled in discerning when the process should be used as it is to be skilled in the process of analyzing errors. A good thinker, for example, accepts some information simply because of the source or accepts certain claims as a matter of faith.

> "Isn't it amazing how often we need to analyze errors? Before they began learning about this process, my fourth-grade students were easily convinced by other people's persuasive writing. Now, they really concentrate on whether or not the information they are receiving is in line with what they already know."
>
> —A teacher in Arkansas

4. Provide students with graphic organizers or representations to help them understand and use the process of analyzing errors.

Figure 3.11 is a graphic representation of the process of analyzing errors. It helps students see how the steps of the process interact. It can also be used as an organizer as students are engaged in the process.

FIGURE 3.11

GRAPHIC ORGANIZER FOR ANALYZING ERRORS

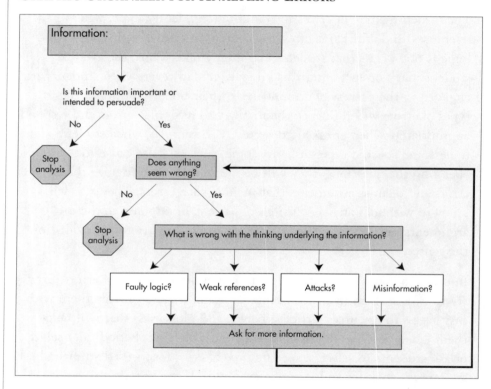

5. Use teacher-structured and student-structured tasks.

At first students will need tasks that are highly structured to help focus their learning on specific types of errors in thinking. You might present the information and ask students to find a specific type of error. You should then ask your students to identify an appropriate response (e.g., ask for clarification or request additional information). For example, during a unit on energy, a teacher might read to the class an editorial about an issue related to the use of resources in the community. She might ask students to listen for errors that reflect misunderstandings and confirmatory bias. (See the section "Types of Errors in Thinking," pages 173-176, for definitions of these types of errors.)

Gradually, students should begin to identify errors without being cued. You might limit your prompting to suggesting that they look for errors in thinking that influence the topic or unit of study. Ideally students should begin to identify errors in thinking even when it is not a stated objective of the unit.

Types of Errors in Thinking

The following four sections briefly describe some types of errors in thinking people make as a result of using

- faulty logic,
- attacks,
- weak references, and
- misinformation.

Faulty Logic

a. **Contradiction.** *Contradiction* occurs when someone presents conflicting information. For example, if a politician says she is for a tax increase, and then a little later says she is against a tax increase, she has committed the *fallacy* of contradiction.

b. **Accident.** An *accident* occurs when someone fails to recognize that an argument is based on an exception to a rule. Concluding that the letter *e* always comes before the letter *i* after observing the spelling of the words *neighbor* and *weigh* is an example of accident.

c. **False Cause.** *False cause* occurs when someone confuses a temporal (time) order of events with causality or when someone oversimplifies a very complex causal network. For example, if someone concludes that the decision to place a man on the moon was prompted by America's failed attempt to send a satellite into orbit, he is confusing temporal order with causality. This is not to say that temporal order does not play a part in causality; it is simply to emphasize that the causes of an event usually include more than the events that immediately preceded it. Similarly, if a person acknowledges only one or two causes of the Civil War, he is making the error of false cause because the reasons for the Civil War were numerous and complexly related.

d. **Begging the question (circularity).** *Begging the question* involves making a claim and then arguing for the claim by using statements that are simply the equivalent of the original claim. For example, if you say, "That product is not very useful," and then back up your assertion by saying, "You can't do anything with it" or "It has no apparent application," your argument is circular. You are backing up one statement with others that mean just about the same thing.

e. ***Evading the issue.*** *Evading the issue* is sidestepping an issue by changing the topic. For example, someone evades the issue if, when asked about his involvement in arms trade to foreign countries, he changes the topic of conversation to the necessity of weapons.

f. ***Arguing from ignorance.*** Arguing that a claim is justified simply because its opposite cannot be proven is called *arguing from ignorance*. For example, arguing that there is no intelligent life beyond the planet Earth because we cannot prove that extraterrestrial life exists is arguing from ignorance.

g. ***Composition and division.*** *Composition* is asserting about a whole something that is true of its parts. *Division* is asserting about all of the parts something that is true of the whole. For example, you are making an error of composition if you assume that all members of a family are intelligent because a single member of the family is (e.g., everyone in the Ewy family must be smart because Robert is). On the other hand, you are making an error of division if you conclude that a specific city in the state of Washington receives a lot of rain simply because the state as a whole is noted for its rainfall.

Attacks

h. ***Poisoning the well.*** Being committed to your position to such an extent that you explain away absolutely everything that is offered in opposition to your position is referred to as *poisoning the well*. This type of attack is not signaled so much by a specific type of information as by a person's unwillingness to listen to or consider anything contradictory to her opinion.

i. ***Arguing against the person.*** Rejecting a claim on the basis of derogatory facts (real or alleged) about the person who is making the claim is referred to as *arguing against the person*. If a politician rejects another politician's stance on nuclear disarmament by attacking the person's heritage, he is arguing against the person.

j. ***Appealing to force.*** *Appealing to force* is the use of threats to establish the validity of a claim. Telling someone that you will not like him anymore unless he takes your side on an issue is an example of appealing to force.

Weak References

k. ***Using sources that reflect habitual and confirmatory biases.***
Sometimes information comes only from sources that were selected as a result of a hidden or obvious bias. In general, biases fall into one of two broad categories: *habitual biases* and *confirmatory biases*. Habitual biases sometimes are unconsciously built into our thinking and are specific to certain people, places, things, and events. For example, we might have a bias toward rejecting ideas from a specific radio talk show host or accepting ideas from a specific magazine. Confirmatory bias is evident when we only accept information that supports what we think or feel and reject information that is contrary to our position. For example, we might receive positive information about a politician but ignore it because we have already decided that we do not like him.

l. ***Using sources that lack credibility.*** Information relevant to a topic or issue might come from sources that lack credibility. Although determining credibility may be subjective, there are some characteristics of sources that most people agree damage credibility (e.g., when the source is known to be biased, has a reputation for communicating false information or rumors, or has little knowledge of the topic).

m. ***Appealing to authority.*** *Appealing to authority* refers to invoking authority as the last word on an issue. For example, someone appeals to authority if he says something is true (or false) simply because it is stated by a superior. This is a weak reference because someone in a position of authority does not necessarily know if something is true or false.

> "Because I'm the mother, that's why."

n. ***Appealing to the people.*** *Appealing to the people* is an attempt to justify a claim on the basis of its popularity. Supporting the claim that "staying up late does not affect my schoolwork" by stating that everyone in school stays up late is an example of appealing to the people.

> "But, Mom, everyone is going."

o. ***Appealing to emotion.*** Using an emotion-laden story, or "sob story," as proof for a claim is referred to as *appealing to emotion*. For example, when a speaker tries to convince people to vote for a particular political candidate by relating a story about the death of the candidate's family in a tragic accident, he is appealing to emotion.

Misinformation

p. ***Confusing the facts.*** It is not uncommon for people to use information that seems to be factual but has been distorted or modified and is no longer accurate. This happens when, for example, events are described out of order or when important facts are left out.

q. ***Misapplying a concept or generalization.*** Errors can be made when a concept or generalization is misunderstood and, therefore, inappropriately applied to explain a situation or to support a claim. For example, if someone claims that protesters at a rally at city hall should be arrested because they are committing "treason," this represents a misunderstanding of the concept of treason.

Classroom Examples

The following classroom examples are offered to stimulate reflection on how to apply the ideas covered in this section of Dimension 3 in your classroom.

Mr. Hagadorn's second-grade health education students were learning practices concerning injury prevention and safety. When they got to the portion of the class devoted to learning refusal skills (e.g., refusing to get in a car with a stranger, not giving in to peer pressure), he constructed a task to help students extend and refine their understanding of errors in thinking, such as faulty logic, attacks, and misinformation. Mr. Hagadorn created scenarios in which students might need to take precautions and use refusal skills.

Mr. Hagadorn had students act out the scenarios and then analyze the situations for any errors in thinking. For example, in one scenario a group of children was trying to convince Sam, another student, to eat earthworms. Students identified several types of errors in thinking. The group of children "begged the question" when they claimed that "earthworms are good for you" and supported this assertion by saying, "Cool things happen to you when you eat earthworms." They used an "appeal to force" when they threatened to stop hanging out with Sam if he didn't eat worms. They used an "appeal to authority" and "used sources that lack credibility" when they said that everyone should eat worms because the captain of the high school football team ate worms. As Mr. Hagadorn's students learned to practice refusal skills, they also learned to identify errors in thinking.

• • •

Mrs. Browning's sixth-grade art class was learning about the factors that contribute to artwork becoming valuable in the marketplace. To extend students' understanding, she constructed a task in which she asked students to examine the advertising campaign of a local technology institute. The institute's ads claimed that computer-generated artwork had become as valuable as individually created artwork. Mrs. Browning asked her students to consider what they had been learning in class to analyze this claim and expose any errors in the thinking that the institute used in its argument (e.g., appeals to authority and begging the question).

• • •

Mrs. Kominami and Mr. McColl collaborated to create an integrated unit for their science and language arts students to end the year. The unit focused on having students learn about the degree to which people use scientific information and valid reasoning to understand their world and the degree to which they base their conclusions about their world on faulty information, misconceptions, or flawed reasoning. Earlier in that year, scientists had announced that evidence from a meteorite suggested that life may have existed on Mars more than 3 billion years ago. This motivated Mrs. Kominami and Mr. McColl to construct the following task as a culminating activity for the unit:

Do you believe that life may have once existed or still exists on Mars? Do you believe that life exists on other planets? Why do you believe this? Examine the reasons for your beliefs, and attempt to analyze your reasons and reasoning. In addition, interview several other people to determine their beliefs about the existence of life on other planets, and examine their reasons and reasoning. In your analysis, attempt to determine to what extent your beliefs and those of others result from the use of scientific information, credible sources, and valid reasoning and to what extent those beliefs reveal faulty reasoning, weak sources, and misunderstandings. For example, if you tend to pay attention only to evidence that supports your opinion, you are guilty of "confirmatory bias." If someone tells you he believes that there is life on Mars because scientists have not proven that life does not exist there, he is guilty of the fallacy of "arguing from ignorance."

Draw some conclusions about the degree to which beliefs are based on scientific information, strong sources, and valid reasoning. Support your conclusions with as many specific examples as possible.

Analyzing Perspectives

> *Analyzing perspectives is the process of identifying multiple perspectives on
> an issue and examining the reasons or logic behind each. Stated more simply,
> it is the process of describing reasons for different points of view.*

**For more on analyzing
perspectives:**

Fisher & Ury (1981) *Getting
to Yes*

Paul (1984) "Critical
Thinking"

Paul (1987) "Critical
Thinking and the Critical
Person"

One of the most powerful thinking processes is to analyze your own
perspectives, to consider the positions you take on issues and to understand
the basis for those positions. Just as powerful is analyzing other perspectives,
trying to understand the reasoning or logic underlying very different ways of
looking at an issue. It can be difficult to analyze perspectives—whether they
are your own or someone else's—when you have strong feelings about the
topic. It takes discipline and skill to stop during an argument, for example,
and take enough of a step back to gain an understanding of your own or
another's perspective. This is why it is important for students to develop this
ability in the classroom through the examination of academic issues that are
not emotionally charged. This classroom process helps students not only to
extend and refine their understanding of content but also to develop a skill
they will need when they face highly emotional situations in which they
need the ability to analyze perspectives.

When teaching the process, it is important to emphasize that the goal of
analyzing perspectives is to seek understanding of the reasons or logic
underlying a position. The goal is not to accept, appreciate, or agree with
opposing perspectives, nor is it to change your own perspective. Although
you might alter your point of view, it is just as likely that you might solidify
your original position because you understand it better or because you
understand more clearly why you reject other positions.

The measure of success in analyzing perspectives, then, is that as result of
your analysis, you can articulate and explain the reasons and logic behind
your own and/or others' perspectives. To achieve this success often will
require digging deeper into sources of information, finding additional
sources, or interviewing people. These are the activities that lead to increased
understanding of content and that help students develop important and
related information-accessing skills. As you teach students to analyze
perspectives in a way that extends and refines their knowledge in these ways,
you might use the suggestions and recommendations in the following
sections.

1. Help students understand the process of analyzing perspectives.

Make it a practice to periodically share with students examples of situations in which someone exemplifies the process of analyzing perspectives. This practice helps increase students' understanding of the process of analyzing perspectives and helps them realize the positive effects of analyzing perspectives. Discuss how the situations are influenced when people take the time to understand other people's reasons for their perspectives. Try to make the examples as relevant to students as possible. You might present examples about which students would be likely to have an opinion, such as dress codes at school, curfews, or requirements for sports participation.

Even when students are working on other reasoning processes during a unit, look for opportunities to point out examples of people analyzing perspectives or of situations that would have benefited had someone taken the time to understand another viewpoint. You might point out instances from literature in which characters enhanced their relationships by seeking understanding of differing points of view; you might also use news reports for examples of conflicts between countries that can be traced not just to disagreements about issues but to misunderstandings about perspectives.

2. Give students a model for the process of analyzing perspectives, and create opportunities for them to practice using the process.

a. Give students a model for the process of analyzing perspectives.

Although analyzing perspectives requires more than just following a set of steps, it is more likely that students will gain this ability if they have a process to guide them. A simple model includes the following steps:

> 1. When you are examining an issue about which people disagree, first identify and clearly articulate one perspective.
> 2. Once you have identified a perspective, try to determine the reasons or logic behind it.
> 3. Next, identify and clearly articulate a different perspective.
> 4. Try to describe the reasons or logic behind the different perspective.

The process might be stated in simpler terms for young students:

1. What is one point of view?
2. What are the reasons for this point of view?
3. What is another point of view?
4. What might be some reasons for this other point of view?

b. Create opportunities for students to practice using the process.

To prepare students for practicing the steps of analyzing perspectives, you might set up a hypothetical situation and, through think-aloud, role play a specific person in the situation. Highlight each step as you talk through the situation.

Wait. Before I continue this argument with my friend, I need to establish why I believe. . . . My reasons include. . . . But he feels equally strong. . . . It must be because. . . .

After modeling the steps and perhaps posting them in the classroom, ask students to pair up and do similar think-alouds using situations from their own lives or from hypothetical situations.

3. As students study and use the process of analyzing perspectives, help them focus on critical steps and difficult aspects of the process.

On the surface, analyzing perspectives is one of the simpler reasoning processes. However, there are some important points to keep in mind as you help students understand and use the process.

Key Points

1) Although students should be reinforced for acknowledging and respecting different points of view, the process of analyzing perspectives demands much more from them. Students should be held accountable for the analysis process, for understanding and clearly articulating not just the obvious reasons and logic underlying perspectives but the more subtle and complex reasons. This rigorous analysis leads students to extend and refine academic content knowledge.

2) Using this model of analyzing perspectives demands that students recognize a good reason and trace the logic of an explanation of a perspective. Helping students understand these two concepts, reasons and logic, presents one of the key challenges of teaching this process.

"Students in my class got into an argument one day about whether their parents should use the V-chip to monitor their television watching. I took the opportunity to teach analyzing perspectives. We had a great discussion while we were identifying the reasons for and against the chip."

—A high school teacher in Colorado

Reasons are those pieces of evidence that support a given point of view or perspective. A common mistake when identifying reasons is to simply restate or rephrase a position, perhaps with more passion (e.g., "I believe seat belt laws are a good idea because it is really important."), rather than providing specific reasons. By logic we mean the strength of the argument when you combine all of the evidence. A common mistake here is to present evidence but to fail to organize it into a coherent argument. To decrease these types of mistakes and to increase understanding of these concepts, students may need the opportunity to examine many examples (both good and bad) of reasons and logical explanations of perspectives.

3) It is important for students to understand that most issues have multiple perspectives. It is easy to develop the mistaken impression that issues have only two perspectives: their own and the opposing viewpoint. Whenever students are analyzing perspectives, provide them with or encourage them to identify more than two. Identifying and analyzing perspectives that are beyond the obvious can increase students' understanding of the issue itself and of the process of analyzing perspectives.

4) Finally, as stated earlier, students need to understand that the goal of analyzing perspectives is not to accept, appreciate, or agree with different perspectives. To keep the focus on honing skills of analysis rather than on changing people's viewpoints, it is best to limit applications of the process to academic content that is not emotionally charged.

4. Provide students with graphic organizers or representations to help them understand and use the process of analyzing perspectives.

Below are two matrices that can help students organize their thoughts as they learn to analyze perspectives. Figure 3.12, a Perspective Examination Matrix, can be used when students are focused on establishing the reasons or logic for their own perspective. Figure 3.13, a Conflict Clarification Matrix, can help students organize their thoughts when they are examining an issue that includes their personal perspective. Using a matrix cues students to record their response to each step and thus allows them to go back and reexamine their ideas once they have completed the process.

FIGURE 3.12

PERSPECTIVE EXAMINATION MATRIX

Statement or Concept	Assigned Value	Reasoning or Logic Behind My Value
A 75-mph speed limit	I think this is a good idea.	
The new rule that all students have to wear a common uniform	I think this is not a very good idea.	

FIGURE 3.13

CONFLICT CLARIFICATION MATRIX

Issue	A new mass transit system for the city
Personal perspective	I think this is a good idea for the city.
Reasons/logic behind my personal perspective	Mass transit is a good idea because ...
Different perspective	Someone could think that mass transit is a bad idea for the city.
Reasons/logic behind different perspective	The reasons they might give are ...
Conclusion/awareness	From this I learned that ...

5. Use teacher-structured and student-structured tasks.

There will be times when you will want to present students with highly structured tasks in which you have identified both the issue and the perspectives and then ask them to identify the reasons and logic for each. For example, during a unit on Western Europe in a secondary class, the teacher might present students with two or three very specific perspectives on particular issues related to unification; the goal of this structured task might be to increase students' understanding of ways in which people and cultures hold on to the past yet look for changes in the future. During a unit about whales, an elementary teacher might focus on the issues surrounding whale hunting. The teacher might make sure that many perspectives are identified and analyzed, including those of hunters, their families, environmentalists, and scientists.

Over time, students can begin to structure their own tasks that require analyzing perspectives. They might identify issues from their own life, such as differing perspectives on types of music or sports-related topics. However, ideally, they should begin recognizing issues in academic content that are worth analyzing. For example, during health class, to help students understand how complex the issues can be, you might periodically encourage them to identify the issues that interest them and about which people disagree. Then have students describe and analyze different perspectives. Even when students are identifying the issues and the perspectives, your role is to hold them to standards of rigorous analysis. This ensures that even tasks that are completely structured by students will help them to extend and refine their knowledge.

Classroom Examples

The following classroom examples are offered to stimulate reflection on how to apply the ideas covered in this section of Dimension 3 in your classroom.

Mr. Pine and Ms. Shikes created an interdisciplinary task for their science and social studies students. Students gathered information about the reintroduction of wolves into Yellowstone National Park, identified various perspectives about the issue (e.g., those held by farmers, animal rights advocates, wildlife biologists, and park rangers), and described the reasons that each group holds its particular views. Mr. Pine and Ms. Shikes then asked students to select another current issue that interested them and apply a similar process.

● ● ●

Mrs. Snow was trying to engage her sixth-grade students in the study of music, specifically, in developing an understanding of the criteria that affect the quality (e.g., use of elements that create unity, tension/release) and effectiveness (e.g., expressive impact). She knew her students were quickly losing interest, so she decided to tap into their experiences and biases. She asked each student to analyze possible perspectives on whether "rap" should be considered music that should be taken seriously as an art form. Some people, for example, think "rap" is simply verses that rhyme, with noise in the background. Others believe it is a new form of music. Students had to articulate two perspectives and offer reasons and logic that reflected their understanding of the criteria that they had been studying.

• • •

In his civics class, Mr. Williams shared with his students a dinner conversation he had with his in-laws about attempts to include England in the unification efforts in Europe. The couple, who was from England, became quite upset during the conversation. It became clear that they were bitterly opposed to bringing England into European economic and political alliances. Mr. Williams said that Mary, a friend who was at the dinner, later commented, "They are just stuck in their old ways. They can't face the future. They should realize that their old way of life is gone, the monarchy clearly is in disarray, their economy is in need of a boost, and if they don't face reality, their future is doomed." Mr. Williams asked students to prepare a response to Mary by presenting at least two perspectives on the issue of whether England should be brought into unification efforts. Their job was to convince Mary that the position that the British couple had taken was not simply irrational or emotional. Students were required to present defensible reasons and logic that would support their own perspective, as well as at least one other opposing perspective, and then present both perspectives in a role play.

Unit Planning: Dimension 3

Planning for Dimension 3 requires asking and answering the following overarching question:

What will be done to help students extend and refine knowledge?

What follows is a step-by-step process that will guide you in answering this question. Each step asks you to answer a key question or provide specific information. There is a place on the planning guide (see page 188) in which to record your decisions about the knowledge that will be extended and refined (Step 1) and descriptions of planned activities (Step 3). A sample planning guide has been filled out for a hypothetical social studies unit about Colorado. (This unit topic was chosen because, with some changes, it could be used for a unit about any state or region and at any developmental level. You will find the entire unit in Chapter 6, "Putting It All Together.")

Step 1

> What knowledge will students be **extending and refining**? Specifically, students will be extending and refining their understanding of. . . .

As you clearly identify the knowledge that students will be extending and refining, remember that the goal of extending and refining knowledge is to deepen and broaden students' understanding of important information. Therefore, the knowledge that you identify here will be the important declarative knowledge identified in the unit. Further, because it is unlikely that students need to increase their understanding of specific facts, the knowledge they are extending and refining will probably be at the more general level of generalizations, principles, and concepts.

The planning guide has two places on each page for planning Dimension 3 activities. This does not imply that there must be exactly two activities. The number of activities depends on the length of the unit and the amount of important knowledge that students need to understand.

As you plan these extending and refining activities, consider whether students already have learned how to use the reasoning processes that the activities require. You may need to limit the number of new reasoning processes that you will teach students during the unit.

Step 2

| What reasoning process will students be using? |

Selecting a reasoning process is important because the type of reasoning that students apply to knowledge significantly influences what they learn. It is sometimes difficult to determine which reasoning process is best suited to the knowledge that you want students to extend and refine. We have, therefore, provided some questions to stimulate your thinking as you consider each process during planning.

Comparing

- Would it be useful to show how things are similar and/or different?

- Would it be useful for students to focus on identifying how similar things are different and how different things are similar?

- Would it be helpful to have students describe how comparing things affects their knowledge or opinions related to those things?

Classifying

- Would it be helpful to have students group things?

- Would it be beneficial for students to generate a number of ways to group the same list of things?

Abstracting

- Is there an abstract pattern that could be applied?

- Could something complex or unfamiliar be understood better by generating an abstract pattern and applying it to something simple or more familiar?

- Are there seemingly different things that could be connected through the generation of an abstract pattern?

Inductive Reasoning

- Are there important unstated conclusions that could be generated from observations or facts?

- Are there situations for which probable or likely conclusions could be generated?

- Are there issues or situations for which students could examine the inductive reasoning used?

Deductive Reasoning

- Are there generalizations (or rules or principles) that could be applied to reach conclusions and make predictions?

- Are there topics or issues for which students could examine the validity of the deductive reasoning used?

Constructing Support

- Are there important claims to be refuted or supported?

- Would it be important to examine existing arguments that support or refute a claim?

Analyzing Errors

- Are there situations in which it would be beneficial to identify errors in reasoning?

Analyzing Perspectives

- Would it be useful to identify and understand the reasoning or logic behind a perspective on a topic or issue?

- Would it be useful to analyze opposing perspectives on a topic or issue?

Step 3

Describe what will be done.

The type of extending and refining activities that you create will vary greatly. Students might be answering a question, constructing a matrix, drawing some conclusions, or gathering information. Clearly describe what students will be doing and how they will be applying the reasoning process.

Dimension 3 Planning Guide

Unit: <u>Colorado</u>

Step 1	Step 2	Step 3
What knowledge will students be **extending and refining?** Specifically, they will be extending and refining their understanding of . . .	What reasoning process will students be using?	Describe what will be done.
Topography, natural resources, and climate influence settlement patterns in a region.	☐ **Comparing** ☑ **Classifying** ☐ **Abstracting** ☐ **Inductive Reasoning** ☐ **Deductive Reasoning** ☐ **Constructing Support** ☐ **Analyzing Errors** ☐ **Analyzing Perspectives** ☐ **Other** _____	*So far we have been focused on understanding how topography, natural resources, and climate influence the "appearance" of settlements. Shift your focus now and examine how these factors influence the "disappearance" of settlements. You will be given descriptions of situations where populations thrived and then disappeared (e.g., Anasazi Indians, several ghost towns, dinosaurs, and the "dust bowl") and the reasons for their demise. Classify each description according to whether the disappearance had more to do with topography, natural resources, or climate. If more than one possible reason is given, you may have to place the example in more than one category.*

Step 1	Step 2	Step 3
What knowledge will students be **extending and refining?** Specifically, they will be extending and refining their understanding of . . .	What reasoning process will students be using?	Describe what will be done.
Topography, natural resources, and climate influence the culture of a region.	☐ **Comparing** ☐ **Classifying** ☐ **Abstracting** ☑ **Inductive Reasoning** ☐ **Deductive Reasoning** ☐ **Constructing Support** ☐ **Analyzing Errors** ☐ **Analyzing Perspectives** ☐ **Other** _____	*Several times during this unit we will, as a class, select articles from "USA Today" that reflect the culture of a place with which we are unfamiliar. Based on what we learn from the article about the culture of the place (e.g., issues or problems people face, their celebrations), we will try to induce specific facts about the topography, natural resources, and climate of the location.*

Dimension **4**

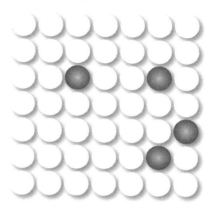

Dimension 4
Use Knowledge Meaningfully

Introduction

The purpose of acquiring knowledge is to be able to use it meaningfully. For example, we might want to learn all that we can about stereos or computers before deciding which brand and model to buy. We might learn a lot about genetics if we are trying to project what will happen in the future as a result of research in genetic engineering. Similarly, we would probably learn a great deal about social security if we were trying to invent a new retirement system. In short, when we use knowledge to deal with specific issues that we care about, we become truly immersed in learning. Dimension 4 emphasizes this important part of learning: the process of *using knowledge meaningfully*.

The challenge is to engage learners in using knowledge in a context that is meaningful *to them*. Many students will complete tasks simply because they have been assigned. But when students perceive tasks as meaningful and relevant, they are motivated to acquire the knowledge needed to complete the task. As a result, they may achieve a higher level of understanding and proficiency related to that knowledge. In addition, because their level of engagement can increase when they use knowledge meaningfully, students are more likely to demonstrate what they have learned. Tasks that require students to use knowledge meaningfully, therefore, are a powerful method—and potentially a more accurate method—of assessing learning.

Teachers can help students become highly engaged in tasks, whether students perceive the key knowledge as meaningful or not. When it is quite obvious to students that the knowledge they are learning is meaningful—

Fred Newmann discusses the importance of distinguishing between projects that ask students to *reproduce* knowledge and those that ask students to *produce* knowledge such as solutions, decisions, clarifications, explanations, and insights. For further reading, see Newmann et al. (1995) *A Guide to Authentic Instruction and Assessment.*

that is, when they see clearly that they need the knowledge in life—it is easy to construct tasks that are meaningful to them; mathematics and language arts are examples of content areas in which it is relatively easy to construct tasks that are meaningful to students. When it is less obvious to students that the knowledge is important and relevant to them, tasks can be constructed in a way that increases their meaningfulness and relevance. By asking students to use knowledge in authentic contexts or in intriguing situations, for example, or by allowing students to be involved in the construction of the tasks, meaningfulness and relevance—and, therefore, students' level of engagement—can increase.

Helping Students Develop Complex Reasoning Processes

As is true with the processes needed to extend and refine knowledge (Dimension 3), using knowledge meaningfully requires students to engage in thinking and reasoning that is quite different from that required when they are asked to simply recall, restate, recognize, recollect, reiterate, or otherwise reproduce knowledge. *Using* knowledge requires students to engage in complex thinking and reasoning processes as they complete long-term, meaningful tasks. Six of these reasoning processes have been identified and defined in this dimension. They are

- *Decision making:* Generating and applying criteria to select from among seemingly equal alternatives

- *Problem solving:* Overcoming constraints or limiting conditions that are in the way of pursuing goals

- *Invention:* Developing unique products or processes that fulfill perceived needs

- *Experimental inquiry:* Generating and testing explanations of observed phenomena

- *Investigation:* Identifying and resolving issues about which there are confusions or contradictions

- *Systems analysis:* Analyzing the parts of a system and the manner in which they interact

When students are engaged in tasks that require them to use the processes listed above—to make decisions, clarify confusions, create new products and ideas, solve problems, and analyze systems—they must also use their content knowledge. When constructing tasks, there are several things to keep in mind.

- Each of these processes crosses content boundaries. Although there are sometimes content-specific versions of the processes (e.g., a problem-solving process in economics), each of those identified above has been used in multiple content areas. If teachers across content areas consistently use these reasoning processes—or those from a similar list a district may generate—students are more likely to become comfortable and proficient with these types of processes and, thus, better able to use increasingly complex content knowledge, whether in content-specific or integrated tasks.

To help students appreciate the usefulness of the complex reasoning processes, a team of middle school teachers invited business leaders from the local community to meet with students. Each of them shared an incident that illustrated how a specific reasoning process had contributed—in the past week alone—to the success of his or her business.

- When the knowledge students are using is *procedural knowledge* (i.e., skills or processes), a task may simply ask students to perform the procedure within a meaningful context; that is, it may not require students to use one of the reasoning processes identified in this dimension. However, many teachers have found that using the reasoning processes to provide a focus for these types of task helps to provide a meaningful context for the demonstration of the procedural knowledge. Students may be required, for example, to use their procedural content knowledge to make a decision, to conduct an experiment, or to generate ideas for an invention. Students are then held accountable for demonstrating their proficiency in using the content-specific skill or process as well as their ability to engage in the targeted reasoning process.

- When the knowledge students are using is *declarative knowledge*—that is, when students are using and developing their understanding of concepts, principles, or generalizations—these reasoning processes should be used to provide a means by which they can apply the knowledge to the task. In the planning section of Dimension 4, at the end of this chapter, you will find questions (identified for each process) that can help you decide which reasoning process would provide the context in which students can demonstrate their understanding of the targeted content knowledge. (For example, if there is a phenomenon that needs to be clarified, then experimental inquiry is most appropriate; if something new needs to be created or improved, then an invention task is needed.) If students are clear about what reasoning process a task requires, they are likely to spend more energy *thinking* about the declarative knowledge than *creating a product* that looks impressive.

- In this age of technology, some educators have complained that students are using software and online sources to produce reports and research papers simply by electronically cutting and pasting text or even by downloading entire papers. Plagiarism, they report, although always a concern, seems to be increasing. Thus, it is increasingly important to hold students accountable for *using knowledge meaningfully*, no matter how it is accessed. One way to combat these abuses of technology, or any form of plagiarism, is to hold students accountable for complex reasoning and for the rigorous *use* of the information they have collected.

- These processes can be used by students at all developmental levels. Younger students will need more guidance and modeling, and, of course, the content must be developmentally appropriate. However, even older students need time to practice using the processes with simple content at first.

For each of the six processes identified in Dimension 4, the following sections are included:

1. *Help students understand the process.* This section discusses how to introduce the process to students and how to help them understand the function or goal of the process.

2. *Give students a model for the process, and create opportunities for them to practice using the process.* This section introduces the complex reasoning process itself: the model and the steps involved in using the process. Examples of specific ways to guide students through the thinking involved in the process are presented.

3. *As students study and use the process, help them focus on critical steps and difficult aspects of the process.* This section identifies critical steps and difficult components of the process as well as specific examples and suggestions about how to deal with these elements.

4. *Provide students with graphic organizers or representations of the model to help them understand and use the process.* Graphic organizers and representations help students understand and visualize the process. Examples of these organizers or representations are included in this section.

5. *Use teacher-structured and student-structured tasks.* This section addresses the importance of modeling and guiding the use of the process, first through the use of teacher-structured tasks. Suggestions are provided for how to move from teacher-structured to student-structured tasks, shifting students from highly structured tasks to tasks that students create as they become more proficient and confident at using the process.

It is important to note that although six mental processes are identified in Dimension 4, tasks that require students to use knowledge meaningfully can be constructed with reasoning processes other than these six. For example, once students become familiar with the nature and purpose of the eight Dimension 3 complex reasoning processes, you can ask them to perform *combination tasks* that require them to do more than simply extend and refine their knowledge. The following task is an example of a combination task that requires students to apply two reasoning processes from Dimension 3 as they use their knowledge from a unit on the Navajo and Hispanic cultures in New Mexico.

> *Consider these aspects of the two cultures:*
>
> * *the types of dwellings they built*
> * *the types of food they ate*
> * *their religion*
> * *their mobility*
> * *their family patterns*
>
> *Then <u>induce</u> at least one generalization about both cultures and explain the specific information that you used to draw this conclusion. Finally, identify and <u>abstract</u> a pattern from one of the cultures and identify another culture or situation to which it applies.*

Decision Making

> **Decision making** *is the process of generating and applying criteria to select from among seemingly equal alternatives. Stated more simply, it is the process of developing and using criteria to select from choices that seem to be equal.*

Decisions that we make every day, whether they are relatively unimportant or critical choices in life, are driven by criteria. Whether you are deciding which movie you will see Friday night or which college you would like to attend, your selection will depend on what you see as important or valuable at the time. When selecting which movie to see, you might loosely verbalize your criteria, for example, "Do I want to laugh, cry, be frightened, or be informed?" When selecting a college, you might write down your criteria related to cost, location, and academic offerings, for example, and then carefully apply each criterion to each alternative you are considering. Although these examples are similar in that they rely on the application of criteria, they are quite different because the choice of which college you would like to attend needs to be made using a process that is methodical and rigorous. Learning to engage in decision making means learning to use a process for applying criteria when the stakes are high—when there is this need to be methodical and rigorous.

As students learn to use a decision-making process and apply it to everyday decisions, they will quickly discover that the process demands that they have a great deal of knowledge related both to the criteria and to the alternatives in the decision-making situation. Likewise, asking students to apply a decision-making process to academic content requires that they demonstrate extensive content knowledge—or seek it out—to complete the task. Just as it would be impossible to use the process to select a college without extensive knowledge about each alternative, students could not apply criteria to decisions in chemistry, for example, without the scientific knowledge needed. This is why engaging students in decision-making tasks not only teaches them a useful process but enhances their learning by requiring that they understand content well enough to use it.

If students are asked to complete decision-making tasks, they will need multiple opportunities to develop their understanding of and ability to use the process. The following suggestions are offered for structuring these opportunities for students.

For more on decision making:

Ehrenberg, Ehrenberg, & Durfee (1979) *BASICS: Teaching/Learning Strategies*

Halpern (1984) *Thought and Knowledge: An Introduction to Critical Thinking*

Wales & Nardi (1985) "Teaching Decision Making"

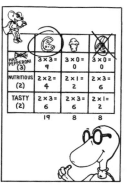

1. Help students understand the process of decision making.

One way to help students begin to understand that decision making requires applying criteria to alternatives is to describe examples of decisions you have made. Try to differentiate between decisions that were fairly trivial (e.g., where to go for the weekend) and those that required a more rigorous process (e.g., deciding how to vote in an important election). For each example identify the criteria and how each alternative measured up to those criteria. The goal is to develop students' understanding of the concepts *criteria* and *seemingly equal alternatives* and to help them understand the process of applying criteria to alternatives.

Another way of increasing students' understanding of the decision making process is to help them understand that this is often the process used when awards are given or distinguished performance is recognized. Students should be familiar with common examples of awards ceremonies or well-publicized honors bestowed on people, such as the presentation of the Academy Awards or Nobel Prizes, the selection of the most valuable player in a sport or game, or a publication's selection of "the person of the year" or "the best and worst dressed." Help students see that in each case criteria are generated and applied to make the selection. Take advantage of current awards shows, special publications, sports awards, or honors programs to discuss with students the criteria that might have been used and how they were applied in the selection process.

2. Give students a model for the process of decision making, and create opportunities for them to practice using the process.

a. Give students a model for the process of decision making.

Presenting an explicit model for decision making is a good way to help students become comfortable with the process. One powerful and useful model includes the following steps:

1. Identify a decision you wish to make and the alternatives you are considering.
2. Identify the criteria you consider important.
3. Assign each criterion an importance score.
4. Determine the extent to which each alternative possesses each criterion.
5. Multiply the criterion scores by the alternative scores to determine which alternative has the highest total points.
6. Based on your reaction to the selected alternative, determine if you want to change importance scores or add or drop criteria.

You may want to describe the process in simpler terms for young students:

1. What am I trying to decide?
2. What are my choices?
3. What are important criteria for making this decision?
4. How important is each criterion?
5. How well does each of my choices match my criteria?
6. Which choice matches best with the criteria?
7. How do I feel about the decision? Do I need to change any criteria and try again?

b. Create opportunities for students to practice using the process.

Most students at first will be unsure of their ability to follow the steps of this process. It is helpful if you begin teaching the process by illustrating each step. Walk students through a highly structured decision-making task using content-area information. For example, let's assume you want to use material from a social studies class. Your demonstrations and explanations might include the following:

My first step is to identify and state a decision question. We have been studying world leaders in class. An interesting question that would help us use what we have been learning might be, "Who, from the past or present, would be the best national leader if the entire world were at peace?"

Next, I have to identify the alternatives to be considered in the decision-making process. Who should we consider? (Allow students to help in this step.) *How about Margaret Thatcher, Martin Luther King, Jr., and Anwar Sadat?*

My next step is to identify the criteria that will be used to decide among the three alternatives. These might be (again, let students help during this step)

- *Good negotiation skills*

- *Charismatic leadership*

- *Extensive knowledge of other cultures*

- *Extensive knowledge of international finance*

It would help me if I use a matrix to organize my alternative and criteria. It might look like this. (Show students an organizer similar to Figure 4.1.)

FIGURE 4.1

DECISION-MAKING GRAPHIC ORGANIZERS

Criteria	Alternatives		
	Thatcher	*King*	*Sadat*
good negotiation skills (1)	1 × ☐	1 × ☐	1 × ☐
charismatic leader (3)	3 × ☐	3 × ☐	3 × ☐
extensive knowledge of other cultures (2)	2 × ☐	2 × ☐	2 × ☐
extensive knowledge of international finance (3)	3 × ☐	3 × ☐	3 × ☐
TOTALS	☐	☐	☐

• Assign importance scores.

Criteria	Alternatives		
	Thatcher	*King*	*Sadat*
good negotiation skills (1)	1 × 2 ☐	1 × 3 ☐	1 × 3 ☐
charismatic leader (3)	3 × 1 ☐	3 × 3 ☐	3 × 3 ☐
extensive knowledge of other cultures (2)	2 × 2 ☐	2 × 2 ☐	2 × 3 ☐
extensive knowledge of international finance (3)	3 × 3 ☐	3 × 1 ☐	3 × 2 ☐
TOTALS	☐	☐	☐

• Determine the extent to which each alternative possesses each criterion.

Criteria	Alternatives		
	Thatcher	*King*	*Sadat*
good negotiation skills (1)	1 × 2 │ 2	1 × 3 │ 3	1 × 3 │ 3
charismatic leader (3)	3 × 1 │ 3	3 × 3 │ 9	3 × 3 │ 9
extensive knowledge of other cultures (2)	2 × 2 │ 4	2 × 2 │ 4	2 × 3 │ 6
extensive knowledge of international finance (3)	3 × 3 │ 9	3 × 1 │ 3	3 × 2 │ 6
TOTALS	18	19	24

• Calculate quality points.

Now that I have the decision question, the alternatives, and the criteria identified, I am ready to weight the criteria by assigning each an importance score. I will use a three-point numeric weight, or importance score. So, if I consider a criterion to be very important, I give it a 3; if I consider it to be not very important, I give it a 1. I give a criterion a 2 if I consider it to be somewhere between "very important" and "not very important." I will assign the importance score, or weight, to each criterion on my matrix. (See, for example, the first organizer in Figure 4.1. At this stage of your demonstration, allow students to help you assign the weights, emphasizing that they must explain the reasoning behind those weights. Make sure students are using sound reasoning when they suggest importance scores.)

Next, I'll need to determine the degree to which each alternative possesses each of the criteria and justify the assignment as I do. Again, I will use a numeric scale: 0 = the alternative does not possess the criterion at all; 1 = possesses it a little bit; 3 = possesses it totally; 2 = somewhere between 1 and 3. (The second organizer in Figure 4.1 depicts a possible ranking of the alternatives in terms of the extent to which they possess each criterion, but you and the students may rank them differently.)

Finally, I will calculate the quality points each alternative has in relation to each criterion. I will do this by multiplying the criterion weights by the alternative weights. (Demonstrate the process of multiplying the number in each cell by the number at the beginning of each row and then enter that product in each cell, as shown in the third organizer in Figure 4.1.)

In this example, Thatcher has two quality points for the criterion "good negotiation skills," three quality points for the criterion "charismatic leader," four quality points for the criterion "extensive knowledge of other cultures," and nine quality points for the criterion "extensive knowledge of international finance."

My next step is to tally the quality points for each alternative and determine which alternative has the most. In my matrix, Anwar Sadat has the most quality points. It would appear, then, that Anwar Sadat would be the best choice for a peacetime leader, based on the information in the decision-making matrix.

But wait. The final step of the process is to ask myself if I am comfortable with the decision. It is legitimate to change the weights that have been assigned or to add or drop criteria. In my example here, for instance, I think that the criterion of good negotiation skills should receive a weight of

3 rather than 1. (This last step is important. You might want to make the point that it is not about changing points arbitrarily. It is about attending to your initial reaction to the decision and thoughtfully reexamining criteria and importance scores, if appropriate.)

After taking students through the steps of the process, give them the opportunity to practice with nonacademic content or with current events. You might create hypothetical situations or ask them to select criteria and alternatives for the "best" football player or television show. Be sure to hold them accountable for generating and thoughtfully and consistently applying criteria to each alternative.

3. As students study and use the process of decision making, help them focus on critical steps and difficult aspects of the process.

As students use the decision-making process, they should gradually be increasing their understanding of and ability to use the process. The following key points describe some of the challenges and important points to keep in mind while you are guiding students through learning the decision-making process.

Key Points

1) Perhaps the most critical concept that needs to be developed as students are engaged in decision making is the concept of a *criterion*. The quality of everyday decisions, as well as those made using academic content, depends on developing criteria that are clearly stated and that accurately identify the conditions that the selected alternative need to meet.

Rarely can a criterion be expressed in one word. Push students to articulate the meaning of a criterion with phrases or sentences that ensure that the criterion can be applied consistently to each alternative. For example, if students are setting up criteria for selecting powerful characters in literature, they should define a weak criterion like "interesting" more clearly, such as "characters had qualities with which I could identify."

In addition, unlike the process of comparing, in which characteristics are stated in neutral language, criteria must be stated with a clearly defined preference or value. For example, a newspaper might objectively compare political candidates on the characteristic of "their plan for taxation." However, if you were deciding which political candidate to vote for, your

"I realize that often when I have asked students to engage in a decision-making task, I have simply looked to see if the decision seems logical. I really have not held students accountable for the criteria. Now that I am holding them accountable, I have discovered many misconceptions that had not surfaced when the focus was on the alternatives."

—A high school biology teacher

criteria would be more subjective and reflect what you prefer or value; for example, you might rate each candidate on the "extent to which he or she will fight property tax decreases." As students practice generating criteria for decision making, provide them with examples of both characteristics and criteria in order to help them understand the difference.

2) Although a decision-making matrix is a common and clear format to use when engaged in decision making, its ease of use can create the misconception that decision making is an exercise in filling out squares in a matrix. The most important aspect of this process is the level of dialogue that occurs as students are using the matrix. Thus, the matrix functions as an enabling tool for thoughtful dialogue and precise thinking. Following the steps of the process does result in placing numbers into boxes, but students must be held accountable for assigning those numbers (importance scores and quality scores) by carefully considering the relative importance of criteria and thoughtfully determining the extent to which the alternatives meet those criteria. Holding students accountable for rigorously using the process will increase the likelihood that they will use academic knowledge meaningfully, as well as increase their proficiency in decision making.

3) Engaging in the decision-making process can create the need for students to use the knowledge they have acquired. It can also help students gain new insights into, and make new connections with, information they have learned, as well as provide a motivation for acquiring additional knowledge. The following are some suggestions for helping students to realize these benefits:

- Once students have made a selection on their matrix, ask them to go back and alter the criteria so that one or two of the alternatives that scored few points score more. This forces students to look at different attributes of the alternatives. For example, using the "best national leader" example above, you could add a criterion of "fought for human rights" and remove the criterion of "extensive knowledge of international finance." This could change the total points for each alternative.

- Begin a unit of study by asking students to make a decision for which they have a limited understanding of the alternatives and the criteria. For example, you might ask students to select "the best national leader" using only what they already know about each of the alternatives. Then halfway through the unit and again at the end of the unit, ask them to go back and determine if they need to change any scores, add or delete criteria, or consider different alternatives in light of their new knowledge. This reinforces the idea that decisions are significantly influenced by the knowledge we have related to the alternatives considered and the extent to which we understand the criteria.

- Lead the class through a decision-making task using the information provided in the unit. Then have them do a similar task that requires them to access the new information in an independent study. For example, as students study criteria relevant to a particular art form, guide them through the process of applying the criteria to examples within that form; then have them set up a matrix that uses criteria and examples from a very different form of their choice.

4. Provide students with graphic organizers or representations to help them understand and use the process of decision making.

When students are following the identified steps of the decision-making process, using the decision-making matrix becomes a necessity (see page 198). A matrix organizes the large quantity of information needed to generate criteria and alternatives and to apply each criterion to each alternative.

As students become comfortable with the process of decision making, you may want to encourage them to create their own graphic organizer to facilitate the process. There are a number of available software programs that students could use to go through the steps. For example, one high school science teacher uses a software program that reports the totals for each alternative in the form of a bar graph. This program also allows students to change the importance scores and to quickly obtain a new printout showing the new results.

5. Use teacher-structured and student-structured tasks.

Once students understand the general process of decision making, you can start giving them fairly well-structured tasks that will let them practice the decision-making process to become more familiar with it. In fact, any time that there is a clear academic goal, you may want to structure all or part of the task. As you develop teacher-structured tasks, you may decide to do all or some of the following for students:

- Clearly state the decision question.

- Clearly identify the choices or alternatives to be considered.

- Clearly identify the criteria on which the alternatives will be judged.

- Monitor students closely as they weight the alternatives and the criteria.

- Have students focus on very specific knowledge as they explain how they reached their decisions.

To illustrate, an elementary teacher presents students with the following structured decision-making task:

> *You are Queen Isabella and must decide whether you should give Columbus funds for an ocean voyage. You may not use what you know now but must work only with what was available to Queen Isabella at the time. Your criteria should reflect your primary concern as Queen to keep the public treasury sound and to work for the public good. However, you should also consider in your criteria your interest in establishing new trade routes. In making your decision, you also should consider the amount of money that might be involved and the number of lives that might be lost. There are no guarantees of success. Make your choice and defend it.*

Gradually, students should be able to generate their own decision-making tasks; that is, they should recognize situations in which the process is applicable and be able to specify many parts of the task. To move toward this goal, reduce the amount of structure that you provide for them and begin to act more as a facilitator of the process. Some suggestions for doing this include the following:

- Suggest a general topic about which students can make a decision, or pose an interesting question. Encourage students to generate similar topics or questions that interest them.

- Suggest some choices to consider, and encourage them to use only some of yours or, when appropriate, to generate their own completely different choices.

- Suggest some criteria to consider, but begin to hold students accountable for criteria that are clear and meaningful.

- Have students apply the criteria to each alternative, and provide feedback only when students request it or when you notice misconceptions that need to be clarified.

- Ask students to explain how they reached their decisions and articulate what they learned from the decision-making process.

To illustrate, the elementary teacher in the above example might encourage students throughout the year to look for situations similar to Queen Isabella's in which an historic decision could be analyzed to increase their understanding of the past. This could be applied, for example, during lessons in science, the arts, geography, or health education.

Classroom Examples

The following classroom examples are offered to stimulate reflection on how to apply the ideas covered in this section of Dimension 4 in your classroom.

Mrs. Flores gives her second-grade students the following task in order to meaningfully use their understanding of mathematics problem-solving strategies:

> *Ben is 43 inches tall. Keisha is 66 inches tall. How many different methods can you use to figure out how much taller Keisha is than Ben? Make a list of the important characteristics of a method for solving a problem (e.g., the time it takes, the number of steps involved). Then make a chart of the methods and important features that will help you to decide which method is the best.*

• • •

Students in Mrs. Wong's middle school class had been studying about the factors that influence people's decisions to emigrate to another country. To pique students' interest, she read aloud several letters from people who had immigrated to the United States from different European countries. These letters explained the hardships they encountered and the reasons they left their homelands. Some left because of war or economic depression; others were excited about exploring a new country; and still others fled because of religious persecution. Mrs. Wong explained that throughout the year, whenever students encounter situations in which people are emigrating, they will examine the factors that influenced people's decisions. At the end of the year, students will look at each matrix and draw a conclusion about the factors that are most common and how that pattern has changed throughout history.

• • •

A large urban high school was planning its annual Career Exploration Fair. The planning committee discussed the fact that, in the past, students typically took notes as they explored each career, but that it was unclear how useful these notes had been. The committee decided that this year each student planning to participate would generate a decision-making matrix. During home-room time, teachers helped those who did not already know the process of decision making to learn to use the steps of the process. All students were then given the time and guidance that they needed to generate criteria and assign importance scores that reflected what they believed was important in a career. This matrix was their ticket for entry to the fair. When committee members observed the students using their matrices and talked to students, they concluded that more than any note-taking technique previously used at the fair, the matrix helped students to focus on the criteria they considered to be important in a career. As a result, students asked better questions of the career representatives than they had in the past, then used the information they received to change and refine their criteria and, in some cases, to rethink their priorities.

Problem Solving

> **Problem solving** *is the process of overcoming constraints or limiting conditions that are in the way of pursuing goals. Stated more simply, it is the process of overcoming limits or barriers that are in the way of reaching goals.*

Most people agree that the ability to engage in problem solving is fundamental to success in life. However, even when people agree that students need to be good problem solvers, achieving the goal is difficult because there are so many different types of problems. To facilitate the discussion here, we have divided problems into two basic types: *unstructured problems* and *structured problems*. Unstructured problems are the kind you face in real life: They often have unclear constraints and require unidentified resources; sometimes the goal is not even clear. Unstructured problems also typically have more than one solution. Trying to improve efficiency (in this case, the goal needs clarification) in a workplace that is steeped in traditions that must not be violated (the constraint needs further elaboration) is an example of an unstructured problem.

Structured problems are the type we usually find in textbooks, games, and puzzles. They generally have clear goals and specify the resources available to accomplish the goals. In addition, structured problems usually have one right answer. For example, if the problem you are trying to solve is how to put the pieces of a puzzle together to form a certain picture, the goal is fairly clear (make the picture) and so are the available resources (the pieces of the puzzle). And there is only one correct way of putting the pieces together to form the picture.

It may confuse and frustrate students if they are taught a problem-solving process only to find that it does not help them with a completely different type of problem. The best course, therefore, is to clearly designate for students what type of problems they are learning to solve. For this reason, it is important to understand that the definition and process for problem solving in this section will focus on only one particular type: *unstructured academic problems*. These are problems for which there are multiple solutions and for which one or more of the following may need to be identified:

- the goal,
- the constraints or limiting conditions that hinder the achievement of the goal, and
- the alternative ways of achieving the goal.

The advantage of focusing on unstructured academic problems is that they are more like the unstructured problems we encounter in everyday life. For

For more on problem solving:

Anderson (1982) "Acquisition of Cognitive Skills"

Anderson (1983) *The Architecture of Cognition*

Gourley (1981) "Adapting the Varsity Sports Model to Nonpsychomotor Gifted Students"

Gourley & Micklus (1982) *Problems, Problems, Problems*

White (1983) "Sources of Difficulty in Understanding Newtonian Dynamics"

"We only think when we
are confronted with a
problem."

—John Dewey

instance, a parent has to find a way to give three children a nutritious dinner, even though the children's sports and activities pose limits on the time available for preparing and eating the meal. Or, a corporate task force has to come up with a process for increasing production without raising costs. Notice that both of these real-life situations have the defining characteristics of unstructured academic problems; that is, there is a need to identify the goal, the constraints or limiting conditions, and/or the alternative ways of achieving the goal. Because unstructured problems like these exist in real life, as students improve their ability to use this process with academic problems in the classroom, they will also develop a useful life skill.

In addition to gaining a life skill and increasing their ability to solve academic problems, students engaged in solving unstructured academic problems should also be using knowledge meaningfully. Problem-solving tasks should not only require students to demonstrate their understanding of important knowledge but should also provide motivation for seeking new knowledge that may be needed to clarify the goal, understand the constraints or limiting conditions, or identify available resources. As with other complex reasoning processes, it is helpful to guide students through a series of activities to ensure that they fully understand the process and how and when to use it.

1. Help students understand the problem-solving process.

Because students are also frequently exposed to *structured* academic problems, it is important for them to understand that the process in this section is designed to help them solve *unstructured* problems. Begin by reviewing with them the distinctions:

> ***Structured problems*** *have clear goals, specific resources available to achieve the goal, and one right answer.*

> ***Unstructured problems****, whether academic or real life, need clarification of the goal, the constraints or limiting conditions, and the resources available. There are multiple solutions to each problem.*

Emphasize with students that the process provided here will help them to solve unstructured problems. It might help them to understand they are answering questions that include "What is my goal?", "What constraints or limits are hindering my achieving the goal?", and "What are some different ways I might overcome these constraints or limits?"

Identify with them both academic and real-life problems that require answering some or all of these questions. For example, if a person has to be at work by 9:00 a.m., but at 8:05 a.m. finds that the car will not start, she has to determine the goal (getting to work or starting the car), identify the obstacle (e.g., public transportation isn't running today or jumper cables are missing), and identify how to overcome the obstacle (call a neighbor or push the car to jump-start it). To generate academic examples, ask students to identify assignments in which students are asked to build something (goal needs to be clarified) with only certain materials (limiting conditions).

In order to emphasize that problem solving requires the meaningful use of knowledge, help students to identify what knowledge is needed to solve each problem that is discussed. They should realize that knowledge is needed to clarify the goal, to understand the constraints and limiting conditions, and to generate solutions to the problem. Once you have presented examples, ask students to describe and analyze problems they have had or problems they have heard or read about.

2. Give students a model for the process of problem solving, and create opportunities for them to practice using the process.

a. *Give students a model for the process of problem solving.*

Providing a model is a good way to help students feel comfortable with the problem-solving process. The steps in the process might be stated as follows:

1. Identify the goal you are trying to accomplish.
2. Identify the constraints or limiting conditions.
3. Determine exactly how these constraints or limiting conditions are preventing you from reaching your goal.
4. Identify different ways of overcoming the constraints or meeting the limiting conditions.
5. Select and try out the alternative that appears to be the best.
6. Evaluate the effectiveness of the alternative you have tried. If appropriate, try a different alternative or identify additional ways of overcoming the constraints or limiting conditions.

You may want to present the process in simpler terms for young students:

1. What am I trying to accomplish?
2. What are the limits or barriers that are in the way?
3. What are some solutions for overcoming the limits or barriers?
4. Which solution will I try?
5. How well did it work? Should I try another solution?

b. **Create opportunities for students to practice using the process.**

To illustrate the steps in the problem-solving process, walk students through a content-area example, preferably a situation that has a clear constraint. You might use a think-aloud while involving students in the example. For instance, your demonstration might include the following:

*Salt has been used for centuries to cure meat, fish, and other foods because it kills microorganisms. How could I produce the same effect on meat, fish, and other foods without using salt or any of its basic elements **and** keep the food at room temperature?*

First, I need to restate the goal. (Alternatively, ask students to restate it.) *I want to treat meat, fish, and other foods with something that will kill the microorganisms even when the food is kept at room temperature.*

Next, I need to identify the constraints or limiting conditions. In this case, there are two constraints: (1) that neither salt nor any of its basic properties can be used and (2) the food must stay at room temperature (i.e., it cannot be frozen or heated).

Next, I need to examine exactly how these constraints are limiting me. (Ask students to help with this step.) *Let's see. The salt kills microorganisms, and dropping the temperature of meat below freezing stops the organic processes that produce microorganisms. Therefore, I must either think of different ways of killing microorganisms or stopping the processes that allow their growth.*

What are some possible ways of doing this, and what are the pluses and minuses of each? Some sort of vacuum packing or drying process might be used to prevent bacteria from growing. (Have students help you with this step. Be sure to discuss with them the extent to which each alternative helps to overcome the constraints. If you have adequate time and resources, the class can try one or more alternatives and discuss the results.)

After you have modeled the various steps in the process, give students opportunities to practice in pairs or small groups beginning with easy academic problems or lighthearted real-life situations.

3. As students study and use the process of problem solving, help them focus on critical steps and difficult aspects of the process.

Gaining confidence in using this problem-solving process with unstructured academic problems will, of course, require practice. As you give students problems to solve, you may want to focus attention on specific parts of the process. As you plan for these lessons, keep in mind the following suggestions and key points related to problem solving.

Key Points

1) The first step of the process—identifying the goal—may sometimes be provided for students. However, students also need to practice identifying the goal. Provide them with situations in which the goal is not clear, and ask them to clearly verbalize it. As they compare their goal statements with those of other students, they may also discover that in any situation there might be several possible goals. For example, if your car will not start in the morning, your first reaction might be that the goal is to get the car started; however, perhaps the goal should be to get to work on time. If parents are complaining about students' test scores at their children's school, should the school's goal be to increase test scores or to decrease the complaining by clearing up misconceptions? It is important for students to practice framing and reframing goal statements to see the effect that different versions have on the other steps of the problem-solving process.

2) Students may be anxious to get to the steps of the problem-solving process in which solutions are generated. However, it is important to make sure that students take time to focus on step 3: analyzing whatever is in the way of achieving the goal. (*Note*: This is step 2 in the simplified language suggested for young students). When students understand exactly how the constraints or barriers hinder the achievement of the goal, the various solutions will be more focused on overcoming those constraints and barriers. For example, you might ask students to construct a vehicle, but give them the constraint of using only certain types of materials. Before students generate solutions, it might be important for them to know if these limitations influence the strength, power, or aerodynamics of the project.

"The beginning of wisdom is the definition of terms."

—Socrates

"Although many of the tasks I've assigned over the years certainly have been challenging and interesting, I've never clearly identified the reasoning process that they require. For example, at times I've called the same task a decision-making task one day and a problem-solving task the next. Consequently, my students didn't focus on the reasoning process; they focused on the product."

—A high school algebra teacher

"No problem can withstand
the assault of sustained
thinking."

Another reason to ensure that students carefully analyze the constraints and barriers is that this is a step in which learning can be enhanced. For example, a primary teacher might create a problem-solving task by asking students to draw a picture of a busy city without using any circles. If students stop to determine how the constraint of using no circles limits them, they may gain a better understanding of the importance of shapes (or the importance of geometry) in their lives.

3) When students get to step 5 (select and try out the alternative that appears to be the best), they may find the need for decision making or invention, two other processes identified in Dimension 4. For example, when they are able to identify many possible solutions, the process of decision making may help them select the one most likely to succeed; when they are unable to generate any solutions, they may conclude that something new must be invented. If students are familiar with these complex reasoning processes, they should be able to shift quite easily to them during this step of problem solving. If they are unfamiliar with these processes, this would be a good time for them to learn about them. In either situation, understanding how these processes support one another can help students appreciate the usefulness of each.

4) It is important for students to understand that the problem-solving process is a way of finding the *best* solution, not simply any solution. Step 6 reinforces this point because it requires evaluating the success of the solution and, based on the evaluation, determining whether further action may be needed. If the first solution, for example, does not work, it might be necessary to go back to one or more of the previous steps. For instance, a failed solution might mean that the goal needs to be reframed (step 1), the constraint needs to be reevaluated (step 3), or different solutions need to be generated or tried (steps 4 or 5). If the solution is successful, it is still beneficial to consider returning to previous steps to find solutions that are the most effective and, in the classroom, to learn more about the problem situation. If students use problem solving in this way, their learning of the content and the problem-solving process should be greatly enhanced.

"In great attempts, it is
glorious even to fail."

4. Provide students with graphic organizers or representations to help them understand and use the process of problem solving.

For some students, organizing information graphically as they perform the steps will help them to use the process. Figure 4.2 provides an example that might be helpful to students.

FIGURE 4.2

GRAPHIC ORGANIZER FOR PROBLEM SOLVING

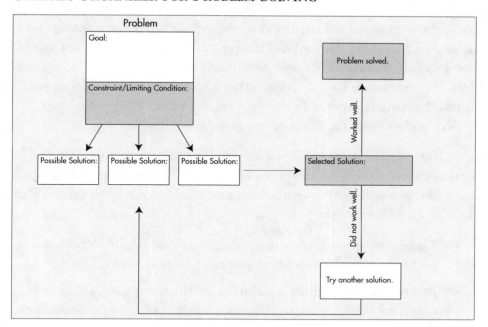

5. Use teacher-structured and student-structured tasks.

As they are first learning the problem-solving process, or any time there is a very specific academic goal, students should engage in well-structured problem-solving tasks. Some suggestions for constructing teacher-structured tasks include the following:

- Identify a situation in your content area in which there is already a constraint or some limiting condition to examine or in which a constraint or limiting condition could be imposed (a hypothetical situation or a simulation).

- Clearly identify the desired goal, perhaps explaining different ways of perceiving the goal.

- Clearly identify the constraint or limiting condition.

- Analyze with students the effect of the constraining element or limiting condition.

- Collaborate with students to generate ways of overcoming the constraint or limiting condition.

- Provide the necessary information and resources for students to try their alternatives.

"Problems are opportunities
in work clothes."

—Henry J. Kaiser

- Have students evaluate the effectiveness of their solutions and then respond appropriately.

To illustrate, an art teacher knows that pastel colors are commonly used to convey soft tones in paintings. She decides to use pastels as the constraint; that is, she tells students that they cannot use pastels in their paintings for this project. She states the goal and the constraint as follows: "I want you to paint a picture that conveys a tone of softness, but you cannot use any pastel colors." Students then have to devise other ways of creating the feeling of softness that pastels commonly convey. Students must then try out their solutions and evaluate the effectiveness of those solutions.

As students become more comfortable with the problem-solving process, encourage them to develop their own tasks. When students are setting up these tasks, you will need to decide how much guidance is appropriate. You might do all or some of the following:

- Suggest a general topic within which students might identify a problem, and ask students to generate additional ideas.

- Ask students to identify a situation in which some constraint or condition has been imposed or a situation in which a constraint or condition might be imposed. Provide suggestions, as appropriate.

- Have students clearly state the goal or the desired outcome. Hold them accountable for clarity and, when appropriate, encourage them to consider other ways of framing the goal.

- Ask students to describe the function of the constrained element, or have them describe the limitations imposed by the conditions. You might find it helpful to provide them with feedback at this point because it may influence the remainder of the process.

- Have students generate ways of accomplishing what the constrained element would have accomplished or have them generate ways of accomplishing the goal within the limiting conditions. Clarify misconceptions and provide advice when appropriate.

- Provide students with the time to access information and other necessary resources to try out their solutions. Offer help and advice when this will help students use their time and resources more efficiently.

- Have students evaluate the effectiveness of their solutions and report on their conclusions. Make sure that students include in their reports the knowledge that helped them understand and solve the problem.

To illustrate, to help her art students begin to structure their own tasks, the teacher might first present the painting task and then ask students to identify another commonly used material or process in painting (e.g., students might select a particular type of brush or brush stroke), determine what the material or the process accomplishes, and then try to accomplish the same thing without using that material or process.

Classroom Examples

The following classroom examples are offered to stimulate reflection on how to apply the ideas covered in this section of Dimension 4 in your classroom.

A teacher designed the following task for students in her family and consumer studies class. Her goal was for students to learn to plan and prepare meals that meet the nutritional needs and dietary restrictions of different people.

> *It's Thanksgiving. For most families this is a simple matter of buying a turkey, whipping up some mashed potatoes, buying a few cans of cranberry sauce, and baking some pies. But your family is different. Your dad has diabetes; your sister is lactose intolerant; your brother is a vegetarian; your mother is on a low-fat diet.*
>
> *How can you create a Thanksgiving meal that incorporates all of the needs of your family members, while still maintaining the appropriate nutritional levels and the traditional foods that most people associate with a good Thanksgiving feast? Develop an outline of what you want the menu to include. Identify the limitations of various dishes and explore alternatives you could use. Try a few different alternatives to see which one might be the most flavorful and nutritious. Continue to try different alternatives until you have come up with a menu that achieves the outlined objectives.*

• • •

Mrs. Brokaw, a middle school English teacher, loved grammar. Her students, however, did not share her passion. To increase their appreciation for the usefulness of grammar and to determine how well they understood how adjectives are used, she assigned the following task as a sort of "reverse psychology":

> *Write a rave review of a movie or book. You may use the articles—a, an, the— freely. You may, however, use adjectives only four times.*

• • •

You have been given a job by a small theater company to design the sets for its next production. The budget is tight, but their facility has one strength: the lighting capabilities. In fact, the producer wants you to use your understanding of the visual and aural elements of an environment (place, time, atmosphere, and mood) to design the sets using only lights.

Invention

> ***Invention*** *is the process of developing unique products or processes that fulfill perceived needs. Stated more simply, it is the process of developing original products or processes that meet specific needs.*

For more on invention:

Amabile (1983) *The Social Psychology of Creativity*

Applebee (1984b) "Writing and Reasoning"

Crabbe (1982) "Creating a Brighter Future"

Marzano (1991) *Cultivating Thinking in English and the Language Arts*

Moffett (1968) *Teaching the Universe of Discourse*

Nickerson, Perkins, & Smith (1985) *The Teaching of Thinking*

Perkins (1986) *Knowledge as Design*

von Oech (1983) *A Whack on the Side of the Head*

"No army can withstand the strength of an idea whose time has come."

—Victor Hugo

We all have encountered the kind of frustrating situations that make us stop and think, "There has to be a better way to. . . ." or "They ought to make a better. . . ." These are the situations in which the process of invention is needed, the process with the explicit purpose of creating products or processes to meet perceived needs. Whether making up a game or devising a better way to move students in and out of the lunch room, you are engaged in invention because you are answering such questions as, "How can I do this better or more efficiently?" or "What can I create that is new?" This creative aspect of invention is probably why many students see it as a reasoning process that is a challenge but is also fun. Students are excited when they are free to brainstorm new ideas and gratified when they realize that the process of invention can help them to create a product or a process that did not exist before.

This freedom and creativity associated with invention highlights how it differs from the problem-solving process. Although both processes involve achieving a goal, problem solving is driven by constraints and conditions, whereas invention is driven by standards or criteria. Constraints and conditions are imposed from the outside; standards and criteria are set by the inventor. For example, while inventing a better way to move students in and out of the lunch room, you might decide that your new process will be quieter and will take less time than the process that is currently being used. These standards are imposed by you, the inventor. They do not necessarily have to be accomplished; the goal of creating a better way of cycling students in and out of the lunchroom could be achieved with very different specific standards. Constraints and limiting conditions, on the other hand, usually come with the problem-solving situation, and the problem solver has little control over them.

Although invention allows for a great deal of freedom, the inventor must identify a clear goal. The identification of the goal is guided by an understanding of the situation that created the need for an invention in the first place. Without this knowledge, the resulting product or process might be unique but might fail to improve the situation. Likewise, in the classroom, when are students given invention tasks related to academic content, they must have the knowledge necessary to complete the task. Engaging students in invention, then, not only helps them develop their ability to use the process, it requires them to use their knowledge meaningfully. The recommendations in the following section are offered as ways of helping students develop their understanding of and ability to use the process of invention.

1. Help students understand the process of invention.

To help students develop an understanding of invention, generate with them a list of inventions that have significantly influenced society and their own lives. You might include inventions from the past as well as those that are currently changing our world. After you have an adequate list, present the definition of invention and then, for several inventions, ask students, "What was the perceived need that motivated the invention?" or "What were the inventors trying to improve?" This will give you an opportunity to emphasize that successful inventions are not just unique; they must have some value or use. Students should be able to identify inventions that were so valuable and useful that people's lives were changed, often for the better. You might get even more interest from some students if you identify which inventions were so successful at meeting a need that the inventor built an entire career or business around his or her invention.

If students are also learning (or already have learned) the problem-solving process, it might help their understanding of both problem solving and invention if you take the time to compare the two processes. For example, you might explain to students that if you asked them to build a bridge across a stream but allowed them to use only 2" × 4" boards that were no longer than four feet, they would have a problem. They would have a clear goal but a major constraint to overcome. On the other hand, if you asked them to build a bridge that is as strong as possible, and told them that they could use any materials that they wanted to use, they would be involved in invention because the goal is clear but there are no constraints or limiting conditions. The task does, however, come with standards—to build a strong bridge—and the inventor might even identify more specific standards, for example, that the bridge must be able to hold at least five people. With invention, standards are set by the inventor; they are an ideal to strive for. With problem solving, limiting conditions and constraints usually come with the situation and determine what you cannot do or cannot use.

Explain to students that understanding the distinction between problem solving and invention—in fact, understanding the distinctions among all of the reasoning processes—is important because when you begin a task and know which process is needed, you are much more likely to achieve the objective of the task.

"There should be a museum dedicated to human inventive failure. The only problem it would face would be its overnight success."

—R.S. Wurman (1989)
Information Anxiety,
p. 200.

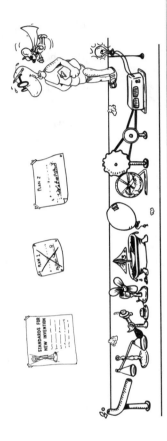

2. Give students a model for the process of invention, and create opportunities for them to practice using the process.

   a. *Give students a model for the process of invention.*

   Providing a model of the steps involved in invention will help students understand and use the process. The steps for invention might be outlined in the following way:

   Choice
   1. Identify a situation you want to improve or a need to which you want to respond.
   2. State your purpose or goal; write or say it several times in several different ways to look at it from different perspectives.

   Drafting
   3. Identify specific standards for your invention. What specifically do you want it to do?
   4. Make a model, sketch, or outline of your invention.
   5. Start developing your product. Keep looking for alternatives and even better ways of creating your product. Don't be too easily satisfied.
   6. Occasionally set your partially completed product aside so you can be more objective when you return to it.

   Revising
   7. Keep going over your invention with attention to detail.
   8. Stop when you have reached a level of completeness consistent with the norms and standards you have set.

   You may want to present the steps in simpler terms for young students:

   1. What do I want to make, or what do I want to make better?
   2. What standards do I want to set for my invention?
   3. What is the best way to make a rough draft of my invention?
   4. How can I improve on my rough draft?
   5. Does my invention meet the standards I have set?

   b. *Create opportunities for students to practice using the process.*

   When first introducing the invention process, walk students through a clear example using a think-aloud strategy and involving them when possible. For instance, while teaching a unit on maps, you might demonstrate in this way:

*People get frustrated when they have to use different maps for each different
purpose, for example, a topographical map to look at terrain or a political
map to examine boundaries. What I think is needed is to have a map that
combines information of various types like political, economic, and
demographic. So my goal is this: I want to create a type of map that combines
information about the economics, terrain, and politics of a region.*

*Now that my goal is set, I have to identify the standards that this map is
going to meet. First, I need to identify how much specific information I can
include. I want to include economic factors (like imports and average
incomes), terrestrial features (like lakes, rivers, and elevations), and political
elements (like alliances and territorial relationships). My goal is to display
all of this information and design a key that will make it easy for users to
find the type of information they want. The map must appear organized and
uncluttered.* (You might allow students to elaborate on your standards
and suggest others.)

Next, I need to do some rough sketches of this map. (Ask students to
develop rough sketches or models of their ideas for the map. As you
work, describe some of the problems you foresee as a result of
making your rough draft and ask students to do the same.)

*I have my draft; now I am ready to create the map. As I work, I'll share
with you some issues that arise during the construction of my invention.* (You
might prepare a finished product before you do this demonstration
or actually create the map with the students. Students can be
simultaneously creating their own maps and sharing with one
another the problems or issue that arise.)

*OK, I like what I have created. Does it meet the standards that I set? Yes,
but how could I put some finishing touches on it to make it better?* (You
could ask groups of students to determine if their maps meet the
identified standards. Then encourage them to add finishing touches,
giving them adequate time to make sure their maps meet the
standards they initially set and encouraging them to make their
products as polished as possible.)

Provide students with opportunities to practice these steps by creating
products and processes that are not necessarily linked to academic content.
They might even try inventing Rube Goldberg-type devices. Discuss each of
the steps as students progress through them and provide feedback to help
them understand the process. For instance, while students are making drafts
of their invention, you could remind them to keep their standards in mind.
You might also post the steps in a prominent place so that students can refer
to them as they work.

"To invent, you need a good
imagination and a pile of
junk."

—Thomas Edison

3. As students study and use the process of invention, help them focus on critical steps and difficult aspects of the process.

Students often become very involved in their projects when they are inventing something because they are so clearly using their own ideas to create something new. As they are working, however, it is important to remember that we not only want them to complete their projects, we want them to improve their ability to engage in the process of invention. What follows are some suggestions and important points to keep in mind as you monitor students' work and provide them with feedback.

Key Points

1) Attending to the first phase of invention, choice, is important to the ultimate success of a new product or process. During this phase, students need to identify exactly what need they are addressing with their invention. A clear, concise explanation of the situation that needs improving will enable them to generate standards and begin the outlines, sketches, or models during the drafting phase of the process. As students are learning to use the invention process, you may give them the opportunity to invent fun, even silly, products or processes as a way of practicing the steps in a nonthreatening environment. However, as soon as possible, begin emphasizing the importance of clearly identifying a need that the invention is going to meet.

   Identifying the perceived need is also the part of the process in which academic knowledge is first used. For example, if students are devising a new process for solving boundary disputes among countries, they must understand the present process and its apparent weaknesses. Without this understanding, students will not be able to define a clear purpose for the invention. Thus, holding students accountable for explaining the perceived need for the invention also demands that they have an in-depth understanding of important academic content.

2) The drafting phase includes one of the pivotal aspects of the invention process, *setting standards for the invention*. The identification of standards answers the questions, "What product or process will this invention provide that does not exist now?" or "How will this invention improve on what exists now?" Not only do the standards determine how the identified need will be met, they guide the work in the drafting and revising stages because the inventor continuously evaluates the extent to which the invention is meeting, or exceeding, the identified standards. For this reason, even when students are anxious to begin creating their

Thomas Edison is reported to have used the following analogy to stimulate his thinking about a motion picture machine: "I want to create a machine that does for the eye what the phonograph does for the ear."

"I love to construct invention tasks for my students now. This process keeps them focused on the standards they are setting so that the final product is useful, not just 'creative'."

—A teacher in Montana

invention, it is important to discourage them from proceeding until clear, rigorous standards are set. Additionally, during this standard-setting phase, keep students focused on the academic content that has provided the context for the invention. This is, along with the choice phase, a part of the process that requires students to use their knowledge meaningfully.

3) The work done during the revising stage will determine if the invention satisfies the identified need and meets the standards that have been set. Students need to understand that most successful inventions were created as a result of numerous drafts and constant revisions. Because these are the phases that are less creative and involve more hard work, students may need a good deal of feedback and reinforcement to keep them engaged in a cycle of drafting, evaluating, revising, checking back on or even modifying the standards, revising again, and polishing. Try to instill in them that the goal is for the completed product or process to meet, or exceed, the standards.

> "Failure is the opportunity to begin again more intelligently."
>
> —Henry Ford

4. Provide students with graphic organizers or representations to help them understand and use the process of invention.

For some students, graphic organizers help them to use the steps of invention and organize their ideas while they work. Figure 4.3 depicts a possible organizer that they might use.

FIGURE 4.3

GRAPHIC ORGANIZER FOR INVENTION

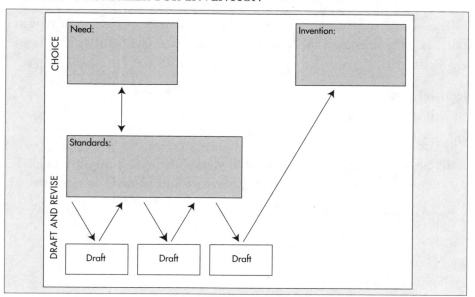

"An invention doesn't have
to be bigger than a
breadbox; it can be an idea."

5. Use teacher-structured and student-structured tasks.

As students are becoming familiar with the process of invention, and any time there is very specific academic content that students are to use in their invention, you may want to present students with very structured invention tasks. When developing these teacher-structured invention tasks, you might include all or some of the following steps:

1. Clearly state the purpose of the invention.

2. Clearly identify the standards that the invention should meet.

3. Provide students with access to the necessary materials and information to develop the invention.

4. Provide extensive feedback as students are developing a model, sketch, or outline of the invention. Make sure they understand the purpose and standards that should be driving their work.

5. Monitor students closely as they are developing and producing their invention.

6. Encourage or, when appropriate, push students to revise the invention until it meets, and hopefully exceeds, the standards that have been identified.

To illustrate, a mathematics teacher asks students to create a new way of performing multiplication. She also sets standards for the invention. These might be the following:

- *Your process should make it easier to identify errors that are made.*

- *Your process should not require much more time than the current process.*

Students would then work alone or in cooperative groups, drafting the initial models and then revising them until they met the standards that have been identified.

Ultimately, students should initiate and develop their own invention tasks. You will still need to provide some guidance and structure, however. You might do all or some of the following:

- Suggest a topic or area related to your content that might include a context or situation in which students could identify an unmet need.

- Ask students to identify an unmet need or something to improve.

- Ask students to state clearly the purpose of their invention, giving them a good deal of choice during this step. Provide direction only if their stated purpose reflects misconceptions related to the content that is providing the context for the invention.

- As students identify the standards for their invention, provide feedback only on the clarity and rigor of their standards.

- As students create a model, sketch, or outline of the invention, provide minimal feedback. If their initial drafts are weak, they will discover that for themselves during the drafting and revising phases.

- While students are working on creating their process or product, ask questions that will help them maintain a focus on their original purpose and standards.

- Encourage and reinforce students as they are revising their inventions.

To illustrate, if a mathematics teacher wants to use a multiplication task to stimulate student-structured invention, she would simply suggest that it would be useful to have a way of doing multiplication that makes it easier to identify possible errors being made. She would then invite students to identify other mathematics procedures that could be improved. Next, students would select their procedures and carry out the invention process.

Classroom Examples

The following classroom examples are offered to stimulate reflection on how to apply the ideas covered in this section of Dimension 4 in your classroom.

In conjunction with Presidents' Day, Ms. Bennis's primary class was studying the concept of symbols, specifically American symbols (e.g., the bald eagle, Uncle Sam, the Stars and Stripes). At about the same time, the school's parent-teacher organization announced a student contest to design a school flag. Ms. Bennis decided that the contest was a perfect opportunity for her students to use their understanding of symbols. She first taught students the phases of invention and then led them through the first phase, setting the standards for the flag. Together they generated some initial ideas that they thought should be represented with a symbol on the flag, such as learning, reading, writing, math, cooperation, and kids. Ms. Bennis then let students work in pairs to design a flag that had symbols of important ideas from the class list or other ideas that they thought of with their partners. After students completed their flags, each pair presented its flag to the class and explained each symbol. Each of the flags was then entered into the contest.

• • •

Mr. Gregorio realized that his physical education students did not understand the importance of engaging in proper warm-up and cool-down techniques when exercising or playing sports. As a result, he decided to spend some concentrated class time modeling the techniques and discussing their benefits and importance. To help students meaningfully use their knowledge of these techniques, he then asked students to use that knowledge to complete the following task:

> *You have been asked by a local television station to design a new routine for a half-hour health and fitness show. The previous routine was criticized by audiences because it did not allow enough warm-up and cool-down time to increase and decrease the heart rate.*
>
> *Using your knowledge of the cardiovascular impact of exercise, toning, and warm-up and cool-down techniques, create an exercise routine that appropriately increases and decreases heart rate. Begin by specifying the standards that you want the routine to meet. Next, outline the exercises you will use as well as the specific warm-up techniques (e.g., static stretches, walking or slow jogging, and calisthenics) and cool-down techniques (e.g., gradual reduction of exercise and stretches similar to those used in warm-up) that will be in your routine. Specify the time you will allot for each of these phases. Continue to develop your routine, exploring alternative combinations of exercises and warm-up and cool-down techniques. Run through the routine with several students, checking pulse rates before, during, and after they exercise. Adjust your routine until it meets the standards you have set. Present your routine to the class, explaining how it meets the standards you set and what adjustments you had to make from your original routine.*

• • •

Ms. DuBois wanted her eleventh-grade science students to use their knowledge of electrically charged materials and the attractive forces between them in creative and meaningful ways. She designed the following task to complete the unit on the electrical forces that exist between objects and within atoms:

> *Your mom ran out of those dryer sheets that keep your socks from clinging to your pants when you take them out of the dryer. Since you don't like the way those dryer sheets smell anyway, and you think they are just clogging up our landfills, you decide to invent a reusable anti-static-cling device for your mom.*
>
> *Using your knowledge of the electrical forces that exist between objects and within atoms, think about how clothes get static charges while they are in the dryer. Create a reusable device that will prevent static electricity in the dryer. Specify the standards you want the anti-static-cling device to meet (e.g., it should not melt in the high heat cycle). Make a model or sketch of your*

invention, and begin developing your product. Test your product as you develop it, making adjustments and changes to your original design as necessary until it meets the standards you have set. Present your completed device to your mother for Mother's Day and explain to her, in terms she can understand, how your product works.

• • •

Students in Mrs. Roser's communications class were discussing various reasons that people attend to or ignore important messages (e.g., messages that could influence their health or safety) and methods that are used to get people's attention. One student shared his experience on a recent family vacation that involved flying to another city. He noticed that many people did not pay attention to the flight attendant during the safety demonstration. Students speculated about why people do not attend to such critically important information. As a result of the class discussion, Mrs. Roser assigned each student the task of using everything they had learned about sending and receiving information to either (1) create a new or better way to communicate airline safety messages or (2) improve another situation in which people commonly ignore important information.

Experimental Inquiry

> **Experimental inquiry** *is the process of generating and testing explanations of observed phenomena. Stated more simply, it is the process of developing and testing explanations of things we observe.*

For more on experimental inquiry:

Gilovich (1991) *How We Know What Isn't So*

Turner & Greene (1977) *The Construction of a Propositional Text Base*

Tweney (1980) *Scientific Thinking*

Experimental inquiry is a process that is as useful to anyone trying to understand what they have observed as it is to the scientist or the researcher. For example, a family from Denver on a vacation in Maine makes the following observations on their trip:

> Maria, their first grader, is surprised and frustrated when she notices that the towels and swimming suits they use on one day are still very wet the next day, even though they hang them outside to dry. After all, towels hung outside on a line in Denver dry in a matter of hours. But then she remembers something she learned in science class during a unit on weather. She decides to use that knowledge to figure out "the towel mystery."

> Maria's parents observe, happily, that their children fight much less on vacation than at home. They wonder if it is because they are all just too busy and tired to fight or if the undivided attention that the children are getting from Mom and Dad accounts for the increased peace. They get out the book they just bought on parenting and try to figure it out.

Both Maria and her parents are engaged in trying to explain what they have observed. They will now use the knowledge available to them to generate clear explanations, predict what might happen if their explanations are accurate, and then set up experiments to test their predictions. While Maria is applying her scientific knowledge and her parents are using what they know about the psychology of children's behavior, both are trying to address the four questions basic to experimental inquiry:

- What do I observe?

- How can I explain what I observe?

- What do I predict based on my explanations?

- How can I test my prediction?

These same questions drive the inquiry process, whether it is performed by nuclear physicists in a lab, by teachers in the classroom, or by children trying to make sense of their world.

Experimental inquiry is a fairly common activity in science classes but is less common in the humanities, liberal arts, and fine arts. This is unfortunate because the same process that is applied to physical phenomena in the sciences can be applied to psychological phenomena. If students are trying to explain why people react to specific literature, music, or visual arts, for example, they will have to use their knowledge to explain the reactions they observe, predict reactions in other situations, and set up experiments, perhaps using surveys or questionnaires, to test their predictions and validate or invalidate their explanations. Clearly, the process of experimental inquiry is a powerful way to use and expand knowledge, no matter what the subject matter.

As with the other complex reasoning processes for using knowledge meaningfully, it is important to introduce the process of experimental inquiry with examples, model the steps in the process so that students learn to perform them rigorously, and then gradually have students use the process independently. As you teach students to use the process of experimental inquiry in a way that uses their knowledge meaningfully, you might use the suggestions and recommendations in the following sections.

1. Help students understand the process of experimental inquiry.

Relating a famous example of experimental inquiry or discussing an experiment you were involved in is a good way to introduce experimental inquiry. You might describe an experiment that you did in high school or college; or you might describe aspects of the many experimental inquiry tasks conducted by Thomas Edison or Benjamin Franklin. As you do so, ask students to identify what they consider to be key aspects of the experimental inquiry process, guiding them to the awareness that experimental inquiry involves answering the questions: "What do I observe?", "How can I explain what I observed?", "What do I predict based on my explanation?", and "How can I test my prediction?" Be sure to emphasize that researchers have to go back many times and try different explanations when their experiments fail to validate their explanations.

Wilhelm Roentgen, the discoverer of X-rays, when asked what he thought they were, reportedly replied, "I do not think; I experiment."

In addition to helping students understand the process, share stories that exemplify how our lives are influenced by discoveries resulting from the process of experimental inquiry (e.g., Jonas Salk's experiments that led to the polio vaccine). Ask students to describe other famous or important examples of experimental inquiry or some current situations in which it might be beneficial for someone to use experimental inquiry. In each case, ask them to describe what knowledge the researcher must have had—both of the scientific process and of the topic being researched—to conduct the experiments.

A team of middle-school science teachers was concerned that students' science fair projects were more focused on elaborate or "glitzy" displays of knowledge. "We realized," said one teacher, "that we were encouraging students to engage in the experimental inquiry process but that we were not holding them accountable for engaging in the process."

2. Give students a model for the process of experimental inquiry, and create opportunities for them to practice using the process.

a. Give students a model for the process of experimental inquiry.

As with all complex reasoning processes, students should be provided with the steps involved in the process. Those steps might be described as follows:

1. Observe something that interests you, and describe what has occurred.
2. Explain what you have observed. What theories or rules could explain what you have observed?
3. Based on your explanation, make a prediction.
4. Set up an experiment or activity to test your prediction.
5. Explain the results of your experiment in light of your explanation. If necessary, revise your explanation or prediction or conduct another experiment.

The process of experimental inquiry might be stated in simpler terms for young students:

1. What do I see or notice?
2. How can I explain it?
3. Based on my explanation, what can I predict?
4. How can I test my prediction?
5. What happened? Is it what I predicted? Do I need to try a different explanation?

b. Create opportunities for students to practice using the process.

To illustrate the process to students, demonstrate each step in a concrete way. You might first use a think-aloud presentation (involving students as you use each step) of a physical phenomenon that students can easily understand, such as the following:

I am going to drop a rock and a feather simultaneously from the same height to demonstrate something I have noticed. I see that the rock falls to the ground faster. I wonder why that is.

I have one idea. I know that gravity makes things fall and that rocks weigh more than feathers. Maybe gravity pulls on things harder if they weigh more. (As an alternative, you might ask students to develop an explanation for what they observe.)

OK. If I am right, then any object that weighs more should fall faster than one that weighs less, and any two objects that weigh the same should fall at the same rate. Let me see. I could then make the following predictions:

- *A piece of paper crumpled into a tight ball will fall at the same rate as a piece of paper loosely crumpled or a flat sheet of paper.*

- *A pound of feathers in a pillow and a small one-pound lead weight should fall at the same rate.*

(You might instead ask students to make their own predictions or to add more predictions to yours.)

My next step is to figure out how the predictions could be tested. I think I will carry out an activity or experiment for one of these predictions. (Demonstrate an experiment, or provide materials for students to set up experiments.)

Based on what I just observed in my experiment, do I have corroboration for my explanation or do I need to change it? The tightly crumpled paper and the lead ball both fell faster even though they were the same weight as their paired object (the loosely crumpled paper and the feathers). My original explanation did not hold up. Maybe it isn't the weight that affects the falling; maybe it has to do with the density or how compact the object is. My new hypothesis is. . . . (You might demonstrate this last step, or allow students to use the think-aloud process for their own experiments.)

Once students have become familiar with the experimental inquiry process, provide multiple opportunities for them to practice and talk through the steps as a class, in small groups, or in pairs using light-hearted situations or interesting current events. Because each step requires understanding concepts, such as prediction and explanation, and an increasing ability to perform the steps, students' early experiences should not simultaneously require them to use complex content knowledge.

3. As students study and use the process of experimental inquiry, help them focus on critical steps and difficult aspects of the process.

Engaging in experimental inquiry provides an opportunity for students not only to use their knowledge but to produce new knowledge in the form of explanations and clarifications of phenomena. If the process is to realize its potential, students must have carefully monitored experiences that increase their understanding of and ability to use the steps of the process. As you plan these experiences, keep the following key points in mind.

Key Points

1) Engaging in the process of experimental inquiry is a complex and demanding undertaking. Because the process can be quite challenging to students, they should be examining phenomena that interest them or that have significant meaning to them personally. A major goal of all the tasks in Dimension 4 is for students to use knowledge in ways that are meaningful *to them*, but the more complex the process, the more important it is for students to care about the outcome of the task. Student interest and engagement can result from presenting them with phenomena that are intriguing or that pique their curiosity. This can also be achieved by allowing students to choose the phenomena they will research and to determine the manner in which they will explore the phenomena. Additional suggestions for increasing students' interest in tasks and their perception of the value of tasks can be found in Dimension 1 (pages 30-32).

2) In the second step of the experimental inquiry process, students are asked to offer an explanation of the phenomenon they are examining. This is a critical point in the process because students have to bring their prior knowledge and experience to the task. In addition, because this is a very *deductive* part of the process—that is, because it requires students to apply general theories and rules to novel, specific situations—students must bring with them an understanding of the concepts, generalizations, and principles that could help explain the phenomenon. Even when they are interested in clarifying the phenomenon, students also must have the knowledge needed to attempt the explanation. It is the responsibility of the teacher, therefore, not only to encourage and prompt students, but to provide opportunities for them to learn the knowledge that they are being asked to use in this part of the inquiry process.

3) When students are asked to make a prediction (step 3) and to set up an experiment (step 4), they are facing the same challenge as researchers who have spent a lifetime learning to generate hypotheses and set up powerful, elegant experiments. These are the steps of the process during which students may need a great deal of modeling and guidance. Although it is important for students to become proficient at independently setting up experiments, it sometimes is appropriate to offer a great deal of help during these steps, especially when the primary goal of the assignment is for students to use their content knowledge meaningfully.

4) As students are analyzing the results of their experiments (step 5), they may begin to understand the interactive nature of the steps of the experimental inquiry process. As experienced researchers know, obtaining

"Our science teachers have helped us to better understand the experimental inquiry process so that we can use it across the disciplines."

—A principal in
New Mexico

the results of the experiment does not represent an end; it simply provides direction for what needs to be done next. When the experiment suggests, for example, that the explanation was *incorrect*, the researcher must decide whether to try a different explanation or set up an alternative experiment. When the experiment indicates that the explanation of the phenomenon was *correct*, it is equally important to go back and set up additional experiments or even consider different explanations.

Although experienced researchers understand this quality of experimental inquiry, it is important to help students gain this understanding as well. It may sometimes be sufficient for them simply to accept that, although they have completed their assignment by analyzing the results of their experiment, there are many more experiments that could and should be done to explore the topic. Other times, you may need to persuade students to continue their inquiry with multiple experiments. The more interested they are in the topic, the more likely they will be to continue their research.

4. **Provide students with graphic organizers or representations to help them understand and use the process of experimental inquiry.**

Figure 4.4 is a graphic representation of the experimental inquiry process. It helps students see how the steps of the process interact. It may also be used as an organizer as they are engaged in the process.

FIGURE 4.4

GRAPHIC ORGANIZER FOR EXPERIMENTAL INQUIRY

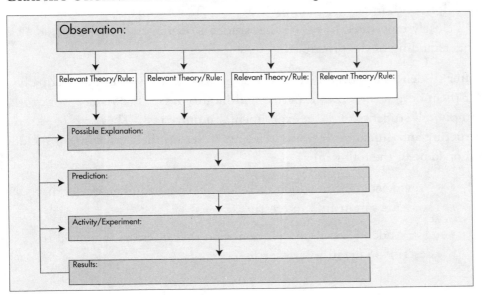

"The great tragedy of science—the slaying of a beautiful hypothesis by an ugly fact."

—Thomas Huxley

5. Use teacher-structured and student-structured tasks.

Once students understand the process of experimental inquiry, you might assign fairly well-structured tasks that give students some guided practice in using the process. When setting up these structured tasks, it important to do all or some of the following:

- Provide a clear demonstration or description of some phenomenon (physical or psychological) in the content area.

- Ask students to explain the phenomenon. You might suggest or require them to use specific content that will help them provide the explanation.

- Using the explanations generated, suggest possible predictions and accompanying experiments or activities to test those predictions and/or provide feedback as students do this.

- Provide the necessary information and resources for students to set up their experiments or activities.

- Upon completion of their experiments, have students review their original explanation in light of the results of the experiments and report on their conclusions and next steps.

A visual arts teacher, for example, might present a task that requires students to demonstrate their understanding of the principles of light and color as applied in painting. For example, students initially might be asked to observe how color affects the way people respond to selected paintings, then apply specific principles of the use of light and color to explain these reactions, and, finally, make and test a prediction to determine if the principles did, in fact, explain the reactions. This task is highly structured and closely monitored to ensure that students demonstrate their level of understanding of the principles.

After students have been given some structured tasks, you might gradually let them design their own experimental inquiry tasks. It does not work to simply tell students to do an experimental inquiry task. They still need some structure and guidance. Helping students to set up their tasks might include all or some of the following:

- Provide content in which there are unexplained phenomena that students might find interesting.

- Ask students to select a phenomenon that interests them and to describe in detail what they observe.

- Have students suggest a possible explanation for the phenomenon they observed, providing feedback as needed.

- Have students make a prediction based on their explanation.

- As students devise and carry out an activity or experiment to test their predictions, give them the responsibility of accessing necessary information and resources.

- Provide an opportunity for students to explain the results of their experiment to an appropriate audience and to describe the steps they would then take.

For example, in a psychology class, a teacher asks students to observe, over time, the way people behave in an elevator. She then asks students to identify some phenomenon that is interesting to them and apply a principle from psychology to explain the phenomenon. With only limited prompting and feedback from the teacher, students are engaging in the inquiry process on their own.

Classroom Examples

The following classroom examples are offered to stimulate reflection on how to apply the ideas covered in this section of Dimension 4 in your classroom.

Mr. McIntyre, a primary level teacher, decided to introduce to his young students the concepts of supply and demand and consumers and producers. He provided very concrete examples of each concept and the relationships among them but was not sure his students understood the ideas. Then during a class discussion, one student said, "Last Christmas, everyone wanted a Tickle Me Elmo doll, but there weren't any. Santa couldn't even get them. I thought you said when more consumers want something, that producers make more." The discussion that followed was heartening to Mr. McIntyre as other students chimed in. "I didn't get a new Nintendo game," said one student, "because there weren't any. My mom said that the company made them difficult to get so that people would want them even more." Mr. McIntyre prompted students to continue their discussion about how limited supply might increase demand. He then helped them set up an experiment to determine what happens when consumers perceive that there is a limited supply of an item.

The class decided to hold a cookie sale near the entrance to the school. Each day students secretly selected one kind of cookie and placed only a few on the display plate. Next to it was a sign: "Hurry! Almost sold out!" Each time they sold one of these cookies, they quickly replaced it so that there were always a few on the plate. Each day they kept a tally of how many they sold of each cookie type so they could determine if they sold more of the cookies that students perceived to be in limited supply. They discovered that when students thought that there were only a few of one type of cookie, they did, in fact, buy more of them. They concluded that this might have been what happened with the Christmas toys.

• • •

Mrs. Carey overheard her American Literature students complaining about how difficult William Faulkner's works were to read and understand. One of the students suggested that it was because Faulkner wrote long, complex sentences which are harder to understand than short sentences. Mrs. Carey asked students whether they wanted to test this hypothesis. The students became excited about conducting an experiment to test the hypothesis. They designed an experiment in which other students in the school read one of two passages that contained identical information. One version was composed of long sentences and the other of short sentences. The experimenters predicted that the students who had the long-sentence version would not understand the information as well and would therefore do more poorly when tested on their understanding of the information in the passage. The students were surprised to find that readers of the long- and short-sentence passages performed equally well. As a result of their findings, they reviewed their Faulkner readings again to see if they could come up with another possible explanation for their difficulty in reading and understanding his works.

• • •

Students in an applied science and technology class were learning about energy types, sources, and conversions. Their teacher created the following task for them to use and apply their understanding that energy cannot be created or destroyed:

> *You have just dashed into Otto's Auto Shop to purchase a new battery for your car when you overhear a man in the store talking about an experience he once had with a battery. The man tells his buddy that he once purchased a new battery for his car, but it went dead before he could install it because he left it sitting on the concrete floor of his garage. You are concerned because it will be a week or so before you will be able to install the new battery in your own car, so you decide to ask Otto about this when you pay for the battery. Unfortunately, Otto is not in the best of moods this afternoon, and he only growls to you that with today's batteries you don't have to worry about that happening anymore. As you leave the store, you become more curious about the whole idea of a concrete*

*floor causing a new battery to lose its charge. You decide to inquire a little
further into the matter.*

*Based on your understanding that energy can never be created or destroyed, how
might you explain the fact that a battery lost its charge just by sitting on a
garage floor? Conduct some research, if necessary, to familiarize yourself with
how batteries work. Review any theories or rules we have learned that might
explain how this could happen. Then come up with your explanation, and make
a prediction based on that explanation. Design and conduct an experiment to
test your prediction. Confirm or revise your prediction based on the results of
your experiment, and be prepared to report your findings to the class.*

For more on investigation:

Applebee (1981) *Writing in the Secondary School*

Applebee (1984a) *Contexts for Learning to Write*

Applebee (1984b) "Writing and Reasoning"

Kentucky Institute for Education Research (1995) *An Independent Evaluation of the Kentucky Instructional Results Information System (KIRIS): Executive Summary*

Investigation

> **Investigation** *is the process of identifying and resolving issues about which there are confusions or contradictions. Stated more simply, it is the process of suggesting and defending ways to clear up confusions about ideas or events.*

We all have read or listened to stories in the media that are the product of investigative reporting. This type of reporting requires digging deeper into a story when the available information contains contradictions, inconsistencies, or other indications that the entire truth has not been exposed. When reporters are engaged in an investigation in an attempt, for example, to explain an event, they first look for as much information as possible from as many different resources as possible. They then construct a sequence of events that seems the most accurate. This process of investigation, as demanding as it sounds, is the same process used by parents to try to find out why a conflict erupted between their children when they were out of the room or by a teenager struggling to define the concept of *friend*. The goal of investigation—whether conducted by a trained reporter or by an untrained individual—is to gather and use information to clear up inconsistencies and confusions or to uncover or generate information that is missing or otherwise unknown.

Just as the investigative reporter's job is different from that of the news reporter, requiring students to engage in investigation provides a different challenge than asking them to simply gather information for an independent study. One major difference is the selection of the topic. When engaged in investigation, students are focused on topics not because they are confused about them but because there are confusions and contradictions in the available information related to that topic. A second major difference is that students cannot simply go to a resource and find the answer. They must use resources to construct a resolution to a confusion or contradiction. For example, a student might decide to do an independent study to understand the customs in the country of Iraq; this would not qualify as an investigation. However, if during that study he realized that there was confusion about the definition of the concept of *the Third World*, then investigation would be needed. He would need to use the appropriate resources to construct such a definition.

At first it may seem that there are limited opportunities to engage students in investigation. However, when this process is more regularly used in the classroom, teachers and students begin to notice topics that have confusions and contradictions that they might have missed before they were familiar with the process. They will be even more likely to recognize the uses of the process if they understand all three types of investigation: *definitional investigation*, *historical investigation*, and *projective investigation*. These types of investigation can be defined in the following way:

Definitional Investigation	Constructing a precise definition of a concept for which there is no generally agreed-upon definition; for example, defining *civil disobedience*.
Historical Investigation	Constructing a scenario for an event or situation from the past for which there is no agreed-upon explanation or sequence of events; for example, determining Columbus's route to the New World.
Projective Investigation	Constructing a scenario for a future event or for a hypothetical past event; for example, predicting what would have happened if Mahatma Gandhi or President Lincoln had not been assassinated or what might happen if genetic engineering continues on its present course.

The entertaining book *Legends, Lies, & Cherished Myths of American History* (Shenkman, 1988) is one man's attempt at investigating numerous historical events about which there are confusions and disagreements.

A limitation of investigation is that even when the investigation has been skillfully completed, the constructed definition or scenario may or may not be accurate. The usefulness of the product of investigation will depend on the ability of the investigator to use the process. The following sections offer suggestions and recommendations for helping students to gain this ability.

1. Help students understand the process of investigation.

To help students understand each type of investigation, provide examples of the three types of investigation and the types of questions that the investigator in each example is trying to answer.

Try focusing your discussion of *definitional investigation* on the Supreme Court's attempts to define the boundaries of free speech by examining, for example, the question of whether burning the American flag in protest of government policy falls within these boundaries. Explain that during definitional investigation, the focusing questions are "What are the important features of. . . ?" or "What are the defining characteristics of. . . ?"

Explain that *historical investigation* is motivated by questions like "What really happened?" or "Why did this happen?" You might describe, for instance, people's efforts to find out exactly who was involved in the assassination of President John F. Kennedy in 1963 and how the assassination was planned. Point out that the movie *JFK* was the result of Oliver Stone's attempt at investigation but that others have constructed very different scenarios as a result of their investigations. Emphasize that examining past events to find out what happened or why something happened will result in only one possible scenario based on information used by the investigator.

Finally, help students understand *projective investigation* by explaining that the movie *It's a Wonderful Life* is an example of someone constructing a scenario for a hypothetical past event and that the book *1984* was George Orwell's prediction of the future. Both types of projective investigation—describing a hypothetical past event and predicting a future event—are trying to answer the questions, "What would have happened if. . . ?" or "What would happen if. . . ?" Provide examples of and ask students to suggest topics for projective investigation. For example, the controversy over the greenhouse effect and the resulting global warming is a good example of a possible future scenario about which people disagree. Explain that some scientists say that global warming will never happen, others say it will surely happen, and still others say it is already happening.

Ask students to generate other possible topics for investigation by using the questions associated with each type. Throughout the year, look for issues and topics that lend themselves to investigation and encourage students to do the same.

To recap, the following questions are associated with the different types of investigation:

Definitional Investigation

What are the important features of. . . ?

What are the defining characteristics of. . . ?

Historical Investigation

What really happened?

Why did this happen?

Projective Investigation

What would happen if. . . ?

What would have happened if. . . ?

2. Give students a model for the process of investigation, and create opportunities for them to practice using the process.

a. *Give students a model for the process of investigation.*

Although different in intent, the three types of investigation all follow the same basic process:

> 1. Clearly identify
>   - the concept to be defined (Definitional Investigation), or
>   - the past event to be explained (Historical Investigation), or
>   - the hypothetical event to be defined or explained (Projective Investigation).
> 2. Identify what is already known or agreed upon.
> 3. Identify and explain the confusion or contradiction.
> 4. Develop and defend a plausible resolution to the confusion or contradiction.

The process might be stated in simpler terms for young students:

> 1. What event or idea do I want to explain?
> 2. What do people already know?
> 3. What confusions do people have about the idea or event?
> 4. What suggestions do I have for clearing up these confusions?
> 5. How can I defend my suggestions?

b. *Create opportunities for students to practice using the process.*

Before engaging students in using the steps of investigation, walk them through the steps using a clear example of one of the types of investigation. Let's say you have decided to model the process of projective investigation using the issue of the possible effect of the decaying ozone layer. Your modeling might include the following:

My first step is to clearly identify the hypothetical event I wish to investigate. My issue is the decaying ozone layer. My specific question is, "What will happen over the next ten years if the ozone layer continues to decay at its present rate?"

The next step is to identify what is already known about the topic. I have here articles and newspaper clippings that I have collected about the decay of the ozone layer. (Provide these for students to review.) Determining what is already known is going to challenge my ability to access and use information. Specifically, this process will challenge my ability to know

- *how and when to use primary sources,*

- *how to separate opinions from facts in the sources being used,*

- *how to cite the sources I am using, and*

- *how to use media centers to locate a variety of sources.*

(Give students time to review the articles and newspaper clippings.)

Now I want you (students) *to help me list the important information on the board and identify any confusions, contradictions, or opposing theories that seem to be part of what is currently known about the ozone layer.* (Emphasize that identifying these confusions, contradictions, and opposing theories is basic to the process of each type of investigation.)

Finally, I am ready to begin clearing up the confusions, contradictions, or differences in theories. This is the difficult step. I must go back over the information I have collected, use everything I know about the issue, perhaps talk to other people and get some ideas, then carefully construct the most plausible scenario. (You might want to give individual students or small groups time to construct their own scenarios. It is important for them to understand that when investigating a topic, different people using exactly the same information can construct very different scenarios. Investigation results in *one* solution to the confusions or contradictions, not *the* solution.)

After appropriately modeling the process, ask students to first practice the steps with content they are comfortable with or with everyday real or hypothetical situations or concepts. For example, students might use one of the following questions to begin practicing the steps:

- What is tattling?

- What happened on the playground yesterday?

- What will happen if school uniforms are required?

As students become more comfortable with the process, have them begin to apply the process to more complex academic content.

3. As students study and use the process of investigation, help them focus on critical steps and difficult aspects of the process.

As students begin to use investigation, it may be helpful for you to provide some additional modeling and specific feedback as they use the process with increasingly complex content. As you are planning for instruction, you might keep the following key points in mind.

Key Points

1) Topics for investigation are sometimes difficult to identify. Although topics for more typical research reports may include anything the student chooses to study independently or any topic important to the content, topics for investigation are identified only when it is discovered that there are confusions and contradictions within the literature and when it is determined that it would be beneficial to clear up these confusions or contradictions. One problem is that you and the students may, at first, not even be aware that there are confusions and contradictions related to concepts or events that you are studying. And, even when possible topics for investigation surface when information is being studied, they may be missed because students are not accustomed to looking for confusions and contradictions among sources of information. In fact, they may ignore confusions and contradictions they do notice because their goal is so often to simply take in the information. Even with these difficulties, there are some things that can be done to begin identifying topics appropriate for investigation.

In order to help students become more accustomed to looking for topics that could benefit from investigation, introduce the process to students with an initial goal of helping them understand the three types of investigation (definitional, historical, and projective). Then, in order to increase their understanding of each of these types of investigation, begin a class list of

- concepts that seem to have no agreed-upon definition,

- historical events about which there are confusions or contradictions, and

- hypothetical past events or future scenarios that might be constructed.

Generating this list will accomplish two things. First, it trains students, and you, to look for and notice topics that need investigation. Second, it can be used later as a resource for ideas for investigation assignments.

> "Whenever students are working on research reports, I remind them to attend to confusions or disagreements within and among sources."
>
> —A middle school teacher in Wyoming

Once you and your students are more accustomed to looking for these topics, you may be surprised at how often the process of investigation is needed.

2) When students are engaged in an independent study that requires simply gathering information about a topic, they are commonly required to use a number of sources for their information. However, in an independent study requiring investigation, the number of sources is not as important; the challenge is to find the specific sources that help the student perform steps 2 and 3 of the process, that is, to identify what is agreed upon or already known about a topic and then to define the confusions or contradictions. These steps often require the students to access and use a wide variety of sources including information taken from primary sources, from interviews, and from hard-to-find documents tracked down through the use of technology.

Because investigation demands such extensive use of a wide variety of sources, you may need to help students learn how to access and use sources. Younger students and students who are just beginning to engage in investigation may need to begin by investigating topics for which the necessary sources of information are readily available in the classroom. Their focus is then on using the sources appropriately. As students become more comfortable with the process and more proficient at finding and accessing sources, you can expect them to take increasing responsibility for the investigation. Keep in mind that whether you are providing resources or having students access their own, you may need to do careful planning with the media specialists in your building so that they understand the purpose of investigation and are aware of the kinds of sources that may need to be available.

3) Many students will perceive the final step of the investigation process—offering a plausible resolution to the confusion or contradiction—as the most creative and stimulating part of the task. It is exciting when students become engaged in crafting and defending their resolution, that is, when they are taking ownership of the task rather than simply completing an assignment for a grade. Encourage and reinforce this ownership by looking for opportunities for students to share their ideas. For example, encourage students to submit their products for publication, to present their ideas to experts in the field, or to add their work to the materials you regularly use in the classroom with all students.

4. Provide students with graphic organizers or representations to help them understand and use the process of investigation.

Students could use a graphic organizer like that depicted in Figure 4.5 while engaged in any of the three types of investigation. You might also encourage students to develop their own graphic organizers.

FIGURE 4.5

GRAPHIC ORGANIZER FOR INVESTIGATION

Concept/Scenario:	
Known or Agreed Upon:	Confusions or Contradictions:
• • •	• • •
Resolution:	

5. Use teacher-structured and student-structured tasks.

Once students understand the general process of investigation, they can begin to practice it. Tightly structured tasks will help them become comfortable with the process. When developing such teacher-structured investigation tasks, you might follow some or all of the following guidelines:

- Clearly identify the concept (definitional investigation), past event (historical investigation), or hypothetical event (projective investigation) to be explained.

- Clearly identify the sources you want students to use, and make these available to them. Encourage students to search for and use other sources as well.

- Specify the issues (confusions, contradictions, and opposing theories) you want students to address, but encourage them to look for others as they engage in the investigation.

- Ask students to generate their own resolution for the issues and to be ready to explain what they learned. When appropriate, hold students accountable for demonstrating their understanding of specific content knowledge.

To illustrate, let's say you are creating a teacher-structured definitional investigation task for the concept of *democracy*. You might specify that you want students to use the writings of Thomas Jefferson, Benjamin Franklin, and Samuel Adams. You might even identify specific works written by these men that you want students to consult. Next, you should identify the specific issue you want students to address: whether the primary focus of a democracy should be the rights and freedoms of the individual or the common good of the people. Students should then develop and defend their positions on this issue using the sources you have identified and others that they consider important.

Students eventually should create their own investigation tasks, as appropriate. As you are planning for shifting this responsibility to the students, you may want to follow some or all of the following guidelines:

- Suggest a general topic or issue that students might like to investigate, but encourage them to find their own topics.

- As students begin to search for various resources, monitor their work and provide guidance when it will contribute to their knowledge and to their efficient use of time.

- As students identify what is known about the topic and describe the contradictions and confusions, check for misconceptions and provide appropriate feedback.

- Monitor students as they generate their resolutions to the issues. When necessary, push them to generate thoughtful and creative solutions.

- As students prepare to share work, whether in writing or orally, make sure they understand the expectations for presenting and defending their resolution.

To illustrate using these guidelines, if you were to use the concept of *democracy* to help students structure their own definitional investigation task, you would simply offer the concept as an illustration of a topic about which there are still confusions. You might then ask the class to identify related concepts that need clarification, for example, *liberal* and *conservative*. Students might select one of these concepts or identify another concept they would like to investigate. Your job from this point on would be to monitor and provide appropriate feedback to ensure that the process is increasing students' understanding of relevant social studies concepts.

Classroom Examples

The following classroom examples are offered to stimulate reflection on how to apply the ideas covered in this section of Dimension 4 in your classroom.

Definitional Investigation

Students in Mrs. Watson's high school language arts class were complaining about the list of books on the class syllabus. Mrs. Watson justified the titles by explaining that the goal was for students to study the classics in literature. One student challenged her further, "What is a classic, anyway?" Fortunately the bell rang signaling the end of class. Mrs. Watson spent the afternoon talking to colleagues, some of whom were college professors, to identify the characteristics of a classic. To her surprise, there was no general agreement.

The next day, Mrs. Watson confessed to students that it seemed there was no agreed-upon definition. Some people she talked to emphasized that the literature must be old. But how old? Some said it must be of high quality, but could not define what that meant. Mrs. Watson challenged students to remedy this obvious contradiction by working throughout the year to craft a definition of a classic in literature. She promised to submit all the definitions to a literary magazine that she respected and to ask the magazine to solicit reactions to the definitions from their readers. She also promised that she would use the class definitions to review and, if necessary, to modify her syllabus for future years. The students accepted her challenge.

• • •

At the beginning of a unit on microbes, Ms. Abraham gave her students the following task to work on periodically throughout the unit:

> *Are viruses living things? Some people say "yes," and some say "no." Some say they are a highly complex piece of inorganic matter. Some say that they are the simplest type of organic matter. Offer a resolution to this disagreement.*

Historical Investigation

*In an eighth-grade unit on exploration and invention in America, Ms. Lindquist decided to digress from her usual approach. She wanted her students to become familiar with specific individuals from history, but she also wanted them to begin to understand that exploration and invention are ongoing processes that involve many people. "It is rare that one day a person suddenly experiences 'Eureka! I've done it!',"
she told them. As a history buff, Ms. Lindquist had many documents, articles, and books about historical discoveries and inventions. She had always been fascinated by the fact that there were so many disagreements about the specific events surrounding these discoveries and inventions and even about who made the discoveries or created the inventions. She designed a task in which students would break into groups, then select a topic from her list (or a topic of their choosing) and use the resources she would*

supply (or any others they could find) to engage in historical investigation. She wanted them to focus more on why there are disagreements and misconceptions than on crafting the perfect resolution. She asked students to pretend that they were producing a movie that would explain the reasons for the disagreements or misconceptions about the topic and offer a resolution (much like Oliver Stone did in the movie JFK). Her list of topics included the following:

- *Did Columbus discover America?*
- *Did Vasco Núñez de Balboa discover the Pacific Ocean?*
- *Did Admiral Peary discover the North Pole?*
- *Did Eli Whitney invent the cotton gin?*
- *Did George Pullman invent the sleeper car?*
- *Did Henry Ford invent the assembly line?*

Students became more involved in their projects than they had been with previous assignments that had asked them simply to write a report about an inventor.

• • •

In Mrs. Martino's advanced placement literature class, students were discussing the idea that many authors write great things because they have lives or personal characteristics that are interesting, even bizarre. Their own lives, the students mused, seemed so everyday, so mundane. How could they ever write great works? Mrs. Martino, explained that many legends about these authors have been generated over the years, after—and perhaps because—their works became famous. In fact, if the students were to do a little digging, she told them, they might find that people disagree about many of the facts surrounding the lives of these authors. For example, there is general disagreement about the extent to which Henry David Thoreau was actually a recluse, about whether Edgar Allan Poe was mentally unstable, and whether Shakespeare engaged in rampant plagiarism. Mrs. Martino created a task for students to work on sometime during the year. Students were to select an author, identify points of disagreement or misconception, and then try to clear these up. She was confident that students would discover that the lives of many authors were not so unique and that they simply drew on everyday, mundane events to craft great works.

Projective Investigation

Students in Mr. Achbach's high school economics class were learning how the progressive tax system in the United States works. In particular, they were studying how taxation, spending, and assistance programs affect people and businesses. Students were calculating federal, state, property, and FICA tax liabilities for hypothetical individuals and businesses. Students discovered that progressive taxes take a larger proportion of income or wealth from higher income families and individuals. The class discussed the pros and cons of the progressive tax system. As a way to stimulate their thinking, Mr. Achbach proposed a task in which students would investigate an alternative to the current tax system.

Some politicians claim that a flat tax of 17% will raise nearly as much money as the current tax system and provide the American people with a modest tax cut. Opponents of the flat tax claim that it will create high inflation, devalue homes, and cause people to lose their jobs. Identify what is already known about the flat tax and explain the confusions or contradictions generated by the debate (e.g., it protects the country from a higher deficit, spurs productive investment and economic growth, and raises unemployment). What do you think would happen if the United States adopted a flat tax system? In essay form, develop a plausible description of what you think might happen and defend this with logical arguments and mathematical calculations.

• • •

Mr. Ballard wanted to more thoroughly assess how much his high school advanced geography students really understood about how a country's future might be impacted by patterns of consumption, production, and population growth. Although he had spent a great deal of time helping students develop a knowledge base about the concepts of growth and change, his assessments had only evaluated whether students had memorized facts and information and not whether they could apply information in a meaningful context. Mr. Ballard constructed the following task which demanded much more of students and gave him a more accurate picture of their understanding.

Latin American countries currently are experiencing rapid population growth. Statistics suggest that some of these countries will double their current populations within 20-30 years. It is likely that this population growth will have a severe impact on employment, education, housing, poverty, and land use within these countries.

To investigate the possible future effects of this enormous population growth, Latin American countries have established a special investigative committee. As a member of this committee, you have been asked to select a specific Latin American country and identify what is already known about the current problems it faces related to rapid population growth. Identify any questions or confusions regarding how these current problems may relate to future population growth problems in this country. Based on the information you have gathered, project how this country might be affected by a population twice its current size. Construct a scenario of the future in which you clearly describe the effects of overpopulation on the country. Be prepared to support your scenario with evidence from your research.

Systems Analysis

> *Systems analysis is the process of analyzing the parts of a system and the manner in which they interact. Stated more simply, it is the process of describing how the parts of a system work together.*

One of the most powerful types of thinking we can engage in is systems analysis. As the name implies, when we engage in this type of thinking we are analyzing the parts of a system and the manner in which they interact. Although this seems straightforward, it is not. One of the hardest things to do is identify systems. This is because they are frequently so transparent that we do not recognize them even though they are all around us. For example, a school district can be viewed as a system that has interacting parts: the students, the school board, the teachers in the district, the administrators, and so on. A family can be viewed as a system. An engine can be viewed as a system. A fish tank can be viewed as a system. The human body can be viewed as a system. In short, the world around us can be viewed as multiple layers of systems interacting with one another.

Although there are certainly many different types of systems, they all appear to have some similar traits. For example, all systems have parts that might be made up of individual units or groups of units. A school when viewed as a system has parts. Some of those parts are composed of groups of individuals. To illustrate, one working part of a school is the teachers taken as a group. Parents as a group can be considered another part of the school, as can the students. Some of the parts of the school are made up of individual units. To illustrate, one part of a school might be the school secretary. The school principal might be considered another part composed of an individual. Each part receives something from and/or gives something to the other parts. Commonly the "something" that is given or received involves information. For example, the principal provides information to the school secretary and receives information from the school secretary. The parents receive information from the school secretary, the students, and teachers; the students receive information from the teachers and give information to the teachers, and so on. All systems are affected when one of the working parts is impacted. For example, if the teachers stop giving information to the principal, everyone else in the system is affected. In summary, although there are many different types of systems that make up the world around us, all systems seem to have similar characteristics and behave in similar ways.

Because our world consists of many types of systems interacting in complex ways, systems analysis is one of the most complex and important thinking and reasoning processes of our time. It can be used to study the interrelations of a group of family members planning a vacation or the interactions of a set of countries involved in a dispute over oil.

1. Help students understand the process of systems analysis.

The first step in helping students understand the process of systems analysis is to help them understand the concept of a *system*. In very basic terms, a system is a collection of parts that interact with each other to function as a whole. Specifically, students should have a basic understanding of the following:

   a.   A system involves working parts that interact with one another.

   b.   What one part in a system does affects all the other parts.

   c.   The world around us is made up of many systems interacting with one another.

The best way to demonstrate *a* and *b* is by simulation. Luckily, there are a number of computer programs that do this quite effectively. For example, Stella II, by High Performance Systems, Inc., is a powerful computer simulation that can be used with virtually any type of system. If there is no access to a computerized program, a teacher might be able to find a simple example of a system in the classroom or the school. For example, the manner in which air temperature is controlled in the classroom is a good example of a system that can be demonstrated in the classroom. The parts of that system are

- the air temperature,

- a furnace,

- an air conditioning unit, and

- a thermostat.

The teacher might point out these parts and then demonstrate how changing one part affects all the others. For example, decreasing the air temperature by opening a window on a cold day makes the thermostat send a message to the furnace, which then turns on and increases the air temperature until it reaches the level specified by the thermostat.

Another way to help students understand the concept of a system is to design a simulation that actively involves students. For example, a simple assembly line is a good illustration of a system. Students can be organized into small groups, each of which has a specific role to play in putting together a particular object, a gingerbread house, for example. Each group might be responsible for constructing a certain aspect of the object (e.g., the roof) and passing that part on to another group. While students are in the groups constructing their particular part of the object, the teacher might change the task of a group by instructing them to add something to what they are making (e.g., she might ask students to add a porch on to the front of the house) or to use different materials. This, in turn, will alter the job of other groups. The change in the system should be introduced only after the groups have started to work effectively as a group so that the effects on the system when one group changes what it is doing are pronounced. After the simulation, students can describe and discuss what they noticed.

Once students have a general idea about the nature of systems, you can guide them in identifying some of the systems that they encounter in their daily lives. The more systems that are identified, the stronger will be the message that the world around us is made up of many systems that interact with one another. Systems that students might identify include

- their families,

- their sports leagues, and

- ecosystems.

2. Give students a model for the process of systems analysis, and create opportunities for them to practice using the process.

a. Give students a model for the process of systems analysis.

Once students have a basic understanding of the nature and function of systems, you can guide them in constructing a model for systems analysis. The first step in helping students construct a model for this process is to describe systems analysis as the process of identifying and describing a system. It is also useful to explain that this type of thinking can be quite complex and challenging. There have been many attempts to describe the steps involved in systems analysis. Some of those attempts can be found in the following works:

Systems One: An Introduction to Systems Thinking (1980), by Draper L. Kauffman, Jr.

Stella II: An Introduction to Systems Thinking (1992), by High Performance Systems, Inc.

Here we use a very simple model. (Readers should consult other sources, such as those above, for more complex versions of systems analysis.) The steps of systems analysis might be stated as follows:

1. Identify the parts of the system.
2. Describe the boundaries of the system.
3. Describe how parts affect each other.
4. Identify various parts of the system and for each explain what would happen if this part changed or stopped working.

This process might be stated in simpler terms for young students:

1. What are the parts of the system?
2. What are things that are related to the system but are not part of it?
3. How do the parts affect each other?
4. What would happen if various parts stopped or changed their behavior?

b. *Create opportunities for students to practice using the process.*

You might present these steps directly to students or guide them in discovering the steps. In either case, you should present a strong, verbal model of the process as you go through the steps. For example, you might use school as an example of a system. You would then answer the question, "What are the parts of this system?" As you answer the question, you would also comment on your thinking, explaining how you arrived at your conclusions. Demonstrate each step of the process in this think-aloud fashion. Your explanations might include the following:

Let's see. What's a system we're familiar with? I know. Our school is a system. What are the parts of the system? (Ask students to help with this step and with the other steps as well.) *There are the parents, the principal, the teachers, the students, and the support staff (that is, the custodians, the office personnel, etc.).*

What are the boundaries of the system—our school? That's kind of hard. It could be our attendance area, but we have students and parents from outside our attendance area so maybe it's the whole district.

How do the parts affect one another? (Give students an opportunity to give their ideas.) *If the principal announces that school is closing early, every part of the system would be affected, wouldn't it? The students would go home early; the*

"I know right now it is popular in the corporate world to talk about 'systems thinking.' This process made that whole idea much more real to me. I can't teach 'systems thinking,' but I can teach the process of systems analysis."

—A teacher in Michigan

parents would have to make arrangements to be home for the students or set up child care; and the support staff would go home early too. The parents affect the principal, the teachers, and the students; if they like what's happening in the school, they give their support. If they don't like something that's happening, they may go to the school board or to the newspaper to get that something to change.

What would happen if one part of the system stopped or changed its behavior? (Again, ask for students' ideas.) *Let's see. If the principal went to a workshop on cooperative learning and liked it and started teaching the teachers how to use it in the classroom, we would probably have lots of cooperative learning lessons in classrooms, which would affect the teachers, students, and parents. If the support staff stopped coming to work, that would affect all parts of the system because all of us depend on their work to get our jobs done.*

Once students are familiar with systems and the steps in the systems analysis process, give them several opportunities to identify systems and then, in groups and individually, have them analyze those systems. Begin with familiar, simple systems, and work toward more complex systems that relate to classroom content.

3. As students study and use the process of systems analysis, help them focus on critical steps and difficult aspects of the process.

As students use the systems analysis process, they should gradually be increasing their understanding of and ability to use the process. The following key points describe some of the challenges and important points to keep in mind while you are guiding students through learning the process.

Key Points

1) Because systems analysis is a very complex reasoning process, all of the steps can be challenging. Identifying the parts of a system can be difficult because one working part might consist of a number of elements. Identifying the boundaries of a system might be difficult because it is hard to precisely determine all of the working parts of the system. In general, however, the most critical step in systems analysis is the third: determining which parts affect each other and how they affect each other. This is the core of systems analysis.

Determining which parts affect each other and how is a difficult step because there are many different ways in which one part might affect another. One part of a system might provide a resource needed by another part; for example, a unit on an automobile assembly line provides a component that is used by another unit to complete its job. One part of a system might provide physical energy to another part; for example, a girl on a bicycle (which together represent a system) provides energy to the peddle. One part of a system might provide information to another part of the system; for example, the principal in a school provides information about schedules to the other members of the school.

2) Another critical aspect of the third step in systems analysis is determining the exact nature of the relationship. Is it always the case that the more resources, energy, or information that one part provides to another, the better? For example, is it always the case that the more information the principal provides to the teachers, the secretaries, and so on, the better? Is it always the case that the more energy the girl provides to the peddle, the better? Technically, this aspect of step three is called identifying the *functional relationship* between one part of a system and another. There are many types of functional relationships. As the flow of resources, information, or energy increases, so might the productivity of the part of the system to which it is flowing. However, it might also be the case that flow of resources, information, or energy increases the productivity of the receiving part up to a certain point. After that point, the receiving part may become less efficient or even break down. Some teachers find it highly useful to use graphs during this stage of the systems analysis process to study the nature of such functional relationships. Again, a powerful and highly recommended tool to this end is a computer simulation like the Stella II program.

4. Provide students with graphic organizers or representations to help them understand and use the process of systems analysis.

Graphic organizers and representations are excellent ways to help students understand the concept of a system and the process of systems analysis. The basic convention used when illustrating a system is an arrow depicting the flow of information or resources from one part of a system to another. Obviously, the more parts that a system has and the more complex the flow of information or resources, the more intricate the diagram. Figure 4.6 shows two possible graphic representations of the concept of a system.

FIGURE 4.6

GRAPHIC REPRESENTATIONS OF A SYSTEM

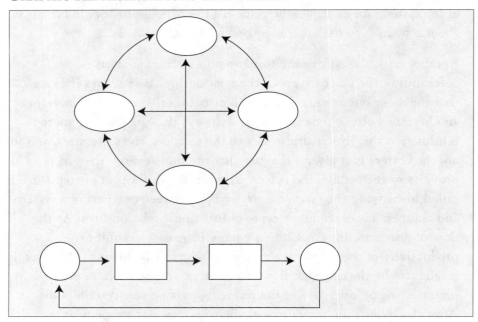

A graphic organizer for a system focuses on the identification of the parts and the manner in which they interact. The emphasis, when considering the process of systems analysis, should be on ensuring that no steps have been left out of the process. If the steps are followed, a student quite naturally will attend to the various parts of a system and how those parts interact.

5. Use teacher-structured and student-structured tasks.

When students are just beginning to use the systems analysis process and whenever you have a very specific academic goal in mind, you might give students highly structured tasks. A teacher-structured task presents students with information about the parts of the system and how the component parts affect one another. Students then determine what would happen if specific parts stopped or changed their behavior. When the analysis is completed, students are asked to summarize what they learned. For example, during a unit on the human body, students would study the different systems that make up the larger system of the human body. Students might then be asked to explain how a breakdown in the circulatory system might affect the nervous system, the reproductive system, the skeletal system, and so on. This process would be structured for students to make sure that they meaningfully use their knowledge of the systems of the human body.

When students have become adept at using the process of systems analysis, have them structure their own tasks. You might ask them to identify the component parts of the circulatory system. Students should then work independently or in groups to identify how the parts affect one another and what might happen if one part, for example the heart, stopped functioning or started working differently. Even though students are working more independently, you might still need to monitor their work to make sure they are rigorously engaged in analysis tasks that will enhance their learning of important content knowledge.

Classroom Examples

The following classroom examples are offered to stimulate reflection on how to apply the ideas covered in this section of Dimension 4 in your classroom.

Students in Mr. Hash's second-grade language arts class were working on general skills and strategies for reading literature. Specifically, students were studying the interactions among setting, plot, and character in texts. In addition, Mr. Hash had also been helping students understand systems and how parts of a systems influence each other. It occurred to him that elements of literature are also a system. He designed the following task to emphasize the systemic nature of the elements.

Plot, setting, and characters form a system:

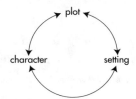

Also, each element is a system. Let's see how the characters in a story, together, are a system. The characters in Cinderella, for example, have feelings about each other, which might be represented as shown below:

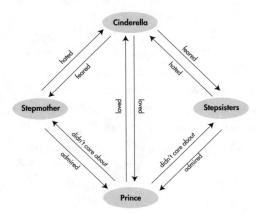

What might happen if you change these feelings? Try it. Change one or two of the feelings (e.g., the stepsisters love Cinderella, or Cinderella doesn't like the Prince). What other relationships would be changed? Now, look back at the system of plot, setting, and characters. If the characters' feelings for each other changed, how would the plot and setting be influenced? Now, get a partner and choose a different story. Change something in the system of relationships among the characters, and explain how the plot and the setting might be affected.

• • •

Mrs. Anzaldúa created a science task for her fifth-grade students to help them meaningfully use their knowledge of ecosystems. Students had been learning how species depend on one another and on the environment for survival and how variations in resources, climate, and organisms affect an entire ecosystem. The task, which served as the culmination of her unit on ecosystems, focused on analyzing the parts of a specific ecosystem and the ways in which these parts interact. The task had two parts. The first section was done by students individually.

> *The most obvious parts of an ecosystem are an oak tree, a squirrel, a brown bear and her cub, a family of field mice, a barn owl, a coyote, a black snake, a grove of rhododendron, and a large patch of wild raspberries. Identify other features that may be a part of this ecosystem. Explain how these features are interrelated with the obvious parts.*

Mrs. Anzaldúa then split the class into groups to work cooperatively on the remainder of the task:

> *What will happen within your ecosystem if various parts change their behavior (e.g., what if the brown bear becomes a vegetarian, if rain does not fall for a month, or if, instead of eating mice, the snake eats only raspberries)?*

• • •

Ms. Switzer's tenth-grade civics students were studying the protection of individual rights within the American judicial system. To provide an opportunity for students to apply their knowledge of the jury system, she constructed a task in which students analyzed the system of a trial.

As students began the process of systems analysis, they found that identifying the parts of the system of "a trial" was difficult because of the many different elements involved. They decided to limit their analysis to the interactions among the human parts of the system (e.g., the judge, the jury, the defense team, and the prosecutor). Determining which parts affect each other and the ways in which they affect each other enhanced their understanding of the relationships. For example, as they identified the functional relationship between a defense lawyer and the defendant, they discovered that a greater flow of information from the client to the lawyer is not always productive. In addition, students examined how changes in the functions or roles of various people might affect the system (e.g., if only 9 out of 12 jurors were required to find a defendant guilty in a criminal trial, or if a defendant is presumed guilty rather than innocent).

Unit Planning: Dimension 4

Planning for Dimension 4 requires asking and answering the following overarching question:

What will be done to help students use knowledge meaningfully?

What follows is a step-by-step process that will guide you in answering this question. Each step asks you to answer a key question or provide specific information. There is a place on the planning guide (see page 259) in which to record the responses to the planning questions and a description of the task that is constructed for the unit. A sample planning guide has been filled out for a hypothetical social studies unit about Colorado. (This unit topic was chosen because, with some changes, it could be used for a unit about any state or region and at many developmental levels. You will find the entire unit in Chapter 6, "Putting It All Together.")

Although this process is presented in a step-by-step sequence, the reality is that the person planning a task for Dimension 4 may not begin with Step 1 (see below), but instead begin with an idea for the context or purpose of the task or with the goal of using a particular reasoning process. The sequence of steps presented here, however, works for many situations. The first two steps emphasize the importance of focusing the task on the knowledge that is being used and on the reasoning process that is being applied in the task.

Step 1

> What **knowledge** will students be **using meaningfully**?
>
> Specifically, students will be demonstrating their understanding of or ability to. . . .

The knowledge that students will be using might be declarative or procedural. If students are to demonstrate their understanding of declarative knowledge, identify the important generalizations, principles, or concepts they will use in the task, and, when appropriate, describe the types of specific information they might need. If students are to demonstrate their ability to use procedural knowledge, clearly identify the skill or process that they will be using in the task. Because tasks that are designed to encourage the meaningful use of knowledge are often the focus of the unit and because completing the task often takes a relatively large amount of time, careful consideration should be given to ensure that the knowledge students are asked to use is knowledge that is worth the time and attention.

Step 2

> What reasoning process will students be using?
>
> ❏ **Decision Making**
> (selecting from seemingly equal alternatives or examining the decisions of others)
>
> ❏ **Problem Solving**
> (seeking to achieve a goal by overcoming constraints or limiting conditions
>
> ❏ **Invention**
> (creating something to meet a need or improve on a situation)
>
> ❏ **Experimental Inquiry**
> (generating an explanation for a phenomenon and testing the explanation)
>
> ❏ **Investigation**
> (resolving confusions or contradictions related to the defining characteristics of something, a historical event, or a hypothetical past or future event)
>
> ❏ **Systems Analysis**
> (analyzing the parts of a system and how they interact)
>
> ❏ **Other** _____

If students are using declarative content knowledge, identify a reasoning process to provide the context and purpose for the task and to ensure that students will be using the knowledge thoughtfully. Notice that this is the second step of constructing the task; this emphasizes the importance of planning how students will be thinking during the task before planning what product they will be handing in.

If students are using procedural knowledge, the reasoning process they are using may be embedded in the skill or process itself, for example, representing data with a mathematical equation. When constructing tasks that use only procedural content knowledge, it might not be necessary to identify any other type of reasoning; students are already applying the knowledge thoughtfully. However, it is worth considering the reasoning processes included within Dimension 4 as a way of enriching the task or providing a meaningful context or purpose for using the skill or process.

As you decide which reasoning process will focus the task, the following questions might help you to consider each process identified here:

Decision Making

- Is there an unresolved decision important to the unit?
- Is there an unresolved issue about who or what is the best or worst?
- Is there an unresolved issue about who or what has the most or least?

Problem Solving

- Is there a situation or process that has some major constraint or limiting condition?
- Is there a situation or process that could be better understood if constraints or limiting conditions were placed on it?

Invention

- Is there a situation that can and should be improved on?
- Is there something new that should be created?

Experimental Inquiry

- Is there an unexplained phenomenon (physical or psychological) for which students could generate explanations that can be tested?

Investigation

- Is there an unresolved issue about the defining characteristics or defining features of something? (Definitional)
- Is there an unresolved issue about how something occurred? (Historical)
- Is there an unresolved issue about why something happened? (Historical)
- Is there an unresolved issue about what would happen if . . . or what would have happened if . . . (Projective)?

Systems Analysis

- Are there parts of a system or the interactions of the parts of a system that could be analyzed?
- Is there something that could be examined in terms of how it behaves or works within a system?

Step 3

Describe what will be done.

As you construct the task, you need to consider the following questions:

- What specifically does the task require students to do? Make sure that the task requires students to use the identified knowledge in order to complete the task.

- What makes the task meaningful to the student?

  - Does it have an authentic context or purpose?

  - Is it intellectually stimulating and interesting?

  - Does it allow for artistic expression?

  - Does it allow for student choice?

- To what extent will students be working alone or in groups?

- What product will students turn in?

- How will the criteria for evaluation be communicated to the students?

Dimension 4 Planning Guide

Unit: _Colorado_

Step 1	Step 2	Step 3
What **knowledge** will students be **using meaningfully?** Specifically, they will be demonstrating their understanding of and ability to. . .	What reasoning process will they be using?	Describe what will be done.

Step 1

The concepts of topography, natural resources, climate, and culture

Topography, natural resources, and climate influence settlement patterns.

Step 2

☐ **Decision Making**
(selecting from seemingly equal alternatives or examining the decisions of others)

☐ **Problem Solving**
(seeking to achieve a goal by overcoming constraints or limiting conditions)

☐ **Invention**
(creating something to meet a need or improve on a situation)

☑ **Experimental Inquiry**
(generating an explanation for a phenomenon and testing the explanation)

☐ **Investigation**
(resolving confusions or contradictions related to a historical event, a hypothetical past or future event, or to the defining characteristics of something)

☐ **Systems Analysis**
(analyzing the parts of a system and how they interact)

☐ **Other** _____

Step 3

We have discussed in class that Colorado's population is growing very rapidly. In fact, compared to many other states, a relatively large number of people who live in Colorado moved from somewhere else. There are actually not that many "Colorado natives." Why have so many people moved to Colorado, and why is the population still growing so rapidly?

One explanation is that aspects of the topography, natural resources, climate, and culture attract people to Colorado. Let's find out if that helps explain it. If it is true, we should be able to trace people's reasons for moving to Colorado to these characteristics of the state.

Set up an activity—for example, surveys or interviews—that would help to determine to what extent people have moved to Colorado because of factors related to topography, natural resources, climate, and culture. You will need to set up the activity, plan for analyzing your results, and be ready to report your findings to the class. Any member of your group may be asked to explain what you found out about the influence of each concept you are considering: topography, natural resources, climate, and culture.

259

Dimension 5

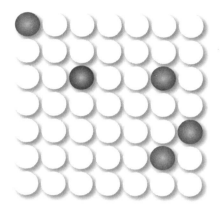

Dimension 5
Habits of Mind

Introduction

Dimension 5, Habits of Mind, identifies productive mental habits that, along with attitudes and perceptions, form the backdrop of the learning process. Students benefit in two principal ways when they develop productive mental habits. First, developing such habits of mind can enhance students' learning of academic content knowledge. When students consistently demonstrate productive mental habits as they approach academic assignments—when, for example, they consistently seek clarity and accuracy—they learn more from those assignments. Second, productive mental habits will serve students well in the future because these habits should increase their abilities to learn in any situation. Although we cannot predict exactly what knowledge students will need, we can predict with a great deal of confidence that in almost every phase of their lives they will need to continue learning. Productive mental habits help students to be successful learners in whatever circumstances they encounter.

The dispositions identified in Dimension 5 are called *habits* because it is important to increase the frequency with which students display them, just as it is important to instill in students good study habits or listening habits. However, the term *habit* can suggest exhibiting behavior so automatically that it is almost unconscious. It is important to emphasize with students that we want them to demonstrate their ability to use productive mental habits *consciously*; more specifically, we want them to demonstrate that they understand when and why the specific habits are needed.

> "Mark Twain once said, 'Nothing so needs reforming as other people's habits.' I remembered that quote after I became so excited about introducing the habits of mind to my students. I decided to slow down and take the time to determine whether I use the habits myself before I tried to teach them to my students."
>
> — A middle school teacher in Texas

The habits of mind identified in the Dimensions of Learning model fall into three general categories: critical thinking, creative thinking, and self-regulated thinking.

Ennis (1985, 1987, 1989) and Paul et al. (1986, 1989) suggest that other mental habits make our learning more critical in nature.

If you have mental habits that exemplify *critical thinking*, you tend to

- Be accurate and seek accuracy

- Be clear and seek clarity

- Maintain an open mind

- Restrain impulsivity

- Take a position when the situation warrants it

- Respond appropriately to others' feelings and level of knowledge

A different set of mental habits characterizes creativity (Amabile, 1983; Perkins, 1984, 1985).

If you have mental habits that exemplify *creative thinking*, you tend to

- Persevere

- Push the limits of your knowledge and abilities

- Generate, trust, and maintain your own standards of evaluation

- Generate new ways of viewing a situation that are outside the boundaries of standard conventions

Certain mental habits render our thinking and actions more self-regulated according to Flavell (1976a, 1976b, 1977) and Brown (1978, 1980).

If you have mental habits that exemplify *self-regulated thinking*, you tend to

- Monitor your own thinking

- Plan appropriately

- Identify and use necessary resources

- Respond appropriately to feedback

Costa (1991a, 1991b) *Developing Minds*

- Evaluate the effectiveness of your actions

This list of mental habits reflects the work of a number of educators. However, it is not meant to be an exhaustive list or a list that is appropriate for everyone. Users of the Dimensions of Learning model are encouraged to change this list, if necessary, to make it most useful to them. Some districts, schools, and classrooms have made additions, deletions, and modifications; others have replaced the list entirely with their own list of habits of mind. You may also want to encourage individual students to build their own personal list of mental habits that they believe enhance their learning.

It is important to understand that the mental habits identified in Dimension 5 are part of the backdrop of the Dimensions of Learning model because they influence the thinking processes identified in the other dimensions. For example, as students try to establish positive attitudes and perceptions for learning (Dimension 1), they may consider the resources available to make the classroom a safe and orderly place. While acquiring and integrating knowledge (Dimension 2), students should seek accuracy. While extending and refining knowledge through induction (Dimension 3), students may need to work on resisting impulsivity. Finally, a key to helping students engage in tasks that require them to use knowledge meaningfully (Dimension 4) is to reinforce appropriate habits of mind at the same time; for example, you can help students to push the limits of their knowledge and ability during problem solving. The habits of mind in Dimension 5, then, provide a foundation that should increase students' success while they are using the processes identified in any of the dimensions.

We perhaps should explain how our treatment of critical and creative thinking may differ from others'. Those familiar with the research and theory on critical thinking are aware that skills and processes such as error analysis and decision making are commonly considered to be aspects of critical thinking. Similarly, creative thinking is commonly understood to include skills and processes such as abstracting and invention. Why, then, are they not included in Dimension 5? We recognize that what we call habits of mind requires the use of various skills and mental processes, but we have chosen to classify skills and processes in other parts of the model. We consider analyzing errors and abstracting as ways to extend and refine knowledge (Dimension 3). Decision making and invention are included in Dimension 4. Although one cannot be a good critical thinker or creative person without being able to do these things, knowing how is not enough. Dimension 5 is concerned with one's determination to be a critical thinker, a creative thinker, and a self-regulated thinker. The commitment to live up to high standards—to be concerned with the quality of one's thinking—is what finally distinguishes Dimension 5 from the other aspects of thinking.

There are many approaches that can help students develop and use productive habits of mind in the classroom. These approaches include direct teaching of the habits, modeling and expecting them in the classroom, and reinforcing students who are exhibiting them. However, to assure the success of any of these approaches, teachers and students need to understand the specific mental habits they are trying to develop. This chapter, therefore, includes classroom strategies and practices that teachers can use to help students develop productive habits of mind, whether the habits are those identified in the Dimensions of Learning model or habits identified by students. In addition, you will find definitions, explanations, and examples of each habit of mind to help you plan activities to address the habits of mind identified in the Dimensions of Learning model.

Helping Students Develop Productive Habits of Mind

Many students will be positively influenced to develop productive habits of mind when classroom teachers and parents model and reinforce good mental habits. However, students may need more than modeling and reinforcement; they may need the habits of mind to be defined, explained, discussed, and rewarded. The following subsections include strategies and activities that can be used by classroom teachers who are interested in overtly and intentionally helping students develop productive habits of mind.

1. Help students understand habits of mind.

The goal of the following suggested activities is to help students gain an understanding of the habits of mind and how they affect learning.

Facilitate classroom discussion of each habit. Whether you are using the list of habits identified in this model or a customized list, provide students with the time to label, define, and talk about each habit so that they can associate the habits with specific behavior. You might then ask students to discuss the possible benefits of having a particular habit and the possible consequences of lacking such a habit. For example, you might have students brainstorm what they think it means to "generate, trust, and maintain your own standards of evaluation." As students begin to develop their understanding of each habit, they should identify the specific behavior of people who exemplify this habit. You might give them examples; for instance, you might say that students who generate their own standards do not constantly ask the teacher, "Is this OK? Is this done?"

Use examples from literature and current events of people who are using the habits in different situations. Whenever you come across a character in literature or a person in the news who exemplifies using a powerful mental habit or who lacks an important habit, bring it to the students' attention. For example, you might use Romeo and Juliet or Peter Rabbit as examples of those who lacked the ability to restrain impulsivity and, therefore, suffered significant consequences. In addition to pointing out examples for students, establish a culture that encourages them to recognize and share examples that they encounter in television programs, movies, books, or personal experiences.

"My mother said to me, 'If you become a soldier, you'll be a general; if you become a monk, you'll end up as Pope.' Instead, I became a painter and wound up as Picasso."

—Pablo Picasso

Share personal anecdotes that relate to a habit. When the situation warrants it, share personal examples of when and why a particular habit was beneficial or when and why the lack of one was problematic. For example, "By planning my time, I saved time and money because I completed my advanced degree in two years." Conversely, "It cost me twice as much time and money to complete my degree because I was unable to plan my time effectively."

Notice and label student behavior that demonstrates a particular habit. When you notice students displaying a particular habit, use it as an opportunity to introduce the habit and acknowledge the behavior. Make sure that students understand exactly what they did and why their behavior exemplifies the habit of mind. For example, when a student engages intensely in a task, acknowledge what she has done and ask her if she can explain how she disciplined herself to work so hard.

Ask students to identify personal heroes or mentors and describe the extent to which they exemplify specific habits of mind. Periodically provide a time for students to identify a fictional or real-life hero or mentor or someone else whom they admire and respect. Ask them to describe the mental habits that these people exemplify. Emphasize that this person might be famous or glamorous but might also be the neighbor upstairs or a mom or dad.

Have students create posters that illustrate their understanding of the habits. As students become familiar with each habit of mind, have them depict it in a poster or drawing that shows someone using the habit in a specific situation.

2. Help students identify and develop strategies related to the habits of mind.

After students understand and appreciate productive habits of mind, they will discover that they must develop strategies for learning, maintaining, and successfully using the habit. People who tend to be clear and seek clarity, for example, may have a process of rigorously editing all written communications to ensure that their messages are clear; they may use paraphrasing or questioning techniques during oral communications to make sure that they understand others correctly. There are a number of ways to help students identify and begin to develop personal strategies.

Use think-aloud to demonstrate specific strategies. Demonstrate a strategy while students listen to you talk through the mental steps. For example, reinforce the habit of planning by reviewing aloud the steps you might

Pushing the Limits ...

follow while planning a research paper. You may say things like, "Let's see. Before I jump into this, I need to state my goal clearly. I should identify types of work that need to be done and then set deadlines. I'll use a calendar to record my plan and keep it in the front of my notebook."

Ask students to share their own strategies. When you notice that students are using or have used a habit, ask them to explain the strategy they used. For example, if a student's project reflects the effective use of available resources, ask the student to tell you or the class what strategies helped him to identify and seek out those resources.

Encourage students to find examples of strategies mentioned in literature and current events. Ask students to look for examples of strategies that relate to the habits of mind as they read literature, newspapers, or magazine articles and as they view or use other media and technologies. Ask them to record these examples in their learning logs and, when appropriate, to share these examples with the class. For example, students might read about the Wright Brothers and conclude that these inventors were exhibiting creative thinking as they engaged intensely even when their airplanes failed to fly.

Ask students to interview others (e.g., parents, friends, or neighbors) to identify strategies. As you help students to develop a specific habit, ask them to identify people who they believe exemplify the habit and then interview them to learn what strategies these people use. For example, while studying the habit of "taking a position when the situation warrants it," students could interview people whom they respect for standing up for their beliefs. They should write down questions they might ask, such as, "How do you decide when it is time to take a position? If you ever find yourself backing off a position too soon, how do you deal with that?"

Each quarter or semester, ask students to identify and focus on a habit of mind they would like to develop. Successfully developing productive habits of mind takes time. By asking students to focus on developing one habit of mind at a time, you can help them to make the most efficient use of their time. You might suggest some strategies for them to use or allow them to identify and develop their own. As you monitor their progress, you may find that you need to make some suggestions. If, for example, a student wants to be more open-minded because his friends have accused him of not listening to others' opinions, you might share Edward DeBono's Plus-Minus-Interesting (PMI) strategy with him and then periodically check to see if it is working. The PMI strategy is designed to help students suspend judgment about an idea until they have listed the pluses (P), minuses (M), and interesting (I) points or possible outcomes of the idea.

de Bono (1983) "The Cognitive Research Trust (CoRT) Thinking Program"

3. Create a culture in the classroom and the school that encourages the development and use of the habits of mind.

Culture is expressed in the language, behavior, and customs that reflect what people believe to be important or valuable. There are many ways to assure that the culture of the classroom and the school communicates to students, in what they see, hear, and experience, that developing productive habits of mind is expected and valued by all members of the school community.

Model the habits. Students know what teachers value by observation. If we want students to develop productive habits of mind, we must consciously and overtly use them ourselves as we go about our tasks and interact with students. For example, if we want students to be responsive to the feedback they receive, then we must deliberately model being responsive to the feedback we receive from them.

Integrate the habits into the daily routines and activities of the classroom. Helping students develop productive habits of mind should not require major changes in the classroom. You can probably use previously planned routines and activities to help students focus on particular habits. Below are suggestions for reinforcing each cluster of the habits of mind (critical, creative, and self-regulated thinking) as students are engaged in typical classroom activities.

Critical Thinking

Debate is a fairly common activity in classrooms and is one of the best arenas in which to reinforce the habits of critical thinking. During a debate, information is presented, defended, attacked, and so on, setting up the need to be clear and seek clarity or to respond appropriately to others' feelings and levels of knowledge. Periodically have groups of three or four students prepare to debate an issue related to the content you are teaching. Then set them up to debate in a "fish bowl" format: Have two groups debate in the middle of the room while the other students in the class observe and pay particular attention to whether the debaters are displaying the habits of critical thinking. At the end of the debate, ask the observers to give feedback to the debate teams. In particular, have them point out specific instances in which team members used one or more of the habits of critical thinking.

Creative Thinking

Solving structured problems is an excellent way to reinforce the habits of creative thinking because almost all types of structured problems require their use to some extent. Structured problems are those that have relatively clear goals; they are found in textbooks, games magazines, and

An elementary teacher asked students to debate the issue of banning fur sales. He taped the debate and then played back the tape, asking students to comment on the use of the habits of critical thinking.

One elementary principal lines the hallways of her school with "interactive bulletin boards" that contain structured problems. As students solve the problems, the principal reinforces specific habits of mind.

A high school principal met with individual students throughout the year to lend his support in setting and meeting goals. "As long as it is legal and moral," he told each student, "I will help you achieve any goal you set."

puzzle books. (See Chapter 4 for further discussion of structured problems.) You might give students structured problems at the beginning or end of class periods or during slow times. While students are working on these problems, ask them to concentrate on one or more specific habits of creative thinking. For example, while they are working on problems that require them to invent something, you might have them focus on the habit of generating new ways of viewing situations outside the boundaries of standard convention.

Self-Regulated Thinking
Having students identify and pursue long-term goals is an excellent way to reinforce the mental habits of self-regulated thinking and to explain that they can be used as tools for accomplishing goals. For example, a student might identify the goal of joining a particular athletic team. You might encourage her to use the habit of planning (by setting up a practice schedule for herself) or of being responsive to feedback (by identifying a way to measure her progress in the skills necessary to earn a position on the team).

To initiate the goal-setting process, you might first have students identify goals that excite them and that they can accomplish within the year, semester, or quarter. Have students write down their goals and identify objectives or milestones. At least once every two weeks, students should meet with a teacher, counselor, or their peers to report on their progress. At the end of the agreed-upon period (e.g., at the end of the semester), ask students to report on their goals, their progress, and what they learned about the mental habits of self-regulated thinking.

Develop and display posters, icons, and other visual representations to express the importance of productive habits of mind. Besides serving as reminders to students, displaying posters of the habits of mind can become easy references to help students identify the mental habits they need for various learning situations. Below is the graphic from the poster that was developed for the Dimensions of Learning habit of mind *Restrain Impulsivity*. We have reproduced the posters for the other habits of mind in the margins throughout this section.

When appropriate, cue students to focus on specific mental habits or ask them to identify habits that would help them while working on difficult tasks. Sometimes students simply need a reminder to use the mental habits while they are working. Before a test you might encourage students to be aware of their thinking and suggest that they replace any negative self-talk with positive self-talk. When assigning a long-term project, you might ask students to select a habit from self-regulated thinking that could help them be successful.

4. Provide positive reinforcement to students who exhibit the habits of mind.

Besides labeling and acknowledging students' use of the habits, offer praise, specific feedback, and rewards, as appropriate. You might offer reinforcement through verbal praise, specific comments or ratings on progress reports and grade cards, or positive notes and telephone calls to parents. The ultimate goal, of course, is for students to begin to experience the intrinsic rewards of increased success and achievement that result from having good mental habits. However, until they have experienced these benefits, immediate and positive reinforcement from teachers and peers may help to motivate and focus them as they work on developing productive habits of mind. Such reinforcement also communicates to students that habits of mind are important. The following are suggestions for specific ways to provide positive reinforcement.

Appoint "process observers," students who watch for positive examples of other students who are demonstrating the habits. Assigning this role benefits the observer and the student who is exhibiting the habit. You can use the process observer role in a variety of ways. For example, you might assign the role regularly during small-group or cooperative learning activities or rotate the role for general classroom activities, with a different student assuming responsibility each week or month.

Ask students to self-assess their use of specific habits. Students will benefit most in the long run if they learn to independently use productive habits of mind. To encourage this independence, periodically ask students to self-assess. Ask students to reflect on their use of the habits in a journal or learning log. Probes for this reflection might be highly structured (e.g., "How often do you evaluate the effectiveness of your own actions?" "How do you act on your evaluation?") or unstructured (e.g., "Evaluate your effectiveness in using any of the habits of mind during the past week.").

Give students feedback on a report card or progress report. Some schools give formal feedback to students and parents on students' development and use of the habits of mind. Figure 5.1 shows a portion of a sample progress report.

FIGURE 5.1

PORTION OF SAMPLE PROGRESS REPORT: HABITS OF MIND

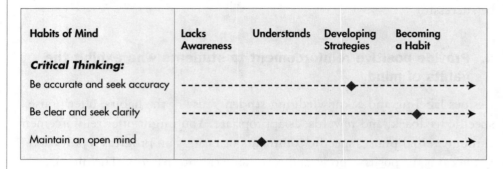

Habits of Mind	Lacks Awareness	Understands	Developing Strategies	Becoming a Habit
Critical Thinking:				
Be accurate and seek accuracy			◆	
Be clear and seek clarity				◆
Maintain an open mind		◆		

Classroom Examples

The following classroom examples for critical, creative, and self-regulated thinking are offered to stimulate reflection on how to apply the ideas covered in Dimension 5 in your classroom.

Critical Thinking

At their monthly meeting, a team of K-5 teachers discussed how beneficial it would be if students began to exhibit the habit of restraining impulsivity. At first the primary teachers thought it might be difficult to introduce this habit in the early grades. However, they realized that many of the stories they read with students were perfect opportunities for increasing students' understanding of this habit. They used stories such as <u>Peter Rabbit</u> and <u>Goldilocks and the Three Bears</u> as examples of the consequences of not restraining impulsive behavior.

● ● ●

When Mr. Foseid, a Spanish teacher, first learned about the habits of mind, he thought they were important but decided that he did not have much time to teach them in his class. Later, as he was preparing lessons for helping students understand other cultures, he realized how important the critical thinking habits are when people from different cultures interact. He then crafted an assignment in which he asked each student to select a specific habit of critical thinking, explain why it would be important when people from different cultures interact, and develop a strategy for its use. After students completed the task, he asked them to present their explanations and strategies in Spanish to the class.

● ● ●

Mr. Johnson decided to design a unit in which students would debate issues related to the presidential election. In addition to teaching them about the elections, he had another goal in mind. He had observed that the students in this particular class were quite opinionated and closed-minded when they discussed the elections. Further, when expressing their opinions they showed little regard for accuracy and clarity. He decided that it was time to introduce and emphasize the critical thinking habits of mind.

Although he was excited about the unit, as Mr. Johnson sat down to plan the lessons he realized that teaching the critical thinking habits of mind would take time. He began to reconsider the goal of teaching the habits of mind. However, as he continued to plan, he reflected on how many units throughout the year would be better if students had an increased understanding of these mental habits. He renewed his commitment to plan lessons focused on students' learning about the critical thinking habits of mind.

The culminating project of the unit was a mock presidential debate in which each student was responsible for clearly and accurately representing a candidate's views and ideas. After each debate, Mr. Johnson and the other classmates gave feedback to the debaters on the accuracy and clarity of their arguments and on the extent to which they demonstrated the ability to strike a balance between taking and defending a position yet maintaining an open mind. Throughout the unit, students recorded in their learning logs any insights they gained about critical thinking and any confusions or questions that they still had about these habits of mind.

Creative Thinking

A team of primary teachers realized that many of their students' favorite stories were wonderful examples of the habits of mind. For example, <u>The Little Engine That Could</u> offered a perfect opportunity to discuss perseverance. Using the language of the habits of mind when reading stories was a great way to help students more fully understand the habits.

• • •

Mrs. Henderson noticed that although her third-graders were intelligent, quick thinking, and often clever, they put forth only a minimum amount of effort in much of their school work, gave up quickly if an answer or solution was not obvious, and constantly asked if their work was what the teacher wanted rather than holding themselves to their own high standards. Mrs. Henderson decided that she might be able to contribute something important to these learners by teaching them about the habits involved in creative thinking. Before introducing the habits, she gave students word puzzles and other entertaining, but increasingly difficult, problems. She noticed that with these activities, almost all of her students seemed to want to do well and were eager for each day's puzzle. After several weeks, Mrs. Henderson introduced the creative thinking habits by putting up a poster that illustrated the habits with a cartoon-like character. She asked the students to explain what they thought each of the habits meant and what it might look like if someone was using or not using the habit. She then asked students to think about the puzzles they had been solving and how these habits related to what they were doing. She asked them to think about and discuss in small groups how they used, or did not use, these habits and how being aware of them now might influence their behavior in the future. As a result of the discussion, the class decided to make a commitment to increasing their understanding and use of the creative thinking habits of mind.

• • •

Mathematics students in a secondary school published a weekly newsletter that contained perplexing problems that they had designed themselves. The newsletter was distributed to every teacher and student in the school. Weekly and monthly competitions were held to solve the problems. After learning about the creative thinking habits of mind, the students decided to modify their awards. They designed a certificate that highlighted the habits of mind that were needed to solve the problems; for example, some problems required generating new ways of viewing situations, whereas others were more divergent and required generating one's own standards of evaluation.

Self-Regulated Thinking

At the beginning of each year, Mrs. Brooks has her elementary students identify academic, social, and physical goals for themselves. She helps each student record and develop a plan for each goal. Once a week, Mrs. Brooks asks students to meet in support groups to discuss their progress and help one another solve difficult problems or roadblocks they are encountering as they work to achieve their goals.

• • •

For three full class periods, Ms. Green had her elementary students work on identifying strategies and techniques that can be used with each of the mental habits of self-regulated thinking. She set up five small groups that students would work in cooperatively. During the first two periods, each of the groups worked on one of the habits of mind. During the third period, each group made a class presentation on the strategies and techniques its members had developed.

• • •

After discussing the mental habits of self-regulated thinking with his social studies students, Mr. Eckhardt, a middle school teacher, decided it was time to give students feedback on their ability to exhibit these habits. He created a decision-making task for students in which he asked them to generate and apply criteria to determine which of the first ten amendments to the U.S. Constitution seems most important in today's society. He also asked students to use the strategies they had talked about in class to develop a plan for completing the task and to submit with it a list of resources they would need. As students worked on the task, Mr. Eckhardt gave them feedback on their use of content knowledge and on whether they were demonstrating self-regulated thinking. When students turned in their final decision-making matrix, Mr. Eckhardt asked them to write a summary of what they noticed about the habits of self-regulated thinking and to self-assess the degree to which they exhibited the habits.

• • •

As a high-school counselor, Mr. Jordan helps students set personal goals. He emphasizes to students that their goals should "make life exciting." To stimulate their thinking, he makes it a practice to ask students, "What would you try to accomplish this year if you knew you would not fail?"

• • •

Ms. Barton, a high school English teacher, decided that it would be beneficial to explicitly and intentionally address self-regulated thinking with students in her AP English class. She believed that these habits were important to her largely college-bound class. She introduced the habits by briefly explaining each and asking her students to discuss them in small groups. She encouraged students to share personal examples of their use of the habits of mind. She then explained that throughout the semester she would ask them to identify characters in literature who use one or more of the habits and to note a positive benefit for having done so.

The Dimensions of Learning Habits of Mind: A Resource for Teachers

The following sections are offered as a resource for teachers who are preparing to provide students with explanations and examples of the specific habits of mind identified in the Dimensions of Learning model. Over time, you will undoubtedly generate your own examples to use with students; however, the following suggestions can help you get started. Each habit of mind is followed by

1. a brief explanation of the habit,

2. examples of situations in which it might be beneficial to have the habit of mind, and

3. examples of strategies recommended by people who exhibit the habit.

Critical Thinking

Be Accurate and Seek Accuracy

Ennis (1985) "Goals for a Critical Thinking Curriculum"

Ennis (1989) "Critical Thinking and Subject Specificity: Clarification and Needed Research"

When you check to make sure that your work is correct or precise and when you expect precision from others' work, you are exhibiting the habit of being accurate and seeking accuracy. *Being accurate* means making accuracy a goal and then using a variety of techniques for checking accuracy as you work. *Seeking accuracy* from information you are receiving acknowledges that it is the responsibility of the receiver of information—as well as the sender—to set and expect high standards of accuracy.

Examples of situations in which it might be beneficial to be accurate and seek accuracy

- When reviewing or preparing documents related to money (e.g., credit card bills, bank statements, tax returns, or loan applications), checking the calculations can help you save money or avoid serious monetary consequences. Mistakes occur even when companies use computerized services.

- Budgeting for a major expense (e.g., buying a house or taking a vacation) is something virtually everyone needs to do at some point. Although estimating can be helpful, it is more likely that you will have sufficient funds if, instead of working from a rough estimate, you create a specific budget to help you reach your goal.

- When someone gives or asks for directions, being accurate and seeking accuracy increases the chance that the traveler will reach the desired destination.

- Any time you receive information that appears suspicious or inaccurate, you should take the time to check for accuracy or ask for additional information. However, circumstances often arise when you are reluctant to check for accuracy because the information is complex or even intimidating (for example, when a report includes complicated statistics). You might be particularly reluctant to check for accuracy if the information is presented in a way that makes it look accurate. If information seems contrary to experience or hard to believe, you should find ways to check it for accuracy, even if it is difficult to do so.

- There are many situations involving your health and well-being that could be affected by your ability to be accurate and seek accuracy. The consequences of being inaccurate can be significant in situations like measuring dosages of medicine or following a specific, prescribed course of physical therapy.

- Advertisers often use media to present information in a way that is engaging, humorous, or provocative. Whether you are listening to the radio, watching television, or reading a newspaper, it is easy to be absorbed in the presentation and forget to consider the accuracy of the information presented. Developing the habit of seeking accuracy can help you become a more informed consumer, one who is more likely to make sound choices.

Examples of strategies recommended by people who exhibit the habit of being accurate and seeking accuracy

- When preparing detailed documents, read them at least once with the clear, single-focused goal of checking for accuracy. If you read for meaning, clarity, and accuracy simultaneously, you might miss errors.

- Use available reference materials, both in print and technology formats (e.g., a dictionary, the spell-check function, a thesaurus, and an encyclopedia) to achieve accuracy in your communications.

- When proofreading documents, try reading each sentence starting from the end of the document to catch typographical errors that you might miss when you read the document for meaning.

Costa (1984) "Mediating the Metacognitive"

Presseisen (1987) *Thinking Skills Throughout the Curriculum*

Paul (1990) *Critical Thinking*

Why? What?
When? Where?

- Ask one or more people to check your work for accuracy. Someone who is unfamiliar with and less invested in the product is more objective and, thus, more likely to find mistakes.

Be Clear and Seek Clarity

Clear communication is a fundamental component of success in nearly every area of life. Yet there are many roadblocks to clear communication: Language is full of ambiguity and connotation; body language is difficult to interpret; intonation can change understanding.

All communication is influenced by the extent to which the parties involved, whether senders or receivers, try to overcome these roadblocks. Confusion and misinterpretation can lead to significant negative consequences; thus, there must be a shared responsibility between sender and receiver to ensure that there is clear communication.

It is particularly important for students to learn to be clear and seek clarity in the classroom. Sometimes when students are working on an assignment, they are more focused on simply "getting it done" than on monitoring themselves to make sure they understand the information presented. The earlier in their learning that students develop this habit, the more likely it is that they will succeed in school.

Examples of situations in which it might be beneficial to be clear and seek clarity

- Throughout their school years, students frequently confront subjects or issues that, at first, appear unclear. Learning is enhanced when students consistently monitor the extent to which they understand information they are receiving and then try to clarify anything that is confusing.

- People often find themselves in situations in which someone is trying to persuade them to do or buy something. At such times, it is important to ask for clarification about claims that sound too good to be true, anything that is confusing, or information that might be incomplete. The ability to seek clarity can help you make informed decisions and commitments.

- Being clear when giving a presentation, especially one that contains complex or detailed information, is challenging because there are often limited opportunities to receive immediate feedback. When people are confused early in a presentation, they may tune out; the opportunity to inform or persuade may be lost.

- Employers appreciate those who seek clarity before jumping into an assignment, particularly one that is complex. Although some people may be reluctant to admit that they do not understand an assignment or a communication, experience shows that seeking clarity can lead to the more efficient use of time and money.

Examples of strategies recommended by people who exhibit the habit of being clear and seeking clarity

- When you are unsure about what you want to express or are afraid that others might misunderstand you, write down exactly what you want to say. Then read it or practice saying it until you can express yourself clearly.

- When presenting important information, occasionally stop and check for understanding by asking the receiver to relate what he understands so far.

- When listening to information that does not make sense, take notes and then, when appropriate, use the notes to ask questions.

- Before giving a written communication to an audience, ask several people to read it, explain what they understand it to say, and point out any parts that are confusing.

- Make it a practice in emotionally charged situations to ask another person who is not emotionally involved to be an active listener. A good listener can often clarify issues just by repeating what was said or by asking good questions.

- When engaged in important conversations, use phrases like, "Did I hear you say that. . . ?" or "I think I understood you to say that. . . ." Using phrases such as these communicates a concern for clarity and helps to immediately identify and clarify any potential misconceptions.

Maintain an Open Mind

Developing the ability to maintain an open mind can enhance learning and increase the likelihood of success in a diverse society. Open-mindedness enhances learning because it requires listening to different perspectives and ideas with the goal of understanding them. Even if we ultimately reject other views, just hearing them gives us additional information that might increase our knowledge about a subject or issue. Open-mindedness helps us live in a diverse society because it enhances communication among people who live and work with others who have different backgrounds, opinions, philosophies, and interests. Being open-minded enough to understand

Paul (1990) *Critical Thinking*

Ennis (1985) "Goals for a Critical Thinking Curriculum"

Ennis (1989) "Critical Thinking and Subject Specificity: Clarification and Needed Research"

Presseisen (1987) *Thinking Skills Throughout the Curriculum*

Hmmm ...
I never thought
about it that way.

diverse views and approaches to life does not necessarily lead to changing our beliefs or perspectives or even to accepting the reasons for others' perspectives. It does, however, mean respecting others' views enough to listen to them. Open-mindedness helps create a society in which even those with very different perspectives can live together productively and respectfully.

Being close-minded means that a person rejects ideas and perspectives without even really listening. A close-minded person habitually engages in self-talk such as, "I don't have to hear this because I'm not going to go along with it anyway," "We've already tried that. It didn't work, so I won't listen," or "My ideas are fine. I don't need to hear others." People who are close-minded cut themselves off from potentially valuable information and suggestions.

For students to learn how to be open-minded, they need to understand why and when this habit of mind is appropriate and develop strategies for maintaining an open mind when it would be beneficial to do so.

Examples of situations in which it might be beneficial to maintain an open mind

- It is not unusual in daily life to have a knee-jerk negative response to particular ideas or potential changes (e.g., an employer proposes a major relocation, a child announces a dramatic shift in education plans, or a spouse suggests a change in lifestyle). In times like these the ability to maintain an open mind—at least long enough to explore the possibilities—can help you to avoid conflict and take advantage of new opportunities.

- You may have had the experience of avoiding or rejecting someone who has different perspectives about life. However, if you seek to maintain an open mind, you might discover new friends and enjoy stimulating conversations.

- Maintaining an open mind can be beneficial when traveling to places that are unfamiliar or culturally or socially different. It can help you view the experience as exciting or challenging instead of uncomfortable and upsetting.

- Whether as an employer or an employee, people are exposed to proposals, ideas, suggestions, and opinions in the workplace. Knowing how and when to maintain an open mind can contribute to being seen as a valued colleague, team player, or dynamic leader.

"Education's purpose is to replace an empty mind with an open one."

—Malcolm Forbes

Examples of strategies recommended by people who exhibit the habit of maintaining an open mind

- When you notice yourself reacting negatively to a suggested change, observe others who are responding positively. Carefully listen to what they are saying and "try on" their point of view.

- Ask questions in a sincere effort to gather information and to understand the reasons for others' opinions. Remember that the goal of being open-minded is not necessarily to change your perspective; it is to seek understanding of others' perspectives.

- When someone makes a suggestion or proposal and you notice that you immediately react a particular way, force yourself to sit down and list the positive and negative things that could happen if the suggestion or proposal were accepted. The act of clearly articulating different perspectives can stimulate reflection and force a deeper level of analysis than just thinking about the issue or idea. It can be helpful to talk to yourself by asking, "Have I listened actively to the different perspectives?", "Have I considered the positives and negatives?", or "What am I missing?"

Restrain Impulsivity

"Wait. Let me think about this." This is the self-talk of someone who recognizes when it might be a good idea to delay a decision or an action until she can gather more information or until there has been time to carefully consider the available information. It is the kind of self-talk that is characteristic of someone who knows when and how to restrain impulsivity.

Restraining impulsivity is a mental habit that involves much more than simply "keeping your hands to yourself" or refraining from making inappropriate comments in the classroom. It includes understanding the kinds of situations in which restraint is needed and then knowing how to stop yourself from acting too quickly. Even if acting on impulse might be desirable at times, the ability to restrain impulsivity appropriately can save relationships, jobs, and even lives.

Examples of situations in which it might be beneficial to restrain impulsivity

- The ability to restrain impulsivity and delay gratification has been associated by researcher Daniel Goleman (1995) with increased academic ability and performance.

Costa (1984) "Mediating the Metacognitive"

Ennis (1985) "Goals for a Critical Thinking Curriculum"

Ennis (1989) "Critical Thinking and Subject Specificity: Clarification and Needed Research"

Goleman (1995) *Emotional Intelligence*

I'll think this through before I answer.

- It is normal in life to feel frustrated at times and to think about lashing out. Controlling this impulse increases the chance that the situation will be resolved through negotiation, cooperation, and compromise.

- Although it is normal to want to contribute to a conversation, sometimes it is better to be a listener first, to learn from what others are saying, and then to analyze the situation and determine how best to contribute.

- A democratic society thrives when citizens are involved in decision making. Yet many issues are complex and media reports and analyses are often conflicting or designed to generate an emotional response. Thus, our initial conclusions might not always be the best. Restraining impulsivity can help us to be more effective participants in the democratic process.

- When a friend faces a problem, you may feel like jumping in impulsively to give advice or to help solve the problem. Regardless of how sincere you are, your behavior might be perceived as meddling or might make the situation worse. Stopping to think in such situations is sometimes the best approach.

- Life is full of opportunities for new adventures and new activities. However, in general it is best to weigh the advantages and disadvantages and consider the risks before rushing in to try something new.

Examples of strategies recommended by people who exhibit the habit of restraining impulsivity

- Use self-talk phrases such as, "Look before you leap," "Think before you speak," or "Wait a minute. Think." as cues to restrain impulsive tendencies. Ask yourself questions such as, "Do I understand this?", "Should I respond yet?", or "Do I have any questions before I say what I think is true?"

- Ask another person with whom you interact to give you feedback about whether you are impulsive in your personal interactions and then, if necessary, help you identify strategies to use to reduce impulsive reactions.

- Allow people who are speaking to finish their thoughts before you respond. Remind yourself how you feel when someone interrupts you.

- Try counting to ten or saying the alphabet to yourself when you notice you are ready to pounce on an idea, a question, a comment, or a proposed solution.

Take a Position When the Situation Warrants It

The complementary habit to maintaining an open mind and restraining impulsivity is taking a position when the situation warrants it. Like the other productive habits of mind, developing this ability requires understanding which situations call for taking a position and knowing how to take a position or stance.

Taking a position is appropriate when we have strong feelings about an issue and have taken the time to examine the arguments and evidence and to construct support for our position. This approach contrasts sharply with taking a position simply because others have, sometimes referred to as taking a "copycat" position. It is also quite different from waffling or switching positions impulsively—even as often as every few minutes—either as a function of the latest argument or to please someone.

Committing to a position with confidence requires the ability to evaluate evidence and construct support. At times it also may include the ability to communicate clearly and the willingness to accept the risk of rejection from others with different positions.

Examples of situations in which it might be beneficial to take a position

- When you are listening as friends debate an issue, you might notice that a particular position in which you believe strongly is not being addressed. In this case, it might be appropriate to express and defend it.

- Most people have faced pressure from peers or others to act in ways that violate their beliefs or values. Sometimes it is appropriate simply to walk away from such pressure. At other times it is important to express a position clearly, no matter how unpopular that may be at the moment. The ability to take a position in this case may influence others and serve as a much-needed role model to people who are not confident enough to resist the pressure.

- There may be times when friends or colleagues take a stand on an issue and ask you to support them publicly. If you agree with their position, you need to be ready to stand strong and verbalize that support.

- As citizens, when we see or experience injustices or controversies, we may decide to make a concerted effort to improve the situation by stating and defending our beliefs.

Costa (1984) "Mediating the Metacognitive"

Ennis (1985) "Goals for a Critical Thinking Curriculum"

Ennis (1989) "Critical Thinking and Subject Specificity: Clarification and Needed Research"

Presseisen (1987) *Thinking Skills Throughout the Curriculum*

Examples of strategies recommended by people who exhibit the habit of taking a position when the situation warrants it

- Develop the habit of asking yourself questions like "Is it time for me to express and support my opinion?" or "What else do I need to know before I take a position?"

- Find examples from current events in which someone whom you admire has taken a position and defended it. Investigate the strategy used, the actions taken, and the outcome of the action.

- Before taking a position, investigate various sides of the issue to help solidify your commitment to that position. When you are confident about your position, you will be more likely to stick to it and express it clearly.

- Become familiar with common fallacies and types of weak arguments. This knowledge will help you listen to diverse positions and construct a strong argument for your own position.

Respond Appropriately to Others' Feelings and Level of Knowledge

Paul (1990) *Critical Thinking*

Whether interacting with people to inform, to persuade, or to share ideas, a good critical thinker watches for implicit and explicit messages that reflect others' feelings and level of knowledge. Assessing what others are feeling and thinking, and then adapting a situation or message based on that assessment, communicates respect for others and increases the chances that goals dependent on collaboration and cooperation will be achieved.

A primary challenge in developing this habit is achieving an appropriate balance between being sensitive to others and achieving the goals of the interaction. For example, being sensitive to others' feelings means respecting them without indulging them and without allowing them to distract inappropriately from the goals of the interaction. Likewise, responding appropriately to others' levels of knowledge means first assessing and then responding in a way that ensures the achievement of the goal, even when people have little or no knowledge about an issue or when people have a great deal of knowledge and seek to dominate. Striking a balance in these situations requires skill and understanding, which are developed over time as a result of experiences in a variety of situations.

Examples of situations in which it might be beneficial to respond appropriately to others' feelings and level of knowledge

- When you are trying to express an opinion, others are more likely to listen if you assess and respond appropriately to their feelings and level of knowledge.

- Even if you have a different perspective on an issue (e.g., the environment, political candidates, or health care), responding with empathy when people are expressing their opinions may improve the situation, especially if they seem troubled or stressed.

- Responding appropriately to others' feelings and levels of knowledge can increase the chances of successful communication with people from different cultures or backgrounds.

Examples of strategies recommended by people who exhibit the habit of responding appropriately to others' feelings and level of knowledge

- In a group situation, people often are reluctant to share their feelings or level of knowledge. There are communication strategies you can use to find out what people are feeling or thinking without making them feel cornered or uncomfortable. One strategy for inviting others into conversation is to ask, "Have you ever had that kind of experience?" or "What have you found?"

- When an interaction is not going well and you find yourself feeling frustrated, stop and think about whether you are reading the situation carefully and responding appropriately. Taking a break or going for a walk can give you time to think over a situation. You can then come back to it feeling more empathetic and understanding.

- Body language and gestures are an important part of communication. However, people from different cultures can interpret a gesture in very different ways. Educating yourself on the nuances and conventions of diverse cultures will help to enhance communication and increase your ability to accurately assess others' feelings and level of knowledge.

- Try to put yourself in the other person's shoes. How might you feel if you were in his or her situation?

Creative Thinking

Persevere

Csikszenthmihalyi (1975)
Beyond Boredom and Anxiety

Covey (1990) *The 7 Habits of Highly Effective People*

From time to time, we all face tasks or problems, whether academic or in the course of daily life, for which the answer or solution is not immediately apparent. Even after putting considerable effort into a task, we may have made little or no progress. The ability to persevere—to stick to the task, to remain engaged in or committed to finding the answer—can be the key to success in these situations. In the classroom, the ability to persevere can help students learn more from academically challenging tasks and can help prepare them for the workplace. In daily life, perseverance is often associated with the work ethic. Thus, many people consider the ability to persevere to be the key to achieving success.

The fact that this mental habit is part of the cluster called "creative thinking" emphasizes that engaging intensely in tasks does not mean simply refusing to give up on a task. It means looking for appropriate help, finding and trying different ways to approach a task, examining it from different viewpoints, taking it apart and putting it back together, and comparing it to other similar problems. These are all qualities critical to creative thinking.

Examples of situations in which it might be beneficial to persevere

- When you persevere, you are more likely to gain knowledge and skills that at first may seem too difficult to understand or master.

- Every job presents challenges. Being self-confident about your ability to seek answers and solutions may increase your willingness to accept challenges and, thus, make you a more valuable employee.

- There are examples of people in almost any field of work who have contributed something important because of their ability to persevere. Perhaps they found a way to provide better service, increase sales, cure a patient, or defend a client. Even when faced with difficult problems, they did not give up until they found a solution.

- The result of meeting a goal sometimes can significantly affect others (e.g., a team or a class). In these situations, your ability to stay engaged and continue trying to find solutions can contribute to others' seeing you as a valuable group leader or role model.

"Success is the ability to go from one failure to another with no loss of enthusiasm."
—Winston Churchill

Examples of strategies recommended by people who exhibit the habit of persevering

- Before beginning a complicated or difficult task, set small goals that will lead to the accomplishment of the larger task. Tackle one small goal at a time, and reward yourself after completing each one.

- When you continually fail at a task, identify aspects of the task that might be contributing to your failure and generate alternative ways to accomplish that part of the task.

- Identify people in your life you should seek out when you are tempted to give up on a task as well as those you should avoid. Some people are good at providing motivation and inspiration to others; some, unfortunately, contribute to a "give it up" attitude.

- Generate and keep in mind a clear picture of solving the problem or generating an answer. Visualizing success can renew your commitment.

- When you feel burned-out in a job or task, step back from it. Take a walk, play some music, or visit with a colleague. People who have the habit of persevering report that the best solutions often occur to them during these breaks.

Push the Limits of Your Knowledge and Abilities

Pushing your limits means more than simply accepting challenges. It means seeking out new challenges even when you know that they could be risky, both physically and psychologically. It means more than working hard. It means attempting things you are not sure you can do. Pushing your limits takes more than perseverance or commitment; it takes the courage to try and to accept failure. However, as long as reason and caution prevail, the benefits of pushing yourself should outweigh the risks, especially if those benefits include excitement, expanded knowledge and abilities, increased confidence, and a willingness to accept and learn from setbacks and failures.

Although pushing limits is listed here as a mental habit, the emphasis is on developing the *tendency and ability* to push your limits, not on habitually doing so. Like many of the other habits of mind, the emphasis is on using it thoughtfully.

"I thought about it all the time."

—Sir Isaac Newton on how he discovered the law of gravity

"Courage and perseverance have a magical talisman before which difficulties disappear and obstacles vanish into thin air."

—John Quincy Adams

Perkins (1981) *The Mind's Best Work*

Harman & Rheingold (1984) *Higher Creativity*

Covey (1990) *The 7 Habits of Highly Effective People*

Csikszenthmihalyi (1975) *Beyond Boredom and Anxiety*

"Ah, but a man's reach should exceed his grasp, or what's a heaven for?"

—Robert Browning

"You must do the thing you think you cannot do."

—Eleanor Roosevelt

Knowledge and Abilities

"Behold the turtle. He makes progress only when he sticks his neck out."

—James Conan Bryant

Examples of situations in which it might be beneficial to push the limits of your knowledge and abilities

- When you have been working at the same job for a long time and find that you are "coasting" through the day using as little energy as possible or avoiding challenging tasks, it may be time to seek ways to push the limits of your knowledge and abilities in some aspect of your responsibilities. This could increase your energy, your excitement, and, ultimately, your salary.

- When you find that you are falling into a routine in your daily life, pushing your limits can turn routines back into challenging and interesting tasks. Pushing your limits can be as simple as playing a golf course you have considered too difficult, redecorating your home in a style you have always admired, making unique Halloween costumes instead of recycling old ideas, making and tossing your own pizza crust, or running in a marathon.

- Learning to push the limits of your knowledge and abilities can be particularly important when the stakes or rewards are high. Continued employment, rehabilitation from illness, saving a relationship, or staying in school can depend on this ability.

Examples of strategies recommended by people who exhibit the habit of pushing the limits of their knowledge and abilities

- When you are involved in a task, set a goal that will challenge you to complete aspects of a task within a shorter amount of time than usual. Then push yourself to meet the time limit.

- To discover potential new challenges, make it a practice to ask others what they do to push their limits. Their experiences can help you to identify personal challenges.

- When you find phrases or sayings that inspire or motivate you to push your limits, write them down and keep them where you will see them regularly, for example, in your personal calendar, framed in your office, or taped to the refrigerator.

- Identify people in your life who help you to push yourself and let them know that you may call on them when you are tempted to simply coast. Conversely, identify those people you want to avoid because they talk you out of trying things or because they mindlessly err on the side of caution.

Generate, Trust, and Maintain Your Own Standards of Evaluation

Although your work often will be evaluated by others, you will function more efficiently and effectively if you consistently apply your own standards of evaluation as you work. When you generate your own set of standards, you might consider the standards that others will use to evaluate your work. However, you may decide to include only some of these standards, reject or adapt others, and add some that are important only to you. If you have rigorously generated your standards, trusting them and doing what is necessary to meet them should follow naturally.

People who exhibit this mental habit become self-directed as learners and workers. Their achievements and growth are not limited by others who do not share their visions and aspirations. They are the people who set new standards in whatever field they pursue.

Examples of situations in which it might be beneficial to generate, trust, and maintain your own standards of evaluation

- You may know how to get the highest grade from a teacher. However, a good learner also will set his own standards when necessary to maximize learning.

- There are many examples of inventors who have built successful, lucrative careers around new products or ideas (e.g., Mrs. Fields and Bill Gates). Successful inventions often are the result of people who generated and applied their own standards of evaluation.

- History is full of examples of individuals who set new standards that influenced people and societies. For example, Martin Luther King and Mahatma Gandhi were both known for setting standards that influenced the behavior of people who wanted to challenge the status quo.

- The books *In Search of Excellence* (Peters & Waterman, 1982) and *A Passion for Excellence* (Peters & Austin, 1985), both best-sellers, document many examples of businesses and schools enjoying unprecedented successes because individuals generated, trusted, and maintained uncommonly high standards in their products and services.

Perkins (1986) *Knowledge as Design*

Perkins (1984) "Creativity by Design"

Finally ...
I got it the way I want it!

Examples of strategies recommended by people who exhibit the habit of generating, trusting, and maintaining their own standards of evaluation

- Whenever you are engaged in setting personal standards, ask yourself questions like, "If I were evaluating this, what would I want to see?" and "How would I know that I put forth my best effort?" This kind of self-talk might motivate you to establish high standards.

- When you feel bored, unchallenged, or uninterested in a project or task, generate and commit to higher standards as a way of increasing your interest and making the task more challenging.

- Take the time to write down your standards. This serves two purposes. First, it forces you to clearly define your standards. Second, you can display the list or review it regularly to focus your work.

- Try setting your standards using a *rubric*, a set of criteria that describes performance at levels that meet, exceed, and miss the standard. The process of generating the rubric can force you to articulate your criteria in even greater detail. Once you have created the rubric, it can provide you with a way of evaluating the extent to which you are maintaining your standards.

Generate New Ways of Viewing a Situation That Are Outside the Boundaries of Standard Conventions

Amabile (1983) *The Social Psychology of Creativity*

Perkins (1986) *Knowledge as Design*

Whether solving a problem, analyzing an issue, clarifying a confusing idea, making a decision, exploring a phenomenon, or inventing a new product, sometimes we need a completely different way of looking at a task. Even when we know this, it can be difficult to bring a fresh perspective to a task, especially when we have been immersed in it for a long time. Deciding that we need to generate a new way of viewing a situation is only the first step; actually viewing it differently takes strategies and practice.

For some people, the tendency to view situations in unique or uncommon ways comes naturally. Unfortunately, people like this sometimes are considered a bit strange when they share their views and, consequently, may learn to keep their visions to themselves. Other people, conversely, find it very difficult to view something from a different angle. Although they may realize that they are constrained by standard conventions, they may not know how to break out of these constraints. People who do this naturally discover that their ability is an asset that serves them well throughout life. Those who struggle learn that with modeling and practice, they, too, can develop this mental habit.

Examples of situations in which it might be beneficial to generate new ways of viewing a situation that are outside the boundaries of standard conventions

- When academic assignments seem uninteresting or mundane, you can change your experience by looking at the assignment in a new way. The result may be a more creative final product, a better grade, and, hopefully, an increase in learning.

- When faced with everyday, complex problems, try to mentally move away from the situation and view it in a different way. You may feel less stressed as a result of seeing that the problem is not so overwhelming, or you may discover more creative solutions.

- Corporations often put together "think tanks," groups of people who sometimes spend days or weeks trying to come up with new ideas or products. You can be a major asset to the company if you are able to lead these groups through exercises that help them generate new ideas.

Examples of strategies recommended by people who exhibit the habit of generating new ways of viewing a situation that are outside the boundaries of standard conventions

- Use analogies and metaphors to help you see things in a different way.

- Use brainstorming techniques to force yourself to go beyond your first idea.

- When attempting to create a solution or a new product or process, generate your initial ideas, leave them alone for a while, and then come back to them later.

- Ask yourself questions like, "What unnecessary constraints am I putting on my thinking?" or "How would a child see this situation?"

- Seek out people (e.g., your child, a parent, or a friend) who have no knowledge or experience with the situation and ask them to react or respond. Sometimes a naive or innocent question or comment will help you get out of your mental rut.

"I'd get real close to him and breathe on his goggles."
—Johnny Kerr, former NBA player and coach, on how he would guard Kareem Abdul-Jabbar

Hanson, Silver, & Strong (1986) *Teaching Styles and Strategies*

One approach to metaphoric thinking is synectics. See Gordon (1961) *Synectics* and Gordon (1971) "Architecture—The Making of Metaphors."

von Oech (1983) *A Whack on the Side of the Head*

Bandura & Schunk (1981) "Developing Competence, Self-efficacy and Intrinsic Interest Through Proximal Self-motivation"

Paris, Lipson, & Wixson (1983) "Becoming a Strategic Reader"

Self-Regulated Thinking

Monitor Your Own Thinking

Being aware of our thinking can help us to be more efficient, make fewer mistakes, and learn from what is working and what is not. When we are aware of our thinking, we periodically stop and monitor the mental strategies we have been using, what we have been saying to ourselves, and what we are picturing in our minds. This process might include asking questions like, "What am I saying to myself right now?" and "What am I seeing in my mind?", or saying things like, "My mind keeps wandering. I need to focus on this task" or "If I did that, then I must have been thinking. . . ."

Examples of situations in which it might be beneficial to monitor your own thinking

- When you are not doing well at any task, it might be helpful to stop and attend to what you are mentally saying to yourself or what you are seeing in your mind. If necessary, change the words and pictures to make them positive.

- When you are learning new information or skills, it is important to be aware of how and what you are thinking. When you are trying to understand something, for example, check to see if you are using effective strategies (e.g., talking to yourself, generating images, and linking new information to old information). Consciously using different kinds of thinking can enhance your learning by increasing your understanding and retention of new information.

- Many Olympic athletes are very aware of their own thinking because they realize how much it influences their performance. An integral part of practicing is monitoring their thinking to keep it as positive as possible.

- Research has identified ways that help people to improve their test-taking and public-speaking skills just by helping them to be aware of and change their own thinking during these stressful situations. Any time you face a situation in which you feel self-conscious or nervous, monitoring your thinking could help to reduce your anxieties.

Examples of strategies recommended by people who exhibit the habit of monitoring their own thinking

- When you are doing a difficult task, set a timer to beep every fifteen minutes as a cue to stop and ask yourself, "What am I thinking right now? Is my thinking hurting me or helping me? What do I want to change?"

- When you are attempting a new skill or solving a difficult problem, keep a piece of paper near you to write down the mental strategies that work for you so that you can repeat your successes next time.

- Keep a journal that includes reflections on what you are thinking during various activities of the day (e.g., when you are taking an exam or working on a project). Reflect on what was helpful, what was detrimental, and what you learned.

- For some people, having a list of personally motivating or inspiring sayings is a useful resource during difficult times. When you come across a particularly compelling saying or phrase on a poster, in a book, from a mentor, at your place of worship, from a movie, or from a relative, write it down and occasionally read it to keep the idea fresh in your mind.

"Change your thoughts and you change your world."
—Norman Vincent Peale

Plan Appropriately

One habit that teachers obviously want students to develop is planning. Planning can be fairly loose or it can involve a process. This process might include methodically defining a goal, identifying the steps needed to achieve the goal, anticipating potential problems, assigning responsibilities, and creating a time line with checkpoints.

Schank & Abelson (1977) *Scripts, Plans, Goals and Understanding*

In school and in daily life, we learn that taking time to create a plan increases the chances that goals—whether individual or group goals—will be achieved. Those who have studied goal setting assert that planning means more than simply keeping the steps in mind; to be most effective, plans should be verbalized or written down. The challenge is to understand when a plan is needed and take the time to verbalize or record the plan so that it will be used to achieve goals.

Examples of situations in which it might be beneficial to plan appropriately

"It wasn't raining when Noah built the ark."
—Howard Ruff

- In school or in day-to-day life, there can be periods of time during which you face many demands all at once. Careful planning can decrease your stress and maximize your effectiveness.

"He who does not look
ahead remains behind."

—Spanish Proverb

- Planning can be especially helpful when working on any kind of long-term project by helping to ensure that things are not put off until the end. For a group project, planning is especially critical in making sure that each person knows his or her responsibilities.

- Over the course of a lifetime, there are milestones that require planning. Going to college, getting married, having a family, and retiring are examples of critical turning points that can, of course, be influenced by luck, coincidence, or whimsy. However, most people would agree that planning for these important milestones increases the chances for positive outcomes.

- In almost any job, you can become involved in major projects. The ability to create and implement detailed plans can not only contribute to the project, it can also increase your value as an employee as you become known for the ability to design and implement complex plans.

- The ability to plan can actually turn into a career. Financial planners, party planners, and construction project planners are all examples of people who have combined their planning abilities with other interests and skills to carve out financially rewarding careers.

Examples of strategies recommended by people who exhibit the habit of planning appropriately

- Make sure that any plan has a clearly identified goal. It is difficult to plan or to know if a plan worked when the identified outcome is fuzzy. For example, "I am going to lose weight" or "We are going to help our students think better" are goals that are too general. Being as specific as possible helps to direct the plan; for example, you might restate your goals by saying, "I am going to lose ten pounds by June 1" or "We are going to help students improve their inductive reasoning when reading from their textbooks."

- Using a particular format, planner, or an organizer for writing down the plan can ensure that it is complete and easy to use. In its simplest form, an organizer might include the following components:

What needs to be accomplished?	By when?	By whom?

- When you have long-term projects or goals, identify short-term objectives or checkpoints to be achieved and to celebrate along the way. You might use symbols or checkmarks to note objectives accomplished.

- Because original plans often have to be revised, it is a good idea to review your plan regularly, assess how the plan is working, and then make necessary revisions.

- When creating a plan for a complex project, seek out others who have been involved in similar projects and have them review your plan. Ask specific questions related to your concerns and encourage them to reflect on what they would have done differently in their project, what cautions they would offer, and what they would be sure to do again.

- Office supply stores carry planners for almost any project and time frame. If you are not particularly skilled at designing your own planner, buy one.

- There are courses offered to help people learn to be better planners. If you are weak in this area, enroll in one.

Identify and Use Necessary Resources

When we encourage students to work hard, to push their limits, and to believe in themselves, we also might need to remind them that success frequently depends on seeking help, that is, seeking the human, financial, material, and information resources that will contribute to completing a task or achieving a goal. Successful people often attribute much of their success to the resources—both human and nonhuman—that contributed to their efforts along the way.

Schunk (1990) "Goal Setting and Self-efficacy During Self-regulated Learning"

Covey (1990) *The 7 Habits of Highly Effective People*

Being aware of necessary resources involves a cycle of assessing what resources are needed, determining their availability, accessing them, using them appropriately, and continually reassessing to identify additional resources as you work. In the technological society we now enjoy, each step of this cycle can be enhanced with the use of communication and information systems.

Examples of situations in which it might be beneficial to identify and use necessary resources

- Every day in school, it is important to use the numerous resources available to you under one roof: teachers, books, equipment, peers, counselors, electronic media, and, especially, time.

- People who have been successful in almost any field have faced many situations that required them to rely not just on their own personal resources but on other people's money, time, support, and ideas. Sports figures often describe their search for the ideal coach; entertainers and artists have stories of receiving backing from patrons of the arts; authors dedicate works to key mentors from whom they have received support and ideas.

- There are many times when identifying necessary resources will help you fulfill your responsibilities as a family member. Most experienced parents, for example, could describe numerous times that they had to identify and seek help and advice as they raised their children. People who face caring for aging parents sometimes have a need to look for suggestions, professional help, or psychological support.

- One of life's major goals, maintaining your own health, increasingly depends on finding and making use of resources, whether it is seeking second opinions on health matters, finding an exercise buddy, or hiring a personal trainer.

Examples of strategies recommended by people who exhibit the habit of identifying and using necessary resources

- When involved in any complex task or situation, start by making a list that includes what is needed, what is available, what is not available, and other resources that could replace what is not available.

- Before beginning a project or task, seek out others who have been involved in similar types of projects and find out what they needed. This can help you to make sure you have not overlooked some important resources and can provide ideas for obtaining the resources you have already identified.

- Regularly ask yourself, "What else is available to me, or what can I make available, that will contribute to this process?" This self-talk can help you to be alert to resources that you might otherwise miss.

Respond Appropriately to Feedback

Seeking out and responding to feedback communicates that you care about being successful and that you acknowledge that self-assessment, although necessary, might not be sufficient for maximum success. It means you listen to others' remarks with an open mind because you value their input and want to improve your performance. However, being sensitive to feedback does not mean that you must agree with or act on every suggestion; it does mean that you listen, reflect, and take appropriate action, which might include dismissing the advice.

Examples of situations in which it might be beneficial to respond appropriately to feedback

- When you are engaged in a repetitious task, you might find yourself getting into a rut. It can be helpful to solicit or listen to someone else's ideas about how to improve performance or prevent careless mistakes.

- If you have a school project to complete or a plan to implement, it can be useful to ask someone to give you feedback. This can help you make the project more focused, thorough, and accurate. Just the process of asking for feedback can help you to stay focused.

- If you are speaking to an audience, you can get feedback from the audience. Watch body language, elicit responses during the speech, and adapt accordingly.

- When you are striving to accomplish any long-term, complex task (e.g., debugging your computer), it is important to actively seek feedback. Being sensitive to the feedback can help keep you on course, allow you to correct if things are not going well, and increase the likelihood of your success.

Examples of strategies recommended by people who exhibit the habit of responding appropriately to feedback

- When you are involved in a difficult task, occasionally stop and ask another person for his or her opinion about your progress. Be sure to ask specific questions such as, "How do you think this is working?", "What would you change about the way that I'm dealing with this?", and "Tell me what I am doing best and which component of the task you think is most important." Direct, specific questions will elicit advice that is most useful.

Resnick (1987) *Education and Learning to Think*

Pressley & Levin (1983b) *Cognitive Strategy Research: Psychological Foundations*

Pressley & Levin (1983a) *Cognitive Strategy Research: Educational Applications*

- When you are creating an action plan to meet a specific goal (e.g., training for a long bike ride), include in your plan exactly when and from whom you will seek feedback. Include people who have some experience in the area so that they can help you identify the signals or signposts that should let you know whether or not you are headed in the right direction.

- When you are creating a new plan at work, ask colleagues for feedback. As you listen, take notes. Avoid accepting or rejecting the feedback until later when you have a chance to reflect on the ideas from each person.

- There are times when you may need to prepare yourself to receive feedback. For example, if you know that you tend to be defensive about feedback in particular situations or from specific people, prepare yourself by trying to be as open as possible.

Evaluate the Effectiveness of Your Actions

Covey (1990) *The 7 Habits of Highly Effective People*

Hansen (1992) "Literacy Portfolios: Helping Students Know Themselves"

Resnick (1987) *Education and Learning to Think*

When you are evaluating the effectiveness of your actions, you are acting as your own process observer. This type of self-assessment involves continually stepping out of your work, looking at what you are accomplishing, and then evaluating how successfully you are accomplishing the task or goal. You might be asking yourself questions, validating or rethinking your approach, deciding whether to maintain your plan of action or start over, and learning if and how you would change your approach the next time. Exhibiting this habit of mind takes discipline and a commitment to high standards.

Examples of situations in which it might be beneficial to evaluate the effectiveness of your actions

- Any time you are starting something new or trying to do something for the first time, evaluating your actions along the way helps you learn from mistakes and can change the way that you perform in the future.

- When you are teaching someone else how to do something, you may find that you need to evaluate your own actions in order to be able to influence others.

- When you are successful at some kind of task, such as organizing large functions, it is useful to evaluate the effectiveness of your decisions and actions so that you will be able to duplicate those successes.

- If you are involved in a project that includes many people, by articulating how you evaluate the effectiveness of your part of the work, you may be able to give others an opportunity to do the same, thereby contributing to the performance of the group as a whole.

Examples of strategies recommended by people who exhibit the habit of evaluating the effectiveness of their actions

- As soon as you have finished working on a challenging, long-term project, ask yourself, "What would I do differently next time? What would I do the same?" Using self-talk is one of the most common approaches to self-assessment.

- As discussed earlier, writing out your plan is a good practice to use during any project. It also allows you to go back and methodically evaluate each phase. This written record is then available to you in future similar endeavors.

- After you have completed a project or task (e.g., painting a room), seek out the strategies other people have used to be successful in that area (e.g., successful painters) and compare your tactics with theirs. Look for ways that you could change your behavior to be more successful in the future.

- When you are trying to improve your ability to use a complex process, it is always useful to break the process down into small parts. This allows you to evaluate each part, rather than examining the whole, and decreases the potential for feeling overwhelmed by the improvements you need to make.

"When you're through changing, you're through."

—Bruce Barton

Unit Planning: Dimension 5

Planning for Dimension 5 requires asking and answering the following overarching question:

What will be done to help students develop productive habits of mind?

What follows is a step-by-step process that will guide you in answering this question. Each step asks you to answer a key question or provide specific information. There is a place on the planning guide (see page 302) in which to record your ideas, notes, decisions, and planned activities. A sample planning guide has been filled out for a hypothetical social studies unit about Colorado. (This unit topic was chosen because, with some changes, it could be used for a unit about any state or region and at any developmental level. You will find the entire unit in Chapter 6, "Putting It All Together.")

Step 1

Are there any goals or concerns related to students' **habits of mind?**
  - in general?
  - related to this specific unit?

To answer these questions, do the following:

- Identify anything you have noticed, in general, about students' awareness of or use of the habits of mind. For example, you might have observed that students rarely stop to identify the necessary resources before planning or that they are reluctant to say anything when things are not clear to them.

- Think about the activities, experiences, and tasks that will be included in the unit, and identify any mental habits that will contribute to students' performance or level of learning. For example, there might be a particularly difficult task in Dimension 4 that will challenge students to push themselves or there might be a class debate during which students need to listen to each other carefully.

Step 2

> What will be done to address these goals or concerns?

This question has two parts, as follows:

Step 2a

> Specifically, will anything be done to help students. . .
>
> **Critical Thinking**
> ❑ be accurate and seek accuracy?
> ❑ be clear and seek clarity?
> ❑ maintain an open mind?
> ❑ restrain impulsivity?
> ❑ take a position when the situation warrants it?
> ❑ respond appropriately to others' feelings and level of knowledge?
>
> **Creative Thinking**
> ❑ persevere?
> ❑ push the limits of their knowledge and abilities?
> ❑ generate, trust, and maintain their own standards of evaluation?
> ❑ generate new ways of viewing a situation that are outside the boundaries of standard conventions?
>
> **Self-regulated Thinking**
> ❑ monitor their own thinking?
> ❑ plan appropriately?
> ❑ identify and use necessary resources?
> ❑ respond appropriately to feedback?
> ❑ evaluate the effectiveness of their actions?

Identify the specific habits of mind that will help you to address your goals and concerns.

Step 2b

> Describe what will be done.

Describe the specific action you will take or the activities and strategies will use. You might want to consider the strategies suggested earlier in this section of the manual. They are as follows:

1. **Help students understand habits of mind.**

   - Facilitate classroom discussion of each habit.

   - Use examples from literature and current events of people who are using the habits in different situations.

   - Share personal anecdotes that relate to a habit.

   - Notice and label student behavior that demonstrates a particular habit.

   - Ask students to identify personal heroes or mentors and describe the extent to which they exemplify specific habits of mind.

   - Have students create posters that illustrate their understanding of the habits.

2. **Help students identify and develop strategies related to the habits of mind.**

   - Use think-aloud to demonstrate specific strategies.

   - Ask students to share their own strategies.

   - Encourage students to find examples of strategies mentioned in literature and current events.

   - Ask students to interview others (e.g., parents, friends, or neighbors) to identify strategies.

   - Each quarter or semester, ask students to identify and focus on a habit of mind they would like to develop.

3. **Create a culture in the classroom and the school that encourages the development and use of the habits of mind.**

   - Model the habits.

   - Integrate the habits into the daily routines and activities of the classroom.

- Develop and display posters, icons, and other visual representations to express the importance of productive habits of mind.

- When appropriate, cue students to focus on specific mental habits or ask them to identify habits that would help them while working on difficult tasks.

4. **Provide positive reinforcement to students who exhibit the habits of mind.**

- Appoint "process observers," students who watch for positive examples of other students who are demonstrating the habits.

- Ask students to self-assess their use of specific habits.

- Give students feedback on a report card or progress report.

Dimension 5 Planning Guide

Step 1	Step 2
Are there any goals or concerns related to students' habits of mind • in general? • related to this specific unit?	**What will be done to address these goals or concerns?**
	Specifically, will anything be done to help students. . .
	Critical Thinking ❑ be accurate and seek accuracy? ❑ be clear and seek clarity? ❑ maintain an open mind? ❑ restrain impulsivity? ❑ take a position when the situation warrants it? ❑ respond appropriately to others' feelings and level of knowledge?	Describe what will be done.
It's that time of year. Students are really slacking off. Energy is low; only the minimum is being done— even from my good students	**Creative Thinking** ☑ persevere? ☑ push the limits of their knowledge and abilities? ❑ generate, trust, and maintain their own standards of evaluation? ❑ generate new ways of viewing a situation that are outside the boundaries of standard conventions?	_I am going to try to energize them a little bit by verbally reinforcing students when they push their limits or persevere. I think it is time to give out a few certificates of achievement when students exhibit these habits._
Students know you should plan before you begin, but they do not consistently or efficiently do this. The experimental inquiry task will be dependent on careful planning and follow-through.	**Self-Regulated Thinking** ❑ monitor their thinking? ☑ plan appropriately? ❑ identify and use necessary resources? ❑ respond appropriately to feedback? ❑ evaluate the effectiveness of their actions?	_I am going to give students a planning form to keep on their desks. I will use it to lead some discussions about planning and then to demonstrate how to use the form. Every few days I am going to have students write in their learning logs about how their planning is going._

Putting It All Together

PUTTING IT
ALL TOGETHER

Putting It All Together

As explained in the introduction to this manual, one of the primary uses of the Dimensions of Learning model is as a structure for planning units of instruction. At the end of the chapter for each dimension, a process for unit planning is explained and examples are provided of a social studies unit about the state of Colorado. Units of study planned using the Dimensions of Learning model might be short—that is, implemented over a period of only three or four days—or long—extending over two or more weeks. The length will be influenced by a number of factors, including how much knowledge is being targeted, the age of the students, and the level of interest of the students. This section, "Putting It All Together," addresses how a teacher might integrate five issues that must be considered in relationship to one another for a unit to truly be effective. The issues are (1) the content that will be covered, (2) how students will be assessed, (3) how grades will be assigned, (4) how instruction will be sequenced, and (5) how conferences will be used.

Content

Whether a unit is short or long, deals with mathematics or social studies, or is targeted for the first grade or the twelfth grade, the planning process requires the curriculum planner to consider each of the five dimensions. The primary questions that have been identified for each dimension include the following:

Dimension 1

What will be done to help students develop positive attitudes and perceptions?

- Are there any goals or concerns related to students' attitudes and perception
  - in general?
  - related to this specific unit?

- What will be done to address these goals or concerns?

- Specifically, will anything be done to help students
  - feel accepted by teachers and peers?
  - experience a sense of comfort and order?
  - perceive tasks as valuable and interesting?
  - believe they have the ability and resources to complete tasks?
  - understand and be clear about tasks?

Dimension 2: *Declarative*

What will be done to help students acquire and integrate declarative knowledge?

- What declarative knowledge will students be in the process of acquiring and integrating? As a result of this unit, students will know or understand. . . .

- What experiences or activities will be used to help students acquire and integrate this knowledge?

- What strategies will be used to help students construct meaning for, organize, and/or store this knowledge?

Dimension 2: *Procedural*

What will be done to help students acquire and integrate procedural knowledge?

- What procedural knowledge will students be in the process of acquiring and integrating? As a result of this unit, students will be able to...

- What strategies will be used to help students construct models for, shape, and internalize the procedural knowledge?

Dimension 3

What will be done to help students extend and refine knowledge?

- What knowledge will students be extending and refining? Specifically, students will be extending and refining their understanding of. . . .

- What reasoning process will students be using?

Dimension 4

What will be done to help students use knowledge meaningfully?

- What knowledge will students be using meaningfully? Specifically, students will be demonstrating their understanding of or ability to. . . .

- What reasoning process will students be using?

Dimension 5

What will be done to help students develop productive habits of mind?

- Are there any goals or concerns related to students' habits of minds
  - in general?
  - related to this specific unit?

- What will be done to address these goals or concerns? Specifically, will anything be done to help students
  - be accurate and seek accuracy?
  - be clear and seek clarity?
  - maintain an open mind?
  - restrain impulsivity?
  - take a position when the situation warrants it?
  - respond appropriately to others' feelings and level of knowledge?
  - persevere?
  - push the limits of their knowledge and abilities?
  - generate, trust, and maintain their own standards of evaluation?
  - generate new ways of viewing a situation that are outside the boundaries of standard conventions?
  - monitor their own thinking?
  - plan appropriately?
  - identify and use necessary resources?
  - respond appropriately to feedback?
  - evaluate the effectiveness of their actions?

The entire unit plan for the Colorado unit, in which each of the primary questions for each dimension is answered, can be found at the end of this chapter.

Although these questions are presented in a step-by-step sequence, planning is, in reality, rarely a linear process. A person planning a unit might start with Dimension 4, then plan Dimensions 2 and 3, and then, because of decisions made in Dimensions 2 and 3, go back and change decisions initially made in Dimension 4. Perhaps the only fairly consistent approach to planning is that the questions related to attitudes and perceptions (Dimension 1) and habits of mind (Dimension 5) are answered last. This is because many of the goals and concerns in these dimensions are not apparent until Dimensions 2, 3, and 4 have been planned.

Even though there is great variation in the order in which people plan the dimensions, it is critical to the planning process to ask and answer the questions for each dimension. This guarantees that each part of the learning process is carefully considered during planning. However, it would be a mistake to conclude that each dimension has an equal role in each unit. Sometimes when you are asking yourself the questions related to a particular dimension, you will decide that nothing or not much will be done to address that dimension during the unit. Because of the specific focus of a unit, one dimension might dominate or be deemphasized. Below are explanations of three models of planning, each representing a different focus and, therefore, a different emphasis on the individual dimensions.

Model 1: Focus on Knowledge

When using Model 1, the teacher focuses on Dimension 2, acquiring and integrating declarative and procedural knowledge. This means that specific concepts, generalizations/principles, skills, or processes are the focus of the unit. Everything that happens in the classroom "serves" these learning goals. Thus, the teacher selects extending and refining activities (Dimension 3) and tasks that require students to use the identified knowledge meaningfully (Dimension 4). The planning sequence for this model might include the following steps:

Step 1

Identify the declarative and procedural knowledge (Dimension 2) that will be the focus of the unit.

Step 2

Create extending and refining activities (Dimension 3) that will reinforce and deepen students' understanding of the declarative and procedural knowledge identified in Step 1.

Step 3

Design a task that requires students to use knowledge meaningfully (Dimension 4). The targeted knowledge should be the declarative and procedural knowledge identified in Step 1.

Model 1 has these general characteristics:

- The knowledge identified in Dimension 2 is selected because the planner considers it to be important for all students or because it is important knowledge related to district or state standards and benchmarks.

- When declarative knowledge is the focus, concepts and generalizations/principles (as opposed to discrete facts) should be identified. When the focus is on procedural knowledge, important declarative knowledge that is related to those procedures also should be identified.

- Both Dimension 3 and Dimension 4 tasks are means of enhancing students' understanding of, or proficiency with, the identified knowledge.

- Usually, only one task that requires students to use knowledge meaningfully (Dimension 4) is included in the units, and the teacher makes sure that students know that the task requires them to use the knowledge identified in Step 1.

Model 2: Focus on Issues

When using this model, you focus on Dimension 4, the meaningful use of knowledge. Specifically, you identify an issue related to the general theme of the unit and decide what kind of task might be associated with the issue. For example, if there is an issue about how or why something happened, then historical investigation becomes the focus of the unit. If there is a phenomenon to be studied, then experimental inquiry becomes the focus of the unit, and so on. Once you have identified the issue and its related task, you identify the declarative and procedural knowledge (Dimension 2) and any extending and refining activities (Dimension 3) needed to complete the task. Work in Dimensions 2 and 3 supports the task that you have selected. The planning process for Model 2 might be represented in this way:

Step 1

Identify an important issue and its related task that requires students to use knowledge meaningfully (Dimension 4).

Step 2

Identify the declarative and procedural knowledge (Dimension 2) needed to complete the task.

Step 3

Identify the extending and refining activities (Dimension 3) needed to enhance students' understanding of the declarative and procedural knowledge.

Model 2 has these general characteristics:

- The unit contains only one task that requires students to use knowledge meaningfully. In the primary grades, an extending and refining activity (Dimension 3) may be used instead because this kind of activity is often more appropriate for young students.

- The identified declarative and procedural knowledge is selected because students need that knowledge to complete the identified Dimension 4 task.

- Extending and refining activities might be deemphasized because the Dimension 4 task will serve to enhance students' understanding of, and proficiency with, the identified knowledge.

Model 3: Focus on Student Exploration

Model 3 most closely resembles the developers' original concept of the workings of the Dimensions of Learning framework. As in Model 1, you first identify the declarative and procedural knowledge (Dimension 2) that will be highlighted in the unit. You also identify the extending and refining activities (Dimension 3) that will reinforce that knowledge. In a departure from both models 1 and 2, however, you do not identify a task that requires students to use knowledge meaningfully (Dimension 4) but ask students to select their own tasks, or projects, for making meaningful use of knowledge. Your job is to assist students in choosing a project and to encourage them to explore issues and interesting questions that arise naturally in the unit. In effect, students have the freedom to study issues that are beyond the scope of the declarative and procedural knowledge you have identified. The only requirement is that students use important knowledge in ways that are meaningful to them. Using this model, the planning process might be delineated in the following way:

Step 1

Identify the declarative and procedural knowledge (Dimension 2) to be highlighted in the unit.

Step 2

Identify extending and refining activities (Dimension 3) that will deepen students' understanding of the declarative and procedural knowledge.

Step 3

Identify ways to help students select tasks in which they use knowledge meaningfully (Dimension 4).

Model 3 has these general characteristics:

- The types of tasks or projects undertaken by students are very diverse.

- A greater portion of class time is devoted to these projects (Dimension 4) because students develop their own projects.

Assessment

Dimensions of Learning can help teachers identify and clarify what they will teach—the content of a unit of instruction. In addition, Dimensions of Learning can be a powerful model for organizing classroom assessment.

What to Assess

Traditionally, classroom assessment has been focused exclusively on the acquisition of information and skills—declarative and procedural knowledge as represented in Dimension 2. The Dimensions of Learning model suggests that, in addition to the content-specific knowledge of Dimension 2, other types of information and skills are important for students to learn and can be assessed, specifically the information and skills involved in Dimensions 3, 4, and 5. In other words, the bias of the Dimensions of Learning model is to assess Dimensions 2, 3, 4, and 5 as opposed to just the information and skills in Dimension 2. Why?

First, even if we could agree that only content-specific information and skills (Dimension 2) are important, most educators would admit that they want students to have more than a surface-level grasp of important declarative and procedural knowledge. Thus, it is important to teach students processes that help them to extend and refine that knowledge—that is, go into more depth, make new connections, have new insights, and correct misconceptions. The Dimension 3 complex reasoning processes accomplish this purpose but must be taught and assessed if students are to learn and use them.

Similarly, most people recognize the necessity for students to apply important information and skills to real-life settings and problems. Again, the Dimension 4 complex reasoning processes provide an opportunity for students to do this. They, too, must be taught and assessed if students are to value them and learn to use them.

Finally, most people concur that having certain dispositions makes it more likely that students will learn content more effectively and function more successfully in the world. The habits of mind in Dimension 5 are the kinds of dispositions that many people believe students need in order to learn effectively in school and to succeed in life. Again, these habits of mind can and must be taught and assessed if students are to learn them.

Dimension 1, it might be noticed, has not been mentioned in this discussion of assessment. Although the different aspects of Dimension 1 may be assessed, primarily through teacher observation or student self-assessment, most people refrain from such assessment because the elements are largely attitudinal.

To summarize, then, we recommend that the various components of Dimensions 2, 3, 4, and 5 be taught and assessed for the many reasons discussed above.

Assessment Techniques: Tools and Techniques for Collecting Data

One of the keys to effectively assessing Dimensions 2, 3, 4, and 5 in the classroom is to have a wide variety of assessment techniques. Here we consider five types of assessment that all classroom teachers can use: (1) forced-choice items, (2) essay questions, (3) performance tasks and portfolios, (4) teacher observation, and (5) student self-assessment. The utility of these five types of assessment for each dimension is depicted in Figure 6.1. As Figure 6.1 illustrates, some types of assessment are much more flexible than others in the number of dimensions they address.

FIGURE 6.1

TYPES OF ASSESSMENT FOR DIFFERENT TYPES OF KNOWLEDGE

	Forced-Choice Items	Essay Questions	Performance Tasks/Portfolios	Teacher Observation	Student Self-Assessment
Dimension 2: Specific Declarative Knowledge	X	X	X	X	X
Dimension 2: General Declarative Knowledge		X	X	X	X
Dimension 2: Specific Procedural Knowledge	X	X	X	X	X
Dimension 2: General Procedural Knowledge		X	X	X	X
Dimension 3 & 4: Complex Reasoning Processes		X	X	X	X
Dimension 5: Habits of Mind			X	X	X

Forced-Choice Items

As described by assessment expert Richard Stiggins (1994), forced-choice items are those found in what we think of as conventional, objective tests. They include multiple-choice items, true/false items, matching exercises, and short, fill-in-the-blank items. The student is asked to select or give the correct or best answer.

Although forced-choice items can be used to assess declarative knowledge—from the general (concepts and generalizations) to the specific (facts about people, places, events)—they are best suited for information at the factual level and when simple recall or recognition of information is the goal. For procedural knowledge, such items are appropriate for assessing whether students have mastered basic algorithms such as adding or subtracting.

Essay Questions

Essay questions have been used by classroom teachers for many years. They are effective for assessing both declarative and procedural knowledge (Dimension 2) as well as the complex reasoning processes (Dimensions 3 and 4). Relative to Dimension 2, essay questions are appropriate for assessing students' understanding of general levels of declarative knowledge (concepts and generalizations, big ideas and their relationships) as well as determining students' proficiency with procedural knowledge (by having students explain or critique a procedure). When a complex reasoning process is applied to declarative knowledge in an essay, students must demonstrate an understanding of the declarative knowledge as well as competence in using the reasoning process.

Performance Tasks and Portfolios

Good essay questions are closely related to performance tasks. In fact, an essay question that uses one of the Dimension 3 or 4 reasoning processes is a type of performance task. Performance tasks require students to construct responses that demonstrate that they can analyze and/or apply knowledge. As indicated in Figure 6.1, performance tasks may be used to assess declarative and procedural knowledge (Dimension 2), complex reasoning processes (Dimensions 3 and 4), and habits of mind (Dimension 5). In addition, performance tasks promote student engagement, a deeper understanding of the content being studied, and an opportunity for students to meaningfully apply that content knowledge.

A model for constructing performance tasks based on the Dimensions of Learning model includes the following steps adapted from *Assessing Student Outcomes* (Marzano, Pickering, & McTighe, 1993):

1. Identify important declarative or procedural knowledge that will be assessed in the task. (Dimension 2: Declarative knowledge should be at the concept, generalization, or "big idea" level of generality.)

2. Structure the task around one of the complex reasoning processes in Dimensions 3 or 4. (This may not be necessary when procedural knowledge from Dimension 2 is selected. Instead, the skill or process may be placed in a real-life, real-use context.)

3. Write a first draft of the performance task, incorporating the information identified in steps 1 and 2.

4. Identify dispositions from the habits of mind (Dimension 5) to include in the task. Revise the task to include them.

5. Identify specific aspects of communication, information processing, and/or cooperation/collaboration, if desired, and build them into the task.

The performance task shown in Figure 6.2 was developed using the above steps. (These steps were adapted from a task from *Assessing Student Outcomes.*) To make the task most effective as an assessment tool, rubrics should be provided for students. (For a discussion of rubrics, see the upcoming section "The Important Role of Judgment.") General rubrics for all the dimensions can be found in the book *Assessing Student Outcomes.*

FIGURE 6.2

DEFINITIONAL INVESTIGATION TASK

Grade-level range: Junior high—high school

Although the term Third World is often used by newscasters, economists, and authors, its meaning is unclear to many people. There is no common understanding of precisely what the Third World is or where the term originated. In your small group, locate descriptions of, or allusions to, the Third World or to another regional term of your choice (e.g., underdeveloped nations, the Far East) that provide information or insights into the characteristics represented by the terms and an explanation of why the term is used.

Construct a definition of the term, and determine if its characteristics focus primarily on political, sociological, topographical, or religious distinctions. Use a consensus process to reach agreement on the definition. You will present your findings in a panel discussion format, so be prepared to defend your definition. You will be assessed on and provided rubrics for the following:

Declarative Knowledge (Dimension 2): Social Studies

1. Your ability to distinguish differing definitions of regions: those based primarily on politics, sociological elements, topography, religions, etc.

Complex Reasoning Process (Dimension 3/4): Definitional Investigation

1. Your ability to define or describe something for which there is no readily available or accepted definition.

2. Your ability to develop and defend a logical and plausible resolution to the confusion, uncertainty, or contradiction about the concept.

Habit of Mind (Dimension 5): Critical Thinking

1. Your ability to take a position when the situation warrants it.

Portfolios are intimately tied to performance tasks. In fact, they usually contain products from a series of performance tasks. They also might contain examples of various stages of a particular performance task to show development and growth. An important aspect of a portfolio is the student's description of the process of creating a product, why certain decisions were made, and a judgment about his or her own effort. Portfolios are often accompanied by exhibitions, that is, presentations or defenses of student work.

Teacher Observation

Perhaps the most direct way of collecting assessment data is to informally observe students. To do this, a teacher commonly makes notes as he observes students demonstrating their understanding of information or their use of a skill. This is done unobtrusively as students engage in classroom activities. As depicted in Figure 6.1, teacher observation can be used to assess Dimensions 2, 3, 4, and 5. Recording data over an extended period of time (e.g., a quarter or a semester) gives a teacher enough information to reliably judge each student's performance on any of the four dimensions that are the focus of assessment.

Student Self-Assessment

This technique is particularly powerful because the assessment data comes directly from students. Usually students are given specific questions, probes, or rubrics to guide them in their self-assessment. They might write their responses to questions or probes in a learning log or journal. They might also respond to surveys and questionnaires. Self-assessments can be used to gather assessment data for any and all of the dimensions of learning. They are particularly appropriate for the habits of mind from Dimension 5 because many of the habits are not easily observed but must be inferred by the teacher.

The Important Role of Judgment

With the exception of forced-choice items, the assessment techniques described above cannot be reduced to responses that can be scored as correct or incorrect. Therefore, teachers using this expanded array of assessment techniques must shift their perspective from one of adding up the number of correct responses a student obtains to one of making judgments about a student's level of performance on specific types of information and skill. One of the best tools for making these types of judgments is a rubric, a set of criteria that describes the characteristics of performance at difference levels of competency. A rubric provides a scale, usually represented by numbers (e.g., 4, 3, 2, and 1 for a 4-point scale) or descriptive terms (e.g., advanced, proficient, developing or basic, and novice). Rubrics provide a structure for making judgments about students' levels of performance. This is especially true for essays, performance tasks, portfolios, teacher observations, and student self-assessments.

Teachers and students who use rubrics attest to their power to improve student performance. Rubrics answer the question that students ask, "What's expected of me?" Grant Wiggins, director of programs for the Center on Learning, Assessment, and School Structure, in describing the usefulness of rubrics, suggests that they are like road signs. Rubrics provide information that lets students know where they are, where they need to be, and what they need to do to get from where they are to where they need to be. Rubrics help students self-assess, self-correct, and be more self-reliant.

The rubrics shown in Figures 6.3 and 6.4 can be used to assess students' performance relative to declarative knowledge, procedural knowledge, complex reasoning processes, and habits of mind. They can be tailored to assignments and tasks by substituting assignment- or task-specific language for the generic terms.

FIGURE 6.3

GENERIC RUBRICS FOR DECLARATIVE AND PROCEDURAL KNOWLEDGE

Declarative

4   Demonstrates a thorough understanding of the important information; is able to exemplify that information in detail and articulate complex relationships and distinctions.

3   Demonstrates an understanding of the important information; is able to exemplify that information in some detail.

2   Demonstrates an incomplete understanding of the important information, but does not have severe misconceptions.

1   Demonstrates an incomplete understanding of the important information along with severe misconceptions.

Procedural

4   Carries out the major processes/skills inherent in the procedure with relative ease and automaticity.

3   Carries out the major processes/skills inherent in the procedure without significant error but not necessarily at an automatic level.

2   Makes a number of errors when carrying out the major processes and skills important to the procedure but still accomplishes the basic purpose of the procedure.

1   Makes so many errors when carrying out the process and skills important to the procedure that it fails to accomplish its purpose.

FIGURE 6.4

RUBRIC FOR THE COMPLEX REASONING PROCESS "COMPARING" ADAPTED FROM GENERIC PROCEDURAL KNOWLEDGE RUBRIC

4 Carries out the steps in the process of comparing completely, accurately, and effectively, and with relative ease and automaticity.

3 Carries out the steps in the process of comparing effectively and without significant error, but not necessarily at an automatic level.

2 Makes a number of errors when carrying out the steps of the process of comparing, but still accomplishes the basic purpose of the comparison.

1 Makes so many errors when carrying out the steps important to the process of comparing that it fails to accomplish its purpose.

Note: The generic procedural knowledge rubric may be similarly adapted to any and all of the Dimension 3 and 4 complex reasoning processes.

RUBRIC FOR THE HABIT OF MIND "RESTRAINS IMPULSIVITY"

4 Carefully considers a situation to determine whether more study is required before acting. When further study is required, gathers thorough and detailed information before acting.

3 Considers a situation to determine whether more study is required before acting. When further study is required, gathers sufficient information before acting.

2 Considers, in a cursory manner, whether more study is required before acting. When further study is required, gathers some information before acting.

1 Does not consider a situation to determine whether more study is required before acting.

Note: See Marzano, Pickering, & McTighe (1993) Assessing Student Outcomes, for rubrics for all of the Habits of Mind.

Grading

Once decisions have been made about the criteria for students' levels of performance on specific dimensions and the types of assessment tools that will be used, the next concern is how to assign grades.

To do this, teachers must stop thinking of a grade as a compilation of scores on tests, assignments, and activities to which points are assigned, and begin to think in terms of levels of performance on (1) the important declarative and procedural knowledge (Dimension 2) specific to a class or subject area, (2) the particular Dimension 3 and 4 complex reasoning processes students are learning and using in the classroom, and (3) the habits of mind (Dimension 5) that have been addressed.

For example, within a unit of study on Colorado (which has been used in the planning sections throughout this manual), the teacher might address a great deal of knowledge (identified in Dimension 2), which can be clustered under the following benchmarks:

Students will...

>*Benchmark 1:* understand the interactions of human and physical characteristics of a regions

>*Benchmark 2:* understand the reasons for human movement within and among regions

>*Benchmark 3:* be able to use thematic maps

Students' abilities to engage in complex reasoning processes and to exhibit habits of mind (skills which may or may not be identified in benchmarks within a district) are also addressed in the unit. Specifically, students use three complex reasoning processes—classifying, inductive reasoning, and experimental inquiry—in the Colorado unit. In addition, the teacher has targeted two creative thinking habits of mind (persevere and push limits) and one self-regulated thinking habit of mind (plan appropriately).

Figure 6.5 shows a sample page from a grade book that might be kept by a teacher using this unit of study. This type of grade book is manageable when the declarative and procedural knowledge is organized under specific benchmarks. If benchmarks are not used, only the most important pieces of knowledge should be included in the grade book; recording separate grades for each piece of knowledge would not be realistic. Each portion of the grade book is explained below.

FIGURE 6.5

SAMPLE PAGE FROM A GRADEBOOK

Assignment Key:				
A. *Quiz*	**E.** *Quiz*	**I.** _____		
B. *Induction Task*	**F.** *Exper. Inq. Task*	**J.** _____		
C. *Reg. cake (HW)*	**G.** *Unit Test*	**K.** **Student Self-Assessment**		
D. *Classify Task*	**H.** *Map Assign (HW)*	**L.** **Observations**		

Standards/Benchmarks: / Students		*Geo S1B2 humans/ physical environment*	*Geo S2B5 human movement/ regions*	*Geo S6B1 use thematic maps*	*Dim 3 & 4 complex reasoning*	*Dim 5 habits of mind*
Al Einstein	A	3				
	B	3			3	
	C	3				
	D		3		3	
	E		3			
	F	3	3		3	2
	G	4	3	2		
	H			1		
	I					
	J					
	K	4	3	2	3	3
	L	4 → 4	3, 3+ → 3	2 → 2	3	2, 2 → 2
Marie Curie	A	2				
	B	3			2	
	C	2				
	D		1		2	
	E		1			
	F	2	2		1	1
	G	1	1	1		
	H			1		
	I					
	J					
	K	3	2	2	2	2
	L	2 → 2	1, 1 → 1	2 → 1	2 → 2	2, 2 → 2
George Carver	A	4				
	B	3			2	
	C	4				
	D		4		4	
	E		4			
	F	4	3		3	3
	G	4	3	3		
	H			4		
	I					
	J					
	K	4	4	4	3	4
	L	3 → 4	3, 4, 3 → 3	4 → 4	3 → 3	4, 4 → 4

The assignment key at the top of the grade book can be used by the teacher to list the various assessment techniques, activities, and assignments used for grading. A page from our sample grade book has room for ten items, student self-assessment, and teacher observations. Eight items have been filled in on this sample page.

A. Quiz

B. Induction Task

C. Regional cake assignment (Homework)

D. Classify Task

E. Quiz

F. Experimental Inquiry Task

G. Unit Test

H. Map Assignment (Homework)

I. _____

J. _____

K. Student Self-Assessment

L. Observation

At the top of each column (where assignments are recorded in more conventional grade books) are categories of knowledge for which grades are recorded during this unit. The first three columns are for three of the benchmarks from the unit; these are followed by a column for complex reasoning processes (Dimensions 3 and 4) used in the unit and a column for habits of mind (Dimension 5) used in the unit.

Note that in this marking period the teacher gave two graded homework assignments, two quizzes, two Dimension 3 tasks, one Dimension 4 task, and a unit test. Each box below each benchmark has room for the teacher to enter a number reflecting his or her judgment about an individual student's performance on a specific assessment, activity, homework assignment, and so on. For example, consider Al Einstein's scores for the first benchmark. This box has a number of rows, each preceded by a letter. The letter in each row represents the assignment, the test, or the event for which the teacher has made judgments about Al's performance. The number represents the teacher's judgment about Al's performance on each of the assessments for each applicable benchmark, reasoning process, or habit of mind.

Note that most of the assessments address more than one benchmark. For example, consider assessment *F*, the Experimental Inquiry Task. The task provides assessment information for students' performance on two content benchmarks, the complex reasoning process, and the habits of mind targeted in the unit.

Row *K* is used to record the individual student's self-assessment for his or her performance relative to each dimension. (The teacher enters this into the grade book at the time of a teacher/student assessment conference. During the conference, each student provides the teacher with his or her personal judgment and the evidence for those judgments.)

Row *L* is used to record the teacher's informal observations on the student's performance relative to each dimension. For example, the teacher assigned a score of 2 on one occasion and a score of 3 on the other occasion.

Numbers ranging from 1 to 4 are used throughout the grade book. These refer to the levels of performance achieved by the student during a single assignment that related to the declarative or procedural knowledge, Dimension 3 or 4 processes, and habits of mind. (Sample rubrics were presented earlier in this section that might be used to assess students' performance relative to the different dimensions.) What does a teacher do, however, when a single assignment or test relates to more than one component in a category of declarative or procedural knowledge (e.g., understanding the concepts of topography, natural resources, climate, and culture are all components of "understanding interactions between human and physical systems") or more than one complex reasoning process or habit of mind (e.g., a single task could assess both comparing and inductive reasoning)? The rubric shown in Figure 6.6 can be used to summarize performance on multiple aspects of a category of declarative or procedural knowledge, multiple complex reasoning processes in Dimensions 3 and 4, or multiple habits of mind.

FIGURE 6.6

RUBRIC SUMMARIZING PERFORMANCE ON MULTIPLE COMPONENTS

4   Advanced performance in some of the components of this objective
3   Proficient performance in the majority of components of this objective
2   Proficient or higher performance in some components of this objective
1   Basic or lower performance in the majority of components within this objective

At the end of the grading period, the teacher assigns a score representing the student's performance for each type of knowledge assessed. This is entered in the white box in the lower portion of each column of the grade book. This score is not intended to be an average of all of the student's scores for that type of knowledge. Many educators believe that it does not matter how long it takes for students to learn the targeted knowledge. The score is intended to reflect the level of performance the student has attained during the grading period.

Once the teacher has assigned a score for each type of knowledge being assessed, more than likely she must combine these into an overall grade. Each type of knowledge might be weighted according to its importance. For example, the declarative and procedural knowledge pieces might be given a weight of 2, the complex reasoning processes a 2, and the habits of mind a 1. The student's scores (representing levels of performance) are multiplied by the assigned weight in order to calculate quality points. The quality points are then added; the sum of the quality points is divided by the sum of the weights to arrive at an average score, as shown in Figure 6.7. Finally, the student's average score is converted into a grade based on the following conversion:

3.26-4.00	=	A
2.76-3.25	=	B
2.01-2.75	=	C
1.50-2.00	=	D
1.49 or below	=	F

FIGURE 6.7

CALCULATING SCORES

Sample Student: Al Einstein			
	Student's Scores	Weight	Quality Points
Content benchmark score 1	4	× 2	8
Content benchmark score 2	3	× 2	6
Content benchmark score 3	2	× 2	4
Complex reasoning score	3	× 2	6
Habits of mind performance	2	× 1	2
Total		9	26
Al Einstein's average score for the quarter: 26 divided by 9 = 2.89			
Al Einstein's grade for the quarter: B			

Using a single overall letter grade is not the ideal for several reasons. First, the apparently arbitrary nature of cut-off scores is a weakness in many respects. Second, a single grade does not provide specific information on performance in the variety of areas it represents. Finally, a single letter grade is an oversimplification of the complex array of information and skills presented, learned, and assessed in a course of study. However, letter grades have a wide appeal and carry with them a particular mystic: People seem to think they mean more than they actually adequately represent. Nonetheless, letter grades probably are here to stay for a while. For a fuller discussion of grading issues, see Marzano and Kendall (1996), *A Comprehensive Guide to Designing Standards-Based Districts, Schools, and Classrooms.* In conclusion, judgments about students' levels of performance on specific benchmarks can be used to assign letter grades in a manner that conveys information to students about specific dimensions of learning.

Sequencing Instruction

A unit of instruction based on Dimensions of Learning quite obviously encompasses many different activities. Students, for example, are engaged in projects based on Dimensions 3 and 4; teachers and students are meeting individually and in small groups; and students sometimes are out of the classroom gathering resources. Given the variety of activities, day-to-day classes also might vary. We recommend that teachers think of instruction in terms of at least two different types of classes: presentation classes and workshop classes.

Presentation Classes

Presentation classes are geared toward Dimensions 2: acquiring and integrating knowledge. Classes devoted to this dimension tend to be more teacher directed. This does not mean that the teacher "dictates" or "lectures" while the students "listen attentively." Nor does it mean that the teacher necessarily "presents" information. Presentation classes include guest speakers, films, and even field trips; information is being "presented" to students in some way. As you can see in Chapter 2, many strategies in Dimension 2 emphasize inquiry and encourage students to actively participate in learning. The general direction of learning, however, is still guided by the teacher.

Although presentation classes certainly differ from subject to subject, certain instructional techniques are used frequently in all presentation classes.

- *Stimulating interest:* Providing some personal anecdote or interesting story to help students become interested in the activity designed to help them acquire and integrate knowledge (Dimension 2).

- *Stating goals:* Explicitly identifying the purpose or goal of the activities that will be used.

- *Making linkages:* Demonstrating how the learning activities relate to what has occurred in previous classes or, better yet, having students make these linkages.

- *Demonstrating:* Clearly explaining or modeling key aspects of the activities that will be used.

- *Providing closure:* Asking students to make summary statements and evaluations about the learning experience.

It is important to note that these five techniques should not be thought of as a "lesson design"—steps that must be used in all presentation classes and performed in a set order. It is also important to note, however, that these five aspects of presentation classes should be systematically addressed.

Workshop Classes

In contrast to presentation classes, the flow of activity in workshop classes is more student directed. This is because workshop classes focus on extending and refining knowledge (Dimension 3) or using knowledge meaningfully (Dimension 4). Workshop classes are a perfect vehicle for helping students to design and work on complex reasoning tasks. You might think of the differences between presentation and workshop classes in this way: During presentation classes the teacher "carries the ball" and students react to what the teacher does; during workshop classes, the students carry the ball and the teacher reacts to what the students do. Workshop classes are commonly divided into three parts: the mini-lesson, the activity period, and the sharing period.

The Mini-Lesson

As its name implies, the mini-lesson is short (five to ten minutes). It commonly, but not necessarily, occurs at the beginning of the workshop and, for the most part, is a vehicle for providing guidance and assistance to students as they work on two types of tasks: those that help them to extend and refine knowledge and those that require them to use knowledge meaningfully.

During a typical mini-lesson a teacher might

- model some strategy or technique that students can use as they work on their projects (e.g., a specific aspect of decision making to help students in their decision-making project); and

- demonstrate or explain resources that students can use in the projects (e.g., preview a book or article that students can use in their decision-making projects).

The mini-lesson, then, is a time for the teacher to provide whole-class support and guidance for student projects.

The Activity Period

The activity period typically lasts between twenty and forty-five minutes. During this time, students work independently or in cooperative groups on their projects. The teacher acts as a coach or guide while students work on their projects. The teacher's main vehicle for doing this is conferencing, which is discussed later in this chapter.

The Sharing Period

The sharing period usually is quite short, perhaps lasting only five to ten minutes. Although it can occur at any time, the sharing period frequently is at the end of the workshop. Students commonly share

- what they learned from the mini-lesson or activity period,

- new insights they have had, and

- perplexing issues they are facing in their projects.

If students are expected to include demonstrations with their projects, then the sharing period is quite long. This usually occurs at the end of a unit.

Integrating Presentation and Workshop Classes

It is important to integrate presentation and workshop classes into a unit of study. Further, all of the presentation classes should not be scheduled at the beginning of the unit and all of the workshop classes at the end. Rather, within a four-week unit of study, presentation and workshop classes might be distributed as shown in Figure 6.8. In this example, there is a gradual shift from an emphasis on presentation classes to an emphasis on workshop classes. In other words, there is a gradual shift from an emphasis on Dimension 2 (acquiring and integrating knowledge) to an emphasis on Dimension 3 (extending and refining knowledge) and Dimension 4 (using knowledge meaningfully). Dimension 1 (positive attitudes and perceptions) and Dimension 5 (productive habits of mind) permeate both presentation and workshop classes. It is the careful sequencing of presentation and workshop classes that makes a unit of study a holistic learning experience, with teacher and students trading off control of learning and the two types of classes supporting each other at strategic points. The four questions below will help you properly sequence your classes and integrate the five dimensions of learning:

1. **What strategies and activities will be used to support Dimensions 1 and 5?**

   For example, the teacher planning the unit on Colorado decided to use the following strategies and activities to support Dimensions 1 and 5:

   • Work on more frequently restating and rephrasing questions (Dimension 1).

   • Give students the opportunity to apply knowledge to regions of their choice (Dimension 1).

   • Verbally reinforce students when they push their limits or persevere (Dimension 5).

   • Help students learn how to plan; have them reflect on planning in their learning logs (Dimension 5).

2. **How many days of the unit will be devoted to presentation classes, and when will they occur?**

   To answer this question, you must determine

   • how to sequence the direct and indirect learning experiences in the presentation classes, and

   • where to build in time for students to practice skills and processes.

FIGURE 6.8

SEQUENCE OF CLASSES

	Monday	Tuesday	Wednesday	Thursday	Friday
Week 1	P	P	P	P	P
Week 2	W	P	P	P	W
Week 3	W	P	W	W	W
Week 4	P	W	W	W	

To illustrate, the teacher planning the unit on Colorado might sequence the presentation and workshop classes as shown in Figure 6.9. The circled letter *P* signifies presentation classes; *W* signals workshop classes. She has decided to use the presentation format for the entire first week, during which she will introduce key concepts from the unit and the procedural knowledge related to reading maps. During the second week, she will present generalizations and facts about the Colorado Gold Rush; she will also include two workshop classes. During the third and fourth weeks, the number of presentation classes decreases as the number of workshop classes increases.

FIGURE 6.9

SEQUENCE OF CLASSES: COLORADO UNIT

	Monday	Tuesday	Wednesday	Thursday	Friday
Week 1	topography, natural resources—read text (P)	construct models and shape for reading physical maps, natural resource maps (P)	• See film—begin both pictographs • climate—read text assign regional cakes (P)	culture, read text, and presentations (P)	culture, read text, and presentations; learn note-taking strategy (P)
Week 2	induction task—demonstrate steps, do some together as class (cakes start coming in this week) (W)	topography, etc. influence culture—discussion using graphic organizer; present information on important people from Colorado history. (P)	topography, etc. influence settlement patterns—read text, handout—use organizer (quiz) (P)	guest speaker on Gold Rush, students use timeline for notes. (P)	classifying task—students already know how to classify, but I will review steps before they start (quiz) (W)
Week 3	introduce experimental inquiry task—teach steps of process—demonstrate planning; students begin work (W)	field trip (P)	experimental inquiry: students work on task, I conference (W)	induction task—students work with newspapers in groups, I conference (W)	• experimental inquiry task—students work on project, I conference, demonstrate planning • review map reading, homework (W)
Week 4	renewable, nonrenewable, etc. film, concept attainment, graphic organizer (P)	experimental inquiry—students work, I conference (W)	experimental inquiry—I will conference (W)	student presentations of results from experimental inquiry task (W)	unit test

3. **How many workshop classes will be needed in the unit?**

An important issue to consider is what you will be doing during the mini-lessons. If, for example, you want students to learn a new complex reasoning process to carry out a Dimension 3 or 4 task, then you need enough time to introduce and model the process. As indicated in Figure 6.9, the teacher has determined that nine periods will be workshop classes.

4. **What sequence of presentation and workshop classes will provide an integrated unit of instruction?**

Students need a certain amount of knowledge before they can effectively direct their own projects. This is why most presentation classes occur at the beginning of the unit—so students can acquire that knowledge. The number of presentation classes diminishes as students start using the knowledge they have acquired to pursue projects in workshop classes. Periodically, students may need small doses of information—presentation classes—to be able to continue their projects, but as Figure 6.8 shows, over the four weeks of a typical unit there is a gradual shift from an emphasis on presentation classes to an emphasis on workshop classes.

In determining the sequence of classes for a unit, you should make sure each class builds on the previous classes and stagger the two types of classes so that you have ample time to give students guidance on their projects. One notable side benefit of properly staggered classes is that students do not have a chance to become bored with the same old routine.

Conferences

Conferences provide the opportunity and format for teacher and students to interact on a more personal basis and break the pattern of teacher as leader and presenter of information and student as follower and receiver of information. In conferences, teacher and student become coinvestigators, colearners.

A conference may last anywhere from three or four minutes to ten or fifteen minutes. The teacher may meet with one student or a small group of students; group conferencing can help the teacher rotate through the class relatively frequently. Although every conference has one basic function—to establish a line of communication between teacher and student—it is useful to think about two different focuses that might be used: projects and assessment.

Project Focus: When a conference focuses on projects, its purpose is to provide guidance for students' work on their Dimension 3 or 4 projects. In project conferences, the teacher and student discuss progress on the project and any problems the student might be having. They also jointly plan next steps for the project.

Assessment Focus: The purpose of the assessment conference is for teachers and students to share their perceptions about how students are doing related to each of the dimensions addressed in the unit. If students have been self-assessing, they report their evaluations to the teacher during the assessment conference. If the teacher and student disagree on their assessment of the student's performance, they try to reconcile those differences during the assessment conference. This type of teacher/student interaction can be a very powerful and empowering learning experience for both the student and the teacher.

In Conclusion

This chapter has addressed important issues that influence the planning and implementation of a unit of study. The sample unit on Colorado, which has been used throughout this manual, was again used to illustrate major points in this chapter. What follows is the entire Colorado unit plan. We recommend that you look through this unit plan to get a clearer, more holistic picture of the planning process.

As you review this sample unit, you will recognize many of the pages as those that appeared in the planning sections at the end of the chapters on each Dimension. You will notice that, although only one page for declarative knowledge was shown in the planning section for Dimension 2 (page 92), in the entire unit there are a number of pages for declarative knowledge, which reflects the quantity of declarative knowledge included in this unit.

Keep in mind that this is a sample unit that focuses on a single content area: social studies. This type of unit was created as a sample unit so that simple examples could be presented to illustrate complex ideas from the Dimensions of Learning model. You should not infer that we are recommending that you use only units like the Colorado Unit. Hopefully, we have made it clear that the planning process lends itself to interdisciplinary units and units that are both shorter and longer than the sample Colorado Unit.

Finally, remember that the Dimensions of Learning model does not have to be used to plan units of study. Educators should use the model, and the resources associated with it, to set and achieve their goals for student learning. The purpose of any model is to help people understand something that is very complex. Because there are few things as complex as human learning, the Dimensions of Learning model is offered as a tool for educators to help them better understand the process of learning. If this understanding is achieved, the ultimate goal of the model should be realized: the enhancement of student learning.

Colorado Unit

Geography Standard 3, Benchmark 2(D): Understand characteristics and locations of renewable and nonrenewable resources

Concepts: Renewable resources, nonrenewable resources, flow resources

Facts describing Colorado's resources will be used as examples of each of these concepts.

Process by which fossil fuels are created will be used to explain a nonrenewable resource.

Geography Standard 2, Benchmark 5(D): Understand the reasons for human movement within and among regions

Generalizations/Principles: Topography, natural resources, and climate influence settlement patterns

Cause-effect examples from Colorado (e.g., Mountains stopped some pioneers, which then caused cities such as Denver and Colorado Springs.)

Geography Standard 6, Benchmark 1(P): Use thematic maps

Knows how to read and interpret a physical map

Knows how to read and interpret a natural resource map

Geography Standard 1, Benchmark 2(D): Understand the interactions among humans and their physical environment within a region

Concepts: Topography, natural resources, climate, culture.

Facts describing Colorado will be used as examples of each of these concepts.

Generalizations/Principles: Topography, natural resources, and climate influence the culture of a region.

Cause-effect examples from Colorado (e.g., Mountains and snow influence winter sport culture.)

Facts: Descriptions of how Molly Brown, Zebulon Pike, Alfred Packer interacted with their physical environments

Vocabulary Terms: tourism, plateau

Other declarative knowledge not related to benchmarks:

Time sequences: The story of the Colorado Gold Rush, 1859-1900

Dimension 1 Planning Guide

Are there any goals or concerns related to students' **attitudes and perceptions** • in general? • related to this specific unit?	What will be done to address these goals or concerns?	
	Specifically, will anything be done to help students. . .	Describe what will be done.
I think I have been in a rut lately when responding both to students' incorrect answers and to their correct or thoughtful answers. The last field trip was not fun for anyone; it seemed unorganized and many rules for bus behavior were forgotten.	**Classroom Climate** ☑ feel accepted by teachers and peers? ☑ experience a sense of comfort and order?	I am going to work on slowing down and giving students a chance to answer my questions; I need to do more restating and rephrasing of the questions. I will go over the rules of bus behavior and the general rules for field trips; I think I'll have students generate some additional rules and suggestions for making the field trip successful.
Students might be getting tired of studying Colorado.	**Classroom Tasks** ☑ perceive tasks as valuable and interesting? ☐ believe they have the ability and resources to complete tasks? ☐ understand and be clear about tasks?	The assignments will give students the opportunity to apply knowledge to regions of their choice.

Dimension 2 Planning Guide: Declarative Knowledge

What **declarative knowledge** will students be in the process of **acquiring and integrating**? As a result of this unit, students will know or understand. . .	What **experiences** or **activities** will be used to help students acquire and integrate this knowledge?	What strategies will be used to help students **construct meaning** for, **organize**, and/or **store** this knowledge?	Describe what will be done.
Concept: Topography —Natural and artificial features including land forms, bodies of water, roads, bridges, etc. Facts describing Colorado's topography will deal with the Rocky Mountains, sand dunes, rivers, plains, plateaus, canyons.	Text, pp. 8-10	K-W-L	On a class K-W-L chart, we all will generate the K and the W related to topography. We will then read the text, watch the film, and read physical maps. After each experience, we will fill out the L of the chart. We will use the information from the K-W-L to start a class pictograph of examples of topography.
	Film: "From Sea to Shining Sea"		
	Read physical maps	Physical/pictographic representation	
	Independent study: Regional cake		Each student will make a cake depicting topography from a region of his or her choice. Students will find information independently. After the regional cake assignment, as a class, we will add to our pictograph.
Concept: Natural Resources —Materials found in nature that are useful, necessary, or attractive. Facts describing Colorado's natural resources will deal with snow, gold, soil, sunshine, forests, oil, mountains.	Film: "From Sea to Shining Sea"	3-minute pause	Several times during the film, I will stop and ask students to identify one type of natural resource. After the film, I will ask them to try to create mental pictures of examples of natural resources and identify what they see, smell, feel, etc. We then will start our pictographs of natural resources, a class one and individual ones. After reading the natural resource maps, we will add information to the pictographs.
		Uses all senses	
	Read natural resource maps	Pictograph	
	Field Trip: Argo Gold Mine		During the field trip, students will have their pictographs with them so they can add examples of the natural resources that we observe.

Dimension 2 Planning Guide: Declarative Knowledge

What **declarative knowledge** will students be in the process of **acquiring and integrating?** As a result of the unit, the student will know or understand. . . .	What **experiences** or **activities** will be used to help students acquire and integrate this knowledge?	What strategies will be used to help students **construct meaning** for, **organize,** and/or **store** the knowledge?	Describe what will be done.
Concept: Climate —Patterns of weather including temperature, rainfall, etc. Facts describing Colorado's climate such as four seasons, very hot and very cold periods, large snowfall, low humidity.	Read text, p. 13 Discuss handout	3-minute pause	_This will be a review for most students; climate is a concept learned in earlier grades. We will read the pages in the text and a handout I received from the local television station discussing weather and climate in general and in Colorado. I will stop students periodically and simply ask them to verbalize what they understand about climate._
Concept: Culture —Beliefs, customs, values, recreation, housing, etc. of a group of people. Facts describing Colorado's culture will be used	Read text, pp. 3-7 Presentation	Reciprocal teaching Notetaking using graphic organizer	_Because culture is a new concept for them and because it is so abstract, we will begin by reading and discussing the information, using the reciprocal teaching strategy. I will guide students through the notetaking strategy to ensure that they record notes and then develop an organizer about what we have learned. I will then do a presentation showing my collection of pictures and souvenirs that depict various aspects of culture from other countries. I will help students add to their notes and continue to develop their organizers, making sure they are including critical characteristics of culture._

Dimension 2 Planning Guide: Declarative Knowledge

What **declarative knowledge** will students be in the process of **acquiring and integrating?** As a result of the unit, the student will know or understand. . .	What **experiences** or **activities** will be used to help students acquire and integrate this knowledge?	What strategies will be used to help students **construct meaning** for, **organize**, and/or **store** the knowledge?	Describe what will be done.
Generalization: Topography and natural resources influence the culture of a region. _Cause-effect examples from Colorado: Mountains and snow influence winter sport culture, etc._	_Discussion_ _Field Trip: Argo Gold Mine_	_Graphic organizer_	_We will use several copies of a blank graphic organizer to make connections between topography, natural resources, climate, and culture for Colorado, then do the same for several other regions of the students' choice. On the field trip, we will fill out the organizer for Colorado. Back in class, students will work in groups to fill it out for other regions._
Generalization: Topography, natural resources, and climate influence settlement patterns. _Cause-effect scenarios from Colorado's history will be used as examples along with examples from other regions_	_Text, pp. 12-16_ _Discussion_ _Handout_	_3-minute pause_ _Advance organizer questions_	_The text and handout discuss the connections between topography, natural resources, and climate and settlement patterns by telling stories of how the mountains contributed to the settlement of Colorado Springs and Denver, how gold caused mining towns to thrive, and how the climate contributed to resort towns emerging when so much snow attracted skiers. Students will receive advance organizer questions to focus them as they read each scenario. They will answer the questions during 3-minute pauses._

Dimension 2 Planning Guide: Declarative Knowledge

What **declarative knowledge** will students be in the process of **acquiring and integrating?** As a result of the unit, the student will know or understand. . .	What **experiences** or **activities** will be used to help students acquire and integrate this knowledge?	What strategies will be used to help students **construct meaning** for, **organize,** and/or **store** the knowledge?	Describe what will be done.
Concept: Renewable resources —Can be replaced (e.g., timber, soy beans)	_Discussion_ _Film: "Sources of our Resources"_	_Inquiry model— concept attainment_	_Using the concept attainment strategy, I will provide students with examples and nonexamples of each of the three types of resources to see if they can figure out the characteristics of each._ _We will then view the film and verify or correct the characteristics of the three types._
Concept: Nonrenewable resources —Cannot be replaced (e.g., minerals, fossil fuels)			
Concept: Flow resources —Must be used when and where they occur (running water, sunshine) _Facts describing Colorado's resources will be used_		_Graphic organizer_	_We will develop a concept graphic organizer together on the overhead, focusing on examples from Colorado. I will then make a copy for each student._

334

Dimension 2 Planning Guide: Declarative Knowledge

Unit: <u>Colorado</u>

What **declarative knowledge** will students be in the process of **acquiring and integrating**? As a result of the unit, the student will know or understand. . .	What **experiences** or **activities** will be used to help students acquire and integrate this knowledge?	What strategies will be used to help students **construct meaning** for, **organize**, and/or **store** the knowledge?	Describe what will be done.
Time sequence: The story of the Colorado Gold Rush, 1859–1900	*Guest speaker*	*Use all senses* *Timeline graphic organizer*	*Mr. Jacobs, a great storyteller and historian, will come to share the story of the Colorado Gold Rush. Each student will use a timeline to record the major events.* *When we go on the field trip to the Argo Gold Mine, we will be at the site of part of the actual story. I will ask students to create mental images and report what they see, hear, smell as they picture the events of the story.*
Vocabulary terms: Tourism, urban, rural, plateau	*Class discussion*	*Vocabulary strategy*	*For each vocabulary term, students will work in groups and go through the steps of the vocabulary strategy. They will then take turns presenting to the class the images and experiences they used to exemplify the terms.*

Dimension 2 Planning Guide: Procedural Knowledge

What **procedural knowledge** will students be in the process of **acquiring and integrating?** As a result of this unit, students will be able to. . .	What will be done to help students **construct models** for, **shape,** and **internalize** the knowledge?	Describe what will be done.
read and interpret physical maps.	_Note: These strategies will be used to teach both types of maps._	_I will talk through the steps of reading a map, demonstrating the steps with each type. I will give them a set of written steps for reading any map._
read and interpret natural resource maps.	_Think-aloud_ _Set of written steps_ _Practice with variations_ _Internalizing is not a goal._	_Working in groups, students will receive several variations in format (taken from different textbooks) for both physical and natural resource maps. There will be questions for the group and then for individual students to answer as a way of becoming familiar with each variation. This assignment also will reinforce the learning of the concepts of topography and natural resources._

Dimension 3 Planning Guide

Unit: _Colorado_

What knowledge will students be **extending and refining**? Specifically, they will be extending and refining their understanding of. . .	What reasoning process will students be using?	Describe what will be done.
Topography, natural resources, and climate influence settlement patterns in a region.	☐ **Comparing** ☑ **Classifying** ☐ **Abstracting** ☐ **Inductive Reasoning** ☐ **Deductive Reasoning** ☐ **Constructing Support** ☐ **Analyzing Errors** ☐ **Analyzing Perspectives** ☐ **Other** _____	_So far we have been focused on understanding how topography, natural resources, and climate influence the "appearance" of settlements. Shift your focus now and examine how these factors influence the "disappearance" of settlements. You will be given descriptions of situations where populations thrived and then disappeared (e.g., Anasazi Indians, several ghost towns, dinosaurs, and the "dust bowl") and the reasons for their demise. Classify each description according to whether the disappearance had more to do with topography, natural resources, or climate. If more than one possible reason is given, you may have to place the example in more than one category._

What knowledge will students be **extending and refining**? Specifically, they will be extending and refining their understanding of. . .	What reasoning process will students be using?	Describe what will be done.
Topography, natural resources, and climate influence the culture of a region.	☐ **Comparing** ☐ **Classifying** ☐ **Abstracting** ☑ **Inductive Reasoning** ☐ **Deductive Reasoning** ☐ **Constructing Support** ☐ **Analyzing Errors** ☐ **Analyzing Perspectives** ☐ **Other** _____	_Several times during this unit we will, as a class, select articles from "USA Today" that reflect the culture of a place with which we are unfamiliar. Based on what we learn from the article about the culture of the place (e.g., issues or problems people face, their celebrations), we will try to induce specific facts about the topography, natural resources, and climate of the location._

Unit: _Colorado_

What **knowledge** will students be **using meaningfully?** Specifically, they will be demonstrating their understanding of and ability to. . .	What reasoning process will they be using?	Describe what will be done.
The concepts of topography, natural resources, climate, and culture _Topography, natural resources, and climate influence settlement patterns._	☐ **Decision Making** (selecting from seemingly equal alternatives or examining the decisions of others) ☐ **Problem Solving** (seeking to achieve a goal by overcoming constraints or limiting conditions) ☐ **Invention** (creating something to meet a need or improve on a situation) ☑ **Experimental Inquiry** (generating an explanation for a phenomenon and testing the explanation) ☐ **Investigation** (resolving confusions or contradictions related to a historical event, a hypothetical past or future event, or to the defining characteristics of something) ☐ **Systems Analysis** (analyzing the parts of a system and how they interact) ☐ **Other** _____	_We have discussed in class that Colorado's population is growing very rapidly. In fact, compared to many other states, a relatively large number of people who live in Colorado moved from somewhere else. There are actually not that many "Colorado natives." Why have so many people moved to Colorado, and why is the population still growing so rapidly?_ _One explanation is that aspects of the topography, natural resources, climate, and culture attract people to Colorado. Let's find out if that helps explain it. If it is true, we should be able to trace people's reasons for moving to Colorado to these characteristics of the state._ _Set up an activity—for example, surveys or interviews—that would help to determine to what extent people have moved to Colorado because of factors related to topography, natural resources, climate, and culture. You will need to set up the activity, plan for analyzing your results, and be ready to report your findings to the class. Any member of your group may be asked to explain what you found out about the influence of each concept you are considering: topography, natural resources, climate, and culture._

Dimension 5 Planning Guide

Are there any goals or concerns related to students' **habits of mind** • in general? • related to this specific unit?	What will be done to address these goals or concerns?
	Specifically, will anything be done to help students. . .	Describe what will be done.
	Critical Thinking ❑ be accurate and seek accuracy? ❑ be clear and seek clarity? ❑ maintain an open mind? ❑ restrain impulsivity? ❑ take a position when the situation warrants it? ❑ respond appropriately to others' feelings and level of knowledge?	
It's that time of year. Students are really slacking off. Energy is low; only the minimum is being done—even from my good students	**Creative Thinking** ☑ persevere? ☑ push the limits of their knowledge and abilities? ❑ generate, trust, and maintain their own standards of evaluation? ❑ generate new ways of viewing a situation outside the boundaries of standard conventions?	*I am going to try to energize them a little bit by verbally reinforcing students when they push their limits or persevere. I think it is time to give out a few certificates of achievement when students exhibit these habits.*
Students know you should plan before you begin, but they do not consistently or efficiently do this. The experimental inquiry task will be dependent on careful planning and follow-through.	**Self-Regulated Thinking** ❑ monitor their thinking? ☑ plan appropriately? ❑ identify and use necessary resources? ❑ respond appropriately to feedback? ❑ evaluate the effectiveness of their actions?	*I am going to give students a planning form to keep on their desks. I will use it to lead some discussions about planning and then to demonstrate how to use the form. Every few days I am going to have students write in their learning logs about how their planning is going.*

References

Amabile, T. M. (1983). *The Social Psychology of Creativity*. New York: Springer-Verlag.

Anderson, J. R. (1982). "Acquisition of Cognitive Skills." *Psychological Review, 89,* 369- 406.

Anderson, J. R. (1983). *The Architecture of Cognition*. Cambridge, MA: Harvard University Press.

Anderson, J. R. (1990). *Cognitive Psychology and its Implications* (3rd ed.). New York: W. H. Freeman.

Anderson, J. R. (1993). *Rules of the Mind*. Hillsdale, NJ: Lawrence Erlbaum.

Anderson, J. R. (1995). *Learning and Memory: An Integrated Approach*. New York: John Wiley & Sons.

Anderson, L., Evertson, C., & Emmer, E. (1980). "Dimensions in Classroom Management Derived from Recent Research." *Journal of Curriculum Studies, 12,* 343-356.

Applebee, A. N. (1981). *Writing in the Secondary School*. Urbana, IL: National Council of Teachers of English.

Applebee, A. N. (1984a). *Contexts for Learning to Write*. Norwood, NJ: Ablex.

Applebee, A. N. (1984b). "Writing and Reasoning." *Review of Educational Research, 54,* 577-596.

ASCD. (1992). Dimensions of Learning Videotape Series. Alexandria, VA: Author.

Ausubel, D. P. (1968). *Educational Psychology: A Cognitive View*. New York: Holt, Rinehart & Winston.

Bandura, A., & Schunk, D. H. (1981). "Developing Competence, Self-efficacy and Intrinsic Interest Through Proximal Self-motivation." *Journal of Personality and Social Psychology, 41*(3), 586-598.

Beyer, B. K. (1988). *Developing a Thinking Skills Program*. Boston: Allyn & Bacon.

Billmeyer, R. (1996). *Teaching Reading in the Content Areas: If Not Me, Then Who?* Aurora, CO: McREL.

Brookover, W., Beady, C., Flood, P., Schweitzer, J., & Wisenbar, J. (1979). *School Social Systems and Student Achievement*. New York: Praeger.

Brooks, J. G., & Brooks, M. G. (1993). *In Search of Understanding: The Case for Constructivist Classrooms*. Alexandria, VA: ASCD.

Brophy, J. (1982). *Classroom Organization and Management*. Washington, DC: National Institute of Education.

Brophy, J., & Good, T. L. (1986). "Teacher Behavior and Student Achievement." In M. C. Wittrock (Ed.), *Handbook of Research on Teaching* (3rd ed.). New York: Macmillan.

Brown, A. L. (1978). "Knowing When, Where and How to Remember: A Problem of Metacognition." In R. Glaser (Ed.), *Advances in Instructional Psychology* (Vol. 1, pp. 77-165). Hillsdale, NJ: Lawrence Erlbaum.

Brown, A. L. (1980). "Metacognitive Development and Reading." In R. J. Spiro, B. C. Bruce, & W. F. Brewer (Eds.), *Theoretical Issues in Reading Comprehension*. Hillsdale, NJ: Lawrence Erlbaum.

Brown, J. L. (1995). *Observing Dimensions of Learning in Classrooms and Schools*. Alexandria, VA: ASCD.

Bruner, J. S., Goodnow, J., & Austin, G. A. (1956). *A Study of Thinking*. New York: Wiley.

Canfield, J., & Wells, H. C. (1976). *100 Ways to Enhance Self-concept in the Classroom*. Englewood Cliffs, NJ: Prentice-Hall.

Carbo, M., Dunn, R., & Dunn, K. (1986). *Teaching Students to Read Through Their Individual Learning Styles*. Englewood Cliffs, NJ: Prentice-Hall.

Carkhuff, R. R. (1987). *The Art of Helping* (6th ed.). Amherst, MA: Human Resource Development Press.

Combs, A. W. (1982). *A Personal Approach to Teaching: Beliefs That Make a Difference*. Boston: Allyn & Bacon.

Copi, I. M. (1972). *Introduction to Logic*. New York: Macmillan.

Costa, A. (1984). "Mediating the Metacognitive." *Educational Leadership, 42,* 57-62.

Costa, A. L. (Ed.). (1991a). *Developing Minds: A Resource Book for Teaching Thinking* (Rev. Ed., Vol. 1). Alexandria, VA: ASCD.

Costa, A. L. (Ed.). (1991b). *Developing Minds: A Resource Book for Teaching Thinking* (Rev. Ed., Vol. 2). Alexandria, VA: ASCD.

Covey, S. R. (1990). *The 7 Habits of Highly Effective People*. New York: Simon & Schuster.

Covington, M. V. (1985). "Strategic Thinking and the Fear of Failure." In J. W. Segal, S. F. Chipman, & R. Glaser (Eds.), *Thinking and Learning Skills: Vol. 1, Relating Instruction to Research* (pp. 389-416). Hillsdale, NJ: Lawrence Erlbaum.

Covington, M. V., Crutchfield, R. S., Davies, L., & Olton, R. M. (1974). *The Productive Thinking Program: A Course in Learning to Think*. Columbus, OH: Merrill.

Crabbe, A. B. (1982). "Creating a Brighter Future: An Update on the Future Problem-Solving Program." *Journal for the Education of the Gifted, 5*, 2-11.

Csikszenthmihalyi, M. (1975). *Beyond Boredom and Anxiety*. San Francisco: Jossey-Bass.

Dale, E. (Comp.). (1984). *The Educator's Quotebook*. Bloomington, IN: Phi Delta Kappa.

de Bono, E. (1983). "The Cognitive Research Trust (CoRT) Thinking Program." In W. Maxwell (Ed.), *Thinking: An Expanding Frontier*. Philadelphia: Franklin Institute Press.

Dunn, R., & Dunn, K. (1978). *Teaching Students Through Their Individual Learning Styles*. Englewood Cliffs, NJ: Prentice-Hall.

Edmonds, R. R. (1982). "Programs of School Improvement: An Overview." *Educational Leadership, 40*(3), 4-11.

Ehrenberg, S. D., Ehrenberg, L. M., & Durfee, D. (1979). *BASICS: Teaching/Learning Strategies*. Miami Beach, FL: Institute for Curriculum and Instruction.

Emmer, E. T., Evertson, C. M., & Anderson, L. (1980). "Effective Management at the Beginning of the School Year." *Elementary School Journal, 80*, 219-231.

Ennis, R. H. (1985). "Goals for a Critical Thinking Curriculum." In A. Costa (Ed.), *Developing Minds: A Resource Book for Teaching Thinking* (pp. 54-57). Alexandria, VA: ASCD.

Ennis, R. H. (1987). "A Taxonomy of Critical Thinking Dispositions and Abilities." In J. Baron & R. Sternberg (Eds.), *Teaching Thinking Skills: Theory and Practice*. New York: Freeman.

Ennis, R. H. (1989). "Critical Thinking and Subject Specificity: Clarification and Needed Research." *Educational Researcher, 18*(3), 4-10.

Evertson, C. M., Emmer, E. T., Clements, B. S., Sanford, J. P., Worsham, M. E., & Williams, E. L. (1981). *Organizing and Managing the Elementary Classroom*. Austin, TX: Research and Development Center for Teacher Education, University of Texas.

Fisher, C. W., Filby, N., Marliave, R. S., Cahen, L. S., Dishaw, M. M., Moore, J. E., & Berliner, D. C. (1978). *Teaching Behaviors, Academic Learning Time and Student Achievement*. Final Report of Phase III-B. Beginning Teacher Evaluation Study. San Francisco: Far West Laboratory for Educational Research and Development.

Fisher, R., & Ury, W. (1981). *Getting to Yes*. New York: Penguin Books.

Fitzhenry, R. (Ed.). (1993). *The Harper Book of Quotations* (3rd ed.). NY: Harper Collins.

Flavell, J. H. (1977). *Cognitive Development*. Englewood Cliffs, NJ: Prentice-Hall.

Flavell, J. H. (1976a). "Metacognitive Aspects of Problem Solving." In L. B. Resnick (Ed.), *The Nature of Intelligence*. Hillsdale, NJ: Lawrence Erlbaum.

Flavell, J. H. (1976b). "Metacognition and Cognitive Monitoring: A New Area of Psychological Inquiry." *American Psychologist, 34*, 906-911.

Gagne, R. M. (1989). *Studies of Learning: 50 Years of Research*. Tallahassee, FL: Learning Systems Institute, Florida State University.

Gardner, H. (1983). *Frames of Mind: The Theory of Multiple Intelligence*. New York: Basic Books.

Gardner, H. (1993). *Multiple Intelligences: The Theory in Practice*. New York: Basic Books.

Gick, M. L., & Holyoak, K. J. (1980). "Analogical Problem Solving." *Cognitive Psychology, 12*, 306-355.

Gick, M. L., & Holyoak, K. J. (1983). "Schema Induction and Analogical Transfer." *Cognitive Psychology, 6*, 270-292.

Gilovich, T. (1991). *How We Know What Isn't So*. New York: Free Press.

Goleman, D. (1995). *Emotional Intelligence: Why It Can Matter More Than IQ*. New York: Bantam Books.

Goldman, J. L., Berquist, G. F., & Coleman, W. E. (1989). *The Rhetoric of Western Thought*. Dubuque, IA: Kendall/Hunt.

Good, T. L. (1982). "How Teachers' Expectations Affect Results." *American Education, 18*(10), 25-32.

Gordon, W. J. J. (1961). *Synectics*. NY: Harper & Row.

Gordon, W. J. J. (1971). "Architecture—The Making of Metaphors." *Main Currents in Modern Thought, 28*(1).

Gourley, T. J. (1981). "Adapting the Varsity Sports Model to Nonpsychomotor Gifted Students." *Gifted Child Quarterly, 25,* 164-166.

Gourley, T. J., & Micklus, C. S. (1982). *Problems, Problems, Problems. Discussion and Activities Designed to Enhance Creativity.* Glassboro, NJ: Creative Publications.

Grayson, D. A., & Martin, M. D. (1985). *Gender Expectations and Student Achievement: Participant Manual.* Downey, CA: Los Angeles County Office of Education.

Gregorc, A. (1983). *Student Learning Styles and Brain Behavior.* Reston, VA: NASSP (monograph).

Halpern, D. F. (1984). *Thought and Knowledge: An Introduction to Critical Thinking.* Hillsdale, NJ: Lawrence Erlbaum.

Hansen, J. (1992). "Literacy Portfolios: Helping Students Know Themselves." *Educational Leadership, 49*(8), 66-68.

Hanson, R. J., Silver, H. F., & Strong, R. W. (1986). *Teaching Styles and Strategies.* Moorestown, NJ: Hanson, Silver, Strong & Associates.

Harman, W., & Rheingold, H. (1984). *Higher Creativity: Liberating the Unconscious for Breakthrough Insights.* Los Angeles: Jeremy P. Tarcher.

Harrison, F. C. (Comp.). (1989). *Spirit of Leadership: Inspiring Quotations for Leaders.* Columbia, TN: Leadership Education and Development, Inc.

Hayes, J. R. (1981). *The Complete Problem Solver.* Philadelphia: Franklin Institute.

Healy, J. M. (1990). *Endangered Minds: Why Our Children Don't Think.* New York: Simon & Schuster.

Heimlich, J. E., & Pittelman, S. D. (1988). *Semantic Mapping: Classroom Applications.* Newark, DE: International Reading Association.

High Performance Systems, Inc. (1992). *Stella II: An Introduction to Systems Thinking.* Hanover, NH: Author.

Holland, J. H., Holyoak, K. J., Nisbett, R. E., & Thagard, P. R. (1987). *Induction: Processes of Inference, Learning and Discovery.* Cambridge, MA: MIT Press.

Hunter, M. (1969). *Teach More Faster!* El Segundo, CA: TIP Publications.

Hunter, M. (1976). *Improved Instruction: Take One Staff Development Meeting as Directed by Madeline Hunter.* El Segundo, CA: TIP Publications.

Hunter, M. (1982). *Mastery Teaching.* El Segundo, CA: TIP Publications.

Johnson, D., Johnson, R., & Holubec, E. (1994). *New Circles of Learning: Cooperation in the Classroom.* Alexandria, VA: Association for Supervision and Curriculum Development.

Johnson-Laird, P. N. (1983). *Mental Models.* Cambridge, MA: Harvard University Press.

Johnson-Laird, P. N. (1985). "Logical Thinking: Does It Occur in Daily Life?" In S. F. Chipman, J. W. Segal, & R. Glaser (Eds.), *Thinking and Learning Skills, Vol. 2: Research and Open Questions* (pp. 293-318). Hillsdale, NJ: Lawrence Erlbaum.

Jones, B. F., Amiran, M., & Katims, M. (1985). "Teaching Cognitive Strategies and Text Structures Within Language Arts Programs." In J. W. Segal, S. F. Chipman, & R. Glaser (Eds.), *Thinking and Learning Skills, Vol. 1: Relating Instruction to Research* (pp. 259-295). Hillsdale, NJ: Lawrence Erlbaum.

Joyce, B., & Weil, M. (1986). *Models of Teaching.* Englewood Cliffs, NJ: Prentice-Hall.

Kagan, S. (1994). *Cooperative Learning Structures* (Rev. Ed.). San Juan Capistrano, CA: Kagan Cooperative Learning.

Kauffman, Jr., D. L. (1980). *Systems One: An Introduction to Systems Thinking.* Minneapolis, MN: S. A. Carlton.

Kentucky Institute for Education Research, The. (1995). *An Independent Evaluation of the Kentucky Instructional Results Information System (KIRIS): Executive Summary.* Frankfort, KY: Author.

Kerman, S., Kimball, T., & Martin, M. (1980). *Teacher Expectations and Student Achievement.* Bloomington, IN: Phi Delta Kappa.

Kinneavy, J. L. (1991). "Rhetoric." In J. Flood, J. M. Jensen, D. Lapp, & J. R. Squire (Eds.), *Handbook of Research on Teaching the English Language Arts* (pp. 633-642). New York: Macmillan.

Klenk, V. (1983). *Understanding Symbolic Logic.* Englewood Cliffs, NJ: Prentice-Hall.

Lindsay, P. H., & Norman, D. A. (1977). *Human Information Processing.* New York: Academic Press.

Lipman, M., Sharp, A. M., & Oscanyan, F. S. (1980). *Philosophy in the Classroom.* Philadelphia: Temple University Press.

Markus, H., & Ruvulo, A. (1990). "Possible Selves: Personalized Representations of Goals." In L. Pervin (Ed.), *Goal Concepts in Psychology* (pp. 211-241). Hillsdale, NJ: Lawrence Erlbaum.

Markus, H., & Wurf, E. (1987). "The Dynamic Self-concept: A Social Psychological Perspective." *Annual Review of Psychology, 38,* 299-337.

Marzano, R. J. (1991). *Cultivating Thinking in English and the Language Arts.* Urbana, IL: National Council of Teachers of English.

Marzano, R. J. (1992). *A Different Kind of Classroom: Teaching with Dimensions of Learning.* Alexandria, VA: ASCD.

Marzano, R. J., & Arredondo, D. E. (1986). *Tactics for Thinking.* Alexandria, VA: ASCD.

Marzano, R. J., & Kendall, J. S. (1996). *A Comprehensive Guide to Designing Standards-Based Districts, Schools, and Classrooms.* Aurora, CO: McREL.

Marzano, R. J., & Marzano, J. S. (1988). *A Cluster Approach to Elementary Vocabulary Instruction.* Newark, DE: International Reading Association.

Marzano, R. J., Pickering, D. J., Arredondo, D. E., Blackburn, G. J., Brandt, R. S., & Moffett, C. A. (1992). *Implementing Dimensions of Learning.* Alexandria, VA: ASCD.

Marzano, R. J., Pickering, D. J., Arredondo, D. E., Blackburn, G. J., Brandt, R. S., Moffett, C. A., Paynter, D. E., Pollock, J. E., & Whisler, J. S. (1997). *Dimensions of Learning Trainer's Manual.* Aurora, CO: McREL.

Marzano, R. J., Pickering, D. J., & McTighe, J. (1993). *Assessing Student Outcomes: Performance Assessment Using the Dimensions of Learning.* Alexandria, VA: ASCD.

Maslow, A. H. (1968). *Toward a Psychology of Being.* New York: Van Nostrand Reinhold.

McCarthy, B. (1980). *The 4MAT System: Teaching to Learning Styles with Right/Left Mode Techniques.* Oak Brook, IL: Excel.

McCarthy, B. (1990). "Using the 4MAT System to Bring Learning Styles to Schools." *Education Leadership,* 48(2), 31-37.

McCombs, B. L., & Whisler, J. S. (1997). *The Learner-Centered Classroom and School.* San Francisco: Jossey-Bass.

Mervis, C. B. (1980). "Category Structure and the Development of Categorization." In R. J. Sprio, B. C. Bruce, & W. F. Brewer (Eds.), *Theoretical Issues in Reading Comprehension* (pp. 279-307). Hillsdale, NJ: Lawrence Erlbaum.

Moffett, J. (1968). *Teaching the Universe of Discourse.* Boston: Houghton Mifflin.

Mullis, I. V. S., Owen, E. H., & Phillips, G. W. (1990). *America's Challenge: Accelerating Academic Achievement (A Summary of Findings from 20 Years of NAEP).* Princeton, NJ: Educational Testing Service.

National Association of Secondary School Principals (NASSP). (1996). *Breaking Ranks: Changing an American Institution.* Reston, VA: Author.

Negin, G. (1987). *Inferential Reasoning for Teachers.* Dubuque, IA: Kendall/Hunt.

Newmann, F. M., Secado, W. G., & Wehlage, G. G. (1995). *A Guide to Authentic Instruction and Assessment: Vision, Standards and Scoring.* Madison, WI: Wisconsin Center for Educational Research, University of Wisconsin.

Nickerson, R. S., Perkins, D. N., & Smith, E. E. (1985). *The Teaching of Thinking.* Hillsdale, NJ: Lawrence Erlbaum.

Ogle, D. (1986). "K-W-L: A Teaching Model That Develops Active Reading of Expository Text," *The Reading Teacher 39,* 564-576.

Ortony, A. (1980). "Metaphor." In R. J. Spiro, B. C. Bruce, & W. F. Brewer (Eds.), *Theoretical Issues in Reading Comprehension.* Hillsdale, NJ: Lawrence Erlbaum.

Palincsar, A. S., & Brown, A. L. (1985). "Reciprocal Teaching: Activities to Promote Reading with Your Mind." In T. L. Harris & E. J. Cooper (Eds.), *Reading, Thinking and Concept Development: Strategies for the Classroom.* New York: College Board.

Palincsar, A. S., Ogle, D. C., Jones, B. F., & Carr, E. D. (1986). *Teaching Reading as Thinking* (Facilitator's Manual). Alexandria, VA: ASCD.

Paris, S. G., Lipson, M. Y., & Wixson, K. K. (1983). "Becoming a Strategic Reader." *Contemporary Educational Psychology,* 8(3), 293-316.

Paul, R. W. (1984). "Critical Thinking: Fundamental to Education for a Free Society." *Educational Leadership,* 42(1), 4-14.

Paul, R. W. (1987). "Critical Thinking and the Critical Person." In *Thinking: Report on Research.* Hillsdale, NJ: Lawrence Erlbaum.

Paul, R. (1990). *Critical Thinking: What Every Person Needs to Survive in a Rapidly Changing World*. Rohnert Park, CA: Center for Critical Thinking and Moral Critique, Sonoma State University.

Paul, R., Binker, A. J. A., & Charbonneau, M. (1986). *Critical Thinking Handbooks: K-3. A Guide for Remodeling Lesson Plans in Language Arts, Social Studies, and Science*. Rohnert Park, CA: Sonoma State University, Center for Critical Thinking and Moral Critique.

Paul, R., Binker, A. J. A., Martin, D., Vetrano, C., & Kreklau, H. (1989). *Critical Thinking Handbook: Grades 6-9*. Rohnert Park, CA: Center for Critical Thinking and Moral Critique.

Perkins, D. N. (1981). *The Mind's Best Work*. Cambridge, MA: Harvard University Press.

Perkins, D. N. (1984). "Creativity by Design." *Educational Leadership, 42*(1), 18-25.

Perkins, D. N. (1985). *Where Is Creativity?* Paper presented at University of Iowa Second Annual Humanities Symposium, Iowa City, IA.

Perkins, D. N. (1986). *Knowledge as Design*. Hillsdale, NJ: Lawrence Erlbaum.

Perkins, D. N., Allen, R., & Hafner, J. (1983). "Difficulties in Everyday Reasoning." In W. Maxwell (Ed.), *Thinking: The Expanding Frontier*. Philadelphia: Franklin Institute Press.

Peters, T. J., & Austin, N. K. (1985). *A Passion for Excellence: The Leadership Difference*. New York: Random House.

Peters, T. J., & Waterman, R. H. (1982). *In Search of Excellence*. New York: Harper & Row.

Presseisen, B. Z. (1987). *Thinking Skills Throughout the Curriculum*. Bloomington, IN: Phi Lamda Theta.

Pressley, M., & Levin, J. R. (Eds.). (1983a). *Cognitive Strategy Research: Educational Applications*. New York: Springer-Verlag.

Pressley, M., & Levin, J. R. (1983b). *Cognitive Strategy Research: Psychological Foundations*. New York: Springer-Verlag.

Purkey, W. (1978). *Inviting School Success*. Belmont, CA: Wadsworth.

Reeve, R., Palincsar, A., & Brown, A. L. (1987). "Everyday and Academic Thinking: Implications for Learning and Problem Solving." *Journal of Curriculum Studies, 19*(2).

Resnick, L. B. (1987). *Education and Learning to Think*. Washington, DC: National Academy Press.

Richardson, A. (1983). "Images, Definitions and Types." In A. A. Sheikh (Ed.), *Imagery: Current Theory, Research, and Application*. New York: John Wiley & Sons.

Robinson, F. P. (1961). *Effective Study* (Rev. Ed.). New York: Harper & Row.

Rosenshine, B. (1983). "Teaching Functions in Instructional Programs." *Elementary School Journal, 83*(4), 335-351.

Rosenthal, R., & Jacobson, L. (1968). *Pygmalion in the Classroom: Teacher Expectation and Pupils' Intellectual Development*. New York: Holt, Rinehart & Winston.

Ross, J., & Lawrence, K. A. (1968). "Some Observations on Memory Artifice." *Psychonomic Science, 13,* 107-108.

Rowe, M. (1974). "Wait-time and Rewards as Instructional Variables, Their Influence on Language, Logic and Fate Control. Part 1 Wait-time." *Journal of Research in Science Teaching, 11,* 81-94.

Sadker, M., & Sadker, D. (1994). *Failing at Fairness: How America's School Cheat Girls*. New York: Macmillan.

Schank, R. C., & Abelson, R. (1977). *Scripts, Plans, Goals and Understanding*. Hillsdale, NJ: Lawrence Erlbaum.

Schunk, D. H. (1990). "Goal Setting and Self-efficacy During Self-regulated Learning." *Educational Psychologist, 25*(1), 71-86.

Shaw, V. (1992). *Building Community in the Classroom*. San Juan Capistrano, CA: Kagan Cooperative.

Shenkman, R. (1988). *Legends, Lies, & Cherished Myths of American History*. New York: Morrow & Company.

Slavin, R. (1983). *Cooperative Learning*. New York: Longman.

Smith, E. E., & Medin, D. L. (1981). *Categories and Concepts*. Cambridge, MA: Harvard University Press.

Smuin, S. (1978). *Turn-ons: 185 Strategies for the Secondary Classroom*. Belmont, CA: David S. Lake Publishers.

Stahl, R. J. (1985). "Cognitive Information Processes and Processing Within a Uniprocess Superstructure/Microstructure Framework: A Practical Information-based Model." Unpublished manuscript, Tucson: University of Arizona.

Stiggins, R. J. (1994). *Student-Centered Classroom Assessment*. New York: Merrill.

Strong, R., Silver, H. F., & Robinson, A. (1995). "What Do Students Want?" *Educational Leadership 53*(1), 8-12.

Suhor, C. (1984). "Toward a Semiotics-based Curriculum." *Journal of Curriculum Studies, 16,* 247-257.

Taba, H. (1967). *Teacher's Handbook for Elementary Social Studies*. Reading, MA: Addison-Wesley.

Toulmin, S. (1958). *The Uses of Argument*. Cambridge, MA: Cambridge University Press.

Toulmin, S., Rieke, R., & Janik, A. (1981). *An Introduction to Reasoning*. New York: Macmillan.

Turner, A., & Greene, E. (1977). *The Construction of a Propositional Text Base*. Boulder, CO: Institute for the Study of Intellectual Behavior, The University of Colorado at Boulder.

Tweney, R. D. (1980). *Scientific Thinking: New Possibilities for Enhancing Education*. Paper presented at the Wingspread Conference on Thinking, Racine, WI.

Tweney, R. D., Doherty, M. E., & Mynatt, C. R. (1981). *On Scientific Thinking*. New York: Columbia University Press.

van Dijk, T. A. (1980). *Macrostructures*. Hillsdale, NJ: Lawrence Erlbaum.

von Oech, R. (1983). *A Whack on the Side of the Head*. New York: Warner Books.

Wales, C. E., & Nardi, A. H. (1985). "Teaching Decision-making: What to Teach and How to Teach it." In A. L. Costa (Ed.), *Developing Minds: A Resource Book for Teaching Thinking*. Alexandria, VA: ASCD.

Wason, P. C., & Johnson-Laird, P. N. (1972). *Psychology of Reasoning: Structure and Content*. Cambridge, MA: Harvard University Press.

Whisler, J. S., & Marzano, R. J. (1988). *Dare to Imagine: An Olympian's Technology*. Aurora, CO: McREL.

Whisler, J. S., & McCombs, B. L. (1992). *Middle School Advisement Program*. Aurora, CO: McREL Institute.

White, B. Y. (1983). "Sources of Difficulty in Understanding Newtonian Dynamics." *Cognitive Science, 7*, 41-65.

Wlodkowski, A., & Ginsberg, M. (1995). *Diversity and Motivation: Culturally Responsive Teaching*. San Francisco: Jossey-Bass.

Wurman, R. S. (1989). *Information Anxiety*. New York: Bantam Books.

Yussen, S. R. (Ed.). (1985). *The Growth of Reflection in Children*. New York: Academic Press.

Index

Limit-pushing, as habit of mind, 285–286
Link strategy, used with symbols and substitutes, 75–76

Macroprocesses, and procedural knowledge, 49
Massed practice, for new skills, 102–103, 103f
Mental habits. *See* Habits of Mind (Dimension 5)
Mental rehearsal, of new skill or process, 96
Mind, habits of. *See* Habits of Mind (Dimension 5)
Mini-lessons, during workshop classes, 323–324
Misinformation, as error in thinking, 175–176
Mnemonics, and information storage, 80
Monitoring of thinking, as habit of mind, 290–291
Movement, physical, use of in classroom, 23

Negative self-talk, student use of, 33
New information
    advance organizer questions for, 68–69
    student discovery of, 56–58
Nonexamples vs. examples, 57
Note-taking strategies, using graphic representations, 70, 70f
Number/key word method, of information storage, 77–79
Number/picture method, of information storage, 79

Observation, by teachers, as assessment technique, 314
Open mind, maintenance of, as habit of mind, 277–279

Perceptions and Attitudes. *See* Attitudes and Perceptions
    (Dimension 1)
Performance levels, standards of, 36, 36f
Performance tasks, as assessment technique, 312, 313f
Perseverance, as habit of mind, 284–285
Personality, appeal through, as persuasion technique, 164
Perspective examination matrix, 181, 182f
Perspectives, analyzing. *See* Analyzing perspectives, as
    complex reasoning process
Physical movement, use of in classroom, 23
Physical representations of information, 71, 71f
Pictographic representations of information, 71, 71f
Planning. *See also* Unit planning
    models for, 306–309
Planning appropriately, as habit of mind, 291–293
Poisoning the well, as example of attack in argument, 174
Portfolios, as assessment technique, 313
Position-taking, as habit of mind, 281–282
Positive reinforcement
    and habits of mind, 269–270
    variation of, in response to correct responses, 19–20
Positive response, to incorrect responses, 19

Positive self-talk, student use of, 33
Practice schedules, for new skills, 102–103, 103f
Predicting, and reciprocal teaching strategy, 59–60
Presentation classes
    instructional techniques for, 322–323
    integrated with workshop classes, 324–327, 325f–326f
Principles/generalizations, as declarative knowledge, 47–48
    advance organizer questions for, 69
    graphic organizer for, 65, 68f
Problem solving, as complex reasoning process, 191, 205–213
    classroom examples of, 213
    critical aspects of, 209–210
    graphic organizers for, 210, 211f
    model for, 207–208
    opportunities to practice, 208–209
    teacher- and student-structured tasks for, 211–213
Procedural knowledge, 43–45, 49, 192
    acquisition and integration of, 49–50, 50f, 93–105
        classroom examples of, 104–105
        and content to be covered, 304
        summary of strategies for, 111
        unit planning for, 106–108
    construction of models for, 93–96
    internalization of, 101–103
    rubric for assessing, 315f
    shaping of, 97–100
    with standards and benchmarks, 107, 110f
    without standards and benchmarks, 107, 109f
Procedures and rules, in classroom, and sense of comfort
    and order, 24–25, 25f
Process/cause-effect relationships, as declarative
    knowledge, 47
    advance organizer questions for, 69
    graphic organizer for, 64
Process observers, for habits of mind, 269
Progress habits, for habits of mind, 270, 270f
Project focus, of teacher-student conferences, 327
Projective investigation, 235–236
    classroom examples of, 244–245
Pushing limits, as habit of mind, 285–286

Questioning, and reciprocal teaching strategy, 59
Questions, advance, for organizing new information, 68–69

Reason, appeal through, as persuasion technique, 164–165
Reasoning
    deductive. *See* Deductive reasoning
    inductive. *See* Inductive reasoning
Reasoning processes. *See* Complex reasoning processes,
    development of

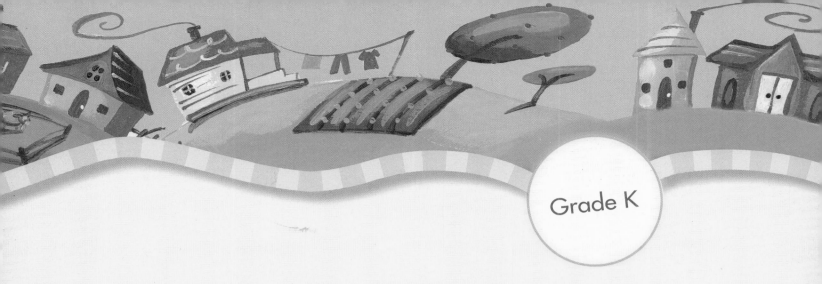

Grade K

First Stop
on Reading Street

PEARSON

Glenview, Illinois • Boston, Massachusetts • Chandler, Arizona
Shoreview, Minnesota • Upper Saddle River, New Jersey

ISBN-13: 978-0-328-50444-2
ISBN-10:   0-328-50444-0

2 3 4 5 6 7 8 9 10 V064 14 13 12 11 10
CC1

Any Path, Any Pace

"Welcome to
Reading Street!
Bienvenidos too."

PEARSON

Find Your Place on Reading Street!

Who leads the way on

YOU ARE HERE!

My Teaching Library
The ultimate find-your-place case! It stores all your Teacher's Editions in one space.

First Stop on Reading Street
It's your how-to guide, coach, and roadmap. Find your place on *Reading Street*.

- Research into Practice
- Teacher Resources
- Professional Development
- Pacing Charts
- Reteach Lessons (and more!)

"Start here, go there, you see a chicken anywhere?"

Print • Online • CD/DVD • School to Home • English/Spanish

Reading Street?

Teachers Do.

How can something be slim and chunky?

The Teacher's Edition is slim, so it won't weigh you down. It's chunky, because it "chunks" the curriculum in manageable, three-week increments.

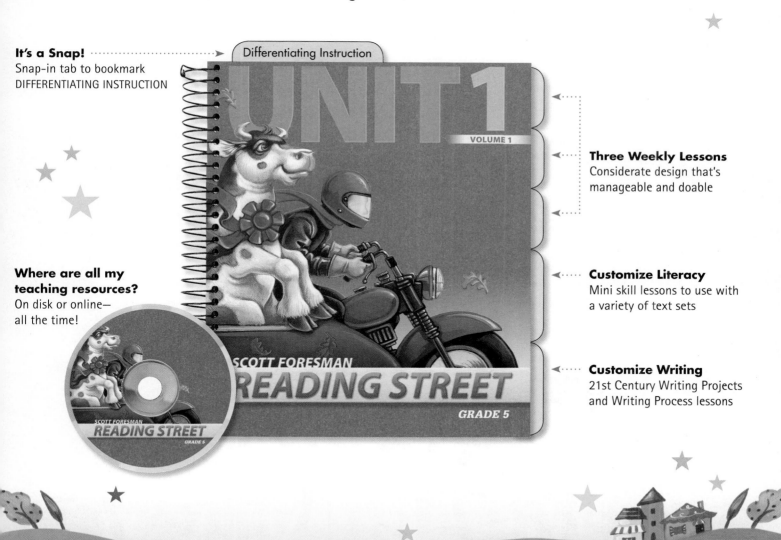

It's a Snap!
Snap-in tab to bookmark
DIFFERENTIATING INSTRUCTION

Where are all my teaching resources?
On disk or online—
all the time!

Three Weekly Lessons
Considerate design that's manageable and doable

Customize Literacy
Mini skill lessons to use with a variety of text sets

Customize Writing
21st Century Writing Projects and Writing Process lessons

Any Path, Any Pace

Who thrives on

All Children.

Every Child.

Every Single One.

"Hey, what about chickens? You didn't mention chickens!"

PEARSON

SCOTT FORESMAN

Print • Online • CD/DVD • School to Home • English/Spanish

Reading Street?

Let's read it and write it and think it and do it!

Let's Go Digital
See It! Hear It! Do It!

Let's Write
Weekly Writing

Let's Learn
Application and Transfer

SCOTT FORESMAN
READING STREET
1ST

Let's Listen
Phonemic Awareness

Let's Talk
Oral Vocabulary/ Amazing Words

Let's Envision
Visual Skills and Strategies

Let's Think
Personalized Reading Coach

"Oh, Chicky wicky, don't be so picky."

Any Path, Any Pace

What makes Reading Street

"A sweet, humble Cow. Now that's a WOW! So long, Chicky."

A day, a week, a unit, and a year!
Connect and scaffold learning

On *Reading Street* everything is neat. The unit concepts connect the curriculum from start to finish, scaffolding children's prior knowledge. Sustained concept and language development accelerates children's ability to comprehend, discuss, and write about what they're reading. Neat? *Sweeeeet.*

"Build your unit around one idea with power, an idea that helps learners make sense of otherwise isolated content."

Grant Wiggins
Coauthor with Jay McTighe of
Understanding by Design
Exclusive Pearson Consulting Author

PEARSON Rules!

strong?

Sustained Concept and Language Development.

Big Ideas
Consider
big questions

Language
Hear and use
sophisticated
language

Envision It
Envision new ways
of thinking

**Unit
Concept**

Team Talk
Share information
every day

Writing
Write to share what
you know

**Science and
Social Studies**
Transfer concepts
and language to
content areas

Text Sets
Read related
text sets

Print • Online • CD/DVD • School to Home • English/Spanish   Any Path, Any Pace

What makes Reading Street

PRIORITY SKILL	SUCCESS PREDICTOR
PHONEMIC AWARENESS	Blending and Segmenting
PHONICS	Word Reading
FLUENCY	Words Correct per Minute
VOCABULARY	Word Knowledge
COMPREHENSION	Retelling

2 **Don't Wait Until Friday!**
Prevent misunderstandings
right away with on-the-spot
reteaching and prescriptions.

1 **Monitor Progress with Success Predictors**
Check students' progress of each priority skill with
research-based predictors of reading success.

Print • Online • CD/DVD • School to Home • English/Spanish

work?

The Right Skills at the Right Time.

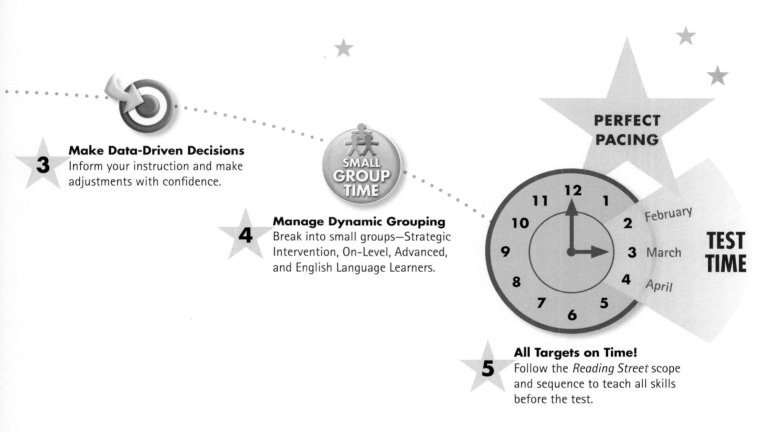

3 **Make Data-Driven Decisions**
Inform your instruction and make adjustments with confidence.

SMALL GROUP TIME

4 **Manage Dynamic Grouping**
Break into small groups—Strategic Intervention, On-Level, Advanced, and English Language Learners.

PERFECT PACING

February
March
April

TEST TIME

5 **All Targets on Time!**
Follow the *Reading Street* scope and sequence to teach all skills before the test.

"Sure a cow can talk the talk, but can a cow ride a bike?"

PEARSON   SCOTT FORESMAN

Any Path, Any Pace

What do readers read

Funny Stories   Myths   **Caldecott Winners**   Classic Literature

Multicultural Literature   E-mails   Big Books

Online Directories   Trucktown Readers   **Adventure Stories**

Nonfiction   Online Sources   Informational Text

Little Big Books   Concept Literacy Readers   Biographies

Narrative Fiction   Decodable Readers   Newbery Winners

Poetry   **Trade Books**   **Mysteries**   Realistic Fiction

English Language Development Readers   Historical Fiction   **Blogs**

Legends   Recipes   Search Engines   News Stories

Pourquoi Tales   Fables   Tall Tales   **Fantasy Stories**

Nursery Rhymes   Web Sites   Drama   Trickster Tales

"I prefer doggy stories over chicky stories."

Print • Online • CD/DVD • School to Home • English/Spanish

on Reading Street?

Kindergarten Literature Selections

"I like horse stories. Say, Chicky,
do you have any spare hay?"

Any Path, Any Pace

What do writers write

Narrative Poems Invitations **Research Papers**

Blogs Classroom Newsletters Realistic Stories

Adventure Stories Compare and Contrast Essays Lists

Friendly Letters Online Journals Online Forums

Persuasive Essays Formal Letters Steps in a Process

Expository Compositions Podcasts Captions

Personal Narratives Multi-paragraph Essays

Drama Scenes E-mail Pen Pals

Fiction Peer Revisions Responses to Prompts

"A writer notices things. Now where's that chicken?"

Print • Online • CD/DVD • School to Home • English/Spanish

on Reading Street?

Customize Your Writing

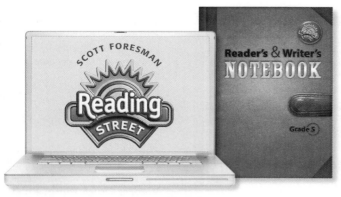

21st Century Writing Projects
The writing section in your Teacher's Edition also provides collaborative writing projects that use the Internet to develop new literacies. Go digital! You choose.

Writing Process
Turn to the writing tab in your Teacher's Edition. A writing process lesson helps children learn the process of writing. Use as a Writing Workshop or customize to your needs.

The Internet Guy
Donald Leu, Ph.D.

The Write Guy
Jeff Anderson, M.Ed.

"Chicken stories are for the birds. I'll write about acorns."

Any Path, Any Pace

Who said so?

The Leading Researchers,

Program Authors

Peter Afflerbach, Ph.D.
Professor
Department of Curriculum
and Instruction
University of Maryland
at College Park

Camille L. Z. Blachowicz, Ph.D.
Professor of Education
National-Louis University

Candy Dawson Boyd, Ph.D.
Professor
School of Education
Saint Mary's College of California

Elena Izquierdo, Ph.D.
Associate Professor
University of Texas at El Paso

Connie Juel, Ph.D.
Professor of Education
School of Education
Stanford University

Edward J. Kame'enui, Ph.D.
*Dean-Knight Professor of
Education and Director*
Institute for the Development of
Educational Achievement and
the Center on Teaching and Learning
College of Education
University of Oregon

Donald J. Leu, Ph.D.
*John and Maria Neag Endowed
Chair in Literacy and Technology
Director, The New Literacies
Research Lab*
University of Connecticut

Jeanne R. Paratore, Ed.D.
Associate Professor of Education
Department of Literacy and
Language Development
Boston University

P. David Pearson, Ph.D.
Professor and Dean
Graduate School of Education
University of California, Berkeley

Sam L. Sebesta, Ed.D.
Professor Emeritus
College of Education
University of Washington, Seattle

Deborah Simmons, Ph.D.
Professor
College of Education and
Human Development
Texas A&M University

Alfred W. Tatum, Ph.D.
*Associate Professor and Director
of the UIC Reading Clinic*
University of Illinois at Chicago

Sharon Vaughn, Ph.D.
*H. E. Hartfelder/Southland
Corporation Regents Professor
Director, Meadows Center for
Preventing Educational Risk*
University of Texas

Susan Watts Taffe, Ph.D.
Associate Professor in Literacy
Division of Teacher Education
University of Cincinnati

Karen Kring Wixson, Ph.D.
Professor of Education
University of Michigan

Consulting Authors

Jeff Anderson, M.Ed.
Author and Consultant
San Antonio, Texas

Jim Cummins, Ph.D.
Professor
Department of Curriculum,
Teaching and Learning
University of Toronto

Lily Wong Fillmore, Ph.D.
Professor Emerita
Graduate School of Education
University of California, Berkeley

Georgia Earnest García, Ph.D.
Professor
Language and Literacy Division
Department of Curriculum
and Instruction
University of Illinois at
Urbana-Champaign

George A. González, Ph.D.
Professor (Retired)
School of Education
University of Texas-Pan American,
Edinburg

Valerie Ooka Pang, Ph.D.
Professor
School of Teacher Education
San Diego State University

Sally M. Reis, Ph.D.
*Board of Trustees Distinguished
Professor*
Department of Educational
Psychology
University of Connecticut

Jon Scieszka, M.F.A.
*Children's Book Author
Founder of GUYS READ
Named First National Ambassador
for Young People's Literature 2008*

Grant Wiggins, Ed.D.
Educational Consultant
Authentic Education
Concept Development

Lee Wright, M.Ed.
Pearland, Texas

xvi

Practitioners, and Authors.

Consultant

Sharroky Hollie, Ph.D.
Assistant Professor
California State University
Dominguez Hills, CA

Teacher Reviewers

Dr. Bettyann Brugger
*Educational Support Coordinator—
Reading Office*
Milwaukee Public Schools
Milwaukee, WI

Kathleen Burke
K–12 Reading Coordinator
Peoria Public Schools, Peoria, IL

Darci Burns, M.S.Ed.
University of Oregon

Bridget Cantrell
District Intervention Specialist
Blackburn Elementary School
Independence, MO

**Tahira DuPree Chase,
M.A., M.S.Ed.**
*Administrator of Elementary
English Language Arts*
Mount Vernon City School District
Mount Vernon, NY

Michele Conner
Director, Elementary Education
Aiken County School District
Aiken, SC

Georgia Coulombe
*K–6 Regional Trainer/
Literacy Specialist*
Regional Center for Training and
Learning (RCTL), Reno, NV

Kelly Dalmas
Third Grade Teacher
Avery's Creek Elementary, Arden, NC

Seely Dillard
First Grade Teacher
Laurel Hill Primary School
Mt. Pleasant, SC

Jodi Dodds-Kinner
Director of Elementary Reading
Chicago Public Schools, Chicago, IL

Dr. Ann Wild Evenson
District Instructional Coach
Osseo Area Schools, Maple Grove, MN

Stephanie Fascitelli
Principal
Apache Elementary, Albuquerque
Public Schools, Albuquerque, NM

Alice Franklin
*Elementary Coordinator, Language
Arts & Reading*
Spokane Public Schools, Spokane, WA

Laureen Fromberg
Assistant Principal
PS 100, Queens, NY

Kimberly Gibson
First Grade Teacher
Edgar B. Davis Community School
Brockton, MA

Kristen Gray
Lead Teacher
A.T. Allen Elementary School
Concord, NC

Mary Ellen Hazen
State Pre-K Teacher
Rockford Public Schools #205
Rockford, IL

Patrick M. Johnson
Elementary Instructional Director
Seattle Public Schools, Seattle, WA

Theresa Jaramillo Jones
Principal
Highland Elementary School
Las Cruces, NM

Sophie Kowzun
*Program Supervisor, Reading/
Language Arts, PreK-5*
Montgomery County Public Schools
Rockville, MD

David W. Matthews
Sixth Grade Teacher
Easton Area Middle School
Easton, PA

Ana Nuncio
Editor and Independent Publisher
Salem, MA

Joseph Peila
Principal
Chappell Elementary School
Chicago, IL

Ivana Reimer
Literacy Coordinator
PS 100, Queens, NY

Sally Riley
Curriculum Coordinator
Rochester Public Schools
Rochester, NH

Dyan M. Smiley
*English Language Arts Program
Director, Grades K-5*
Boston Public Schools, Literacy
Department, Boston, MA

Michael J. Swiatowiec
Lead Literacy Teacher
Graham Elementary School
Chicago, IL

Dr. Helen Taylor
Director of Reading/English Education
Portsmouth City Public Schools
Portsmouth, VA

Carol Thompson
Teaching and Learning Coach
Independence School District
Independence, MO

Erinn Zeitlin
Kindergarten Teacher
Carderock Springs Elementary School
Bethesda, MD

Any Path, Any Pace

Any Path, Any Pace

Find Your Place on Reading Street!

"On Reading Street, you can do anything and go anywhere."

PEARSON

SCOTT FORESMAN

"Tell me and I forget. Teach me and I remember. Involve me and I learn."

—Benjamin Franklin

Welcome! You've arrived on Reading Street

You're about to take your class on a rich instructional journey. As children explore the world that reading opens to them, they will look to you for guidance and support. You, as their teacher, can make the difference in their literacy experience. To help you, *Scott Foresman Reading Street* has paved the way with solid, research-based instruction. This support will be your clear path to success.

Now it's time to discover what you can expect in the materials and professional support that *Reading Street* offers. It's time to make your *First Stop on Reading Street!*

First Stop on
Reading Street: Kindergarten

From Our Authors...

Dear Kindergarten Teacher,

Thank you for teaching kindergarten. Please know that my words are sincere and are based on a career's worth of experiences teaching kindergarten children, observing kindergarten instruction, and designing kindergarten curriculum. And designing literacy materials is by far the simplest of these three! I have been privileged to visit extraordinary kindergarten classrooms where teachers like you epitomize the talents of orchestra conductors, the empathy of psychologists, the encouragement of life coaches, the acumen of event coordinators, and the stamina of Olympic athletes. On top of that, you are charged with what I consider the all-important professional responsibility of *teaching children to read.* When I leave kindergarten classrooms, I am thankful; I am astonished; I am exhausted.

Have you ever considered how astute Robert Fulghum was when he authored *All I Really Need to Know I Learned in Kindergarten?* When he offered the basic principles of sharing, being kind to one another, always flushing, and cleaning up after yourself, he indeed captured characteristics and habits that would serve people for a lifetime. Perhaps there is one more essay he should add as a postscript to his best-seller: *Develop a love and capacity for the written word.* After all, kindergarten represents the critical window of opportunity where the world of print is formally introduced to most children and when learning trajectories are largely established. Perhaps Fulghum was not so far off in his estimation of the importance of kindergarten.

Deborah Simmons, Ph.D.

...you have accepted the mission of transforming lives—

As a kindergarten teacher, you have accepted the mission of transforming lives—of changing children from nonreaders to readers. As children enter your classroom door, they come with a range of experiences and knowledge. Some have the benefit of hundreds of hours of shared book reading, while others have never turned the pages of a book. The opportunity that lies in the 180 instructional days in the kindergarten year (give or take one for the field trip to the pumpkin patch and another for Bring-Your-Parent-to-School Day) is to teach children "as quickly as you can but as slowly as you must." I wish I knew the author of that instructional mantra, as I would readily credit that teacher for such sage advice. For some children, your role will be to enrich and extend. For others, your job will be to develop and accelerate. Fortunately, there are established language-arts standards that serve as benchmarks and programs to help you.

For example, at the end of kindergarten, children should:

- recognize, name, and write all letters of the alphabet;

- blend and segment the phonemes in words;

- read simple one-syllable words and common high-frequency words;

- use and expand vocabulary as they describe common objects and events;

- retell familiar stories and identify characters, settings, and important events in narrative text;

- ask and answer questions about informational text;

- spell and write consonant-vowel-consonant words.

Literacy demands are higher today than ever before...

This progressive level of literacy development reflects the higher demands for literacy necessary for today's informational and technological society. Literacy demands are higher today than ever before, and development formally begins in kindergarten.

Although you must assume the roles of conductor, counselor, and coach, you need not also serve as the architect of materials and curriculum. For years as a speech/language specialist, I pieced and pulled together materials, never quite sure whether I had enough of some parts or too much of others. Fortunately, today we have programs that focus on the construction of tasks, activities, and text, enabling you to focus on instruction, to "breathe life" into the curriculum, personalizing and enabling potential.

In closing, thank you for your efforts, your smarts, your best intentions, and your life-changing ability as a teacher of kindergarten children. I wish you much success and joy in your professional career.

With every best wish,

Deborah Simmons

Deborah Simmons, Ph.D.
Professor, Texas A&M University

Research into Practice on Reading Street

Section 1 is your tour of the daily lessons on
Scott Foresman Reading Street. When you make each of these stops, your kindergarten instruction is successful.

- Get Ready to Read

- Read and Comprehend

- Language Arts

- Wrap Up Your Day

Along the way, you'll learn more about Oral Language, Phonemic Awareness, and other research building blocks of literacy. You'll discover that every activity and routine in the daily lesson is there because research has shown that it's important for your teaching practice.

This Research into Practice section presents a representative sample of lesson pages for one week of instruction. Where pages from the Teacher's Edition are not shown for a given week, those pages are listed with references to research supporting the instruction.

The Building Blocks of Research in Literacy

Oral Language

Phonemic Awareness

Phonics

Decodable Text

Fluency

Oral Vocabulary

Language Arts

Reading Vocabulary

Comprehension

Academic Vocabulary

Informational Text

21st Century Skills

Writing

Differentiated Instruction

English Language Learners

Success Predictors

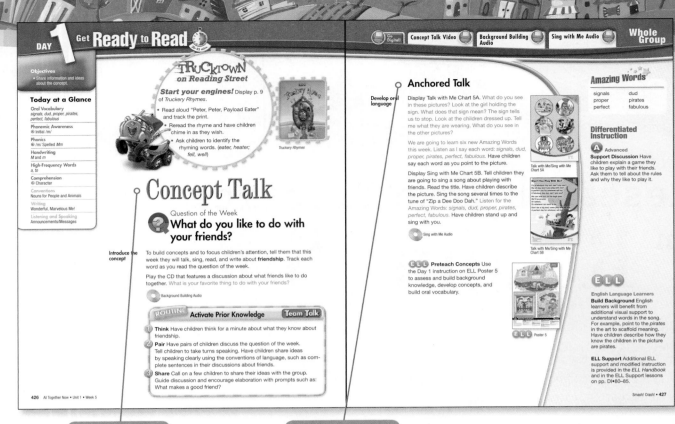

Objectives
• Share information and ideas about the concept.

Today at a Glance

Oral Vocabulary
signals, dud, proper, pirates, perfect, fabulous

Phonemic Awareness
⊕ Initial /m/

Phonics
⊕ /m/ Spelled Mm

Handwriting
M and m

High-Frequency Words
a, to

Comprehension
⊕ Character

Conventions
Nouns for People and Animals

Writing
Wonderful, Marvelous Me!

Listening and Speaking
Announcements/Messages

TRUCKTOWN on Reading Street

Start your engines! Display p. 9 of Truckery Rhymes.

• Read aloud "Peter, Peter, Payload Eater" and track the print.
• Reread the rhyme and have children chime in as they wish.
• Ask children to identify the rhyming words. (eater, heater; fell, well)

Truckery Rhymes

Concept Talk

Question of the Week

What do you like to do with your friends?

Introduce the concept! To build concepts and to focus children's attention, tell them that this week they will talk, sing, read, and write about **friendship**. Track each word as you read the question of the week.

Play the CD that features a discussion about what friends like to do together. What is your favorite thing to do with your friends?

Background Building Audio

ROUTINE Activate Prior Knowledge | Team Talk

1. **Think** Have children think for a minute about what they know about friendship.
2. **Pair** Have pairs of children discuss the question of the week. Tell children to take turns speaking. Have children share ideas by speaking clearly using the conventions of language, such as complete sentences in their discussions about friends.
3. **Share** Call on a few children to share their ideas with the group. Guide discussion and encourage elaboration with prompts such as: What makes a good friend?

426 All Together Now • Unit 1 • Week 5

Anchored Talk

Develop oral language

Display Talk with Me Chart 5A. What do you see in these pictures? Look at the girl holding the sign. What does that sign mean? The sign tells us to stop. Look at the children dressed up. Tell me what they are wearing. What do you see in the other pictures?

We are going to learn six new Amazing Words this week. Listen as I say each word: signals, dud, proper, pirates, perfect, fabulous. Have children say each word as you point to the picture.

Display Sing with Me Chart 5B. Tell children they are going to sing a song about playing with friends. Read the title. Have children describe the picture. Sing the song several times to the tune of "Zip a Dee Doo Dah." Listen for the Amazing Words: signals, dud, proper, pirates, perfect, fabulous. Have children stand up and sing with you.

Sing with Me Audio

Talk with Me/Sing with Me Chart 5A

Talk with Me/Sing with Me Chart 5B

ELL Preteach Concepts Use the Day 1 instruction on ELL Poster 5 to assess and build background knowledge, develop concepts, and build oral vocabulary.

ELL Poster 5

Amazing Words

signals   dud
proper   pirates
perfect   fabulous

Differentiated Instruction

Ⓐ Advanced

Support Discussion Have children explain a game they like to play with their friends. Ask them to tell about the rules and why they like to play it.

ELL

English Language Learners
Build Background English learners will benefit from additional visual support to understand words in the song. For example, point to the pirates in the art to scaffold meaning. Have children describe how they know the children in the picture are pirates.

ELL Support Additional ELL support and modified instruction is provided in the ELL Handbook and in the ELL Support lessons on pp. DI•80–85.

Smash! Crash! • 427

····· ORAL LANGUAGE ·····

In Reading Street

Concept Talk A brief, whole-class, rich, oral language experience about the Question of the Week guides children to activate prior knowledge and develop new knowledge and understanding of the unit concept.

Because Research Says

▶ Linking of previous knowledge and experience to new material is a crucial part of the researching and learning process and affirms the importance of conversation rather than silence in young children's learning.
—(Wray and Lewis, 1996)

▶ Text discussions should go beyond answering comprehension questions. Discussing text with students requires that teachers understand that meaning is not in text per se, but is to be found in the text and the experiences the reader brings to it. —(Tatum, 2005)

····· ORAL LANGUAGE ·····

In Reading Street

Anchored Talk Multiple approaches help to activate prior knowledge build background for the concept of the week. On Day 1, children are introduced to a set of conceptually related Amazing Words through pictures found on the Talk With Me Chart. A Sing With Me Audio CD provides songs that children sing using the Amazing Words.

Because Research Says

▶ For optimum learning to occur, children should think about what they already know about a topic and gather new information to facilitate their understanding of new ideas that will be encountered in the new text. —(Duke and Pearson, 2002)

Objectives
- Listen initial /m/.
- Identify words with initial /m/.
- Discriminate words with initial /m/.
- Segment words into syllables.

Check Phonemic Awareness
SUCCESS PREDICTOR

My Skills Buddy, pp. 92–93

○ **Phonemic Awareness**
Initial /m/

Introduce
Today we will learn a new sound. Listen carefully: /m/ /m/ /m/. Say it with me: /m/ /m/ /m/. Display the *moon* Picture Card. *Moon* begins with /m/ /m/ /m/, *moon*. What sound does *moon* begin with? Repeat the routine using the *mitten, moose, man,* and *mug* Picture Cards.

Model
Have children look at the picture on pp. 92–93 of *My Skills Buddy*. Tell them that they will be listening for a new sound—/m/. I see a *marching* band. What sound do you hear at the beginning of *marching*? I hear /m/ at the beginning of *marching*. The first sound in *marching* is /m/. What other things do you see that begin with that sound?

Picture Card

Guide practice
As children name example words from the picture, guide them in stating that /m/ is the beginning sound. Discuss with children some of the bulleted items on p. 92 of *My Skills Buddy*. Save the other bulleted items for discussion on Day 2.

Corrective feedback
If... children have difficulty naming words with /m/, then... say *marching* again, stretching the beginning sound—/m/ /m/ /m/, *marching*.

428 All Together Now • Unit 1 • Week 5

Discriminate sounds
Display the *moon* and *cat* Picture Cards. This is the *moon*. This is a *cat*. *Moon* begins with /m/. *Cat* begins with /k/. Does *cat* begin with the same sound as *moon*? Say the words and sounds with me: *moon*, /m/; *cat*, /k/. No, *moon* and *cat* do not begin with the same sound. Continue the activity with the following pairs of Picture Cards: *moose, pan; man, map; fox, mask; mitten, goose; mug, mop.*

Listen as I say a word. If the word begins with /m/, pat your head. If it does not begin with /m/, keep your hands in your lap. Listen carefully: *melt* (pat head), *bird* (hands in lap), *park* (hands in lap), *make* (pat head). Continue with the following words: *mud, pen, mitt, mad, pig, ten, mug, dog, mat.*

Corrective feedback
If... children cannot discriminate initial /m/, then... have them enunciate /m/ as they say *moon*.

When you say the first sound in *moon*, you press your lips together. Say /m/ with me: /m/ /m/ /m/. Are your lips together? Say *moon* with me: *moon*. Repeat the activity with *make, mat,* and *mug*.

Segment
Say the word *moon* as you clap one time. How many parts, or syllables, does the word *moon* have? How many claps do you hear? Say the word *mountain* as you clap two times. Repeat the questions. Then have children say each word and clap the number of syllables with you. Continue with the words *mug, music, mother, man, museum,* and *mop.*

MONITOR PROGRESS ○ **Check Phonemic Awareness** Words with Initial /m/

Say *bear* and *mouse*. Have children identify the word that begins with /m/. Continue with *seal, mug; mother, top; monster, pillow; house, map.*

If... children cannot discriminate /m/ words, then... use the small-group Strategic Intervention lesson, p. DI•69, to reteach /m/.

Day 1 Check Phonemic Awareness	Day 2 Check Sound-Spelling/ Retelling	Day 3 Check Word Reading	Day 4 Check Letter Recognition	Day 5 Check Oral Vocabulary

Differentiated Instruction

SI **Strategic Intervention**
Identify /m/ Words Have children draw a picture of something that begins with /m/. Then have them use this sentence frame to identify the initial /m/ sound: _____ begins with /m/.

ELL

English Language Learners
Support Phonemic Awareness Point to the images in the pictures on pp. 92–93 of *My Skills Buddy* as you say the corresponding words. To clarify understanding, have children point to the image as you say the word.

429 Success Predictor

11

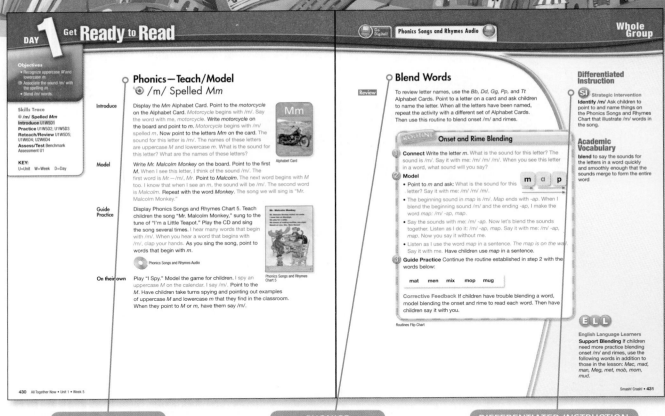

Objectives
- Recognize uppercase *M* and lowercase *m*.
- Associate the sound /m/ with the spelling *m*.
- Blend /m/ words.

Skills Trace
/m/ Spelled *Mm*
Introduce U1W5D1
Practice U1W5D2; U1W5D3
Reteach/Review U1W5D5; U1W6D4; U2W6D4
Assess/Test Benchmark Assessment U1

KEY:
U=Unit W=Week D=Day

Phonics—Teach/Model
/m/ Spelled *Mm*

Introduce Display the *Mm* Alphabet Card. Point to the *motorcycle* on the Alphabet Card. *Motorcycle* begins with /m/. Say the word with me, *motorcycle*. Write *motorcycle* on the board and point to *m*. *Motorcycle* begins with /m/ spelled *m*. Now point to the letters *Mm* on the card. The sound for this letter is /m/. The names of these letters are uppercase *M* and lowercase *m*. What is the sound for this letter? What are the names of these letters?

Alphabet Card

Model Write *Mr. Malcolm Monkey* on the board. Point to the first *M*. When I see this letter, I think of the sound /m/. The first word is *Mr.*—/m/, *Mr.* Point to *Malcolm*. The next word begins with *M* too. I know that when I see an *m*, the sound will be /m/. The second word is *Malcolm*. Repeat with the word *Monkey*. The song we will sing is "Mr. Malcolm Monkey."

Guide Practice Display Phonics Songs and Rhymes Chart 5. Teach children the song "Mr. Malcolm Monkey," sung to the tune of "I'm a Little Teapot." Play the CD and sing the song several times. I hear many words that begin with /m/. When you hear a word that begins with /m/, clap your hands. As you sing the song, point to words that begin with *m*.

Phonics Songs and Rhymes Audio

Phonics Songs and Rhymes Chart 5

On their own Play "I Spy." Model the game for children. I spy an uppercase *M* on the calendar. I say /m/. Point to the *M*. Have children take turns spying and pointing out examples of uppercase *M* and lowercase *m* that they find in the classroom. When they point to *M* or *m*, have them say /m/.

Blend Words

Review To review letter names, use the *Bb, Dd, Gg, Pp,* and *Tt* Alphabet Cards. Point to a letter on a card and ask children to name the letter. When all the letters have been named, repeat the activity with a different set of Alphabet Cards. Then use this routine to blend onset /m/ and rimes.

ROUTINE Onset and Rime Blending

1. **Connect** Write the letter *m*. What is the sound for this letter? The sound is /m/. Say it with me: /m/ /m/ /m/. When you see this letter in a word, what sound will you say?

2. **Model**
   - Point to *m* and ask: What is the sound for this letter? Say it with me: /m/ /m/ /m/.
   - The beginning sound in *map* is /m/. *Map* ends with *-ap.* When I blend the beginning sound /m/ and the ending *-ap,* I make the word *map:* /m/ *-ap, map.*
   - Say the sounds with me: /m/ *-ap, map.* Now let's blend the sounds together. Listen as I do it: /m/ *-ap, map.* Say it with me: /m/ *-ap, map.* Now you say it without me.
   - Listen as I use the word *map* in a sentence. *The map is on the wall.* Say it with me. Have children use *map* in a sentence.

   m a p

3. **Guide Practice** Continue the routine established in step 2 with the words below:

   mat   men   mix   mop   mug

Corrective Feedback If children have trouble blending a word, model blending the onset and rime to read each word. Then have children say it with you.

Routines Flip Chart

Differentiated Instruction

SI Strategic Intervention

Identify /m/ Ask children to point to and name things on the Phonics Songs and Rhymes Chart that illustrate /m/ words in the song.

Academic Vocabulary

blend to say the sounds for the letters in a word quickly and smoothly enough that the sounds merge to form the entire word

ELL English Language Learners

Support Blending If children need more practice blending onset /m/ and rimes, use the following words in addition to those in the lesson: *Mac, mad, man, Meg, met, mob, mom, mud.*

PHONICS

In Reading Street

Alphabetic Knowledge To ensure that children learn how spoken language maps onto written language, letter knowledge and phonological awareness are taught together. Daily lessons begin with the teacher displaying the letter and identifying the letter sound. The teacher models the connection between the sound and letter name. Application continues throughout the week with decoding and blending activities.

Because Research Says

Both letter knowledge and phonological awareness are needed in combination for young children to acquire the alphabetic principle. —(Snow, Burns, and Griffin, 1998)

Systematic and explicit instruction in decoding, with a focus on how sounds in words are represented by letters, is essential for children to learn to read. —(Gaskins, 2003)

PHONICS

In Reading Street

Blend Words This routine provides explicit instruction for sound-spellings and word parts. Children develop an understanding of the alphabetic principle as they are led to use and point to letters as words are written, and then to blend, or sound out, words.

Because Research Says

Segmenting words into phonemes and blending phonemes into words contributes more to learning to read than any other phonological awareness skills. —(Vaughn and Linan-Thompson, 2004)

DIFFERENTIATED INSTRUCTION

In Reading Street

Strategic Intervention Children who are struggling receive more explicit, intensive instruction, more scaffolding, more practice with critical skills, and more opportunities to respond. Children who perform at an advanced level may receive instruction to enhance the skills taught in the core lesson, provide exposure to more challenging reading and vocabulary, and incorporate independent investigative work.

Because Research Says

A consistent finding in meta-analyses examining effective instructional practices for students with reading and learning disabilities is that a combination of explicit and systematic instruction that provides modeling and feedback is associated with improved academic outcomes. —(Vaughn and Linan-Thompson, 2003)

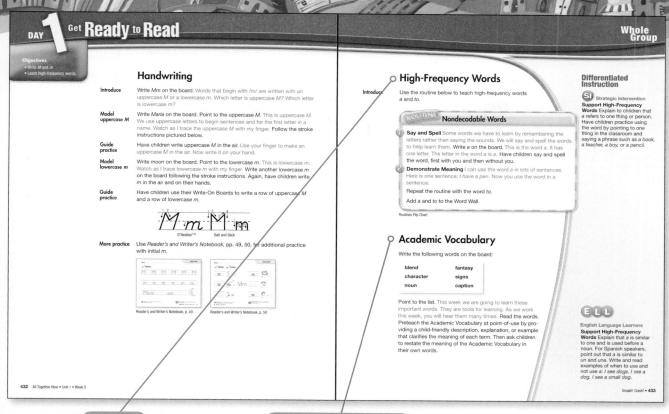

PHONICS

In Reading Street

High-Frequency Words Children learn two to seven high-frequency words each week. The teacher presents the words in connected text. The teacher guides children to say and spell each word and demonstrate meaning. Additional practice opportunities help children read the words fluently.

Because Research Says

Not all words can be read through decoding. For example, in irregular words, some or all of the letters do not represent their most commonly used sound. Children should encounter some of these words in texts for beginning readers, and will need to identify them by sight or automatically. To help children learn these words, teachers should introduce them in a reasonable order, and cumulatively review the ones that have been taught. —(Vaughn and Linan-Thompson, 2004)

ACADEMIC VOCABULARY

In Reading Street

Academic Vocabulary During the week, teachers directly teach a limited number of academic vocabulary words related to genres of reading and content-area reading. Lessons also offer multiple strategies for developing an understanding of this academic vocabulary.

Because Research Says

When choosing words for direct instruction, include those that lead to conceptual understanding. Students need to understand these words beyond the sense of the general concept and be able to provide precision and specificity in describing the concept. The most productive direct vocabulary instruction aims at words that are of high frequency for mature language users and are found across a variety of domains. —(Beck, McKeown, and Kucan, 2002)

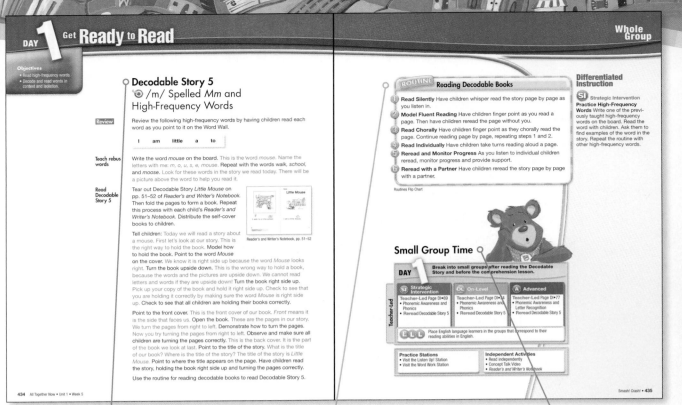

PHONICS

In Reading Street

Decodable Text Each week, children practice the target phonics skills by reading decodable texts. On Day 1 children read a Decodable Story, and on Day 2 they read a Decodable Book.

Because Research Says

Learning letter-sound relationships in isolation is necessary, but not enough. Children must know how to apply their knowledge to reading text. They should begin by reading decodable text comprised largely of words containing previously taught letter-sound relationships and gradually move to less controlled text as their ability and confidence grow. —(Vaughn and Linan-Thompson, 2004)

FLUENCY

In Reading Street

Reading Decodable Books On Days 1 and 2, children engage in repeated oral reading as the teacher monitors fluency and provides guidance and feedback.

Because Research Says

Perhaps the best known of the strategies designed to support fluency development is that of repeated readings. Generally, the children involved in using this strategy enjoy seeing the gains they make through their tracking of the changes in their reading and experience gratification when making visible improvement over a short period of time. —(Kuhn, 2003)

DIFFERENTIATED INSTRUCTION

In Reading Street

Small Group Time Group instruction is based on the 3-Tier Reading Model developed at the University of Texas. At the start of the school year, use the Baseline Group Test to make initial instructional decisions: Children with below-level performance are given Strategic Intervention instruction, those performing at grade level are placed in the On-Level group, and those who perform above grade level are given Advanced instruction.

Because Research Says

The components of effective reading instruction are the same whether the focus is prevention or intervention. By coordinating research evidence from effective classroom reading instruction with effective small-group and one-on-one reading instruction, teachers can meet the literacy needs of all children. —(Foorman and Torgesen, 2001)

Objectives
◗ Identify characters.

Skills Trace
● **Character**
Introduce U1W1D1; U1W5D1; U4W4D1; U6W2D1
Practice U1W1D2; U1W1D3; U1W1D4; U1W5D2; U1W5D3; U1W5D4; U4W4D2; U4W4D3; U4W4D4; U6W2D2; U6W2D3; U6W2D4
Reteach/Review U1W1D5; U1W2D4; U1W5D5; U3W4D4; U4W4D5; U5W4D4; U6W2D5
Assess/Test Benchmark Assessment U1; U6

KEY:
U=Unit W=Week D=Day

My Skills Buddy, pp. 94–95

○ **Listening Comprehension**
◉ Character

Introduce

Envision It!

A story may be about one or more than one person or animal. The people or animals that a story is about are called **characters**. Good readers pay attention to the characters in a story because it helps them understand who the story is about.

Have children turn to pp. 94–95 in *My Skills Buddy* and look at the pictures. Tell children the story of "The Tortoise and the Hare."

• Who are the characters in this story? (the tortoise and the hare)

• Are the characters people or animals? (The characters are animals.)

Model

Today I will read a story about friends who like to dance. Read **"Dancing Together"** and model how to identify characters.

Think Aloud When I read a story, I pay attention to the people or animals in the story. These are the characters. In "Dancing Together" the characters are the three children, Amy, Will, and Kim.

436 All Together Now • Unit 1 • Week 5

Guide practice Ask children who the characters in the story are. Amy, Will, and Kim are the characters. How do we know that these characters are good friends? (The story tells us that they like to spend time together and that they share what they learn in their dance classes.)

More practice Display Big Book *Plaidypus Lost.* Page through the story. Help children recall and describe the characters in the story. For example, after they identify the girl, ask them to describe her. She loves to take Plaidypus everywhere, but she is forgetful.

Connect to everyday life Imagine you and your best friend are characters in a story. What do you look like? What are you doing?

Differentiated Instruction

Ⓐ **Advanced**

Access Prior Knowledge Ask children who know the story "The Tortoise and the Hare" well to tell the story to their classmates.

Academic Vocabulary

character a person or animal in a story, book, poem, or play

ELL

English Language Learners
Oral Comprehension To prepare English learners for the Read Aloud, use the modified Read Aloud in the ELL Support lesson.

Read Aloud

Dancing Together

Amy's house has a big back porch. Amy and her friends Will and Kim like to dance on the porch. As the music plays, Amy leaps, Will twirls, and Kim jigs. They pretend they are dancing on a stage.

One day Amy says, "Guess what! My mom says I can go to dance class."

Will and Kim are happy for Amy. They want to take dance classes too. They talk to their parents. The next day they have news.

"I'm going to dance class!" says Will.

"I'm going to dance class!" says Kim.

Now when the friends listen to music together, they show one another what they have learned in their dance classes. Amy jigs, Will leaps, and Kim twirls.

Smash! Crash! • 437

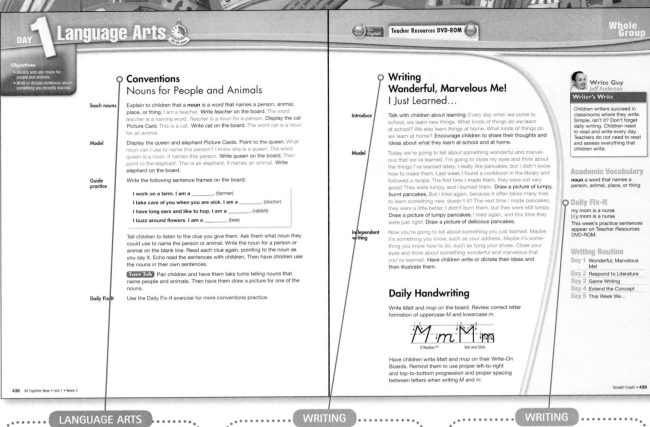

Conventions
Nouns for People and Animals

Teach nouns Explain to children that a **noun** is a word that names a person, animal, place, or thing. I am a teacher. Write *teacher* on the board. The word *teacher* is a naming word. *Teacher* is a noun for a person. Display the *cat* Picture Card. This is a cat. Write *cat* on the board. The word *cat* is a noun for an animal.

Model Display the *queen* and *elephant* Picture Cards. Point to the queen. What noun can I use to name this person? I know she is a queen. The word *queen* is a noun. It names this person. Write *queen* on the board. Then point to the elephant. This is an elephant. It names an animal. Write *elephant* on the board.

Guide practice Write the following sentence frames on the board:

> I work on a farm. I am a _____. (farmer)
> I take care of you when you are sick. I am a _____. (doctor)
> I have long ears and like to hop. I am a _____. (rabbit)
> I buzz around flowers. I am a _____. (bee)

Tell children to listen to the clue you give them. Ask them what noun they could use to name the person or animal. Write the noun for a person or animal on the blank line. Read each clue again, pointing to the noun as you say it. Echo read the sentences with children. Then have children use the nouns in their own sentences.

Team Talk Pair children and have them take turns telling nouns that name people and animals. Then have them draw a picture for one of the nouns.

Daily Fix-It Use the Daily Fix-It exercise for more conventions practice.

Writing
Wonderful, Marvelous Me!
I Just Learned…

Introduce Talk with children about learning. Every day when we come to school, we learn new things. What kinds of things do we learn at school? We also learn things at home. What kinds of things do we learn at home? Encourage children to share their thoughts and ideas about what they learn at school and at home.

Model Today we're going to tell about something wonderful and marvelous that we've learned. I'm going to close my eyes and think about the things I've learned lately. I really like pancakes, but I didn't know how to make them. Last week I found a cookbook in the library and followed a recipe. The first time I made them, they were not very good! They were lumpy, and I burned them. Draw a picture of lumpy, burnt pancakes. But I tried again, because it often takes many tries to learn something new, doesn't it? The next time I made pancakes, they were a little better. I didn't burn them, but they were still lumpy. Draw a picture of lumpy pancakes. I tried again, and this time they were just right! Draw a picture of delicious pancakes.

Independent writing Now you're going to tell about something you just learned. Maybe it's something you know, such as your address. Maybe it's something you know how to do, such as tying your shoes. Close your eyes and think about something wonderful and marvelous that you've learned. Have children write or dictate their ideas and then illustrate them.

Daily Handwriting

Write *Matt* and *mop* on the board. Review correct letter formation of uppercase *M* and lowercase *m*.

D'Nealian™   Ball and Stick

Have children write *Matt* and *mop* on their Write-On Boards. Remind them to use proper left-to-right and top-to-bottom progression and proper spacing between letters when writing *M* and *m*.

Write Guy
Jeff Anderson

Writer's Write

Children writers succeed in classrooms where they write. Simple, isn't it? Don't forget daily writing. Children need to read and write every day. Teachers do not need to read and assess everything that children write.

Academic Vocabulary

noun a word that names a person, animal, place, or thing

Daily Fix-It

my mom is a nurse
My mom is a nurse.
This week's practice sentences appear on Teacher Resources DVD-ROM.

Writing Routine

Day 1 Wonderful, Marvelous Me!
Day 2 Respond to Literature
Day 3 Genre Writing
Day 4 Extend the Concept
Day 5 This Week We…

• • • • • LANGUAGE ARTS • • • • •

In Reading Street

Conventions Every week, children are introduced to a grammar skill. The grammar skill is practiced and applied in children's writing throughout the week.

Because Research Says

▸ If grammar is to make a more visible and viable contribution to writing improvement, we need to teach not so much "rules of grammar" but "principles of writing." —(Noguchi, 2002)

• • • • • WRITING • • • • •

In Reading Street

Writing In daily routines, teachers introduce, model, guide student practice, and encourage independent practice of various writing activities, including storytelling, responding to literature, genre writing, and extending the weekly concept.

Because Research Says

▸ Writing has a central role in early reading development. Increasingly, we see the synergistic relationship between learning to write and learning to read. —(National Writing Project and Nagin, 2003)

• • • • • WRITING • • • • •

In Reading Street

Daily Fix-It Practice sentences provide opportunities for reviewing conventions, such as spelling, grammar, and punctuation. Each sentence contains errors in previously taught skills.

Because Research Says

▸ Students need to edit anonymous copy where there is no vested interest, and where errors are easier to spot because the writing is someone else's. This warm-up leaves them more prepared to work on their own text. —(Spandel, 2005)

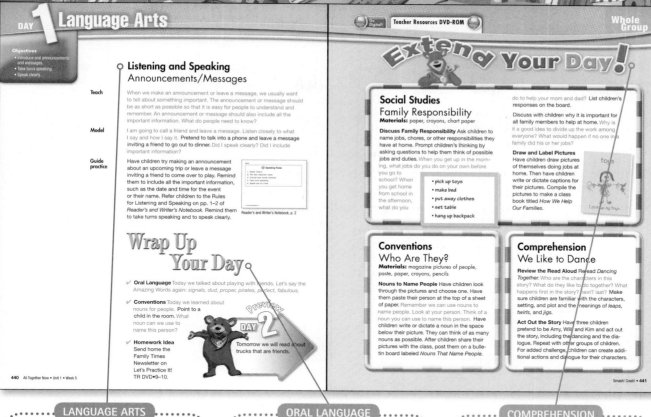

In Reading Street

Listening and Speaking Each week children practice an important listening or speaking behavior while relating their own personal experiences. The teacher models the behavior, and then children apply the behavior during a classroom or partner activity. Listening and speaking, combined with reading and writing, create an integrated language arts curriculum.

Because Research Says

In order to learn language, children need opportunities to talk and be heard. Listening is not a natural, innate ability. Instead, it is learned through the guidance and teaching of parents, teachers, and other people in young children's environment.
—(Seefeldt and Wasik, 2006)

In Reading Street

Wrap Up Your Day This end-of-the-day routine reviews the day's skill instruction, encourages discussion about shared literature and the week's concepts, and previews what's to come.

Because Research Says

For children to develop rich vocabularies, they need to have many interactions with adults. It is from these interactions that they will develop the words they need to negotiate their world. —(Stahl and Stahl, 2004)

In Reading Street

Extend Your Day Additional activities give teachers the opportunity to integrate science, social studies, and math concepts, as well as engage children in additional practice of the week's literacy skills.

Because Research Says

When learning experiences are integrated with other content areas, children are better able to make connections between facts and ideas, develop an understanding of abstract concepts, and develop higher-order thinking strategies.
—(Seefeldt and Wasik, 2006)

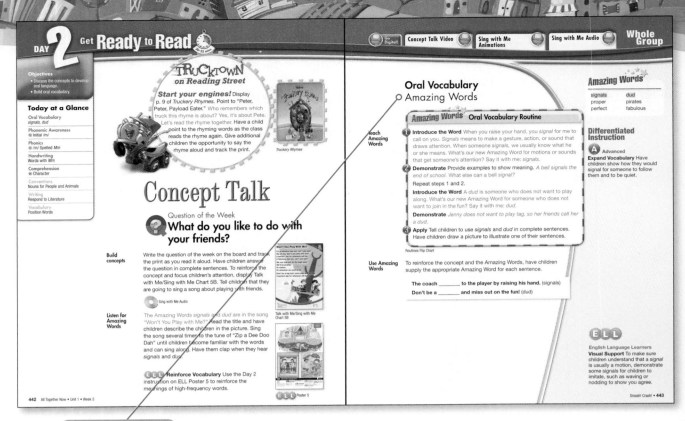

ORAL VOCABULARY

In Reading Street

Amazing Words Each week children learn a set of conceptually related Amazing Words selected from literature and reinforced in songs. The teacher provides direct instruction for each Amazing Word during Oral Vocabulary Routines throughout the week.

Because Research Says

Although a great deal of vocabulary is learned indirectly through shared storybook reading, teachers need to provide more explicit vocabulary instruction. It is important to provide multiple exposures of target words and carefully scheduled review and practice.
—(Armbruster and Osborn, 2001; Coyne, Simmons, and Kame'enui, 2004)

Pages 20–21 are based on the same research as pages 4–5. Pages 22–23 are based on the same research as pages 6–7. Pages 24–25 are based on the same research as pages 8–9. Pages 26–27 are based on the same research as pages 10–11.

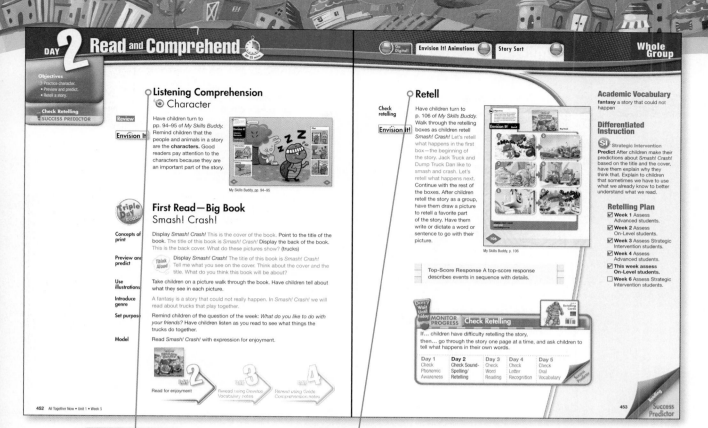

In Reading Street

Listening Comprehension
Before reading the trade book selection, children review the comprehension skill, discuss concepts of print, preview the selection, and make predictions. After the class walks through the book and describes what they see, the children use the Question of the Day to set a purpose for reading.

Because Research Says

Good readers typically look over the text before they read, noting such things as the structure that might be most relevant to their reading goals. —(Duke and Pearson, 2002)

In Reading Street

Retelling After reading the selection for enjoyment on Day 2, children retell the narrative with the assistance of the retelling strip in the Student Edition.

Because Research Says

Oral retelling provides information as a process and a product. It allows teachers to assess what students remember about what they read without direct questioning or support from a teacher. —(Paratore and McCormack, 2005)

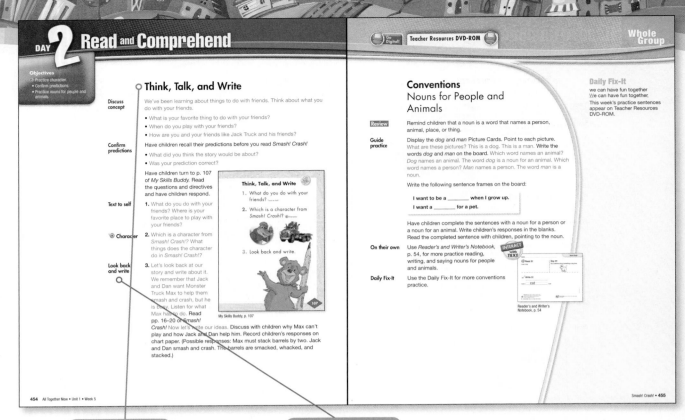

Objectives
- Practice character.
- Confirm predictions.
- Practice nouns for people and animals.

Think, Talk, and Write

Discuss concept
We've been learning about things to do with friends. Think about what you do with your friends.
- What is your favorite thing to do with your friends?
- When do you play with your friends?
- How are you and your friends like Jack Truck and his friends?

Confirm predictions
Have children recall their predictions before you read *Smash! Crash!*
- What did you think the story would be about?
- Was your prediction correct?

Have children turn to p. 107 of *My Skills Buddy*. Read the questions and directives and have children respond.

Text to self
1. What do you do with your friends? Where is your favorite place to play with your friends?

Character
2. Which is a character from *Smash! Crash!*? What things does the character do in *Smash! Crash!*?

Look back and write
3. Let's look back at our story and write about it. We remember that Jack and Dan want Monster Truck Max to help them smash and crash, but he is busy. Listen for what Max has to do. Read pp. 16–20 of *Smash! Crash!* Now let's write our ideas. Discuss with children why Max can't play and how Jack and Dan help him. Record children's responses on chart paper. (Possible responses: Max must stack barrels by two. Jack and Dan smash and crash. The barrels are smacked, whacked, and stacked.)

Think, Talk, and Write
1. What do you do with your friends? ___
2. Which is a character from *Smash! Crash!*? ___
3. Look back and write.

My Skills Buddy, p. 107

Conventions
Nouns for People and Animals

Review
Remind children that a noun is a word that names a person, animal, place, or thing.

Guide practice
Display the *dog* and *man* Picture Cards. Point to each picture. What are these pictures? This is a dog. This is a man. Write the words *dog* and *man* on the board. Which word names an animal? *Dog* names an animal. The word *dog* is a noun for an animal. Which word names a person? *Man* names a person. The word *man* is a noun.

Write the following sentence frames on the board:

> I want to be a _____ when I grow up.
> I want a _____ for a pet.

Have children complete the sentences with a noun for a person or a noun for an animal. Write children's responses in the blanks. Read the completed sentence with children, pointing to the noun.

On their own
Use *Reader's and Writer's Notebook,* p. 54, for more practice reading, writing, and saying nouns for people and animals.

Daily Fix-It
Use the Daily Fix-It for more conventions practice.

Reader's and Writer's Notebook, p. 54

Daily Fix-It
we can have fun together
We can have fun together.

This week's practice sentences appear on Teacher Resources DVD-ROM.

COMPREHENSION

In Reading Street

Think, Talk, and Write After reading the selection, children talk about the weekly concept and its application to the selection. They also check the predictions they made about the book.

Because Research Says

By creating opportunities for students to read and respond in the company of others, teachers foster their students' ability to make sense of text worlds and lived worlds. —(Galda and Beach, 2004)

WRITING

In Reading Street

Look Back and Write Children recall the Question of the Day after reading the selection. The teacher lists children's responses to the question and then tracks the print as the class reads the list together.

Because Research Says

Writing is a complex activity; more than just a skill or talent, it is a means of inquiry and expression for learning in all grades and disciplines. —(National Writing Project and Nagin, 2003)

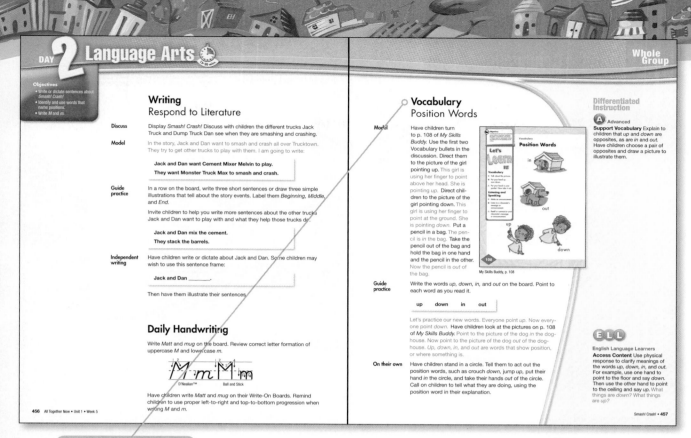

In Reading Street

Vocabulary Skill This activity helps to expand children's word knowledge by introducing them to basic concept words. The teacher uses a word from the selection and provides examples of other words that are related to the same concept, such as position words or temperature words.

Because Research Says

Given beginning readers' word identification limitations, the text materials used in the early phases of learning to read should comprise words children know from oral language, that is, Tier One words like *run* and *ball*. Indeed, learning to read is learning a new representation for the language young children know from speech. —(Beck, McKeown, and Kucan, 2002)

Pages 34–35 are based on the same research as pages 16–17. Pages 36–37 are based on the same research as page 2 and page 19. Pages 38–39 are based on the same research as pages 4–5. Pages 40–41 are based on the same research as pages 6–7. Pages 42–43 are based on the same research as pages 10–11.

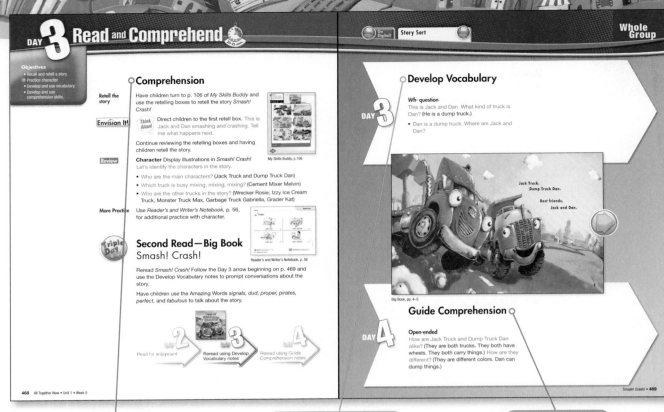

Story Sort

Whole Group

Objectives
• Recall and retell a story.
• Practice character.
• Develop and use vocabulary.
• Develop and use comprehension skills.

Comprehension

Retell the story
Have children turn to p. 106 of *My Skills Buddy* and use the retelling boxes to retell the story *Smash! Crash!*

Envision It! | **Think Aloud** Direct children to the first retell box. This is Jack and Dan smashing and crashing. Tell me what happens next.

Continue reviewing the retelling boxes and having children retell the story.

Review | **Character** Display illustrations in *Smash! Crash!* Let's identify the characters in the story.

• Who are the main characters? (Jack Truck and Dump Truck Dan)
• Which truck is busy mixing, mixing, mixing? (Cement Mixer Melvin)
• Who are the other trucks in the story? (Wrecker Rosie, Izzy Ice Cream Truck, Monster Truck Max, Garbage Truck Gabriella, Grader Kat)

More Practice Use *Reader's and Writer's Notebook*, p. 56, for additional practice with character.

My Skills Buddy, p. 106

Reader's and Writer's Notebook, p. 56

Triple Day

Second Read—Big Book
Smash! Crash!

Reread *Smash! Crash!* Follow the Day 3 arrow beginning on p. 469 and use the Develop Vocabulary notes to prompt conversations about the story.

Have children use the Amazing Words *signals, dud, proper, pirates, perfect,* and *fabulous* to talk about the story.

DAY 2 Read for enjoyment
DAY 3 Reread using Develop Vocabulary notes
DAY 4 Reread using Guide Comprehension notes

Develop Vocabulary

DAY 3

Wh- question
This is Jack and Dan. What kind of truck is Dan? (He is a dump truck.)
• Dan is a dump truck. Where are Jack and Dan?

Jack Truck.
Dump Truck Dan.
Best friends.
Jack and Dan.

Big Book, pp. 4–5

Guide Comprehension

DAY 4

Open-ended
How are Jack Truck and Dump Truck Dan alike? (They are both trucks. They both have wheels. They both carry things.) How are they different? (They are different colors. Dan can dump things.)

468 All Together Now • Unit 1 • Week 5

Smash! Crash! • 469

In Reading Street

Comprehension On Day 3, children revisit the Trade Book selection from the previous day. They begin by retelling or summarizing the story or selection. Next they review the target comprehension skill by applying it to the story or selection.

Because Research Says

Teachers can ask children to retell stories or information books and examine the detail and vocabulary to gain an idea about children's oral language and comprehension development. —(Beck, McKeown, and Kucan, 2002)

In Reading Street

Develop Vocabulary On Day 3, the selection is reread with a focus on developing vocabulary. The teacher uses the Develop Vocabulary notes to ask questions about the words from the selection, giving children an opportunity to use the words, and then reinforcing the meanings in context to build understanding. This approach is called Dialogic Reading. Children are encouraged to use the week's Amazing Words in their discussion.

Because Research Says

Dialogic reading is based on the theory that practice using language, feedback regarding language, and appropriately scaffolded adult-child interactions in the context of picture book reading facilitate young children's language development. —(Zevenenbergen and Whitehurst, 2003)

In Reading Street

Guide Comprehension On Day 4, the selection is read for a third time, with a focus on greater understanding. The teacher uses the Guide Comprehension notes to give children the opportunity to gain a more complete understanding of the selection.

Because Research Says

More effective teachers engage children in more higher-level responses to text (both in discussions and written assignments) as part of what the researchers labeled a framework of instruction promoting cognitive engagement during reading. —(Taylor, Pearson, Peterson, and Rodriguez, 2005)

Pages 46–59 are based on the same research as pages 44–45. Pages 60–61 are based on the same research as pages 14–15.

Objectives
- Practice announcements and messages.
- Take turns speaking.

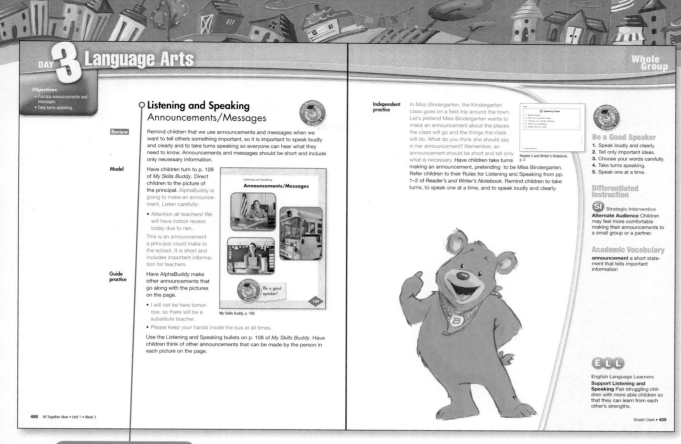

○ **Listening and Speaking**
Announcements/Messages

Review Remind children that we use announcements and messages when we want to tell others something important, so it is important to speak loudly and clearly and to take turns speaking so everyone can hear what they need to know. Announcements and messages should be short and include only necessary information.

Model Have children turn to p. 109 of *My Skills Buddy*. Direct children to the picture of the principal. AlphaBuddy is going to make an announcement. Listen carefully:

- Attention all teachers! We will have indoor recess today due to rain.

This is an announcement a principal could make to the school. It is short and includes important information for teachers.

Guide practice Have AlphaBuddy make other announcements that go along with the pictures on the page.

- I will not be here tomorrow, so there will be a substitute teacher.
- Please keep your hands inside the bus at all times.

Use the Listening and Speaking bullets on p. 108 of *My Skills Buddy*. Have children think of other announcements that can be made by the person in each picture on the page.

My Skills Buddy, p. 109

Independent practice In *Miss Bindergarten*, the Kindergarten class goes on a field trip around the town. Let's pretend Miss Bindergarten wants to make an announcement about the places the class will go and the things the class will do. What do you think she should say in her announcement? Remember, an announcement should be short and tell only what is necessary. Have children take turns making an announcement, pretending to be Miss Bindergarten. Refer children to their Rules for Listening and Speaking from pp. 1–2 of *Reader's and Writer's Notebook*. Remind children to take turns, to speak one at a time, and to speak loudly and clearly.

Reader's and Writer's Notebook, p. 2

Be a Good Speaker
1. Speak loudly and clearly.
2. Tell only important ideas.
3. Choose your words carefully.
4. Take turns speaking.
5. Speak one at a time.

Differentiated Instruction

SI Strategic Intervention
Alternate Audience Children may feel more comfortable making their announcements to a small group or a partner.

Academic Vocabulary

announcement a short statement that tells important information

ELL English Language Learners
Support Listening and Speaking Pair struggling children with more able children so that they can learn from each other's strengths.

••••• 21ST CENTURY SKILLS •••••

In Reading Street

Listening and Speaking Each week children have direct instruction for the listening and speaking skills needed to perform and be an audience for brief oral presentations. Children demonstrate these skills with others during Team Talk activities.

Because Research Says

Social learning strategies will become increasingly important. Helping children learn effective literacy strategies from one another will prepare them for their futures where workplaces require these collaborative learning skills. —(Leu and Kinzer, 2000)

Pages 64–65 are based on the same research as pages 16–17. Pages 66–67 are based on the same research as page 2 and page 19. Pages 68–69 are based on the same research as pages 4–7.

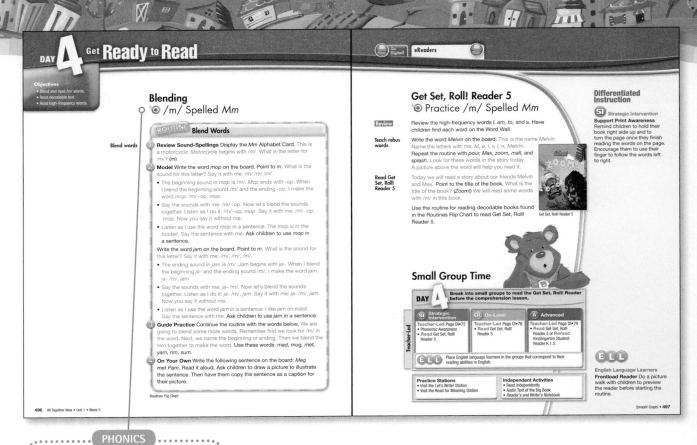

In Reading Street

Blending The routine provides explicit instruction in connecting sounds to letters. Children develop an understanding of the alphabetic principle.

Because Research Says

Grapheme-phoneme knowledge, also referred to as alphabetic knowledge, is essential for literacy acquisition to reach a mature state. It is important to include spelling as well as reading in this picture, because learning to read and learning to spell words in English depend on processes that are tightly interconnected. —(Ehri, 1992)

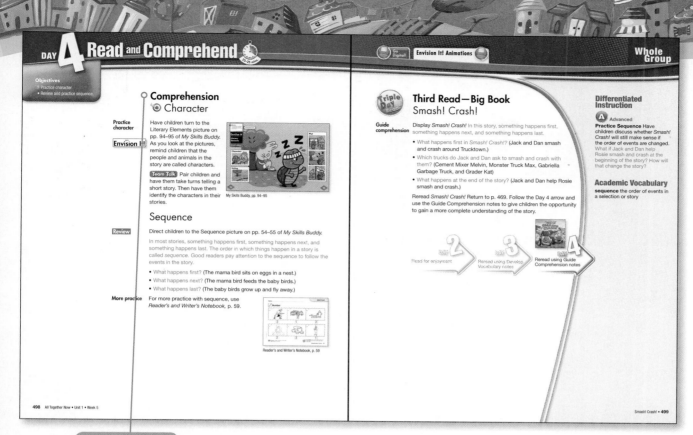

Pages 74–75 are based on the same research as pages 14–15. Pages 76–77 are based on the same research as pages 16–17.

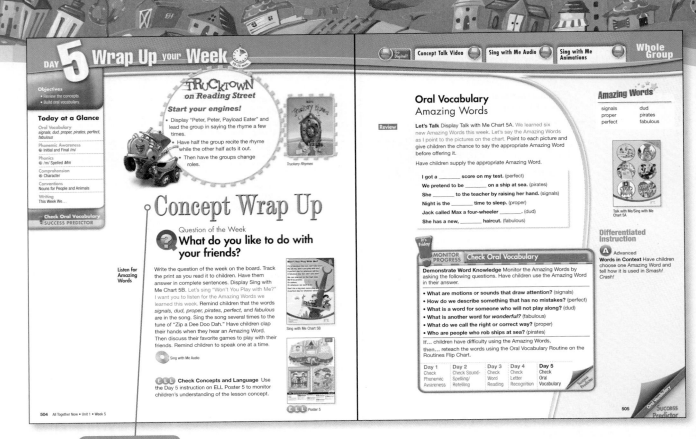

TRUCKTOWN on Reading Street

Start your engines!

- Display "Peter, Peter, Payload Eater" and lead the group in saying the rhyme a few times.
- Have half the group recite the rhyme while the other half acts it out.
- Then have the groups change roles.

Truckery Rhymes

Concept Wrap Up

Listen for Amazing Words

Question of the Week
What do you like to do with your friends?

Write the question of the week on the board. Track the print as you read it to children. Have them answer in complete sentences. Display Sing with Me Chart 5B. Let's sing "Won't You Play with Me?" I want you to listen for the Amazing Words we learned this week. Remind children that the words *signals, dud, proper, pirates, perfect,* and *fabulous* are in the song. Sing the song several times to the tune of "Zip a Dee Doo Dah." Have children clap their hands when they hear an Amazing Word. Then discuss their favorite games to play with their friends. Remind children to speak one at a time.

Sing with Me Audio

ELL **Check Concepts and Language** Use the Day 5 instruction on ELL Poster 5 to monitor children's understanding of the lesson concept.

Won't You Play with Me?

Sing with Me Chart 5B

ELL Poster 5

504 All Together Now • Unit 1 • Week 5

Concept Talk Video | Sing with Me Audio | Sing with Me Animations | **Whole Group**

Oral Vocabulary
Amazing Words

Review

Let's Talk Display Talk with Me Chart 5A. We learned six new Amazing Words this week. Let's say the Amazing Words as I point to the pictures on the chart. Point to each picture and give children the chance to say the appropriate Amazing Word before offering it.

Have children supply the appropriate Amazing Word.

I got a _____ score on my test. (perfect)

We pretend to be _____ on a ship at sea. (pirates)

She _____ to the teacher by raising her hand. (signals)

Night is the _____ time to sleep. (proper)

Jack called Max a four-wheeler _____. (dud)

She has a new, _____ haircut. (fabulous)

It's Friday

MONITOR PROGRESS Check Oral Vocabulary

Demonstrate Word Knowledge Monitor the Amazing Words by asking the following questions. Have children use the Amazing Word in their answer.

- What are motions or sounds that draw attention? (signals)
- How do we describe something that has no mistakes? (perfect)
- What is a word for someone who will not play along? (dud)
- What is another word for *wonderful?* (fabulous)
- What do we call the right or correct way? (proper)
- Who are people who rob ships at sea? (pirates)

If... children have difficulty using the Amazing Words, then... reteach the words using the Oral Vocabulary Routine on the Routines Flip Chart.

| Day 1 Check Phonemic Awareness | Day 2 Check Sound-Spelling/ Retelling | Day 3 Check Word Reading | Day 4 Check Letter Recognition | **Day 5** Check Oral Vocabulary |

Amazing Words

signals   dud
proper   pirates
perfect   fabulous

Talk with Me/Sing with Me Chart 5A

Differentiated Instruction

A Advanced
Words in Context Have children choose one Amazing Word and tell how it is used in *Smash! Crash!*

505   Success Predictor

Pages 80–81 are based on the same research as pages 4–7.

Assess
- Identify words that begin with /m/.
- Read high-frequency words.

○ **Assessment**
Monitor Progress

/m/ Spelled Mm

Whole Class Have children number a sheet of paper from 1 to 6. Read the list of words below. For each word, have children write an *m* next to the corresponding number if the word begins with /m/ or an X if it does not.

| 1. duck | 2. middle | 3. car |
| 4. moon | 5. lizard | 6. melon |

MONITOR PROGRESS — **Check Sound Discrimination and Word Reading**

If... children cannot complete the whole-class assessment,
then... use the Reteach lesson in *First Stop.*

If... you are unsure of a child's grasp of this week's skills,
then... use the assessment below to obtain a clearer evaluation of the child's progress.

/m/ Spelled Mm and high-frequency words

One-on-One To facilitate individual progress monitoring, assess some children on Day 4 and the rest on Day 5. While individual children are being assessed, the rest of the class can reread this week's books and look for words with /m/ and high-frequency words.

Phonemic Awareness Initial /m/

Use the pictures on reproducible p. 509 to assess each child's ability to identify initial /m/ words. We're going to identify pictures whose names begin with /m/. I'll do the first one. This is a *mop. Mop* begins with /m/. For each child, record any problems.

Word reading

Use the words on reproducible p. 509 to assess each child's ability to read high-frequency words. Have each child read the words aloud.

Record scores

Monitor children's accuracy by recording their scores using the Sound Discrimination and Word Reading Chart for this unit in *First Stop.*

508 All Together Now • Unit 1 • Week 5

Name _____

Name the Sound

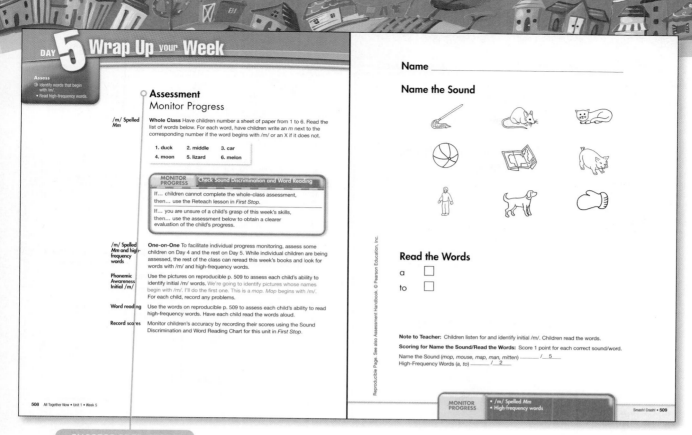

Read the Words

a ☐

to ☐

Note to Teacher: Children listen for and identify initial /m/. Children read the words.

Scoring for Name the Sound/Read the Words: Score 1 point for each correct sound/word.

Name the Sound (*mop, mouse, map, man, mitten*) _____ /__5__
High-Frequency Words (*a, to*) _____ /__2__

MONITOR PROGRESS
- /m/ Spelled Mm
- High-frequency words

Smash! Crash! • 509

In Reading Street

Assessment The assessment begins with a whole-class activity that assesses phonics. If the teacher is unsure of a child's grasp of the phonics skill, the teacher can use the individual assessment to obtain a clearer evaluation of the child's progress. The teacher then administers the reproducible assessment.

Because Research Says

Systematic evaluation of each student's progress is characteristic of classrooms in which students make the most progress. —(Gaskins, 2003)

Pages 84–85 are based on the same research as pages 12–13.

Objectives
• Review weekly concept.
• Review character.

Wrap Up Your Week!

Amazing Words
You've learned
0 0 6
words this week!
You've learned
0 3 0
words this year!

Illustrate character

Question of the Week
What do you like to do with your friends?

This week we talked about things we like to do with our friends. We read about Jack Truck and Dump Truck Dan.

• Make a word web like the one shown and have children fill it with characters from *Smash! Crash!*
• These trucks are the characters in the story. Which truck is your favorite?
• Have children draw a picture of their favorite truck and something that truck does with his or her friends in the story. Then have children draw a picture of themselves and a friend doing something together.

Trucks — Jack Truck

Next Week's Question
How do machines help people work?

Discuss next week's question. Talk with children about how people use machines to help them do work.

Preview
NEXT WEEK
Tell children that next week they will read about machines that help people do their work.

Extend Your Day!

Social Studies
Good Friends
Materials: chart paper, markers

Discuss Qualities of a Good Friend Talk with children about what makes someone a good friend. Explain that we choose friends because of what they are like.

• What are your friends like?
• What makes them good friends?
• Why do you like to play with them?
• What makes you a good friend?
• How do you learn how to be a good friend?

Make a list of the qualities that children suggest.

Good Friends
good listener   nice
share toys   play with me
make me laugh   help me do things

Draw a Picture Have children draw a picture of themselves playing with friends. Tell them to write or dictate a word or phrase that tells about a good quality in a friend.

Phonics
Match *m* to /m/
Materials: Picture Cards—*kite, map, mitten, moon, mop, pig, rock, seal;* four index cards with *m* written on them

Identify /m/ Words Mix the Picture Cards and place them face up in a row. Have a child take an index card and place it on a picture whose name begins with /m/. Continue until all the index cards are matched with /m/ Picture Cards. Collect the cards and begin a new game.

Conventions
Name My Job

Guess Nouns for People Review with children that we use nouns to name people. Together, generate a list of nouns that name people's jobs, such as *teacher, doctor, carpenter, actor, truck driver,* and *store clerk,* and write them on the board. Have a child secretly choose a job from the list and either pantomime doing the job or give clues about it while classmates try to guess the person's job.

········· **ORAL LANGUAGE** ·········

In Reading Street

Wrap Up Your Week In this end-of-the-week routine, the class revisits the Question of the Week one last time. Children have the opportunity to apply a previously learned comprehension skill to the concept of the week. The teacher also connects the concept of the week to the concepts children will encounter the following week.

Because Research Says

When we truly understand, we can explain via generalizations or principles, providing justified and systematic accounts of phenomena, facts, and data; make insightful connections; and provide illuminating examples or illustrations. —(Wiggins and McTighe, 2006)

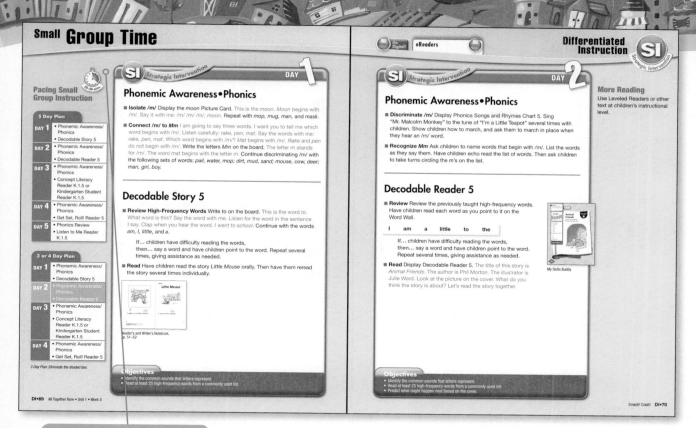

eReaders

Differentiated Instruction

Pacing Small Group Instruction

5 Day Plan

DAY 1
• Phonemic Awareness/ Phonics
• Decodable Story 5

DAY 2
• Phonemic Awareness/ Phonics
• Decodable Reader 5

DAY 3
• Phonemic Awareness/ Phonics
• Concept Literacy Reader K.1.5 or Kindergarten Student Reader K.1.5

DAY 4
• Phonemic Awareness/ Phonics
• Get Set, Roll! Reader 5

DAY 5
• Phonics Review
• Listen to Me Reader K.1.5

3 or 4 Day Plan

DAY 1
• Phonemic Awareness/ Phonics
• Decodable Story 5

DAY 2
• Phonemic Awareness/ Phonics
• Decodable Reader 5

DAY 3
• Phonemic Awareness/ Phonics
• Concept Literacy Reader K.1.5 or Kindergarten Student Reader K.1.5

DAY 4
• Phonemic Awareness/ Phonics
• Get Set, Roll! Reader 5

3 Day Plan: Eliminate the shaded box.

SI Strategic Intervention — DAY 1

Phonemic Awareness•Phonics

■ **Isolate /m/** Display the *moon* Picture Card. This is the *moon*. *Moon* begins with /m/. Say it with me: /m/ /m/ /m/, *moon*. Repeat with *mop, mug, man,* and *mask*.

■ **Connect /m/ to *Mm*** I am going to say three words. I want you to tell me which word begins with /m/. Listen carefully: *rake, pen, mat.* Say the words with me: *rake, pen, mat.* Which word begins with /m/? *Mat* begins with /m/. *Rake* and *pen* do not begin with /m/. Write the letters *Mm* on the board. The letter *m* stands for /m/. The word *mat* begins with the letter *m.* Continue discriminating /m/ with the following sets of words: *pail, water, mop; dirt, mud, sand; mouse, cow, deer; man, girl, boy.*

Decodable Story 5

■ **Review High-Frequency Words** Write *to* on the board. This is the word *to.* What word is this? Say the word with me. Listen for the word in the sentence I say. Clap when you hear the word. *I went to school.* Continue with the words *am, I, little,* and *a.*

> If... children have difficulty reading the words,
> then... say a word and have children point to the word. Repeat several times, giving assistance as needed.

■ **Read** Have children read the story *Little Mouse* orally. Then have them reread the story several times individually.

Reader's and Writer's Notebook, pp. 51–52

Objectives
• Identify the common sounds that letters represent.
• Read at least 25 high-frequency words from a commonly used list.

SI Strategic Intervention — DAY 2

Phonemic Awareness•Phonics

■ **Discriminate /m/** Display Phonics Songs and Rhymes Chart 5. Sing "Mr. Malcolm Monkey" to the tune of "I'm a Little Teapot" several times with children. Show children how to march, and ask them to march in place when they hear an /m/ word.

■ **Recognize *Mm*** Ask children to name words that begin with /m/. List the words as they say them. Have children echo read the list of words. Then ask children to take turns circling the *m's* on the list.

Decodable Reader 5

■ **Review** Review the previously taught high-frequency words. Have children read each word as you point to it on the Word Wall.

I	am	a	little	to	the

> If... children have difficulty reading the words,
> then... say a word and have children point to the word. Repeat several times, giving assistance as needed.

■ **Read** Display Decodable Reader 5. The title of this story is *Animal Friends.* The author is Phil Morton. The illustrator is Julie Ward. Look at the picture on the cover. What do you think the story is about? Let's read the story together.

My Skills Buddy

Objectives
• Identify the common sounds that letters represent.
• Read at least 25 high-frequency words from a commonly used list.
• Predict what might happen next based on the cover.

More Reading
Use Leveled Readers or other text at children's instructional level.

DI•69   All Together Now • Unit 1 • Week 5

Smash! Crash!   DI•70

DIFFERENTIATED INSTRUCTION

In Reading Street

Strategic Intervention

Instruction Daily Small Group Time lessons provide struggling readers with more intensive instruction, more scaffolding, more practice with critical skills, and more opportunities to respond.

Because Research Says

In a year-long detailed class-room analysis of four first-grade classrooms, differentiated instruction had the most payoffs for students. Students who most needed letter-sound instruction got more of it than students who did not. The teacher's feedback was responsive to their individual understanding of letters and sounds. —(Juel, 2005)

Pages DI•71–DI•73 are based on the same research as pages DI•69–DI•70. Page DI•74 is based on the same research as pages DI•75–DI•76.

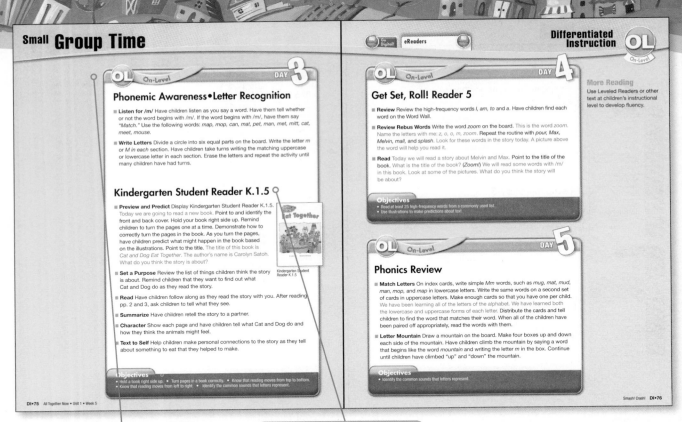

eReaders

OL On-Level — DAY 3

Phonemic Awareness • Letter Recognition

■ **Listen for /m/** Have children listen as you say a word. Have them tell whether or not the word begins with /m/. If the word begins with /m/, have them say "Match." Use the following words: *map, mop, can, mat, pet, man, met, mitt, cat, meet, mouse.*

■ **Write Letters** Divide a circle into six equal parts on the board. Write the letter *m* or *M* in each section. Have children take turns writing the matching uppercase or lowercase letter in each section. Erase the letters and repeat the activity until many children have had turns.

Kindergarten Student Reader K.1.5

■ **Preview and Predict** Display Kindergarten Student Reader K.1.5. Today we are going to read a new book. Point to and identify the front and back cover. Hold your book right side up. Remind children to turn the pages one at a time. Demonstrate how to correctly turn the pages in the book. As you turn the pages, have children predict what might happen in the book based on the illustrations. Point to the title. The title of this book is *Cat and Dog Eat Together.* The author's name is Carolyn Satoh. What do you think the story is about?

■ **Set a Purpose** Review the list of things children think the story is about. Remind children that they want to find out what Cat and Dog do as they read the story.

■ **Read** Have children follow along as they read the story with you. After reading pp. 2 and 3, ask children to tell what they see.

■ **Summarize** Have children retell the story to a partner.

■ **Character** Show each page and have children tell what Cat and Dog do and how they think the animals might feel.

■ **Text to Self** Help children make personal connections to the story as they tell about something to eat that they helped to make.

Eat Together

Kindergarten Student Reader K.1.5

Objectives
• Hold a book right side up. • Turn pages in a book correctly. • Know that reading moves from top to bottom.
• Know that reading moves from left to right. • Identify the common sounds that letters represent.

DI•75   All Together Now • Unit 1 • Week 5

OL On-Level — DAY 4

Get Set, Roll! Reader 5

■ **Review** Review the high-frequency words *I, am, to* and *a.* Have children find each word on the Word Wall.

■ **Review Rebus Words** Write the word *zoom* on the board. This is the word *zoom.* Name the letters with me: *z, o, o, m, zoom.* Repeat the routine with *pour, Max, Melvin, mall,* and *splash.* Look for these words in the story today. A picture above the word will help you read it.

■ **Read** Today we will read a story about Melvin and Max. Point to the title of the book. What is the title of the book? (*Zoom!*) We will read some words with /m/ in this book. Look at some of the pictures. What do you think the story will be about?

Objectives
• Read at least 25 high-frequency words from a commonly used list.
• Use illustrations to make predictions about text.

OL On-Level — DAY 5

Phonics Review

■ **Match Letters** On index cards, write simple *Mm* words, such as *mug, mat, mud, man, mop,* and *map* in lowercase letters. Write the same words on a second set of cards in uppercase letters. Make enough cards so that you have one per child. We have been learning all of the letters of the alphabet. We have learned both the lowercase and uppercase forms of each letter. Distribute the cards and tell children to find the word that matches their word. When all of the children have been paired off appropriately, read the words with them.

■ **Letter Mountain** Draw a mountain on the board. Make four boxes up and down each side of the mountain. Have children climb the mountain by saying a word that begins like the word *mountain* and writing the letter *m* in the box. Continue until children have climbed "up" and "down" the mountain.

Objectives
• Identify the common sounds that letters represent.

Smash! Crash!   DI•76

More Reading
Use Leveled Readers or other text at children's instructional level to develop fluency.

DIFFERENTIATED INSTRUCTION

In Reading Street

On-Level Instruction Daily Small Group Time lessons focus on appropriate instructional strategies for children reading at grade level.

Because Research Says

Smaller group ratios increase the likelihood of academic success through student-teacher interactions, individualization of instruction, student on-task behavior, and teacher monitoring of student progress and feedback. —(Vaughn, et al., 2003)

DIFFERENTIATED INSTRUCTION

In Reading Street

On-Level Readers Instructional-level fiction and nonfiction books are provided for readers at the Strategic Intervention, On-Level, and Advanced levels. These books relate to weekly concepts and offer children opportunities to read texts and practice targeted skills and strategies in small groups at their individual instructional levels. Teachers also use progress monitoring to move children along a continuum to independent reading.

Because Research Says

One of the five components of the model of explicit comprehension instruction best supported by research is guided practice with gradual release of responsibility. —(Duke and Pearson, 2002)

Pages DI•77–DI•78 are based on the same research as page DI•79.

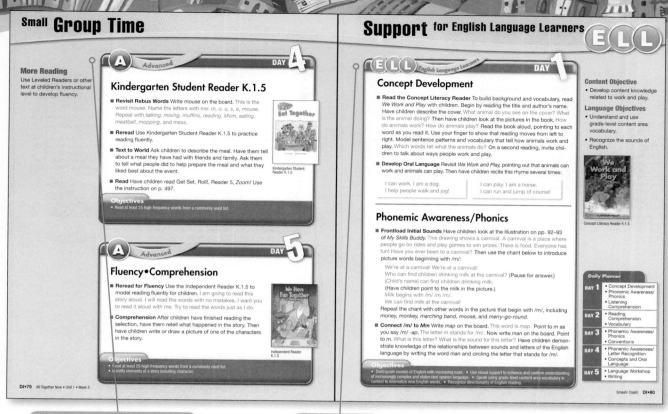

More Reading Use Leveled Readers or other text at children's instructional level to develop fluency.

A · Advanced · DAY 4

Kindergarten Student Reader K.1.5

■ **Revisit Rebus Words** Write *mouse* on the board. This is the word *mouse*. Name the letters with me: *m, o, u, s, e, mouse*. Repeat with *talking, mixing, muffins, reading, Mom, eating, meatball, mopping,* and *mess.*

■ **Reread** Use Kindergarten Student Reader K.1.5 to practice reading fluently.

■ **Text to World** Ask children to describe the meal. Have them tell about a meal they have had with friends and family. Ask them to tell what people did to help prepare the meal and what they liked best about the event.

■ **Read** Have children read Get Set, Roll!, Reader 5, *Zoom!* Use the instruction on p. 497.

Kindergarten Student Reader K.1.5

Objectives
• Read at least 25 high-frequency words from a commonly used list.

A · Advanced · DAY 5

Fluency•Comprehension

■ **Reread for Fluency** Use the Independent Reader K.1.5 to model reading fluently for children. I am going to read this story aloud. I will read the words with no mistakes. I want you to read it aloud with me. Try to read the words just as I do.

■ **Comprehension** After children have finished reading the selection, have them retell what happened in the story. Then have children write or draw a picture of one of the characters in the story.

Independent Reader K.1.5

Objectives
• Read at least 25 high-frequency words from a commonly used list.
• Identify elements of a story including character.

DI•79 All Together Now • Unit 1 • Week 5

ELL · English Language Learners · DAY 1

Concept Development

■ **Read the Concept Literacy Reader** To build background and vocabulary, read *We Work and Play* with children. Begin by reading the title and author's name. Have children describe the cover. What animal do you see on the cover? What is the animal doing? Then have children look at the pictures in the book. How do animals work? How do animals play? Read the book aloud, pointing to each word as you read it. Use your finger to show that reading moves from left to right. Model sentence patterns and vocabulary that tell how animals work and play. Which words tell what the animals do? On a second reading, invite children to talk about ways people work and play.

■ **Develop Oral Language** Revisit *We Work and Play*, pointing out that animals can work and animals can play. Then have children recite this rhyme several times:

I can work. I am a dog.
I help people walk and jog!

I can play. I am a horse.
I can run and jump of course!

Phonemic Awareness/Phonics

■ **Frontload Initial Sounds** Have children look at the illustration on pp. 92–93 of *My Skills Buddy*. This drawing shows a carnival. A carnival is a place where people go on rides and play games to win prizes. There is food. Everyone has fun! Have you ever been to a carnival? Then use the chant below to introduce picture words beginning with /m/:

We're at a carnival! We're at a carnival!
Who can find children drinking milk at the carnival? (Pause for answer.)
(Child's name) can find children drinking milk.
(Have children point to the milk in the picture.)
Milk begins with /m/ /m/ /m/.
We can find milk at the carnival!
Repeat the chant with other words in the picture that begin with /m/, including *money, monkey, marching band, moose,* and *merry-go-round.*

■ **Connect /m/ to Mm** Write *map* on the board. This word is *map*. Point to *m* as you say /m/ -*ap*. The letter *m* stands for /m/. Now write *man* on the board. Point to *m*. What is this letter? What is the sound for this letter? Have children demonstrate knowledge of the relationships between sounds and letters of the English language by writing the word *man* and circling the letter that stands for /m/.

Objectives
• Distinguish sounds of English with increasing ease. • Use visual support to enhance and confirm understanding of increasingly complex and elaborated spoken language. • Speak using grade-level content area vocabulary in context to internalize new English words. • Recognize directionality of English reading.

Smash! Crash! DI•80

Concept Literacy Reader K.1.5

Content Objective
• Develop content knowledge related to work and play.

Language Objectives
• Understand and use grade-level content area vocabulary.
• Recognize the sounds of English.

Daily Planner

DAY 1	• Concept Development • Phonemic Awareness/Phonics • Listening Comprehension
DAY 2	• Reading Comprehension • Vocabulary
DAY 3	• Phonemic Awareness/Phonics • Conventions
DAY 4	• Phonemic Awareness/Letter Recognition • Concepts and Oral Language
DAY 5	• Language Workshop • Writing

DIFFERENTIATED INSTRUCTION

In Reading Street

Advanced Instruction Daily Small Group Time lessons for children reading above grade level enhance the skills taught in the core lesson, provide exposure to more challenging reading and vocabulary, and incorporate independent investigative work. Activities provide advanced readers additional opportunities to engage in critical and creative thinking, and to focus on problem-solving skills.

Because Research Says

In general, grouping academically talented students together for instruction has been found to produce positive achievement outcomes when the curriculum provided to students in different groups is appropriately differentiated. In other words, it is the instruction that occurs within groups that makes grouping an appropriate instructional strategy. —(Reis, et al., 2003)

ELL SUPPORT

In Reading Street

ELL Instruction English learners receive extra support to allow them to successfully participate in and progress through the daily lessons of the basic program with their peers.

Because Research Says

Given the diversity in our society, it is imperative to recognize that young children may differ considerably in their inventory of skills and abilities, and these differences should not be treated as reflecting deficiencies in ability. —(Wong Fillmore and Snow, 2002)

Pages DI•81–DI•82 are based on the same research as page DI•80.

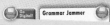
ELL English Language Learners — DAY 3

Phonemic Awareness/Phonics

■ **Isolate Initial and Final /m/** Say *am*, and then model segmenting sounds in the word by saying /a/ /m/. Emphasize the final sound in the word. Repeat with initial and final /m/ in *Sam, man, mom,* and *jam*. Help children hear /m/ in each word.

■ **Connect /m/ to Mm** Write the words *am, mom,* and *Sam* on the board. As you read the words aloud, point to the *m* when you say the last sound. What is the last sound you hear in each word? Yes, /m/. What letter spells /m/? Yes, the letter *m* spells /m/. Help children recognize that these words end with the same sound and the same letter.

Conventions: Nouns for People and Animals

■ **Provide Scaffolding** Display the *cat, dog, frog, pig,* and *robin* Picture Cards. These are pictures of animals. What are the names of these animals? Point to each card as children identify the animals. Write the words on the board. Read the list with children. These words are naming words. They name the animal in each picture. Naming words are called *nouns*. What are naming words called?

Display the *man* and *woman* Picture Cards and the *Bb* Alphabet Card. These are pictures of people. Have children identify names for each picture as you point to it. (man, dad, woman, mom, baby) Write the words on the board. These words are nouns too. They are nouns that name people.

■ **Practice** What other nouns can you think of that name animals? Have children work in pairs or groups to think of nouns that name animals. Encourage children to think of pets they have or animals they have seen at the zoo or at the park. What other nouns can you think of that name people? Encourage children to think of people they live with, go to school with, or see in the neighborhood. Write the words on the board. Have children choose one noun and use it in this sentence frame: _____ is a noun that names a _____ (person/animal).

Beginning/Intermediate Have children name an animal and pretend to be that animal. As each child acts out an animal, have the other children say: *I see a _____.* Repeat until all children have an opportunity to be an animal.
Advanced/Advanced-High Have children act out each animal and narrate their actions.

Content Objective
• Use learning strategies.

Language Objectives
• Connect /m/ to *Mm*.
• Use nouns for people and animals.

Transfer Skills
Pronounce /m/ Children's familiarity with /m/ in home language words will help them recognize /m/ in English. For example, Spanish speakers are likely to know the cognate *mucho* (much).

Use Learning Strategies
Explain that *a* is similar to one and is used before nouns. *I see a dog. I see a man. I see a horse.*

Objectives
• Monitor oral language production and employ self-corrective techniques or other resources. • Distinguish sounds of English with increasing ease. • Monitor understanding of spoken language during classroom instruction and interactions. • Narrate with increasing specificity and detail as more English is acquired.

DI•83 All Together Now • Unit 1 • Week 5

ELL English Language Learners — DAY 4

Phonemic Awareness/Letter Recognition

■ **Review Initial Sounds** Say these words: *dad, mom, man.* As you say each word, emphasize the initial sound. After you say each word, repeat the initial sound, say the word again, and ask: What sound does this word begin with? Then have children tell whether the following word pairs begin with the same initial sound: *dad, mom; mom, man; dad, man.*

■ **Letter Names** Display the *Aa* Alphabet Card. Point to and name uppercase *A.* What is the name of this letter? Repeat with lowercase *a.* Then repeat the routine with the other Alphabet Cards to help children review all of the letters in alphabetical order.

Concepts and Oral Language

■ **Revisit Talk with Me Chart 5A** Display the chart. Point to the picture of the girl holding the stop sign. This girl signals to someone to stop. The sign and her hand give a signal to stop. A signal is a sign or action that tells something. Have you seen a stop sign before? What color is it? What does it tell you to do? Continue reviewing the other words on the chart.

■ **Develop Oral Vocabulary** Discuss the vocabulary words on Talk with Me Chart 5A. Let's talk about signals. When you signal, you don't say anything. You use actions to tell what you mean. We signal many things while we are in school. Raise your hand. We raise our hands in school. What does raising our hands mean? Have children explain the signal using this sentence frame: *Raising my hand means _____.* Demonstrate other signals, such as waving, using one finger by your mouth to indicate "shhh," and motioning with one hand to "come here." Then have children practice each signal. Remind them not to say words but to use gestures.

Beginning Have children repeat the sentences other children say. Then have them point to the picture that shows a signal. Have children imitate it.
Intermediate Have children think of how they can signal they are happy.
Advanced/Advanced-High Encourage children to use prior knowledge to think of other ways to signal.

Content Objectives
• Develop oral language.
• Use learning strategies.

Language Objectives
• Discriminate initial sounds.
• Review letter names.

Use Learning Strategies
Work with children to draw pictures of something fabulous or proper. Have them keep their drawings for reference.

Talk with Me Chart 5A

Objectives
• Use prior experiences to understand meanings in English. • Use strategic learning techniques to acquire grade-level vocabulary. • Use contextual support to enhance and confirm understanding of increasingly complex and elaborated spoken language.

Smash! Crash! DI•84

ELL SUPPORT

In Reading Street

ELL Leveled Support Teachers use a variety of instructional activities to support English language learners at different levels of proficiency. Different techniques can be chosen as the teacher observes which children need more support or more challenging language activities. At the beginning level, techniques include gesturing and having children draw. For more advanced levels, children are encouraged to speak in more complex sentences and use a wider range of vocabulary.

Because Research Says

Often beginning and intermediate English language learners may not understand what their classroom teachers say or read aloud in English. When it becomes clear from students' actions and responses that they understand what is being said, teachers can vary their strategies. —(García, 2010)

ELL SUPPORT

In Reading Street

Oral Language Lessons provide teachers ways to engage English language learners in authentic use of social language. Children learn and use fixed English expressions such as *run away* and *throw it to* while teachers model language and correct their usage so that children's English sounds natural.

Because Research Says

The most effective activities provide English language learners ample opportunity to hear English and to use it productively in meaningful communication. Children must be able to participate to the extent possible in discussions with classmates who are more proficient in English, but only teachers can ensure that English language learners get access to the kind of language needed for literacy development. —(Wong Fillmore, 2010)

Page DI•85 is based on the same research as pages DI•83–DI•84.

Research Bibliography

Anderson, Jeff. *Mechanically Inclined: Building Grammar, Usage, and Style into Writer's Workshop.* Stenhouse Publishers, 2005.

Anderson, R., E. Hiebert, J. Scott, and I. Wilkinson. "The Report of the Commission on Reading." *Becoming a Nation of Readers.* The National Institute of Education, 1985.

Armbruster, B. B., F. Lehr and J. Osborn. *Put Reading First: The Research Building Blocks for Teaching Children to Read.* Partnership for Reading, 2001.

Beck, Isabel L., Margaret G. McKeown, Rebecca L. Hamilton, and Linda Kucan. *Bringing Words to Life: Robust Vocabulary Instruction.* The Guilford Press, 2002.

Blachowicz, Camille and Peter J. Fisher. *Teaching Vocabulary in All Classrooms,* 2nd ed. Merrill Prentice Hall, 2002.

Block, Cathy Collins and Michael Pressley. "Best Practices in Comprehension Instruction." *Best Practices in Literary Instruction.* The Guilford Press, 2003.

Coyne, Michael D., Deborah C. Simmons, and Edward J. Kame'enui. "Vocabulary Instruction for Young Children at Risk of Experiencing Reading Difficulties." *Vocabulary Instruction: Research to Practice.* The Guilford Press, 2004.

Cummins, Jim. "The Three Pillars of English Language Learning." *Pearson Scott Foresman EL Handbook Teacher's Manual,* 2010.

Duke, Nell K. and P. David Pearson. "Effective Practices for Developing Reading Comprehension." *What Research Has to Say About Reading Instruction,* 3rd ed. International Reading Association, 2002.

Duke, Nell K., V. Susan Bennett-Armistead, Ebony M. Roberts. "Bridging the Gap Between Learning to Read and Reading to Learn." *Literacy and Young Children: Research-Based Practices.* The Guilford Press, 2003.

Ehri, Linnea C. and Simone R. Nunes. "The Role of Phonemic Awareness in Learning to Read." *What Research Has to Say About Reading Instruction,* 3rd ed. International Reading Association, 2002.

Ehri, Linnea C., M. R., and S. A. Stahl. "Fluency: A Review of Developmental and Remedial Practices." *Journal of Educational Psychology,* vol. 95, 2003.

Ehri, Linnea C. "Grapheme-Phoneme Knowledge Is Essential for Learning to Read Words in English." *Word Recognition in Beginning Literacy.* Lawrence Erlbaum Associates, 1992.

Foorman, B. R., and J. Torgesen. "Critical Elements of Classroom and Small-Group Instruction Promote Reading Success in All Children." *Learning Disabilities Research and Practice,* vol. 16, November 2001.

Galda, Lee, and Richard Beach. "Response to Literature as a Cultural Activity." *Theoretical Models and Processes of Reading,* 5th ed. International Reading Association, 2004.

García, Georgia Earnest. "English Learners and Literacy: Best Practices." *Pearson Scott Foresman EL Handbook Teacher's Manual,* 2010.

Gaskins, Irene W. "A Multidimensional Approach to Beginning Literacy." *Literacy and Young Children: Research-Based Practices.* The Guilford Press, 2003.

Ivey, Gay. "Building Comprehension When They're Still Learning to Read the Words." *Comprehension Instruction: Research-Based Best Practices.* The Guilford Press, 2002.

Juel, Connie. "Impact of Early School Experiences," *Handbook of Early Literacy Research,* 2nd ed. The Guilford Press, 2005.

Kaplan, S. "Reading Strategies for Gifted Readers." *Teaching for High Potential,* vol. 1, no. 2, 1999.

Kuhn, M. R., and S. A. Stahl. "Fluency: A Review of Developmental and Remedial Practices." *Journal of Educational Psychology,* vol. 95, 2003.

Kuhn, Melanie. "How Can I Help Them Pull It All Together? A Guide to Fluent Reading Instruction." *Literacy and Young Children: Research-Based Practices.* The Guilford Press, 2003.

Krashen, Stephen D., and Tracy D. Terrell. *The Natural Approach: Language Acquisition in the Classroom.* Alemany Press, 1983.

Leu, D. J. Jr., C. K. Kinzer, J. Coiro, and D. Cammack. "Toward a Theory of New Literacies Emerging from the Internet and Other Information and Communication Technologies." *Theoretical Models and Processes of Reading,* 5th ed. International Reading Association, 2004.

Leu, Donald and Charles Kinzer. "The Convergence of Literary Instruction with Networked Technologies for Information and Communication." *Reading Research Quarterly,* vol. 35, no. 1, January/February/March 2000.

Leu, Donald. "The New Literacies: Research on Reading Instruction With the Internet." *What Research Has to Say About Reading Instruction,* 3rd ed., International Reading Association, 2002.

McKee, Judith and Donna Ogle. *Integrating Instruction, Literacy and Science.* The Guilford Press, 2005.

Morrow, Lesley Mandel and Linda Gambrell. "Literature-Based Instruction in the Early Years." *Handbook of Early Literacy Research.* The Guilford Press, 2002.

Morrow, L. M., "Story Retelling: A Discussion Strategy to Develop and Assess Comprehension." *Lively Discussions! Fostering Engaged Reading.* International Reading Association, 1996.

National Reading Panel. *Teaching Children to Read.* National Institute of Child Health and Human Development. 1999.

National Writing Project and Carl Nagin. *Because Writing Matters.* Jossey-Bass, 2003.

Noguchi, Rei R. *The English Record.* Winter, 2002.

Ogle, D. and C. L. Blachowicz. "Beyond Literature Circles: Helping Students Comprehend Informational Texts." *Comprehension Instruction: Research-Based Best Practices.* The Guilford Press, 2002.

Paratore, Jeanne and Rachel McCormack. *Teaching Literacy in Second Grade.* The Guilford Press, 2005.

Pearson, P. D., L. R. Roehler, J. A. Dole, and G. G, Duffy. "Developing Expertise in Reading Comprehension." *What Research Says About Reading Instruction,* 2nd ed. International Reading Association, 1992.

Pearson, P. David and Nell K. Duke. "Comprehension Instruction in the Primary Grades." *Comprehension Instruction: Research-Based Best Practices.* The Guilford Press, 2002.

Pressley, M., and C. C. Block. "Summing Up: What Comprehension Instruction Could Be." *Comprehension Instruction: Research-Based Best Practices.* The Guilford Press, 2002.

Pressley, M. "Metacognition and Self-Regulated Comprehension." *What Research Has to Say About Reading Instruction,* 3rd ed. International Reading Association, 2002.

Reis, Sally M., E. Jean Gubbins, Christine Briggs, Fredric J. Schreiber, Susannah Richards, Joan Jacobs, Rebecca D. Eckert, Joseph S. Renzulli, and Margaret Alexander. *Reading Instruction for Talented Readers: Case Studies Documenting Few Opportunities for Continuous Progress* (RM03184). The National Research Center on the Gifted and Talented, University of Connecticut, 2003.

Reis, Sally M., and Joseph S. Renzulli. "Developing Challenging Programs for Gifted Readers." *The Reading Instruction Journal,* vol. 32, 1989.

Samuels, S. J. "Reading Fluency: Its Development and Assessment." *What Research Has to Say About Reading Instruction,* 3rd ed. International Reading Association, 2002.

Seefeldt, Carol and Barbara A. Wasik. *Early Education: Three-, Four-, and Five-Year Olds Go to School,* 2nd ed. Pearson Merrill Prentice Hall, 2006.

Smith, Sylvia B., Deborah C. Simmons, and Edward J. Kame'enui. "Phonological Awareness: Instructional and Curricular Basics and Implications." *What Reading Research Tells Us About Children With Diverse Learning Needs: Bases and Basics.* Lawrence Erlbaum Associates, 1998.

Snow, Catherine E., M. Susan Burns, and Peg Griffin, eds. *Preventing Reading Difficulties in Young Children.* National Research Council, 1998.

Spandel, Vicki. "Assessing With Heart." National Staff Development Council, vol. 27, no. 3. Summer 2006.

_____. *Creating Writers Through 6-Trait Writing Assessment and Instruction.* 2nd ed. Merrill Prentice Hall, 2002.

_____. *Creating Writers Through 6-Trait Writing Assessment and Instruction.* 3rd ed. Addison Wesley Longman, 2001.

_____. *Creating Writers Through 6-Trait Writing Assessment and Instruction.* 4th ed. Allyn and Bacon, 2004.

Stahl, Steven A. and Katherine A. Dougherty Stahl. "Word Wizards All! Teaching Word Meanings in Preschool and Primary Education." *Vocabulary Instruction: Research to Practice.* The Guilford Press, 2004.

Tatum, Alfred. *Teaching Reading to Black Adolescent Males.* Stenhouse Publishers, 2005.

Taylor, Barbara M., P. David Pearson, Debra S. Peterson, and Michael C. Rodriguez. "The CIERA School Change Framework: An Evidence-Based Approach to Professional Development and School Reading Improvement." *Reading Research Quarterly,* vol. 40, no. 1, January/February/March 2005.

VanTassel-Baska, J. "Effective Curriculum and Instructional Models for Talented Students." *Gifted Child Quarterly,* vol. 30, 1996.

Vaughn, Sharon and Sylvia Linan-Thompson. *Research-Based Methods of Reading Instruction.* Association for Supervision and Curriculum Development, 2004.

_____. "Group Size and Time Allotted to Intervention: Effects for Students with Reading Difficulties." *Preventing and Remediating Reading Difficulties: Bringing Science to Scale.* Baltimore York Press, 2003.

Vaughn, Sharon, Sylvia Linan-Thompson, Kamiar Kouzekanani, Diane Pedrotty, Shirley Dickson, and Shelly Blozis. "Reading Instruction Grouping for Students with Reading Difficulties." *Remedial and Special Education,* vol. 24, no. 5, September/October 2003.

Weaver, Constance. *Grammar for Teachers: Perspectives and Definitions.* NCTE, 1979.

Wiggins, Grant and Jay McTighe. *Understanding by Design.* Pearson Education, Inc., 2006.

Wilkinson, L. C. and E. R. Silliman. "Classroom Language and Literacy Learning." *Handbook of Reading Research,* vol. III. Lawrence Erlbaum Associates, 2000.

Wong Fillmore, Lily and Catherine E. Snow. "What Teachers Need to Know About Language." *What Teachers Need to Know About Language.* The Center for Applied Linguistics and Delta Systems Co., Inc., 2002.

Wong Fillmore, Lily. "Preparing English Language Learners for Assessment." *Pearson Scott Foresman EL Handbook Teacher's Manual,* 2010.

Wray, David and Maureen Lewis. "But Bonsai Tress Don't Grow in Baskets: Young Children's Talk During Authentic Inquiry." *Lively Discussions! Fostering Engaged Reading.* International Reading Association, 1996.

Zevenenbergen, Andrea and Grover Whitehurst. *On Reading Books to Children: Parents and Teacher.* Lawrence Erlbaum Associates, 2003.

Guide to
Reading Street

Section 2

Kindergarten children are energetic! It's rewarding to channel their energy and enthusiasm into rich learning experiences. In this easy guide to *Reading Street*, you'll find suggestions on how to set up your classroom and manage it effectively. Stop here when you need suggestions and background information for teaching these critical elements of literacy:

- Phonemic Awareness

- Phonics

- Comprehension

- Language Arts

- Differentiated Instruction

- Assessment

- Writing

This section ends with a visit with the distinguished authors whose research is the foundation of *Scott Foresman Reading Street* so they can answer some of your questions.

Setting Up Your Classroom

How Should I Organize My Classroom?

Setting up your classroom can be an overwhelming task! Your goal is to create an environment where children feel safe and secure. With young children the most effective approach seems to be dividing the classroom into smaller work areas. The focal point of the classroom should be the area you use for whole-group instruction. Create a print-rich environment by labeling items throughout the classroom such as the clock, the calendar, tables, practice stations, windows, and doors.

Whole-Group Area

At times throughout the day you'll have all children gather in this classroom area. You may wish to have a rug large enough for all children to sit comfortably. This is a perfect spot to take attendance, discuss the calendar, and read stories. Use this area as a meeting place during transition time. It is also helpful to have easy access to a chalkboard or large chart.

Independent Work Area

Kindergarten children are busy people. They have work to do. The quiet work area should be positioned strategically to minimize distractions. Each child should have a spot labeled with his or her name. It may be helpful to have a basket on each table with pencils, crayons, glue, and scissors for children. If children bring their own supplies, put their things in resealable plastic bags labeled with their names and then place them in a basket.

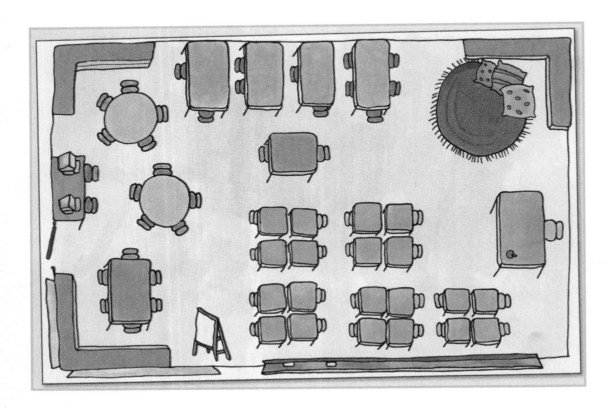

Small-Group Area

Set up an area in your classroom where you can work with small groups of five to six children. Choose a distraction-free area where you can easily see the entire classroom.

Practice Stations

Set up a variety of practice stations in your classroom. You can set up a system so children know which station they are supposed to work at each day. A large chart with station names and children's names listed below is often the simplest and most effective tool. *Scott Foresman Reading Street* offers weekly activities through the Practice Stations, along with weekly suggestions in the Teacher's Edition that support the use of stations in your classroom. It is usually best to set up six stations a week and have children rotate through them during the week.

Kindergarten Practice Stations

Listening Station	Writing Station
Book Corner	Crosscurricular Station
Word Work	Social Studies, Science, Math
Art	

Helping Children Take Responsibility

With a little coaching, children can learn to take responsibility for completing their independent work. Setting up routines and rules at the beginning of the year can go a long way toward making group time successful. During group time, use a work plan that outlines the activities you expect children to complete. For additional guidance, *Scott Foresman Reading Street* provides the *Practice Stations Management Handbook.*

Getting to Know Kindergarten Children

Kindergarten children enter the classroom wanting to read. You are their guide to the world of literacy they are eager to explore. Typically children enter kindergarten with a wide range of abilities. As you talk to children individually as well as in small and large group settings, you will gain a better understanding of each child's personality and how each child contributes to the class as a whole.

What Are the Best Tools?

Throughout the kindergarten year you will see children develop emotionally, socially, and academically. The *Baseline Group Test* is a formal assessment tool that will provide more information to help you discover each child's readiness for kindergarten. Administering the *Reading Street Unit Benchmark Assessments* and collecting samples of children's work will help you understand each child's strengths and challenges. Observe how children interact with each other, listen to their vocabulary, and watch them play to give you a deeper understanding of their social and emotional development.

It is important to be flexible with your grouping. Depending on how quickly a child is learning, move him or her to a faster or slower paced group. You can screen children throughout the lessons. During the week monitor the progress of each child using the Monitor Progress: Success Predictors in the Teacher's Edition.

You, as the kindergarten teacher, have the wonderful job of opening the world of literacy to children. You will guide children as they build the foundation of their reading and writing skills. When children leave your classroom, they will be readers and writers. You will help children expand their comprehension of text and how it applies to other areas in their lives. You will help children expand their oral vocabulary and apply it to other areas of learning. Above all, you will instill in them a love of learning and exploring.

Oral Vocabulary

Daily instruction is organized into three chunks: Get Ready to Read, Read and Comprehend, and Language Arts. Routines help you expose children to the richness of the English language and to engage children in the kind of talk that develops their language and expands their understanding of concepts.

Trucktown on Reading Street

The Big Noisy Book of Truckery Rhymes welcomes kindergarten children each morning to the world of language with a fanciful collection of well-known nursery rhymes with a twist. The characters in the rhymes are the delightful trucks from *Jon Scieszka's Trucktown.* Children listen and chime in as you read and reread the rhymes—a perfect vehicle for developing oral language and listening comprehension skills.

Question of the Week

Write the Question of the Week in a location where children can read it with you. On days 1 and 5, you help children focus on the question of the week by listening to and singing songs. On days 2, 3, and 4, the question will connect to the weekly concept. Encourage children to answer and discuss the questions in complete sentences.

Oral Vocabulary/Amazing Words

Developing oral vocabulary is especially important in kindergarten. Children should be learning words and concepts that they will need as they progress in school. *Reading Street* provides explicit and systematic routines to help children develop and expand their oral vocabulary.

Research tells us that children learn vocabulary directly and indirectly. Kindergarten children expand their vocabularies by listening to adults read to them, and by engaging in daily oral language activities. Every week children are introduced to six "Amazing Words." The Amazing Words are not words most five- or six-year-old children use in their daily conversation. The Amazing Words are words to expand and enhance children's vocabularies, and ultimately their comprehension of text and the world around them. The words come directly from the main selection for the week. Children hear and interact with the words through the literature and the Talk with Me/Sing with Me Charts.

Phonemic Awareness

What Are First Steps on the Way to Reading?

phonological awareness	>>	an awareness of the sounds that make up spoken language
phonemic awareness	>>	one kind of phonological awareness, which includes the ability to hear individual sounds in words and to identify and manipulate those sounds

Kindergarten opens the world of sounds and letters to children. Many children are aware of sounds and letters around them but few understand how sounds and letters connect to form words. You have the rewarding job of helping children make that connection. *Scott Foresman Reading Street* provides you with tools and activities that open the world of words for your kindergarteners.

To learn to read, children must understand that spoken language is made up of a series of sounds. They develop **phonological awareness.** The early levels of phonological awareness include:

- segmenting words into syllables
- identifying words that begin with the same sound
- blending onset and rime into a word and segmenting words into onset and rime
- progress monitoring opportunities

Phonological awareness skills can be sequenced into several levels of development. **Phonemic awareness** is the most complex of these levels. It is one of the strongest predictors of a child's future reading ability.

When Do Children Develop Phonemic Awareness?

Beginning in week five, every lesson begins with a phonemic awareness activity. These activities focus on the target sounds of the week. Children practice isolating and discriminating the target sounds. At this level children develop the skills they need to benefit from phonics instruction. They learn to

- isolate individual sounds at the beginning, middle, or end of words
- blend individual sounds to make words
- segment a spoken word into its individual sounds
- add, delete, and substitute sounds in spoken words

How Can I Make Phonemic Awareness Fun?

When children are busy imitating sounds and connecting sounds to pictures and words, they are engaged. Phonemic awareness lessons in *Scott Foresman Reading Street* help children have fun as you introduce, model, and guide their practice. You support children working at the phonemic awareness level by having them

- blend individual sounds to form words. For example, if you say /b/ /a/ /th/, they say *bath.*

- segment spoken words into individual sounds. For example, if you say *me,* they say /m/ /ē/.

- add or delete sounds from spoken words. For example, *Say late without the /l/. Say ear with /n/ at the beginning.*

- change a sound in a spoken word to make a new word. For example, *Change the first sound in ham to /j/. Change the last sound in ham to /d/.*

The program offers picture cards and a phonemic awareness lesson in *My Skills Buddy* as aids in teaching phonemic awareness. The *My Skills Buddy* lesson features a series of lively scenes where children name images that match sounds they are learning. Tips for providing corrective feedback occur often so that all children are learning these critical skills to become good readers.

Phonics

How Do Children Learn Phonics?

When we help children relate the sounds of spoken language to the spellings of written language, we are teaching phonics. Phonics instruction helps children understand the systematic relationships between sounds and spellings. Becoming familiar with sound-spelling relationships helps children become successful readers and writers. In *Scott Foresman Reading Street* you will find explicit teaching of sound-spellings in a carefully developed, clearly defined sequence.

In the kindergarten program every **phonemic awareness** lesson is tied to the phonics lesson that follows it. For example, if the day's phonics instruction is short *a,* the phonemic awareness lesson that precedes it focuses on blending or segmenting short *a* words. Children benefit most from phonemic awareness instruction that connects sounds to letters. This connection is a built-in feature in *Scott Foresman Reading Street.*

Blending Sounds to Decode

Your phonics instruction begins with introducing letter-sounds in isolation. You quickly move children from recognizing sounds to blending sounds to decoding words. It's an exciting moment for children when they "crack the code" and read words with meanings they understand!

At each step, you use teaching routines to make instruction explicit. Children learn to blend the sounds into words when you use this teaching routine.

> **Phonics Routine**
> ## Sound-by-Sound Blending
>
> 1. Write the word *sat* or spell it with letter cards.
> 2. Put your hand under *s* and say /s/. Move your hand to *a* and say /a/. Move to *t* and say /t/.
> 3. Then move your hand below the word *sat* from left to right and blend the sounds sequentially, with no pause between letter-sounds, /sat/.
> 4. Then pronounce the word normally.
> 5. Have children repeat the blending process for *sat*, first with you, and then as a group.

> **What is a new word? Is the new word a word you know? Does it make sense in the sentence?**
>
> Ask these questions to help children make sense of written symbols they decode. As children respond to your questions, they reevaluate and adapt until they are successful. That "on my own" success encourages them to ask *themselves* the same questions when they read independently. You're teaching them an important lesson: they can expect written symbols to make sense.

When and What Do Children Read?

Children can quickly use what they learn to read real stories on their own. With *Scott Foresman Reading Street,* practice is exciting as children read a new Decodable Reader each week. They use different senses by singing, listening, and gesturing when they practice new skills with the Phonics Songs and Rhymes Charts. Your phonics instruction is effective because it's supported by a variety of engaging practice opportunities.

The Decodable Books in *My Skills Buddy* reinforce and apply the target sound-spellings each week. Use the Reading Decodable Books routine to incorporate reading silently, modeling, choral reading, and individual reading into your teaching. These research-based practices help children become confident, successful readers.

The Kindergarten Student Readers apply target sound-spellings and high-frequency words. The books for weeks one to five of each unit have continuing characters. The book for week six in each unit is a realistic fiction or a nonfiction selection. The readers have 100% potential for accuracy.

Every week on day 4, children are treated to a Get Set, Roll! Reader from the world of *Jon Scieszka's Trucktown.* These books are specifically aimed at the reluctant reader. The books practice the weekly target sound-spellings and high-frequency words. There is 100% potential for accuracy . . . and fun!

Read and Comprehend

Why is comprehension important? It's the ultimate goal of your reading instruction. **Comprehension** is the process of making meaning from text. It involves not just reading words accurately, but drawing on prior knowledge, making inferences, making connections, and using strategies to make sense of text. In kindergarten, **comprehension skills and strategies** should be taught through both listening and reading.

Why Is Listening Comprehension Important?

Research has shown that instruction in listening comprehension transfers to reading comprehension. Even before children are able to read complex literature on their own, you can develop their higher-level thinking skills by using read-alouds and shared reading. *Scott Foresman Reading Street* has theme-related read-alouds and shared readings built into the program. All kindergarten comprehension skills are introduced with text that is read aloud. Use this text to model how good readers use comprehension skills and strategies.

How Can I Help Children Become Good Readers?

On day 2 of each week, you will read the main story or selection for the purpose of enjoyment for children. After the initial reading children are asked to retell the selection. Research tells us that good readers can retell stories and summarize selections they have listened to. Every week you will find a Retelling or Summarizing Rubric to use in monitoring children's retelling and summarizing skills. Then children return to the Question of the Week and write together to answer the question. As children think, talk, and write about the literature they become good readers!

Good readers understand and apply what they read to other areas of their lives. To meet this goal, *Scott Foresman Reading Street* introduces a target comprehension skill each week. The target skill is practiced and applied to the current literature as well as the previously read literature.

> **Good readers are active!**
>
> You can help children become involved in conversations about the literature all week long. *Scott Foresman Reading Street* provides many opportunities for children to expand their vocabulary and understanding of the selection.

What Is Dialogic Reading?

On day 3 of each week, you will read the main story or selection. The notes in Develop Vocabulary are based on Dr. Grover J. Whitehurst's dialogic reading model.

In dialogic reading, you read a story multiple times. The first time is for enjoyment, as done on day 2. In subsequent readings, you engage children in a conversation about the book through questions and prompts. Respond to children's answers by using their response in a complete sentence. Continue the conversation by asking more questions. Use the Develop Vocabulary notes on day 3 in the Teacher's Edition to prompt conversations.

Each week children build new vocabulary through photographs, discussion, explicit instruction, and literature. On day 4 children use their new vocabulary to discuss and comprehend the story or selection. Use the Guiding Comprehension notes on day 4 to prompt children with comprehension questions.

> Dialogic reading is an approach that develops children's oral language skills and makes reading interactive and engaging. Each Develop Vocabulary and Guiding Comprehension note in *Scott Foresman's Reading Street* reflects Dr. Whitehurst's research.
>
> **Completion** Leave a blank in the question for children to fill in.
> **Recall** Ask questions about what happened in the book.
> **Open-ended** Have children tell more about an illustration or idea in the book.
> ***Wh-* Questions** Ask *Who, What, When, Where, Why,* and *How* questions.
> **Distancing** Ask questions to encourage children to relate the book to their own lives.

Language Arts

Just as with reading, children need explicit and systematic instruction, as well as meaningful practice, to become fluent writers. *Scott Foresman Reading Street* has daily writing instruction and practice activities.

Conventions

Every week children will be introduced to a grammar skill. They will practice the skill all week.

Daily Fix-It

The Daily Fix-It gives children practice with capitalization, punctuation, and grammar every day.

Writing

Children will have many opportunities to write throughout the week. Each day brings a slightly different focus to the writing lesson.

- **Wonderful, Marvelous Me!** On Day 1, writing focuses on children's emotions, imaginations, self-esteem, and personal growth. The "Wonderful, Marvelous Me!" shared writing lessons provide children the opportunity to express themselves on a variety of topics.

- **Respond to Literature** On Day 2, children respond to literature in a modeled writing lesson that engages and challenges them. The lesson provides opportunities for children to express ideas about a range of literature and text.

- **Genre Writing** On Day 3, a modeled writing lesson introduces various forms of writing to children. Children have many opportunities to practice these genres.

- **Extend the Concept** On Day 4, a shared writing lesson guides children to extend and connect new ideas to themselves, to other texts, and to the world around them.

- **Writing Process** Week 6 of every unit is devoted to writing process lessons that provide an in-depth study and application of the five stages of the writing process: plan, draft, revise, edit, and share. These lessons cover a variety of genres within the narrative and expository modes of writing.

Listening and Speaking

Children will be introduced to a speaking and listening skill every week. The skill will be introduced and practiced throughout the week. Each day children also learn and discuss two new Amazing Words.

Wrap Up Your Day!

The parent of every kindergarten child asks, "What did you do at school today?" This quick wrap-up will help children remember their day.

Extend Your Day

Integrate literacy with social studies, science, math, and other content areas through fun, focused activities. *Scott Foresman Reading Street* helps you extend the day's concepts and skill instruction with a variety of activities that connect to the week's concepts and skills.

Differentiated Instruction

When you differentiate instruction, you use lessons and strategies to meet the needs of all students. You begin by flexibly grouping children according to their instructional needs. Keep flexible groups small, no more than five children per group. This enables you to provide either additional intensive instruction and practice or more challenging work depending on children's performance. Regroup when necessary.

Which Children Make Up the Strategic Intervention Group?

Identifying kindergarten children who need strategic intervention is essential since reading accomplishments in kindergarten set the stage for much of the learning that follows. Children who are at risk for problems in reading may exhibit one or more of these characteristics:

- **Lack of Phonemic Awareness** Deficits in phonemic abilities are the basis of some reading disabilities. Intense phonemic training should be part of any preventative or remedial program for at-risk children.

- **Difficulty Connecting Sounds and Letters** Children may struggle when identifying sounds and applying them to letters. Providing children with intensive, systematic, and explicit phonics instruction along with additional practice and teacher feedback are essential components of *Scott Foresman Reading Street.*

How Do I Meet All Children's Needs?

Scott Foresman Reading Street integrates into the core program daily extra support strategies for children at the Strategic Intervention level as well as for On-Level and Advanced. You'll find these point-of-use supports for English language learners also.

For comprehensive instructional materials to address the needs of your flexible groups, turn to the daily lessons and pacing that *Reading Street* provides. Daily lessons are designed specifically for each group—Strategic Intervention, On-Level, and Advanced—and for English Language Learners.

During group time, children will need independent literacy activities to complete while you meet with small groups. The Small Group Time pages in each Teacher's Edition will tell you where to find instruction for each group and independent activities recommended for that day.

Assessment

How Can I Make Regrouping Decisions?

As you travel on your kindergarten teaching journey, you'll use a variety of assessment tools along the way. At the beginning of the year, use the *Baseline Group Test* to help identify children's needs. Assessment is a key tool for determining when you want to regroup children. You may want to group them according to ability levels, skills, interests, or strategy instruction.

Throughout the week, you'll often assess children with regular progress monitoring. *If . . . then* is corrective feedback integrated in the Teacher's Edition lessons in *Reading Street.* The "Don't Wait Until Friday" assessments help you monitor progress regularly during the week. On day 5 you assess children to determine their mastery of the target weekly skills. You have multiple, consistent opportunities to assess children during your literacy instruction. At the end of longer periods of instruction, or whenever you choose, use these observations and reliable data for making your regrouping decisions.

The *Reading Street* Authors answer the most Frequently Asked Questions

Here's "the scoop" on *Reading Street!*

1. **What's the underlying "story" of *Reading Street*?**
   Reading Street provides explicit, systematic, high-quality instruction focusing on the five critical elements of reading identified by research: phonemic awareness, phonics, fluency, vocabulary, and text comprehension, as well as an emphasis on concept and oral language development.

2. **How is *Reading Street* different from other basal programs?**
   Reading Street is built around the "Understanding by Design" model of instruction. Each unit focuses on a "big question" that connects reading, vocabulary, and writing for a full six weeks. Children expand their higher order thinking skills and conceptual understanding by exploring different aspects of the "big question" and a series of related sub-questions each week, creating a culture of engaging inquiry around ideas and texts.

3. **Is there a Spanish program? Are the same resources available in Spanish?**
   Calle de la Lectura is *Reading Street's* fully aligned Spanish literacy system. It provides parallel Spanish instruction, as well as integrated language and concept development.

4. **How are the Student and Teacher's editions organized?**
   Student Editions include six units of integrated reading, writing, skill, and vocabulary development organized under a unit concept. Weekly paired texts further develop each concept and are aligned to either Science or Social Studies.

   Our Teacher's Editions have a unique delivery system of 12 slim, manageable volumes, allowing for greater pacing flexibility while keeping the integrity of our validated scope and sequence. Teachers will find opportunities to customize grade level lesson plans to serve all learners for both reading and language arts instruction.

5. **Is *Reading Street* for all students? What about below and above level learners, English Language Learners, and other learners?**
   One of the key goals of *Reading Street* is to support and meet the individualized needs of all learners. Focused differentiated group work provides targeted and explicit instruction that helps all learners participate alongside their peers.

6. **Why is there a student book at Kindergarten?**
   Young children respond to lively, interactive print materials as they are building a sense of themselves as readers and learners. *My Skills Buddy,* designed to be a companion to the classroom content, serves as a handbook children can visit to apply and practice newly acquired skills.

7. **How does *Reading Street* help teachers assess students?**
   Reading Street's assessment plan helps teachers assess their students both formally and informally. Daily Success Predictors help teachers monitor priority skills by assessing predictors of reading success. Weekly Assessment Checkpoints provide a more formal way of identifying students' understanding of key concepts and skills.

8. **Are there digital resources that go with this program (or an online version)?**
   Reading Street provides a robust digital path that aligns with each week of instruction. Digital components such as animations, songs, videos, and interactive games support instruction and make the content relevant, motivating, and accessible to all learners.

9. **What other products and support materials come with the program?**
   Reading Street provides a wide array of text products, digital products, and interactive products that support the varying modalities and levels of all children.

Assessment on Reading Street

Your journey is a safe one when you have a guide who knows the way. For your kindergarten teaching journey, assessment can be your trusted guide.

With *Scott Foresman Reading Street*, you have assessment planning and tools at your fingertips. The **Section 3** overview shows how each type of assessment is ready for you to use when you need it. You'll see at a glance how you can make decisions about the focus, pacing, and grouping for your instruction throughout your lesson and week and at other key times through the year.

You'll also learn more about the assessment tools. They provide the data-driven instruction you need for your kindergarteners on *Reading Street.* Use these tools to set your kindergarteners on the path to reading success.

Assessment and Grouping

What Makes Grouping and Assessment Effective?

At the beginning of the year, you want know your kindergarteners' interests, learning styles, and academic needs. When you use the right assessments at the right times, you get to know children quickly. The next step, determining your groups for effective instruction, becomes easier. All along the way, you monitor children's progress and use that information to regroup them.

When and How Is It Best to Assess?

In order to know your kindergarteners, you need critical information all through the year. This data comes through a 4-step process:

1. Diagnose and Differentiate
2. Monitor Progress
3. Assess and Regroup
4. Summative Assessment

① Diagnose and Differentiate

At the beginning of the year, it is important to diagnose children's instructional needs. Use the Baseline Group Test or another initial placement test such as the DIBELS. Then you can plan your groups.

Why Is Diagnosing a Critical Step? Diagnosis gives you a picture of where each child is at that moment. When you diagnose early, you have data to identify who is at risk of failing and needs extra support. It also helps you determine which children have not mastered the previous year's standards. You also find out who is performing on level or above level.

How Do I Provide Differentiated Instruction for Different Abilities? After you diagnose, you can turn to *Scott Foresman Reading Street* for lessons and pacing designed for three levels.

If children assess at the **SI** level, use the regular instruction and the daily **Strategic Intervention** small group lessons.

If children assess at the **OL** level, use the regular instruction and the daily **On Level** small group lessons.

If children assess at the **A** level, use the regular instruction and the daily **Advanced** small group lessons.

The lessons focus on target strategies and skills as they help you offer intensive, explicit, and advanced instructional approaches. When it's time for children to read, you can match them to a wide array of books at their instructional and independent reading levels. With leveled books, children are continually challenged and engaged.

For more support for struggling readers, you can also use the Strategic Intervention lessons in the Teacher's Edition and the Reading Street Intervention Kit for children who need intensive intervention.

② Monitor Progress

Each week you can assess at the lesson level by taking time to monitor targeted skills and strategy instruction. Using a variety of these "during-the-lesson" and weekly assessments, you are consistently aware of how children change and develop throughout the year. You are equipped with performance data so you can meet individual needs.

Scott Foresman Reading Street offers tools that allow you to pause for assessment at different critical points of instruction.

During lesson instruction, pause for spiral review and *if…, then…* corrective feedback. They help you quickly track children's understanding of key instruction. You can use Don't Wait Until Friday checklists to assess children's progress in phonemic awareness, word reading, retelling, and oral vocabulary. At various points during instruction, you can use Reader's and Writer's Notebook activities as assessment tools.

At the end of the week, monitor children's phonics and comprehension progress with the Weekly Assessment on Day 5. Weekly Tests give you data on children's progress as you teach target skills.

Now that you have data, you can plan your whole-group and small-group instruction. The *Reading Street* program has suggestions and pacing to guide you as these questions come to mind.

- Which skills and strategies do children need to develop? How can I make these the focus of instruction?
- Which children can be grouped together for skill instruction or reteaching?
- Which children can be grouped together in reading groups?
- Which children need additional instruction and perhaps intensive intervention?

When you teach the weekly skills and strategies, you don't want to wait until the weekly tests on Friday, or even later, to find if your teaching has been effective for all children. An effective practice is to monitor children's progress at key times during the week. These informal assessments are guides that help you identify children who need extra support as well as those who will benefit from challenge activities.

❸ Assess and Regroup

A clearer picture of each kindergartener is coming into focus as a result of your assessment throughout the weekly lessons. The initial groups you formed were based on data from diagnosis at the beginning of the year. As children change and develop throughout kindergarten, you will need to regroup them for differentiated instruction.

When Is It Best to Regroup? Regrouping is a part of the assessment process, so you rely on assessments to help you determine new groups. Recommendations in *Scott Foresman Reading Street* guide teachers to begin by recording the results of the Weekly Assessments. Then they use the data from retelling and phonics to track progress. *Reading Street's* Unit Benchmark Test results are important to include. This summative assessment reveals how children are achieving mastery of the unit skills.

Other assessments, such as DIBELS, may recommend regrouping at other times during the year.

These assessments keep the goal of mastery reachable for all children because you quickly identify children in need of additional practice or reteaching. Responsive individual or group instruction will return children to on-level learning. Begin to think about regrouping as you near the end of the second unit of instruction, and then regroup for subsequent units.

❹ Summative Assessment

At fixed times, you should check children's progress toward skills and standards. These assessments show the effectiveness of your instruction. The Unit Benchmark Tests measure children's mastery of target skills taught throughout the unit. The End-of-Year test measures children's mastery of target skills taught throughout the six units of the program.

Use the Differentiated Instruction suggestions in the Teacher's Edition and the Reteach Lessons in *First Stop on Reading Street* to meet individual needs. The Small Group Time lessons provide flexible ways for pacing the instruction for Strategic Intervention, On-level, and Advanced levels of instruction throughout the week.

Grouping Throughout the Year

Initial Grouping	Diagnose using the Baseline Group Test. Use the same groups for Units 1 and 2.
Regroup	for Unit 3
Regroup	for Unit 4
Regroup	for Unit 5
Regroup	for Unit 6

Teacher Form

Narrative Retelling Chart

Unit _____ Selection Title _____ Name _____ Date _____

Retelling Criteria/Teacher Prompt	Teacher-Aided Response	Student-Generated Response	Rubric Score (Circle one.)
Connections Did you like this book? Why or why not? How does this story remind you of other stories?			4 3 2 1
Author's Purpose What was the author trying to teach us?			4 3 2 1
Characters Describe _____ (character's name).			4 3 2 1
Setting Where and when did the story happen?			4 3 2 1
Plot Tell me what happened in the story.			4 3 2 1

Summative Retelling Score 4 3 2 1

Comments _____

See also *Assessment Handbook* | © Pearson Education, Inc.

See also *Assessment Handbook* | © Pearson Education, Inc.

Teacher Form

Expository Summarizing Chart

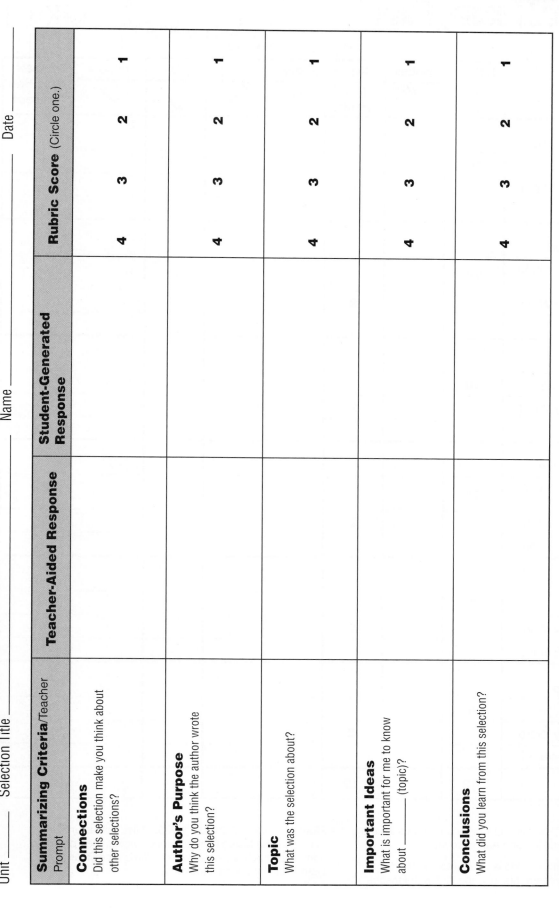

Unit _____ Selection Title _____

Name _____ Date _____

Summarizing Criteria/Teacher Prompt	Teacher-Aided Response	Student-Generated Response	Rubric Score (Circle one.)			
Connections Did this selection make you think about other selections?			4	3	2	1
Author's Purpose Why do you think the author wrote this selection?			4	3	2	1
Topic What was the selection about?			4	3	2	1
Important Ideas What is important for me to know about _____ (topic)?			4	3	2	1
Conclusions What did you learn from this selection?			4	3	2	1

Summative Summarizing Score   4   3   2   1

Comments _____

Name _____

Letter/Word Reading Chart

USE WITH GRADE K UNIT 1

S = Satisfactory
N = Needs practice

	Letter Recognition		High-Frequency		Comprehension		Reteach	Reassess: Number Correct
	Total Letters	Letters Correct	Total Words	Words Correct	S ✔	N ✔	✔	
Week 1 *The Little School Bus*								
Aa, Bb, Cc, Dd, Ee	10							
High-Frequency Words			2					
Character								
Week 2 *We Are So Proud*								
Ff, Gg, Hh, Ii, Jj, Kk, Ll, Mm, Nn	18							
High-Frequency Words			2					
Setting								
Week 3 *Plaidypus Lost*								
Oo, Pp, Qq, Rr, Ss	10							
High-Frequency Words			2					
Sequence								
Week 4 *Miss Bindergarten*								
Tt, Uu, Vv, Ww, Xx, Yy, Zz	15							
High-Frequency Words			2					
Classify and Categorize								
Week 5 *Smash! Crash!*								
/m/Mm	5							
High-Frequency Words			2					
Character and Setting								
Week 6 *Dig Dig Digging*								
/t/Tt	4							
High-Frequency Words			2					
Classify and Categorize								
Unit Scores	62		12					

- **RECORD SCORES** Use this chart to record scores for the Day 5 Letter/Word Reading Assessment.

- **RETEACH SKILLS** If the child is unable to successfully complete the assessments, use the Reteach lessons in *First Stop*.

- **PRACTICE HIGH-FREQUENCY WORDS** If the child is unable to read all the tested high-frequency words, then provide additional practice for the week's words. Use Routine Card 5 for Nondecodable Words.

See also Assessment Handbook | © Pearson Education, Inc.

Word/Sentence Reading Chart

USE WITH GRADE K UNIT 2

S = Satisfactory
N = Needs practice

	Phonics		High-Frequency		Comprehension		Reteach	Reassess:
	Total Words	Words Correct	Total Words	Words Correct	S ✔	N ✔	✔	Words Correct
Week 1 *Flowers*								
Short *a*	6							
High-Frequency Words			4					
Compare and Contrast								
Week 2 *Nature Spy*								
/s/*Ss*	5							
High-Frequency Words			4					
Setting								
Week 3 *Animal Babies in Grasslands*								
/p/*Pp*	7							
High-Frequency Words			5					
Main Idea								
Week 4 *Bear Snores On*								
/k/*Cc*	7							
High-Frequency Words			5					
Realism and Fantasy								
Week 5 *A Bed for the Winter*								
Short *i*	8							
High-Frequency Words			4					
Sequence								
Week 6 *Jack and the Beanstalk*								
Short *i*	8							
High-Frequency Words			4					
Realism and Fantasy								
Unit Scores	41		26					

- **RECORD SCORES** Use this chart to record scores for the Day 5 Word Reading Assessment.

- **RETEACH SKILLS** If the child is unable to successfully complete the assessments, use the Reteach lessons in *First Stop*.

- **PRACTICE HIGH-FREQUENCY WORDS** If the child is unable to read all the tested high-frequency words, then provide additional practice for the week's words. Use Routine Card 5 for Nondecodable Words.

- **REASSESS** Use two different sentences for reassessment.

Name _____

Word/Sentence Reading Chart

S = Satisfactory
N = Needs practice

	Phonics		High-Frequency		Comprehension		Reteach	Reassess: Words Correct
	Total Words	Words Correct	Total Words	Words Correct	S ✔	N ✔	✔	
Week 1 *Little Panda*								
/b/Bb; /n/Nn	14							
High-Frequency Words			5					
Compare and Contrast								
Week 2 *Little Quack*								
/r/Rr	9							
High-Frequency Words			5					
Plot								
Week 3 *George Washington Visits*								
/d/Dd; /k/Kk	15							
High-Frequency Words			4					
Cause and Effect								
Week 4 *Farfallina and Marcel*								
/f/Ff	10							
High-Frequency Words			4					
Plot								
Week 5 *Then and Now*								
Short o	11							
High-Frequency Words			5					
Draw Conclusions								
Week 6 *The Lion and the Mouse*								
Short o	11							
High-Frequency Words			5					
Main Idea								
Unit Scores	70		28					

- **RECORD SCORES** Use this chart to record scores for the Day 5 Letter/Word Reading Assessment.

- **RETEACH SKILLS** If the child is unable to successfully complete the assessments, use the Reteach lessons in *First Stop*.

- **PRACTICE HIGH-FREQUENCY WORDS** If the child is unable to read all the tested high-frequency words, then provide additional practice for the week's words. Use Routine Card 5 for Nondecodable Words.

- **REASSESS** Use two different sentences for reassessment.

See also Assessment Handbook | © Pearson Education, Inc.

Word/Sentence Reading Chart

USE WITH GRADE **K** UNIT **4**

S = Satisfactory
N = Needs practice

	Phonics		High-Frequency		Comprehension		Reteach	Reassess:
	Total Words	Words Correct	Total Words	Words Correct	S ✔	N ✔	✔	Words Correct
Week 1 *Rooster's Off to See the World*								
/h/Hh	11							
High-Frequency Words			5					
Sequence								
Week 2 *My Lucky Day*								
/l/Ll	11							
High-Frequency Words			5					
Cause and Effect								
Week 3 *One Little Mouse*								
Consonant Blends	9							
High-Frequency Words			7					
Sequence								
Week 4 *Goldilocks*								
/g/Gg	9							
High-Frequency Words			7					
Character, Setting, Plot								
Week 5 *If You Could Go to Antarctica*								
Short e	13							
High-Frequency Words			5					
Classify and Categorize								
Week 6 *Abuela*								
Short e	13							
High-Frequency Words			5					
Setting								
Unit Scores	66		34					

- **RECORD SCORES** Use this chart to record scores for the Day 5 Word/Sentence Reading Assessment.

- **RETEACH SKILLS** If the child is unable to successfully complete the assessments, use the Reteach lessons in *First Stop*.

- **PRACTICE HIGH-FREQUENCY WORDS** If the child is unable to read all the tested high-frequency words, then provide additional practice for the week's words. Use Routine Card 5 for Nondecodable Words.

- **REASSESS** Use two different sentences for reassessment.

Name _____

Word/Sentence Reading Chart

USE WITH GRADE K UNIT 5

S = Satisfactory
N = Needs practice

	Phonics		High-Frequency		Comprehension		Reteach	Reassess: Words Correct
	Total Words	Words Correct	Total Words	Words Correct	S ✔	N ✔	✔	
Week 1 *Max Takes the Train*								
/w/Ww; /j/Jj	11							
High-Frequency Words			5					
Realism and Fantasy								
Week 2 *Mayday! Mayday!*								
/ks/Xx	11							
High-Frequency Words			5					
Cause and Effect								
Week 3 *Trucks Roll!*								
/u/Uu	13							
High-Frequency Words			5					
Compare and Contrast								
Week 4 *The Little Engine*								
/u/Uu	13							
High-Frequency Words			5					
Plot								
Week 5 *On the Move!*								
/v/Vv; /z/Zz	14							
High-Frequency Words			4					
Main Idea								
Week 6 *This Is the Way We Go to School*								
/y/Yy; /kw/Qq	14							
High-Frequency Words			4					
Draw Conclusions								
Unit Scores	76		28					

- **RECORD SCORES** Use this chart to record scores for the Day 5 Word/Sentence Reading Assessment.

- **RETEACH SKILLS** If the child is unable to successfully complete the assessments, use the Reteach lessons in *First Stop*.

- **PRACTICE HIGH-FREQUENCY WORDS** If the child is unable to read all the tested high-frequency words, then provide additional practice for the week's words. Use Routine Card 5 for Nondecodable Words.

- **REASSESS** Use two different sentences for reassessment.

See also *Assessment Handbook* | © Pearson Education, Inc.

Word/Sentence Reading Chart

USE WITH GRADE K UNIT 6

S = Satisfactory
N = Needs practice

	Phonics		High-Frequency		Comprehension		Reteach	Reassess:
	Total Words	Words Correct	Total Words	Words Correct	S ✔	N ✔	✔	Words Correct
Week 1 *Building With Dad*								
Short *a;* Short *i*	12							
High-Frequency Words			10					
Compare and Contrast								
Week 2 *Old MacDonald*								
Short *o*	12							
High-Frequency Words			10					
Character								
Week 3 *Building Beavers*								
Short *e*	12							
High-Frequency Words			10					
Main Idea								
Week 4 *Allistair and Kips Great Adventure*								
Short *u*	12							
High-Frequency Words			10					
Plot								
Week 5 *The House That Tony Lives In*								
Short vowels *a, e, i, o, u*	12							
High-Frequency Words			10					
Setting								
Week 6 *Ants and Their Nests*								
Short vowels *a, e, i, o, u*	12							
High-Frequency Words			10					
Draw Conclusions								
Unit Scores	72		60					

- **RECORD SCORES** Use this chart to record scores for the Day 5 Word/Sentence Reading Assessment.

- **RETEACH SKILLS** If the child is unable to successfully complete the assessments, use the Reteach lessons in *First Stop*.

- **PRACTICE HIGH-FREQUENCY WORDS** If the child is unable to read all the tested high-frequency words, then provide additional practice for the week's words. Use Routine Card 5 for Nondecodable Words.

- **REASSESS** Use two different sentences for reassessment.

Unit 1
Assess and Regroup

FYI In Kindergarten there are opportunities for regrouping every six weeks—at the end of Units 2, 3, 4, and 5. These options offer sensitivity to each child's progress although some teachers may prefer to regroup less frequently.

Regroup for Unit 2
To make regrouping decisions at the end of Unit 1, consider children's end-of-unit scores for
- Unit 1 Day 5 Assessments
- Unit 1 Benchmark Assessment

Group Time

On-Level	Strategic Intervention	Advanced
To continue On-Level or to move into the On-Level group, children should	Children would benefit from Strategic Intervention if they	To move to the Advanced group, children should
• score 80% or better on their cumulative Unit Scores on the Day 5 Assessment	• score 60% or lower on their cumulative Unit Scores on the Day 5 Assessment	• score 100% on their cumulative Unit Scores for the Day 5 Assessment
• score Developing on 3 or 4 skill strands of the Unit 1 Benchmark Assessment	• score Emerging on 2 or more skill strands of the Unit 1 Benchmark Assessment	• score Proficient on at least 4 skill strands of the Unit 1 Benchmark Assessment
• be capable of working in the On-Level group based on teacher judgment	• are struggling to keep up with the On-Level group based on teacher judgment	• read above grade level material fluently. You may try them out on the Independent Leveled Reader.
		• be capable of handling the work of the Advanced group based on teacher judgment
		• score 4 on retelling in this unit and demonstrate ease of language in their retellings

Questions to Consider
- What types of test questions did the child miss? Are they specific to a particular skill or strategy?
- Does the child have adequate background knowledge to understand the test passages or selections for retelling?

- Has the child's performance met expectations for daily lessons and assessments with little or no reteaching?
- Is the child performing more like children in another group?
- Does the child read for enjoyment, different purposes, and with varied interests?

Unit Scores
Weighted
100% = 74
80% = 59
60% = 44

Unit 2
Assess and Regroup

FYI In Kindergarten there are opportunities for regrouping every six weeks—at the end of Units 2, 3, 4, and 5. These options offer sensitivity to each child's progress although some teachers may prefer to regroup less frequently.

Regroup for Unit 3
To make regrouping decisions at the end of Unit 2, consider children's end-of-unit scores for
- Unit 2 Day 5 Assessments
- Unit 2 Benchmark Assessment

Group Time

On-Level	Strategic Intervention	Advanced
To continue On-Level or to move into the On-Level group, children should	Children would benefit from Strategic Intervention if they	To move to the Advanced group, children should
• score 80% or better on their cumulative Unit Scores on the Day 5 Assessment	• score 60% or lower on their cumulative Unit Scores on the Day 5 Assessment	• score 100% on their cumulative Unit Scores for the Day 5 Assessment
• score Developing on 3 or 4 skill strands of the Unit 2 Benchmark Assessment	• score Emerging on 2 or more skill strands of the Unit 2 Benchmark Assessment	• score Proficient on at least 4 skill strands of the Unit 2 Benchmark Assessment
• be capable of working in the On-Level group based on teacher judgment	• are struggling to keep up with the On-Level group based on teacher judgment	• read above grade level material fluently. You may try them out on the Independent Leveled Reader.
		• be capable of handling the work of the Advanced group based on teacher judgment
		• score 4 on retelling in this unit and demonstrate ease of language in their retellings

Questions to Consider

- What types of test questions did the child miss? Are they specific to a particular skill or strategy?
- Does the child have adequate background knowledge to understand the test passages or selections for retelling?

- Has the child's performance met expectations for daily lessons and assessments with little or no reteaching?
- Is the child performing more like children in another group?
- Does the child read for enjoyment, different purposes, and with varied interests?

Unit Scores
Weighted

100% =	67
80% =	54
60% =	40

Unit 3
Assess and Regroup

FYI In Kindergarten there are opportunities for regrouping every six weeks—at the end of Units 2, 3, 4, and 5. These options offer sensitivity to each child's progress although some teachers may prefer to regroup less frequently.

Regroup for Unit 4

To make regrouping decisions at the end of Unit 3, consider children's end-of-unit scores for
- Unit 3 Day 5 Assessments
- Unit 3 Benchmark Assessment

Group Time

On-Level	**Strategic Intervention**	**Advanced**
To continue On-Level or to move into the On-Level group, children should	Children would benefit from Strategic Intervention if they	To move to the Advanced group, children should
• score 80% or better on their cumulative Unit Scores on the Day 5 Assessment	• score 60% or lower on their cumulative Unit Scores on the Day 5 Assessment	• score 100% on their cumulative Unit Scores for the Day 5 Assessment
• score Developing on 3 or 4 skill strands of the Unit 3 Benchmark Assessment	• score Emerging on 2 or more skill strands of the Unit 3 Benchmark Assessment	• score Proficient on at least 4 skill strands of the Unit 3 Benchmark Assessment
• be capable of working in the On-Level group based on teacher judgment	• are struggling to keep up with the On-Level group based on teacher judgment	• read above grade level material fluently. You may try them out on the Independent Leveled Reader.
		• be capable of handling the work of the Advanced group based on teacher judgment
		• score 4 on retelling in this unit and demonstrate ease of language in their retellings

Questions to Consider

- What types of test questions did the child miss? Are they specific to a particular skill or strategy?
- Does the child have adequate background knowledge to understand the test passages or selections for retelling?

- Has the child's performance met expectations for daily lessons and assessments with little or no reteaching?
- Is the child performing more like children in another group?
- Does the child read for enjoyment, different purposes, and with varied interests?

Unit Scores

Weighted

100% = 98
 80% = 78
 60% = 59

Unit 4
Assess and Regroup

FYI In Kindergarten there are opportunities for regrouping every six weeks—at the end of Units 2, 3, 4, and 5. These options offer sensitivity to each child's progress, although some teachers may prefer to regroup less frequently.

Regroup for Unit 5

To make regrouping decisions at the end of Unit 4, consider children's end-of-unit scores for
- Unit 4 Day 5 Assessments
- Unit 4 Benchmark Assessment

Group Time

On-Level	Strategic Intervention	Advanced
To continue On-Level or to move into the On-Level group, children should	Children would benefit from Strategic Intervention if they	To move to the Advanced group, children should
• score 80% or better on their cumulative Unit Scores on the Day 5 Assessment	• score 60% or lower on their cumulative Unit Scores on the Day 5 Assessment	• score 100% on their cumulative Unit Scores for the Day 5 Assessment
• score Developing on 3 or 4 skill strands of the Unit 4 Benchmark Assessment	• score Emerging on 2 or more skill strands of the Unit 4 Benchmark Assessment	• score Proficient on at least 4 skill strands of the Unit 4 Benchmark Assessment
• be capable of working in the On-Level group based on teacher judgment	• are struggling to keep up with the On-Level group based on teacher judgment	• read above grade level material fluently. You may try them out on the Independent Leveled Reader.
		• be capable of handling the work of the Advanced group based on teacher judgment
		• score 4 on retelling in this unit and demonstrate ease of language in their retellings

Questions to Consider

- What types of test questions did the child miss? Are they specific to a particular skill or strategy?
- Does the child have adequate background knowledge to understand the test passages or selections for retelling?

- Has the child's performance met expectations for daily lessons and assessments with little or no reteaching?
- Is the child performing more like children in another group?
- Does the child read for enjoyment, different purposes, and with varied interests?

Unit Scores

Weighted

100% = 100
80% = 80
60% = 60

Unit 5
Assess and Regroup

FYI In Kindergarten there are opportunities for regrouping every six weeks—at the end of Units 2, 3, 4, and 5. These options offer sensitivity to each child's progress although some teachers may prefer to regroup less frequently.

Regroup for Unit 6

To make regrouping decisions at the end of Unit 5, consider children's end-of-unit scores for
- Unit 5 Day 5 Assessments
- Unit 5 Benchmark Assessment

Group Time

On-Level

To continue On-Level or to move into the On-Level group, children should

- score 80% or better on their cumulative Unit Scores on the Day 5 Assessment
- score Developing on 3 or 4 skill strands of the Unit 5 Benchmark Assessment
- be capable of working in the On-Level group based on teacher judgment

Strategic Intervention

Children would benefit from Strategic Intervention if they

- score 60% or lower on their cumulative Unit Scores on the Day 5 Assessment
- score Emerging on 2 or more skill strands of the Unit 5 Benchmark Assessment
- are struggling to keep up with the On-Level group based on teacher judgment

Advanced

To move to the Advanced group, children should

- score 100% on their cumulative Unit Scores for the Day 5 Assessment
- score Proficient on at least 4 skill strands of the Unit 5 Benchmark Assessment
- read above grade level material fluently. You may try them out on the Independent Leveled Reader.
- be capable of handling the work of the Advanced group based on teacher judgment
- score 4 on retelling in this unit and demonstrate ease of language in their retellings

Questions to Consider

- What types of test questions did the child miss? Are they specific to a particular skill or strategy?
- Does the child have adequate background knowledge to understand the test passages or selections for retelling?

- Has the child's performance met expectations for daily lessons and assessments with little or no reteaching?
- Is the child performing more like children in another group?
- Does the child read for enjoyment, different purposes, and with varied interests?

Unit Scores

Weighted

100%	= 104
80%	= 83
60%	= 62

Unit 6
Assess and Regroup

 **FYI** In Kindergarten there are opportunities for regrouping every six weeks—at the end of Units 2, 3, 4, and 5. These options offer sensitivity to each child's progress although some teachers may prefer to regroup less frequently.

Regroup for First Grade
To help the next teacher make grouping decisions, consider children's end-of-unit scores for
- Unit 6 Day 5 Assessments
- Unit 6 Benchmark Assessment

Group Time

On-Level

To continue On-Level or to move into the On-Level group, children should

- score 80% or better on their cumulative Unit Scores on the Day 5 Assessment
- score Developing on 3 or 4 skill strands of the Unit 6 Benchmark Assessment
- be capable of working in the On-Level group based on teacher judgment

Strategic Intervention

Children would benefit from Strategic Intervention if they

- score 60% or lower on their cumulative Unit Scores on the Day 5 Assessment
- score Emerging on 2 or more skill strands of the Unit 6 Benchmark Assessment
- are struggling to keep up with the On-Level group based on teacher judgment

To move to the Advanced group, children should

- score 100% on their cumulative Unit Scores for the Day 5 Assessment
- score Proficient on at least 4 skill strands of the Unit 6 Benchmark Assessment
- read above grade level material fluently. You may try them out on the Independent Leveled Reader.
- be capable of handling the work of the Advanced group based on teacher judgment
- score 4 on retelling in this unit and demonstrate ease of language in their retellings

Questions to Consider

- What types of test questions did the child miss? Are they specific to a particular skill or strategy?
- Does the child have adequate background knowledge to understand the test passages or selections for retelling?

- Has the child's performance met expectations for daily lessons and assessments with little or no reteaching?
- Is the child performing more like children in another group?
- Does the child read for enjoyment, different purposes, and with varied interests?

Unit Scores
Weighted

100% =	132
80% =	106
60% =	79

Differentiate Instruction on Reading Street

Kindergarten children all seem to have boundless energy and enthusiasm. Once you get to know your new class, you'll recognize that they also have differences. Some will need more support and others will need more challenges.

Section 4 explains the multiple options *Scott Foresman Reading Street* offers for differentiating instruction.

- Strategic Intervention

- On-Level

- Advanced

- English Language Learners

Academic success depends on learning to read well. In turn, learning to read well depends on rich language knowledge. In this section, you'll see how the plans for small groups in *Reading Street* are carefully designed so that all children experience that rich language environment. Use them to help children meet your high expectations.

Differentiated Instruction for Group Time

How Can I Use Flexible Groups for Instruction?

The Baseline Group Test, published by Scott Foresman, will help identify children's needs at the beginning of the year. Throughout the year, use the results of regular progress monitoring to make regrouping decisions.

Reading Street provides weekly plans and daily lessons for these types of small group instruction: Strategic Intervention, On-level, Advanced, and English Language Learners. Keep flexible groups small with no more than five children per group.

SI Strategic Intervention

OL On-Level

A Advanced

ELL English Language Learners

Reading Street follows the Response to Intervention model (RTI) to help you reach your goal of meeting the instructional needs of all children. It offers a process that monitors children's progress throughout the year so you can support on-level and advanced children and identify struggling readers early. More support is in the Response to Intervention Kit, which addresses the five core areas of reading instruction: phonemic awareness, phonics, fluency, vocabulary, and comprehension. As you work with struggling readers in small groups, you can use the kit for additional teacher modeling, more scaffolding, and multiple opportunities for practice. You have the strategies and tools you need to prevent these children from falling behind.

How Do I Use Practice Stations to Manage Small Groups?

During group time, children will need independent literacy activities to complete while you meet with small groups. Paired reading for fluency practice, journal writing, and activities at practice stations are all good activities for this time. The weekly Differentiated Instruction pages in each Teacher's Edition tell you where to find instruction for each group and provides *If . . . Then . . .* activities to support individual children.

Spend time at the beginning of the year coaching children on how to take responsibility for completing their independent work. Establish expectations, routines, and rules. Discuss rules with children and post them. Make sure children know what to do if they run out of materials or finish early. Support them in solving problems that may arise during this time.

The Scott Foresman Reading Street Practice Stations Kit contains grade level Practice Stations Flipcharts and a Management Handbook that includes lesson-specific reproducible work plans for children.

The Practice Stations Kit provides suggestions for six practice stations each week. The station activities support the week's skills and expand the week's concepts. Informal, ongoing assessments are an important means of guiding classroom instruction, and station activities provide excellent opportunities for ongoing assessments. Rubrics, portfolios, and other informal observation ideas are included in the Practice Stations Kit.

Differentiated Instruction for Strategic Intervention

Identifying your kindergarteners who need intervention is essential. Reading accomplishments in kindergarten set the stage for much of the learning that follows. Observe children who are at risk of problems in learning to read and plan early for intervention. These children will exhibit one or more of these characteristics:

- **Lack of phonemic awareness.** It has been found that deficits in phonemic abilities are the basis of some reading disabilities. Explicit, intense phonemic training should be part of any preventive or remedial program for children who are at-risk for reading problems.

- **Difficulties in connecting sounds and letters.** Children may struggle when identifying sounds and applying them to letters. Providing children with intensive, systematic, explicit phonics instruction along with additional practice and teacher feedback are essential components of *Reading Street*.

How Can I Help Children with a Very Low Reading Ability?

Some children come to kindergarten with lower basic skills than other children in the Strategic Intervention group. To provide them additional support in skills and concepts, the Small Group Instruction lessons for Strategic Intervention include the Concept Literacy Leveled Readers. Each book is written at a lower level than the Below-Level Reader for the week. The books align with the weekly concepts in each unit and provide struggling readers with a way to practice independent reading as they build understanding and develop concept knowledge. The Concept Literacy Readers play a role in the instruction for the Strategic Intervention group, but they can be used for independent reading practice for any struggling reader.

As necessary, use a variety of approaches and equipment aids in your classroom. They'll allow all children to succeed using *Reading Street.*

What Is Strategic Intervention?

Scott Foresman Reading Street integrates into the core program daily extra support strategies for strategic intervention—the differentiated instruction that children who are struggling need. You have comprehensive guidance and effective, efficient, and explicit instruction for readers who struggle. This extra support includes

- materials to reinforce and extend the daily lessons.

- instructional opportunities to increase background knowledge and reteach prerequisite skills.

- preteaching and reteaching of lesson skills.

- additional practice in key skills and strategies taught in the lesson.

- additional opportunities for vocabulary and concept development.

- more frequent opportunities to read and respond with teacher feedback.

- additional opportunities for checking understanding.

Differentiated Instruction for Advanced Learners

How Do Advanced Learners Differ from Other Learners?

Research suggests that advanced learners learn faster, identify and solve problems more easily, and understand and make connections among abstract concepts. Advanced readers show these characteristics:

- They enjoy reading. They read for knowledge and seek depth and complexity in their reading. They tend to prefer nonfiction and pursue interest-based reading opportunities.

- They read early and above-level. These learners read at least one-and-a-half to two grade levels above their chronological grade placement.

- They have advanced processing skills in reading. They retain large amounts of information and analyze and synthesize ideas quickly.

- They have advanced language skills. They enjoy the subtleties of language and use an expansive vocabulary.

Reading Street integrates daily instruction for advanced learners into the core program. The Advanced lessons include these strategies to meet advanced learners' needs:

- acceleration of the curriculum to provide more advanced work
- creative or critical thinking activities and advanced inquiry projects
- opportunities for independent study
- recommendations for advanced trade books on the week's theme
- interest-based reading opportunities
- small group instruction

All children should have opportunities to participate in appropriately challenging learning experiences. Advanced lessons will ensure that all learners make continuous progress in reading.

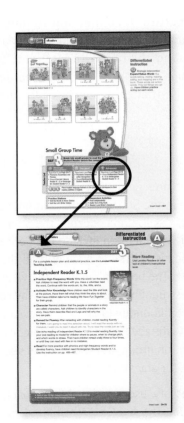

Differentiated Instruction for English Language Learners

How Do English Language Learners Differ from Other Learners?

Academic success depends on learning to read well. Learning to read well depends on rich language knowledge—which presents unique challenges for English language learners and others who have not acquired academic English.

A lack of reading and language skills should not be taken as a sign that children have a language or reading deficit, but rather that their language experiences haven't included sufficient academic instruction. In order for English language learners to participate fully in reading/language arts instruction and thrive as readers and writers, these language needs must be provided for.

How Do I Meet the Needs of English Language Learners?

Daily support for English language learners can be found in the Differentiated Instruction feature in the *Reading Street* Teacher's Edition, as well as daily lessons for your ELL group. They offer pacing suggestions for the week and scaffolded instruction for the week's target skills and strategies.

English language learner support is designed to enable you to "front-load," or preteach, the core instruction. It is also beneficial to children as reteaching. Activities address various levels of proficiency of English language learners, writing, science and history-social science, vocabulary, and transfer skills.

Support for English Language Learners on *Scott Foresman Reading Street* includes

ELL Posters

- Large-format posters that support tested vocabulary and weekly concepts
- Daily structured talk for practice of speaking and listening skills

ELL/ELD Readers

- Weekly accessible readers specifically developed to support English language learners
- Readers that reinforce the weekly concept and vocabulary while building language and fluency

ELL Handbook

- Additional materials including grammar and phonics lessons, transference notes, reproducible pages for additional practice, language activities, and articles by notable experts in the English language learner community

Differentiated Instruction for On-Level Learners

The main instruction in *Reading Street* is designed for children who need instruction right at the kindergarten level. While your small groups for Strategic Intervention, Advanced, and English Language Learners are engaged at their levels, your on-level children will benefit from small-group instruction that expands their knowledge of skills and strategies and provides on-level reading opportunities.

Reading Street integrates daily instruction for on-level children into the core program. On-level children are ready to expand what they learned in whole group lesson. The On-Level lessons provide multiple opportunities for children to talk and explore concepts in more depth.

- They expand their background knowledge of literature selections.
- They expand their understanding of the weekly concept by connecting it to a weekly question.
- They expand comprehension through focused activities.
- They expand their knowledge of vocabulary and word structure.

The On-Level daily lessons also offer

- opportunities for in-depth review of skills and strategies.
- on-level readers with practice for skills and strategies.
- multiple opportunities for retelling and fluency practice.
- writing response activities that extend reading skills and strategies.

Use the on-level lessons and choose from 5-Day and 3- or 4-Day pacing plans as a guide to ensure success.

How Do I Support Children with Different Needs in the Groups?

To form groups, it's necessary to give them labels. But never lose awareness that each child within a group is an individual with unique abilities and challenges. Small group time presents teachers the opportunity to become aware of children's needs and how best to support those needs. You can gain insight into children with special needs who may be in an advanced, on-level, or strategic intervention group. For these children, you can also use *Reading Street* materials to help them express their abilities and demonstrate their competence. These and many other activities can be used for children with different special needs:

Dyslexia—Guide the child's hand in forming letters or writing legibly.

Hearing Impairment—Pair children with others who can repeat explicit instructions.

Physical Disabilities—Suggest procedural or equipment modifications, such as modified computers, keyboards, scanners, and spell checkers.

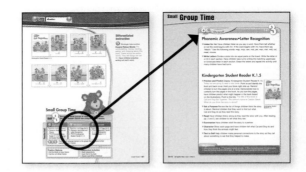

English Language Learners on Reading Street

Your kindergarten classroom and school may be a mirror of others across the United States that are welcoming increasing numbers of English language learners. ELLs make up the fastest growing K–12 student population in the United States.

Section 5 shows how you successfully can support kindergarten children whose first language is not English. The wide array of English language learning resources in *Scott Foresman Reading Street* will ensure that you'll engage them as you teach.

As you read the research and practical tips from renowned researchers, you'll feel that expert partners are at your side, guiding you in best practices for English language learners.

Use these proven instructional approaches to help ELLs excel.

Essentials of ELL Instruction in Scott Foresman Reading Street

Identify and Communicate Content Objectives and Language Objectives

Frontload the Lesson

Provide Comprehensible Input

Enable Language Production

Assess for Content and Language Understanding

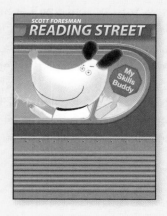

Overview of English Language Learners

Imagine children from diverse language backgrounds communicating in English on the playground. It's easy to think that they are fluent English speakers, but they may still be at the beginning stage of using English for learning purposes. Research proves that it takes at least five years of exposure to academic English to catch up with native-speaker proficiency in school.

How Do English Language Learners Differ from Other Learners?

ELLs face challenges because they have not acquired academic English. Children's reading and language skills may seem deficient because their language experiences have lacked academic instruction. ELLs need targeted instruction to participate fully in reading/language arts lessons with their peers. Helping ELLs achieve academically is critically important because they must meet the same state and federal grade-level standards as other children. Their academic success depends on learning to read well, and this depends on rich language knowledge.

> **Academic Language** is the language of classroom talk. It's used for academic purposes, not social or personal ones.

Essentials of ELL Instruction

The following five essential practices take into account language and academic needs of English language learners. They are incorporated into *Reading Street* as common-sense, everyday strategies that help you build an effective learning relationship between you and your ELL children.

Identify and Communicate Content Objectives and Language Objectives English language learners need instruction for the same grade-level skills and strategies as children whose first language is English. Deliver your instruction with clear, simple language. Provide extra support for academic vocabulary. Provide direct instruction for the academic language that children need to use to complete classroom tasks successfully.

Frontload the Lesson When new information arrives as a blur to ELL children, they are lost at the beginning of a lesson. Taking time to frontload, or preteach, lesson elements will bring them into mainstream instruction. Activating prior knowledge, building background, previewing, and setting a purpose for reading are frontloading methods that remove learning obstacles. Asking children to make personal connections helps them see relationships and gives you insight into their experiences and backgrounds.

Provide Comprehensible Input The instruction and content you present to ELL children may be unclear because of language barriers. Using visual supports, multimedia, examples of real items, and demonstrations are a few ways to provide comprehensible instruction. Communicating through non-linguistic methods such as gestures, props, dramatization, and others can be an effective approach. Hands-on activities and multiple exposures to new concepts can lessen confusion.

Enable Language Production The listening, speaking, reading, and writing ELLs do for school is different from the language they use in everyday conversation. In school, ELLs need ample opportunities to demonstrate their use of English. Two critical methods for enabling children's English language production are direct instruction and modeling the use of a skill in a comprehensible way. Create scaffolds so that children can read and hear English language patterns and build on them to express their own thoughts. Paraphrasing, restatements, cloze sentences, writing prompts, and templated forms for note-taking are other useful supports. Responding to children's strengths and needs by modifying instruction gives them opportunities to express themselves in an academic setting and gain proficiency in English.

Assess for Content and Language Understanding Since ELLs are required to achieve the same high standards as mainstream children, you need assessment tools that help you plan how to support ELLs' strengths and address their challenges. Keep in mind that children are at different stages for learning English language and literacy skills. Asking these questions frequently and using assessments will help you determine how to modify your instruction for different proficiency levels.

- Where are ELL children in their **acquisition of English** language proficiency?
- Where are they in their **acquisition of literacy** skills?

Just as for all children, you will rely on diagnostic, formative, and summative assessments for ELLs. Consistently integrate informal assessment into your lessons to target specific problem areas for learning, adapt your instruction, and intervene earlier rather than later.

You can modify both formal and informal assessments so that ELLs show their proficiency in literacy skills with a minimal amount of negative impact. These modifications include time extensions, use of bilingual dictionaries and glossaries, repeated readings of listening passages, use of dual-language assessments, and allowing written responses in the first language.

To meet ELLs at their own level of English acquisition, teachers use instructional supports and tools. Through scaffolding and modifying instruction you can lead ELLs to achieve the same instructional goals that mainstream children do. The ELL strategies and supports in *Reading Street* have the five essential principles of ELL as their foundation. Use them throughout your instruction to modify or scaffold core instruction. With ELL Leveled Support activities, you meet children where they are—from beginning to advanced levels of English proficiency. The features provide on-the-spot information for vocabulary, writing, and language transfer information.

Tips for Providing Comprehensible Input

- Face children when speaking.
- Use vocabulary-rich visuals such as ELL Posters.
- Use teaching techniques that involve the senses.
- Use ELL Readers and other materials with ELL supports.

Other English language learner resources include:

Student Edition The kindergarten student edition builds every child's reading and language skills.

Teacher's Edition The teacher's edition has ELL instructional strategies built into the lesson plans. The ELL weekly lessons have pacing plans to help you carefully integrate instruction. The lessons guide you in using sheltered techniques and routines for teaching academic vocabulary, listening comprehension, phonics, vocabulary, comprehension, and writing.

ELL Readers ELL readers develop English learners' vocabulary and comprehension skills.

ELL Posters ELL posters contain high-quality illustrations and five days of activities supporting key oral vocabulary, selection vocabulary, and lesson concepts.

English Language Support These supports are all provided as reproducible masters: English Language Support resource books with comprehension skill practice, selection vocabulary word cards, multilingual summaries of Student Edition literature, study guides for ELL Readers, and multilingual vocabulary charts. The English selection summaries and vocabulary charts are accompanied by translations in Spanish and in several other languages.

Ten Important Sentences The Ten Important Sentences reproducibles help children focus on comprehension while they expand their English proficiency.

ELL Handbook The ELL Handbook supports teachers' professional development and children's transition to advanced levels of proficiency.

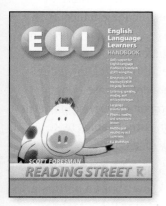

The Three Pillars of English Language Learning

Dr. Jim Cummins, the University of Toronto

In order to understand how English learners develop second-language literacy and reading comprehension, we must distinguish between three different aspects of language proficiency:

Conversational fluency This dimension of proficiency represents the ability to carry on a conversation in face-to-face situations. Most native speakers of English have developed conversational fluency by age 5. This fluency involves use of high-frequency words and simple grammatical constructions. English learners generally develop fluency in conversational English within a year or two of intensive exposure to the language in school or in their neighborhood environments.

Discrete language skills These skills reflect specific phonological, literacy, and grammatical knowledge that students can acquire in two ways—through direct instruction and through immersion in a literacy-rich and language-rich environment in home or in school. The discrete language skills acquired early include:

- knowledge of the letters of the alphabet
- knowledge of the sounds represented by individual letters and combinations of letters
- the ability to decode written words

Children can learn these specific language skills concurrently with their development of basic English vocabulary and conversational fluency.

Academic language proficiency This dimension of proficiency includes knowledge of the less frequent vocabulary of English as well as the ability to interpret and produce increasingly complex written language. As students progress through the grades, they encounter:

- far more low-frequency words, primarily from Greek and Latin sources
- complex syntax (for example, sentences in passive voice)
- abstract expressions

Acquiring academic language is challenging. Schools spend at least 12 years trying to teach all students the complex language associated with academic success. It is hardly surprising that research has repeatedly shown that English language learners, on average, require *at least* 5 years of exposure to academic English to catch up to native-speaker norms.

Effective instruction for English language learners is built on three fundamental pillars.

English Learners

Activate Prior Knowledge/ Build Background	Access Content	Extend Language

Activate Prior Knowledge/ Build Background

No learner is a blank slate. Each person's prior experience provides the foundation for interpreting new information. In reading, we construct meaning by bringing our prior knowledge of language and of the world to the text. The more we already know about the topic in the text, the more of the text we can understand. Our prior knowledge enables us to make inferences about the meaning of words and expressions that we may not have come across before. Furthermore, the more of the text we understand, the more new knowledge we can acquire. This expands our knowledge base (what cognitive psychologists call *schemata*, or underlying patterns of concepts). Such comprehension, in turn, enables us to understand even more concepts and vocabulary.

It is important to *activate* students' prior knowledge because students may not realize what they know about a particular topic or issue. Their knowledge may not facilitate learning unless that knowledge is brought to consciousness.

Teachers can use a variety of strategies to activate students' prior knowledge:	
Brainstorming/Discussion	Visual stimuli
Direct experience	Student writing
Dramatization	Drawing

When students don't already have knowledge about a topic, it is important to help them acquire that knowledge. For example, in order to comprehend texts such as *The Midnight Ride of Paul Revere*, students need to have background knowledge about the origin of the United States.

Access Content

How can teachers make complex academic English comprehensible for students who are still in the process of learning English?

We can *scaffold* students' learning by modifying the input itself. Here are a variety of ways of modifying the presentation of academic content to students so that they can more effectively gain access to the meaning.

Using Visuals Visuals enable students to "see" the basic concepts we are trying to teach much more effectively than if we rely only on words. Among the visuals we can use are:

- *pictures/diagrams*
- *real objects*
- *vocabulary cards*
- *graphic organizers*
- *maps*

Dramatization/Acting Out For beginning English learners, *Total Physical Response*, in which they follow commands such as "Turn around," can be highly effective. The meanings of words can be demonstrated through *gestures* and *pantomime*.

Language Clarification This category of teaching methods includes language-oriented activities that clarify the meaning of new words and concepts. *Use of dictionaries*, either bilingual or English-only, is still the most direct method of getting access to meaning.

Making Personal and Cultural Connections We should constantly search for ways to link academic content with what students already know or what is familiar to them from their family or cultural experiences. This not only validates children's sense of identity, but it also makes the learning more meaningful.

Extend Language

A systematic exploration of language is essential if students are to develop a curiosity about language and deepen their understanding of how words work. Students should become *language detectives* who investigate the mysteries of language and how it has been used throughout history to shape and change society.

Students also can explore the building blocks of language. A large percentage of the less frequently heard academic vocabulary of English derives from Latin and Greek roots. Word formation follows predictable patterns. These patterns are very similar in English and Spanish.

When students know rules or conventions of how words are formed, it gives them an edge in extending vocabulary. It helps them figure out the meanings of words and how to form different parts of speech from words. The exploration of language can focus on meaning, form, or use:

Focus on meaning Categories that can be explored within a focus on meaning include:

- *home language equivalents or cognates*
- *synonyms, antonyms, and homonyms*
- *meanings of prefixes, roots, and suffixes*

Focus on form Categories that can be explored within a focus on form include:

- *word families*
- *grammatical patterns*
- *words with same prefixes, roots, or suffixes*

Focus on use Categories that can be explored within a focus on use include:

- *general uses*
- *idioms*
- *metaphorical use*
- *proverbs*
- *advertisements*
- *puns and jokes*

The Three Pillars

- Activate Prior Knowledge/ Build Background
- Access Content
- Extend Language

establish a solid structure for the effective instruction of English language learners.

English Learners and Literacy: Best Practices

Dr. Georgia Earnest García, the University of Illinois at Urbana-Champaign

Like other children, English language learners come to school with much oral language knowledge and experience. Their knowledge and experience in languages other than English provide skills and world knowledge that teachers can build on.

Making literacy instruction comprehensible to English language learners is essential. Many of the teaching strategies developed for children who are proficient in English can be adapted for English learners, and many strategies from an English as a Second Language curriculum are also useful in "mainstream" reading education.

Building on Children's Knowledge

It is vital to learn about each student's literacy development and proficiency in the home language. School personnel should ask parents:

- How many years of school instruction has the child received in the home language?
- Can the child read and write in that language?
- Can the child read in any other language?

Students can transfer aspects of home-language literacy to their English literacy development, such as phonological awareness and reading (or listening) comprehension strategies. If they already know key concepts and vocabulary in their home languages, then they can transfer that knowledge to English. For the vocabulary concepts they already know in their home languages, they only need to learn the English labels. Not all English learners automatically transfer what they have learned in the home language to their reading in English. Teachers can help facilitate relevant transfer by explicitly asking English learners to think about what they have learned about a topic in the home language.

A teacher need not speak each student's home language to encourage English language learners to work together and benefit from one another's knowledge. Students can communicate in their home languages and English, building the content knowledge, confidence, and English skills that they need to participate fully in learning. Devising activities in which students who share home languages can work together also allows a school to pool resources, such as bilingual dictionaries and other books, as well as home-language tutors or aides.

Sheltering Instruction in English

Often, beginning and intermediate English language learners may not understand what their classroom teachers say or read aloud in English. These students benefit when teachers shelter, or make comprehensible, their literacy instruction.

Sheltered techniques include using:

- consistent, simplified, clearly enunciated, and slower-paced oral language to explain literacy concepts or activities
- gestures, photos, illustrations, drawings, real objects, dramatization, and/or physical action to illustrate important concepts and vocabulary
- activities that integrate reading, writing, listening, and speaking, so students see, hear, read, and write new vocabulary, sentence structures, and content

When it is clear from students' actions and responses that they understand what is being said, teachers can vary their strategies. As students' comprehension expands, teachers can gradually curtail their use of adapted oral language and of gestures, illustrations, and dramatizations.

Adapting Literacy Activities

Teachers can use many instructional activities developed for native English speakers with English language learners. For example, teacher read-alouds, shared reading, and paired reading can allow an English learner to follow the text during a reading. Such techniques greatly improve students' learning skills and comprehension.

Similarly, interactive journal writing, in which the teacher and student take turns writing entries, allows students to explore topics and ask questions. It also allows teachers to engage in ongoing authentic assessment of student proficiency and to pinpoint areas of misunderstanding.

Small group instruction and discussion also are helpful. Beginning English language learners benefit from the repeated readings of predictable texts with illustrations, especially when the teacher has provided a brief preview of each text to introduce the topic of the story and preview new vocabulary.

Repeated reading aloud of such predictable, patterned, illustrated texts provides English language learners with multiple opportunities to match the text they read with the words they hear. When students participate in shared reading and echo the spoken text or read the words aloud chorally, anxiety about pronunciation or decoding errors is reduced. When teachers choose texts that are culturally familiar and ask English language learners personal questions related to the text, the result is a lower-risk learning environment and an increased opportunity for students to make accurate inferences.

Examples of Teaching Strategies

Before students read content material, provide them with hands-on or visual experience directly related to the content. Then, have them use a graphic organizer to map what they have learned or seen about the topic. Let pairs or small groups of students brainstorm for words that are related to the concept. Then introduce other related words, including vocabulary from the reading. Illustrate new concepts or vocabulary with drawings, photographs, or artifacts that represent the concepts. The hands-on experience and graphic organizer that precede the reading help introduce students to new concepts. Students will thus be familiar with the selection's subject before they begin to read.

Semantic Mapping Working with graphic organizers can help teach vocabulary and concepts in subject areas.

For example, before a reading on the subject of baby animals, have students help you to complete a semantic map showing pictures of animals and the names of baby animals. Ask them to volunteer the names for animal babies in their home language and transcribe their responses. Then, show students examples of the different forms of writing. Ask students to meet in small groups to identify the examples. They may do this in English or their home language. If they use the home language, the teacher needs to write the English labels on the board for each form of writing. Then, students need to enter the words for the different forms of writing, with drawings or home language equivalents, into a vocabulary notebook.

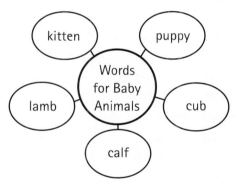

Summarizing After reading, students can dictate what they remember from their reading to the teacher. Students can then illustrate their summaries, and label the illustrations with vocabulary from the reading.

Preparing English Language Learners for Assessment

Dr. Lily Wong Fillmore, the University of California, Berkeley

Under federal and state law, all students—including English learners—must be assessed annually on their progress toward mastery of academic standards in reading, math, and science. Many questions arise when such assessments are used with ELLs, because their test scores are never easy to interpret when they are assessed in English. The most critical question is this: What do test scores mean when they are based on instruction and assessments given in a language students have not yet mastered? Although difficult to interpret, these assessments are required of all students, so we must consider how to help ELLs perform as well as possible.

Addressed in this essay

- What can teachers do to fast-track their ELL students' mastery of the language and content needed to perform as well as possible in required assessments?
- What language and literacy skills are needed?
- What learning strategies can teachers promote to facilitate language and literacy development?

Three types of assessments are vital to reading instruction for all students, including ELLs.

1. Ongoing informal assessments

The assessments that provide teachers the most useful and important information about English learners are those used as part of the instructional process. How well do children understand the materials they are working with, and what needs adjustment or modification in instruction? These are built into these instructional materials and help teachers keep an ongoing record of student progress over time. Such assessments do not need to

be elaborate. Asking children what they think is happening in a text can reveal how well they comprehend what they are reading. Asking children what they think words or phrases mean can show whether they are trying to make sense of text. These types of questions are highly useful to teachers since they allow them to monitor participation levels and help them discover who understands the materials and who needs more attention and support.

2. Diagnostic assessments

A second type of assessment that some ELLs may require is diagnostic, and it is needed when individuals are not making the progress expected of them. The school must determine where student problems lie (e.g., skill development, perception or awareness of English sounds, vocabulary, or grammar) before teachers can provide the corrective help needed.

3. Standardized assessments

The type of assessments that cause teachers of ELLs the greatest concern are the standards-based tests of English Language Arts and content area tests (especially in Math). These state tests are required of all students and are recognized as "high stakes" tests for students and for schools. They are often used to evaluate the effectiveness of a curriculum, the teacher, or the instructional approach used.

What's involved in reading?

Reading skills are built on several types of knowledge: linguistic, symbolic, experiential, and strategic. Each is crucial and is linked with the others. *Language is fundamental*; it is the medium through which meaning—information, story, knowledge, poetry, and thought—is communicated from writer to reader. Unlike speech, what is communicated by written language is indirect and *encoded in symbols* that must be deciphered before access to meaning is possible.

But reading goes beyond mere decoding. Texts call for readers to apply what they know about how language is used to convey thought and ideas to interpret what they are reading. Having *experienced reading as a sense-making activity*, readers will seek meaning as they learn to read. This calls for *special strategies:* they look for meaning if they assume it is to be found in texts. If they do not know the language in which the texts are written, they will recognize that learning the code is the key to unlocking meaning. They will pay attention to the language, and ask: What is this saying? What does this mean? How does this relate to what I already know about the way the language works?

English learners have an easier time learning to read in English if they have already learned to read in their first language. Without question, a language barrier makes learning to read a more difficult task. But if students have already learned to read in their primary language, they know what is involved, what to expect, and thus, they are in a better position to deal with learning to read in the new language in order to access meaning.

Can children learn to read in a language before they are fully proficient in that language?

Can they in fact learn the language through reading? *Yes, but only with ample instructional assistance that supports the development of both.* Ideally, reading instruction in English comes after ELLs have gained some familiarity with the sounds and patterns of spoken English. Children need to hear the sounds of the new language before they can connect symbols to those sounds. For example, in order for children to gain confidence relating the many vowel sounds of English to the 5 vowel symbols used to "spell them" they need help hearing them and differentiating them in words.

Similarly, many ELLs need help dealing with the ways consonants pile up at the beginning and at the ends of syllables and words in English, which may be quite different than the way consonants are used in their primary language. Most crucially, ELLs need help in connecting the words they are learning to decode from the text to their referents. Using pictures, demonstrations, diagrams, gestures, and enactments, teachers can help ELLs see how the words, phrases, and sentences in the reading selections have meaning that can be accessed through the language they are learning.

Helping ELLs become successful readers

The most important way to help ELLs perform well in mandated reading assessments is by giving them the instructional support they need to become successful readers. This involves help in:

- Learning English
- Discovering the purpose of reading
- Becoming active learners
- Gaining access to academic language

Learning English

The more proficient children are in the language they are reading, the more readily they learn to read. For ELLs, support for learning English is support for learning to read. The most effective kind of help comes in content-focused language instruction, where learners are engaged in grade-level-appropriate instructional activities and their participation is scaffolded and supported as needed.

The most effective activities provide ELLs ample opportunity to hear English and to use it productively in meaningful communication. Teachers play a vital role in creating a supportive classroom environment. ELLs must be able to participate to the extent possible (again, with as much support as needed) in discussions with classmates who are more proficient in English. Peers can offer practice and support, but only teachers can ensure that ELLs get access to the kind of language needed for literacy development.

Purpose of reading

The greatest dangers ELLs face in learning to read in English before they are proficient in that language is that the effort involved in decoding takes precedence in their minds over all else. Connections between words and referents, between words and structures, and between text and meaning are overlooked when children focus on sounding out, figuring out symbols, and figuring out sounds. This is especially likely to happen when there is too little emphasis placed on reading as a sense-making activity in instructional programs. If meaning—no matter how difficult it is to come by—is not constantly emphasized in reading instruction, children end up believing that decoding is reading, and that there is nothing missing when they read without understanding. Decoding

becomes an end in itself, and the real purpose of reading is lost. Unfortunately, this is the outcome for many ELLs, who even after having learned English do not perform well in reading assessments.

Literacy in English begins as deciphering for ELLs—they must first figure out how the code in which the text is written works. It is not until the reader engages in an interpretive process in which the thoughts, information, concepts, situations, and relations encoded in the texts are manifested as meanings that there is real reading. This is true for both ELLs and for native English speakers. ELLs, however, will need a lot of guidance and instructional support from teachers to do that. Once children have gained enough familiarity with English to participate even at a rudimentary level in discussions about reading selections and content, they begin to learn that the materials they are reading have something to say to them and that hearing what they have to say is the real purpose of learning to read.

Active readers

Helping children become active learners of English and users of the literacy skills they are acquiring is a key to their becoming successful students and performing well in the assessments they have to take. This is accomplished by encouraging children to take an active role in instructional activities, asking questions, seeking answers, and trying to make sense of what they are studying in school.

Both teachers and students can have many preconceived ideas about the roles they play as teachers and learners. Children sometimes come to school believing that learning is something that will be done to them, rather than something they must take an active role in doing. In their view, the role of the teacher is active and the role they play as learners is passive. When teachers share that belief, there is little likelihood of active or independent learning. Instruction is most effective when teachers are knowledgeable about the subject matter they are teaching and they create a classroom environment in which learners can take an active role in discovering how things work, what things mean, and how to get and make sense of information.

Academic English

Teachers are aware that the language used in written texts is sufficiently different from everyday spoken language to constitute a barrier to children who are not already familiar with it. Academic English is not just another name for "standard English." It is, instead, the special forms of standard English used in academic discourse and in written texts. It makes use of grammatical constructions, words, and rhetorical conventions that are not often used in everyday spoken language.

Paradoxically, academic language is both a prerequisite for full literacy and the outcome of it. Some children arrive at school with a running start in acquiring it. Children who come from homes where family members engage in frequent discussions of books and ideas are already familiar with it, and thus have an advantage learning to read.

It should be noted that the language used at home does *not* have to be English for children to benefit from such experiences. Teachers can provide their students, irrespective of background, experiences with academic language by reading to them and discussing readings, instructional activities, and experiences. By drawing children into instructional conversations focused on the language they encounter in their school texts and other materials, teachers get children to notice language itself and to figure out how it works.

Supporting language and literacy development for ELLs

Teachers support language development by engaging children as active participants in making sense of the texts they are working on. They do it by drawing the English learners into discussions relating to the texts. Even relative newcomers are able to participate in these discussions as long as ample scaffolding is provided:

It says here, "Her teacher picked up the paper and studied it carefully."

Hector, what does the text tell us Vashti's teacher did first?

Yes, she picked up the paper first.

Take a look at the picture. Marta, can you show us, which part of the sentence tells us what the teacher is doing?

Can you tell us what she is doing?

Yes! She is studying the paper carefully.

Teachers draw attention to words, phrases, and sentences, asking: "Let's see if we can figure out what that means!" By relating language to meaning, they help students gain access to meaning by demonstrating, referring to illustrations and diagrams, and by paraphrasing in simpler language.

Instructional conversations about the texts they are reading are as essential for newcomers as they are for ELLs who have already gained some proficiency in English. It is vital to their literacy development to realize that what they are "reading" can be understood, even if its meaning is not immediately available to them as it would be to readers who are fully proficient in English. Without such help, ELLs sometimes come to believe that decoding without access to meaning is an empty exercise one does in school, and except for that, it has little relevance to their lives.

Teachers can help students discover how the language works and how to extract meaning from texts by considering how the language they encounter can convey information, ideas, stories, feelings, and images. This cannot wait until the learners are fully proficient in the language they are reading. It can enhance language development if done from the start, as soon as ELLs are introduced to English reading.

Strategies for supporting language and literacy development and preparing ELLs for assessment

The most effective support comes in the form of instructional conversations in which ELLs are drawn into discussions of reading selections and content. By hearing their teachers and other classmates discuss the materials they are reading, they gradually learn how the language works in texts and in conversation.

- Draw attention to the language used in reading selections and other text materials—words, phrases, and sentences— and relate them to meaning that is discussed and commented on, both locally and globally, to help ELLs learn how to get at meaning in texts.

- Provide students ample opportunity to use the language of texts in speaking (during discussions of the reading selections, for example) and in writing (in response to writing prompts).

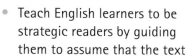

- Teach English learners to be strategic readers by guiding them to assume that the text should make sense and that meaning can be accessed by figuring out what the words, phrases, and sentences mean.

- Teach students to ask questions about meaning as it unfolds in the text. Help them recognize that some parts of texts provide background knowledge while other parts reveal new information.

- Teach children how to relate new information presented in a text to what is already known. Train students to make inferences about meaning based on the words and phrases used in a text.

- Expect ELLs to make progress, and then ensure it by providing ample grade level discussion of content. At the same time, recognize that it takes time to learn English, and that learners may differ in the amount and kind of help they need in order to make progress.

- Recognize that the most crucial kind of preparation for assessment is in helping children develop the **language and literacy skills** that are essential to successful performance in tests and for academic progress itself.

- Call children's attention to words, phrases, and constructions that often figure in text items. For example, words such as *both, not,* and *best* may not seem to be noteworthy, but their uses in test questions prove otherwise. ELLs need help in seeing how such words frame and constrain the ideas expressed in sentences in which they appear.

- Teach children the logic of test questions. Use released test items or models of test items (both of which are likely to be available online from your state department of education or district web sites). Show children, for example, that the question, "Which of the following is NOT a sentence?" entails that all of the listed options except one *are* sentences.

- Teach children to read carefully. Children who are fully proficient in English may occasionally benefit from test-taking strategies such as reading the test question and answer options first and then skimming the test passage to find information that will aid in the selection of the

correct answer to the question. This tactic does not serve English learners well. They need to read and understand the passage carefully, and then consider how to answer the questions asked.

- Teach children when the text calls for activation of prior knowledge. All children have such knowledge, but English learners need help in deciding where it is called for and how they should bring what they already know to interpret the texts they are reading.

- Expand children's horizons by reading them texts that may be too difficult to handle on their own. Help them make sense of such materials by commenting on meaning, drawing attention to how language is used in them, and engaging children in discussions about aspects of the texts.

The texts that are read to children, and the ones they read themselves, provide reliable access to the academic language they need for literacy and for assessment, provided teachers call their attention to language, and help children see how it works. Teachers do this by identifying interesting (not just new) phrases and commenting on them, inviting children to try using the phrases, and providing scaffolds as needed; they model the uses of language from texts in subsequent instructional activities; they encourage children to remember and keep records of words they learn from texts; they remind them when words and phrases encountered earlier show up again in different contexts.

The Concept of Transfer

Dr. Elena Izquierdo, the University of Texas at El Paso

Research continues to support the critical role of the child's first language (L1) in literacy development and its effect on literacy in (L2) English. Strong (L1) literacy skills facilitate the *transfer* into English literacy, and students ultimately progress rapidly into learning in English. In reality, the concept of transfer refers to the child's facility in appropriating knowledge from one language to the other. *Children do not know they know, but they know.* They are constantly and indirectly, unconsciously and automatically, constructing the knowledge that is inherent in the contexts for which each of these languages can function. The effective transfer of skills transpires as students develop their metalinguistic and metacognitive skills and as they engage in a contrastive analysis of the two languages (Cummins, 2007).

Matters of transfer occur within essentials of language that are (1) *common* to L1 and L2; (2) *similar*, but not exact in both languages; and (3) *specific* to each language and not applicable to the other language. In essence, children develop a special awareness of language and its function; learn that some sounds are the same in both languages; and also learn that there are certain boundaries for specific sounds depending on the language.

Children who have developed an awareness for phonemes, phonics, vocabulary building, and reading comprehension skills, can transfer these skills to English. They develop an enhanced awareness of the relationship between their L1 and English, which leads them to successfully appropriate strategies of transfer in similar types of word recognition processing; searching for cognates; making reference to prior knowledge, inferencing, questioning, and monitoring. Facilitating these cognitive skills in children will support their success in English literacy and their learning in English.

Introduction to Linguistics
How People Speak

All languages have both consonants and vowels. Consonants are made with some obstruction of the vocal tract, either a complete stoppage of air or enough constriction to create friction. Vowels are produced with the vocal tract more open, with no constriction that might cause friction.

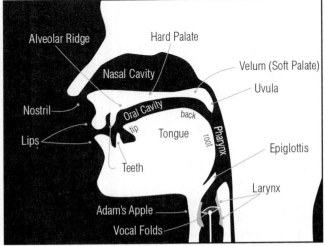

Figure 1: The human vocal tract makes the sounds of speech.

Manner of Articulation This is the type or degree of constriction that occurs in an articulation. For example, the /t/ sound completely stops the airflow with the tongue tip at the alveolar ridge, but /s/ allows air to pass noisily through a small opening.

Consonants

Every consonant can be described by noting three characteristics: voicing, place of articulation, and manner of articulation.

Voicing Many sounds of language, including all vowels, employ vibration of the vocal folds in the larynx. This creates more resonance and energy for the sound. All speech sounds are characterized as either voiced (with vocal fold vibration) or voiceless (with no vocal fold vibration). Feeling the vibration around the Adam's apple can help you understand this difference. If you say "sssss" and then "zzzzz," you can feel the distinction: /s/ is voiceless and /z/ is voiced.

Place of Articulation This is the location in the vocal tract where the air stream may be constricted. The /s/ sound, for example, is made with the tongue tip close to the alveolar ridge (see Figure 1).

Vowels

Vowels are open, sonorous sounds. Each vowel can be uniquely described by noting the position of the tongue, the tension of the vocal tract, and the position of the lips. Vowels are described by *height,* where the tongue is relative to the roof of the mouth. They can be high, mid, or low. Tongue backness tells if the tongue articulation is in the front or back of the mouth. Tense vowels are more common around the world. In English, they are longer and include an expansion of the throat at the pharynx. Lax vowels are shorter with a more neutral pharynx. An example is the tense long *e* as in *meet* versus the lax short *i* as in *mitt.* The lips either can be in a spread or neutral position, or they can be rounded and protrude slightly.

Speaking English

English is the third most widely spoken native language in the world, after Mandarin and Spanish. There are about 330 million native speakers of English and 600 million who speak it as a foreign language.

English Consonant Sounds

The following chart gives the International Phonetic Alphabet (IPA) symbol for each English consonant along with its voicing, place, and manner of articulation. This information can be used to understand and help identify problems that non-native speakers may encounter when learning to speak English.

Consonants of English		
IPA	Articulation	Example
p	voiceless bilabial stop	pit
b	voiced bilabial stop	bit
m	voiced bilabial nasal stop	man
w	voiced labio-velar approximant	win
f	voiceless labio-dental fricative	fun
v	voiced labio-dental fricative	very
θ	voiceless interdental fricative	thing
ð	voiced interdental fricative	there
t	voiceless alveolar stop	time
d	voiced alveolar stop	dime
n	voiced alveolar nasal stop	name
s	voiceless alveolar fricative	soy
z	voiced alveolar fricative	zeal
ɾ	voiced alveolar tap	butter
l	voiced alveolar lateral approximant	loop
ɹ	voiced alveolar central approximant	red
ʃ	voiceless palato-alveolar fricative	shallow
ʒ	voiced palato-alveolar fricative	vision
ʧ	voiceless palato-alveolar affricate	chirp
ʤ	voiced palato-alveolar affricate	joy
j	voiced palatal approximant	you
k	voiceless velar stop	kite
g	voiced velar stop	goat
ŋ	voiced velar nasal stop	king
h	voiceless glottal fricative	hope

English Vowel Sounds

Most languages in the world have around five vowel sounds. English has 13 common vowel sounds, which means that many students of English must learn more vowel distinctions than there are in their native language. The lax vowels are most difficult. Some vowels are diphthongs, meaning the tongue is in one position at the beginning of the sound, and it moves to another position by the end of it.

Vowels of English		
IPA	Sound	Example
i	ē	beat
ɪ	ĭ	bit
e	ā	bait
ɛ	ĕ	bet
æ	ă	bat
u	o͞o	boot
ʊ	o͝o	could
o	ō	boat
ɔ	aw	law
ɑ	ŏ	hot
ə	ə	about
ʌ	ŭ	cut
ɝ	er	bird
ɑ ʊ	ow	house
ɔ ɪ	oy	boy
ɑ ɪ	ī	bite

Figure 2 is a schematic of the mouth. The left is the front of the mouth; the right is the back. The top is the roof of the mouth and the bottom is the floor. Placement of the vowel shows where the tongue reaches its maximum in the English articulation.

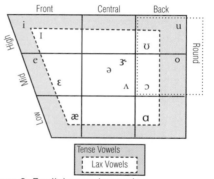

Figure 2: English vowel sounds

Introduction to Linguistics
Transference

Pronunciation

All languages build on the same fundamentals. All languages contrast voiced and voiceless sound, and have stops and fricatives. Many languages use the same places of articulation for consonants as well. The majority of sounds will easily transfer from another language to English.

However, there will always be some sounds that are not found in a person's native language that can pose a challenge to the English language learner. English has a few relatively rare sounds, such as the interdental sounds spelled with *th*, /θ/ and /ð/. The /r/ sound in English is also a very rare type of sound. Most other languages use a tap or trill articulation for an /r/ sound.

In some languages, the /l/ and /r/ sounds belong to one psychological category. This means that they count as the same sound in that language. In this case, it is not the articulation that is difficult, but the perception of the difference and consistent use of one versus the other in any word context. This type of psychological category is called a *phoneme*, and multiple speech sounds all can be categorized as the same phoneme in that language.

This is true for English as well, where, for example, the alveolar lateral /l/ as in *lob* and the velarized lateral /ɫ/ as in *ball* are both counted as the same sound—an l—to native speakers of English. It is important to keep in mind that both the phonetic articulation of a sound and its psychological, phonemic category factor into the learning of a new language.

Grammar

Pronouncing English is not the only stumbling block for English learners. The grammar and usage, or syntax, of English may present distinctions that are unique to the language. For example, English syntax requires adjectives to precede the nouns they modify, as in *the tall girl*. In other languages, such as Spanish, Hmong, and Vietnamese, adjectives follow nouns, as in *la chica alta* (literally *the girl tall* in Spanish). This may cause word-order problems, particularly for less advanced English learners.

Other syntactic differences are less obvious and may cause problems even for advanced learners. For example, many East Asian languages (such as Mandarin, Cantonese, and Korean) do not mark agreement between subject and verb. Speakers of these languages may therefore leave out agreement markers such as the *-s* in *The girl like cats*.

The use of articles varies across languages. For instance, Spanish uses the definite article more often than English, while Mandarin and Cantonese do not have articles. A Spanish-speaking English learner might say *The girl likes the cats* instead of *The girl likes cats*, and a Mandarin or Cantonese speaker might say *Girl like cat*.

Plural marking is another potential trouble spot: Vietnamese, Filipino, Cantonese, and Mandarin do not add plural markers to nouns. Learners speaking these languages may have difficulty with English plurals, saying *cat* instead of *cats*.

> **Grammar Hot Spots**
> Look for Grammar Hot Spots on the following pages for tips on the most common syntax errors by speakers of languages other than English.

Common First Languages

In the Common First Languages section, you will find details of some common non-English languages spoken in the United States. They are:

- Spanish
- Vietnamese
- Cantonese
- Hmong
- Filipino
- Korean
- Mandarin

You can use the fundamentals of speech articulation already covered to help you understand where the languages differ from English. Differences in the spoken language and in the writing systems are explored as well. These sections pinpoint common trouble spots specific to learners of English.

> **Culture Clues**
> Look to Culture Clues for insights into the cultural differences of each language learner as well as ideas for ways to embrace students' diversity.

Linguistic Contrastive Analysis

The Linguistic Contrastive Analysis Charts provide a quick reference for comparing English sounds with those of other languages. The charts allow you to check at a glance which sounds have equivalents in other languages. For those sounds that don't have equivalents, you can find the closest sound used as a substitute and suggestions for helping someone gain a native English articulation.

In these charts, the sounds are notated using the International Phonetic Alphabet (IPA). This is the most widely recognized and used standard for representing speech sounds in any language. A guiding principle of the IPA across all languages is that each sound is uniquely represented by one symbol, and each symbol represents only one sound.

The chart has columns for each native language with rows corresponding to each English phoneme. Each cell in the chart gives an example word using that sound in the native language, a definition in parenthesis, and transference tips below. If there is no sound equivalent to English, a common substitution used by speakers of that language may be provided.

> **Transference Tips**
> Transference tips give you ideas of how the sound will be produced by the learner. Cells in bold note where the English learner will have particular difficulty with the English sound.

Common First Languages
Spanish

Background Spanish is the second most widely spoken language in the world. There are more than 400 million native Spanish speakers in 20-plus countries on three continents. Spanish vocabulary and pronunciation differ from country to country. While most dialect differences in English are in vowel sounds, Spanish dialects differ in their consonants.

Spoken Spanish sounds are similar to those found in English, so there is a strong foundation for the native Spanish speaker learning English. However, there are three key differences between English and Spanish consonants:

> **Culture Clues**
>
> The Spanish language covers many countries, dialects, and cultures. Always encourage students to share special things about their culture, such as foods, festivals, or social customs.

1. Most of the alveolar sounds in English, such as /t/, /d/, and /n/ are produced farther forward in the mouth in Spanish. Instead of the tongue touching the alveolar ridge as in English, in Spanish it touches the back of the teeth.

2. Another difference is that the /r/ sound in English is not found in Spanish. There are two /r/ sounds in Spanish. One is the tap /ɾ/, which occurs in English as the quick sound in the middle of the name *Betty*. Psychologically, this tap sound is a kind of /t/ or /d/ sound in English, while in Spanish it is perceived as an /r/. The other /r/ sound in Spanish is a trill, or series of tongue taps on the alveolar ridge. This does not occur in English.

3. The third key difference between English and Spanish can be found in the English production of the voiceless stops /p/, /t/, and /k/. In English these sounds are aspirated, with an extra puff of air at the end, when the sound occurs at the beginning of a word or stressed syllable. So, /p/ is aspirated in *pit*. Learners can add a puff of air to such sounds to sound more like native English speakers.

There are five vowels in Spanish, which are a subset of the English vowels. Spanish vowels include tense vowel sounds /a/ /e/ /i/ /o/ /u/. Lax vowel sounds in English are the problematic ones for native Spanish speakers.

Written Like English, written Spanish uses the Roman alphabet, so both writing systems are similar. There are a few orthographic differences to note, however:

- The letter *h* in Spanish is silent, but the sound /h/ is written as *j* or *g*.

- A single letter *r* in Spanish represents a tap, while the double *rr* represents a trill.

- Accents are used to show the stress on a syllable when the stress is different from the usual rules. In some cases, words change meaning according to the accents. For example, *el* means *the* while *él* means *he*.

Written Spanish vowels are pronounced like the symbols in the IPA. So, the Spanish "i" is pronounced with the long ē as in the word *beat*. The IPA and Spanish symbol for this letter is the same: i.

> **Grammar Hot Spots**
> - Double negatives are part of standard grammar in Spanish. Stress the single negative construction in English.
> - English prepositions are a common stumbling block for Spanish speakers.

Vietnamese

Background Approximately eighty million people in Vietnam speak Vietnamese. The northern dialect is the standard, though central and southern dialects also exist. Most Vietnamese speakers in the United States are from southern Vietnam and speak the southern dialect.

Spoken Vietnamese is a tonal language, so each syllable is pronounced with a distinctive tone that affects meaning. Vietnamese has a complex vowel system of 12 vowels and 26 diphthongs. Its consonants are simpler, but Vietnamese syllable structure allows few possibilities for final consonants.

Students may need help noticing and learning to reproduce final consonant sounds in English words and syllables. Vietnamese syllable structure allows for limited combinations of initial consonants. Students also may need help with the more complex initial consonant clusters of English words and syllables.

Written Since the 1600s, Vietnamese has used a Romanized alphabet. Many characters written in Vietnamese have sounds different from their English counterparts, such as *d, x, ch, nh, kh, g, tr, r,* and *e.*

> **Culture Clues**
>
> In traditional Vietnamese education, there is a strict division between the roles of student and teacher. Students may be confused if asked to direct a part of their own study, so encourage group work.

> **Grammar Hot Spots**
>
> - Like English, Vietnamese uses Subject-Verb-Object (SVO) syntax, or word order.
> - Vietnamese does not use affixes; instead, syntax expresses number, case, and tense.

Cantonese

Background Cantonese is one of the seven major Chinese languages, not all of which are mutually intelligible. Cantonese is mostly spoken in China's southern provinces, Hong Kong, and Macau by about 66 million people. It is a tonal language, and the same sequence of letters can have different meanings depending on their pitch.

Spoken Cantonese has six stops, aspirated and non-aspirated /p/, /t/, /k/; three fricatives /f/, /s/, /h/, and two affricates /ts/, /tsʰ/. Some sounds which do not exist in Cantonese can be difficult for the English language learner. The /v/ often gets pronounced as /f/ or /w/; the /z/ is often said as /s/; the sounds spelled with *th* are often said as /t/, /d/, or /f/. Cantonese speakers have difficulty distinguishing between /l/ and /r/, since /r/ is not present in their language. They tend to produce an /l/-like sound for both English sounds in words such as *ride* and *lied.*

Cantonese has 11 vowels and 10 diphthongs. One of the major problems for Cantonese speakers is distinguishing between English tense and lax vowels, because the distribution of Cantonese short and long vowels is determined by the sound context.

Syllables in Cantonese don't have consonant clusters. English consonant clusters are often deleted or broken up by vowel insertion (e.g., *list* becomes *lis*). This may be especially problematic when producing English past tense (e.g., *baked*).

Written Cantonese is written with standard Chinese characters known as *Hànzi* where each character represents a syllable and has a meaning. Additional Cantonese-specific characters were also added. Cantonese speakers may have difficulty with sound-letter correspondences in English.

> **Grammar Hot Spots**
>
> - English articles and prepositions are difficult for Cantonese speakers. *In, on,* and *at,* for instance, can be translated as the same pronoun in Cantonese.
> - Plurals, tenses, and gerund endings are difficult for Cantonese speakers to transfer to English.

Common First Languages

Hmong

Background Hmong is a group of approximately 18 languages within the Hmong-Mien family. There are roughly four million speakers of Hmong, including 200,000 in the United States. They are mainly from two groups with mutually intelligible dialects—Hmong Daw and Mong Leng.

Spoken Hmong vowels are few and simple, but its consonants are complex and differ from those of English. Notable features of Hmong phonology absent from English include consonantal pre-nasalization (the /m/n/ŋ/ sound before a consonant) and the contrast between nasalized and non-nasalized vowels. Hmong is tonal. Each syllable is pronounced with a distinctive pitch.

Written The Romanized Popular Alphabet (RPA), developed in the 1950s, is the usual way of transcribing Hmong. Syllable-final consonants are absent in pronunciation but are used to represent orthographically the tonal value of a given syllable. Students may need particular help in identifying and learning to reproduce the final consonant sounds of English words and syllables.

> **Culture Clues**
>
> In traditional Hmong culture, learning takes place through hands-on experience. Students may find it difficult to adjust to the use of graphics or print media. Competition, personal achievement, and self-directed instruction may be unfamiliar concepts, so students may prefer group work.

> **Grammar Hot Spots**
>
> - Like English, Hmong is an SVO language. Personal pronouns are marked for number, including inflection for singular, dual, and plural, though they are not marked for case.
> - Because Hmong and English prepositions often have different semantic qualities, students may need help mastering uses of English prepositions. For example, it is correct to say "think <u>about</u> [something]" rather than "think <u>on</u> [something]."

Filipino

Background Filipino and English are the official languages of the Philippines, where 175 languages are spoken. There are about 24 million native speakers of Filipino, and more than 50 million people speak Filipino as a second language. You may hear the terms Filipino and Tagalog being used interchangeably.

Spoken Filipino has many similar speech sounds to English. The notable exceptions are the lack of the consonant sounds /f/, /v/, and those spelled with *th*. Of these, the English /f/ and /v/ cause the most difficulty for learners. The distinction between long *e* (as in *beat*) and short *i* (as in *bit*) is also a trouble spot. Filipino does not allow consonant clusters at the end of syllables, so *detect* may be simplified to just one final consonant (*detec*).

Written The Filipino alphabet has 28 letters and is based on the Spanish alphabet, so the English writing system poses little problem.

> **Culture Clues**
>
> Most people from the Philippines can speak Filipino, but for many it is not their first language. Ask Filipino students about other languages they speak. Because English is used alongside Filipino as the language of instruction in the Philippines, most Filipinos are familiar with English.

> **Grammar Hot Spots**
>
> - Filipino word order is Verb-Subject-Object (VSO), which does not transfer well to English.
> - Inflectional verb endings, such as *-s, -en, -ed,* and *-ing* do not exist in Filipino, so it is common to leave out the third person singular verb marker (*"He walk,"* not *"He walks"*).

Korean

Background Korean is spoken by 71 million people in North and South Korea. Standard Korean is based on the speech in and around Seoul.

Spoken Korean does not have corresponding sounds for English /f/, /v/, /θ/, /ð/, and /ʤ/. In word-initial position, all Korean stops are voiceless. Voiced stops /b/, /d/, and /g/ are only produced between two vowels. Korean speakers may have difficulty producing /s/, /ʃ/, and /z/ in some contexts, in addition to English /r/ and /l/ sounds (e.g., *rock* and *lock*). They may have problems in producing English consonant clusters (e.g., *str-, sk-*). These problems can often be eliminated by vowel insertion or consonant deletion. In addition, the distinction between English tense and lax vowels (e.g., /i/ as in *beat* vs. /ɪ/ as in *bit*) may be problematic for Korean speakers.

> **Culture Clues**
>
> Korean uses a complex system of honorifics, so it is unusual for Korean students to use the pronoun *you* or call their teachers by their first name.

Written Modern Korean uses the Korean alphabet *(Hangul)* or a mixed script of *Hangul* and Chinese. *Hangul* is an alphabetic script organized into syllabic blocks.

> **Grammar Hot Spots**
>
> - In contrast to English, Korean word order is Subject-Object-Verb (SOV). The verb always comes at the end of a sentence.
> - Korean syllable stress is different, so learners may have difficulties with the rhythm of English.

Mandarin

Background Chinese encompasses a wide range of dialects and is the native language of two-thirds of China. There are approximately 870 million Mandarin speakers worldwide. North Mandarin, as found in Beijing, is the basis of the modern standard language.

Spoken Mandarin Chinese and English differ substantially in their sound structure. Mandarin lacks voiced obstruent consonants (/b/, /d/, /g/, /ʤ/), causing difficulty for speakers in perceiving and producing English voiced consonants (e.g., *buy* may be pronounced and perceived as *pie*). The sounds spelled with *th* are not present in Mandarin, so they are often substituted with /s/ or /t/ causing, for example, *fourth* to be pronounced as *fours*. Mandarin Chinese has five vowels. Due to the relatively small vowel inventory and contextual effects on vowels in Mandarin, many English vowels and tense/lax distinctions present problems for speakers of Mandarin Chinese. Mandarin allows only a very simple syllable structure, causing problems in producing consonant clusters in English. Speakers may drop consonants or insert vowels between them (e.g., *film* may become /filəm/). The use of tones in Mandarin may result in the rising and falling of pitch when speaking English.

Written Chinese is written with characters known as Hànzi. Each character represents a syllable and also has a meaning. A Romanized alphabet called Pinyin marks pronunciation of characters. Chinese speakers may have problems mastering letter-sound correspondences in written English, especially for sounds that are not present in Mandarin.

> **Grammar Hot Spots**
>
> - The non-inflected nature of Chinese causes Mandarin speakers to have problems with plurals, past-tense markers, and gerund forms *(-s, -ed, -ing)*.
> - Mastering English tenses and passive is difficult. Students should be familiarized with correct lexical and syntactic features as well as appropriate situations for the use of various tenses and passives.

Linguistic Contrastive Analysis Chart
The Consonants of English

IPA	ENGLISH	SPANISH	VIETNAMESE	CANTONESE
p	**p**it Aspirated at the start of a word or stressed syllable	**p**ato (duck) Never aspirated	**p**in (battery)	**p**ʰa (to lie prone) Always aspirated
b	**b**it	**b**arco (boat) Substitute voiced bilabial fricative /ə/ in between vowels	**b**a (three) Implosive (air moves into the mouth during articulation)	NO EQUIVALENT Substitute /p/
m	**m**an	**m**undo (world)	**m**ot (one)	**m**a (mother)
w	**w**in	agua (water)	NO EQUIVALENT Substitute word-initial /u/	**w**a (frog)
f	**f**un	**f**lor (flower)	**ph**uʼoʼng (phoenix) Substitute sound made with both lips, rather than with the lower lip and the teeth like English /f/	**f**a (flower) Only occurs at the beginning of syllables
v	**v**ery	NO EQUIVALENT Learners can use correct sound	**V**iệt Nam (Vietnam)	NO EQUIVALENT Substitute /f/
θ	**th**ing Rare in other languages. When done correctly, the tongue will stick out between the teeth.	NO EQUIVALENT Learners can use correct sound	NO EQUIVALENT Substitute /tʰ/ or /f/	NO EQUIVALENT Substitute /tʰ/ or /f/
ð	**th**ere Rare in other languages. When done correctly, the tongue will stick out between the teeth.	ca**d**a (every) Sound exists in Spanish only between vowels; sometimes substitute voiceless θ.	NO EQUIVALENT Substitute /d/	NO EQUIVALENT Substitute /t/ or /f/
t	**t**ime Aspirated at the start of a word or stressed syllable English tongue-touch. Is a little farther back in the mouth than the other languages.	**t**ocar (touch) Never aspirated	**t**ám (eight) Distinguishes aspirated and non-aspirated	**t**ʰa (he/she) Distinguishes aspirated and non-aspirated
d	**d**ime English tongue-touch is a little farther back in the mouth than the other languages.	**d**os (two)	Ðō**ng** (Dong = unit of currency) Vietnamese /d/ is implosive (air moves into the mouth during articulation)	NO EQUIVALENT Substitute /t/
n	**n**ame English tongue-touch is a little farther back in the mouth than the other languages.	**n**ube (cloud)	**n**am (south)	**n**a (take)
s	**s**oy	**s**eco (dry)	**x**em (to see)	**s**a (sand) Substitute sh– sound before /u/ Difficult at ends of syllables and words
z	**z**eal	NO EQUIVALENT Learners can use correct sound	**r**òi (already) In northern dialect only Southern dialect, substitute /y/	NO EQUIVALENT Substitute /s/
ɾ	bu**tt**er Written 't' and 'd' are pronounced with a quick tongue-tip tap.	**r**ana (toad) Written as single r and thought of as an /r/ sound.	NO EQUIVALENT Substitute /t/	NO EQUIVALENT Substitute /t/

HMONG	FILIPINO	KOREAN	MANDARIN
peb (we/us/our) Distinguishes aspirated and non-aspirated	**p**aalam (goodbye) Never aspirated	**p**al (sucking)	**pʰ**ei (cape) Always aspirated
NO EQUIVALENT Substitute /p/	**b**aka (beef)	**NO EQUIVALENT** /b/ said between vowels Substitute /p/ elsewhere	**NO EQUIVALENT**
mus (to go)	**m**abuti (good)	**m**al (horse)	**m**ei (rose)
NO EQUIVALENT Substitute word-initial /u/	**w**alo (eight)	g**we** (box)	**we**n (mosquito)
faib (to divide)	**NO EQUIVALENT** Substitute /p/	**NO EQUIVALENT** Substitute /p/	**f**a (issue)
Vaj ('Vang' clan name)	**NO EQUIVALENT** Substitute /b/	**NO EQUIVALENT** Substitute /b/	**NO EQUIVALENT** Substitute /w/ or /f/
NO EQUIVALENT Substitute /tʰ/ or /f/	**NO EQUIVALENT** Learners can use correct sound, but sometimes mispronounce voiced /ð/.	**NO EQUIVALENT** Substitute /t/	**NO EQUIVALENT** Substitute /t/ or /s/
NO EQUIVALENT Substitute /d/	**NO EQUIVALENT** Learners can use correct sound	**NO EQUIVALENT** Substitute /d/	**NO EQUIVALENT** Substitute /t/ or /s/
them (to pay) Distinguishes aspirated and non-aspirated	**t**akbo (run) Never aspirated	**t**al (daughter)	**t**a (wet) Distinguishes aspirated and non-aspirated
dev (dog)	**d**eretso (straight)	**NO EQUIVALENT** Substitute /d/ when said between vowels and /t/ elsewhere.	**NO EQUIVALENT** Substitute /t/
noj (to eat)	**n**aman (too)	**n**al (day)	**n**i (you) May be confused with /l/
xa (to send)	**s**ila (they)	**s**al (rice) Substitute *shi*– sound before /i/ and /z/ after a nasal consonant	**s**an (three)
NO EQUIVALENT Learners can use correct sound	**NO EQUIVALENT** Learners can use correct sound	**NO EQUIVALENT** Learners can use correct sound	**NO EQUIVALENT** Substitute /ts/ or /tsʰ/
NO EQUIVALENT Substitute /t/	**r**in/**d**in (too) Variant of the /d/ sound	Only occurs between two vowels Considered an /l/ sound	**NO EQUIVALENT**

Linguistic Contrastive Analysis Chart
The Consonants of English (continued)

IPA	ENGLISH	SPANISH	VIETNAMESE	CANTONESE
l	*loop* English tongue-touch is a little farther back in the mouth than the other languages. At the ends of syllables, the /l/ bunches up the back of the tongue, becoming velarized /ɫ/ or dark-l as in the word *ball*.	*libro* (book)	*cú lao* (island) /l/ does not occur at the ends of syllables	*lau* (angry) /l/ does not occur at the ends of syllables
ɹ	*red* Rare sound in the world Includes lip-rounding	NO EQUIVALENT Substitute /r/ sound such as the tap /ɾ/ or the trilled /r/	NO EQUIVALENT Substitute /l/	NO EQUIVALENT Substitute /l/
ʃ	*shallow* Often said with lip-rounding	NO EQUIVALENT Substitute /s/ or /tʃ/	*sieu thị* (supermarket) Southern dialect only	NO EQUIVALENT Substitute /s/
ʒ	*vision* Rare sound in English	NO EQUIVALENT Substitute /z/ or /dʒ/	NO EQUIVALENT Substitute /s/	NO EQUIVALENT Substitute /s/
tʃ	*chirp*	*chico* (boy)	*chính phủ* (government) Pronounced harder than English *ch*	NO EQUIVALENT Substitute /ts/
dʒ	*joy*	NO EQUIVALENT Sometimes substituted with /ʃ/ sound Some dialects have this sound for the *ll* spelling as in *llamar*	NO EQUIVALENT Substitute /c/, the equivalent sound, but voiceless	NO EQUIVALENT Substitute /ts/ Only occurs at beginnings of syllables
j	*you*	*cielo* (sky) Often substitute /dʒ/	*yeu* (to love)	*jau* (worry)
k	*kite* Aspirated at the start of a word or stressed syllable	*casa* (house) Never aspirated	*com* (rice) Never aspirated	*kʰa* (family) Distinguishes aspirated and non-aspirated
g	*goat*	*gato* (cat)	NO EQUIVALENT Substitute /k/	NO EQUIVALENT Substitute /k/
ŋ	*king*	*mango* (mango)	*Ngũyen* (proper last name)	*phaŋ* (to cook)
h	*hope*	*gente* (people) Sometimes substitute sound with friction higher in the vocal tract as velar /x/ or uvular /χ/	*hoa* (flower)	*ha* (shrimp)

HMONG	FILIPINO	KOREAN	MANDARIN
*p*eb (we/us/our) Distinguishes aspirated and non-aspirated	*p*aalam (goodbye) Never aspirated	*p*al (sucking)	*pʰei* (cape) Always aspirated
NO EQUIVALENT Substitute /p/	*b*aka (beef)	NO EQUIVALENT /b/ said between vowels Substitute /p/ elsewhere	NO EQUIVALENT
*m*us (to go)	*m*abuti (good)	*m*al (horse)	*m*ei (rose)
NO EQUIVALENT Substitute word-initial /*u*/	*w*alo (eight)	*gw*e (box)	*w*en (mosquito)
*f*aib (to divide)	NO EQUIVALENT Substitute /p/	NO EQUIVALENT Substitute /p/	*f*a (issue)
*V*aj ('Vang' clan name)	NO EQUIVALENT Substitute /b/	NO EQUIVALENT Substitute /b/	NO EQUIVALENT Substitute /w/ or /f/
NO EQUIVALENT Substitute /tʰ/ or /f/	NO EQUIVALENT Learners can use correct sound, but sometimes mispronounce voiced /ð/.	NO EQUIVALENT Substitute /t/	NO EQUIVALENT Substitute /t/ or /s/
NO EQUIVALENT Substitute /d/	NO EQUIVALENT Learners can use correct sound	NO EQUIVALENT Substitute /d/	NO EQUIVALENT Substitute /t/ or /s/
*th*em (to pay) Distinguishes aspirated and non-aspirated	*t*akbo (run) Never aspirated	*t*al (daughter)	*t*a (wet) Distinguishes aspirated and non-aspirated
*d*ev (dog)	*d*eretso (straight)	NO EQUIVALENT Substitute /d/ when said between vowels and /t/ elsewhere.	NO EQUIVALENT Substitute /t/
*n*oj (to eat)	*n*aman (too)	*n*al (day)	*n*i (you) May be confused with /l/
*x*a (to send)	*s*ila (they)	*s*al (rice) Substitute *shi*– sound before /i/ and /z/ after a nasal consonant	*s*an (three)

Linguistic Contrastive Analysis Chart
The Vowels of English

IPA	ENGLISH	SPANISH	VIETNAMESE	CANTONESE
i	*beat*	*hijo* (son)	*di* (to go)	*si* (silk)
ɪ	*bit* Rare in other languages Usually confused with /i/ (*meat* vs. *mit*)	NO EQUIVALENT Substitute /ē/	NO EQUIVALENT Substitute /ē/	*sik* (color) Only occurs before velars Substitute /ē/
e	*bait* End of vowel diphthongized—tongue moves up to /ē/ or short *e* position	*eco* (echo)	*kê* (millet)	*se* (to lend)
ɛ	*bet* Rare in other languages Learners may have difficulty distinguishing /ā/ and /e/ (short *e*): *pain* vs. *pen*	NO EQUIVALENT Substitute /ā/	NO EQUIVALENT Substitute /ā/	*seŋ* (sound) Only occurs before velars; difficult to distinguish from /ā/ in all positions
æ	*bat* Rare in other languages Learners may have trouble getting the tongue farther forward in the mouth	NO EQUIVALENT Substitute mid central /u/ (short *u*) or low front tense /o/ (short *o*)	*ghe* (boat)	NO EQUIVALENT Hard to distinguish between /æ/ and /ā/
u	*boot*	*uva* (grape)	*mua* (to buy)	*fu* (husband)
ʊ	*could* Rare in other languages Learners may have difficulty distinguishing the vowel sounds in *wooed* vs. *wood*	NO EQUIVALENT Substitute long *u*	NO EQUIVALENT Substitute long *u* (high back unrounded)	*suk* (uncle) Only occurs before velars Difficult to distinguish from long *u* in all positions
o	*boat* End of vowel diphthongized—tongue moves up to long *u* or ʊ position	*ojo* (eye)	*cô* (aunt)	*so* (comb)
ɔ	*law*	NO EQUIVALENT Substitute long *o* or short *o* Substituting long *o* will cause confusion (*low* vs. *law*); substituting short *o* will not	*cá* (fish)	*hok* (shell) Only occurs before velars Difficult to distinguish from long *o* in all positions
ɑ	*hot*	*mal* (bad)	*con* (child)	*sa* (sand)
ɑ ʊ	*house* Diphthong	*pauta*	*dao* (knife)	*sau* (basket)
ɔ ɪ	*boy* Diphthong	*hoy* (today)	*ròi* (already)	*soi* (grill)
ɑ ɪ	*bite* Diphthong	*baile* (dance)	*hai* (two)	*sai* (to waste)
ə	*about* Most common vowel in English; only in unstressed syllables Learners may have difficulty keeping it very short	NO EQUIVALENT Substitute short *u* or the full vowel from the word's spelling	*mua* (to buy)	NO EQUIVALENT
ʌ	*cut* Similar to schwa /ə/	NO EQUIVALENT Substitute short *o*	*giờ'* (time)	*san* (new)
ɝ	*bird* Difficult articulation, unusual in the world but common in American English Learners must bunch the tongue and constrict the throat	NO EQUIVALENT Substitute short *u* or /er/ with trill	NO EQUIVALENT Substitute /ɨ/	*hæ* (boot)

HMONG	FILIPINO	KOREAN	MANDARIN
ib (one)	*ikaw* (you) This vowel is interchangeable with /ɪ/; hard for speakers to distinguish these	zɪːʃaŋ (market)	*ti* (ladder) Sometimes English /i/ can be produced shorter
NO EQUIVALENT Substitute /ē/	*limampu* (fifty) This vowel is interchangeable with /ē/; hard for speakers to distinguish these	**NO EQUIVALENT** Substitute /ē/	**NO EQUIVALENT**
tes (hand)	*sero* (zero)	*beːda* (to cut)	*te* (nervous) Sometimes substitute English schwa /ə/
NO EQUIVALENT Substitute /ā/	*sero* (zero) This vowel interchanges with /ā/ like *bait*; not difficult for speakers to learn	*thɛːdo* (attitude)	**NO EQUIVALENT**
NO EQUIVALENT Substitute short *e*	**NO EQUIVALENT** Substitute short *o* as in *hot*	**NO EQUIVALENT**	**NO EQUIVALENT** Substitute /ə/ or short *u*
kub (hot or gold)	*tunay* (actual) This vowel interchanges with vowel in *could*; not difficult for speakers to learn	*zuːbag* (watermelon)	*lu* (hut) Sometimes English long *u* can be produced shorter
NO EQUIVALENT Substitute a sound like long *e* (mid central with lips slightly rounded)	*gumawa* (act) This vowel interchanges with long *u* like *boot*; not difficult for speakers to learn	**NO EQUIVALENT**	**NO EQUIVALENT**
NO EQUIVALENT	*ubo* (cough)	*boːzu* (salary)	*mo* (sword) This vowel is a little lower than English vowel
Yaj (Yang clan name)	**NO EQUIVALENT** Spoken as short *o*, as in *hot*	**NO EQUIVALENT**	**NO EQUIVALENT** Substitute long *o*
mov (cooked rice)	*talim* (blade)	*maːl* (speech)	*ta* (he/she) Sometimes substitute back long *o* or *u*
plaub (four)	*ikaw* (you)	**NO EQUIVALENT**	**NO EQUIVALENT**
NO EQUIVALENT	*apoy* (fire)	**NO EQUIVALENT**	**NO EQUIVALENT**
qaib (chicken)	*himatay* (faint)	**NO EQUIVALENT**	**NO EQUIVALENT**
NO EQUIVALENT	**NO EQUIVALENT** Spoken as short *o*, as in *hot*	**NO EQUIVALENT** Difficult sound for learners	**NO EQUIVALENT**
NO EQUIVALENT	**NO EQUIVALENT** Spoken as short *o*, as in *hot*	**NO EQUIVALENT**	**NO EQUIVALENT**
NO EQUIVALENT Substitute diphthong /əɨ/	**NO EQUIVALENT** Spoken as many different vowels (depending on English spelling) plus tongue tap /ɾ/	**NO EQUIVALENT**	**NO EQUIVALENT**

Comparative Oral Language Proficiency Chart

Levels of Proficiency	Level 1	Level II	Level III	Level IV	Level V
	Entering	Beginning	Developing	Expanding	Bridging
	Beginning	Early Intermediate	Intermediate	Early Advanced	Advanced
	Beginning	**Intermediate**		**Advanced**	**Advanced High**
Characteristics of the English Language Learner	• Minimal comprehension • May be very shy • No verbal production • Non-English speaker • Silent period (10 hours to 3 months) • Uses gestures and actions to communicate	• Limited comprehension • Gives one- or two-word responses • May use two- or three-word phrases • Stage may last 6 months to 2 years	• Comprehension increases • Errors still occur in speech • Simple sentences • Stage may last 2 to 4 years	• Good comprehension • Sentences become more complex • Engages in conversation • Errors in speech are more complex	• Few errors in speech • Orally proficient • Near-native vocabulary • Lacks writing skill • Uses complex sentences
What They Can Do: Performance Indicators	• Listen • Point • Illustrate • Match • Choose	• Name • List and group • Categorize • Label • Demonstrate	• Compare and contrast • Recall and retell • Summarize • Explain	• Higher-order thinking skills • Analyze, debate, justify	• All performance indicators
Instructional Ideas for Teachers	• Visual cues • Tape passages • Pair students • Total Physical Response activities • Concrete objects • Graphic organizers	• Short homework assignments • Short-answer quizzes • Open-ended sentences	• Graphs • Tables • Group discussions • Student-created books • Cloze activities	• Group panels • Paraphrasing • Defending and debating	• Lessons on writing mechanics • Free reading of appropriate books • Cooperative learning groups

Customize Literacy
on Reading Street

When kindergarten children burst into the classroom, you're eager to welcome them—and the different literacy experiences they bring with them. You appreciate that not all children learn at the same rate or level.

You customize your literacy program because it's a responsive and rewarding way to teach. Like many teachers, you want to use different approaches as you develop children's strengths and support their needs. At the same time, you carefully balance your plan to build in required skills.

Section 6 shows how *Scott Foresman Reading Street* provides just what you need to organize and carry out your customized literacy program. You'll find planning guides and instructional lessons to help you plan and implement your lessons. You can select from a rich array of readers to match texts to your kindergarteners.

Keep your expectations high as you customize your literacy program. *Reading Street* is here to help!

What Are Goals for Customizing a Literacy Program?

When you customize literacy, you create a program that balances direct skill instruction with a variety of approaches to meet children's needs. Your goal is to allow children to be increasingly in charge of their own learning, so you use flexible grouping and organize your literacy materials and practice stations in specific ways. The decisions you make about setting up your classroom and your use of a variety of assessments support the overall goals you've set. You want to know the most effective ways to:

- assess children to determine their strengths and learning needs.
- meet state standards for reading, writing, speaking, and listening.
- plan lessons to focus on areas of instructional need, based on assessment.
- match books to meet readers at their instructional level.
- build a community of learners.

How Can You Customize Literacy with *Reading Street*?

Lesson plans can be thought out in broad strokes in advance. Yet, if instruction is to be truly effective, lesson plans need to be revised constantly to accommodate new assessment information, and lessons need to be customized to suit the learning needs of individual children. At the same time, your plan must include district and state standards.

How Should You Group Children for Reading Instruction?

As you conduct a variety of assessments, you learn about children as individuals. You come to know a great deal about their achievement levels, their interests, and their ability to interact with other children. The results of these observations and performance-based assessments help you determine children's instructional needs and make grouping decisions. Your flexible groups will vary depending on the different instructional purpose you want to address for each. You may address DRA2 Level instruction, strategy and skill instruction, children's interests, or their social abilities. Your guided reading groups may be based on specific areas of need from the DRA2 continuum and Focus for Instruction.

Grouping to Meet Children's Needs	
Grouping Pattern	**Instructional Purpose**
Strategy/Skill Instruction	To work with children who need instruction on a specific reading strategy
Interest	To provide an opportunity for children with the same interests to learn together
Social Skills	To give children an opportunity to build and practice skills for collaboration and cooperation

How Do I Connect with DRA2 Results When I Customize Literacy?

As you customize your literacy program, detailed planning is needed for grouping children based on DRA2 Levels or strategy and skill instruction. For DRA2 Levels, use the chart that begins on the following page to determine the DRA2 instructional strand you plan to teach. The accompanying Focus for Instruction is shown along with the DRA benchmark levels. You'll also want to use lessons in *Reading Street* and leveled readers for practicing the key skills. Those materials are listed for you as well.

What Tools Help Me Teach Skills and Strategies?

For other groups, you may want to teach based on comprehension skill and strategy instruction. The chart that begins on the next page will help you choose leveled readers based on comprehension skill and strategy instruction for these groups. This chart also shows the Fountas and Pinnell leveling criteria, the corresponding DRA benchmark levels, and the genres and content connections of the leveled readers available on *Reading Street*.

The Customize Literacy section in the *Reading Street* Teacher's Edition provides strategies and support as you plan groups, pacing, and the purpose of your instruction. You'll always be able to match your young readers with the right books. To be assured you are providing consistent instruction, you can incorporate the routines from the Teacher Edition in your customized lessons. The flexibility of *Reading Street* resources provides the structure you need when you customize your literacy program. Overall, you're in the driver's seat, always doing your own thinking and planning.

A Rich Array of Leveled Text Sets

You choose the texts when you customize your literacy program. Select from Below-Level, On-Level, and Advanced Readers in *Reading Street*. Specific text sets are also available for your ELD and ELL groups. For struggling readers who need to practice independent reading as they build understanding and develop concept knowledge, choose the Concept Literacy Leveled Readers.

Grade K Alignment with DRA2

Many educators use the Developmental Reading Assessment, or DRA2, to assess students' reading achievement. This chart shows how *Reading Street* aligns with DRA2.

Kindergarten Instructional Strand	Focus for Instruction	DRA2 Benchmark	*Reading Street* Unit/ Week Lesson Plan	Materials
Print Awareness				
	Model and support directionality	A–4	Taught throughout U1	DI pages: K1v1 DI1–DI11 K1v1 DI18–DI28 K1v1 DI35–DI45 K1v2 DI52–DI62 K1v2 DI69–DI79 K1v2 DI86–DI96 Leveled Readers*
	Model and support concept of a letter and a word	A–4	Taught throughout U1	DI pages: K1v1 DI1–DI11 K1v1 DI18–DI28 K1v1 DI35–DI45 K1v2 DI52–DI62 K1v2 DI69–DI79 K1v2 DI86–DI96 Leveled Readers*
	Model and support concept of first and last letter of a word	A–4	Taught throughout U1	DI pages: K1v1 DI1–DI11 K1v1 DI18–DI28 K1v1 DI35–DI45 K1v2 DI52–DI62 K1v2 DI69–DI79 K1v2 DI86–DI96 Leveled Readers*
	Model and support one to one correspondence	A–4	Taught throughout U1	DI pages: K1v1 DI1–DI11 K1v1 DI18–DI28 K1v1 DI35–DI45 K1v2 DI52–DI62 K1v2 DI69–DI79 K1v2 DI86–DI96 Leveled Readers*
	Model and support language structure	A–4	Taught throughout U1	DI pages: K1v1 DI1–DI11 K1v1 DI18–DI28 K1v1 DI35–DI45 K1v2 DI52–DI62 K1v2 DI69–DI79 K1v2 DI86–DI96 Leveled Readers*
	Model parts of a book and turning pages	A–4	Taught throughout U1	DI pages: K1v1 DI1–DI11 K1v1 DI18–DI28 K1v1 DI35–DI45 K1v2 DI52–DI62 K1v2 DI69–DI79 K1v2 DI86–DI96 Leveled Readers*

* See following pages for a list of Leveled Readers.

Kindergarten Instructional Strand	Focus for Instruction	DRA2 Benchmark	*Reading Street* Unit/ Week Lesson Plan	Materials
Phonics				
	Identify letter sounds	A–4	Taught throughout the year	DI pages: K1v1 DI1–K6v2 DI96 Leveled Readers*
	Teach upper and lowercase letter names	A–4	1/1–1/4	DI pages: K1v1 DI1–DI11 K1v1 DI18–DI28 K1v1 DI35–DI45 K1v2 DI52–DI62 Leveled Readers*
	Teach how to blend onsets and rimes to make one-syllable words	A–4	Begins in U2, continues throughout the year	DI pages: K2v1 DI1–K6v2 DI96 Leveled Readers*
	Teach to identify syllables in spoken words	A–4	1/2, 1/3	DI pages: K1v1 DI18–DI28 K1v1 DI35–DI45 Leveled Readers*
	Teach sentence structure	A–4	3/6, 4/3, 6/3	DI pages: K3v2 DI86–DI96 K4v1 DI35–DI45 K6v1 DI35–DI45 Leveled Readers*
	Teach how to segment and blend sounds	A–4	Taught throughout the year	DI pages: K1v1 DI1–K6v2 DI96 Leveled Readers*
	Teach to identify and read high–frequency words	A–4	Taught throughout the year	DI pages: K1v1 DI1–K6v2 DI96 Leveled Readers*
Vocabulary				
	Model sorting pictures into categories	A–4	1/2, 2/1, 3/1	DI pages: K1v1 DI18–DI28 K2v1 DI1–DI11 K3v1 DI1–DI11 Leveled Readers*
	Teach to identify naming words	A–4	1/4, 2/5, 3/2, 3/3, 4/5	DI pages: K1v2 DI52–DI62 K2v2 DI69–DI79 K3v1 DI18–DI28 K3v1 DI35–DI45 K4v2 DI69–DI79 Leveled Readers*

* See following pages for a list of Leveled Readers.

Kindergarten Instructional Strand	Focus for Instruction	DRA2 Benchmark	*Reading Street* Unit/ Week Lesson Plan	Materials
Comprehension				
	Model holding a book while previewing	A–4	Taught throughout U1	DI pages: K1v1 DI1–DI11 K1v1 DI18–DI28 K1v1 DI35–DI45 K1v2 DI52–DI62 K1v2 DI69–DI79 K1v2 DI86–DI96 Leveled Readers*
	Teach the elements of a good retelling	3–4	Taught throughout the year	DI pages: K1v1 DI1–K6v2 DI96 Leveled Readers*
	Use character names during retelling	3–4	Taught throughout the year	DI pages: K1v1 DI1–K6v2 DI96 Leveled Readers*
	Model retelling a story	3–4	Taught throughout the year	DI pages: K1v1 DI1–K6v2 DI96 Leveled Readers*
	Model how to use and monitor visual information	3–4	1/4, 1/5, 3/3	DI pages: K1v2 DI52–DI62 K1v2 DI69–DI79 K3v1 DI35–DI45 Leveled Readers*

* See following pages for a list of Leveled Readers.

Leveled Reader Skills Chart

How do I find the right reader for every student?

The books in this list were leveled using the criteria suggested in Matching Books to Readers *and* Leveled Books for Readers, Grades 3–6 *by Irene C. Fountas and Gay Su Pinnell. For more on leveling, see the* Reading Street Leveled Readers Leveling Guide. *Complete books may also be found on* the Leveled Readers Database.

Grade K — Title	Level*	DRA Level*	Genre	Target Comprehension Skill	
Max the Duck	A	1	Fantasy	Character	
Fun for Us	B	2	Informational Text	Setting	
Nick the Fix-It Man	B	2	Informational Text	Sequence	
Red and Blue	B	2	Realistic Fiction	Classify and Categorize	
We Have Fun Together	B	2	Fantasy	Character	
Two or Three?	B	2	Realistic Fiction	Classify and Categorize	
Buds for Mom	B	2	Realistic Fiction	Compare and Contrast	
A Walk in the Forest	B	2	Realistic Fiction	Setting	
Looking for Animals	B	2	Realistic Fiction	Main Idea	
Skip and Run	C	3	Fantasy	Realism and Fantasy	
A Winter Home	C	3	Informational Text	Sequence	
A Yard for All	C	3	Fantasy	Realism and Fantasy	
The Fawn	C	3	Realistic Fiction	Compare and Contrast	
We Can Do It!	C	3	Realistic Fiction	Plot	
Fun with Gram	C	3	Realistic Fiction	Cause and Effect	
They Will Grow	C	3	Realistic Fiction	Plot	
What Can You Do?	C	3	Informational Text	Draw Conclusions	
Sad and Glad	C	3	Realistic Fiction	Main Idea	
The Trip	C	3	Informational Text	Sequence	
Pigs	C	3	Informational Text	Cause and Effect	
Frog's New Home	C	3	Informational Text	Sequence	
Five Bears	C	3	Fantasy	Character	
My Walk in Antarctica	C	3	Realistic Fiction	Classify and Categorize	
A Trip to Washington, D.C.	C	3	Informational Text	Setting	
The Bus Ride	C	3	Realistic Fiction	Realism and Fantasy	
The Boat Ride	C	3	Realistic Fiction	Cause and Effect	
Ming on the Job	C	3	Realistic Fiction	Compare and Contrast	
The Big Train	D	4	Realistic Fiction	Plot	
Get On the Bus!	D	4	Realistic Fiction	Main Idea	
Catch the Ball!	D	4	Realistic Fiction	Draw Conclusions	
Homes	D	4	Informational Text	Compare and Contrast	
The Best Club Hut	D	4	Realistic Fiction	Character	
A Small Trip	D	4	Informational Text	Main Idea	
The Box	D	4	Informational Text	Plot	
Our Camping Trip	D	4	Realistic Fiction	Setting	
Safe Places for Animals	D	4	Informational Text	Draw Conclusions	

* Suggested Guided Reading level. Use your knowledge of children's abilities to adjust levels as needed.

Additional Comprehension Instruction	Comprehension Strategy	Vocabulary	Content Connection
N/A	Recall/Retell	N/A	Culture
N/A	Recall/Retell	N/A	Citizenship
N/A	Recall/Retell	N/A	Citizenship
N/A	Recall/Retell	N/A	Citizenship
N/A	Recall/Retell	N/A	Citizenship
N/A	Recall/Retell	N/A	Citizenship
N/A	Recall/Retell	N/A	Citizenship
N/A	Recall/Retell	N/A	Life Science
N/A	Recall/Retell	N/A	Life Science
N/A	Recall/Retell	N/A	Life Science
N/A	Recall/Retell	N/A	Life Science
N/A	Recall/Retell	N/A	Life Science
N/A	Recall/Retell	N/A	Life Science
N/A	Recall/Retell	N/A	Earth Science
N/A	Recall/Retell	N/A	Life Science
N/A	Recall/Retell	N/A	Life Science
N/A	Recall/Retell	N/A	Life Science
N/A	Recall/Retell	N/A	Life Science
N/A	Recall/Retell	N/A	Life Science
N/A	Recall/Retell	N/A	Life Science
N/A	Recall/Retell	N/A	Life Science
N/A	Recall/Retell	N/A	Culture
N/A	Recall/Retell	N/A	Culture
N/A	Recall/Retell	N/A	Geography
N/A	Recall/Retell	N/A	Culture
N/A	Recall/Retell	N/A	Culture
N/A	Recall/Retell	N/A	Citizenship
N/A	Recall/Retell	N/A	History
N/A	Recall/Retell	N/A	Culture
N/A	Recall/Retell	N/A	Physical Science
N/A	Recall/Retell	N/A	Culture
N/A	Recall/Retell	N/A	Physical Science
N/A	Recall/Retell	N/A	Life Science
N/A	Recall/Retell	N/A	Citizenship
N/A	Recall/Retell	N/A	Culture
N/A	Recall/Retell	N/A	Life Science

Leveled Reader Skills Chart (*continued*)

Need more choices? Look ahead to Grade 1.

Grade 1 — Title	Level*	DRA Level*	Genre	Target Comprehension Skill	
Bix the Dog	A	1	Realistic Fiction	Plot	
Time for Dinner	B	2	Realistic Fiction	Main Idea and Details	
Sam	B	2	Realistic Fiction	Character and Setting	
Mack and Zack	B	2	Realistic Fiction	Character and Setting	
The Sick Pets	B	2	Realistic Fiction	Plot	
On the Farm	B	2	Realistic Fiction	Character and Setting	
At Your Vet	B	2	Realistic Fiction	Main Idea and Details	
Fun in the Sun	B	2	Expository Nonfiction	Cause and Effect	
We Are a Family	B	2	Nonfiction	Sequence	
Where They Live	C	3	Realistic Fiction	Character and Setting	
Which Fox?	C	3	Realistic Fiction	Main Idea and Details	
Which Animals Will We See?	C	3	Realistic Fiction	Cause and Effect	
Let's Go to the Zoo	C	3	Nonfiction	Sequence	
A Play	C	3	Realistic Fiction	Cause and Effect	
A Class	C	3	Nonfiction	Cause and Effect	
Here in My Neighborhood	C	3	Nonfiction	Author's Purpose	
Look at My Neighborhood	C	3	Realistic Fiction	Author's Purpose	
Look at Dinosaurs	C	3	Expository Nonfiction	Sequence	
Around the Forest	C	3	Nonfiction	Author's Purpose	
Learn About Worker Bees	C	3	Expository Nonfiction	Compare and Contrast	
In My Room	C	3	Nonfiction	Sequence	
Hank's Song	C	3	Fantasy	Compare and Contrast	
Gus the Pup	C	3	Realistic Fiction	Fact and Opinion	
What Animals Can You See?	D	4	Expository Nonfiction	Main Idea and Details	
The Dinosaur Herds	D	4	Expository Nonfiction	Sequence	
People Help the Forest	D	4	Expository Nonfiction	Author's Purpose	
Honey	D	4	Nonfiction	Compare and Contrast	
Let's Build a Park!	D	4	Fiction	Sequence	
Mac Can Do It!	D	4	Fantasy	Compare and Contrast	
The Seasons Change	D	4	Nonfiction	Author's Purpose	
Animals Change and Grow	D	4	Nonfiction	Fact and Opinion	
Ready for Winter?	D	4	Expository Nonfiction	Draw Conclusions	

* Suggested Guided Reading level. Use your knowledge of children's abilities to adjust levels as needed.

Additional Comprehension Instruction	Comprehension Strategy	Vocabulary	Content Connection
Sequence	Summarize	High-Frequency Words	Life Science
Compare and Contrast	Important Ideas	High-Frequency Words	Life Science
Draw Conclusions	Monitor and Clarify	High-Frequency Words	Life Science
Main Idea	Monitor and Clarify	High-Frequency Words	Life Science
Draw Conclusions	Summarize	High-Frequency Words	Life Science/Citizenship
Plot	Visualize	High-Frequency Words	Citizenship
Theme	Story Structure	High-Frequency Words	Citizenship
Author's Purpose	Text Structure	High-Frequency Words	Life Science
Draw Conclusions	Predict and Set Purpose	High-Frequency Words	Culture
Theme and Plot	Visualize	High-Frequency Words	Geography/Culture
Compare and Contrast	Important Ideas	High-Frequency Words	Life Science
Setting and Plot	Text Structure	High-Frequency Words	Life Science
Compare and Contrast	Predict and Set Purpose	High-Frequency Words	Life Science
Main Idea	Monitor and Clarify	High-Frequency Words	Citizenship
Author's Purpose	Monitor and Clarify	High-Frequency Words	Citizenship/Culture
Draw Conclusions	Important Ideas	High-Frequency Words	Citizenship/Culture
Compare and Contrast	Important Ideas	High-Frequency Words	Citizenship
Cause and Effect	Inferring	High-Frequency Words	Life Science
Cause and Effect	Background Knowledge	High-Frequency Words	Life Science
Sequence	Questioning	High-Frequency Words	Life Science
Author's Purpose	Summarize	High-Frequency Words	Life Science
Realism and Fantasy	Inferring	High-Frequency Words	Citizenship
Cause and Effect	Monitor and Clarify	High-Frequency Words	Culture
Compare and Contrast	Text Structure	High-Frequency Words	Life Science
Draw Conclusions	Inferring	High-Frequency Words	Life Science
Cause and Effect	Background Knowledge	High-Frequency Words	Life Science
Draw Conclusions	Questioning	High-Frequency Words	Life Science
Author's Purpose	Summarize	High-Frequency Words	Citizenship
Realism and Fantasy	Inferring	High-Frequency Words	Life Science
Draw Conclusions	Visualize	High-Frequency Words	Life Science
Sequence	Text Structure	High-Frequency Words	Life Science
Sequence	Background Knowledge	High-Frequency Words	Earth Science

Leveled Reader Skills Chart (*continued*)

Grade 1 Title	Level*	DRA Level*	Genre	Target Comprehension Skill	
A Party for Pedro	D	4	Realistic Fiction	Draw Conclusions	
Space Star	D	4	Realistic Fiction	Theme	
Our Leaders	D	4	Nonfiction	Facts and Details	
Grandma's Farm	D	4	Realistic Fiction	Facts and Details	
A New Baby Brother	D	4	Realistic Fiction	Theme	
My Babysitter	D	4	Narrative Nonfiction	Cause and Effect	
What Brown Saw	D	4	Animal Fantasy	Character, Setting, and Plot	
Fly Away Owl!	D	4	Realistic Fiction	Draw Conclusions	
What A Detective Does	D	4	Realistic Fiction	Compare and Contrast	
The Inclined Plane	D	4	Expository Nonfiction	Main Idea and Details	
Using the Telephone	D	4	Expository Nonfiction	Sequence	
A Garden for All	D	4	Nonfiction	Theme	
Big Wishes and Her Baby	E	6–8	Realistic Fiction	Fact and Opinion	
Plans Change	E	6–8	Realistic Fiction	Author's Purpose	
Let's Visit a Butterfly Greenhouse	E	6–8	Nonfiction	Fact and Opinion	
Seasons Come and Go	E	6–8	Expository Nonfiction	Draw Conclusions	
Special Days, Special Food	E	6–8	Expository Nonfiction	Draw Conclusions	
The Art Show	F	10	Realistic Fiction	Theme	
Treasures of Our Country	F	10	Nonfiction	Facts and Details	
A Visit to the Ranch	F	10	Realistic Fiction	Facts and Details	
My Little Brother Drew	F	10	Realistic Fiction	Theme	
The Story of the Kids Care Club	F	10	Expository Nonfiction	Cause and Effect	
Squirrel and Bear	G	12	Animal Fantasy	Character, Setting and Plot	
Puppy Raiser	G	12	Expository Nonfiction	Draw Conclusions	
A Mighty Oak Tree	G	12	Expository Nonfiction	Compare and Contrast	
Simple Machines at Work	G	12	Expository Nonfiction	Main Idea and Details	
Carlos Picks a Pet	H	14	Realistic Fiction	Character and Setting	
That Cat Needs Help!	H	14	Realistic Fiction	Plot	
Loni's Town	H	14	Realistic Fiction	Character and Setting	
Baby Animals in the Rain Forest	H	14	Expository Nonfiction	Main Idea and Details	
Cary and the The Wildlife Shelter	H	14	Realistic Fiction	Main Idea and Details	
Around the World	H	14	Narrative Nonfiction	Cause and Effect	

* Suggested Guided Reading level. Use your knowledge of children's abilities to adjust levels as needed.

Additional Comprehension Instruction	Comprehension Strategy	Vocabulary	Content Connection
Author's Purpose	Monitor and Clarify	High-Frequency Words	Culture
Realism and Fantasy	Visualize	High-Frequency Words	Citizenship/Culture
Cause and Effect	Important Ideas	High-Frequency Words	Government
Plot	Questioning	High-Frequency Words	Culture
Realism and Fantasy	Story Structure	High-Frequency Words	Culture
Main Idea	Predict and Set Purpose	High-Frequency Words	Culture
Realism and Fantasy	Monitor and Clarify	High-Frequency Words	Life Science
Cause and Effect	Background Knowledge	High-Frequency Words	Citizenship
Cause and Effect	Monitor and Clarify	High-Frequency Words	Earth Science/Life Science
Cause and Effect	Summarize	High-Frequency Words	Physical Science
Author's Purpose	Text Structure	High-Frequency Words	Space and Technology
Sequence	Inferring	High-Frequency Words	Citizenship
Setting	Monitor and Clarify	High-Frequency Words	Citizenship
Setting	Visualize	High-Frequency Words	Life Science
Author's Purpose	Text Structure	High-Frequency Words	Life Science
Compare and Contrast	Background Knowledge	High-Frequency Words	Life Science
Author's Purpose	Monitor and Clarify	High-Frequency Words	Culture
Plot	Visualize	High-Frequency Words	Citizenship/Culture
Cause and Effect	Important Ideas	High-Frequency Words	History/Geography
Compare and Contrast	Questioning	High-Frequency Words	Culture
Realism and Fantasy	Story Structure	High-Frequency Words	Citizenship
Author's Purpose	Predict and Set Purpose	High-Frequency Words	Citizenship
Realism and Fantasy	Monitor and Clarify	High-Frequency Words	Citizenship
Main Idea	Background Knowledge	High-Frequency Words	Citizenship
Draw Conclusions	Monitor and Clarify	High-Frequency Words	Life Science
Compare and Contrast	Summarize	High-Frequency Words	Physical Science
Compare and Contrast	Monitor and Clarify	Amazing Words	Life Science
Sequence	Summarize	Amazing Words	Citizenship
Theme	Visualize	Amazing Words	History
Author's Purpose	Important Ideas	Amazing Words	Life Science
Sequence	Story Structure	Amazing Words	Life Science
Main Idea	Text Structure	Amazing Words	Life Science

Leveled Reader Skills Chart *(continued)*

Grade 1 Title	Level*	DRA Level*	Genre	Target Comprehension Skill	
The Communication Story	H	14	Expository Nonfiction	Sequence	
Marla's Good Idea	H	14	Realistic Fiction	Theme	
Rules at School	I	16	Animal Fantasy	Sequence	
School: Then and Now	I	16	Expository Nonfiction	Cause and Effect	
Mom the Mayor	I	16	Realistic Fiction	Author's Purpose	
The Dinosaur Detectives	I	16	Expository Nonfiction	Sequence	
All About Food Chains	I	16	Expository Nonfiction	Author's Purpose	
Bees and Beekeepers	I	16	Expository Nonfiction	Compare and Contrast	
A New Library	I	16	Narrative Nonfiction	Sequence	
Paul's Bed	J	18	Traditional Tales	Compare and Contrast	
Britton Finds a Kitten	J	18	Realistic Fiction	Fact and Opinion	
All About the Weather	J	18	Expository Nonfiction	Author's Purpose	
Learn About Butterflies	J	18	Expository Nonfiction	Fact and Opinion	
Monarchs Migrate South	J	18	Narrative Nonfiction	Draw Conclusions	
Cascarones Are for Fun	J	18	Expository Nonfiction	Draw Conclusions	
Jamie's Jumble of Junk	J	18	Realistic Fiction	Theme	
America's Home	K	20	Nonfiction	Facts and Details	
Go West!	K	20	Legend	Facts and Details	
Double Trouble Twins	K	20	Realistic Fiction	Theme	
What Makes Buildings Special?	K	20	Expository Nonfiction	Cause and Effect	
Grasshopper and Ant	K	20	Fable	Character, Setting, and Plot	
Ways to be a Good Citizen	K	20	Expository Nonfiction	Draw Conclusions	
Great Scientists: Detectives at Work	L	24	Expository Nonfiction	Compare and Contrast	
Simple Machines in Compound Machines	L	24	Nonfiction	Main Idea and Details	
Telephones Over the Years	L	24	Expository Nonfiction	Sequence	
Cody's Adventure	L	24	Realistic Fiction	Theme	

* Suggested Guided Reading level. Use your knowledge of children's abilities to adjust levels as needed.

Additional Comprehension Instruction	Comprehension Strategy	Vocabulary	Content Connection
Compare and Contrast	Text Structure	High-Frequency Words	Space and Technology
Sequence	Inferring	High-Frequency Words	Space and Technology
Character	Predict and Set Purpose	Amazing Words	Citizenship
Draw Conclusions	Monitor and Clarify	Amazing Words	History
Cause and Effect	Important Ideas	Amazing Words	Government
Draw Conclusions	Inferring	Amazing Words	Life Science
Cause and Effect	Background Knowledge	Amazing Words	Life Science
Main Idea	Questioning	Amazing Words	Life Science
Author's Purpose	Summarize	Amazing Words	Citizenship
Character	Inferring	Amazing Words	Citizenship
Setting	Monitor and Clarify	Amazing Words	Life Science
Plot	Visualize	Amazing Words	Earth Science
Cause and Effect	Text Structure	Amazing Words	Life Science
Author's Purpose	Background Knowledge	Amazing Words	LIfe Science
Sequence	Monitor and Clarify	Amazing Words	Culture/History
Character, Setting, and Plot	Visualize	Amazing Words	Culture
Cause and Effect	Important Ideas	Amazing Words	Government
Theme	Questioning	Amazing Words	Culture
Realism and Fantasy	Story Structure	Amazing Words	Citizenship
Draw Conclusions	Predict and Set Purpose	Amazing Words	Culture
Cause and Effect	Monitor and Clarify	Amazing Words	Citizenship
Compare and Contrast	Background Knowledge	Amazing Words	Citizenship
Compare and Contrast	Monitor and Clarify	Amazing Words	Citizenship
Cause and Effect	Summarize	Amazing Words	Physical Science
Draw Conclusions	Text Structure	Amazing Words	Space and Technology
Sequence	Inferring	Amazing Words	Science

Concept Literacy Leveled Reader Chart

Concept Literacy Leveled Readers align with the weekly concepts in each unit. Each book is written at a lower level than the Below-Level Reader for the week to provide struggling readers with a way to practice independent reading as they build understanding and develop concept knowledge. Concept Literacy Readers play a role in the instruction for the Strategic Intervention group, but they can be used for independent reading practice for any struggling readers.

Grade K — Title	Level*	DRA Level*	Concept	Content Connection
Off to School	A	1	All Together Now	Social Studies
I Help	A	1	All Together Now	Citizenship
Families	A	1	All Together Now	Social Studies
Who Helps?	A	1	All Together Now	Citizenship
We Work and Play	A	1	All Together Now	Citizenship
Machines Help	A	1	All Together Now	Physical Science
Parts of a Flower	A	1	Look at Us	Life Science
Look Around	A	1	Look at Us	Science
In the Grasslands	A	1	Look at Us	Life Science
The Bear	A	1	Look at Us	Life Science
Animal Homes	A	1	Look at Us	Life Science
In the Garden	A	1	Look at Us	Life Science
Pandas Grow Up	A	1	Change All Around Us	Life Science
Growing Up	A	1	Change All Around Us	Social Studies
Long Ago and Today	A	1	Change All Around Us	History
Animals Change	A	1	Change All Around Us	Life Science
Old and New	A	1	Change All Around Us	History
What Makes Me Happy?	A	1	Change All Around Us	Culture
What Do I See?	A	1	Let's Go Exploring	Social Studies
My Lucky Day	A	1	Let's Go Exploring	Social Studies
Animal Adventures	A	1	Let's Go Exploring	Life Science
What Can I Do?	A	1	Let's Go Exploring	Social Studies
Antarctic Adventures	A	1	Let's Go Exploring	Life Science
In the City	A	1	Let's Go Exploring	Culture
There It Goes!	A	1	Going Places	Social Studies
We Help	A	1	Going Places	Citizenship
What Carries Loads?	A	1	Going Places	Physical Science
Trains Work Hard	A	1	Going Places	Physical Science
We Travel	A	1	Going Places	Culture
I Go to School	A	1	Going Places	Social Studies
What Do We Need?	A	1	Putting It Together	Economics
We Build a Birdhouse	A	1	Putting It Together	Physical Science
Busy Beavers	A	1	Putting It Together	Life Science
What Can We Make Together?	A	1	Putting It Together	Citizenship
Who Builds a House?	A	1	Putting It Together	Science
Ants Build	A	1	Putting It Together	Life Science

* Suggested Guided Reading level. Use your knowledge of children's abilities to adjust levels as needed.

Concept Literacy Leveled Reader Chart (continued)

Need more choices? Look ahead to Grade 1.

Grade 1 Title	Level*	DRA Level*	Concept	Content Connection
In My Room	A	1	Home and Families	Culture
My Family	A	1	Home and Families	Culture
Outside My Door	A	1	Home and Families	Social Studies
My Friends	A	1	Neighborhoods	Social Studies
My School	A	1	Neighborhoods	Social Studies
Around My Neighborhood	A	1	Neighborhoods	Social Studies
The Dog	A	1	Animal Friends	Life Science
Helping Pets	A	1	Animal Friends	Citizenship
Animals Help	A	1	Animal Friends	Citizenship
We See Animals	A	1	Wild Animals	Life Science
Neighborhood Animals	A	1	Wild Animals	Life Science
Wild Animals	A	1	Wild Animals	Life Science
My Family	A	1	People in Communities	Culture
At School	A	1	People in Communities	Social Studies
In My Neighborhood	A	1	People in Communities	Social Studies
Animals Work Together	A	1	Communities in Nature	Life Science
In the Forest	A	1	Communities in Nature	Life Science
Ants and People	A	1	Communities in Nature	Science
Gardens Change	A	1	Growing and Changing	Life Science
I Can Read	A	1	Growing and Changing	Social Studies
Animals Change	A	1	Growing and Changing	Life Science
Changes in Gardens	A	1	Changes in Nature	Life Science
Caterpillars Change	A	1	Changes in Nature	Life Science
In the Winter	A	1	Changes in Nature	Life Science
Surprise! Surprise!	B	2	Surprising Treasures	Social Studies
Special Stories	B	2	Surprising Treasures	Culture
Our Country's Treasures	B	2	Surprising Treasures	History
Places We Treasure	B	2	Treasures to Share	Social Studies
Treasures We Share	B	2	Treasures to Share	Culture
My Town	B	2	Treasures to Share	Social Studies
Great Ideas	B	2	Clever Solutions	Social Studies
Ways We Learn	B	2	Clever Solutions	Social Studies
Who Likes the Old Tree?	B	2	Clever Solutions	Life Science
Simple Machines	B	2	Ideas That Change Our World	Physical Science
Telephones Help Us Every Day	B	2	Ideas That Change Our World	Space & Technology
Let's Plant A Garden	B	2	Ideas That Change Our World	Life Science

* Suggested Guided Reading level. Use your knowledge of children's abilities to adjust levels as needed.

21ˢᵗ Century Skills on Reading Street

Your kindergarteners are "digital natives." So when you tell them to *Get Online!* they jump at the chance. The world of information and communication technology (ICT) is a natural part of their everyday lives.

In **Section 7**, you'll discover the visually engaging and entertaining Digital Path locations on *Scott Foresman Reading Street.* These exciting, research-based tools motivate children to explore the new literacies of the 21ˢᵗ Century and their own ideas through technology.

The next step is easy. To begin exploring content and features, just visit www.ReadingStreet.com!

21st Century Skills

As a kindergarten teacher, your focus is the whole child. You are providing a learning environment that promotes readiness skills and provides a foundation for future learning. Technology is part of your kindergarten environment. You're teaching while the nature of reading and learning is changing.

The kindergarteners in your classroom now will someday become part of a 21st century workforce. As a teacher of literacy, you will continually adapt your teaching as new technologies appear. Children need these valuable literacy skills as they grow up in this information, media, and information-rich context.

Technology on *Scott Foresman Reading Street* can be used both for enhancing children's classroom learning experiences and preparing them for the future. Throughout the year, you can choose from research-based technology options that enrich your instruction and assist you in the management of classroom learning.

What Are New Literacies?

The Internet and other technologies create new opportunities, new solutions, and new literacies—new ways to make meaning out of what we see and read onscreen. Each new technology for reading, writing, and communicating requires new literacies to take full advantage of its potential. The future calls for new comprehension skills too. Children must adapt and use new reading comprehension skills when they are online. These literacies are increasingly important to our children and our society.

Research has shown that technology is a powerful motivational tool as well as a critical literacy area for the future. It has the power to engage and hold children's attention, maximize time on task, and help you scaffold learning. Child engagement leads to willingness to practice, and practice is "doing." It leads to real learning. To be effective, technology and digital media for literacy learning must be carefully designed to include instructionally effective visuals, audio, and interactivity.

"Locating information on the Internet requires very different reading skills from locating information in a book."
Donald J. Leu, Jr., 2008

How Can I Help Children Adjust to Changing Technology?

Technology is part of our lives, so what we are used to now changes rapidly. New uses for technology are constantly being envisioned, and teachers respond by changing their instruction. They see the benefits of child-centered learning that technology makes possible. In the future, technology will foster even more learner-based instruction. Your kindergarteners don't have to wait for opportunities to control how they will achieve certain learning goals. *Scott Foresman Reading Street* has multiple destinations on its Digital Path that help make the transition to child-centered instruction effective. With these research-based multimedia tools, you can guide children to See It!, Hear It!, and Do It!

Big Question Videos introduce the unit level Big Question that children explore throughout the unit. Children use the Journal activity to capture their questions and ideas in a graphic organizer.

Concept Talk Videos support you in providing critical background building information. Children learn background about text topics before they begin to read. Seeing and hearing concept vocabulary prepares children to talk about the topic with others in the class.

Envision It! Animations make cause and effect, compare and contrast, and other comprehension skills come to life in an animated context. After students watch, they can talk about and understand the skill. The next stop, learning the academic vocabulary for each comprehension skill, comes more easily. Students can click on to retellings, which include concept vocabulary, and access definitions. The picture prompts help students retell. Envision It! also includes a paired selection, with audio, that expands on the theme or topic in a new way.

What Skills Do Children Need for New Literacies?

Five comprehension skill areas are important for children to develop as they read online. These skills build on the decoding, vocabulary, and text comprehension skills that are also necessary for reading on the Internet.

1. **Ask, identify, and generate important questions.**
   What motivates children to read on the Internet? Most begin with a question or another need to find information. Children need to know how to ask important questions. They also need to use the Internet to generate questions.

2. **Use multiple comprehension skills to locate information.**
   Children encounter separate search engines to find information. Then they read search results and make inferences to select the best links for their needs.

3. **Critically evaluate information on the Internet.**
   Children read information that anyone may have published on the Internet, so they must pay attention to accuracy. Children need to determine who created the information and consider why and when it was published. They need to detect bias in the information. They must also know how to use other sources to check if information is accurate for their own purposes.

4. **Synthesize information to create unique answers.**
   Readers on the Internet are putting together a new, or external, text as they find information in different places. A critical new comprehension skill is learning to make wise choices as they select links and add information. Each child's synthesis may be different because different links may be chosen. Children also must learn to create the external text that answers their question, or answers additional questions that arose as they searched.

5. **Communicate the answers to others.**
   Reading and writing are integrated when using the Internet. Children must learn to compose texts through the links that they select during reading. They use blogs, e-mail, text messaging, and other communication technologies to send the new information.

When children follow the Digital Path in *Scott Foresman Reading Street*, they are learning 21st Century literacy skills. As they read Paired eSelections, which extend concepts, vocabulary, and the topic of the main selection, they can select the Read Online feature. This interactive lesson is like a private tutor that teaches children information and communication technology (ICT) comprehension skills and strategies for e-mail, Web sites, and media awareness.

How Does Technology Help Children Acquire Vocabulary?

Have you observed that children who use academic vocabulary in classroom conversations—even before they can read the words—are at an advantage? Later, when children see the words in print, you notice that they comprehend more quickly. Your observations align with what research is pointing to. Children who view images, video, and animation while listening to audio gain important information. But they won't use those sources alone. In the 21st century, children will use multimedia information sources and read traditional text often. The reason is obvious: we can read text far faster than we can listen to or view it. The need for speed and information management will require all readers to depend on a balance of technological and traditional text sources—as well as their expanded knowledge of literacy skills.

When you're on the Digital Path of *Scott Foresman Reading Street* you have a variety of options for online games and activities that build vocabulary and skills. You can choose matching, sorting, word building, and other activities that support your instructional goals in kindergarten.

eReaders Leveled books are available as audio books. Teachers can assign the book matched to each child based on his or her reading profile, or choose another book based on a different instructional purpose.

Grammar Jammer has songs and rhymes that help children remember the weekly conventions skills.

What Makes Technology Powerful?

Watch children as they engage in technology. They have a "Do It!" attitude and seem to be aware that they're actively learning. Your kindergarteners are eager to make choices in response to reading prompts. They become motivated when they receive immediate feedback and are receptive to thought-provoking questions about their use of strategies. Technology is also a powerful tool for the emerging writer. Research shows that technology for writing instruction helps children think as they write, especially when the technology has prompts to support reflection on writing, spelling, and grammar. When you use carefully designed technology, your instruction has more power because it's more child-centered.

While these literacy and learning outcomes are important, new literacies can also lead to important new realizations for children. When you use the Internet, children have the potential to travel across information bridges and interact with authors, experts, communities, and children from around the globe. Meaningful interactions with other children from diverse communities spark new questions about the larger world. As children search for answers, their insights and understanding broaden too.

How Does Technology Support Teachers?

As a teacher in the 21st century, you want to be skilled in the effective use of information and communication technology (ICT) for teaching and learning. You expect a literacy curriculum that integrates the new literacies of ICT into your instructional programs. You need assessment practices in literacy that include reading on the Internet and writing using word-processing. When you go to the Student and Teacher Resources and Download Center in the *Scott Foresman Reading Street* Digital Path, you can choose digital supports for all your needs. The Teacher's Edition is available online, as well as a variety of online assessment tools that help you adjust your instruction and make grouping decisions. You can search by standards or skill key word to find additional resources that target children's needs. Your kindergarteners will get the specific extra practice they need before reassessment. You'll also find many other teacher and student materials in CD and CD-ROM formats.

Story Sort allows children to drag and drop retelling cards and place them in correct order. This interactive sequencing is a visual way to practice retelling stories, a critical comprehension skill. Children build comprehension as they write an Image Essay about one picture.

Decodable eBooks show children word-by-word highlighting as they hear the decodable text read aloud. You can use underlining and highlighting tools for group or one-on-one instruction.

Letter Tile Drag and Drop is a word building game that teachers can use whenever children are ready to practice phonics and word building. They manipulate the familiar yellow tiles that appear in Teacher Edition lessons for word work.

Phonics Songs and Rhymes Audio CDs provide the engaging practice you need to help kindergarten readers practice the phonics skills they are learning.

New Literacies on *Reading Street*

Did you know that many nations are preparing their children for the reading demands of the Internet? Students need to be prepared for a global information economy. The ability to read information online to learn, solve problems, and communicate solutions is central to success.

As our reliance on technology increases, it is essential that children learn digital skills. Starting in First Grade, *Reading Street* weaves these basic digital skills—e-mail, Web sites, parts of a computer—with the core knowledge. More than ever, America's children require an emphasis on 21st century skills and basic digital know-how. Writing e-mail weekly or daily, children practice the comprehension and writing skills taught in *Reading Street*. School projects call students to search engines, online directories, and reference sources that support the research skills taught in *Reading Street* Teacher Editions.

As students progress in school, *Reading Street* teaches increasingly important ways to write e-mail, browse Web sites, research with online directories and search engines, and evaluate online sources using easily understood and fun-to-read selections. *Reading Street* prepares our youth for the success that they deserve as they enter middle school and high school.

You change the world when you teach a child to read. And now, with the new literacies of the Internet, this can happen in profoundly powerful ways. The Internet opens your classroom windows to the world.

Parts of a Computer Using a computer for the first time might be a puzzling experience for children. That's why *Reading Street* provides a "Read Together" selection called "My Computer." Colorful illustrations of a basic desktop point out the essential parts of a computer, including the cursor, mouse, keyboard, printer, CD-ROM, and monitor. In just a few minutes, children will be familiar with a few of the devices that they'll use as they approach higher grades!

E-mail E-mail is one of the quickest and easiest ways to teach young children how to interact with people using the written word. *Reading Street* teaches first and second graders how to write e-mail to family and friends. By writing and mastering e-mail, children practice comprehension and

vocabulary skills, exchange ideas, engage in dialogue with peers, and gain the electronic skills vital to their future.

Web Sites With almost every click of a mouse button, children encounter information on Web sites. Children browse Web sites for fun, for researching school projects, and for learning about other nations and cultures. *Reading Street* shows first and second graders that they can use Web sites for learning more about what they read in class. Browsing the Internet is one of the easiest ways for a child to improve comprehension and develop a thirst for learning. Encourage students to keep on clicking!

Online Directories Students browse online directories when they want to find information about specific topics. Using the same set of skills they hone while browsing Web sites, students punch key words into directories to discover organized information and articles that assist them in research and broaden their view of the environment around them.

Evaluating Online Sources Two questions to listen for from Web-browsing students: *Who wrote that? Can I trust them?* As students learn to research information on the Internet, they also must learn to evaluate online sources. Information on the Internet can be inaccurate or even false. Successful students evaluate online information for accuracy and reliability by checking URL extensions, a crucial step in children's development.

Search Engines When kids use the Internet for research, they are amateur sleuths, clicking links and typing in key words to hunt down the information they need. One of the best tools for Internet information-hunting is the search engine. Learning to use a search engine helps students identify questions and frame information in ways that help them solve problems.

Online Reference Sources Dictionaries, almanacs, encyclopedias: These are the essential tools at our fingertips to complete projects and learn about our world. In *Reading Street*, students learn to access online reference sources to learn about topics in science and social studies. They analyze information to answer questions. By learning to navigate these sources, students gain research skills and learn how to construct better solutions to problems.

Teacher Resources

on Reading Street

Grade K

- Oral Vocabulary: Amazing Words
- Word Lists
- Glossary of Reading Terms
- Handwriting Models
- Reteach Lessons
- Student Edition Pictionary
- Scope and Sequence
- Pacing Charts
- Student Progress Reports
- 21st Century Skills
- Science and Social Studies Connections
- Teacher's Edition Index

Teacher Resources
for Grade K

Oral Vocabulary/Amazing Words

UNIT 1

WEEK 1

fifth
first
fourth
second
sixth
third

WEEK 2

cooperation
creation
float
guide
preparation
proud

WEEK 3

around
found
groceries
lost
market
platypus

WEEK 4

bakery
chaperone
fire station
library
park
post office

WEEK 5

dud
fabulous
perfect
pirates
proper
signals

WEEK 6

gobbling
rumbling
scooping
spinning
squelching
swooshing

UNIT 2

WEEK 1

bloom
buds
fruits
petals
seeds
stem

WEEK 2

acorn
discover
nature
pattern
pod
spy

WEEK 3

calf
cub
foal
grassland
joey
pup

WEEK 4

blustery
cave
sleep
storm
winter
woods

WEEK 5

den
hive
meadow
nest
stump
tree trunk

WEEK 6

beanstalk
lad
lend
magic
naughty
ogre

UNIT 3

WEEK 1

bamboo
curious
explore
healthy
measure
weigh

WEEK 2

brave
duckling
paddle
plunged
pond
proud

WEEK 3

arch
barn
blacksmith
celebration
soldier
sprinted

WEEK 4

butterfly
caterpillar
cocoon
goose
gosling
reflection

WEEK 5

gears
handwritten
headphones
newspapers
phonographs
webcams

WEEK 6

beast
entangled
jungle
nibbling
snarled
trembling

UNIT 4

WEEK 1

homesick
horizon
journey
lonely
trip
world

WEEK 2

cook
filthy
fox
lucky
piglet
scrubber

WEEK 3

comfortable
hollow
nest
shadows
vale
woodland

WEEK 4

bears
big
cottage
middle-sized
porridge
small

WEEK 5

Antarctica
continent
icebergs
penguins
seals
whales

WEEK 6

abuela
adventure
airport
city
flock
harbor

UNIT 5

WEEK 1

ferryboat
jetway
plane
sidecar
subway
tunnel

WEEK 2

mechanic
pilot
rescue
sailor
shimmering
yacht

WEEK 3

cabs
haul
headlight
steering wheel
trailors
truckers

WEEK 4

engine
mountain
passenger
roundhouse
tracks
valley

WEEK 5

dogsled
double-decker bus
kayak
llama
submarine
travel

WEEK 6

cable car
horse-and-buggy
Metro line
skis
trolley
vaporetto

UNIT 6

WEEK 1

foundation
gleaming
groundbreaking
trenches
waterproof
welding

WEEK 2

chisel
drill
file
hammer
saw
screwdriver

WEEK 3

beaver
lake
lodge
paddle
river
stream

WEEK 4

aboard
distant
drifting
gathered
island
voyage

WEEK 5

architect
electricians
landscapers
movers
painters
plumbers

WEEK 6

chambers
colony
pebbles
silk
twigs
underground

You've learned 216 **Amazing Words** this year!

Word Lists for Unit 1

The Little School Bus

Letter Recognition

Aa
Bb
Cc
Dd
Ee

High-Frequency/Tested Words

am
I

We Are So Proud

Letter Recognition

Ff
Gg
Hh
Ii
Jj
Kk
Ll
Mm
Nn

High-Frequency/Tested Words

am
I

Plaidypus Lost

Letter Recognition

Oo
Pp
Qq
Rr
Ss

High-Frequency/Tested Words

little
the

Miss Bindergarten Takes a Field Trip with Kindergarten

Letter Recognition

Tt
Uu
Vv
Ww
Xx
Yy
Zz

High-Frequency/Tested Words

little
the

Smash! Crash!

Consonant /m/ *m*

High-Frequency/Tested Words

a
to

Dig Dig Digging

Consonant /t/ *t*

High-Frequency/Tested Words

a
to

Word Lists for Unit 2

Flowers

Short /a/ *a*

am
at
mat

High-Frequency/Tested Words

have
is

Nature Spy

Consonant /s/ *s*

Sam
sat

High-Frequency/Tested Words

have
is

Animal Babies in Grasslands

Consonant /p/ *p*

Pam   map
pat   sap
           tap

High-Frequency/Tested Words

like
my
we

Bear Snores On

Consonant /k/ *c*

cap   Mac
cat

High-Frequency/Tested Words

like
my
we

A Bed for the Winter

Short /i/ *i*

it
pip
pit
sip
sit
Tim
tip

High-Frequency/Tested Words

for
he

Jack and the Beanstalk

Short /i/ *i*

it
pip
pit
sip
sit
Tim
tip

High-Frequency/Tested Words

for
he

Word Lists for Unit 3

Little Panda

Consonant /b/ *b*

bam	cab
bat	tab
bib	
bit	

Consonant /n/ *n*

nab	an
Nan	ban
nap	bin
Nat	can
	in
	man
	pan
	pin
	tan
	tin

High-Frequency/Tested Words

me
she
with

Little Quack

Consonant /r/ r

ran
rap
rib
Ric
rim
rip

High-Frequency/Tested Words

me
she
with

George Washington Visits

Consonant /d/ *d*

dab	ad
dad	bad
Dan	bid
did	fad
dim	mad
dip	pad
	rid
	sad
	Sid
	Tad

Consonant /k/ *k*

kid
Kim
kin
Kip
kit

High-Frequency/Tested Words

look
see

Farfallina and Marcel

Consonant /f/ *f*

fad
fan
fat
fib
fin
fit
if

High-Frequency/Tested Words

look
see

Then and Now

Short /o/ *o*

Bob	pod
bop	pop
cot	pot
Don	rob
dot	rod
fog	Ron
hog	rot
mob	sob
mom	sod
mop	Tom
nod	top
not	tot
on	

High-Frequency/Tested Words

of
they
you

The Lion and the Mouse

Short /o/ *o*

Bob	pod
bop	pop
cot	pot
Don	rob
dot	rod
fog	Ron
hog	rot
mob	sob
mom	sod
mop	Tom
nod	top
not	tot
on	

High-Frequency/Tested Words

of
they
you

Word Lists for Unit 4

Rooster's Off to See the World

Consonant /h/ _h_

had
ham
hat
hid
him
hip
hit
hop
hot

High-Frequency/Tested Words

are
do
that

My Lucky Day

Consonant /l/ _l_, _ll_

lab
lad
lap
lid
Lil
lip
lit
lob
lop
lot

Al
bill
dill
fill
gal
Hal
hill
ill
mill
pal
pill

High-Frequency/Tested Words

are
do
that

One Little Mouse

Consonant Blends

blab
blob
brim
clam
clap
clip
clod
crab
drill
drip
drop
flat
flip
flop

plan
plop
skin
skip
slab
slam
slap
slid
slim
slip
snap
trap
trim
trip

and
ant
ask
band
camp
cast
fast
fist
hand
lamp
land
last
lift
limp

lint
list
mast
mint
mist
pant
past
raft
sand

High-Frequency/Tested Words

one
two
three
four
five

Goldilocks and the Three Bears

Consonant /g/ *g*

gab	bag	pig
gag	big	rag
gap	brag	rig
gas	dig	sag
gig	drag	snag
Gil	fig	tag
gob	flag	
got	lag	
grim	nag	

High-Frequency/Tested Words

one
two
three
four
five

If You Could Go to Antarctica

Short /e/ *e*

bed	fed	less	rent
beg	fell	let	rest
bell	felt	Meg	sell
Ben	Fred	melt	send
belt	get	men	sent
bend	held	mess	set
bent	help	met	sled
best	hem	Ned	smell
den	hen	nest	spell
dent	kept	net	step
desk	led	Peg	tell
elf	left	pen	ten
elm	leg	pet	tent
end	lend	red	test

High-Frequency/Tested Words

from
here
go

Dig Dig Digging

Short /e/ *e*

bed	fed	less	rent
beg	fell	let	rest
bell	felt	Meg	sell
Ben	Fred	melt	send
belt	get	men	sent
bend	held	mess	set
bent	help	met	sled
best	hem	Ned	smell
den	hen	nest	spell
dent	kept	net	step
desk	led	Peg	tell
elf	left	pen	ten
elm	leg	pet	tent
end	lend	red	test

High-Frequency/Tested Words

from
here
go

Word Lists for Unit 5

Max Takes the Train

Consonant /w/ *w*

wag
web
wed
well
went
wept
west
wet
wig
will
win
wisp
wit

Consonant /j/ *j*

jab   jig
jam   Jill
Jan   Jim
Jed   job
Jeff   jog
Jen   Jon
jest   jot
jet

High-Frequency/Tested Words

blue
green
yellow

Mayday! Mayday!

Consonant /ks/ *x*

ax
box
fax
fix
fox
Lex
Max
mix
ox
sax
six
tax
wax

High-Frequency/Tested Words

blue
green
yellow

Trucks Roll!

Short /u/ *u*

bug   mud
bus   must
but   nut
cub   pup
cup   rub
cut   rug
dug   run
dust   snug
fun   sum
hug   sun
hum   tub
hut   tug
jump   up
just   us

High-Frequency/Tested Words

said
was
what

The Little Engine That Could

Short /u/ *u*

bug	mud
bus	must
but	nut
cub	pup
cup	rub
cut	rug
dug	run
dust	snug
fun	sum
hug	sun
hum	tub
hut	tug
jump	up
just	us

High-Frequency/Tested Words

said
was
what

On the Move!

Consonant /v/ *v*

Val
van
vast
vat
vent
vest
vet
Vic

Consonant /z/ *z, zz*

zap	buzz
zest	fizz
zip	fuzz
	jazz

High-Frequency/Tested Words

come
where

This Is the Way We Go to School

Consonant /y/ *y*

yak
yam
yell
yes
yet
yip
yum

Consonant /kw/ *qu*

quill
Quinn
quit
quiz

High-Frequency/Tested Words

come
where

Word Lists for Unit 6

Building with Dad

Short /a/ *a*	Short /i/ *i*	High-Frequency/Tested Words
am	it	do
at	pip	here
cap	pit	little
cat	sip	what
Mac	sit	with
map	tip	
mat	Tim	
Pam		
pat		
Sam		
sap		
sat		

Old MacDonald had a Woodshop

Short /o/ *o*		High-Frequency/Tested Words
Bob	pod	come
bop	pop	go
cot	pot	is
Don	rob	that
dot	rod	where
fog	Ron	
hog	rot	
mob	sob	
mom	sod	
mop	Tom	
nod	top	
not	tot	
on		

Building Beavers

Short /e/ *e*				High-Frequency/Tested Words
bed	fed	less	rent	from
beg	fell	let	rest	like
bell	felt	Meg	sell	the
Ben	Fred	melt	send	to
belt	get	men	sent	was
bend	held	mess	set	
bent	help	met	sled	
best	hem	Ned	smell	
den	hen	nest	spell	
dent	kept	net	step	
desk	led	Peg	tell	
elf	left	pen	ten	
elm	leg	pet	tent	
end	lend	red	test	

Allistair and Kip's Great Adventure

Short /u/ *u*

bug	mud
bus	must
but	nut
cub	pup
cup	rub
cut	rug
dug	run
dust	snug
fun	sum
hug	sun
hum	tub
hut	tug
jump	up
just	us

High-Frequency/Tested Words

for
my
of
we
yellow

The House That Tony Lives In

Consonants and Short Vowels

and	gift	red
beds	hand	set
best	it	spot
bit	jump	stop
bug	log	tent
bump	Max	up
can	milk	went
cats	nap	wet
club	next	
crab	not	
cub	nut	
drum	on	
fit	pets	
glad	plot	

High-Frequency/Tested Words

blue
four
have
they
two

Ants and Their Nests

Consonants and Short Vowels

bag	jump	pig
bed	lamp	sap
box	leg	sip
crab	let	six
cut	limp	spot
dad	lint	Stan
desk	mask	tab
dog	mud	ten
end	must	web
fan	nod	wet
hand	on	yes
hat	ox	
his	pads	
jug	past	

High-Frequency/Tested Words

look
said
see
three
you

Glossary of Reading Terms

This glossary includes academic language terms used with students as well as reading terms provided for your information and professional use.

abbreviation a shortened form of a word. *Dr.* is an abbreviation for *doctor.*

accuracy reading words in text without errors, an element of fluency

action verb a word that shows action

adjective a word that describes a person, place, or thing. An adjective tells how many, what kind, or which one.

adverb a word that tells how, when, or where something happens. Adverbs also tell how much or how little is meant. Adverbs often end in *–ly.*

affix a prefix, suffix, or inflected ending that is added to a base word to form a new word

alliteration the repetition of a consonant sound in a group of words, especially in poetry

allusion a word or phrase that refers to something else the reader already knows from history, experience, or reading

alphabetical order the arrangement of words according to the letters of the alphabet

animal fantasy a story about animals that talk and act like people

answer questions a reading strategy in which readers use the text and prior knowledge to answer questions about what they are reading

antecedent the noun or nouns to which a pronoun refers

antonym a word that means the opposite of another word

apostrophe punctuation (') that shows where letters have been left out in a contraction or that is used with *s* at the end of a noun to show possession

appositive a word or phrase that explains the word it follows

ask questions a reading strategy in which readers ask themselves questions about the text to help make sense of what they read

author a person who writes books, stories, poems, or plays

author's point of view the author's opinion on the subject he or she is writing about

author's purpose the reason the author wrote the text

autobiography tells about a real person's life written by the person who lived it

automaticity the ability to read words or connected text automatically, with little or no attention to decoding

background knowledge the information and experience that a reader brings to a text

base word a word that can stand alone or take endings, prefixes, and suffixes

biography tells about a real person's life. It is written by another person

blend combine a series of sounds in sequence without pausing between them

cause why something happens

character a person, animal, or personalized object in a story

choral reading reading aloud in unison as a group

chronological order events in a selection, presented in the order in which they occurred

chunking a decoding strategy for breaking words into manageable parts to read them

classify and categorize put things, such as pictures or words, into groups

clause a group of words having a subject and predicate and used as part of a compound or complex sentence

climax the point in a story at which conflict is confronted

collective noun a noun that names a group of persons or things, such as *audience* or *herd*

colon punctuation (:) that may introduce a list or separate hours from minutes to show time

comma punctuation (,) that can be used, for example, to indicate a pause in a sentence or to separate items in a series

comparative adjective an adjective used to compare two people, places, or things. Add *-er* to most adjectives to make them comparative.

compare tell how things are the same

complete predicate all the words in the predicate

complete subject all the words in the subject

complex sentence a sentence made up of one independent clause and one or more dependent clauses

composition a short piece of written work

compound sentence a sentence that contains two or more independent clauses. The clauses are joined either by a comma and a conjunction or by a semicolon.

compound word a word made up of two or more short words

comprehension understanding of text being read—the ultimate goal of reading

comprehension strategy a conscious plan used by a reader to gain understanding of text. Comprehension strategies may be used before, during, or after reading.

conclusion a decision or opinion arrived at after thinking about facts and details and using prior knowledge

conflict the problem or struggle in a story

conjunction a word, such as *and, but,* and *or,* that connects words, phrases, clauses, or sentences

consonant any letter of the alphabet that is not a vowel

consonant blend two or more consecutive consonants, each of which is pronounced and blended with the other, such as *cl* in *clock*

consonant digraph two consecutive consonants, that stand for a single sound, such as *ch, sh, th.* Its pronunciation usually differs from the sound of either individual consonant.

context clue the words, phrases, or sentences near an unknown word that give the reader clues to the word's meaning

continuous sound a sound that can be sustained without distortion, such as /m/, /f/, and /s/

contraction a shorter word formed by combining two words. The omitted letters are replaced with an apostrophe.

contrast tell how things are different

cursive handwriting handwriting in which the letters are joined

declarative sentence a sentence that tells something and ends with a period

decode apply knowledge of sound-spellings and word parts to read a new word

definition the meaning of a word

dependent clause a clause that cannot stand alone as a sentence

details small pieces of information

dialect form of a language spoken in a certain region or by a certain group of people that differs from the standard form of that language

dialogue written conversation

diary a day-to-day record of one's activities and thoughts

digraph two letters that stand for a single sound

diphthong two consecutive vowels whose sounds are pronounced in immediate sequence within a syllable, such as *oi* in *noise*

direct object a noun or pronoun that follows an action verb and tells who or what receives the action of the verb

discussion talking something over with other people

draft the first attempt at a composition. A draft is a rough copy that usually requires revision and editing before publication.

drama a story written to be acted out for others

draw conclusions arrive at decisions or opinions after thinking about facts and details and using prior knowledge

edit the stage in the writing process when a draft is corrected for facts and such mechanical errors as grammar, punctuation, usage, and spelling

Glossary of Reading Terms

effect what happens as the result of a cause

elaborate add more detail to what has already been said or written

entry word the word being defined in a dictionary or glossary. It is printed in boldface type.

etymology an explanation of the origin and history of a word and its meaning

exaggeration a statement that makes something seem larger or greater than it actually is

exclamation mark punctuation (!) following a word, phrase, or sentence that was exclaimed, or spoken with strong feeling

exclamatory sentence a sentence that expresses strong feeling or surprise and ends with an exclamation mark

expository text tells facts about a topic

expression emotion put into words while reading or speaking

fable a story that teaches a lesson

fact piece of information that can be proved to be true

fairy tale a folk story with magical characters and events

fantasy a make-believe story that could never happen in the real world

fiction writing that tells about imaginary people, things, and events

figurative language the use of language that gives words a meaning beyond their usual definitions in order to add beauty or force

flashback an interruption in the sequence of events of a narrative to include an event that happened earlier

fluency the ability to read quickly, accurately, and with expression. Fluent readers can focus their attention on the meaning of the text.

folk tale a story that has been handed down over many years

foreshadowing the use of hints or clues about what will happen later in a story

generalize make a broad statement or rule after examining particular facts

gesture a meaningful movement of the hands, arms, or other part of the body. Gestures may be used instead of words or with words to help express an idea or feeling.

glossary an alphabetical list of words and their definitions, usually found at the back of a book

graphic organizer a drawing, chart, or web that illustrates concepts or shows how ideas relate to each other. Readers use graphic organizers to help them keep track of and understand important information and ideas as they read. Story maps, word webs, Venn diagrams, and K-W-L charts are graphic organizers.

graphic source a chart, diagram, or map within a text that adds to readers' understanding of the text

guide words the words at the top of a dictionary or glossary page that show the first and last entry words on that page

high-frequency words the words that appear most commonly in print. The one hundred most frequent words account for about 50 percent of printed words. They are often called *sight words* since automatic recognition of these words is necessary for fluent reading.

historical fiction realistic fiction that takes place in the past

homograph a word that is spelled the same as another word, but has a different meaning and history. The words may or may not be pronounced the same. *Bass,* meaning a low singing voice, and *bass,* meaning a fish, are homographs.

homophone a word that sounds the same as another word, but has a different spelling, meaning, and history. *Ate* and *eight* are homophones.

humor writing or speech that has a funny or amusing quality

humorous fiction a funny story about imaginary people and events

hyperbole an exaggerated statement not meant to be taken literally, such as *I'm so hungry I could eat a horse.*

idiom a phrase whose meaning differs from the ordinary meaning of the words. *A stone's throw* is an idiom meaning "a short distance."

illustrative phrase or sentence an example showing how an entry word in a dictionary may be used in a sentence or phrase. It is printed in italic type.

illustrator a person who draws the pictures to go with a selection

imagery the use of language to create beautiful or forceful pictures in the reader's mind

imperative sentence a sentence that gives a command or makes a request. It usually ends with a period.

indent to begin the first line of a paragraph farther in from the left margin than the other lines

independent clause a clause that can stand by itself as a sentence

index an alphabetical list of people, places, and things that are mentioned in a book. An index gives the page numbers where each of these can be found. It appears at the end of a book.

indirect object a noun or pronoun that shows to whom or for whom the action of the verb is done

inference conclusion reached on the basis of evidence and reasoning

inflected ending a letter or group of letters added to the end of a base word that does not change the part of speech of the base word. Inflected endings are *-s, -es, -ed, -ing, -er,* and *-est.*

inflection a grammatical change in the form of a word, usually by adding an ending

inform give knowledge, facts, or news to someone

informational text often gives facts about real people, places and events that reflect history or the traditions of communities

interjection a word that is used to express strong feeling, such as *Oh!*

interrogative sentence a sentence that asks a question and ends with a question mark

interview a face-to-face conversation in which someone responds to questions

intonation the rise and fall of a reader's or speaker's voice

introductory paragraph the first paragraph of a composition or piece of writing. It sets up what is to come in the composition.

introductory sentence the first sentence of the first paragraph in a composition or a piece of writing. It sets up what is to come in the paragraph.

irony a way of speaking or writing in which the ordinary meaning of the words is the opposite of what the speaker or writer is thinking; a contrast between what is expected and what actually happens

irregular verb a verb that does not add *-ed* to form the past tense

jargon the language of a special group or profession

legend an old story that tells about the great deeds of a hero

legible clear and easy to read

linking verb a verb that does not show action, such as *is, seem,* and *become*

literary elements the characters, setting, plot, and theme of a narrative text

literary nonfiction tells about a true event or a series of events like a story

long vowel sound a vowel sound that is the same as the name of a vowel letter—*a, e, i, o,* and *u*

main idea the big idea that tells what a paragraph or a selection is mainly about; the most important idea of a text

media often, **the media** print and electronic sources such as newspapers, magazines, TV, radio, the Internet, and other such means of communication

Glossary of Reading Terms

metacognition an awareness of one's own thinking processes and the ability to monitor and direct them to a desired goal. Good readers use metacognition to monitor their reading and adjust their reading strategies.

metaphor a comparison that does not use *like* or *as,* such as *a heart of stone*

meter the pattern of beats or accents in poetry

modulation the variance of the volume, tone, or pitch of one's voice

monitor and clarify a comprehension strategy by which readers actively think about understanding their reading and know when they understand and when they do not. Readers use appropriate strategies to make sense of difficult words, ideas, or passages.

mood the atmosphere or feeling of a written work

moral the lesson or teaching of a fable or story

morpheme the smallest meaningful unit of language, including base words and affixes. There are three morphemes in the word *unfriendly—un, friend,* and *ly.*

motive the reason a character in a narrative does or says something

multiple-meaning word a word that has more than one meaning. Its meaning can be understood from the context in which it is used.

mystery a story about mysterious events that are not explained until the end, so as to keep the reader in suspense

myth an old story that often explains something about nature

narrative a story, made up or true, that someone tells or writes

narrator the character in a selection who tells the story

negative a word that means "no" or "not"

nonfiction writing that tells about real things, real people, and real events

noun a word that names a person, place, animal, or thing

onomatopoeia the use of words that sound like their meanings, such as *buzz* and *hum*

onset the part of a word or syllable that comes before the vowel. In the word *black, bl* is the onset. Also see *rime.*

opinion someone's judgment, belief, or way of thinking

oral rereading repeated reading of text until it can be read fluently

oral vocabulary the words needed for speaking and listening

outcome the resolution of the conflict in a story

pace (in fluency) the speed at which someone reads

paired reading reading aloud with a partner who provides help identifying words and other feedback. Also called *partner reading.*

paragraph a group of sentences about one main idea. Each paragraph begins on a new line and is indented.

paraphrase retell the meaning of a passage in one's own words

parentheses two curved lines ( ) used to set off words or phrases in text

participle a word formed from a verb and often used as an adjective or a noun

period the dot (.) that signifies the end of most sentences or shows an abbreviation, as in *Dec.*

personification a figure of speech in which human traits are given to animals or inanimate objects, as in *The sunbeam danced on the waves.*

persuade convince someone to do or to believe something

phoneme the smallest part of spoken language that makes a difference in the meaning of words. The word *sat* has three phonemes—/s/, /a/, and /t/.

phoneme blending orally combining a series of phonemes in sequence to form a word

phoneme isolation the ability to identify and pronounce an individual phoneme in a word

phoneme manipulation adding, deleting, or substituting phonemes in spoken words, for example, Say *fox* without the /f/: *ox*.

phonemic awareness one kind of phonological awareness. It includes the ability to hear individual sounds in words and to identify and manipulate them.

phonics the study of the relationship between sounds and their spellings

phonogram the part of a one-syllable word comprised of a vowel and all the letters that follow it, as *ack* in *back, crack, track, shack*. Words that share a phonogram are called a *word family*.

phonological awareness an awareness of the sounds that make up spoken language

photo essay a collection of photographs on one theme, accompanied by text

phrasing breaking text into natural thought units when reading

pitch degree of highness or lowness of a sound or of a speaker's voice

play a story that is written to be acted out for an audience

plot a series of related events at the beginning, middle, and end of a story; the action of a story

plural noun a noun that names more than one person, place, or thing

plural possessive noun a noun that shows there are two or more owners of something. Add an apostrophe to a plural noun ending in *-s* to make it a plural possessive noun.

poem an expressive, imaginative piece of writing often arranged in lines having rhythm and rhyme. In a poem, the patterns made by the sounds of the words have special importance.

possessive noun a noun that shows ownership or possession

possessive pronoun a pronoun that shows who or what owns or has something

pourquoi tale a type of folk story that explains why things in nature came to be. *Pourquoi* is a French word meaning "why."

predicate a word or group of words that tells what the subject is or does

predict tell what a selection might be about or what might happen in a text. Readers use text features and information to predict. They confirm or revise their predictions as they read.

prefix a word part added at the beginning of a base word to change its meaning or make another word, such as *un* in *unbutton*

preposition a word that shows the relationship of a noun or pronoun to another word. It is the first word in a prepositional phrase.

prepositional phrase a group of words that begins with a preposition and ends with a noun or pronoun

presentation something that is presented to an audience

preview look over a text before reading it

prewrite an initial stage in the writing process when topics may be brainstormed, ideas may be considered, and planning may occur

prior knowledge the information and experience that a reader brings to a text. Readers use prior knowledge to help them understand what they read.

procedural text a set of directions and graphic features telling how to do something

pronoun a word that can take the place of a noun or nouns

pronunciation key the explanation of the symbols used in a dictionary or glossary

pronunciation the letters and diacritical marks appearing in parentheses after an entry word in a dictionary that show how the word is pronounced

prop an item, such as an object, picture, or chart, used in a performance or presentation

proper noun a word that names a particular person, place, or thing. A proper noun begins with a capital letter.

Glossary of Reading Terms

punctuation the marks used in writing to separate sentences and their elements and to make meaning clear. Periods, commas, question marks, semicolons, and colons are punctuation marks.

question mark a punctuation mark (?) used at the end of a sentence to indicate a question

quotation marks the punctuation marks (" ") used to indicate the beginning and end of a speaker's exact words

reading vocabulary the words we recognize or use in print

realistic fiction a story of imaginary people and events that could happen in real life

r-controlled vowel sound the sound of a vowel immediately followed by *r* in the same syllable. Its sound is neither long nor short.

regular verb a verb that adds *-ed* to form the past tense

repetition the repeated use of some aspect of language

resolution the point in a story where the conflict is resolved

revise the stage in the writing process when a draft may be changed to improve such things as focus, ideas, organization, word choice, or voice

rhyme to end in the same sound(s)

rhythm a pattern of strong beats in speech or writing, especially in poetry

rime the part of a word or syllable that includes the vowel and any following consonants. In the word *black, ack* is the rime. Also see *onset.*

rising action the buildup of conflicts and complications in a story

root a word part, usually of Greek or Latin origin, that cannot stand alone, but is used to form a family of words. *Trans* in *transfer* and *transportation* is a root.

rubric a set of guidelines used to evaluate a product such as writing

run-on sentence two sentences written together without correct punctuation

salutation the words of greeting in a letter that address the person to whom the letter is being written

schwa the vowel sound in an unaccented syllable, such as the sound of *a* in *above*

science fiction a story based on science that tells what life in the future might be like

segment break a spoken word into its individual sounds

semantic map a graphic organizer, often a web, used to display words or concepts that are meaningfully related

semicolon punctuation (;) that indicates a pause between two clauses in a sentence

sensory language the use of words that help the reader understand how things look, sound, smell, taste, or feel

sentence a group of words that tells or asks something; asks a question; or makes a request, a command, or an exclamation

sequence the order of events in a selection or the order of the steps in which something is done

sequence words clue words such as *first, next, then,* and *finally* that signal the order of events in a selection

setting where and when a story takes place

short vowel sound the sound of *a, e, i, o,* and *u* as heard in *bat, bet, bit, box,* and *but*

simile a comparison that uses *like* or *as,* as in as *busy as a bee*

simple predicate the verb in the complete predicate

simple subject the main noun or pronoun in the complete subject

singular noun a noun that names one person, place, or thing

singular possessive noun a noun that shows there is one owner of something. Add an apostrophe and *-s* to a singular noun to make it a singular possessive noun.

sound boxes a graphic consisting of a row of boxes in which each box represents a single phoneme. A marker is placed in a box for each sound heard in a given word. Also called *Elkonin boxes.*

speech a public talk to a group of people made for a specific purpose

stanza a group of lines in a poem

statement a sentence that tells something. A statement ends with a period.

steps in a process the order of the steps in which something is done

stop sound a phoneme that can be said without distortion for only an instant. /b/, /k/, and /g/ are all stop sounds.

story map a graphic organizer used to record the literary elements and the sequence of events in a narrative text

story structure how the characters, setting, and events of a story are organized into a plot

subject a word or group of words that tells whom or what a sentence is about

subject-verb agreement when the subject and verb in a sentence work together, or agree. A sentence with a singular subject must have a verb that works, or agrees, with a singular subject.

suffix a word part added at the end of a word to change its meaning and part of speech, such as *-ly* in *friendly*

summarize give the most important ideas of what was read. Readers summarize important information in the selection to keep track of what they are reading.

superlative adjective an adjective used to compare three or more people, places, or things. Add *-est* to most adjectives to make them superlative.

supporting detail piece of information that tells about the main idea

syllable a word part that contains a single vowel sound

symbolism the use of one thing to suggest something else; often the use of something concrete to stand for an abstract idea

synonym a word with the same or nearly the same meaning as another word

table of contents list of chapters, articles, or stories in a book. It appears at the beginning of the book.

tall tale a story that uses exaggeration

tempo (in speaking) the speed at which someone speaks

text structure the organization of a piece of writing. Text structures of informational text include cause/effect, chronological, compare/contrast, description, problem/solution, proposition/support, and ask/answer questions.

theme the big idea or author's message in a story

think aloud an instructional strategy in which a teacher verbalizes his or her thinking to model the process of comprehension or the application of a skill

timed reading a method of measuring fluency by determining words correct per minute (WCPM)

title the name of a written work; a word or abbreviation that can come before the name of a person, such as *Dr.* or *Mrs.*

tone author's attitude toward the subject or toward the reader

topic the subject of a discussion, conversation, or piece of text

topic sentence the sentence that tells the main idea of a paragraph

verb a word that tells what something or someone does or is

visualize picture in one's mind what is happening in the text. Visualizing helps readers imagine the things they read about.

volume (in speaking) degree of loudness of a speaker's voice

vowel digraph two vowels together that stand for a single sound, such as *oa* in *boat* or *ea* in *leaf*

vowel the letters *a, e, i, o, u,* and sometimes *y*

WCPM words correct per minute; the number of words read correctly in one minute

word analysis decoding a word by using its parts, such as suffixes, prefixes, and syllables

word family a group of words that rhyme and share the same phonogram, such as *fill, still, will*

D'Nealian™ Alphabet

a b c d e f g h i

j k l m n o p q r s t

u v w x y z

A B C D E F G

H I J K L M N O

P Q R S T U V

W X Y Z . , ' ?

1 2 3 4 5 6

7 8 9 10

Manuscript Alphabet

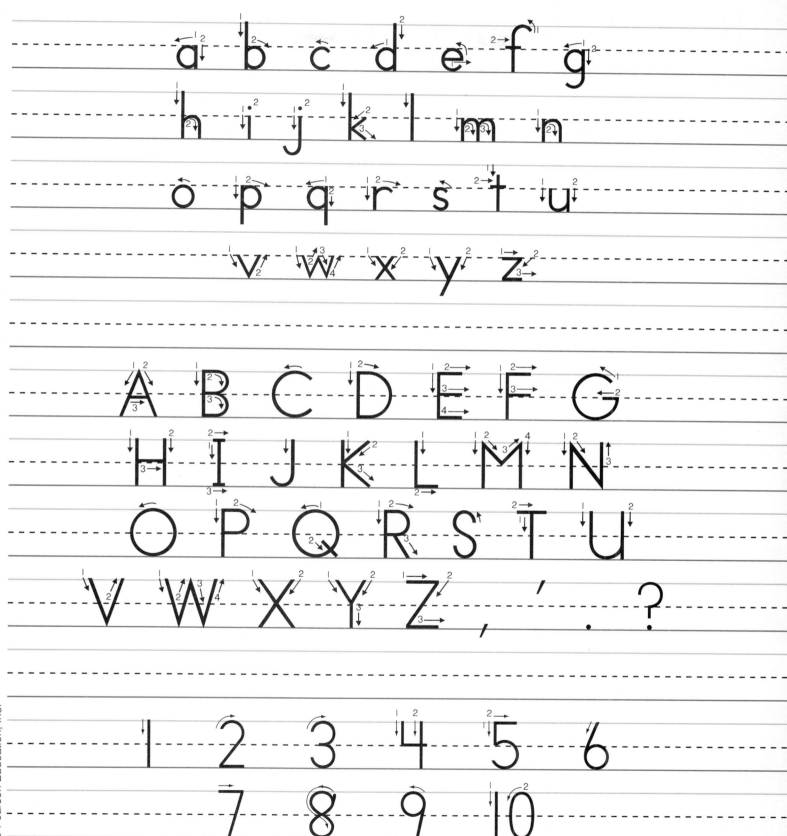

Reteach Lessons: Grade K

Reteach

Reteach Phonics

Reteach
Phonological Awareness

① Rhyming Words

Tell children that words that rhyme have the same middle and ending sounds. Say: *Listen to these words:* hat, bat, cat. *All three words end with* -at. *All three words have the same middle and ending sounds, so the words rhyme:* hat, bat, cat.

I will say three words. I want you to tell me the two words that rhyme. Use sets of words such as these: *met, net, cap; hop, pit, top; ran, rug, mug; hot, not, yes; sun, sip, tip; hen, rod, ten; big, cab, tab; fill, nut, hill.*

② Syllables

Explain to children that syllables are parts of words. Demonstrate how to clap once for each syllable as you say the word *umbrella*. Say: *How many times do I clap when I say* um-brel-la? *I clap three times. The word* umbrella *has three syllables.*

Help children clap and count syllables in words such as these: *kit-ten, coat, oc-to-pus, bub-ble, el-e-va-tor, five, feath-er, as-tro-naut, cat-er-pil-lar, desk, hip-po-pot-a-mus.*

③ Initial Sound Discrimination

Tell children that you want them to listen for words that begin with the same sound. Say: *Listen carefully:* dog, duck, dirt. *Say the words with me:* dog, duck, dirt. *Do all of these words begin with the same sound?* (Yes) *Listen carefully:* cat, cup, dig. *Do all of these words begin with the same sound?* (No) *Which word does not begin like the others?* (Dig does not begin like cat and cup.)

Continue the routine with sets of words such as these: *hot, hand, sad; mug, pack, moon; sock, bug, soap; tape, bag, bib; pot, pipe, race.*

Reteach
Phonemic Awareness

1 Initial and Final Phonemes

Display the *bag* Picture Card. Say: *This is a bag. The word* bag
begins with /b/. Exaggerate /b/ as you say *bag* several times. Say:
Feel where your tongue is when you say /b/. Have children say *bag*
with you, exaggerating /b/. Display the *bed, dog, bat, map, boat,
pig, box, bubble,* and *bus* Picture Cards. Have children say the
picture names and then sort the pictures into two groups—those
whose names begin with /b/ and those whose names do not.
Together say the picture names that begin with /b/, emphasizing
the initial sound.

Repeat the routine for final /b/, using the *crab, mop, tub, rug,
web,* and *cat* Picture Cards.

Use the routine and sets of appropriate Picture Cards to
help children practice discriminating other initial and final
consonant sounds.

2 Segment and Blend Phonemes

Display the *bat* Picture Card. Say: *This is a bat. I will say the
sounds in the word* bat : /b/ /a/ /t/. Have children say the sounds
with you. Then say the sounds again, this time holding up one
finger for each sound. Say: *How many fingers am I holding up?*
(Three) *How many sounds are there in the word bat?* (Three)
Have children say the sounds in bat and hold up three fingers,
one at a time. Next blend the sounds together. Say the sounds
in *bat* quickly, raising each finger as you say a sound. Repeat
this several times and have children imitate you. Finally, hold up
the index finger on one hand and say /b/. Hold up two fingers
on your other hand and say /at/. Say /b/ *-at, bat.* Have children
imitate you as they say *bat.*

Repeat the routine using the *red, wig, mop,* and *sun* Picture
Cards to help children practice segmenting and blending
other phonemes.

Reteach
Letter Recognition

1 Display the *Aa* Alphabet Card. Point to the uppercase letter. Say: *What is the name of this letter? This is uppercase* A. Point to lowercase *a*. Say: *The name of this letter is also* a. *Say it with me. This is an astronaut.* Astronaut *begins with* a. *What letter does it begin with? Why is an astronaut on the* Aa *card?* (The word astronaut begins with the letter *a*.) Have children form the letter on the palm of their hand.

Repeat the routine with the other Alphabet Cards, asking children similar questions about the letters and pictures.

2 Display the *Aa* Alphabet Card and Big Book *Trucktown ABCs*. Have a volunteer identify the two letter forms on the Alphabet Card. Have another volunteer turn to the *Aa* page in *Trucktown ABCs*. Hold the Alphabet Card next to the letters in the book. Say: *Do the letters match?* (Yes) *What picture do you see on the card?* (An astronaut) *What picture do you see in the book?* (action) *Why are these pictures on the* Aa *Alphabet Card and the* Aa *page in the book?* (The picture names astronaut and action begin with the letter *a*.)

Repeat the routine with the other Alphabet Cards and pages in *Trucktown ABCs* to give children practice with identifying those letters.

3 Have small groups of children work with a calendar and identify uppercase and lowercase *a*. Say: *On a calendar you will find both kinds of* a. *When you find one, raise your hand and tell me whether it is uppercase or lowercase.*

Repeat the activity with other letters. If the calendar does not have the letter in question, have the group announce that fact. Remind children to look beyond the names of the months.

Reteach
Consonant
Sound-Spellings

1 Display the *bag* and *doll* Picture Cards. Say: *This is a* bag. *The word* bag *begins with /b/. This is a* doll. *The word* doll *begins with /d/. What is the beginning sound in* bag? *in* doll? Display the *Bb* and *Dd* Alphabet Cards. Say: *The letter for /b/ is* b. *The letter for /d/ is* d. *What is the letter for /b/? for /d/? What is the letter for the beginning sound in* bag? *in* doll? Have children place the appropriate Alphabet Card next to each Picture Card.

Repeat the routine for other pairs of consonant sound-spellings, using Picture Cards and Alphabet Cards: /p/*Pp (pen)*, /m/*Mm (mug)*; /f/*Ff (fox)*, /v/*Vv (van)*; /k/*Cc (cap)*, /t/*Tt (ten)*; /g/*Gg (goat)*, /k/*Kk (kite)*; /j/*Jj (jam)*, /r/*Rr (red)*; /n/*Nn (net)*, /l/*Ll (leaf)*; /w/*Ww (wolf)*, /h/*Hh (hose)*; /s/*Ss (six)*, /z/*Zz (zoo)*.

2 Display page 5 in Big Book *Trucktown ABCs*. Have children identify the character *Big Rig*. Say: *The word* Big *begins with /b/. What is the beginning sound in* Big? Point to the letters Bb. Say: *The letter for /b/ is* b. Big Rig *begins with uppercase* b *because Big Rig is a name. The word* Big *begins with /b/. What is the first letter in* Big? (B) Have children point to the *B* in *Big* and say /b/. Say: Big *begins with /b/. The letter for /b/ is* B: /b/, B, Big.

Repeat the routine for the other consonant sound-spellings using *Trucktown ABCs*.

3 Write the letters *Bb* on the board and have children name both letter forms. Ask a volunteer to find the letter *b* on the ABC Wall. Have the volunteer stand by the *Bb* section of the wall. Read aloud a word in the section that begins with the single consonant *b*. Say: *This word begins with /b/. The letter for /b/ is* b. Have the volunteer point to the *B* or *b* at the beginning of the word as children repeat the word, the sound, and the letter name.

Repeat the routine for the other consonant sound-spellings using words on the ABC Wall.

Reteach
Short Vowel Sound-Spellings

1 Display page 4 in Big Book *Trucktown ABCs*. Say the word *Action*, and have children repeat it. Say: *The word* Action *begins with /a/. What is the beginning sound in* Action*?* Point to the letters *Aa*. Say: *This is uppercase* A. *This is lowercase* a. *What are the names of these letters?* Point to the *A* in *Action*. Say: *The word* Action *begins with uppercase* A. *What letter does* Action *begin with? The letter for /a/ is* A: Action, /a/, A.

Repeat the routine for /e/*Ee*, /i/*Ii*, /o/*Oo*, and /u/*Uu* using pages 8, 11, 17, and 22 in *Trucktown ABCs*.

2 Display the *ant* and *map* Picture Cards. Say *ant* and *map* several times, emphasizing the initial and medial /a/. Have children say the words. Say: *The words* ant *and* map *both have /a/. Which word has /a/ at the beginning,* ant *or* map*? Which word has /a/ in the middle,* ant *or* map*?* Write the words *ant* and *map* on the board. Say: *What is the letter for the beginning /a/ in* ant*?* Have a volunteer circle *a*. Say: *What is the letter for the middle /a/ in* map*?* Have a volunteer circle *a*. Say: *The letter for /a/ is* a.

Repeat the routine using the *egg* and *bed* Picture Cards for /e/ *Ee*, the *inch* and *pig* cards for /i/*Ii*, the *ox* and *top* cards for /o/*Oo*, and the *up* and *sun* cards for /u/*Uu*.

3 Display the *hat* Picture Card. Say: *What is this?* (A hat) Say the word *hat*, emphasizing the medial /a/. Have children say the word. Say: *What sound is in the middle of* hat*?* (/a/) *What is the letter for /a/?* (Aa) Turn the Picture Card to its word side and have children check their answer by naming the middle letter in the word. Say: *Yes,* a *is the letter for /a/ in* hat. Continue with the *jam* and *van* Picture Cards.

Repeat the routine using the *hen, red,* and *web* Picture Cards for /e/*Ee*; the *pig, six,* and *wig* cards for /i/*Ii*; the *dog, fox,* and *mop* cards for /o/*Oo*; and the *bus, mug,* and *tub* cards for /u/*Uu*.

Reteach Comprehension
Character

① Teach

Explain that every story is about somebody, either people or animals. The people or animals in a story are the *characters* of the story. Characters are who the story is about. They can be real or make-believe.

Display the Envision It! pages for Literary Elements in *My Skills Buddy*, Unit 1, pp. 14–15. Have children look at the illustration labeled Characters. Say: *I see here a picture of a tortoise and a hare. The heading says that these are characters in this story, and I know that a story can have animal characters.* Call children's attention to the pictures under Plot and comment that the tortoise and the hare appear in all these pictures as well. Say: *So the story must be about the tortoise and the hare, and they must be the characters of the story. I can tell that these characters are make-believe because they are wearing clothes.*

② Practice

Show children a picture that includes a number of people and animals. Ask:

- If you were going to tell a story about this picture, who or what would be in your story?

- What are their names? What are they like?

- What might happen in the story?

As children tell their stories, list the characters they name. When the storytelling is over, refer to the list and read the names. Tell children: *These are the people and animals that were in your stories. They are your characters.*

Reteach Comprehension
Setting

1 Teach

Explain that the *setting* of a story is the time and place the story happens. Sometimes you can use clues to find out what the setting is. A setting can be real or make-believe.

Display the Envision It! pages for Literary Elements in *My Skills Buddy*, Unit 1, pp. 34–35. Have children look at the illustration labeled Setting. Say: *I know that setting is where the story takes place. I see here a picture of a path, a tree, some grass, and the sun. These are good clues that the setting must be outdoors.* Call children's attention to the pictures under Plot. Say: *It looks like the setting stays the same all the way through, so I was right. The story's setting is outdoors on a path. But it must be a path used for races, because there are* Start *and* Finish *signs. And the time is during the day, because the sun is shining in all the pictures.*

2 Practice

Show children pictures from magazines or family photos from vacations or holidays. For each picture ask:

- Where do you think this is taking place?

- When do you think this is taking place?

- Imagine that you were here when this picture was taken. Tell me about it.

- What was the weather like? How did you feel?

Remind students that every story and real-life event has a time and a place in which it happens.

3 Connect to Everyday Life

Ask children to think about their favorite books or movies and describe the settings.

Reteach Comprehension
Sequence

1 ## Teach

Explain that when things happen, they happen in a certain order. Something happens before, and something happens after. When you think about what happens first, what happens next, and what happens last, you are looking at a *sequence*. It is important to understand what happens first, next, and last in a piece of writing because it will help you understand the writing and remember it better.

Display the Envision It! pages for Sequence in *My Skills Buddy*, Unit 1, pp. 54–55. Say: *I know that sequence means the events happen in order. Let's look at these pictures. First I see a mother bird sitting in her nest with her eggs. In the next picture, the eggs have hatched, and the mother bird is feeding her babies. Finally, the mother bird is waving to her baby birds as they fly away. After looking at the pictures, I ask myself, "Does the sequence of events make sense?" Yes, it does make sense because a mother bird can't feed her babies if she doesn't hatch them, and the baby birds can't grow up and fly away if the mother bird doesn't take care of them. The sequence of the story is important and should make sense.*

2 ## Practice

Ahead of time, prepare three pictures of three stages of a plant's growth. Show a plant after it has sprouted, when it is slightly bigger, and when it is fully grown with a flower.

Display the three pictures out of order. Let volunteers take turns putting the pictures in order to show the way a flower would look as it grows. Explain that putting things in their proper sequence means showing what happens first, next, and last.

3 ## Connect to Everyday Life

Ask children each to share three things they did today in the order they did them.

Reteach Comprehension
Classify and Categorize

1 Teach

Explain that a *group* is a number of people or things. We can put some things together in groups because they are alike in some way. *Alike* means how they are the same.

Display the Envision It! pages for Classify and Categorize in *My Skills Buddy*, Unit 1, pp. 74–75. Say: *What do you suppose the boy is thinking? Maybe something like "What are some groups I can put the toys into? Do some of the toys look like other toys?" Well, I see stuffed animals and blocks. These are two groups I can put the toys in. Now call attention to the picture on the right.* Say: *This must be what the boy thought too. Look, he also grouped his toys into stuffed animals and blocks.*

2 Teach

Show pictures of various animals such as a bear, lion, dog, fish, octopus, kitten, rabbit, turtle, and wolf. Ask: *How are all of these pictures alike? (They are all animals.)* Say: *Let's think of ways to group these animals.*

- Which animals could be pets? *(dog, fish, kitten, rabbit, turtle)*
- Which animals could not be pets? *(bear, lion, wolf, octopus)*
- What are the two groups we used to put the animals in? *(Pets and Not Pets)*

(If you wish, you might suggest other groupings as well, such as water animals or animals that hunt for food.)

3 Connect to Everyday Life

Write this list of activities on the board: *run, sleep, ride a bike, watch television, eat supper, take a bath, go swimming.* Tell children that there are many things we do indoors and outdoors. Have them group these activities as indoor or outdoor activities. (Students might note that some things can be done either indoors or outdoors.)

Reteach Comprehension
Compare and Contrast

① Teach

Explain that some things are alike, and some things are different. *Alike* means things that are the same. *Different* means things that are not the same. When we tell how things are alike, we *compare* them. When we tell how things are different, we *contrast* them.

Display the Envision It! pages for Compare and Contrast in *My Skills Buddy*, Unit 2, pp. 14–15. Say: *When I look for things that are alike and different, I look first to see what things are the same. The bicycles are the same. Both of them are for riding. They both have wheels, a seat, and handlebars. When I look for things that are not the same, I see that the bicycles are also different because the one on the right has training wheels and is a different color. Also, the sun is out on the right side, but there is a cloud on the left side.*

Remind students that comparing and contrasting is a way of telling about likenesses and differences.

② Practice

Show children two different lunch boxes or other common objects. Ask:

- How are the lunch boxes alike? *(They both carry food; they have handles and a latch; they are plastic, etc.)*

- How are the lunch boxes different? *(They have different pictures; they are different colors, sizes, shapes, etc.)*

③ Connect to Everyday Life

Have children compare and contrast a dog and a cat. They can do so by telling their likenesses and then telling their differences.

Reteach Comprehension
Main Idea

1 Teach

Explain that all selections are about one big idea. This idea is the most important thing the author wants to talk about. It is also called the *main idea*.

Display the Envision It! pages for Main Idea in *My Skills Buddy*, Unit 2, pp. 54–55. Say: *I know that the main idea is the big idea. I will try and find one on this poster.* Point to the four surrounding pictures and finally to the school in the center. Say: *When I look at the pictures, I see that a school is in the middle. Maybe the main idea has something to do with school. When I look around the picture, I see a child riding a bike, two children walking, a child in a car, and children on a school bus. Then I ask myself, "Where are all these children going?" Since School is in the middle, maybe they're all going there. That is what all these pictures have in common. It is the one big idea that connects everything: Ways we go to school. That must be the main idea.*

2 Practice

Begin a discussion of favorite animals. Tell children what your favorite animal is and why. Ask children to do the same. (Vary your prompts: *What animal do you think is most special; . . . would you choose for a pet; . . . do you have most fun with?*) Write children's responses on the board. When the discussion is over, read the list and ask:

- What is this list all about? *(favorite animals)*

- If we want to give this list a name, what might we call it? *(Our Favorite Animals)*

Say: *Our Favorite Animals is what our list is all about. That is the main idea of our list.*

3 Connect to Everyday Life

Think about a story or nonfiction selection the class has recently read. Help children determine the main idea of that selection.

Reteach Comprehension
Realism and Fantasy

1 Teach

Explain that a *realistic* story tells about things that could happen in real life. A *fantasy* tells about things that could not happen in real life. It is make-believe.

Display the Envision It! pages for Realism and Fantasy in *My Skills Buddy,* Unit 2, pp. 74–75. Say: *When I am trying to decide what is real and what is fantasy, I ask myself, "Could this happen in real life?" Well, I think the fish on the left looks pretty real because I've seen fish that look just like that, and I know some fish live in bowls. So I think the picture on the left is realistic because it could happen in real life.* Now call attention to the picture on the right. Point to elements in the picture as you talk about them. Say: *When I look at the picture on the right, I ask myself, "Could this happen in real life?" I know I've never seen fish sit at desks, or a fish teach a class or wear a necklace, so I don't think this could ever happen in real life. This picture must be fantasy.*

Remind children that things that could happen in real life are realistic, and things that could never happen in real life are fantasy.

2 Practice

Show pictures from books you have read as a class, both realism and fantasy. Ask children to identify the realistic pictures and the fantasy pictures and explain their choices.

3 Connect to Everyday Life

Have children describe realistic scenes from their school or neighborhood. Then have them change one thing in each scene that will turn it into fantasy.

Reteach Comprehension
Plot

1 Teach

Explain that all stories are made up of events, or things that happen. The *plot* of a story tells the important events that happen one after another. It is what happens at the beginning, middle, and end of the story.

Display the Envision It! pages for Literary Elements in *My Skills Buddy*, Unit 3, pp. 34–35. Call children's attention to the three pictures under the Plot heading. Say: *The plot of the story tells what happens in the story. When I look at the first picture, I see that a tortoise and hare are at the beginning of a race. The next picture shows me that the hare is sleeping, but the tortoise is still racing and is ahead of the hare. The last picture shows that the tortoise has won the race. This is the plot. I know what happens in the beginning, middle, and end of the story.*

2 Practice

Display a picture that shows a number of people in action. Tell children: *Let's make up a story about the picture.* Ask:

- What will happen at the beginning of our story?
- What will happen in the middle of our story?
- What will happen at the end of our story?

Write children's contributions on the board. When children are finished, reread the whole story from beginning to end.

Remind children that a story has things that happen in the beginning, the middle, and the end. Those events are the plot of the story.

3 Connect to Everyday Life

With children, recall one or more books you have read as a class. For each, ask: What is the plot of the story? Have children retell what happened at the beginning, middle, and end of each story.

Reteach Comprehension
Cause and Effect

① Teach

Explain that many things happen because something else makes them happen, or causes them to happen. What happens is called an *effect*. Why it happens is called a *cause*.

Display the Envision It! pages for Cause and Effect in *My Skills Buddy*, Unit 3, pp. 54–55. Say: *To find cause and effect, I look for what happens and why it happens. When I look at the first picture, I see a girl painting. I also see a dog with its paws on a table that has an open paint can on it.* With your finger, trace the arrow from the first to the second picture. Say: *The arrow shows that this* (first picture) *leads to this* (second picture). *Here, the girl looks surprised. Also, the can of paint has fallen on the floor and the dog is covered with paint spots. I ask myself, "Why is the dog covered with paint spots?" The reason must be because the dog tipped over the table that had the paint on it.*

Remind children that when something happens, there is a cause for why it happens. The dog's standing with its paws on the table is the cause for paint spilling on him, the effect.

② Practice

Write these sentence pairs on the board or on sentence strips. Read them aloud. Then have a volunteer come up to draw an arrow from each cause to its effect.

Rain started to fall. Sissy opened her umbrella.
Our dog barked loudly. The mail carrier put letters in the mailbox.
The lunch bell rang. The children got up and formed a line.
Mom turned on the lights in the room. It became dark outside.

③ Connect to Everyday Life

Ask children to suggest possible causes for the following:
I put on a sweater. I ate a snack.
Ask children to suggest possible effects for the following:
I opened a window. I spilled a glass of water.

Reteach Comprehension
Draw Conclusions

1 Teach

Explain that readers can make up their minds about things in a story or selection. A *conclusion* is an understanding you get. To come to a conclusion, you think about what you read and see. Then you add what you already know to figure it out.

Display the Envision It! pages for Draw Conclusions in *My Skills Buddy*, Unit 3, pp. 94–95. Say: *When I look at the picture, I see a smiling girl holding a beautifully wrapped gift. I ask myself, "How is the girl feeling?" Well, I know when I get a gift from someone, I feel very happy and excited. The girl in the picture must be feeling the same way because she has a big smile on her face.* Point to the equal sign and the other elements as you continue: *This is an equal sign. Sometimes we use it for "means." Now we can read this as "The gift and the smile mean the girl is happy, happy, happy." That is my conclusion, and I got it by putting together what's in the picture with what I already know about getting a gift.*

2 Practice

Have children answer these questions by drawing conclusions:

- A teacher and her class are on a field trip. They hear a lion roar and monkeys chatter. Where is the class? *(at a zoo)*

- Your baby brother is in his high chair, laughing and pounding on the tray. A bowl of cereal is upside-down on the floor. How did it get there? *(He threw it down.)*

- Your dad is backing the car out of the driveway when he hears a crash and feels a thump. Getting out, he finds a tricycle under the car. What has happened? *(He ran over it.)*

3 Connect to Everyday Life

Have children draw conclusions about the following:

- In the middle of a thunderstorm, the television goes dead and the lights in the room shut off. What has happened? *(The electricity has gone off.)*

- At a birthday party, you hear a loud *pop!* and turn around to find a boy holding two balloons on strings and a third string dangling with some colored plastic tied to the end. What has happened? *(He had three balloons, but one burst.)*

Student Edition
Pictionary

Words for Things That Go

airplane

bike

truck

car

bus

van

boat

train

Words for Colors

white

purple

brown

green

pink

black

blue

red

yellow

orange

Words for Shapes

square

circle

triangle

rectangle

heart

star

oval

diamond

Words for Places

school

home

park

train station

police station

fire station

post office

library

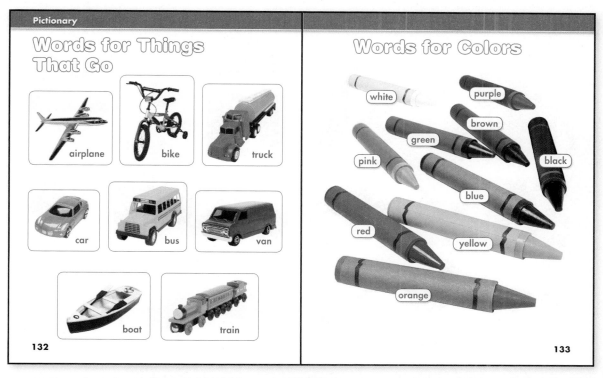
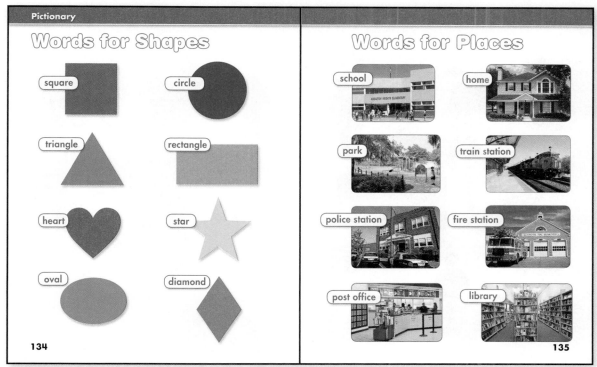

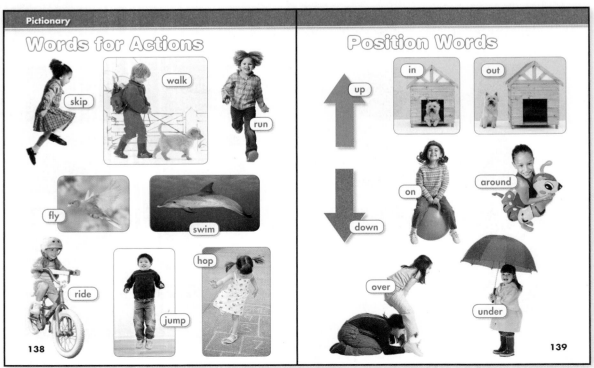

Student Edition
Pictionary

My Classroom

bookcase

easel

books

desk

teacher

toys

paper

chair

blocks

table

markers

crayons

pencils

rug

140

141

Words for Feelings

happy

frightened

worried

excited

angry

proud

sad

surprised

142

My Family

mom
mother

dad
father

sister

grandmother

grandfather

brother

143

167

Scope and Sequence

Reading

Concepts About Print	Pre-K	K	1	2	3	4	5	6
Hold book right side up, turn pages correctly, move from front to back of book	•	•	•					
Identify parts of a book and their functions (front cover, title page/title, back cover, page numbers)	•	•	•					
Identify information that different parts of a book provides (title, author, illustrator)	•	•	•	•				
Know uppercase and lowercase letter names and match them	•	•	•					
Know the order of the alphabet	•	•	•					
Demonstrate one-to-one correspondence between oral words and printed words		•	•					
Identify and distinguish between letters, words, and sentences	•	•	•					
Recognize distinguishing features of a paragraph		•	•					
Recognize environmental print		•	•	•				
Track print (front to back of book, top to bottom of page, left to right on line, sweep back left for next line)	•	•	•					
Recognize first name in print	•	•	•					

Phonological and Phonemic Awareness	Pre-K	K	1	2	3	4	5	6
Phonological Awareness								
Identify and produce rhyming words in response to an oral prompt	•	•	•					
Distinguish rhyming pairs of words from nonrhyming pairs	•	•						
Track and represent changes in simple syllables and words with two and three sounds as one sound is added, substituted, omitted, or changed		•	•					
Count each syllable in a spoken word		•	•					
Segment and blend syllables in spoken words			•					
Segment and blend onset and rime in one-syllable words		•	•					
Recognize and produce words beginning with the same sound	•	•	•					
Phonemic Awareness								
Identify and isolate initial, final, and medial sounds in spoken words	•	•	•	•				
Blend sounds orally to make words or syllables		•	•	•				
Segment a word or syllable into sounds		•	•	•				
Count sounds in spoken words or syllables and syllables in words		•	•	•				
Manipulate sounds in words (add, delete, and/or substitute phonemes)	•	•	•	•				
Distinguish long- and short-vowel sounds in orally stated single-syllable words				•				

Decoding and Word Recognition	Pre-K	K	1	2	3	4	5	6
Read simple one-syllable and high-frequency (sight) words		•T	•T	•T	•			
Phonics								
Understand and apply the *alphabetic principle* that spoken words are composed of sounds that are represented by letters; as letters change, so do sounds	•	•	•					
Know sound-letter relationships and match sounds to letters		•T	•T	•				
Generate sounds from letters and blend those sounds to decode		•	•T	•T	•T			
Consonants, consonant blends, and consonant digraphs		•	•T	•T	•T			
Short and long vowels		•	•T	•T	•T			
r-controlled vowels; vowel digraphs; diphthongs; common vowel patterns			•T	•T	•T			
Phonograms/word families		•	•	•				

• instructional opportunity   **T** tested in standardized test format

Decoding and Word Recognition *continued*	Pre-K	K	1	2	3	4	5	6
Word Structure								
Decode multisyllabic words with common word parts and spelling patterns		•	•T	•T	•T	•T	•T	•T
Base words and inflected endings; plurals			•T	•T	•T	•T	•T	•T
Contractions and compound words			•T	•T	•T	•T	•T	•T
Prefixes and suffixes			•T	•T	•T	•T	•T	•T
Greek and Latin roots						•	•	•
Apply knowledge of syllabication rules to decode words			•T	•T	•T	•T	•T	•T
Recognize common abbreviations			•	•	•			
Decoding Strategies								
Blending strategy: Apply knowledge of sound-letter relationships to decode unfamiliar words		•	•	•	•			
Apply knowledge of word structure to decode unfamiliar words		•	•	•	•	•	•	•
Use context along with sound-letter relationships and word structure to decode		•	•	•	•	•	•	•
Self-monitor accuracy of decoding and self-correct		•	•	•	•	•	•	•
Fluency								
Read aloud grade level text fluently with accuracy, comprehension, appropriate pace/rate; with expression/intonation (prosody); with attention to punctuation and appropriate phrasing			•T	•T	•T	•T	•T	•T
Practice fluency in a variety of ways, including choral reading, partner/paired reading, Readers' Theater, repeated oral reading, and tape-assisted reading		•	•	•	•	•	•	•
Work toward appropriate fluency goals by the end of each grade			•	•	•	•	•	•
Read regularly and with comprehension in independent-level material		•	•	•	•	•	•	•
Read silently for increasing periods of time		•	•	•	•	•	•	•
Vocabulary and Concept Development	Pre-K	K	1	2	3	4	5	6
Recognize and understand selection vocabulary		•	•	•T	•T	•T	•T	•T
Understand content-area vocabulary and specialized, technical, or topical words		•	•	•	•	•	•	•
Word Learning Strategies								
Develop vocabulary through direct instruction, concrete experiences, reading, listening to text read aloud	•	•	•	•	•	•	•	•
Use knowledge of word structure to figure out meanings of words			•	•T	•T	•T	•T	•T
Use context clues for meanings of unfamiliar words, multiple-meaning words, homonyms, homographs			•	•T	•T	•T	•T	•T
Use grade-appropriate reference sources to learn word meanings	•	•	•	•	•T	•T	•T	•T
Use picture clues to help determine word meanings	•	•	•	•				
Use new words in a variety of contexts	•	•	•	•	•	•	•	•
Create and use graphic organizers to group, study, and retain vocabulary			•	•	•	•	•	•
Monitor expository text for unknown words or words with novel meanings by using word, sentence, and paragraph clues to determine meaning						•	•	•
Extend Concepts and Word Knowledge								
Academic language	•	•	•	•	•	•	•	•
Classify and categorize	•	•	•	•	•	•	•	•
Abbreviations			•	•	•			•
Antonyms and synonyms			•	•T	•T	•T	•T	•T
Prefixes and suffixes			•	•	•	•	•	•T

• instructional opportunity   **T** tested in standardized test format

Vocabulary and Concept Development *continued*	Pre-K	K	1	2	3	4	5	6
Homographs and homophones				•	•T	•T	•T	•T
Multiple-meaning words			•	•T	•T	•T	•T	•T
Related words and derivations					•	•	•	•
Compound words				•	•	•	•	•
Figurative language and idioms				•	•	•	•	•
Descriptive words (location, size, color, shape, number, ideas, feelings)	•	•	•	•				
High-utility words (shapes, colors, question words, position/directional words, and so on)	•	•	•	•				
Time and order words	•	•	•	•	•			
Word origins: etymologies/word histories; words from other languages, regions, or cultures						•	•	•
Adages and sayings							•	
Analogies							•	•

Reading Comprehension	Pre-K	K	1	2	3	4	5	6

Comprehension Strategies

	Pre-K	K	1	2	3	4	5	6
Predict and set purpose to guide reading	•	•	•	•	•	•	•	•
Use background knowledge before, during, and after reading	•	•	•	•	•	•	•	•
Monitor and clarify by using fix-up strategies to resolve difficulties in meaning: adjust reading rate, reread and read on, seek help from references sources and/or other people, skim and scan		•	•	•	•	•	•	•
Inferring		•	•	•	•	•	•	•
Questioning before, during, and after reading	•	•	•	•	•	•	•	•
Visualize—use mental imagery		•	•	•	•	•	•	•
Summarize text		•	•	•	•	•	•	•
Recall and retell stories	•	•	•	•	•	•	•	•
Important ideas (nonfiction) that provide clues to an author's meaning				•	•	•	•	•
Text structure (nonfiction—such as cause/effect, chronological, compare/contrast, description)	•		•	•	•	•	•	•
Story structure (fiction—such as plot, problem/solution)	•		•	•	•	•	•	•
Create and use graphic and semantic organizers, including outlines, notes, summaries				•	•	•	•	•
Use strategies flexibly and in combination				•	•	•	•	•

Comprehension Skills

	Pre-K	K	1	2	3	4	5	6
Author's purpose			•T	•T	•T	•T	•T	•T
Author's viewpoint/bias							•T	•T
Categorize and classify	•	•	•	•				
Cause and effect		•	•T	•T	•T	•T	•T	•T
Compare and contrast		•	•T	•T	•T	•T	•T	•T
Draw conclusions and make inferences		•	•T	•T	•T	•T	•T	•T
Facts and details		•	•T	•T	•	•	•	•T
Fact and opinion (statements of fact and opinion)			•T	•T	•T	•T	•T	•T
Follow directions/steps in a process	•	•	•	•	•	•	•	•
Generalize					•T	•T	•T	•

• instructional opportunity   **T** tested in standardized test format

Reading Comprehension *continued*	Pre-K	K	1	2	3	4	5	6
Graphic sources (illustrations, photos, maps, charts, graphs, font styles, etc.)		•	•	•	•	•T	•T	•T
Main idea and supporting details		•T	•T	•T	•T	•T	•T	•T
Paraphrase				•	•	•	•	•
Persuasive devices and propaganda					•	•	•	•
Realism/fantasy	•	•T	•T					
Sequence of events	•	•T	•T	•T	•T	•T	•T	•T
Higher Order Thinking Skills								
Analyze					•	•	•	•
Analyze text with various organizational patterns					•	•	•	•
Describe and connect the essential ideas, arguments, and perspectives of a text			•	•	•	•	•	•
Evaluate and critique ideas and text			•	•	•	•	•	•
Draw inferences, conclusions, or generalizations; support them with textual evidence and prior knowledge		•	•T	•T	•T	•T	•T	•T
Make judgments about ideas and texts			•	•	•	•	•	•
Hypothesize					•	•	•	•
Make connections (text to self, text to text, text to world)	•	•	•	•	•	•	•	•
Organize and synthesize ideas and information			•	•	•	•	•	•T
Literary Response and Analysis	Pre-K	K	1	2	3	4	5	6
Genre and Its Characteristics								
Identify types of everyday print materials (storybooks, poems, newspapers, signs, labels)	•	•	•	•	•	•	•	•
Recognize characteristics of a variety of genre	•	•	•	•	•	•	•	•
Distinguish common forms of literature		•	•	•	•	•	•	•
Identify characteristics of literary texts, including drama, fantasy, traditional tales		•	•	•	•	•	•	•
Identify characteristics of nonfiction texts, including biography, interviews, newspaper articles		•	•	•	•	•	•	•
Identify characteristics of poetry and song, including nursery rhymes, limericks, blank verse	•	•	•	•	•	•	•	•
Literary Elements and Story Structure								
Character	•	•T	•T	•T	•T	•T	•T	•T
Recognize and describe traits, actions, feelings, and motives of characters		•	•	•	•	•	•	•
Analyze characters' relationships, changes, and points of view		•	•	•	•	•	•	•
Analyze characters' conflicts				•	•	•	•	•
Analyze the effect of character on plot and conflict					•	•	•	•
Plot and Plot Structure	•	•T	•T	•T	•T	•T	•T	•T
Beginning, middle, end	•	•	•	•	•	•		
Goal and outcome or problem and solution/resolution		•	•	•	•	•	•	•
Rising action, climax, and falling action/denouement; setbacks						•	•	•
Setting	•	•T	•T	•T	•T	•T	•T	•T
Relate setting to problem/solution		•	•	•	•	•	•	•
Explain ways setting contributes to mood						•	•	•
Theme				•T	•T	•T	•T	•T

• instructional opportunity   **T** tested in standardized test format

Literary Response and Analysis *continued*	Pre-K	K	1	2	3	4	5	6
Use Literary Elements and Story Structure	•	•	•	•	•	•	•	•
Analyze and evaluate author's use of setting, plot, character, and compare among authors				•	•	•	•	•
Identify similarities and differences of characters, events, and settings within or across selections/cultures		•	•	•	•	•	•	•
Literary Devices								
Dialect						•	•	•
Dialogue and narration	•		•	•	•	•	•	•
Identify the speaker or narrator in a selection		•	•	•	•	•	•	•
Exaggeration/hyperbole				•	•	•	•	•
Figurative language: idiom, jargon, metaphor, simile, slang				•	•	•	•	•
Flashback						•	•	•
Foreshadowing						•	•	•
Formal and informal language				•	•	•	•	•
Humor				•	•	•	•	•
Imagery and sensory words			•	•	•	•	•	•
Mood				•	•	•	•	•
Personification						•	•	•
Point of view (first-person, third-person, omniscient)						•	•	•
Puns and word play						•	•	•
Sound devices and poetic elements	•	•	•	•	•	•	•	•
Alliteration, assonance, onomatopoeia	•	•	•	•	•	•	•	•
Rhyme, rhythm, repetition, and cadence	•	•	•	•	•	•	•	•
Word choice		•	•	•	•	•	•	•
Symbolism							•	•
Tone						•	•	•
Author's and Illustrator's Craft								
Distinguish the roles of author and illustrator	•	•	•	•				
Recognize/analyze author's and illustrator's craft or style			•	•	•	•	•	•
Evaluate author's use of various techniques to influence readers' perspectives						•	•	•
Literary Response								
Recollect, talk, and write about books	•	•	•	•	•	•	•	•
Reflect on reading and respond (through talk, movement, art, and so on)	•	•	•	•	•	•	•	•
Ask and answer questions about text	•	•	•	•	•	•	•	•
Write about what is read		•	•	•	•	•	•	•
Use evidence from the text to support opinions, interpretations, or conclusions		•	•	•	•	•	•	•
Support ideas through reference to other texts and personal knowledge				•	•	•	•	•
Locate materials on related topic, theme, or idea				•	•	•	•	•
Make connections: text to self, text to text, text to world			•	•	•	•	•	•
Offer observations, react, speculate in response to text				•	•	•	•	•

• instructional opportunity   **T** tested in standardized test format

Literary Response and Analysis *continued*	Pre-K	K	1	2	3	4	5	6
Literary Appreciation/Motivation								
Show an interest in books and reading; engage voluntarily in social interaction about books	•	•	•	•	•	•	•	•
Choose text by drawing on personal interests, relying on knowledge of authors and genres, estimating text difficulty, and using recommendations of others	•	•	•	•	•	•	•	•
Read a variety of grade-level-appropriate narrative and expository texts		•	•	•	•	•	•	•
Read from a wide variety of genres for a variety of purposes		•	•	•	•	•	•	•
Read independently		•	•	•	•	•	•	•
Establish familiarity with a topic		•	•	•	•	•	•	•
Cultural Awareness								
Comprehend basic plots of classic tales from around the world			•	•	•	•	•	•
Compare and contrast tales from different cultures			•	•	•	•	•	•
Develop attitudes and abilities to interact with diverse groups and cultures	•	•	•	•	•	•	•	•
Connect experiences and ideas with those from a variety of languages, cultures, customs, perspectives	•	•	•	•	•	•	•	•
Compare language and oral traditions (family stories) that reflect customs, regions, and cultures		•	•	•	•	•	•	•
Recognize themes that cross cultures and bind them together in their common humanness		•	•	•	•	•	•	•

Language Arts

Writing	Pre-K	K	1	2	3	4	5	6
Concepts About Print for Writing								
Write uppercase and lowercase letters		•	•					
Print own name and other important words	•	•	•					
Write using pictures, some letters, some phonetically spelled words, and transitional spelling to convey meaning	•	•	•					
Write consonant-vowel-consonant words		•	•					
Dictate messages or stories for others to write	•	•	•					
Create own written texts for others to read; write left to right on a line and top to bottom on a page	•	•	•					
Participate in shared and interactive writing	•	•	•					
Traits of Writing								
Focus/Ideas		•	•	•	•	•	•	•
State a clear purpose and maintain focus; sharpen ideas		•	•	•	•	•	•	•
Use sensory details and concrete examples; elaborate			•	•	•	•	•	•
Delete extraneous information			•	•	•	•	•	•
Use strategies, such as tone, style, consistent point of view, to achieve a sense of completeness						•	•	•
Organization		•	•	•	•	•T	•T	•T
Use graphic organizers to group ideas	•	•	•	•	•	•	•	•
Write coherent paragraphs that develop a central idea and have topic sentences and facts and details			•	•	•	•	•	•
Use transitions to connect sentences and paragraphs and establish coherence			•	•	•	•	•	•

• instructional opportunity **T** tested in standardized test format

Writing *continued*	Pre-K	K	1	2	3	4	5	6
Select an organizational structure, such as comparison and contrast, categories, spatial order, climactic order, based on purpose, audience, length							•	•
Organize ideas in a logical progression, such as chronological order or order of importance	•	•	•	•	•	•	•	•
Write introductory, supporting, and concluding paragraphs					•	•	•	•
Use strategies of note-taking, outlining, and summarizing to impose structure on composition drafts					•	•	•	•
Write a multi-paragraph paper				•	•	•	•	•
Voice			•	•	•	•	•	•
Develop personal, identifiable voice and an individual tone/style			•	•	•	•	•	•
Maintain consistent voice and point of view							•	•
Use voice appropriate to audience, message, and purpose						•	•	•
Word Choice		•	•	•	•T	•T	•T	•T
Use clear, precise, appropriate language		•	•	•	•	•	•	•
Use figurative language and vivid words			•	•	•	•	•	•
Use sensory details, imagery, characterization			•	•	•	•	•	
Select effective vocabulary using word walls, dictionary, or thesaurus		•	•	•	•	•	•	•
Sentences		•	•	•	•T	•T	•T	•T
Combine, elaborate, and vary sentences	•	•	•	•	•T	•T	•T	•T
Write topic sentence, supporting sentences with facts and details, and concluding sentence		•	•	•	•	•	•	
Use correct word order		•	•	•	•	•	•	•
Conventions		•	•	•	•T	•T	•T	•T
Use correct spelling and grammar; capitalize and punctuate correctly		•	•	•	•	•	•	•
Correct sentence fragments and run-ons					•	•	•	•
Use correct paragraph indentation			•	•	•	•	•	•

The Writing Process

	Pre-K	K	1	2	3	4	5	6
Prewrite using various strategies	•	•	•	•	•	•	•	•
Develop first drafts of single- and multiple-paragraph compositions		•	•	•	•	•	•	•
Revise drafts for varied purposes, including to clarify and to achieve purpose, sense of audience, improve focus and coherence, precise word choice, vivid images, and elaboration		•	•	•	•	•	•	•
Edit and proofread for correct conventions (spelling, grammar, usage, and mechanics)		•	•	•	•	•	•	•
Publish own work	•	•	•	•	•	•	•	•

Writing Genres

	Pre-K	K	1	2	3	4	5	6
Narrative writing (such as personal narratives, stories, biographies, autobiographies)	•	•	•T	•T	•T	•T	•T	•T
Expository writing (such as comparison and contrast, problem and solution, essays, directions, explanations, news stories, research reports, summaries)		•	•	•T	•T	•T	•T	•T
Descriptive writing (such as labels, captions, lists, plays, poems, response logs, songs)	•	•	•T	•T	•T	•T	•T	•T
Persuasive writing (such as ads, editorials, essays, letters to the editor, opinions, posters)		•	•	•T	•T	•T	•T	•T
Notes and letters (such as personal, formal, and friendly letters, thank-you notes, and invitations)		•	•	•	•	•	•	•

• instructional opportunity   **T** tested in standardized test format

Writing *continued*	Pre-K	K	1	2	3	4	5	6
Responses to literature			•	•	•	•	•	•
Writing Habits and Practices								
Write on a daily basis	•	•	•	•	•	•	•	•
Use writing as a tool for learning		•	•	•	•	•	•	•
Write independently for extended periods of time			•	•	•	•	•	•
Penmanship								
Gain increasing control of penmanship, including pencil grip, paper position, posture, stroke	•	•	•	•				
Write legibly, with control over letter size and form; letter slant; and letter, word, and sentence spacing		•	•	•	•	•	•	•
Write lowercase and uppercase letters	•	•	•	•	•	•	•	•
Manuscript	•	•	•	•	•	•	•	•
Cursive				•	•	•	•	•
Write numerals	•	•	•					
Written and Oral English Language Conventions	Pre-K	K	1	2	3	4	5	6
Grammar and Usage in Speaking and Writing								
Sentences								
Correct word order in written sentences		•	•	•				
Types (declarative, interrogative, exclamatory, imperative)	•	•	•T	•T	•T	•T	•T	•T
Structure (complete, incomplete, simple, compound, complex, compound-complex)	•	•	•	•T	•T	•T	•T	•T
Parts (subjects/predicates: complete, simple, compound; phrases; clauses)			•	•T	•T	•T	•T	•T
Fragments and run-on sentences		•	•	•	•	•	•	•
Combine and rearrange sentences; use appositives, participial phrases, adjectives, adverbs, and prepositional phrases				•	•	•	•	•
Transitions and conjunctions to connect ideas; independent and dependent clauses				•	•	•	•	•
Varied sentence types and sentence openings to present effective style						•	•	•
Parts of speech: nouns (singular and plural), verbs and verb tenses, adjectives, adverbs, pronouns and antecedents, conjunctions, prepositions, interjections, articles		•	•	•T	•T	•T	•T	•T
Contractions			•	•T	•T	•T	•T	•T
Usage								
Subject-verb agreement		•	•	•T	•T	•T	•T	•T
Pronoun agreement/referents			•	•	•T	•T	•T	•T
Misplaced modifiers							•	•
Misused words					•		•	•
Negatives; avoid double negatives					•	•	•	•
Mechanics in Writing								
Capitalization (first word in sentence, proper nouns and adjectives, pronoun *I*, titles, months, days of the week, holidays, and so on)	•	•	•T	•T	•T	•T	•T	•T
Punctuation (period, question mark, exclamation mark, apostrophe, comma, quotation marks, parentheses, colon, and so on)		•	•T	•T	•T	•T	•T	•T

• instructional opportunity   **T** tested in standardized test format

Written and Oral English Language Conventions *continued*	Pre-K	K	1	2	3	4	5	6
Spelling								
Spell independently by using pre-phonetic knowledge, knowledge of letter names, sounds of the alphabet	•	•	•T	•	•	•	•	•
Consonants: single, double, blends, digraphs, silent letters, and unusual consonant spellings		•	•T	•T	•T	•T	•T	•T
Vowels: short, long, *r*-controlled, digraphs, diphthongs, less-common vowel patterns, schwa		•	•T	•T	•T	•T	•T	•T
Use knowledge of word structure to spell			•	•	•	•	•	•
Base words and affixes (inflections, prefixes, suffixes), possessives, contractions, and compound words			•	•T	•T	•T	•T	•T
Greek and Latin roots, syllable patterns, multisyllabic words			•	•	•	•	•	•
Spell high-frequency, irregular words		•T	•T	•	•	•	•	•
Spell frequently misspelled words correctly, including homophones or homonyms			•	•	•	•	•	•
Use meaning relationships to spell					•	•	•	•
Listening and Speaking	Pre-K	K	1	2	3	4	5	6
Listening Skills and Strategies								
Listen to a variety of presentations attentively and politely	•	•	•	•	•	•	•	•
Self-monitor comprehension while listening, using a variety of skills and strategies, e.g., ask questions	•	•	•	•	•	•	•	•
Listen for a purpose								
For enjoyment and appreciation	•	•	•	•	•	•	•	•
To expand vocabulary and concepts	•	•	•	•	•	•	•	•
To obtain information and ideas	•	•	•	•	•	•	•	•
To follow oral directions	•	•	•	•	•	•	•	•
To answer questions and solve problems	•	•	•	•	•	•	•	•
To participate in group discussions	•	•	•	•	•	•	•	•
To identify and analyze the musical elements of literary language	•	•	•	•	•	•	•	•
To gain knowledge of one's own culture, the culture of others, and the common elements of cultures	•	•	•	•	•	•	•	•
To respond to persuasive messages with questions or affirmations						•	•	•
Determine purpose of listening			•	•	•	•	•	•
Recognize formal and informal language			•	•	•	•	•	•
Connect prior experiences to those of a speaker	•	•	•	•	•	•	•	•
Listen critically to distinguish fact from opinion and to analyze and evaluate ideas, information, experiences		•	•	•	•	•	•	•
Paraphrase, retell, or summarize information that has been shared orally			•	•	•	•	•	•
Evaluate a speaker's delivery; identify tone, mood, and emotion					•	•	•	•
Interpret and critique a speaker's purpose, perspective, persuasive techniques, verbal and nonverbal messages, and use of rhetorical devices; draw conclusions						•	•	•
Speaking Skills and Strategies								
Speak clearly, accurately, and fluently, using appropriate delivery for a variety of audiences, and purposes; sustain audience interest, attention	•	•	•	•	•	•	•	•
Use proper intonation, volume, pitch, modulation, and phrasing		•	•	•	•	•	•	•
Speak with a command of standard English conventions	•	•	•	•	•	•	•	•
Use appropriate language for formal and informal settings	•	•	•	•	•	•	•	•

• instructional opportunity   **T** tested in standardized test format

Listening and Speaking *continued*	Pre-K	K	1	2	3	4	5	6
Use visual aids to clarify oral presentations	•	•	•	•	•	•	•	•
Organize ideas and convey information in a logical sequence or structure with a beginning, middle, and end and an effective introduction and conclusion			•	•	•	•	•	•
Support opinions with detailed evidence and with visual or media displays					•	•	•	•
Emphasize key points to assist listener						•	•	•
Speak for a purpose								
To ask and answer questions	•	•	•	•	•	•	•	•
To give directions and instructions	•	•	•	•	•	•	•	•
To retell, paraphrase, or explain information	•	•	•	•	•	•	•	•
To communicate needs and share ideas and experiences	•	•	•	•	•	•	•	•
To describe people, places, things, locations, events, and actions		•	•	•	•	•	•	•
To participate in conversations and discussions	•	•	•	•	•	•	•	•
To express an opinion	•	•	•	•	•	•	•	•
To recite poems or songs or deliver dramatic recitations, interpretations, or performances	•	•	•	•	•	•	•	•
To deliver oral responses to literature	•	•	•	•	•	•	•	•
To deliver presentations or oral reports (narrative, descriptive, persuasive, problems and solutions, and informational based on research)	•	•	•	•	•	•	•	•
Stay on topic; maintain a clear focus	•	•	•	•	•	•	•	•
Support spoken ideas with details and examples		•	•	•	•	•	•	•
Use appropriate verbal and nonverbal elements (such as facial expression, gestures, eye contact, posture)	•	•	•	•	•	•	•	•

Viewing/Media	Pre-K	K	1	2	3	4	5	6
Interact with and respond to a variety of media for a range of purposes	•	•	•	•	•	•	•	•
Compare and contrast print, visual, and electronic media				•	•	•	•	•
Analyze media						•	•	•
Evaluate media				•	•	•	•	•
Recognize bias and propaganda in media message						•	•	•
Recognize purpose and persuasion in media messages				•	•	•	•	•

Research Skills

Understand and Use Graphic Sources	Pre-K	K	1	2	3	4	5	6
Advertisement				•	•	•	•	•
Chart/table	•	•	•	•	•	•	•	•
Diagram/scale drawing				•	•	•	•	•
Graph (bar, circle, line, picture)			•	•	•	•	•	•
Illustration, photograph, caption, label	•	•	•	•	•	•	•	•
Map/globe	•	•	•	•	•	•	•	•
Poster/announcement	•	•	•	•	•	•	•	•
Schedule						•	•	•
Sign	•	•	•	•		•		•
Time line				•	•	•	•	•

• instructional opportunity   **T** tested in standardized test format

Understand and Use Reference Sources	Pre-K	K	1	2	3	4	5	6
Know and use organizational features and parts of a book to locate information	•	•	•	•	•	•	•	•
Use alphabetical order			•	•		•	•	•
Understand purpose, structure, and organization of reference sources (print, electronic, media, Internet)	•	•	•	•	•	•	•	•
Almanac						•	•	•
Atlas					•	•	•	•
Card catalog/library database					•	•	•	•
Picture Dictionary		•	•	•				•
Dictionary/glossary				•	•T	•T	•T	•T
Encyclopedia				•	•	•	•	•
Magazine/periodical				•	•	•	•	•
Newspaper and newsletter				•	•	•	•	•
Readers' Guide to Periodical Literature						•	•	•
Technology (on- and offline electronic media)		•	•	•	•	•	•	•
Thesaurus					•	•	•	•

Study Skills and Strategies	Pre-K	K	1	2	3	4	5	6
Adjust reading rate				•	•	•	•	•
Clarify directions	•	•	•	•	•	•	•	•
Outline					•	•	•	•
Skim and scan				•	•	•	•	•
SQP3R								
Summarize		•	•	•	•	•	•	•
Take notes, paraphrase, and synthesize				•	•	•	•	•
Use graphic and semantic organizers to organize information		•	•	•	•	•	•	•

Test-Taking Skills and Strategies	Pre-K	K	1	2	3	4	5	6
Understand the question, the vocabulary of tests, and key words				•	•	•	•	•
Answer the question; use information from the text (stated or inferred)	•	•	•	•	•	•	•	•
Write across texts				•	•	•		•
Complete the sentence					•	•	•	•

Technology/New Literacies	Pre-K	K	1	2	3	4	5	6
Non-Computer Electronic Media								
Audiotapes/CDs, videotapes/DVDs		•	•	•	•	•	•	•
Computer Programs/Services: Basic Operations and Concepts								
Use accurate computer terminology		•	•	•	•	•	•	•
Create, name, locate, open, save, delete, and organize files			•	•	•	•	•	•
Use input and output devices (such as mouse, keyboard, monitor, printer, touch screen)	•	•	•	•	•	•	•	•
Use basic keyboarding skills		•	•	•	•	•	•	•
Responsible Use of Technology Systems and Software								
Work cooperatively and collaboratively with others; follow acceptable-use policies	•	•	•	•	•	•	•	•
Recognize hazards of Internet searches					•	•	•	•
Respect intellectual property					•	•	•	•

• instructional opportunity   **T** tested in standardized test format

Technology/New Literacies *continued*

Information and Communication Technologies:

Information Acquisition

	Pre-K	K	1	2	3	4	5	6
Use electronic Web (nonlinear) navigation, online resources, databases, keyword searches				•	•	•	•	•
Use visual and nontextual features of online resources	•	•	•	•	•	•	•	•
Internet inquiry								
Identify questions				•	•	•	•	•
Locate, select, and collect information				•	•	•	•	•
Analyze information				•	•	•	•	•
Evaluate electronic information sources for accuracy, relevance, bias					•	•	•	•
Understand bias/subjectivity of electronic content (about this site, author search, date created)						•	•	•
Synthesize information					•	•	•	•
Communicate findings				•	•	•	•	•
Use fix-up strategies (such as clicking *Back, Forward,* or *Undo;* redoing a search; trimming the URL)					•	•	•	•

Communication

	Pre-K	K	1	2	3	4	5	6
Collaborate, publish, present, and interact with others		•	•	•	•	•	•	•
Use online resources (e-mail, bulletin boards, newsgroups)			•	•	•	•	•	•
Use a variety of multimedia formats			•	•	•	•	•	•

Problem Solving

	Pre-K	K	1	2	3	4	5	6
Use technology resources for solving problems and making informed decisions					•	•	•	•
Determine when technology is useful			•	•	•	•	•	•

The Research Process

	Pre-K	K	1	2	3	4	5	6
Identify topics; ask and evaluate questions; develop ideas leading to inquiry, investigation, and research		•	•	•	•	•	•	•
Choose and evaluate appropriate reference sources		•	•	•	•	•	•	•
Locate and collect information including using organizational features of electronic text	•	•	•	•	•	•	•	•
Take notes/record findings		•	•	•	•	•	•	•
Combine and compare information			•	•	•	•	•	•
Evaluate, interpret, and draw conclusions about key information		•	•	•	•	•	•	•
Paraphrase and summarize information		•	•	•	•	•	•	•
Make an outline			•	•	•	•	•	•
Organize content systematically		•	•	•	•	•	•	•
Communicate information		•	•	•	•	•	•	•
Write and present a report		•	•	•	•	•	•	•
Include citations					•	•	•	•
Respect intellectual property/avoid plagiarism						•	•	•
Select and organize visual aids		•	•	•	•	•	•	•

• instructional opportunity   **T** tested in standardized test format

Pacing

BACK TO SCHOOL!

| | UNIT 1 | | | | | | UNIT 2 | |
	WEEK 1	WEEK 2	WEEK 3	WEEK 4	WEEK 5	WEEK 6	WEEK 7	WEEK 8
Phonological/ Phonemic Awareness	Rhyming Words	Syllables	Discriminate Sounds Segment Syllables	Discriminate Sounds	Isolate /m/ Discriminate Sounds	Isolate /t/ Discriminate Sounds Rhyme	Isolate /a/ Oral Blending	Isolate /s/ Oral Blending
Phonics	Letter Naming: Aa, Bb, Cc, Dd, Ee	Letter Naming: Ff, Gg, Hh, Ii, Jj, Kk, Ll, Mm, Nn	Letter Naming: Oo, Pp, Qq, Rr, Ss	Letter Naming: Tt, Uu, Vv, Ww, Xx, Yy, Zz	Connect /m/ to Mm	Connect /t/ to Tt	Connect /a/ to Aa	Connect /s/ to Ss
High-Frequency Words	I, am	I, am	the, little	the, little	a, to	a, to	have, is	have, is
Listening Comprehension	Character	Setting	Sequence	Classify and Categorize	Character and Setting	Classify and Categorize	Classify and Categorize	Setting
Comprehension Strategies	Preview and Predict, Recall and Retell							

| | UNIT 4 | | | | | | UNIT 5 | |
	WEEK 19	WEEK 20	WEEK 21	WEEK 22	WEEK 23	WEEK 24	WEEK 25	WEEK 26
Phonemic Awareness	Isolate /h/ Oral Blending Segment Phonemes	Isolate /l/ Oral Blending Segment Phonemes	Isolate Blends Discriminate Phonemes Segment Phonemes	Isolate /g/ Segment Phonemes	Segment Phonemes Discriminate Phonemes	Isolate /e/ Segment Phonemes Discriminate Phonemes	Isolate /j/, /w/ Oral Blending Segment Phonemes	Isolate /ks/ Oral Blending Segment Phonemes
Phonics	Connect /h/ to Hh	Connect /l/ to Ll	Consonant Blends	Connect /g/ to Gg	Connect /e/ to Ee	Connect /e/ to Ee	Connect /j/ to Jj and /w/ to Ww	Connect /ks/ to Xx
High-Frequency Words	are, that, do	are, that, do	one, two, three, four, five	one, two, three, four, five	here, go, from	here, go, from	yellow, blue, green	yellow, blue, green
Listening Comprehension	Sequence	Cause and Effect	Sequence	Character	Classify and Categorize	Setting	Realism and Fantasy	Cause and Effect
Comprehension Strategies	Preview and Predict, Recall and Retell							

IT'S TEST TIME!

How do I cover all the skills before the test?

This chart shows the instructional sequence from Scott Foresman Reading Street. *You can use this pacing chart as is to ensure you're following a comprehensive scope and sequence, or you can adjust the sequence to match your school/district focus calendar, curriculum map, or testing schedule.*

UNIT 3

	WEEK 9	WEEK 10	WEEK 11	WEEK 12	WEEK 13	WEEK 14	WEEK 15	WEEK 16	WEEK 17	WEEK 18
	Isolate /p/ Oral Blending	Isolate /k/ Oral Blending	Isolate /i/ Discriminate Sounds Oral Blending	Discriminate Sounds Oral Blending	Isolate /n/, /b/ Oral Blending Segment Phonemes	Isolate /r/ Oral Blending Segment Phonemes	Isolate /d/, /k/ Oral Blending Segment Phonemes	Isolate /f/ Oral Blending Segment Phonemes	Isolate /o/ Oral Blending Segment Phonemes	Oral Blending Segment Phonemes
	Connect /p/ to Pp	Connect /k/ to Cc	Connect /i/ to Ii	Connect /i/ to Ii	Connect /n/ to Nn and /b/ to Bb	Connect /r/ to Rr	Connect /d/ to Dd and /k/ to Kk	Connect /f/ to Ff	Connect /o/ to Oo	Connect /o/ to Oo
	we, my, like	we, my, like	he, for	he, for	me, with, she	me, with, she	see, look	see, look	they, you, of	they, you, of
	Main Idea	Realism and Fantasy	Sequence	Realism and Fantasy	Compare and Contrast	Plot	Cause and Effect	Plot	Draw Conclusions	Main Idea

Preview and Predict, Recall and Retell | Preview and Predict, Recall and Retell

UNIT 6

	WEEK 27	WEEK 28	WEEK 29	WEEK 30	WEEK 31	WEEK 32	WEEK 33	WEEK 34	WEEK 35	WEEK 36
	Isolate /u/ Oral Blending Segment Phonemes	Isolate /u/ Oral Blending Segment Phonemes	Isolate /v/, /z/ Oral Blending Segment Phonemes	Isolate /y/, /kw/ Oral Blending Segment Phonemes	Isolate /a/ and /i/ Blend Phonemes Segment Phonemes	Isolate /o/ Blend Phonemes Segment Phonemes	Isolate /e/ Blend Phonemes Segment Phonemes	Isolate /u/ Blend Phonemes Segment Phonemes	Discriminate Sounds Blend Phonemes Segment Phonemes	Discriminate Sounds Blend Phonemes Segment Phonemes
	Connect /u/ to Uu	Connect /u/ to Uu	Connect /v/ to Vv and /z/ to Zz	Connect /y/ to Yy and /kw/ to qu	Connect /a/ to Aa and /i/ to Ii	Connect /o/ to Oo	Connect /e/ to Ee	Connect /u/ to Uu	Consonants and Short Vowels	Consonants and Short Vowels
	what, said, was	what, said, was	where, come	where, come	Reteach and Review	Reteach and Review	Reteach and Review	Reteach and Review	Reteach and Review	Reteach and Review
	Compare and Contrast	Plot	Main Idea	Draw Conclusions	Compare and Contrast	Character	Main Idea	Plot	Setting	Draw Conclusions

Preview and Predict, Recall and Retell | Preview and Predict, Recall and Retell

WHEN IS YOUR STATE TEST?

Pacing

BACK TO
SCHOOL!

	UNIT 1						UNIT 2	
	WEEK 1	WEEK 2	WEEK 3	WEEK 4	WEEK 5	WEEK 6	WEEK 7	WEEK 8
Speaking, Listening, and Viewing	Follow Directions	Drama—Respond to Literature	Listen for Rhyme and Rhythm	Talk About Me	Announce-ments and Messages	Drama—Respond to Literature	Listen for Sequence	Listen for Directions
Grammar	*Say Our Names*	*Write Our Names*	*What We Look Like*	*What We Can Do*	*Nouns for People and Animals*	*Nouns for Places and Things*	*Nouns for More Than One*	*Proper Nouns*
Writing	Shared, Modeled, Interactive, and Independent							

	UNIT 4						UNIT 5	
	WEEK 19	WEEK 20	WEEK 21	WEEK 22	WEEK 23	WEEK 24	WEEK 25	WEEK 26
Speaking, Listening, and Viewing	Give Directions	Compare and Contrast	Listen for Sequence	Discuss Authors and Illus-trators	Listen for Story Elements: Character	Listen to Poems	Ask and Answer Questions	Drama—Respond to Literature
Grammar	*Subjects (Naming Parts)*	*Predicates (Action Parts)*	*Complete Sentences*	*Telling Sentences*	*Capital Letters and Periods*	*Pronouns I and me*	*Questions*	*Question Marks and Capital Letters*
Writing	Shared, Modeled, Interactive, and Independent							

IT'S TEST TIME!

UNIT 3

WEEK 9	WEEK 10	WEEK 11	WEEK 12	WEEK 13	WEEK 14	WEEK 15	WEEK 16	WEEK 17	WEEK 18
Discussions	Listen for Setting	Give a Description	Listen for Plot	Respond to Literature	Sequence	Recite Rhymes	Oral Presentation	Messages and Letters	Ask and Answer Questions
Adjectives: Colors and Shapes	*Adjectives: Sizes and Numbers*	*Adjectives: Opposites*	*Adjectives*	*Verbs*	*Verbs for Now and the Past*	*Verbs That Add –s*	*Verbs for Now and the Future*	*Meaningful Word Groups*	*Sentences*

Shared, Modeled, Interactive, and Independent   Shared, Modeled, Interactive, and Independent

UNIT 6

WEEK 27	WEEK 28	WEEK 29	WEEK 30	WEEK 31	WEEK 32	WEEK 33	WEEK 34	WEEK 35	WEEK 36
Discuss Literature	Sequence	Oral Presentation—Description	Discuss Literary Elements: Plot	Recite Language	Discuss Fact and Opinion	Interpret Information	Discuss Literary Elements: Character	Oral Presentation—Book Report	Discuss Literary Elements: Setting
Prepositions	*Nouns*	*Nouns in Sentences*	*Verbs*	*Pronouns I and me*	*Prepositional Phrases*	*Telling Sentences*	*Questions*	*Exclamations*	*Complete Sentences*

Shared, Modeled, Interactive, and Independent   Shared, Modeled, Interactive, and Independent

WHEN IS YOUR STATE TEST?

Student Progress Report: Grade K

Name _____

This chart lists the skills taught in this program. On this reproducible chart, record your child's progress toward mastery of the skills covered in this school year here. Use the chart below to track the coverage of these skills.

Skill	Date	Date	Date	Date	Date
Recognize that spoken words can be represented by print for communication.					
Identify upper- and lower-case letters.					
Demonstrate the one-to-one relationship between a spoken word and a printed word in text.					
Recognize the difference between a letter and a printed word.					
Recognize that sentences have words separated by spaces and demonstrate an awareness of those separations.					
Hold a book right side up, turn its pages correctly, and know that reading moves from top to bottom and left to right.					
Identify different parts of a book.					
Identify that a sentence is made up of a group of words.					
Identify syllables in spoken words.					
Say words that rhyme with spoken words.					
Distinguish rhyming pairs of words from non-rhyming pairs.					
Recognize spoken alliteration or groups of words that begin with the same sound.					
Blend spoken onsets and rimes to form simple words.					
Blend spoken sounds to form one-syllable words.					
Isolate the initial sound to one-syllable spoken words.					
Divide one-syllable words into two to three sounds.					

Skill	Date	Date	Date	Date	Date
Identify the common sounds that letters represent.					
Decode regular words in text and independent of content.					
Recognize that new words are created when letters are changed, added, or deleted.					
Identify and read at least 25 high-frequency words from a commonly used list.					
Predict what will happen next based on the cover, title, and illustrations.					
Ask and answer questions about texts that are read aloud.					

Skill	Date	Date	Date
Identify and use words that name actions, directions, positions, sequences, and locations.			
Recognize that compound words are made up of shorter words.			
Identify and sort pictures of objects into conceptual categories.			
Use a picture dictionary to find words.			
Identify elements of a story including setting, character, and key events.			
Discuss the big idea (theme) of a well-known folktale or fable and connect it to personal experience.			
Recognize sensory details.			
Recognize recurring phrases and characters in traditional fairy tales, lullabies, and folktales from various cultures.			
Respond to rhythm and rhyme in poetry through identifying a regular beat and similarities in word sounds.			
Retell a main event from a story read aloud.			

Skill	Date	Date	Date
Describe characters in a story and the reasons for their actions.			
Identify the topic of an informational text heard.			
Identify the topic and details heard or read, and referring to the words and/or illustrations.			
Retell important facts in a text, heard or read.			
Discuss the ways authors group information in text.			
Use titles and illustrations to make predictions about text.			
Follow pictorial directions.			
Identify the meaning of specific signs.			
Identify different forms of media.			
Identify techniques used in media.			
Plan a first draft by generating ideas for writing through class discussion.			
Develop drafts by sequencing the action or details in the story.			
Revise drafts by adding details or sentences.			
Edit drafts by leaving spaces between letters and words.			
Share writing with others.			
Write sentences to tell a story and put the sentences in chronological order.			
Write short poems.			
Dictate or write information for lists, captions, or invitations.			
Understand and use the past and future tenses when speaking.			

Skill	Date	Date	Date
Understand and use nouns when reading, writing, and speaking.			
Understand and use descriptive words when reading, writing, and speaking.			
Understand and use prepositions and simple prepositional phrases when speaking or writing.			
Understand and use pronouns when reading, writing, and speaking.			
Speak in complete sentences to communicate.			
Use complete simple sentences.			
Form upper- and lower- case letters legibly using the basic conventions of print.			
Capitalize the first letter in a sentence.			
Use punctuation at the end of a sentence.			
Use phonological knowledge to match sounds to letters.			
Use letter-sound correspondences to spell consonant-vowel-consonant (CVC) words.			
Write one's own name.			
Ask questions about topics of class-wide interest.			
Decide what sources or people in the classroom, school, library, or at home can answer research questions.			
Gather evidence from provided text sources.			
Use pictures along with writing when documenting research.			
Listen attentively by facing speakers and asking questions to clarify information.			
Follow oral directions that involve a short related sequence of actions.			

Skill	Date	Date	Date
Share information and ideas by speaking clearly and using proper language.			
Follow rules for discussion taking turns and speaking one at a time.			
Discuss the purposes for reading and listening to various texts.			
Ask and respond to questions about the text.			
Monitor and adjust comprehension.			
Make inferences based on the cover, title, illustrations, and plot.			
Retell or act out important events in stories.			
Make connections to own experiences, to ideas in other texts, and to the larger community and discuss textual evidence.			

English/Language Arts and Cross-Disciplinary Connections

Kindergarten

English/Language Arts Standards

Writing

Compose a variety of texts that demonstrate clear focus, the logical development of ideas in well-organized paragraphs, and the use of appropriate language that advances the author's purpose. • Determine effective approaches, forms, and rhetorical techniques that demonstrate understanding of the writer's purpose and audience. • Generate ideas and gather information relevant to the topic and purpose, keeping careful records of outside sources. • Evaluate relevance, quality, sufficiency, and depth of preliminary ideas and information, organize material generated, and formulate thesis. • Recognize the importance of revision as the key to effective writing.	U1W6, U2W6, U3W6, U4W6, U5W6, U6W6

Reading

Locate explicit textual information and draw complex inferences, analyze, and evaluate the information within and across texts of varying lengths. • Use effective reading strategies to determine a written work's purpose and intended audience. • Use text features and graphics to form an overview of informational texts and to determine where to locate information. • Identify explicit and implicit textual information including main ideas and author's purpose. • Draw and support complex inferences from text to summarize, draw conclusions, and distinguish facts from simple assertions and opinions. • Analyze the presentation of information and the strength and quality of evidence used by the author, and judge the coherence and logic of the presentation and the credibility of an argument. • Analyze imagery in literary texts. • Evaluate the use of both literal and figurative language to inform and shape the perceptions of readers. • Compare and analyze how generic features are used across texts. • Identify and analyze the audience, purpose, and message of an informational or persuasive text. • Identify and analyze how an author's use of language appeals to the senses, creates imagery, and suggests mood. • Identify, analyze, and evaluate similarities and differences in how multiple texts present information, argue a position, or relate a theme.	U2W1, U2W3, U2W5, U3W1, U3W3, U3W6, U4W1, U4W3, U4W5, U5W3, U5W6, U6W1, U6W3, U6W4, U6W6
Understand new vocabulary and concepts and use them accurately in reading, speaking, and writing. • Identify new words and concepts acquired through study of their relationships to other words and concepts. • Apply knowledge of roots and affixes to infer the meanings of new words. • Use reference guides to confirm the meanings of new words or concepts.	U1W1, U1W2, U1W3, U1W4, U1W5, U1W6, U2W1, U2W2, U2W3, U2W4, U2W5, U2W6, U3W1, U3W2, U3W3, U3W4, U3W5, U3W6, U4W1, U4W2, U4W3, U4W4, U4W5, U4W6, U5W1, U5W2, U5W3, U5W4, U5W5, U5W6, U6W1, U6W2, U6W3, U6W4, U6W5, U6W6

Describe, analyze, and evaluate information within and across literary and other texts from a variety of cultures and historical periods.	U1W1, U1W2, U1W3, U1W4, U1W5, U1W6, U2W1, U2W2, U2W3, U2W4, U2W5, U2W6, U3W1, U3W2, U3W3, U3W4, U3W5, U3W6, U4W1, U4W2, U4W3, U4W4, U4W5, U4W6, U5W1, U5W2, U5W3, U5W4, U5W5, U5W6, U6W1, U6W2, U6W3, U6W4, U6W5, U6W6

- Read a wide variety of texts from American, European, and world literatures.
- Analyze themes, structures, and elements of myths, traditional narratives, and classical and contemporary literature.
- Analyze works of literature for what they suggest about the historical period and cultural contexts in which they were written.
- Analyze and compare the use of language in literary works from a variety of world cultures.

Speaking

Understand the elements of communication both in informal group discussions and formal presentations (e.g., accuracy, relevance, rhetorical features, and organization of information).	U1W1, U1W2, U1W3, U1W4, U1W5, U1W6, U2W1, U2W2, U2W3, U2W4, U2W5, U2W6, U3W1, U3W2, U3W3, U3W4, U3W5, U3W6, U4W1, U4W2, U4W3, U4W4, U4W5, U4W6, U5W1, U5W2, U5W3, U5W4, U5W5, U5W6, U6W1, U6W2, U6W3, U6W4, U6W5, U6W6

- Understand how style and content of spoken language varies in different contexts and influences the listener's understanding.
- Adjust presentation (delivery, vocabulary, length) to particular audiences and purposes.

Develop effective speaking styles for both group and one-on-one situations.	U1W4, U2W3, U2W5, U3W4, U4W1, U4W4, U5W3, U5W5, U6W2, U6W4, U6W5

- Participate actively and effectively in one-on-one oral communication situations.
- Participate actively and effectively in group discussions.
- Plan and deliver focused and coherent presentations that convey clear and distinct perspectives and demonstrate solid reasoning.

Listening

Apply listening skills as an individual and as a member of a group in a variety of settings (e.g., lectures, discussions, conversations, team projects, presentations, interviews).	U1W3, U2W1, U2W2, U2W4, U2W6, U4W3, U4W5, U4W6

- Analyze and evaluate the effectiveness of a public presentation.
- Interpret a speaker's message; identify the position taken and the evidence in support of that position.
- Use a variety of strategies to enhance listening comprehension (e.g., focus attention on message, monitor message for clarity and understanding, provide verbal and nonverbal feedback, note cues such as change of pace or particular words that indicate a new point is about to be made, select and organize key information).

Listen effectively in informal and formal situations.	U1W3, U1W4, U2W1, U2W2, U2W3, U2W4, U2W5, U2W6, U3W4, U4W1, U4W3, U4W4, U4W5, U4W6, U5W3, U5W5, U6W2, U6W4, U6W5

- Listen critically and respond appropriately to presentations.
- Listen actively and effectively in one-on-one communication situations.
- Listen actively and effectively in group discussions.

Research

Formulate topic and questions.	U4W6, U5W6, U6W6

- Formulate research questions.
- Explore a research topic.
- Refine research topic and devise a timeline for completing work.

Cross-Disciplinary Standards

Key Cognitive Skills

Intellectual curiosity • Engage in scholarly inquiry and dialogue. • Accept constructive criticism and revise personal views when valid evidence warrants.	U2W3, U4W4, U5W3, U6W2, U6W4
Academic behaviors • Self-monitor learning needs and seek assistance when needed. • Use study habits necessary to manage academic pursuits and requirements. • Strive for accuracy and precision. • Persevere to complete and master tasks.	U1W1, U1W2, U1W3, U1W4, U1W5, U1W6, U2W1, U2W2, U2W3, U2W4, U2W5, U2W6, U3W1, U3W2, U3W3, U3W4, U3W5, U3W6, U4W1/ U4W2, U4W3, U4W4, U4W5, U4W6, U5W1, U5W2, U5W3, U5W4, U5W5, U5W6, U6W1, U6W2, U6W3, U6W4, U6W5, U6W6
Work habits • Work independently. • Work collaboratively.	U1W1, U1W2, U1W3, U1W4, U1W5, U1W6, U2W1, U2W2, U2W3, U2W4, U2W5, U2W6, U3W1, U3W2, U3W3, U3W4, U3W5, U3W6, U4W1, U4W2, U4W3, U4W4, U4W5, U4W6, U5W1, U5W2, U5W3, U5W4, U5W5, U5W6, U6W1, U6W2, U6W3, U6W4, U6W5, U6W6

Foundational Skills

Reading across the curriculum • Use effective prereading strategies. • Use a variety of strategies to understand the meanings of new words. • Identify the intended purpose and audience of the text. • Identify the key information and supporting details. • Analyze textual information critically. • Annotate, summarize, paraphrase, and outline texts when appropriate. • Adapt reading strategies according to structure of texts. • Connect reading to historical and current events and personal interest.	U3W3, U5W6, U6W1
Writing across the curriculum • Write clearly and coherently using standard writing conventions. • Write in a variety of forms for various audiences and purposes. • Compose and revise drafts.	U1W1, U1W2, U1W3, U1W4, U1W5, U1W6, U2W1, U2W2, U2W3, U2W4, U2W5, U2W6, U3W1, U3W2, U3W3, U3W4, U3W5, U3W6, U4W1, U4W2, U4W3, U4W4, U4W5, U4W6, U5W1, U5W2, U5W3, U5W4, U5W5, U5W6, U6W1, U6W2, U6W3, U6W4, U6W5, U6W6

Science Connections on Reading Street

Kindergarten

Biology

Classification and taxonomy • Know ways in which living things can be classified based on each organism's internal and external structure, development, and relatedness of DNA sequences.	U2W1, U2W2, U2W6
Systems and homeostasis • Know that organisms possess various structures and processes (feedback loops) that maintain steady internal conditions. • Describe, compare, and contrast structures and processes that allow gas exchange, nutrient uptake and processing, waste excretion, nervous and hormonal regulation, and reproduction in plants, animals, and fungi; give examples of each.	U2W1, U2W2, U2W4, U3W1, U3W4
Ecology • Identify Earth's major biomes, giving their locations, typical climate conditions, and characteristic organisms present in each. • Know patterns of energy flow and material cycling in Earth's ecosystems. • Understand typical forms of organismal behavior. • Know the process of succession.	U2W3, U2W5

Physics

Mechanical Energy • Understand potential and kinetic energy. • Understand conservation of energy. • Understand the relationship of work and mechanical energy.	U1W6

Social Studies Connections on Reading Street

Kindergarten

Interrelated Disciplines and Skills

Spatial analysis of physical and cultural processes that shape the human experience	U3W3, U4W1, U4W2, U4W4, U4W5, U6W1, U6W2

- Use the tools and concepts of geography appropriately and accurately.
- Analyze the interaction between human communities and the environment.
- Analyze how physical and cultural processes have shaped human communities over time.
- Evaluate the causes and effects of human migration patterns over time.
- Analyze how various cultural regions have changed over time.
- Analyze the relationship between geography and the development of human communities.

Periodization and chronological reasoning	U3W5

- Examine how and why historians divide the past into eras.
- Identify and evaluate sources and patterns of change and continuity across time and place.
- Analyze causes and effects of major political, economic, and social changes in U.S. and world history.

Change and continuity of social groups, civic organizations, institutions, and their interaction	U1W2, U1W3, U1W4

- Identify different social groups (e.g., clubs, religious organizations) and examine how they form and how and why they sustain themselves.
- Define the concept of socialization and analyze the role socialization plays in human development and behavior.
- Analyze how social institutions (e.g., marriage, family, churches, schools) function and meet the needs of society.
- Identify and evaluate the sources and consequences of social conflict.

Diverse Human Perspectives and Experiences

Factors that influence personal and group identities, (e.g., race, ethnicity, gender, nationality, institutional affiliations, socioeconomic status)	U3W2, U3W6

- Explain and evaluate the concepts of race, ethnicity, and nationalism.
- Explain and evaluate the concept of gender.
- Analyze diverse religious concepts, structures, and institutions around the world.
- Evaluate how major philosophical and intellectual concepts influence human behavior or identity.
- Explain the concepts of socioeconomic status and stratification.
- Analyze how individual and group identities are established and change over time.

Interdependence of Global Communities

Spatial understanding of global, regional, national, and local communities   U1W1, U5W4, U5W5

- Distinguish spatial patterns of human communities that exist between or within contemporary political boundaries.
- Connect regional or local developments to global ones.
- Analyze how and why diverse communities interact and become dependent on each other.

Effective Communication

Clear and coherent oral and written communication

- Use appropriate oral communication techniques depending on the context or nature of the interaction.
- Use conventions of standard written English.

U1W1, U1W2, U1W3, U1W4, U1W5, U1W6, U2W1, U2W2, U2W3, U2W4, U2W5, U2W6, U3W1, U3W2, U3W3, U3W4, U3W5, U3W6, U4W1, U4W2, U4W3, U4W4, U4W5, U4W6, U5W1, U5W2, U5W3, U5W4, U5W5, U5W6, U6W1, U6W2, U6W3, U6W4, U6W5, U6W6

Index

C

Index

Emerging reading. *See* Print awareness.

Endings. *See* Word analysis, plurals.

End punctuation. *See* Exclamation mark, Period, Question mark.

English, conventions of. *See* Adjectives, Capitalization, Exclamation mark, Nouns, Period, Prepositions and prepositional phrases, Pronouns, Question mark, Sentences, Subject-verb agreement, Verbs.

English language learners. *See* ELL (English Language Learners) suggestions.

Environmental print. *See* Print awareness.

ESL (English as a Second Language). *See* ELL (English Language Learners) suggestions.

Essential message. *See* Main idea and details.

Evaluation. *See* Assessment.

Expository nonfiction. *See* Genres.

Expository text/article. *See* Genres.

F

Fable. *See* Genres.

Fact and fantasy, distinguishing. *See* Realism and fantasy.

Fairy tale. *See* Genres.

Family involvement. *See* School-home connection.

Fantasy. *See* Genres.

Feeling words. *See* Vocabulary strategies.

Fiction. *See* Genres.

Fluency, reading

G

Genres

Graphic and semantic organizers

H

I

J

K

L

M

N

O

W

Web. *See* Graphic and semantic organizers, types.

Word analysis

Word attack skills. *See* Phonics/decoding, Vocabulary strategies, Word analysis.

Word identification. *See* Phonics/decoding, Vocabulary strategies, Word analysis.

Word reading. *See* Fluency, reading.

Word study. *See* Phonics/decoding, Vocabulary strategies, Word analysis.

Writing forms/products

Writing modes

Writing process

Notes

Notes